Go far...without going far from home.
Nearby colleges want to hear from you!

Thomson Peterson's Regional College Survey lets you show colleges in your geographic area what makes you a great applicant. Complete the survey online at www.petersons.com/studentnetworks or return this completed form by mail, indicating which colleges interest you.

New York

First Name: _____ Middle Initial: _____

Last Name: _____

Address: _____

City: _____ State: _____ Zip: _____ - _____

Phone: _____

E-mail Address: _____

DOB: Month _____ Day _____ Year _____ Gender: ❑ Male ❑ Female
(mm/dd/yyyy)

Race/ethnic background—U.S. citizens and permanent residents only (optional):

❑ American Indian or Aleut   ❑ Asian or Pacific Islander
❑ Black or African American   ❑ Caucasian
❑ Latin American or Hispanic   ❑ Mexican American or Chicano
❑ Puerto Rican   ❑ Other

SCHOOL & SCORES
Name and location of your high school:

High School Name: _____

City: _____ State: _____

Expected year of high school graduation: _____

Estimated Current GPA: (4.0 = A) _____

PSAT Scores: Critical Reading_____ Math_____ Writing_____

SAT Scores: Critical Reading_____ Math_____ Writing_____
             or Verbal

PLAN Score: _____ ACT Score: _____

Please indicate your top choice for field of study (Mark only one choice):

❑ Architecture   ❑ Humanities/Humanistic Studies
❑ Art   ❑ Mathematics
❑ Biology   ❑ Music
❑ Business   ❑ Physical Sciences
❑ Communications   ❑ Prelaw Studies
❑ Computer and Information Sciences ❑ Premedical Studies
❑ Dance   ❑ Social Sciences
❑ Education   ❑ Undecided
❑ Engineering
❑ Health Science

ACTIVITIES

For each item, mark an X on the appropriate line if you participate in this activity in high school or expect to participate in it in college.

	HIGH SCHOOL	COLLEGE
Academic interest groups	____	____
Arts	____	____
Community service	____	____
Debate	____	____
Drama and theatrical productions	____	____
Intramural sports	____	____
Junior varsity and varsity athletics	____	____
Music, including chorus, choir, and orchestra	____	____
National Honor Society	____	____
Political/social issues group	____	____
Religious groups	____	____
School spirit organization	____	____
Student government	____	____
Student publications (newspaper, yearbook)	____	____

❑ **Check here to receive information about relevant products and services from Thomson Peterson's and its partners.**

Please mark below the colleges you find most appealing and from which you would like to receive catalogs, viewbooks, and other admission/financial aid material.

NEW YORK

❑ Adelphi University
❑ Bernard M. Baruch College of the City University of New York
❑ Canisius College
❑ Cazenovia College
❑ Clarkson University
❑ D'Youville College
❑ Eugene Lang College, New School University
❑ Fordham University
❑ Hobart and William Smith Colleges
❑ Hofstra University
❑ Ithaca College
❑ Le Moyne College
❑ Manhattan College
❑ Manhattanville College
❑ Molloy College
❑ Mount Saint Mary College
❑ New York School of Interior Design
❑ Niagara University

❑ Purchase College, State University of New York
❑ Queens College of the City University of New York
❑ Rensselaer Polytechnic Institute
❑ Rochester Institute of Technology
❑ St. Bonaventure University
❑ St. John's University
❑ St. Joseph's College, New York
❑ Siena College
❑ State University of New York at Oswego
❑ State University of New York College at Old Westbury
❑ United States Military Academy
❑ Wells College

D1385051

BUSINESS REPLY MAIL
FIRST-CLASS MAIL   PERMIT NO. 4764   TRENTON, NJ

POSTAGE WILL BE PAID BY ADDRESSEE

REGIONAL COLLEGES CONSORTIUM
THOMSON PETERSON'S
PRINCETON PIKE CORPORATE CENTER
2000 LENOX DRIVE
P.O. BOX 67005
LAWRENCEVILLE, NJ 08648-9901

Fold here to return (do not detach)

Please tape closed to mail

PETERSON'S
COLLEGES IN
NEW YORK

2006

THOMSON

PETERSON'S

Australia • Canada • Mexico • Singapore • Spain • United Kingdom • United States

THOMSON

PETERSON'S

About Thomson Peterson's

Thomson Peterson's (www.petersons.com) is a leading provider of education information and advice, with books and online resources focusing on education search, test preparation, and financial aid. Its Web site offers searchable databases and interactive tools for contacting educational institutions, online practice tests and instruction, and planning tools for securing financial aid. Thomson Peterson's serves 110 million education consumers annually.

For more information, contact Thomson Peterson's, 2000 Lenox Drive, Lawrenceville, NJ 08648; 800-338-3282; or find us on the World Wide Web at www.petersons.com/about.

Editor: Fern A. Oram; Production Editor: L. A. Wagner; Copy Editors: Bret Bollmann, Jim Colbert, Michael Haines, Sally Ross, Jill C. Schwartz, Mark D. Snider, Pam Sullivan, Valerie Bolus Vaughan; Research Project Manager: Daniel Margolin; Research Associate: Mary Meyer-Penniston; Programmer: Phyllis Johnson; Manufacturing Manager: Ray Golaszewski; Composition Manager: Linda M. Williams; Client Relations Representatives: Mimi Kaufman, Karen D. Mount, Mary Ann Murphy, Jim Swinarski, Eric Wallace.

ISSN Pending
ISBN 0-7689-1758-1

Printed in the United States of America

10 9 8 7 6 5 4 3 2 1   07 06 05

Twenty-first Edition

CONTENTS

A Note from the Peterson's Editors

Welcome to the world of college decision making. This guide can be an invaluable tool as you think about college and where to apply. You are probably considering at least one college that is relatively near your home. It may surprise you to learn that the majority of all students go to college within a 300-mile radius of where they live. Because of that factor, we publish this series of college guides that focuses on the colleges in each of six regions of the country so that students can easily compare the colleges in their own area. (Two-year public and proprietary colleges are not included because their admission patterns are significantly different from other colleges.)

For advice and guidance in the college search and selection process, just turn the page. "Surviving Standardized Tests" describes the most frequently used test and lists test dates for 2005–06. Of course, part of the college selection process involves visiting the schools themselves and "The Whys and Whats of College Visits" is just the planner you need to make those trips well worth your while. Next, "Applying 101" provides advice on how best to approach the application phase of the process. If you've got questions about transferring, "Successful Transfer" has got the answers you need. "Who's Paying for This? Financial Aid Basics" and the "Financial Aid Programs for Schools in New York" articles provide you with the essential information on how to meet your education expenses. "Searching for Four-Year Colleges Online" gives you all the tips you'll need to integrate the Web into your college search. Lastly, you'll want to read through the "How to Use This Guide" and learn how to use all the information presented in this volume.

Following these articles are the **Profiles of Colleges** sections. The college profiles are easy to read and should give you a good sense of whether a college meets your basic needs and should be considered further. This consistently formatted collection of data can provide a balance to the individual mailings you are likely to receive from colleges.

In a number of the profiles (those marked with a *Sponsor* icon), you will find helpful information about social life, academic life, campus visits, and interviews. These **Special Messages to Students** are written in each case by a college admissions office staff member. You will find valuable insights into what each writer considers special about his or her institution (both socially and academically), what is expected of you during your interview at that college, and how important the interview is there. You will also be alerted to outstanding attractions on campus or nearby so you can plan a productive visit. In many cases travel information (nearest commercial airport and nearest interstate highway) that will be of help on your campus visit is included.

And if you still thirst for even more information, look for the two-page narrative descriptions appearing in the **In-Depth Descriptions of Colleges** sections of the book. These descriptions are written by admissions deans and provide great detail about each college. They are edited to provide a consistent format across entries for your ease of comparison.

The **Indexes** at the back of the book ("Majors and Degrees," "Athletic Programs and Scholarships," and "ROTC Programs") enable you to pinpoint colleges listed in the **Profiles** according to their specific offerings. In addition, there is an "Alphabetical Listing of Colleges and Universities" to enable you to quickly find a school that you may have already determined meets your criteria.

We hope you will find this information helpful. Try to remember that admission directors are as interested in you and the possibility of your attending their college as you are in the possibility of applying. They spend most of their time reaching out to students, explaining their colleges' programs and policies, and easing the application process whenever they can. If you think of them as people who like students and if you can picture them taking the time to carefully provide the information in this book for you, it might help to lessen any anxiety you are feeling about applying.

Our advice is to relax, enjoy high school, and do as well as you can in your courses. Give yourself enough time during the early stages of your search to think about what kind of person you are and what you want to become so you can choose colleges for the right reasons. Read all college materials with an open mind, and visit as many campuses as you can. Plan ahead so you do not rush through your applications. If you can keep yourself in balance during this process, it need not become the panic period you may have seen some friends experience. We urge you to contact admission staff members at any college in which you are interested. They are all willing to help you. In fact, the admission people whose names you will find in this book hope to hear from you. We at Thomson Peterson's wish you success and happiness wherever you enroll.

The College Admissions Process

Surviving Standardized Tests

WHAT ARE STANDARDIZED TESTS?

Colleges and universities in the United States use tests to help evaluate applicants' readiness for admission or to place them in appropriate courses. The tests that are most frequently used by colleges are the ACT Assessment of American College Testing, Inc., and the College Board's SAT. In addition, the Educational Testing Service (ETS) offers the TOEFL test, which evaluates the English-language proficiency of nonnative speakers. The tests are offered at designated testing centers located at high schools and colleges throughout the United States and U.S. territories and at testing centers in various countries throughout the world. The ACT Assessment test and the SAT tests are each taken by more than a million students each year. The TOEFL test is taken by more than 800,000 students each year.

Upon request, special accommodations for students with documented visual, hearing, physical, or learning disabilities are available. Examples of special accommodations include tests in Braille or large print and such aids as a reader, recorder, magnifying glass, or sign language interpreter. Additional testing time may be allowed in some instances. Contact the appropriate testing program or your guidance counselor for details on how to request special accommodations.

College Board SAT Program

Currently, the SAT Program consists of the SAT and the SAT Subject Tests. The SAT is a 3-hour 45-minute test made up of ten sections, primarily multiple-choice, that focuses on college success skills of writing, critical reading, and mathematics. The writing component measures grammar and usage and includes a short, student-written essay. The critical reading sections test verbal reasoning and critical reading skills. Emphasis is placed on reading passages, which are 400–850 words in length. Some reading passages are paired; the second opposes, supports, or in some way complements the point of view expressed in the first. The three mathematics sections test a student's ability to solve problems involving arithmetic, Algebra I and II, and geometry. They include questions that require students to produce their own responses, in addition to questions that

students can choose from four or five answer choices. Calculators may be used on the SAT mathematics sections.

The SAT Subject Tests are 1-hour tests, primarily multiple-choice, in specific subjects that measure students' knowledge of these subjects and their ability to apply that knowledge. Some colleges may require or recommend these tests for placement, or even admission. The Subject Tests measure a student's academic achievement in high school and may indicate readiness for certain college programs. Tests offered include Literature, U.S. History, World History, Mathematics Level IC, Mathematics Level IIC, Biology E/M (Ecological/Molecular), Chemistry, Physics, French, German, Modern Hebrew, Italian, Latin, and Spanish, as well as Foreign Language Tests with Listening in Chinese, French, German, Japanese, Korean, Spanish, and English Language Proficiency (ELPT). The Mathematics Level IC and IIC tests require the use of a scientific calculator.

SAT scores are automatically sent to each student who has taken the test. On average, they are mailed about three weeks after the test. Students may request that the scores be reported to their high schools or to the colleges to which they are applying.

ACT Assessment Program

The ACT Assessment Program is a comprehensive data collection, processing, and reporting service designed to

---

DON'T FORGET TO . . .

- Take the SAT or ACT Assessment before application deadlines.
- Note that test registration deadlines precede test dates by about six weeks.
- Register to take the TOEFL test if English is not your native language and you are planning on studying at a North American college.
- Practice your test-taking skills with **Peterson's Ultimate SAT Tool Kit, Peterson's Ultimate ACT Assessment Tool Kit, The Real ACT Prep Guide** (published by Peterson's), and **Peterson's TOEFL Success** (some available with software).
- Contact the College Board or American College Testing, Inc., in advance if you need special accommodations when taking tests.

assist in educational and career planning. The ACT Assessment instrument consists of four academic tests, taken under timed conditions, and a Student Profile Section and Interest Inventory, completed when students register for the ACT Assessment.

The academic tests cover four areas—English, mathematics, reading, and science reasoning. The ACT Assessment consists of 215 multiple-choice questions and takes approximately 3 hours and 30 minutes to complete with breaks (testing time is actually 2 hours and 55 minutes). They are designed to assess the student's educational development and readiness to handle college-level work. The minimum standard score is 1, the maximum is 36, and the national average is 21. Students should note that beginning in February 2005, an optional writing test was offered.

The Student Profile Section requests information about each student's admission and enrollment plans, academic and out-of-class high school achievements and aspirations, and high school course work. The student is also asked to supply biographical data and self-reported high school grades in the four subject-matter areas covered by the academic tests.

The ACT Assessment has a number of career planning services, including the ACT Assessment Interest Inventory, which is designed to measure six major dimensions of student interests–business contact, business operations, technical, science, arts, and social service. Results are used to compare the student's interests with those of college-bound students who later majored in each of a wide variety of areas. Inventory results are also used to help students compare their work-activity preferences with work activities that characterize twenty-three "job families."

Because the information resulting from the ACT Assessment Program is used in a variety of educational settings, American College Testing, Inc., prepares three reports for each student: the Student Report, the High School Report, and the College Report. The Student Report normally is sent to the student's high school, except after the June test date, when it is sent directly to the student's home address. The College Report is sent to the colleges the student designates.

Early in the school year, American College Testing, Inc., sends registration packets to high schools across the country that contain all the information a student needs to register for the ACT Assessment. High school guidance offices also receive a supply of *Preparing for the ACT Assessment*, a booklet that contains a complete practice test, an answer key, and general information about preparing for the test.

2005–06 ACT ASSESSMENT AND SAT TEST DATES

ACT Assessment
September 24, 2005*
October 22, 2005
December 10, 2005
February 11, 2006**
April 8, 2006
June 10, 2006

All test dates fall on a Saturday. Tests are also given on the Sundays following the Saturday test dates for students who cannot take the test on Saturday because of religious reasons. The basic ACT Assessment registration fee for 2004–05 was $28 ($45 outside of the U.S.). The optional writing test is $14 and is refundable for students who are absent on test day.

*The September test is available only in Arizona, California, Florida, Georgia, Illinois, Indiana, Maryland, Nevada, North Carolina, Pennsylvania, South Carolina, Texas, and Washington.

**The February test date is not available in New York.

SAT
October 8, 2005 (SAT and SAT Subject Tests)
November 5, 2005 (SAT, SAT Subject Tests, and Language Tests with Listening, including ELPT*)
December 3, 2005 (SAT and SAT Subject Tests)
January 28, 2006 (SAT, SAT Subject Tests, and ELPT)
April 1, 2006 (SAT only)**
May 6, 2006 (SAT and SAT Subject Tests)
June 3, 2006 (SAT and SAT Subject Tests)

For the 2004–05 academic year, the basic fee for the SAT was $41.50. The basic fee for the SAT Subject Tests was $17, $18 for the Language Tests with Listening, and $8 each for all other Subject Tests. Students can take up to three SAT Subject Tests on a single date, and a $17 basic registration and reporting fee should be added for each test date. Tests are also given on the Sundays following the Saturday test dates for students who cannot take the test on Saturday because of religious reasons. Fee waivers are available to juniors and seniors who cannot afford test fees.

*Language Tests with Listening (including the English Language Proficiency Test, or ELPT) are only offered on November 5; the ELPT is offered on November 5 and January 28 at some test centers. See the Registration Bulletin for details.

**The April 1 test date is only available in the U.S. and its territories.

Test of English as a Foreign Language (TOEFL)

The TOEFL is used by various organizations, such as colleges and universities, to determine English proficiency. Beginning in September, the new TOEFL (TOEFL iBT) will be offered in the United States and in the rest of the world in 2006. The test will be offered in an Internet-based format. The TOEFL iBT tests students in the areas of speaking, listening, reading, and writing.

The current TOEFL tests students in the areas of listening, structure, reading comprehension, and writing. Score requirements are set by individual institutions. For more information on TOEFL, and to obtain a copy of the Information Bulletin, contact the Educational Testing Service.

Peterson's *TOEFL CBT Success* can help you prepare for the current exam. The CD version of the book includes a TOEFL practice test and adaptive English skill building exercise. An online CBT test can also be taken for a small fee at petersons.com.

Contact your secondary school counselor for full information about the SAT and ACT Assessment programs and the TOEFL test.

The Whys and Whats of College Visits

Dawn B. Sova, Ph.D.

The campus visit should not be a passive activity for you and your parents. Take the initiative and gather information beyond that provided in the official tour. You will see many important indicators during your visit that will tell you more about the true character of a college and its students than the tour guide will reveal. Know what to look for and how to assess the importance of such indicators.

WHAT SHOULD YOU ASK AND WHAT SHOULD YOU LOOK FOR?

Your first stop on a campus visit is the visitor center or admissions office, where you will probably have to wait to meet with a counselor. Colleges usually plan to greet visitors later than the appointed time in order to give them the opportunity to review some of the campus information that is liberally scattered throughout the visitor waiting room. Take advantage of the time to become even more familiar with the college by arriving 15 to 30 minutes before your appointment to observe the behavior of staff members and to browse through the yearbooks and student newspapers that will be available.

If you prepare in advance, you will have already reviewed the college catalog and map of the campus. These materials familiarize you with the academic offerings and the physical layout of the campus, but the true character of the college and its students emerges in other ways.

Begin your investigation with the visitor center staff members. As a student's first official contact with the college, they should make every effort to welcome prospective students and project a friendly image.

- How do they treat you and other prospective students who are waiting? Are they friendly and willing to speak with you, or do they try their hardest to avoid eye contact and conversation?
- Are they friendly with each other and with students who enter the office, or are they curt and unwilling to help?
- Does the waiting room have a friendly feeling or is it cold and sterile?

If the visitor center staff members seem indifferent to *prospective* students, there is little reason to believe that they will be warm and welcoming to current students. View such behavior as a warning to watch very carefully the interaction of others with you during the tour. An indifferent or unfriendly reception in the admissions office may be simply the first of many signs that attending this college will not be a pleasant experience.

Look through several yearbooks and see the types of activities that are actually photographed, as opposed to the activities that colleges promise in their promotional literature. Some questions are impossible to answer if the college is very large, but for small and moderately sized colleges the yearbook is a good indicator of campus activity.

- Has the number of clubs and organizations increased or decreased in the past five years?
- Do the same students appear repeatedly in activities?
- Do sororities and fraternities dominate campus activities?
- Are participants limited to one sex or one ethnic group, or is there diversity?
- Are all activities limited to the campus, or are students involved in activities in the community?

Use what you observe in the yearbooks as a means of forming a more complete understanding of the college, but don't base your entire impression on just one facet. If time permits, look through several copies of the school newspaper, which should reflect the major concerns and interests of the students. The paper is also a good way to learn about the campus social life.

- Does the paper contain a mix of national and local news?
- What products or services are advertised?
- How assertive are the editorials?
- With what topics are the columnists concerned?
- Are movies and concerts that meet your tastes advertised or reviewed?
- What types of ads appear in the classified section?

The newspaper should be a public forum for students, and, as such, should reflect the character of the campus and of the student body. A paper that deals only with seemingly safe and well-edited topics on the editorial page and in regular feature columns might indicate administrative censorship. A lack of ads for restaurants might indicate either a lack of good places to eat or that area restaurants do not welcome student business. A limited mention of movies, concerts, or other entertainment might reveal a severely limited campus social life. Even if ads and reviews are included, you can also learn a lot about how such activities reflect your tastes.

You will have only a limited amount of time to ask questions during your initial meeting with the admissions counselor, for very few schools include a formal interview in the initial campus visit or tour. Instead, this brief meeting is often just a nicety that allows the admissions office to begin a file for the student and to record some initial impressions. Save your questions for the tour guide and for students on campus you meet along the way.

HOW CAN YOU ASSESS THE TRUE CHARACTER OF A COLLEGE AND ITS STUDENTS?

Colleges do not train their tour guides to deceive prospective students, but they do caution guides to avoid unflattering topics and campus sites. Does this mean that you are condemned to see only a sugarcoated version of life on a particular college campus? Not at all, especially not if you are observant.

Most organized campus visits include such campus facilities as dormitories, dining halls, libraries, student activity and recreation centers, and the health and student services centers. Some may only be pointed out, while you will walk through others. Either way, you will find that many signs of the true character of the college emerge if you keep your eyes open.

Bulletin boards in dormitories and student centers contain a wealth of information about campus activities, student concerns, and campus groups. Read the posters, notices, and messages to learn what *really* interests students. Unlike ads in the school newspaper, posters put up by students advertise both on- and off-campus events, so they will give you an idea of what is also available in the surrounding community.

Review the notices, which may cover either campuswide events or events that concern only small groups of students. The catalog may not mention a performance group, but an individual dormitory with its own small theater may offer regular productions. Poetry readings, jam sessions, writers' groups, and other activities may be announced and shows diversity of student interests.

Even the brief bulletin board messages offering objects for sale and noting objects that people want to purchase reveal a lot about a campus. Are most of the items computer related? Or do the messages specify CDs, audio equipment, or musical instruments? Are offers to trade goods or services posted? Don't ignore the "ride wanted" messages. Students who want to share rides home during a break may specify widely diverse geographical locations. If so, then you know that the student body is not limited to only the immediate area or one locale. Other messages can also enhance your knowledge of the true character of the campus and its students.

As you walk through various buildings, examine their condition carefully.

- Is the paint peeling, and do the exteriors look worn?
- Are the exteriors and interiors of the building clean?
- Is the equipment in the classrooms up-to-date or outdated?

Pay particular attention to the dormitories, especially to factors that might affect your safety. Observe the appearance of the structure, and ask about the security measures in and around the dormitories.

- Are the dormitories noisy or quiet?
- Do they seem crowded?
- How good is the lighting around each dormitory?
- Are the dormitories spread throughout the campus or are they clustered in one main area?
- Who has access to the dormitories in addition to students?
- How secure are the means by which students enter and leave the dormitory?

While you are on the subject of dormitory safety, you should also ask about campus safety. Don't expect that the guide will rattle off a list of crimes that have been committed in the past year. To obtain that information, access the recent year of issues of *The Chronicle of Higher Education* and locate its yearly report on campus crime. Also ask the guide about safety measures that the campus police take and those that students have initiated.

- Can students request escorts to their residences late at night?
- Do campus shuttle buses run at frequent intervals all night?
- Are "blue-light" telephones liberally placed throughout the campus for students to use to call for help?
- Do the campus police patrol the campus regularly?

If the guide does not answer your questions satisfactorily, wait until after the tour to contact the campus police or traffic office for answers.

Campus tours usually just point out the health services center without taking the time to walk through. Even if you don't see the inside of the building, you should take a close look at the location of the health services center and ask the guide questions about services.

- How far is the health center from the dormitories?
- Is a doctor always on call?
- Does the campus transport sick students from their dormitories or must they walk?
- What are the operating hours of the health center?
- Does the health center refer students to a nearby hospital?

If the guide can't answer your questions, visit the health center later and ask someone there.

Most campus tours take pride in showing students their activities centers, which may contain snack bars, game rooms, workout facilities, and other means of entertainment. Should you scrutinize this building as carefully as the rest? Of course. Outdated and poorly maintained activity equipment contributes to your total impression of the college. You should also ask about the hours, availability, and cost (no, the activities are usually *not* free) of using the bowling alleys, pool tables, air hockey tables, and other ammenities.

As you walk through campus with the tour, also look carefully at the appearance of the students who pass. The way in which both men and women groom themselves, the way they dress, and even their physical bearing communicate a lot more than any guidebook can. If everyone seems to conform to the same look, you might feel that you would be uncomfortable at the college, however nonconformist that look might be. On the other hand, you might not feel comfortable on a campus that stresses diversity of dress and behavior, and your observations now can save you discomfort later.

- Does every student seem to wear a sorority or fraternity t-shirt or jacket?
- Is everyone of your sex sporting the latest fad haircut?
- Do all of the men or the women seem to be wearing expensive name-brand clothes?
- Do most of the students seem to be working hard to look outrageous with regards to clothing, hair color, and body art?
- Would you feel uncomfortable in a room full of these students?

Is appearance important to you? If it is, then you should consider very seriously if you answer *yes* to any of the above questions. You don't have to be the same as everyone else on campus, but standing out too much may make you unhappy.

As you observe the physical appearance of the students, also listen to their conversations as you pass them? What are they talking about? How are they speaking? Are their voices and accents all the same, or do you hear diversity in

their speech? Are you offended by their language? Think how you will feel if surrounded by the same speech habits and patterns for four years.

WHERE SHOULD YOU VISIT ON YOUR OWN?

Your campus visit is not over when the tour ends because you will probably have many questions yet to be answered and many places to still be seen. Where you go depends upon the extent to which the organized tour covers the campus. Your tour should take you to view residential halls, health and student services centers, the gymnasium or field house, dining halls, the library, and recreational centers. If any of the facilities on this list have been omitted, visit them on your own and ask questions of the students and staff members you meet. In addition, you should step off campus and gain an impression of the surrounding community. You will probably become bored with life on campus and spend at least some time off campus. Make certain that you know what the surrounding area is like.

The campus tour leaves little time to ask impromptu questions of current students, but you can do so after the tour. Eat lunch in one of the dining halls. Most will allow visitors to pay cash to experience a typical student meal. Food may not be important to you now while you are living at home and can simply take anything you want from the refrigerator at any time, but it will be when you are away at college with only a meal ticket to feed you.

- How clean is the dining hall? Consider serving tables, floors, and seating.
- What is the quality of the food?
- How big are the portions?
- How much variety do students have at each meal?
- How healthy are the food choices?

While you are eating, try to strike up a conversation with students and tell them that you are considering attending their college. Their reactions and advice can be eye-opening. Ask them questions about the academic atmosphere and the professors.

- Are the classes large or small?
- Do the majority of the professors only lecture or are tutorials and seminars common?
- Is the emphasis of the faculty career-oriented or abstract?
- Are the teaching methods innovative and stimulating or boring and dull?
- Is the academic atmosphere pressured, lax, or somewhere in between?
- Which are the strong majors? The weak majors?
- Is the emphasis on grades or social life or a mix of both at the college?

- How hard do students have to work to receive high grades?

Current students can also give you the inside line on the true nature of the college social life. You may gain some idea through looking in the yearbook, in the newspaper, and on the bulletin boards, but students will reveal the true highs and lows of campus life. Ask them about drug use, partying, dating rituals, drinking, and anything else that may affect your life as a student.

- Which are the most popular club activities?
- What do students do on weekends? Do most go home?
- How frequently do concerts occur on campus? Which groups have recently performed?
- How can you become involved in specific activities (name them)?
- How strictly are campus rules enforced and how severe are penalties?
- What counseling services are available?
- Are academic tutoring services available?
- Do they feel that the faculty really cares about students, especially freshmen?

You will receive the most valuable information from current students, but you will only be able to speak with them after the tour is over. And you might have to risk rejection as you try to initiate conversations with students who might not want to reveal how they feel about the campus. Still, the value of this information is worth the chance.

If you have the time, you should also visit the library to see just how accessible research materials are and to observe the physical layout. The catalog usually specifies the days and hours of operation, as well as the number of volumes contained in the library and the number of periodicals to which it subscribes. A library also requires accessibility, good lighting, an adequate number of study carrels, and lounge areas for students. Many colleges have created 24-hour study lounges for students who find the residence halls too noisy for studying, although most colleges claim that they designate areas of the residences as "quiet study" areas. You may not be interested in any of this information, but when you are a student you will have to make frequent use of the campus library so you should know what is available. You should at least ask how extensive their holdings are in your proposed major area. If they have virtually nothing, you will have to spend a lot of time ordering items via interlibrary loan or making copies, which can become expensive. The ready answer of students that they will obtain their information from the Internet is unpleasantly countered by professors who demand journal articles with documentation.

Make a point of at least driving through the community surrounding the college, because you will be spending time there shopping, dining, working in a part-time job, or attending events. Even the largest and best-stocked campus will not meet all of your social and personal needs. If you can spare the time, stop in several stores to see if they welcome college students.

- Is the surrounding community suburban, urban, or rural?
- Does the community offer stores of interest, such as bookstores, craft shops, and boutiques?
- Do the businesses employ college students?
- Does the community have a movie or stage theater?
- Are there several types of interesting restaurants?
- Do there seem to be any clubs that court a college clientele?
- Is the center of activity easy to walk to, or do you need a car or other transportation?

You might feel that a day is not enough to answer all of your questions, but even answering some questions will provide you with a stronger basis for choosing a college. Many students visit a college campus several times before making their decision, as you also should. Keep in mind that for the rest of your life you will be associated with the college that you attend. You will spend four years of your life at this college. The effort of spending several days to obtain the information to make your decision is worthwhile.

Dawn B. Sova, Ph.D., is a former newspaper reporter and columnist, as well as the author of more than eight books and numerous magazine articles. She teaches creative and research writing, as well as scientific and technical writing, newswriting, and journalism.

Applying 101

The words "applying yourself" have several important meanings in the college application process. One meaning refers to the fact that you need to keep focused during this important time in your life, keep your priorities straight, and know the dates that your applications are due so you can apply on time. The phrase might also refer to the person who is really responsible for your application—you.

You are the only person who should compile your college application. You need to take ownership of this process. The guidance counselor is not responsible for completing your applications, and your parents shouldn't be typing them. College applications must be completed in addition to your normal workload at school, college visits, and SAT, ACT Assessment, or TOEFL testing.

THE APPLICATION

The application is your way of introducing yourself to a college admissions office. As with any introduction, you want to make a good first impression. The first thing you should do in presenting your application is to find out what the college or university needs from you. Read the application carefully to find out the application fee and deadline, required standardized tests, number of essays, interview requirements, and anything else you can do or submit to help improve your chances for acceptance.

Completing college applications yourself helps you learn more about the schools to which you are applying. The information a college asks for in its application can tell you much about the school. State university applications often tell you how they are going to view their applicants. Usually, they select students based on GPAs and test scores. Colleges that request an interview, ask you to respond to a few open-ended questions, or require an essay are interested in a more personal approach to the application process and may be looking for different types of students than those sought by a state school.

In addition to submitting the actual application, there are several other items that are commonly required. You will be responsible for ensuring that your standardized test scores and your high school transcript arrive at the colleges to which you apply. Most colleges will ask that you submit teacher recommendations as well. Select teachers who know you and your abilities well and allow them plenty of time to complete the recommendations. When all portions of the application have been completed and sent in, whether

FOLLOW THESE TIPS WHEN FILLING OUT YOUR APPLICATION

- **Follow the directions to the letter.** You don't want to be in a position to ask an admissions officer for exceptions due to your inattentiveness.
- **Make a photocopy** of the application and work through a rough draft before you actually fill out the application copy to be submitted.
- **Proofread all parts of your application,** including your essay. Again, the final product indicates to the admissions staff how meticulous and careful you are in your work.
- **Submit your application as early as possible,** provided all of the pieces are available. If there is a problem with your application, this will allow you to work through it with the admissions staff in plenty of time. If you wait until the last minute, it not only takes away that cushion but also reflects poorly on your sense of priorities.

electronically or by mail, make sure you follow up with the college to ensure their receipt.

THE APPLICATION ESSAY

Some colleges may request one essay or a combination of essays and short-answer topics to learn more about who you are and how well you can communicate your thoughts. Common essay topics cover such simple themes as writing about yourself and your experiences or why you want to attend that particular school. Other colleges will ask that you show your imaginative or creative side by writing about a favorite author, for instance, or commenting on a hypothetical situation. In such cases, they will be looking at your thought processes and your level of creativity.

Whereas the other portions of your application—your transcript, test scores, and involvement in extracurricular activities—are a reflection of what you've accomplished up to this point, your application essay is an opportunity to present yourself in the here and now. The essay shows your originality and verbal skills and is very important. Test scores and grades may represent your academic results, but your essay shows how you approach a topic or problem and express your opinion.

Admissions officers, particularly those at small or mid-size colleges, use the essay to determine how you, as a student, will fit into life at that college. The essay, therefore, is a critical component of the application process. Here are some tips for writing a winning essay:

- Colleges are looking for an honest representation of who you are and what you think. Make sure that the tone of the essay reflects enthusiasm, maturity, creativity, the ability to communicate, talent, and your leadership skills.
- Be sure you set aside enough time to write the essay, revise it, and revise it *again*. Running the "spell check" feature on your computer will only detect a fraction of the errors you probably made on your first pass at writing it. Take a break and then come back to it and reread it. You will probably notice other style, content, and grammar problems—and ways that you can improve the essay overall.
- Always answer the question that is being asked, making sure that you are specific, clear, and true to your personality.
- Enlist the help of reviewers who know you well—friends, parents, teachers—since they are likely to be the most honest and will keep you on track in the presentation of your true self.

THE PERSONAL INTERVIEW

Although it is relatively rare that a personal interview is required, many colleges recommend that you take this opportunity for a face-to-face discussion with a member of the admissions staff. Read through the application materials to determine whether or not a college places great emphasis on the interview. If they strongly recommend that you have one, it may work against you to forego it.

In contrast to a group interview and some alumni interviews, which are intended to provide information about a college, the personal interview is viewed both as an information session and as further evaluation of your skills and strengths. You will meet with a member of the admissions staff who will be assessing your personal qualities, high school preparation, and your capacity to contribute to undergraduate life at the institution. On average, these meetings last about 45 minutes—a relatively short amount of time in which to gather information and leave the desired impression—so here are some suggestions on how to make the most of it.

Scheduling Your Visit

Generally, students choose to visit campuses in the summer or fall of their senior year. Both times have their advantages. A summer visit, when the campus is not in session, generally allows for a less hectic visit and interview. Visiting in the fall, on the other hand, provides the opportunity to see what campus life is like in full swing. If you choose the fall, consider arranging an overnight trip so that you can stay in one of the college dormitories. At the very least, you should make your way around campus to take part in classes, athletic events, and social activities. Always make an appointment and avoid scheduling more than two college interviews on any given day. Multiple interviews in a single day hinder your chances of making a good impression, and your impressions of the colleges will blur into each other as you hurriedly make your way from place to place.

Preparation

Know the basics about the college before going for your interview. Read the college viewbook or catalog in addition to this guide. You will be better prepared to ask questions that are not answered in the literature and that will give you a better understanding of what the college has to offer. You should also spend some time thinking about your strengths and weaknesses and, in particular, what you are looking for in a college education. You will find that as you get a few interviews under your belt, they will get easier. You might consider starting with a college that is not a top contender on your list, where the stakes are not as high.

Asking Questions

Inevitably, your interviewer will ask you, "Do you have any questions?" Not having one may suggest that you're unprepared or, even worse, not interested. When you do ask questions, make sure that they are ones that matter to you and that have a bearing on your decision about whether or not to attend that college. The questions that you ask will give the interviewer some insight into your personality and priorities. Avoid asking questions that can be answered in the college literature—again, a sign of unpreparedness. Although the interviewer will undoubtedly pose questions to you, the interview should not be viewed merely as a question-and-answer session. If a conversation evolves out of a particular question, so much the better. Your interviewer can learn a great deal about you from how you sustain a conversation. Similarly, you will be able to learn a great deal about the college in a conversational format.

Separate the Interview from the Interviewer

Many students base their feelings about a college solely on their impressions of the interviewer. Try not to characterize a college based only on your personal reaction, however, since your impressions can be skewed by whether you and your interviewer hit it off. Pay lots of attention to everything else that you see, hear, and learn about a college. Once on campus, you may never see your interviewer again.

In the end, remember to relax and be yourself. Your interviewer will expect you to be somewhat nervous, which will relieve some of the pressure. Don't drink jitters-producing caffeinated beverages prior to the interview, and suppress nervous fidgets like leg-wagging, finger-drumming, or bracelet-jangling. Consider your interview an opportunity to put forth your best effort and to enhance everything that the college knows about you up to this point.

THE FINAL DECISION

Once you have received your acceptance letters, it is time to go back and look at the whole picture. Provided you received more than one acceptance, you are now in a position to compare your options. The best way to do this is to compare your original list of important college-ranking criteria with what you've discovered about each college along the way. In addition, you and your family will need to factor in the financial aid component. You will need to look beyond these cost issues and the quantifiable pros and cons of each college, however, and know that you have a good feeling about your final choice. Before sending off your acceptance letter, you need to feel confident that the college will feel like home for the next four years. Once the choice is made, the only hard part will be waiting for an entire summer before heading off to college!

Successful Transfer

Adrienne Aaron Rulnick

Transfer students need and deserve detailed and accurate information but often lack direction as to where it can be obtained. Few general college guides offer information about transfer deadlines and required minimum grade point averages for transfer admission. College catalogs are not always clear about the specific requirements and procedures for transfer students who may be confused about whether they need to present high school records, SAT or ACT Assessment scores, or a guidance counselor's recommendation, particularly if they have been out of high school for several years. Transfer advisers are not available to those enrolled at a baccalaureate institution; at community and junior colleges, the transfer advising function may be performed by a designated transfer counselor or by a variety of college advisers who are less clearly identified.

The challenge for transfer students is to determine what they need to know in order to make good, informed decisions and identify the individuals and resources that can provide that information. An organized research process is very much at the heart of a successful transfer.

HOW TO BEGIN

Perhaps the most important first step in this process is one of self-analysis. Adopting a consumer approach is appropriate—higher education is a formidable purchase, no matter how it is financed. The reputation of the college from which you obtain your degree may open doors to future jobs and careers; friendships and contacts you make at college can provide a significant network for lifelong social and professional relationships. The environment of a transfer school may be the perfect opportunity for you to test out urban living or the joys of country life, explore a different area of the country, experience college residential living for the first time, or move out of the family nest into your first apartment. Like any major purchase in your life, there are costs and benefits to be weighed. Trade-offs include cost, distance, rigor of academic work, extra time in school required by a cooperative education program, and specific requirements, such as foreign language competence at a liberal arts institution or courses in religion at an institution with a denominational affiliation.

USE EXPERIENCE AS A GUIDE

The wise consumer reflects on his or her own experience with a product (i.e., your initial college or colleges) and then seeks out people who have firsthand experience with the new product being considered. Talk to friends and family members who have attended the colleges you are considering; ask college faculty members you know to tell you about the colleges they attended and how they view these schools. Talk to people engaged in the careers you are considering: what are their impressions of the best programs and schools in their field? Make sure you sample a variety of opinions, but beware of dated experiences. An engineering department considered top-notch when Uncle Joe attended college twenty years ago might be very different today!

THE NITTY-GRITTY

Once your list is reduced to a manageable number of schools, usually fewer than ten, it is important to identify academic requirements, requisite grade point averages for admission, and deadline dates. Most schools admit for both the fall and spring semesters; those on a trimester system may have winter and summer admissions as well. Some schools have rolling admission policies and will process applications as they are received; others, particularly the more selective colleges, have firm deadlines because their admission process involves a committee review, and decisions are made on a competitive basis. It is helpful to know how many transfer students are typically accepted for the semester you wish to begin, whether the minimum grade point average is indicative of the actual average of accepted students (this can vary widely), and whether the major you are seeking has special prerequisites and admission procedures. For example, fine arts programs admission procedures usually require portfolios or auditions. For engineering, computer science, and some business majors, there are specific requirements in mathematics that must be met before a student is considered for admission. Many specialized health-care programs, including nursing, may only admit once a year. Some schools have different standards for sophomore and junior transfers or for in-state and out-of-state students.

Other criteria that you should identify include whether college housing and financial aid are available for transfer students. Some colleges have special transfer scholarships that require separate applications and references, while others simply award aid based on applications that indicate a high grade point average or membership in a nationally recognized junior and community college honor society, such as Phi Theta Kappa. There are also scholarships for transfer students who demonstrate accomplishment in specified academic and performance areas; the latter may be based on talent competitions or accomplishment evidenced in a portfolio or audition.

NONTRADITIONAL STUDENTS

For the nontraditional student, usually defined as anyone beyond the traditional college age of 18 to 23, there may be additional aspects to investigate. Some colleges award credit based on demonstrated life experience; many colleges grant credit for qualifying scores on the CLEP exams or for participation in the DANTES program. Experience in industry may yield college credit as well. If you are ready and able to pursue further college work but are not in a position to attend regular classes at a senior college, there are a variety of distance learning options at fully accredited colleges. Other colleges provide specialized support services for nontraditional students and may allow students the opportunity to attend part-time if they have family and work responsibilities. In some cases, usually at large universities, there may be married student housing or family housing available. More and more schools have established day-care facilities, although the waiting lists are often very long.

APPLYING

Once you have identified the schools that meet the needs you have established as priorities, it is time to begin the application process. Make sure you observe all the indicated deadlines. It never hurts to have everything in early, as there can be consequences, such as closed-out majors and the loss of housing and financial aid, if you submit your application late. Make appointments with faculty members and others who are providing references; make sure they understand what is required of them and when and where their references must be sent. It is your responsibility to follow through to make sure all of your credentials are received, including transcripts from all colleges previously attended, even if you only took one summer course or attended for less than a semester. If you have not yet had the opportunity to visit the schools to which you are applying, now is the time to do so. Arrange interviews wherever possible, and make sure to include a tour of the campus and visits to the department and career offices to gain a picture of the facilities and future opportunities. If you have questions about financial aid, schedule an appointment in the financial aid office, and make sure you are aware of all the deadlines and requirements and any scholarship opportunities for which you are eligible.

MAKING YOUR CHOICE

Congratulations! You have been accepted at the colleges of your choice. Now what? Carefully review the acceptance of your previous college credit and how it has been applied. You are entitled to know how many transfer credits you have received and your expected date of graduation. Compare financial aid packages and housing options. The best choice should emerge from this review process. Then, send a note to the schools you will not be attending. Acknowledge your acceptance, but indicate that you have chosen to attend elsewhere. Carefully read everything you have received from the college of your choice. Return required deposits within the deadline, reserve time to attend transfer orientation, arrange to have your final transcript sent from the college you currently attend, and review the financial picture. This is the time to finalize college loan applications and make sure you are in a position to meet all the costs entailed at this college. Don't forget to include the costs of travel and housing.

You've done it! While many transfer students reflect on how much work was involved in the transfer admission process, those who took the time to follow all of the steps outlined report a sense of satisfaction with their choices and increased confidence in themselves. We wish you an equally rewarding experience.

Adrienne Aaron Rulnick is a Transfer Counselor at Berkshire Community College.

Who's Paying for This? Financial Aid Basics

A college education can be expensive—costing more than $150,000 for four years at some of the higher priced private colleges and universities. Even at the lower cost state colleges and universities, the cost of a four-year education can approach $50,000. Determining how you and your family will come up with the necessary funds to pay for your education requires planning, perseverance, and learning as much as you can about the options that are available to you.

Paying for college should not be looked at as a four-year financial commitment. For most families, paying the total cost of a student's college education out of current savings is usually not realistic. For families that have planned ahead and have financial savings established for higher education, the burden is a lot easier. But for most, meeting the cost of college requires the pooling of current income and assets and investing in longer-term loan options. These family resources, together with possible financial assistance from state, federal, and institutional sources, enable millions of students each year to attend the institution of their choice.

FINANCIAL AID PROGRAMS

There are three types of financial aid:

1. Gift-aid—Scholarships and grants are funds that do not have to be repaid.
2. Loans—Loans must be repaid, usually after graduation; the amount you have to pay back is the total you've borrowed plus any accrued interest. This is considered a source of self-help aid.
3. Student employment—Student employment is a job arranged for you by the financial aid office. This is another source of self-help aid.

The federal government has two major grant programs—the Federal Pell Grant and the Federal Supplemental Educational Opportunity Grant. These grants are targeted to low-to-moderate income families with significant financial need. The federal government also sponsors a student employment program called Federal Work-Study, which offers jobs both on and off campus; and several loan programs, including those for students and for parents of undergraduate students.

There are two types of student loan programs, subsidized and unsubsidized. The Subsidized Stafford Loan and the Federal Perkins Loan are need-based, government-subsidized loans. Students who borrow through these programs do not have to pay interest on the loan until after they graduate or leave school. The Unsubsidized Stafford Loan and the Parent Loan Program are not based on need, and borrowers are responsible for the interest while the student is in school. There are different methods on how these loans are administered. Once you choose your college, the financial aid office will guide you through this process.

After you've submitted your financial aid application and you've been accepted for admission, each college will send you a letter describing your financial aid award. Most award letters show estimated college costs, how much you and your family are expected to contribute, and the amount and types of aid you have been awarded. Most students are awarded aid from a combination of sources and programs. Hence, your award is often called a financial aid "package."

SOURCES OF FINANCIAL AID

More than 14 million people apply for financial aid each year. The largest single source of aid is the federal government, which awarded almost $81.5 billion during 2003–04.

The next largest source of financial aid is found in the college and university community. Institutions award an estimated $23 billion to students each year. Most of this aid is awarded to students who have a demonstrated need based on the Federal Methodology. Some institutions use a different formula, the Institutional Methodology (IM), to award their own funds in conjunction with other forms of aid. Institutional aid may be either need-based or non-need based. Aid that is not based on need is usually awarded for a student's academic performance (merit awards), specific talents or abilities, or to attract the type of students a college seeks to enroll.

Another source of financial aid is from state government, awarding more than $6 billion per year. All states offer grant and/or scholarship aid, most of which is need-based. However, more and more states are offering substantial merit-based aid programs. Most state programs award aid only to students attending college in their home state.

Other sources of financial aid include:

- Private agencies
- Foundations
- Corporations
- Clubs
- Fraternal and service organizations
- Civic associations
- Unions
- Religious groups that award grants, scholarships, and low-interest loans
- Employers that provide tuition reimbursement benefits for employees and their children

More information about these different sources of aid is available from high school guidance offices, public libraries, college financial aid offices, directly from the sponsoring organizations, and on the Web at www.finaid.org.

HOW NEED-BASED FINANCIAL AID IS AWARDED

When you apply for aid, your family's financial situation is analyzed using a government-approved formula called the Federal Methodology. This formula looks at five items:

1. Demographic information of the family.
2. Income of the parents.
3. Assets of the parents.
4. Income of the student.
5. Assets of the student.

This analysis determines the amount you and your family are expected to contribute toward your college expenses, called your Expected Family Contribution or EFC. If the EFC is equal to or more than the cost of attendance at a particular college, then you do not demonstrate financial need. However, even if you don't have financial need, you may still qualify for aid, as there are grants, scholarships, and loan programs that are not need-based.

If the cost of your education is greater than your EFC, then you do demonstrate financial need and qualify for assistance. The amount of your financial need that can be met varies from school to school. Some are able to meet your full need, while others can only cover a certain percentage of need. Here's the formula:

Cost of Attendance

– Expected Family Contribution

= Financial Need

The EFC remains constant, but your need will vary according to the costs of attendance at a particular college. In general, the higher the tuition and fees at a particular college, the higher the cost of attendance will be. Expenses for books and supplies, room and board, transportation, and other miscellaneous costs are included in the overall cost of attendance. It is important to remember that you do not have to be "needy" to qualify for financial aid. Many middle and upper-middle income families qualify for need-based financial aid.

APPLYING FOR FINANCIAL AID

Every student must complete the Free Application for Federal Student Aid (FAFSA) to be considered for financial aid. The FAFSA is available from your high school guidance office, many public libraries, colleges in your area, or directly from the U.S. Department of Education.

Students are encouraged to apply for federal student aid on the Web. The electronic version of the FAFSA can be accessed at http:www.fafsa.ed.gov. Both the student and at least one parent must apply for a federal pin number at http://www.pin.ed.gov. The pin number serves as your electronic signature when applying for aid on the Web.

To award their own funds, some colleges require an additional application, the Financial Aid PROFILE® form. The PROFILE asks supplemental questions that some colleges and awarding agencies feel provide a more accurate assessment of the family's ability to pay for college. It is up to the college to decide whether it will use only the FAFSA or both the FAFSA and the PROFILE. PROFILE applications are available from the high school guidance office and on the Web. Both the paper application and the Web site list those colleges and programs that require the PROFILE application.

If Every College You're Applying to for Fall 2006 Requires Just the FAFSA

. . . then it's pretty simple: Complete the FAFSA after January 1, 2006, being certain to send it in before any college-imposed deadlines. (You are not permitted to send in the 2006-07 FAFSA before January 1, 2006.) Most college FAFSA application deadlines are in February or early March. It is easier if you have all your financial records for the previous year available, but if that is not possible, you are strongly encouraged to use estimated figures.

After you send in your FAFSA, either with the paper application or electronically, you'll receive a Student Aid Report (SAR) that includes all of the information you reported and shows your EFC. If you provided an e-mail address, the SAR is sent to you electronically; otherwise, you will receive a paper copy in the mail. Be sure to review the SAR, checking to see if the information you reported is accurate. If you used estimated numbers to complete the FAFSA, you may have to resubmit the SAR with any corrections to the data. The college(s) you have designated on the FAFSA will receive the information you reported and will use that data to make their decision. In many instances, the colleges you've applied to will ask you to send copies of your and your parents' federal income tax returns for 2005, plus any other documents needed to verify the information you reported.

If a College Requires the PROFILE

Step 1: Register for the Financial Aid PROFILE in the fall of your senior year in high school.

You can apply for the PROFILE online at http://profileonline.collegeboard.com/index.jsp. Registration information with a list of the colleges that require the PROFILE are available in most high school guidance offices. There is a fee for using the Financial Aid PROFILE application ($23 for the first college and $18 for each additional college). You must pay for the service by credit card when you register. If you do not have a credit card, you will be billed.

Step 2: Fill out your customized Financial Aid PROFILE.

Once you register, your application will be immediately available online and will have questions which all students must complete, questions which must be completed by the student's parents (unless the student is independent and the colleges or programs selected do not require parent information), and *may* have supplemental questions needed by one or more of your schools or programs. If required, those will be found in Section Q of the application.

In addition to the PROFILE Application you complete online, you may also be required to complete a Business/Farm Supplement via traditional paper format. Completion of this form is not a part of the online process. If this form is required, instructions on how to download and print the supplemental form are provided. If your biological or adoptive parents are separated or divorced and your colleges and programs require it, your noncustodial parent may be asked to complete the Noncustodial POFILE.

Once you complete and submit your PROFILE Application, it will be processed and sent directly to your requested colleges and programs.

IF YOU DON'T QUALIFY FOR NEED-BASED AID

If you are not eligible for need-based aid, you can still find ways to lessen the burden on your parents.

Here are some suggestions:

- Search for merit scholarships. You can start at the initial stages of your application process. College merit awards are becoming increasingly important as more and more colleges award these grants to students they especially want to attract. As a result, applying to a college at which your qualifications put you at the top of the entering class may give you a larger merit award. Another source of aid to look for is private scholarships that are given for special skills and talents. Additional information can be found at Petersons.com and at www.finaid.org.

- Seek employment during the summer and the academic year. The student employment office at your college can help you locate a school-year job. Many colleges and local businesses have vacancies remaining after they have hired students who are receiving Federal Work-Study financial aid.

- Borrow through the Unsubsidized Stafford Loan programs. These are open to all students. The terms and conditions are similar to the subsidized loans. The biggest difference is that the borrower is responsible for the interest while still in college, although most lenders permit students to delay paying the interest right away and add the accrued interest to the total amount owed. You must file the FAFSA to be considered.

- After you've secured what you can through scholarships, working, and borrowing, your parents will be expected to meet their share of the college bill (the Expected Family Contribution). Many colleges offer monthly payment plans that spread the cost over the academic year. If the monthly payments are too high, parents can borrow through the Federal Parent Loan for Undergraduate Students (PLUS program), through one of the many private education loan programs available, or through home equity loans and lines of credit. Families seeking assistance in financing college expenses should inquire at the financial aid office about what programs are available at the college. Some families seek the advice of professional financial advisers and tax consultants.

HOW IS YOUR EXPECTED FAMILY CONTRIBUTION CALCULATED?

The chart on the next page makes the following assumptions:

- two parent family where age of older parent is 45
- lower income families (under $30,000) will file the 1040A or 1040EZ tax form
- student income is less than $2300
- there are no student assets
- there is only one family member attending college

All figures are estimates and may vary when the complete FAFSA or PROFILE application is submitted.

Approximate Expected Family Contribution

ASSETS / FAMILY SIZE	INCOME BEFORE TAXES								
	$20,000	30,000	40,000	50,000	60,000	70,000	80,000	90,000	100,000
$ 20,000									
3	$ 0	1,180	2,850	5,000	8,100	10,000	13,350	16,700	20,300
4	0	300	1,950	3,750	6,300	8,100	11,500	14,800	18,400
5	0	0	1,100	2,750	4,900	6,400	9,600	13,000	16,600
6	0	0	150	1,800	3,600	4,800	7,600	11,000	14,600
$ 30,000									
3	$ 0	1,180	2,850	5,000	8,100	10,000	13,350	16,700	20,300
4	0	300	1,950	3,750	6,300	8,100	11,500	14,800	18,400
5	0	0	1,100	2,750	4,900	6,400	9,600	13,000	16,600
6	0	0	150	1,800	3,600	4,800	7,600	11,000	14,600
$ 40,000									
3	$ 0	1,180	2,850	5,000	8,600	10,500	13,850	17,200	20,800
4	0	300	1,950	3,750	6,800	8,500	1,200	15,300	18,900
5	0	0	1,100	2,750	5,400	6,900	10,100	13,500	17,100
6	0	0	150	1,800	4,100	5,300	8,100	11,500	15,100
$ 50,000									
3	$ 0	1,180	3,200	5,000	9,100	11,000	14,350	17,700	21,300
4	0	300	2,260	3,750	7,300	9,100	12,500	15,800	19,400
5	0	0	1,400	2,750	5,900	7,400	10,600	14,000	17,600
6	0	0	480	1,800	4,600	5,800	8,600	12,000	15,600
$ 60,000									
3	$ 0	1,180	3,500	6,500	9,600	11,500	14,850	18,200	21,800
4	0	300	2,500	5,250	7,800	9,600	13,000	15,300	19,900
5	0	0	1,700	4,250	6,400	7,900	11,100	14,500	18,100
6	0	0	750	3,300	5,100	6,300	9,200	12,500	16,100
$ 80,000									
3	$ 0	1,180	4,200	7,500	10,600	12,500	15,850	19,200	22,800
4	0	300	3,100	6,250	8,800	10,600	14,000	17,300	20,900
5	0	0	2,200	5,250	7,400	8,900	12,100	15,500	19,100
6	0	0	1,250	4,300	6,100	7,300	10,200	13,500	17,100
$ 100,000									
3	$ 0	1,180	5,000	8,500	11,600	13,500	16,850	20,200	23,800
4	0	300	3,700	7,250	9,800	11,600	15,000	18,300	21,900
5	0	0	2,700	6,250	8,400	9,900	13,100	16,500	20,100
6	0	0	1,800	5,300	7,100	8,300	11,200	14,500	18,100
$ 120,000									
3	$ 0	1,180	5,850	9,500	12,600	14,500	17,850	21,200	24,800
4	0	300	4,400	8,250	10,800	12,600	16,000	19,300	22,900
5	0	0	3,350	7,250	9,400	10,900	14,100	17,500	21,100
6	0	0	2,300	6,300	8,100	9,300	12,200	15,500	19,100
$ 140,000									
3	$ 0	1,180	6,800	10,500	13,600	15,500	18,850	22,200	24,800
4	0	300	5,200	9,250	11,800	13,600	17,000	20,300	23,900
5	0	0	4,000	8,250	10,400	11,900	15,100	18,500	22,100
6	0	0	2,875	7,300	9,100	10,300	13,200	16,500	20,100

Financial Aid Programs for Schools in New York

Each state government has established one or more state-administered financial aid programs for qualified students. The state programs may be restricted to legal residents of the state, or they also may be available to out-of-state students who are attending public or private colleges or universities within the state. In addition, other qualifications may apply.

The programs are described below in alphabetical order, along with information about how to determine eligibility and how to apply. The information refers to awards for 2004–05, unless otherwise stated. Students should write to the address given for each program to request that award details for 2005–06 be sent to them as soon as they are available.

Department of Education Scholarship for Programs in China. Scholarships offered to students who are pursuing Chinese language programs in China. Must be a U.S. citizen enrolled in a CIEE program. Students must have the equivalent of two years study in Chinese language documented. Deadlines are April 15 and November 15. For more details see Web site: http://www.ciee.org. *Academic Fields/Career Goals:* Education. *Award:* Scholarship for use in junior, senior, or graduate year; not renewable. *Award amount:* $500–$6000. *Number of awards:* 10–20. *Eligibility Requirements:* Applicant must be enrolled or expecting to enroll full-time at a four-year institution or university and must have an interest in foreign language. Applicant must have 3.0 GPA or higher. Available to U.S. citizens. *Application Requirements:* Application, essay, financial need analysis, references, transcript. *Deadline:* varies. **Contact:** Scholarship Committee, Council for International Educational Exchange, 7 Custom House Street, 3rd Floor, Portland, ME 04101. *E-mail:* scholarships@ciee.org. *Web site:* www.ciee.org/study.

New York Aid for Part-Time Study (APTS). Renewable scholarship provides tuition assistance to part-time students who are New York residents attending New York accredited institutions. Deadlines and award amounts vary. Must be U.S. citizen. *Award:* Grant for use in freshman, sophomore, junior, or senior year; renewable. *Award amount:* up to $2000. *Number of awards:* varies. *Eligibility Requirements:* Applicant must be enrolled or expecting to enroll part-time at a two-year or four-year institution; resident of New York and studying in New York. Available to U.S. citizens. *Application Requirements:* Application. **Contact:** Student Information, New York State Higher Education Services Corporation, 99 Washington Avenue, Room 1320, Albany, NY 12255. *Phone:* 518-473-3887. *Fax:* 518-474-2839. *Web site:* www.hesc.org.

New York Educational Opportunity Program (EOP). Renewable award for New York resident attending New York college/university for undergraduate study. For educationally and economically disadvantaged students; includes educational assistance such as tutoring. Contact prospective college for information. *Award:* Scholarship for use in freshman, sophomore, junior, or senior year; renewable. *Award amount:* varies. *Number of awards:* varies. *Eligibility Requirements:* Applicant must be enrolled or expecting to enroll full-time at a two-year or four-year institution or university; resident of New York and studying in New York. Available to U.S. citizens. *Application Requirements:* Application, financial need analysis, transcript. **Contact:** Student Information, New York State Higher Education Services Corporation, 99 Washington Avenue, Room 1320, Albany, NY 12255. *Web site:* www.hesc.org.

New York Lottery Leaders of Tomorrow (Lot) Scholarship. The goal of this program is to reinforce the lottery's education mission by awarding four-year scholarships, $1000 per year for up to four years. One scholarship is available to every New York high school, public or private, that awards a high school diploma. *Award:* Scholarship for use in freshman, sophomore, junior, or senior year; renewable. *Award amount:* $1000. *Number of awards:* varies. *Eligibility Requirements:* Applicant must be high school student; planning to enroll or expecting to enroll full-time at a two-year, four-year, or technical institution or university; resident of New York and studying in New York. Applicant must have 3.0 GPA or higher. Available to U.S. citizens. *Application Requirements:* Application, essay, transcript. *Deadline:* varies. **Contact:** Betsey Morgan, Program Coordinator, CASDA-LOT (Capital Area School Development Association), The University at Albany East Campus, One University Place—A-409, Rensselaer, NY 12144-3456. *E-mail:* casdalot@uamail.albany.edu. *Phone:* 518-525-2788. *Fax:* 518-525-2797. *Web site:* www.nylottery.org/lot.

New York State Aid to Native Americans. Award for enrolled members of a New York State tribe and their children who are attending or planning to attend a New York State college and who are New York State residents. Award for full-time-students up to $1550 annually; part-time awards approximately $65 per credit hour. *Award:* Scholarship for use in freshman, sophomore, junior, or senior year; not renewable. *Award amount:* up to $1550. *Number of awards:* varies. *Eligibility Requirements:* Applicant must be American Indian/Alaska Native; enrolled or expecting to enroll full or part-time at a two-year, four-year, or technical institution or university; resident of New York and studying in New York. *Application Requirements:* Application. *Deadline:* July 15. **Contact:** Native American Education Unit, New York State Education Department, New York State Higher Education Services Corporation, EBA Room 374, Albany, NY 12234. *Phone:* 518-474-0537. *Web site:* www.hesc.org.

New York State Tuition Assistance Program. Award for New York state residents attending a New York postsecondary institution. Must be full-time student in approved program with tuition over $200 per year. Must show financial need and not be in default in any other state program. Renewable award of $500-$5000. *Award:* Grant for use in freshman, sophomore, junior, or senior year; renewable. *Award amount:* $500–$5000. *Number of awards:* 350,000–360,000. *Eligibility Requirements:* Applicant must be enrolled or expecting to enroll full-time at a two-year or four-year institution or university; resident of New York and studying in New York. *Application Requirements:* Application, financial need analysis. *Deadline:* May 1. **Contact:** Student Information, New York State Higher Education Services Corporation, 99 Washington Avenue, Room 1320, Albany, NY 12255. *Web site:* www.hesc.org.

New York Vietnam Veterans Tuition Awards. Scholarship for veterans who served in Vietnam. Must be a New York resident attending a New York institution. Renewable award of $500-$1000. Deadline: May 1. Must establish eligibility by September 1. *Award:* Scholarship for use in freshman, sophomore, junior, or senior year; renewable. *Award amount:* $500–$1000. *Number of awards:* varies. *Eligibility Requirements:* Applicant must be enrolled or expecting to enroll full or part-time at a two-year, four-year, or technical institution or university; resident of New York and studying in New York. Applicant must have served in the Air Force, Army, Marine Corp, or Navy. *Application Requirements:* Application, financial need analysis. *Deadline:* May 1. **Contact:** Student Information, New York State Higher Education Services Corporation, 99 Washington Avenue, Room 1320, Albany, NY 12255. *Web site:* www.hesc.org.

Regents Award for Child of Veteran. Award for students whose parent, as a result of service in U.S. Armed Forces during war or national emergency, died; suffered a 40% or more disability; or is classified as missing in action or a prisoner of war. Veteran must be current New York State resident or have been so at time of death. Must be New York resident attending, or planning to attend, college in New York State. Must establish eligibility before applying for payment. *Award:* Scholarship for use in freshman, sophomore, junior, or senior year; not renewable. *Award amount:* $450. *Number of awards:* varies. *Eligibility Requirements:* Applicant must be enrolled or expecting to enroll full-time at a two-year or four-year institution or university; resident of New York and studying in New York. Available to U.S. citizens. Applicant or parent must meet one or more of the following requirements: general military experience; retired from active duty; disabled or killed as a result of military service; prisoner of war; or missing in action. *Application Requirements:* Application, proof of eligibility. *Deadline:* May 1. **Contact:** Student Information, New York State Higher Education Services Corporation, 99 Washington Avenue, Room 1320, Albany, NY 12255. *Web site:* www.hesc.org.

Regents Professional Opportunity Scholarship. Scholarship for New York residents beginning or already enrolled in an approved degree-bearing program of study in New York that leads to licensure in a particular profession. See the Web site for the list of eligible professions. Must be U.S. citizen or permanent resident. Award recipients must agree to practice upon licensure in their profession in New York for 12 months for each annual payment received. Priority given to economically disadvantaged members of minority groups underrepresented in the professions. *Academic Fields/Career Goals:* Accounting; Architecture; Dental Health/Services; Engineering/Technology; Health and Medical Sciences; Interior Design; Landscape Architecture; Law/Legal Services; Nursing; Pharmacy; Psychology; Social Services. *Award:* Scholarship

for use in freshman, sophomore, junior, senior, or graduate year. *Award amount:* $1000–$5000. *Number of awards:* 220. *Eligibility Requirements:* Applicant must be enrolled or expecting to enroll full-time at a two-year or four-year institution or university; resident of New York and studying in New York. Available to U.S. citizens. *Application Requirements:* *Deadline:* May 3. **Contact:** Lewis J. Hall, Coordinator, New York State Education Department, Room 1078 EBA, Albany, NY 12234. *Phone:* 518-486-1319. *Fax:* 518-486-5346. *Web site:* www.highered.nysed.gov.

Regents Professional Opportunity Scholarships. Award for New York State residents pursuing career in certain licensed professions. Must attend New York State college. Priority given to economically disadvantaged members of minority group underrepresented in chosen profession and graduates of SEEK, College Discovery, EOP, and HEOP. Must work in New York State in chosen profession one year for each annual payment. *Award:* Scholarship for use in freshman, sophomore, junior, senior, or graduate year; not renewable. *Award amount:* $1000–$5000. *Number of awards:* 220. *Eligibility Requirements:* Applicant must be enrolled or expecting to enroll full-time at a two-year or four-year institution or university; resident of New York and studying in New York. Available to U.S. citizens. *Application Requirements:* Application. *Deadline:* May 3. **Contact:** Scholarship Processing Unit-New York State Education Department, New York State Higher Education Services Corporation, EBA Room 1078, Albany, NY 12234. *Phone:* 518-486-1319. *Web site:* www.hesc.org.

Scholarship for Academic Excellence. Renewable award for New York residents. Scholarship winners must attend a college or university in New York. 2000 scholarships are for $1500 and 6000 are for $500. The selection criteria used are based on Regents test scores and rank in class. Must be U.S. citizen or permanent resident. *Award:* Scholarship for use in freshman, sophomore, junior, or senior year; renewable. *Award amount:* $500–$1500. *Number of awards:* up to 8000. *Eligibility Requirements:* Applicant must be high school student; planning to enroll or expecting to enroll full-time at a two-year or four-year institution or university; resident of New York and studying in New York. Applicant must have 3.5 GPA or higher. Available to U.S. citizens. *Application Requirements:* Application. *Deadline:* December 19. **Contact:** Lewis J. Hall, Coordinator, New York State Education Department, Room 1078 EBA, Albany, NY 12234. *Phone:* 518-486-1319. *Fax:* 518-486-5346. *Web site:* www.highered.nysed.gov.

Scholarships for Academic Excellence. Renewable awards of up to $1500 for academically outstanding New York State high school graduates planning to attend an approved postsecondary institution in New York State. For full-time study only. Contact high school guidance counselor to apply. *Award:* Scholarship for use in freshman, sophomore, junior, or senior year; renewable. *Award amount:* $500–$1500. *Number of awards:* 8000. *Eligibility Requirements:* Applicant must be high school student; planning to enroll or expecting to enroll full-time at a four-year institution or university; resident of New York and studying in New York. Available to U.S. citizens. *Application Requirements:* Application. *Deadline:* December 19. **Contact:** Student Information, New York State Higher Education Services Corporation, 99 Washington Avenue, Room 1320, Albany, NY 12255. *Web site:* www.hesc.org.

World Trade Center Memorial Scholarship. Renewable awards of up to the average cost of attendance at a State University of

New York four-year college. Available to the families and financial dependents of victims who died or were severely and permanently disabled as a result of the Sept. 11, 2001 terrorist attacks on the U.S. and the rescue and recovery efforts. *Award:* Scholarship for use in freshman, sophomore, junior, or senior year; renewable. *Award amount:* varies. *Number of awards:* varies. *Eligibility Requirements:* Applicant must be enrolled or expecting to enroll full-time at a two-year or four-year institution or university; resident of New York and studying in New York. Available to U.S. citizens. *Application Requirements:* Application. *Deadline:* May 1. **Contact:** HESC Scholarship Unit, New York State Higher Education Services Corporation, 99 Washington Avenue, Room 1320, Albany, NY 12255. *Phone:* 518-402-6494. *Web site:* www.hesc.org.

Searching for Four-Year Colleges Online

The Internet can be a great tool for gathering information about four-year colleges and universities. There are many worthwhile sites that are ready to help guide you through the various aspects of the selection process, including Peterson's College Bound Channel at www.petersons.com/ugchannel.

HOW PETERSON'S COLLEGE BOUND CHANNEL CAN HELP

Choosing a college involves a serious commitment of time and resources. Therefore, it is important to have the most up-to-date information about prospective schools at your fingertips. That is why Peterson's College Bound Channel is a great place to start your college search and selection process.

Find a College

Peterson's College Bound Channel is a comprehensive information resource that will help you make sense of the college admissions process. Peterson's College Bound Channel offers visitors enhanced search criteria and an easily navigable interface. The Channel is organized into various sections that make finding a program easy and fun. You can search for colleges based on name or location for starters, or do a detailed search on the following criteria:

- *Location*
- *Major*
- *Tuition*
- *Size*
- *Student/faculty ratio*
- *Average GPA*
- *Type of college*
- *Sports*
- *Religion*

Once you have found the school of your choice, simply click on it to get information about the institution, including majors, off-campus programs, costs, faculty, admission requirements, location, academic programs, academic facilities, athletics, student life, financial aid, student government, and application information and contacts.

E-mail the School

If, after looking at the information provided on Peterson's College Bound Channel, you still have questions, you can send an e-mail directly to the admissions department of the school. Just click on the "E-mail the School" button and send your message. In most instances, if you keep your questions short and to the point, you will receive an answer in no time at all.

School Web Site

For institutions that have provided information about their Web sites, simply click on the "School Web Site" button and you will be taken directly to that institution's Web page. Once you arrive at the school's Web site, look around and get a feel for the place. Often, schools offer virtual tours of the campus, complete with photos and commentary. If you have specific questions about the school, a visit to a school's Web site will often yield an answer.

Detailed Description

If the schools you are interested in have provided Peterson's with an **In-Depth Description,** you can do a keyword search on that description. Here, schools are given the opportunity to communicate unique features of their programs to prospective students.

Microsite

Several educational institutions provide students access to microsites, where more information about the types of resources and services offered can be found. In addition, students can take campus tours, apply for admissions, and explore academic majors.

Apply

The Apply link gives you the ability to directly apply to the school online.

Add to My List

The *My List* feature is designed to help you with your college planning. Here you can save the list of schools you're interested in, which you can then revisit at any time, access all the features of the site, and be reminded of important dates. You'll also be notified when new features are added to the site.

Get Recruited

HERE'S your chance to stop looking for colleges and let them find you with CollegesWantYou[SM] (www. collegeswantyou.com), the new approach to the search and selection process. Unlike other college search and selection tools, CollegesWantYou[SM] allows you to enter information on your preferences, test scores, and extracurricular activities into the online form, and before you know it, colleges that meet your specifications will be in touch with you. Registration is free, and all you need to do is complete a short profile indicating your preferences and then sit back and wait as colleges contact you directly!

Write Admissions Essays

This year, 500,000 college applicants will write 500,000 different admissions essays. Half will be rejected by their first-choice school, while only 11 percent will gain admission to the nation's most selective colleges. With acceptance rates at all-time lows, setting yourself apart requires more than just blockbuster SAT scores and impeccable transcripts-it requires the perfect application essay. Named "the world's premier application essay editing service" by the New York Times Learning Network and "one of the best essay services on the Internet" by the *Washington Post*, EssayEdge (www.essayedge.com) has helped more applicants write successful personal statements than any other company in the world. Learn more about EssayEdge and how it can give you an edge over hundreds of applicants with comparable academic credentials.

Practice for Your Test

At Thomson Peterson's, we understand that the college admissions process can be very stressful. With the stakes so high and the competition getting tighter every year, it's easy to feel like the process is out of your control. Fortunately, preparing for college admissions tests, like the SAT, ACT, and PSAT, helps you exert some control over the options you will have available to you. You can visit Peterson's Test Prep Channel (www.petersonstestprep.com) to learn more about how Thomson Peterson's can help you maximize your scores—and your options.

USE THE TOOLS TO YOUR ADVANTAGE

Choosing a college is an involved and complicated process. The tools available to you on www.petersons.com/ugchannel can help you to be more productive in this process. So, what are you waiting for? Fire up your computer; your future alma mater may be just a click away!

How to Use This Guide

This article provides an outline of the profile format, describing the items covered. All college information presented was supplied to Thomson Peterson's by the colleges themselves. Any item that does not apply to a particular college or for which no current information was supplied may be omitted from that college's profile. Colleges that were unable to supply usable data in time for publication are listed by name and, if available, address.

PROFILES OF COLLEGES IN NEW YORK

This section presents pertinent factual and statistical data for each college in a standard format for easy comparison.

General Information

The first paragraph gives a brief introduction to the college, covering the following elements.

Type of student body: The categories are *men's* (100 percent of the student body), *primarily men's*, *women's* (100 percent of the student body), *primarily women's*, and *coed*. A college may also be designated as coordinate with another institution, indicating that there are separate colleges or campuses for men and women, but facilities, courses, and institutional governance are shared.

Institutional control: A *public* college receives its funding wholly or primarily from the federal, state, and/or local government. The term *private* indicates an independent, nonprofit institution, that is, one whose funding comes primarily from private sources and tuition. This category includes independent, religious colleges, which may also specify a particular religious denomination or church affiliation. Profit-making institutions are designated as *proprietary*.

Institutional type: A *two-year college* awards associate degrees and/or offers the first two years of a bachelor's degree program. A *primarily two-year college* awards bachelor's degrees, but the vast majority of students are enrolled in two-year programs. A *four-year college* awards bachelor's degrees and may also award associate degrees, but it does not offer graduate (postbachelor's) degree programs. A *five-year college* offers a five-year bachelor's program in a professional field such as architecture or pharmacy but does not award graduate degrees. An *upper-level institution* awards bachelor's degrees, but entering students must have at least two years of previous college-level credit; it may also offer graduate degree programs. A *comprehensive institution* awards bachelor's degrees and may also award associate degrees; graduate degree programs are offered primarily at the master's, specialist's, or professional level, although one or two doctoral programs may also be offered. A *university* offers four years of undergraduate work plus graduate degrees through the doctorate in more than two academic and/or professional fields.

Founding date: This is the year the college came into existence or was chartered, reflecting the period during which it has existed as an educational institution, regardless of subsequent mergers or other organizational changes.

Degree levels: An *associate* degree program may consist of either a college-transfer program, equivalent to the first two years of a bachelor's degree, or a one- to three-year terminal program that provides training for a specific occupation. A *bachelor's* degree program represents a three- to five-year liberal arts, science, professional, or preprofessional program. A *master's* degree is the first graduate degree in the liberal arts and sciences and certain professional fields and usually requires one to two years of full-time study. A *doctoral* degree is the highest degree awarded in research-oriented academic disciplines and usually requires from three to six years of full-time graduate study; the *first professional* degrees in such fields as law and medicine are also at the doctoral level. For colleges that award degrees in one field only, such as art or music, the field of specialization is indicated.

Campus setting: This indicates the size of the campus in acres or hectares and its location.

Academic Information

This paragraph contains information on the following items.

Faculty: The number of full-time and part-time faculty members as of fall 2004 is given, followed by the percentage of the full-time faculty members who hold doctoral, first professional, or terminal degrees, and then the student-faculty ratio. (Not all colleges calculate the student-faculty ratio in the same way; Thomson Peterson's prints the ratio provided by the college.)

Library holdings: The numbers of books, serials, and audiovisual materials in the college's collections are listed.

Special programs: *Academic remediation for entering students* consists of instructional courses designed for students deficient in the general competencies necessary for a regular postsecondary curriculum and educational setting. *Services for LD students* include special help for learning-disabled students with resolvable difficulties, such as dyslexia. *Honors programs* are any special programs for very able students, offering the opportunity for educational enrichment, independent study, acceleration, or some combination of these. *Cooperative (co-op) education programs* are formal arrangements with off-campus employers, allowing students to combine work and study in order to gain degree-related experience, usually extending the time required to complete a degree. *Study abroad* is an arrangement by which a student completes part of the academic program studying in another country. A college may operate a campus abroad or it may have a cooperative agreement with other U.S. institutions or institutions in other countries. *Advanced placement* gives credit toward a degree awarded for acceptable scores on College Board Advanced Placement tests. *Accelerated degree programs* allow students to earn a bachelor's degree in three academic years. *Freshmen honors college* is a separate academic program for talented freshmen. *Tutorials* allow undergraduates to arrange for special in-depth academic assignments (not for remediation), working with faculty members one-on-one or in small groups. *English as a second language (ESL)* is a course of study designed specifically for students whose native language is not English. *Double major* consists of a program of study in which a student concurrently completes the requirements of two majors. *Independent study* consists of academic work, usually undertaken outside the regular classroom structure, chosen or designed by the student with departmental approval and instructor supervision. *Distance learning* consists of credit courses that can be accessed off campus via cable television, the Internet, satellite, videotapes, correspondence courses, or other media. *Self-designed major* is a program of study based on individual interests, designed by the student with the assistance of an adviser. *Summer session for credit* includes summer courses through which students may make up degree work or accelerate their program. *Part-time degree programs* offer students the ability to earn a degree through part-time enrollment in regular session (daytime) classes or evening, weekend, or summer classes. *External degree programs* are programs of study in which students earn credits toward a degree through a combination of independent study, college courses, proficiency examinations, and personal experience. External degree programs require minimal or no classroom attendance. *Adult/ continuing education programs* are courses offered for nontraditional students who are currently working or are returning to formal education. *Internships* are any short-term, supervised work experience, usually related to a student's major field, for which the student earns academic credit. The work can be full- or part-time, on or off campus, paid or unpaid. *Off-campus study* is a formal arrangement with one or more domestic institutions under which students may take courses at the other institution(s) for credit.

Most popular majors: The most popular field or fields of study at the college, in terms of the number of undergraduate degrees conferred in 2004, are listed.

Student Body Statistics

Enrollment: The total number of students, undergraduates, and freshmen (or entering students for an upper-level institution) enrolled in degree programs as of fall 2004 are given.

With reference to the undergraduate enrollment for fall 2004, the percentages of women and men and the number of states and countries from which students hail are listed. The following percentages are also provided: in-state students, international students, and the percentage of last year's graduating class who went on to graduate and professional schools.

Expenses

Costs are given in each profile according to the most up-to-date figures available from each college for the 2004–05 or 2005–06 academic year.

Annual expenses may be expressed as a comprehensive fee (includes full-time tuition, mandatory fees, and college room and board) or as separate figures for full-time tuition, fees, room and board, and/or room only. For public institutions where tuition differs according to residence, separate figures are given for area and/or state residents and for nonresidents. Part-time tuition and fees are expressed in terms of a per-unit rate (per credit, per semester hour, etc.) as specified by the college.

The tuition structure at some institutions is complex in that freshmen and sophomores may be charged a different rate from that for juniors and seniors; a professional or vocational division may have a different fee structure from the liberal arts division of the same institution; or part-time tuition may be prorated on a sliding scale according to the number of credit hours taken. In all of these cases, the average figures are given along with an explanation of the basis for the variable rate. For colleges that report that room and board costs vary according to the type of accommodation and meal plan, the average costs are given. The phrase *no college housing* indicates that the college does not own or operate any housing facilities for its undergraduate students.

Financial Aid

This paragraph contains information on the following items.

Forms of financial aid: The categories of college-administered aid available to undergraduates are listed. College-administered means that the college itself determines the recipient and amount of each award. The types of aid covered are non-need scholarships, need-based scholarships, athletic grants, and part-time jobs.

Financial aid: This item pertains to undergraduates who enrolled full-time in a four-year college in 2003 or 2004. The figures given are the dollar amount of the average financial aid package, including scholarships, grants, loans, and part-time jobs, received by such undergraduates.

Financial aid application deadline: This deadline may be given as a specific date, as continuous processing up to a specific date or until all available aid has been awarded, or as a priority date rather than a strict deadline, meaning that students are encouraged to apply by that date in order to have the best chance of obtaining aid.

Freshman Admission

The supporting data that a student must submit when applying for freshman admission are grouped into three categories: *required for all*, *recommended*, and *required for some*. They may include an essay, a high school transcript, letters of recommendation, an interview on campus or with local alumni, standardized test scores, and, for certain types of schools or programs, special requirements such as a musical audition or an art portfolio.

The most commonly required standardized tests are the ACT Assessment and the College Board's SAT and SAT Subject Tests. TOEFL (Test of English as a Foreign Language) is for international students whose native language is not English.

The application deadline for admission is given as either a specific date or *rolling*. Rolling means that applications are processed as they are received, and qualified students are accepted as long as there are openings. The application deadline for out-of-state students is indicated if it differs from the date for state residents. *Early decision* and *early action* deadlines are also given when applicable. Early decision is a program whereby students may apply early, are notified of acceptance or rejection well in advance of the usual notification date, and agree to accept an offer of admission, the assumption being that only one early application has been made. Early action is the same as early decision except that applicants are not obligated to accept an offer of admission.

Transfer Admission

This paragraph gives the application requirements and application deadline for a student applying for admission as a transfer from another institution. In addition to the requirements previously listed for freshman applicants, requirements for transfers may also include a college transcript and a minimum college grade point average (expressed as a number on a scale of 0 to 4.0, where 4.0 equals A, 3.0 equals B, etc.). The name of the person to contact for

additional transfer information is also given if it is different from the person listed in **For Further Information**.

Transfer Associate Degree Program Admission

This paragraph may be substituted for the **Freshman Admission** paragraph for two-year colleges that offer a college transfer program. The categories and requirements are listed in the same way as in the **Freshman Admission** paragraph.

Terminal Associate Degree Program Admission

This paragraph may also be substituted for the **Freshman Admission** paragraph for two-year colleges. It contains the requirements for admission to a terminal program that provides specific occupational training. The format for this paragraph also follows that of the **Freshman Admission**.

Entrance Difficulty

This paragraph contains the college's own assessment of its *entrance difficulty level*, including notation of an *open admission policy* where applicable. Open admission means that virtually all applicants are accepted without regard to standardized test scores, grade average, or class rank. A college may indicate that open admission is limited to a certain category of applicants, such as state residents, or does not apply to certain selective programs, often those in the health professions.

The five levels of entrance difficulty are: *most difficult*, *very difficult*, *moderately difficult*, *minimally difficult*, and *noncompetitive*.

The final item in this paragraph is the percentage of applicants accepted for the fall 2004 freshman (or entering) class.

For Further Information

The name, title, and mailing address of the person to contact for more information on application and admission procedures are given at the end of the profile. A telephone number, fax number, e-mail address, and Web site are also included in this paragraph for profiles that do not contain this information in the paragraph on interviews and campus visits.

SPECIAL MESSAGE TO STUDENTS

In addition, a number of college admissions office staff members, as part of a major information-dissemination effort, have supplemented their **Profile** with special descriptive information on four topics of particular interest to students.

This section appears only for those colleges that submitted supplementary information and covers the following:

Social Life: This paragraph conveys a feeling for life on campus by addressing such questions as: What are the most popular activities? Are there active fraternities and sororities? What is the role of student government? Do most students live on campus or commute? Does the college have a religious orientation?

Academic Highlights: This paragraph describes some of the special features and characteristics of the college's academic program, such as special degree programs and opportunities for study abroad or internships.

Interviews and Campus Visits: Colleges that conduct on-campus admission interviews describe the importance of an interview in their admission process and what they try to learn about a student through the interview. For those colleges that do not interview applicants individually, there is information on how a student interested in the college can visit the campus to meet administrators, faculty members, and currently enrolled students as well as on what the prospective applicant should try to accomplish through such a visit. This paragraph may also include a list of the most noteworthy places or things to see during a campus visit and the location, telephone number (including toll-free numbers if available), and business hours of the office to contact for information about appointments and campus visits. Also included, when available, is travel information, specifically the nearest commercial airport and the nearest interstate highway, with the appropriate exit.

IN-DEPTH DESCRIPTIONS OF COLLEGES IN NEW YORK

Two-page narrative descriptions appear in this section, providing an inside look at colleges and universities, shifting the focus to a variety of other factors, some of them intangible, that should also be considered. The descriptions presented in this section provide a wealth of statistics that are crucial components in the college decision-making equation—components such as tuition, financial aid, and major fields of study. Prepared exclusively by college officials, the descriptions are designed to help give students a better sense of the individuality of each institution, in terms that include campus environment, student activities, and lifestyle. Such quality-of-life intangibles can be the deciding factors in the college selection process. The absence from this section of any college or university does not constitute an editorial decision on the part of Thomson Peterson's. In essence, this section is an open forum for colleges and universities, on a voluntary basis, to communicate their particular message to prospective college students. The colleges included have paid a fee to Thomson Peterson's to provide this information. The descriptions are edited to provide a consistent format across entries for your ease of comparison and are presented alphabetically by the official name of the institution.

PROFILES AND IN-DEPTH DESCRIPTIONS OF OTHER COLLEGES TO CONSIDER

Do you know that schools sometimes target specific areas of the country for student recruitment, even if those states are not part of a specific region? In this section, you'll find **Profiles** and **In-Depth Descriptions** of schools outside of New York looking to recruit students like you. The format of both the **Profiles** and the **In-Depth Descriptions** in this section matches the format in the previous sections.

INDEXES

Majors and Degrees

This index lists hundreds of undergraduate major fields of study that are currently offered most widely. The majors appear in alphabetical order, each followed by an alphabetical list of the colleges that report offering a program in that field and the degree levels (*A* for associate, *B* for bachelor's) available. The majors represented here are based on the National Center for Education Statistics (NCES) 2000 Classification of Instructional Programs (CIP). The CIP is a taxonomic coding scheme that contains titles and descriptions of instructional programs, primarily at the postsecondary level. CIP was originally developed to facilitate NCES's collection and reporting of postsecondary degree completions, by major field of study, using standard classifications that capture the majority of program activity. The CIP is now the accepted federal government statistical standard for classifying instructional programs. However, although the term "major" is used in this guide, some colleges may use other terms, such as "concentration," "program of study," or "field."

Athletic Programs and Scholarships

This index lists the colleges that report offering intercollegiate athletic programs, listed alphabetically. An *M* or *W* following the college name indicates that the sport is offered for men or women, respectively. An *s* in parentheses following an *M* or *W* indicates that athletic scholarships (or grants-in-aid) are offered by the college for men or women, respectively, in that sport.

ROTC Programs

This index lists the colleges that report offering Reserve Officers' Training Corps programs in one or more branches of the armed services, as indicated by letter codes following the college name: *A* for Army, *N* for Navy, and *AF* for Air Force. A *c* in parentheses following the branch letter code indicates that the program is offered through a cooperative arrangement on another college's campus.

Alphabetical Listing of Colleges and Universities

This index gives the page locations of various entries for all the colleges and universities in this book. The page numbers for the **Profiles** are printed in regular type, those for **Profiles** with **Special Messages** in *italic* type, and those for **In-Depth Descriptions** in **boldface** type. When there is more than one number in **boldface** type, it indicates that the institution has more than one **In-Depth Description**.

DATA COLLECTION PROCEDURES

The data contained in the **Profiles** and **Indexes** were researched between fall 2004 and spring 2005 through *Thomson Peterson's Annual Survey of Undergraduate Institutions* and *Thomson Peterson's Annual Survey of Undergraduate Financial Aid*. Questionnaires were sent to the more than 2,000 colleges and universities that met the outlined inclusion criteria. All data included in this edition have been submitted by officials (usually admissions and financial aid officers, registrars, or institutional research personnel) at the colleges. In addition, many of the institutions that submitted data were contacted directly by the Thomson Peterson's research staff to verify unusual figures, resolve discrepancies, or obtain additional data. All usable information received in time for publication has been included. The omission of any particular item from an index or profile listing signifies that the information is either not applicable to that institution or not available. Because of Thomson Peterson's comprehensive editorial review and because all material comes directly from college officials, we believe that the information presented in this guide is accurate. You should check with a specific college or university at the time of application to verify such figures as tuition and fees, which may have changed since the publication of this volume.

CRITERIA FOR INCLUSION IN THIS BOOK

The term "four-year college" is the commonly used designation for institutions that grant the baccalaureate degree. Four years is the expected amount of time required to earn this degree, although some bachelor's degree programs may be completed in three years, others require five years, and part-time programs may take considerably longer. Upper-level institutions offer only the junior and senior years and accept only students with two years of college-level credit. Therefore, "four-year college" is a conventional term that accurately describes most of the institutions included in this guide, but it should not be taken literally in all cases.

To be included in this guide, an institution must have full accreditation or be a candidate for accreditation (preaccreditation) status by an institutional or specialized accrediting body recognized by the U.S. Department of Education or the Council for Higher Education Accreditation (CHEA). Institutional accrediting bodies, which review each institution as a whole, include the six regional associations of schools and colleges (Middle States, New England, North Central, Northwest, Southern, and Western), each of which is responsible for a specified portion of the United States and its territories. Other institutional accrediting bodies are national in scope and accredit specific kinds of institutions (e.g., Bible colleges, independent colleges, and rabbinical and Talmudic schools). Program registration by the New York State Board of Regents is considered to be the equivalent of institutional accreditation, since the board requires that all programs offered by an institution meet its standards before recognition is granted. A Canadian institution must be chartered and authorized to grant degrees by the provincial government, affiliated with a chartered institution, or accredited by a recognized U.S. accrediting body. This guide also includes institutions outside the United States that are accredited by these U.S. accrediting bodies. There are recognized specialized or professional accrediting bodies in more than forty different fields, each of which is authorized to accredit institutions or specific programs in its particular field. For specialized institutions that offer programs in one field only, we designate this to be the equivalent of institutional accreditation. A full explanation of the accrediting process and complete information on recognized, institutional (regional and national) and specialized accrediting bodies can be found online at www.chea.org or at www.ed.gov/admins/finaid/accred/index.html.

Profiles of Colleges in New York

New York

This map provides a general perspective on New York and shows the major metropolitan areas and its capital.

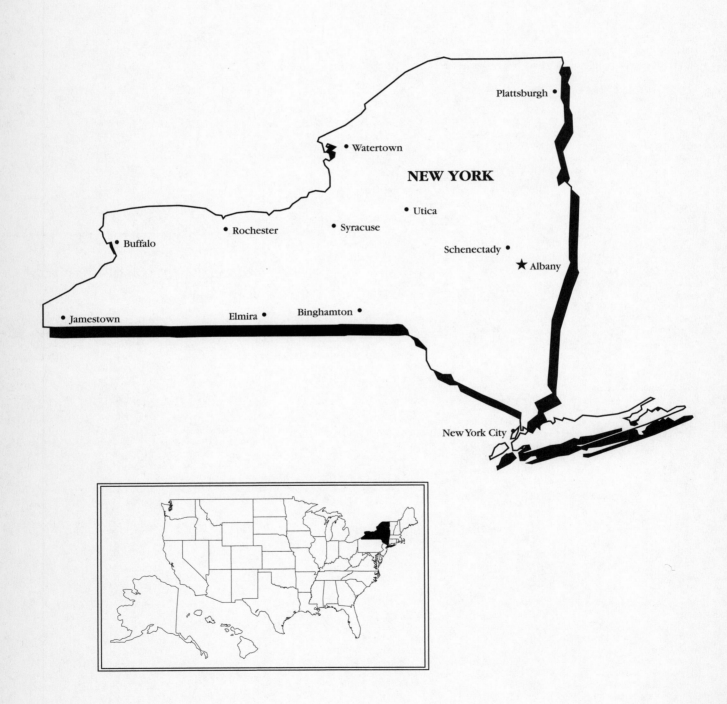

NEW YORK

Plattsburgh •

• Watertown

• Utica

• Rochester   • Syracuse

• Buffalo

Schenectady •

★ Albany

• Jamestown   Elmira •   Binghamton •

New York City

ADELPHI UNIVERSITY
Garden City, New York

SPONSOR
See Front Insert
for Details!

Adelphi is a coed, private university, founded in 1896, offering degrees at the associate, bachelor's, master's, and doctoral levels and post-master's and postbachelor's certificates. It has a 75-acre campus in Garden City near New York City.

Academic Information   The faculty has 751 members (32% full-time). The undergraduate student-faculty ratio is 14:1. The library holds 631,023 titles, 1,642 serial subscriptions, and 44,191 audiovisual materials. Special programs include services for learning-disabled students, an honors program, study abroad, advanced placement credit, accelerated degree programs, Freshman Honors College, double majors, independent study, distance learning, self-designed majors, summer session for credit, part-time degree programs (daytime, evenings, weekends, summer), and internships. The most frequently chosen baccalaureate fields are business/marketing, health professions and related sciences, social sciences and history.

Student Body Statistics   The student body totals 7,592, of whom 4,425 are undergraduates (815 freshmen). 71 percent are women and 29 percent are men. Students come from 38 states and territories and 47 other countries. 92 percent are from New York. 2.9 percent are international students. 41 percent of the 2004 graduating class went on to graduate and professional schools.

Expenses for 2004–05   *Application fee:* $35. *Comprehensive fee:* $27,200 includes full-time tuition ($17,700), mandatory fees ($1000), and college room and board ($8500). Full-time tuition and fees vary according to course level, location, and program. Room and board charges vary according to board plan and housing facility. *Part-time tuition:* $570 per credit. *Part-time mandatory fees:* $520 per year. Part-time tuition and fees vary according to course level, location, and program.

Financial Aid   Forms of aid include need-based and non-need-based scholarships, athletic grants, and part-time jobs. The average aided 2004–05 undergraduate received an aid package worth an estimated $13,450. The priority application deadline for financial aid is March 1.

Freshman Admission   Adelphi requires an essay, a high school transcript, 1 recommendation, SAT or ACT scores, and TOEFL scores for international students. A minimum 3.0 high school GPA and an interview are recommended. 2 recommendations, an interview, and auditions/portfolios for performing and fine arts are required for some. The application deadline for regular admission is rolling and for early action it is December 1.

Transfer Admission   The application deadline for admission is rolling.

Entrance Difficulty   Adelphi assesses its entrance difficulty level as moderately difficult; honors college is very difficult; general studies is minimally difficult. For the fall 2004 freshman class, 70 percent of the applicants were accepted.

SPECIAL MESSAGE TO STUDENTS

Social Life There's a campus full of life beyond the classroom at Adelphi. Resident and commuter students alike enjoy the array of excellent facilities, activities, and regularly scheduled events every semester. These events include theater and dance, sports and speakers, and more than seventy clubs and special interest groups, fraternities, sororities, academic societies, and community service organizations. In the sporting arena, Adelphi boasts both popular intramural and competitive intercollegiate sports programs. Adelphi University (AU) teams compete in eighteen Division I and II men's and women's intercollegiate sports, including soccer, tennis, basketball, lacrosse, baseball, softball, volleyball, golf, swimming, track, and cross-country running. Students can also join cheerleading and dance squads.

Academic Highlights AU offers more than forty programs of undergraduate and graduate study and is comprised of eight schools: the College of Arts and Sciences; the Schools of Business, Education, Social Work, and Nursing; University College; the Gordon F. Derner Institute of Psychological Studies; and the Honors College. Joint-degree programs are offered in computer science, dentistry, engineering, environmental studies, law, optometry, and physical therapy. Other specialized programs include the Learning Disabilities Program, the General Studies Program, and internships in selected disciplines.

Interviews and Campus Visits A personal interview is highly recommended as part of the admission process. Prospective students are encouraged to visit Adelphi's campus, interview with an admission counselor, and tour the campus. During the interview, counselors try to identify the abilities and goals of the applicant by inquiring about their involvement in cocurricular activities, areas of interest in and out of school, and any circumstances that may have affected their high school performance. It is also a time for applicants to have their questions about the University answered. Visitors are invited on a personal guided tour of the campus. Over the past few years, Adelphi has invested millions of dollars in campuswide improvements, renovating and expanding facilities, and upgrading technological infrastructure. Applicants can tour Swirbul Library, which contains a large collection of printed volumes, documents, audio/video and microformat items, an integrated online catalog and circulation system, and a comfortable state-of-the-art Information Commons. Other "must-sees" are Adelphi's Computing Center and specialized multimedia classrooms; the new Laser and Optics Center; the Olmsted Theatre, which houses Adelphi's acclaimed theater, dance, and technical theater/design programs; one of Adelphi's residence halls, all of which were recently renovated; and the Ruth S. Harley University Center—the central meeting place on campus—where students, faculty members, and staff members can browse in the bookstore, refresh themselves, and relax in one of the UC's lounges. A commuter student lounge provides special facilities, including lockers.For information about appointments and campus visits, students should call or visit the Office of University Admissions at 516-877-3050 or 800-ADELPHI (toll-free), Monday through Thursday, 8:30 a.m. to 7 p.m.; Friday, 8:30 a.m. to 5 p.m.; or selected Saturdays. Admissions is located at Adelphi's Garden City Campus, Levermore Hall, Room 114. The nearest commercial airport is John F. Kennedy International.

For Further Information Write to the Office of University Admissions, One South Avenue, Garden City, NY 11530. *Web site:* http://www.adelphi.edu.

ALBANY COLLEGE OF PHARMACY OF UNION UNIVERSITY
Albany, New York

Albany College of Pharmacy is a coed, private, comprehensive unit of Union University (Albany Law School, Albany Medical College, Union College, NY), founded in 1881, offering degrees at the bachelor's and first professional levels. It has a 1-acre campus in Albany.

Academic Information   The faculty has 69 members (91% full-time), 75% with terminal degrees. The undergraduate student-faculty ratio is 14:1. The library holds 16,124 titles, 3,576 serial subscriptions, and 319 audiovisual materials. Special programs include academic remediation, services for learning-disabled students, advanced placement credit, accelerated degree programs, summer session for credit, internships, and arrangement for off-campus study with Hudson-Mohawk Association of Colleges and Universities. The most frequently chosen baccalaureate field is health professions and related sciences.

Student Body Statistics   The student body totals 886, of whom 701 are undergraduates (206 freshmen). 61 percent are women and 39 percent are men. Students come from 10 states and territories and 7 other countries. 88 percent are from New York. 3.6 percent are international students. 10 percent of the 2004 graduating class went on to graduate and professional schools.

Expenses for 2004–05   *Application fee:* $50. *Comprehensive fee:* $23,900 includes full-time tuition ($17,300), mandatory fees ($600), and college room and board ($6000). Room and board charges vary according to board plan and housing facility.

Financial Aid   Forms of aid include need-based and non-need-based scholarships and part-time jobs. The priority application deadline for financial aid is February 1.

Freshman Admission   Albany College of Pharmacy requires an essay, a high school transcript, 2 recommendations, SAT or ACT scores, and TOEFL scores for international students. A minimum 2.0 high school GPA is recommended. An interview is required for some. The application deadline for regular admission is February 1 and for early decision it is November 1.

Entrance Difficulty Albany College of Pharmacy assesses its entrance difficulty level as moderately difficult; most difficult for transfers. For the fall 2004 freshman class, 64 percent of the applicants were accepted.

For Further Information Contact Mr. Robert Gould, Director of Admissions, Albany College of Pharmacy of Union University, 106 New Scotland Avenue, Albany, NY 12208-3425. *Telephone:* 518-445-7221 or 888-203-8010 (toll-free). *Fax:* 518-445-7202. *E-mail:* admissions@acp.edu. *Web site:* http://www.acp.edu/.

ALBERT A. LIST COLLEGE OF JEWISH STUDIES

See The Jewish Theological Seminary.

ALFRED UNIVERSITY

Alfred, New York

Alfred is a coed, private university, founded in 1836, offering degrees at the bachelor's, master's, and doctoral levels and post-master's certificates. It has a 232-acre campus in Alfred near Rochester.

Academic Information The faculty has 212 members (81% full-time), 73% with terminal degrees. The undergraduate student-faculty ratio is 12:1. The library holds 288,137 titles, 1,478 serial subscriptions, and 166,301 audiovisual materials. Special programs include academic remediation, services for learning-disabled students, an honors program, cooperative (work-study) education, study abroad, advanced placement credit, accelerated degree programs, double majors, independent study, self-designed majors, summer session for credit, part-time degree programs (daytime, summer), internships, and arrangement for off-campus study. The most frequently chosen baccalaureate fields are engineering/engineering technologies, business/marketing, visual/performing arts.
Student Body Statistics The student body totals 2,355, of whom 2,057 are undergraduates (506 freshmen). 50 percent are women and 50 percent are men. Students come from 38 states and territories and 32 other countries. 70 percent are from New York. 1.7 percent are international students. 24 percent of the 2004 graduating class went on to graduate and professional schools.
Expenses for 2004–05 *Application fee:* $40. *Comprehensive fee:* $29,434 includes full-time tuition ($19,250), mandatory fees ($810), and college room and board ($9374). *College room only:* $4884. Full-time tuition and fees vary according to program and student level. Room and board charges vary according to board plan and housing facility. *Part-time tuition:* $630 per credit hour. Part-time tuition varies according to course load and program.
Financial Aid Forms of aid include need-based and non-need-based scholarships and part-time jobs. The average aided 2004–05 undergraduate received an aid package worth an estimated $19,364. The application deadline for financial aid is continuous.
Freshman Admission Alfred requires an essay, a high school transcript, 1 recommendation, SAT or ACT scores, and TOEFL scores for international students. An interview is recommended. An interview and a portfolio are required for some. The application deadline for regular admission is February 1 and for early decision it is December 1.
Transfer Admission The application deadline for admission is August 1.
Entrance Difficulty Alfred assesses its entrance difficulty level as moderately difficult; very difficult for ceramic engineering, art and design programs. For the fall 2004 freshman class, 73 percent of the applicants were accepted.

For Further Information Contact Mr. Scott Hooker, Director of Admissions, Alfred University, Alumni Hall, Alfred, NY 14802-1205. *Telephone:* 607-871-2115 or 800-541-9229 (toll-free). *Fax:* 607-871-2198. *E-mail:* admwww@alfred.edu. *Web site:* http://www.alfred.edu/.

AMERICAN ACADEMY MCALLISTER INSTITUTE OF FUNERAL SERVICE

New York, New York

For Information Write to American Academy McAllister Institute of Funeral Service, New York, NY 10019-3602.

AMERICAN ACADEMY OF DRAMATIC ARTS

New York, New York

The Academy is a coed, private, two-year college, founded in 1884, offering degrees at the associate level.

Expenses for 2004–05 *Application fee:* $50. *Tuition:* $15,350 full-time.

For Further Information Contact Ms. Karen Higginbotham, Director of Admissions, American Academy of Dramatic Arts, 120 Madison Avenue, New York, NY 10016. *Telephone:* 800-463-8990 or 800-463-8990 (toll-free). *Fax:* 212-696-1284. *E-mail:* admissions-ny@aada.org. *Web site:* http://www.aada.org/.

ARNOLD & MARIE SCHWARTZ COLLEGE OF PHARMACY AND HEALTH SCIENCES

See Long Island University, Brooklyn Campus.

AUDREY COHEN COLLEGE

See Metropolitan College of New York.

BARD COLLEGE

Annandale-on-Hudson, New York

Bard is a coed, private, comprehensive institution, founded in 1860, offering degrees at the associate, bachelor's, master's, and doctoral levels. It has a 600-acre campus in Annandale-on-Hudson.

Academic Information The faculty has 208 members (62% full-time), 80% with terminal degrees. The undergraduate student-faculty ratio is 9:1. The library holds 350,000 titles, 15,000 serial subscriptions, and 3,200 audiovisual materials. Special programs include services for learning-disabled students, study abroad, advanced placement credit, accelerated degree programs, ESL programs, double majors, independent study, self-designed majors, part-time degree programs (daytime, evenings), adult/continuing education programs, internships, and arrangement for off-campus study with Vassar College, State University of New York at New Paltz. The most frequently chosen baccalaureate fields are social sciences and history, English, visual/performing arts.
Student Body Statistics The student body totals 1,726, of whom 1,484 are undergraduates (398 freshmen). 55 percent are women and 45 percent are men. Students come from 50 states and territories and 51 other countries. 30 percent are from New York. 5.5 percent are international students. 55 percent of the 2004 graduating class went on to graduate and professional schools.
Expenses for 2004–05 *Application fee:* $50. *One-time mandatory fee:* $510. *Comprehensive fee:* $40,160 includes full-time tuition ($29,910), mandatory fees ($832), and college room and board ($9418). *College room only:* $4464. *Part-time tuition:* $935 per credit. *Part-time mandatory fees:* $200 per term.
Financial Aid Forms of aid include need-based and non-need-based scholarships and part-time jobs. The average aided 2004–05 undergraduate received an aid package worth an estimated $23,991. The application deadline for financial aid is February 15 with a priority deadline of February 1.

Freshman Admission   Bard requires an essay, a high school transcript, 3 recommendations, and TOEFL scores for international students. A minimum 3.0 high school GPA, an interview, SAT or ACT scores, and SAT Subject Test scores are recommended. An interview is required for some. The application deadline for regular admission is January 15 and for early action it is November 1.
Transfer Admission   The application deadline for admission is March 15.
Entrance Difficulty   Bard assesses its entrance difficulty level as very difficult. For the fall 2004 freshman class, 36 percent of the applicants were accepted.

For Further Information   Contact Ms. Mary Inga Backlund, Director of Admissions, Bard College, PO Box 5000, 51 Ravine Road, Annandale-on-Hudson, NY 12504-5000. *Telephone:* 845-758-7472. *Fax:* 845-758-5208. *E-mail:* admission@bard.edu. *Web site:* http://www.bard.edu/.

BARNARD COLLEGE

New York, New York

Barnard is a women's, private, four-year college of Columbia University, founded in 1889, offering degrees at the bachelor's level. It has a 4-acre campus in New York.

Academic Information   The faculty has 296 members (62% full-time), 90% with terminal degrees. The student-faculty ratio is 10:1. The library holds 204,906 titles, 543 serial subscriptions, and 17,448 audiovisual materials. Special programs include services for learning-disabled students, an honors program, study abroad, advanced placement credit, accelerated degree programs, double majors, independent study, self-designed majors, internships, and arrangement for off-campus study with Manhattan School of Music, Jewish Theological Seminary of America, Juilliard School, Columbia University School of International and Public Affairs, Spelman College. The most frequently chosen baccalaureate fields are psychology, English, social sciences and history.
Student Body Statistics   The student body is made up of 2,287 undergraduates (553 freshmen). Students come from 50 states and territories and 40 other countries. 34 percent are from New York. 3.1 percent are international students. 24 percent of the 2004 graduating class went on to graduate and professional schools.
Expenses for 2004–05   *Application fee:* $45. *Comprehensive fee:* $39,140 includes full-time tuition ($27,064), mandatory fees ($1276), and college room and board ($10,800). *College room only:* $6566. Room and board charges vary according to board plan and housing facility. *Part-time tuition:* $902 per credit.
Financial Aid   Forms of aid include need-based scholarships and part-time jobs. The average aided 2003–04 undergraduate received an aid package worth $26,045. The application deadline for financial aid is February 1.
Freshman Admission   Barnard requires an essay, a high school transcript, 3 recommendations, SAT and SAT Subject Test or ACT scores, and TOEFL scores for international students. An interview, SAT or ACT scores, and SAT Subject Test scores are recommended. The application deadline for regular admission is January 1 and for early decision it is November 15.
Transfer Admission   The application deadline for admission is April 1.
Entrance Difficulty   Barnard assesses its entrance difficulty level as most difficult. For the fall 2004 freshman class, 27 percent of the applicants were accepted.

For Further Information   Contact Ms. Jennifer Gill Fondiller, Dean of Admissions, Barnard College, 3009 Broadway, New York, NY 10027. *Telephone:* 212-854-2014. *Fax:* 212-854-6220. *E-mail:* admissions@barnard.edu. *Web site:* http://www.barnard.edu/.

BEIS MEDRASH HEICHAL DOVID

Far Rockaway, New York

For Information   Write to Beis Medrash Heichal Dovid, Far Rockaway, NY 11691.

BERKELEY COLLEGE-NEW YORK CITY CAMPUS

New York, New York

Berkeley is a coed, proprietary, primarily two-year college, founded in 1936, offering degrees at the associate and bachelor's levels.

Academic Information   The faculty has 140 members (29% full-time). The student-faculty ratio is 26:1. The library holds 13,164 titles, 138 serial subscriptions, and 949 audiovisual materials. Special programs include academic remediation, cooperative (work-study) education, study abroad, advanced placement credit, ESL programs, distance learning, summer session for credit, part-time degree programs (daytime, evenings, weekends, summer), adult/continuing education programs, internships, and arrangement for off-campus study with Berkeley College, White Plains; Berkeley College, West Paterson. The most frequently chosen baccalaureate field is business/marketing.
Student Body Statistics   The student body is made up of 2,012 undergraduates (503 freshmen). 70 percent are women and 30 percent are men. Students come from 14 states and territories and 66 other countries. 91 percent are from New York. 12.7 percent are international students.
Expenses for 2005–06   *Application fee:* $40. *Tuition:* $16,200 full-time, $395 per credit part-time. *Mandatory fees:* $750 full-time, $75 per term part-time.
Financial Aid   Forms of aid include need-based scholarships and part-time jobs. The priority application deadline for financial aid is May 1.
Freshman Admission   Berkeley requires a high school transcript, SAT or ACT scores, and TOEFL scores for international students. An interview is recommended. The application deadline for regular admission is rolling.
Transfer Admission   The application deadline for admission is rolling.
Entrance Difficulty   Berkeley assesses its entrance difficulty level as minimally difficult. For the fall 2004 freshman class, 87 percent of the applicants were accepted.

For Further Information   Contact Mr. Stuart Siegman, Director, High School Admissions, Berkeley College-New York City Campus, 3 East 43rd Street, New York, NY 10017. *Telephone:* 212-986-4343 Ext. 125 or 800-446-5400 (toll-free). *Fax:* 212-818-1079. *E-mail:* info@berkeleycollege.edu. *Web site:* http://www.berkeleycollege.edu/.

BERKELEY COLLEGE-WESTCHESTER CAMPUS

White Plains, New York

Berkeley is a coed, proprietary, primarily two-year college, founded in 1945, offering degrees at the associate and bachelor's levels. It has a 10-acre campus in White Plains near New York City.

Academic Information   The faculty has 53 members (32% full-time). The student-faculty ratio is 22:1. The library holds 9,526 titles, 66 serial subscriptions, and 777 audiovisual materials. Special programs include academic remediation, services for learning-disabled students, cooperative (work-study) education, study abroad, advanced placement credit, ESL programs, distance learning, summer session for credit, part-time degree programs (daytime, evenings, weekends, summer), adult/continuing education programs, internships, and arrangement for off-campus study with Berkeley College, West Paterson; Berkeley College, New York. The most frequently chosen baccalaureate field is business/marketing.
Student Body Statistics   The student body is made up of 658 undergraduates (225 freshmen). 71 percent are women and 29 percent are men. Students come from 9 states and territories and 28 other countries. 86 percent are from New York. 4 percent are international students.
Expenses for 2005–06   *Application fee:* $40. *Tuition:* $16,200 full-time, $395 per credit part-time. *Mandatory fees:* $750 full-time, $75 per term part-time. *College room only:* $5850.
Financial Aid   Forms of aid include need-based scholarships and part-time jobs. The priority application deadline for financial aid is May 1.

Freshman Admission   Berkeley requires a high school transcript, SAT or ACT scores, and TOEFL scores for international students. An interview is recommended. The application deadline for regular admission is rolling.

Transfer Admission   The application deadline for admission is rolling.

Entrance Difficulty   Berkeley assesses its entrance difficulty level as minimally difficult. For the fall 2004 freshman class, 88 percent of the applicants were accepted.

For Further Information   Contact Mr. David Bertrone, Director of High School Admissions, Berkeley College-Westchester Campus, 99 Church Street, White Plains, NY 10601. *Telephone:* 914-694-1122 Ext. 3106 or 800-446-5400 (toll-free). *Fax:* 914-328-9469. *E-mail:* info@ berkeleycollege.edu. *Web site:* http://www.berkeleycollege.edu/.

BERNARD M. BARUCH COLLEGE OF THE CITY UNIVERSITY OF NEW YORK

New York, New York

Baruch College is a coed, public, comprehensive unit of City University of New York System, founded in 1919, offering degrees at the bachelor's, master's, and doctoral levels and post-master's certificates.

Academic Information   The faculty has 921 members (53% full-time), 65% with terminal degrees. The undergraduate student-faculty ratio is 17:1. The library holds 297,959 titles, 4,038 serial subscriptions, and 1,044 audiovisual materials. Special programs include services for learning-disabled students, an honors program, study abroad, advanced placement credit, accelerated degree programs, ESL programs, double majors, independent study, distance learning, self-designed majors, summer session for credit, part-time degree programs (daytime, evenings, weekends, summer), adult/continuing education programs, and internships. The most frequently chosen baccalaureate fields are business/marketing, computer/information sciences, liberal arts/general studies.

Student Body Statistics   The student body totals 15,537, of whom 12,734 are undergraduates (1,718 freshmen). 56 percent are women and 44 percent are men. Students come from 14 states and territories and 120 other countries. 97 percent are from New York. 9.9 percent are international students.

Expenses for 2005–06   *Application fee:* $70. *State resident tuition:* $4000 full-time, $170 per credit part-time. *Nonresident tuition:* $8640 full-time, $360 per credit part-time. *Mandatory fees:* $300 full-time, $75 per term part-time. Full-time tuition and fees vary according to class time and course load. Part-time tuition and fees vary according to class time and course load.

Financial Aid   Forms of aid include need-based and non-need-based scholarships and part-time jobs. The average aided 2004–05 undergraduate received an aid package worth an estimated $4930. The application deadline for financial aid is April 30 with a priority deadline of March 15.

Freshman Admission   Baruch College requires a high school transcript, a minimum 2.5 high school GPA, 16 academic units, SAT or ACT scores, and TOEFL scores for international students. Recommendations and an interview are required for some. The application deadline for regular admission is April 1; for early decision it is December 13; and for early action it is December 15.

Transfer Admission   The application deadline for admission is May 1.

Entrance Difficulty   Baruch College assesses its entrance difficulty level as very difficult; most difficult for finance computer information systems. For the fall 2004 freshman class, 36 percent of the applicants were accepted.

SPECIAL MESSAGE TO STUDENTS

Social Life Baruch's students benefit from all that a college in one of the world's greatest cities can offer. The College is totally integrated into its midtown Manhattan environs. Although Baruch is primarily a commuter school, its students enjoy a rich collegiate social life. In addition to the city's vast social and cultural resources, Baruch students have access to more than

100 clubs and organizations spanning a wide range of interests and activities—academic, professional, social, religious, cultural, and athletic. From theater to intercollegiate basketball to the radio station, there is something for everyone. Three separate student government organizations represent day-session undergraduates, evening-session undergraduates, and graduate students.

Academic Highlights Baruch College rewards academic excellence by awarding generous scholarships ranging from $16,000 to $20,000 ($4000 or $5000 per year for four years) to entering freshmen each year. Through the honors program, scholarship recipients and other exceptional Baruch students are able to pursue intensive work under the guidance of selected faculty members. Students may spend a semester or two at a university abroad through exchange programs in England, France, Germany, Israel, and Mexico. Closer to home, major speakers and performers from business, politics, and the arts visit the College each semester. Recent programs have featured entertainer and humanitarian, Harry Belafonte; business and government leaders, including Paul Volcker, Jack Welch, and Ralph Lauren; and literary luminaries Tony Kushner, Paul Auster, Edward Albee, and Philip Gourevitch.

Interviews and Campus Visits To learn more about Baruch College, its programs, and requirements for admission, prospective students are encouraged to make an appointment with an admissions counselor. Campus visits are available by appointment. While on a tour, students visit the Information and Technology Building, which houses the technologically advanced William and Anita Newman Library. The library, which seats 1,400, surrounds a six-story atrium. Connection to the burgeoning electronic highway (through CUNY+PLUS and the Internet) makes the world's information resources directly accessible to the Baruch community. Online information services include Dialog, Dow Jones News/Retrieval Service, and LexisNexis. The Baruch Computing and Technology Center (with more than 500 workstations), and the Conference Center also incorporate the latest technological advances. Directly across the street from the Information and Technology Building is the seventeen-floor "Vertical Campus," which opened in 2001. As the hub of the College, this innovative structure houses research facilities, high-technology classrooms, a three-level athletic and recreation center, a theater and recital hall, and other specialized facilities. For information about appointments and campus visits, students should call Undergraduate Admissions at 646-312-1400, Monday through Friday, 9 a.m. to 5 p.m. The office is located at 151 East 25 Street, Room 720. The nearest commercial airport is La Guardia.

For Further Information Write to Mr. James Murphy, Director of Undergraduate Admissions and Financial Aid, Baruch College of The City University of New York, One Bernard Baruch Way, Box H-0720, New York, NY 10010-5518. *E-mail:* admissions@baruch.cuny.edu. *Web site:* http://www.baruch.cuny.edu.

See page 98 for a narrative description.

BETH HAMEDRASH SHAAREI YOSHER INSTITUTE

Brooklyn, New York

For Information   Write to Beth HaMedrash Shaarei Yosher Institute, Brooklyn, NY 11204.

BETH HATALMUD RABBINICAL COLLEGE

Brooklyn, New York

For Information   Write to Beth Hatalmud Rabbinical College, Brooklyn, NY 11214.

BORICUA COLLEGE

New York, New York

Boricua College is a coed, private, comprehensive institution, founded in 1974, offering degrees at the associate, bachelor's, and master's levels.

Academic Information   The faculty has 116 members (44% full-time). The undergraduate student-faculty ratio is 20:1. The library holds 112,600 titles and 780 serial subscriptions. Special programs include an honors program, study abroad, accelerated degree programs, summer session for credit, adult/continuing education programs, and internships.

Student Body Statistics   The student body totals 1,520, of whom 1,468 are undergraduates. 25 percent of the 2004 graduating class went on to graduate and professional schools.

Expenses for 2004–05   *Application fee:* $25. *Tuition:* $7200 full-time. *Mandatory fees:* $100 full-time.

Financial Aid   Forms of aid include need-based scholarships and part-time jobs. The priority application deadline for financial aid is March 1.

Freshman Admission   Boricua College requires a high school transcript, 2 recommendations, an interview, proficiency in English and Spanish, and CAT. The application deadline for regular admission is rolling.

Transfer Admission   The application deadline for admission is rolling.

Entrance Difficulty   Boricua College assesses its entrance difficulty level as moderately difficult. For the fall 2004 freshman class, 47 percent of the applicants were accepted.

For Further Information   Contact Dr. Mercedes Alicea, Director of Registration and Assessment, Boricua College, 3755 Broadway, New York, NY 10032-1560. *Telephone:* 212-694-1000 Ext. 525. *Web site:* http://www.boricuacollege.edu/.

BRAMSON ORT COLLEGE

Forest Hills, New York

For Information   Write to Bramson ORT College, Forest Hills, NY 11375-4239.

BRIARCLIFFE COLLEGE

Bethpage, New York

Briarcliffe is a coed, proprietary, four-year college of Career Education Corporation, founded in 1966, offering degrees at the associate and bachelor's levels. It has an 18-acre campus in Bethpage near New York City.

Academic Information   The faculty has 191 members (20% full-time), 15% with terminal degrees. The student-faculty ratio is 16:1. The library holds 11,834 titles and 191 serial subscriptions. Special programs include academic remediation, services for learning-disabled students, cooperative (work-study) education, advanced placement credit, accelerated degree programs, independent study, distance learning, summer session for credit, part-time degree programs (daytime, evenings, weekends, summer), external degree programs, adult/continuing education programs, and internships. The most frequently chosen baccalaureate fields are business/marketing, visual/performing arts.

Student Body Statistics   The student body is made up of 3,227 undergraduates (843 freshmen). 52 percent are women and 48 percent are men. Students come from 10 states and territories and 7 other countries. 100 percent are from New York. 0.4 percent are international students.

Expenses for 2004–05   *Application fee:* $35. *Comprehensive fee:* $22,358 includes full-time tuition ($13,608), mandatory fees ($1400), and college room and board ($7350). Full-time tuition and fees vary according to course load. Room and board charges vary according to board plan. *Part-time tuition:* $567 per credit. *Part-time mandatory fees:* $375 per term. Part-time tuition and fees vary according to course load.

Financial Aid   Forms of aid include need-based scholarships and part-time jobs. The application deadline for financial aid is continuous.

Freshman Admission   Briarcliffe requires a high school transcript and TOEFL scores for international students. An interview and SAT and SAT Subject Test or ACT scores are recommended. The application deadline for regular admission is rolling.

Transfer Admission   The application deadline for admission is rolling.

Entrance Difficulty   Briarcliffe assesses its entrance difficulty level as moderately difficult. For the fall 2004 freshman class, 85 percent of the applicants were accepted.

For Further Information   Contact Ms. Theresa Donohue, Vice President of Marketing and Admissions, Briarcliffe College, Bethpage, NY 11714. *Telephone:* 516-918-3705 or 888-333-1150 (toll-free in-state). *Fax:* 516-470-6020. *E-mail:* info@bcl.edu. *Web site:* http://www.briarcliffe.edu/.

See page 100 for a narrative description.

BROOKLYN COLLEGE OF THE CITY UNIVERSITY OF NEW YORK

Brooklyn, New York

Brooklyn College is a coed, public, comprehensive unit of City University of New York System, founded in 1930, offering degrees at the bachelor's and master's levels and post-master's and postbachelor's certificates. It has a 26-acre campus in Brooklyn.

Academic Information   The faculty has 1,066 members (48% full-time), 63% with terminal degrees. The undergraduate student-faculty ratio is 15:1. The library holds 1 million titles, 13,500 serial subscriptions, and 21,731 audiovisual materials. Special programs include services for learning-disabled students, an honors program, study abroad, advanced placement credit, Freshman Honors College, ESL programs, double majors, independent study, distance learning, summer session for credit, part-time degree programs (daytime, evenings, weekends, summer), adult/continuing education programs, internships, and arrangement for off-campus study with other units of the City University of New York System. The most frequently chosen baccalaureate fields are business/marketing, computer/information sciences, education.

Student Body Statistics   The student body totals 15,384, of whom 11,172 are undergraduates (1,215 freshmen). 60 percent are women and 40 percent are men. Students come from 25 states and territories and 75 other countries. 99 percent are from New York. 6 percent are international students.

Expenses for 2004–05   *Application fee:* $50. *State resident tuition:* $4000 full-time, $170 per credit part-time. *Nonresident tuition:* $8640 full-time, $360 per credit part-time. *Mandatory fees:* $353 full-time, $139.05 per term part-time.

Financial Aid   Forms of aid include need-based and non-need-based scholarships and part-time jobs. The average aided 2003–04 undergraduate received an aid package worth $5400. The priority application deadline for financial aid is April 1.

Freshman Admission   Brooklyn College requires a high school transcript, a minimum 3.0 high school GPA, SAT or ACT scores, and TOEFL scores for international students. SAT Subject Test scores are recommended. An essay, recommendations, and an interview are required for some. The application deadline for regular admission is rolling.

Entrance Difficulty   Brooklyn College assesses its entrance difficulty level as moderately difficult; most difficult for Scholars Program, 8-year BA/MD, CUNY Honors Program. For the fall 2004 freshman class, 33 percent of the applicants were accepted.

For Further Information   Contact Ms. Marianne Booufall-Tynan, Director of Admissions, Brooklyn College of the City University of New York, 2900 Bedford Avenue, 1103 James Hall, Brooklyn, NY 11210-2889. *Telephone:* 718-951-5001. *Fax:* 718-951-4506. *E-mail:* admingry@brooklyn.cuny.edu. *Web site:* http://www.brooklyn.cuny.edu/.

BRYANT AND STRATTON COLLEGE, AMHERST CAMPUS

Clarence, New York

Bryant & Stratton is a coed, proprietary, primarily two-year college of Bryant and Stratton College, founded in 1977, offering degrees at the associate and bachelor's levels. It has a 12-acre campus in Clarence near Buffalo.

Academic Information The faculty has 38 members (21% full-time), 34% with terminal degrees. The library holds 4,500 titles, 25 serial subscriptions, and 150 audiovisual materials. Special programs include academic remediation, cooperative (work-study) education, advanced placement credit, double majors, independent study, distance learning, summer session for credit, part-time degree programs (daytime, evenings, summer), and internships.

Student Body Statistics The student body is made up of 341 undergraduates (66 freshmen). 71 percent are women and 29 percent are men.

Expenses for 2005–06 *Application fee:* $25. *One-time mandatory fee:* $25. *Tuition:* $10,920 full-time, $394 per credit part-time. *Mandatory fees:* $300 full-time, $100 per term part-time. Full-time tuition and fees vary according to class time, course load, and location. Part-time tuition and fees vary according to class time and course load.

Financial Aid Forms of aid include need-based scholarships and part-time jobs. The application deadline for financial aid is continuous.

Freshman Admission Bryant & Stratton requires a high school transcript, an interview, and TABE, CPAt or ACCUPLACER. SAT or ACT scores are recommended. An essay and an interview are required for some. The application deadline for regular admission is rolling.

Transfer Admission The application deadline for admission is rolling.

Entrance Difficulty Bryant & Stratton assesses its entrance difficulty level as minimally difficult. For the fall 2004 freshman class, 80 percent of the applicants were accepted.

For Further Information Contact Ms. Cathy Oddo, Dean of Students, Bryant and Stratton College, Amherst Campus, 40 Hazelwood Drive, Amherst, NY 14228. *Telephone:* 716-884-9120. *Fax:* 716-691-6716. *Web site:* http://www.bryantstratton.edu/.

BUFFALO STATE COLLEGE, STATE UNIVERSITY OF NEW YORK

Buffalo, New York

Buffalo State College, State University of New York is a coed, public, comprehensive institution, founded in 1867, offering degrees at the bachelor's and master's levels and post-master's certificates. It has a 115-acre campus in Buffalo.

Academic Information The faculty has 715 members (55% full-time), 56% with terminal degrees. The undergraduate student-faculty ratio is 17:1. The library holds 489,069 titles, 2,847 serial subscriptions, and 22,189 audiovisual materials. Special programs include academic remediation, services for learning-disabled students, an honors program, cooperative (work-study) education, study abroad, advanced placement credit, Freshman Honors College, ESL programs, double majors, independent study, distance learning, summer session for credit, part-time degree programs, adult/continuing education programs, internships, and arrangement for off-campus study with Western New York Consortium, National Student Exchange. The most frequently chosen baccalaureate fields are business/marketing, education, social sciences and history.

Student Body Statistics The student body totals 11,072, of whom 9,008 are undergraduates (1,333 freshmen). 60 percent are women and 40 percent are men. Students come from 30 states and territories and 21 other countries. 99 percent are from New York. 0.5 percent are international students. 27.4 percent of the 2004 graduating class went on to graduate and professional schools.

Expenses for 2004–05 *Application fee:* $30. *State resident tuition:* $4350 full-time, $181 per semester hour part-time. *Nonresident tuition:* $10,610 full-time, $442 per semester hour part-time. *Mandatory fees:* $787 full-time,

$32.80 per credit hour part-time. *College room and board:* $6200. *College room only:* $3920. Room and board charges vary according to board plan, housing facility, and student level.

Financial Aid Forms of aid include need-based and non-need-based scholarships and part-time jobs. The average aided 2003–04 undergraduate received an aid package worth $3037. The application deadline for financial aid is continuous.

Freshman Admission Buffalo State College, State University of New York requires a high school transcript, a minimum 3.0 high school GPA, SAT and SAT Subject Test or ACT scores, and TOEFL scores for international students. An essay, recommendations, and an interview are required for some. The application deadline for regular admission is rolling and for early decision it is November 15.

Transfer Admission The application deadline for admission is rolling.

Entrance Difficulty Buffalo State College, State University of New York assesses its entrance difficulty level as moderately difficult. For the fall 2004 freshman class, 51 percent of the applicants were accepted.

For Further Information Contact Ms. Lesa Loritts, Director of Admissions, Buffalo State College, State University of New York, 110 Moot Hall, Buffalo, NY 14222. *Telephone:* 716-878-5519. *Fax:* 716-878-6100. *E-mail:* admissions@buffalostate.edu. *Web site:* http://www.buffalostate.edu/.

CANISIUS COLLEGE

Buffalo, New York

SPONSOR See Front Insert for Details!

Canisius is a coed, private, Roman Catholic (Jesuit), comprehensive institution, founded in 1870, offering degrees at the bachelor's and master's levels and post-master's certificates. It has a 36-acre campus in Buffalo.

Academic Information The faculty has 452 members (45% full-time), 41% with terminal degrees. The undergraduate student-faculty ratio is 15:1. The library holds 328,278 titles, 1,637 serial subscriptions, and 7,710 audiovisual materials. Special programs include academic remediation, services for learning-disabled students, an honors program, study abroad, advanced placement credit, ESL programs, double majors, independent study, distance learning, summer session for credit, part-time degree programs, external degree programs, internships, and arrangement for off-campus study with members of the Western New York Consortium. The most frequently chosen baccalaureate fields are business/marketing, communications/communication technologies, education.

Student Body Statistics The student body totals 5,018, of whom 3,519 are undergraduates (886 freshmen). 56 percent are women and 44 percent are men. Students come from 28 states and territories and 31 other countries. 94 percent are from New York. 2.8 percent are international students. 27.6 percent of the 2004 graduating class went on to graduate and professional schools.

Expenses for 2004–05 *Application fee:* $25. *Comprehensive fee:* $30,206 includes full-time tuition ($20,910), mandatory fees ($901), and college room and board ($8395). *College room only:* $4860. Room and board charges vary according to board plan and housing facility. *Part-time tuition:* $596 per credit. *Part-time mandatory fees:* $20.50 per credit, $18 per term.

Financial Aid Forms of aid include need-based and non-need-based scholarships, athletic grants, and part-time jobs. The average aided 2004–05 undergraduate received an aid package worth an estimated $17,869. The priority application deadline for financial aid is February 15.

Freshman Admission Canisius requires a high school transcript, SAT or ACT scores, and TOEFL scores for international students. An essay, recommendations, and an interview are recommended. An interview is required for some. The application deadline for regular admission is April 1.

Transfer Admission The application deadline for admission is rolling.

Entrance Difficulty Canisius assesses its entrance difficulty level as moderately difficult. For the fall 2004 freshman class, 82 percent of the applicants were accepted.

SPECIAL MESSAGE TO STUDENTS

Social Life Canisius has invested more than $110 million over the last decade to create state-of-the-art residence halls and cultural and recreational spaces on the campus. Canisius' residential population continues to grow significantly, as does its reputation for having a friendly and caring atmosphere on campus. There is something for everyone at Canisius. Students have opportunities to develop leadership skills through involvement in student clubs and organizations, research, and service learning. There are more than 100 student organizations—from the Equestrian Club to the Canisius College Chorale to the sixteen NCAA Division I athletic teams. Since joining the Metro Atlantic Athletic Conference (MAAC) in 1989, men's baseball, basketball, soccer, and softball and women's cross-country have claimed conference titles. In addition to the numerous opportunities on campus at Canisius, the City of Buffalo provides even more. Buffalo is a great college town that has it all: professional sports teams including Buffalo Sabres (NHL), the Buffalo Bills (NFL), and the Buffalo Bisons (AAA baseball); the internationally known Albright-Knox Art Gallery; the Buffalo Zoo and Delaware Park, a 350-acre park with a lake and a golf course located less than a mile from the campus; the Buffalo Philharmonic Orchestra; and the Studio Arena Theatre, which provides a wide variety of theater experiences. Recently, Buffalo was rated fourth in the nation as a top arts destination.

Academic Highlights Simply put, Canisius College offers one of the best in high-quality academic programs and facilities and an outstanding faculty with members who are leaders in their fields. More than seventy majors, minors, and special programs provide students with a wide range of academic options. The newest undergraduate majors include accounting information systems, bioinformatics, digital media arts, and entrepreneurship. The College also offers a wide range of graduate programs in education, business, and organizational communication and development. Academic highlights include the 4+1 Program, an elite, dual-degree program allowing students to complete the bachelor's degree in any field, combined with the Canisius M.B.A; the Early Assurance Program, which ensures superior college students of their acceptance into SUNY at Buffalo Medical or Dental Schools or Upstate Medical University in Syracuse, New York; and joint-degree programs in pharmacy, dentistry, podiatry, optometry, and osteopathic medicine, which allows students to complete their bachelor's and professional degrees in a reduced time period. Students can enhance their academic experience through several exceptional opportunities: the All-College Honors Program; one of many study-abroad programs; internships easily accessible in the City of Buffalo through business, government, or service agencies; or independent research projects supervised closely by a faculty mentor. Technology plays a central role in all aspects of the college experience at Canisius, with ninety technology classrooms and wireless zones in three major academic buildings, the library, and the student center. Canisius students thrive as leaders; in the past few years, 19 students have won Fulbright Fellowships, the U.S. government's premier scholarship providing tuition, fees, travel, and research funds for a full year.

Interviews and Campus Visits Visiting the campus is the best way to explore all that Canisius has to offer. An interview, which is strongly recommended, provides the opportunity to discuss educational plans with a member of the admissions staff and tour the campus with a Canisius student. Families may visit throughout the year. Students should visit the Web site for more information on special visit opportunities. Scheduling a campus visit can be done at the Web site or by calling the Office of Undergraduate Admissions during regular business hours, Monday through Friday, 8:30 a.m. to 5 p.m. The office is located in Lyons Hall on campus. The nearest commercial airport is Buffalo–Niagara International.

For Further Information Write to the Office of Admissions, Canisius College, 2001 Main Street, Buffalo, NY 14208-1098. *Telephone:* 800-843-1517 (toll-free). *Web site:* http://www.canisius.edu/.

See page 102 for a narrative description.

CAZENOVIA COLLEGE
Cazenovia, New York

SPONSOR
See Front Insert for Details!

Cazenovia is a coed, private, four-year college, founded in 1824, offering degrees at the associate and bachelor's levels. It has a 40-acre campus in Cazenovia near Syracuse.

Academic Information The faculty has 138 members (36% full-time), 36% with terminal degrees. The student-faculty ratio is 13:1. The library holds 79,920 titles, 430 serial subscriptions, and 3,736 audiovisual materials. Special programs include academic remediation, services for learning-disabled students, an honors program, cooperative (work-study) education, study abroad, advanced placement credit, independent study, distance learning, self-designed majors, summer session for credit, part-time degree programs (evenings, weekends), adult/continuing education programs, internships, and arrangement for off-campus study. The most frequently chosen baccalaureate fields are business/marketing, protective services/public administration, visual/performing arts.

Student Body Statistics The student body is made up of 1,180 undergraduates (226 freshmen). 81 percent are women and 19 percent are men. Students come from 20 states and territories and 2 other countries. 88 percent are from New York. 0.2 percent are international students.

Expenses for 2005–06 *Application fee:* $25. *Comprehensive fee:* $26,530 includes full-time tuition ($18,940) and college room and board ($7590). *College room only:* $4080. Full-time tuition varies according to course load. Room and board charges vary according to board plan. *Part-time tuition:* $400 per credit. Part-time tuition varies according to class time and course load.

Financial Aid Forms of aid include need-based and non-need-based scholarships and part-time jobs. The average aided 2004–05 undergraduate received an aid package worth an estimated $14,800. The priority application deadline for financial aid is March 15.

Freshman Admission Cazenovia requires a high school transcript and TOEFL scores for international students. SAT and SAT Subject Test or ACT scores are recommended. The application deadline for regular admission is rolling.

Transfer Admission The application deadline for admission is rolling.

Entrance Difficulty Cazenovia assesses its entrance difficulty level as minimally difficult; moderately difficult for transfers. For the fall 2004 freshman class, 85 percent of the applicants were accepted.

SPECIAL MESSAGE TO STUDENTS

Social Life Cazenovia College's small size and residential atmosphere encourage lasting friendships. Cocurricular activities are designed to help students develop leadership skills in planning, organizing, and presenting campus social and cultural events. In addition, students can choose from forty-five clubs and organizations. Residence halls are fully wired for television, telephone, and Internet access. State-of-the-art computer labs are available to all students. The College's athletic center houses its NCAA Division III teams, two gymnasiums, a swimming pool, and a fitness center. The Equine Education Center is home to the College's nationally known equestrian teams.

Academic Highlights Part of what makes Cazenovia unique is the diversity and flexibility of its degree programs. Students select from academic programs that balance liberal arts and sciences competencies necessary for success in modern society with preparation in specific career fields. Cazenovia College offers a wide range of programs in art and design, business and management, communications, criminal justice, early childhood education, elementary education, English, environmental studies, equine studies, fashion design, human services, interior design, liberal studies, photography, psychology, social science, sports management, and visual communication. Practical experiences include internships, volunteer activities, campus leadership roles, community service, and summer jobs. Faculty members serve as academic advisers and mentors. The individual attention provided is critical to supporting student endeavors. Learning Center specialists provide structure and guidance for students seeking to improve grades or study skills. Cazenovia's Career Services Office provides assistance in each phase of a student's career search, employment, or continuing education.

Interviews and Campus Visits An interview and campus tour are key components of the admission process. Applicants discuss education plans and career goals with admission/financial aid counselors; may meet with faculty members, coaches, and students; observe a class; and eat in the dining hall. To arrange a campus visit, students should call 800-654-3210 (toll-free), Monday through Friday, 8:30 a.m. to 5 p.m. The nearest commercial airport is Syracuse-Hancock International.

For Further Information Write to Mr. Robert A. Croot, Dean for Admissions and Financial Aid, Cazenovia College, Cazenovia, NY 13035.

CENTRAL YESHIVA TOMCHEI TMIMIM-LUBAVITCH

Brooklyn, New York

For Information Write to Central Yeshiva Tomchei Tmimim-Lubavitch, Brooklyn, NY 11230.

CITY COLLEGE OF THE CITY UNIVERSITY OF NEW YORK

New York, New York

CCNY is a coed, public unit of City University of New York System, founded in 1847, offering degrees at the bachelor's, master's, and first professional levels and post-master's certificates. It has a 35-acre campus in New York.

Academic Information The faculty has 1,109 members (49% full-time). The undergraduate student-faculty ratio is 11:1. The library holds 1 million titles, 22,027 serial subscriptions, and 38,300 audiovisual materials. Special programs include academic remediation, services for learning-disabled students, an honors program, cooperative (work-study) education, study abroad, advanced placement credit, accelerated degree programs, Freshman Honors College, ESL programs, independent study, self-designed majors, summer session for credit, part-time degree programs (evenings), adult/continuing education programs, internships, and arrangement for off-campus study with other units of the City University of New York System. The most frequently chosen baccalaureate fields are engineering/engineering technologies, architecture, social sciences and history.

Student Body Statistics The student body totals 12,108, of whom 9,117 are undergraduates (1,213 freshmen). 49 percent are women and 51 percent are men. 96 percent are from New York. 12 percent are international students. 14 percent of the 2004 graduating class went on to graduate and professional schools.

Expenses for 2004–05 *Application fee:* $65. *State resident tuition:* $4080 full-time, $170 per credit part-time. *Nonresident tuition:* $8640 full-time, $360 per credit part-time. *Mandatory fees:* $259 full-time. Full-time tuition and fees vary according to class time and program. Part-time tuition varies according to class time, course load, and program.

Financial Aid Forms of aid include need-based and non-need-based scholarships and part-time jobs. The average aided 2004–05 undergraduate received an aid package worth an estimated $5771. The priority application deadline for financial aid is April 1.

Freshman Admission CCNY requires a high school transcript, SAT or ACT scores, and TOEFL scores for international students. The application deadline for regular admission is March 1.

Transfer Admission The application deadline for admission is rolling.

Entrance Difficulty CCNY assesses its entrance difficulty level as moderately difficult; most difficult for biomedical, urban legal studies programs. For the fall 2004 freshman class, 49 percent of the applicants were accepted.

For Further Information Contact Celia Lloyd, Interim Director of Admissions, City College of the City University of New York, Convent Avenue at 138th Street, New York, NY 10031-9198. *Telephone:* 212-650-6977. *Fax:* 212-650-6417. *E-mail:* admissions@ccny.cuny.edu. *Web site:* http://www.ccny.cuny.edu/.

CLARKSON UNIVERSITY

Potsdam, New York

Clarkson is a coed, private university, founded in 1896, offering degrees at the bachelor's, master's, and doctoral levels. It has a 640-acre campus in Potsdam.

Academic Information The faculty has 189 members (91% full-time), 83% with terminal degrees. The undergraduate student-faculty ratio is 16:1. The library holds 257,958 titles, 1,806 serial subscriptions, and 2,058 audiovisual materials. Special programs include services for learning-disabled students, an honors program, cooperative (work-study) education, study abroad, advanced placement credit, accelerated degree programs, ESL programs, double majors, independent study, self-designed majors, summer session for credit, part-time degree programs (daytime, summer), internships, and arrangement for off-campus study with Associated Colleges of the St. Lawrence Valley. The most frequently chosen baccalaureate fields are business/marketing, engineering/engineering technologies, interdisciplinary studies.

Student Body Statistics The student body totals 3,123, of whom 2,736 are undergraduates (659 freshmen). 23 percent are women and 77 percent are men. Students come from 35 states and territories and 23 other countries. 75 percent are from New York. 2.8 percent are international students. 29 percent of the 2004 graduating class went on to graduate and professional schools.

Expenses for 2005–06 *Application fee:* $50. *Comprehensive fee:* $34,930 includes full-time tuition ($25,185), mandatory fees ($400), and college room and board ($9345). *College room only:* $4896. Full-time tuition and fees vary according to course load. Room and board charges vary according to housing facility. *Part-time tuition:* $840 per credit. Part-time tuition varies according to course load.

Financial Aid Forms of aid include need-based and non-need-based scholarships, athletic grants, and part-time jobs. The average aided 2004–05 undergraduate received an aid package worth an estimated $17,163. The priority application deadline for financial aid is March 1.

Freshman Admission Clarkson requires a high school transcript, 2 recommendations, SAT or ACT scores, and TOEFL scores for international students. An interview and SAT Subject Test scores are recommended. The application deadline for regular admission is March 15; for early decision plan 1 it is December 1; and for early decision plan 2 it is January 15.

Entrance Difficulty Clarkson assesses its entrance difficulty level as very difficult. For the fall 2004 freshman class, 86 percent of the applicants were accepted.

SPECIAL MESSAGE TO STUDENTS

Social Life Clarkson offers more than 100 clubs and organizations, a 640-acre tree-covered campus, and 600 major cultural or educational events within a 10-mile radius of the campus each year. More than 75 percent of Clarkson students participate in extracurricular activities, and the 6-million-acre Adirondack Park is only minutes away.

Academic Highlights Academics at Clarkson emphasize rigorous professional preparation; dynamic, real-world learning; flexibility and adaptability; and teamwork that spans disciplines. All degree programs develop communication and collaboration skills, with a focus on practical application of knowledge and creative, open-ended problem solving. Every student majoring in business, for example, gains first-hand experience by actually running a business. Undergraduates customize programs through specialized concentrations and minors that broaden career options. Clarkson's relatively small size encourages personal attention and interactions between students and faculty members, flexibility, and interdisciplinary collaboration in learning and research. Strong advising is a hallmark of the academic environment. The University offers an honors program for high-achieving students, an accelerated three-year bachelor's degree, and co-op education with industry, structured so that participants graduate in four years.

Interviews and Campus Visits Although an interview is not required, Clarkson strongly recommends that students visit the campus for a tour and meeting with representatives. This meeting provides an opportunity for an informal exchange of information between the student and an admission staff member. Students who visit the campus for an interview with an admission counselor receive a fee-waived voucher for a Clarkson application. Clarkson is located in the friendly community of Potsdam, between the beautiful Adirondack Mountains and the St. Lawrence River. The scenic, open campus offers a blend of old and new architecture. New buildings include the Center for Advanced Materials Processing, a new state-of-the-art building for business and liberal arts, and the Cheel Student Center, a combination student union and multipurpose arena facility. There are many prominent sandstone buildings in the community, and the storefronts in Potsdam are an attractive Victorian style. There are also several other colleges in the area. For information about appointments and campus visits, students should call the Office of Undergraduate Admission at 315-268-6479 or 6480 or 800-527-6577 (toll-free), Monday through Friday, 9 a.m. to 4 p.m., or Saturday, 10 a.m. to 2 p.m. The office is located in Holcroft House on campus. The nearest commercial airport is Syracuse-Hancock International.

For Further Information Write to Mr. Brian Grant, Director of Admission, Clarkson University, P.O. Box 5605, Potsdam, NY 13699-5605. *E-mail:* admission@clarkson.edu. *Web site:* http://www.clarkson.edu.

See page 104 for a narrative description.

COCHRAN SCHOOL OF NURSING
Yonkers, New York

Cochran is a coed, primarily women's, private, two-year college, founded in 1894, offering degrees at the associate level. It is located in Yonkers near New York City.

For Further Information Contact Ms. Sandra Sclafani, Registrar, Cochran School of Nursing, 967 North Broadway, Yonkers, NY 10701. *Telephone:* 914-964-4296. *Fax:* 914-964-4796. *E-mail:* ssclafani@riversidehealth.org. *Web site:* http://www.riversidehealth.org/.

COLGATE UNIVERSITY
Hamilton, New York

Colgate is a coed, private, comprehensive institution, founded in 1819, offering degrees at the bachelor's and master's levels. It has a 515-acre campus in Hamilton.

Academic Information The faculty has 300 members (81% full-time), 90% with terminal degrees. The undergraduate student-faculty ratio is 10:1. The library holds 1 million titles, 2,227 serial subscriptions, and 9,161 audiovisual materials. Special programs include services for learning-disabled students, an honors program, study abroad, advanced placement credit, double majors, independent study, self-designed majors, internships, and arrangement for off-campus study with New York State Visiting Student Program. The most frequently chosen baccalaureate fields are English, philosophy, religion, and theology, social sciences and history.
Student Body Statistics The student body totals 2,830, of whom 2,823 are undergraduates (737 freshmen). 52 percent are women and 48 percent are men. Students come from 49 states and territories and 34 other countries. 31 percent are from New York. 5.4 percent are international students. 17 percent of the 2004 graduating class went on to graduate and professional schools.
Expenses for 2004–05 *Application fee:* $55. *Comprehensive fee:* $39,060 includes full-time tuition ($31,230), mandatory fees ($210), and college room and board ($7620). *College room only:* $3680. Full-time tuition and fees vary according to course load. Room and board charges vary according to board plan and housing facility. *Part-time tuition:* $3903 per course. Part-time tuition varies according to course load.
Financial Aid Forms of aid include need-based scholarships, athletic grants, and part-time jobs. The average aided 2004–05 undergraduate received an aid package worth an estimated $26,923. The application deadline for financial aid is February 1.
Freshman Admission Colgate requires an essay, a high school transcript, 3 recommendations, SAT or ACT scores, and TOEFL scores

for international students. The application deadline for regular admission is January 15; for early decision plan 1 it is November 15; and for early decision plan 2 it is January 15.
Transfer Admission The application deadline for admission is March 15.
Entrance Difficulty Colgate assesses its entrance difficulty level as very difficult. For the fall 2004 freshman class, 33 percent of the applicants were accepted.

For Further Information Contact Mr. Gary L. Ross, Dean of Admission, Colgate University, 13 Oak Drive, Hamilton, NY 13346-1383. *Telephone:* 315-228-7401. *Fax:* 315-228-7544. *E-mail:* admission@mail.colgate.edu. *Web site:* http://www.colgate.edu/.

COLLEGE OF AERONAUTICS
See Vaughn College of Aeronautics and Technology.

COLLEGE OF MOUNT SAINT VINCENT
Riverdale, New York

Mount Saint Vincent is a coed, private, comprehensive institution, founded in 1911, offering degrees at the associate, bachelor's, and master's levels and post-master's certificates. It has a 70-acre campus in Riverdale near New York City.

Academic Information The faculty has 150 members (49% full-time), 43% with terminal degrees. The undergraduate student-faculty ratio is 12:1. The library holds 160,696 titles, 362 serial subscriptions, and 5,775 audiovisual materials. Special programs include academic remediation, services for learning-disabled students, an honors program, study abroad, advanced placement credit, accelerated degree programs, Freshman Honors College, ESL programs, double majors, independent study, self-designed majors, summer session for credit, part-time degree programs (daytime, evenings, summer), adult/continuing education programs, internships, and arrangement for off-campus study with Manhattan College. The most frequently chosen baccalaureate fields are business/marketing, communications/communication technologies, health professions and related sciences.
Student Body Statistics The student body totals 1,685, of whom 1,393 are undergraduates (357 freshmen). 75 percent are women and 25 percent are men. Students come from 23 states and territories and 5 other countries. 88 percent are from New York. 0.3 percent are international students. 10 percent of the 2004 graduating class went on to graduate and professional schools.
Expenses for 2005–06 *Application fee:* $35. *Comprehensive fee:* $28,150 includes full-time tuition ($19,900) and college room and board ($8250).
Financial Aid Forms of aid include need-based and non-need-based scholarships and part-time jobs. The priority application deadline for financial aid is February 15.
Freshman Admission Mount Saint Vincent requires an essay, a high school transcript, a minimum 2.0 high school GPA, 1 recommendation, SAT or ACT scores, and TOEFL scores for international students. 2 recommendations and an interview are recommended. An interview is required for some. The application deadline for regular admission is rolling and for early action it is November 15.
Transfer Admission The application deadline for admission is rolling.
Entrance Difficulty Mount Saint Vincent assesses its entrance difficulty level as moderately difficult. For the fall 2004 freshman class, 71 percent of the applicants were accepted.

For Further Information Contact Mr. Timothy Nash, Dean of Admissions and Financial Aid, College of Mount Saint Vincent, 6301 Riverdale Avenue, Riverdale, NY 10471-1093. *Telephone:* 718-405-3268 or 800-665-CMSV (toll-free). *Fax:* 718-549-7945. *E-mail:* admissns@mountsaintvincent.edu. *Web site:* http://www.mountsaintvincent.edu/.

THE COLLEGE OF NEW ROCHELLE

New Rochelle, New York

CNR is a coed, primarily women's, private, comprehensive institution, founded in 1904, offering degrees at the bachelor's and master's levels and post-master's and postbachelor's certificates (also offers a non-traditional adult program with significant enrollment not reflected in profile). It has a 20-acre campus in New Rochelle near New York City.

Academic Information The faculty has 162 members (45% full-time). The undergraduate student-faculty ratio is 7:1. The library holds 220,000 titles, 1,450 serial subscriptions, and 4,350 audiovisual materials. Special programs include academic remediation, services for learning-disabled students, an honors program, cooperative (work-study) education, study abroad, advanced placement credit, accelerated degree programs, double majors, independent study, self-designed majors, summer session for credit, part-time degree programs (daytime, evenings, summer), adult/continuing education programs, internships, and arrangement for off-campus study with Iona College, Concordia College (NY), Marymount College, Dominican College of San Rafael. The most frequently chosen baccalaureate fields are health professions and related sciences, communications/communication technologies, psychology.
Student Body Statistics The student body totals 2,564, of whom 1,080 are undergraduates (152 freshmen). 94 percent are women and 6 percent are men. Students come from 16 states and territories and 10 other countries. 90 percent are from New York. 1.2 percent are international students. 37 percent of the 2004 graduating class went on to graduate and professional schools.
Expenses for 2005–06 *Application fee:* $20. *Comprehensive fee:* $28,476 includes full-time tuition ($20,246), mandatory fees ($350), and college room and board ($7880). Full-time tuition and fees vary according to course load and program. Room and board charges vary according to housing facility. *Part-time tuition:* $682 per credit. *Part-time mandatory fees:* $60 per term. Part-time tuition and fees vary according to course load.
Financial Aid Forms of aid include need-based and non-need-based scholarships and part-time jobs. The average aided 2003–04 undergraduate received an aid package worth $18,052. The application deadline for financial aid is continuous.
Freshman Admission CNR requires a high school transcript, SAT or ACT scores, and TOEFL scores for international students. An essay, 1 recommendation, and an interview are recommended. The application deadline for regular admission is rolling and for early decision it is November 1.
Transfer Admission The application deadline for admission is rolling.
Entrance Difficulty CNR assesses its entrance difficulty level as moderately difficult. For the fall 2004 freshman class, 45 percent of the applicants were accepted.

For Further Information Contact Ms. Stephanie Decker, Director of Admission, The College of New Rochelle, 29 Castle Place, New Rochelle, NY 10805-2339. *Telephone:* 914-654-5452 or 800-933-5923 (toll-free). *Fax:* 914-654-5464. *E-mail:* admission@cnr.edu. *Web site:* http://cnr.edu/.

THE COLLEGE OF SAINT ROSE

Albany, New York

CSR is a coed, private, comprehensive institution, founded in 1920, offering degrees at the bachelor's and master's levels and post-master's and postbachelor's certificates. It has a 28-acre campus in Albany.

Academic Information The faculty has 452 members (38% full-time). The undergraduate student-faculty ratio is 15:1. The library holds 205,938 titles, 925 serial subscriptions, and 1,513 audiovisual materials. Special programs include academic remediation, services for learning-disabled students, study abroad, advanced placement credit, accelerated degree programs, double majors, independent study, self-designed majors, summer session for credit, part-time degree programs (daytime, evenings, weekends, summer), external degree programs, adult/continuing education programs, internships, and arrangement for off-campus study with Hudson-Mohawk Association of Colleges and Universities. The most frequently chosen

baccalaureate fields are communications/communication technologies, computer/information sciences, engineering/engineering technologies.
Student Body Statistics The student body totals 4,971, of whom 2,958 are undergraduates (564 freshmen). 74 percent are women and 26 percent are men. Students come from 20 states and territories. 94 percent are from New York.
Expenses for 2004–05 *Application fee:* $35. *Comprehensive fee:* $24,252 includes full-time tuition ($16,230), mandatory fees ($550), and college room and board ($7472). *College room only:* $3542. Full-time tuition and fees vary according to course load and program. Room and board charges vary according to board plan. *Part-time tuition:* $540 per credit hour. Part-time tuition varies according to class time.
Financial Aid Forms of aid include need-based and non-need-based scholarships, athletic grants, and part-time jobs. The average aided 2003–04 undergraduate received an aid package worth $7095. The priority application deadline for financial aid is March 1.
Freshman Admission CSR requires an essay, a high school transcript, 1 recommendation, SAT or ACT scores, and TOEFL scores for international students. A minimum 3.0 high school GPA and an interview are recommended. An interview is required for some. The application deadline for regular admission is May 1.
Transfer Admission The application deadline for admission is May 1.
Entrance Difficulty CSR assesses its entrance difficulty level as moderately difficult. For the fall 2004 freshman class, 71 percent of the applicants were accepted.

For Further Information Contact Ms. Mary Elizabeth Amico, Director of Undergraduate Admissions, The College of Saint Rose, 432 Western Avenue, Albany, NY 12203. *Telephone:* 518-454-5150 or 800-637-8556 (toll-free). *Fax:* 518-454-2013. *E-mail:* admit@mail.strose.edu. *Web site:* http://www.strose.edu/.

COLLEGE OF STATEN ISLAND OF THE CITY UNIVERSITY OF NEW YORK

Staten Island, New York

CSI is a coed, public, comprehensive unit of City University of New York System, founded in 1955, offering degrees at the associate, bachelor's, and master's levels and post-master's certificates. It has a 204-acre campus in Staten Island near New York City.

Academic Information The faculty has 823 members (42% full-time), 53% with terminal degrees. The undergraduate student-faculty ratio is 18:1. The library holds 220,025 titles, 18,796 serial subscriptions, and 8,076 audiovisual materials. Special programs include academic remediation, services for learning-disabled students, an honors program, cooperative (work-study) education, study abroad, advanced placement credit, accelerated degree programs, Freshman Honors College, ESL programs, double majors, independent study, distance learning, summer session for credit, part-time degree programs (daytime, evenings, weekends, summer), adult/continuing education programs, internships, and arrangement for off-campus study with other units of the City University of New York System. The most frequently chosen baccalaureate fields are business/marketing, liberal arts/general studies, social sciences and history.
Student Body Statistics The student body totals 12,442, of whom 11,130 are undergraduates (2,247 freshmen). 59 percent are women and 41 percent are men. Students come from 5 states and territories and 111 other countries. 99 percent are from New York. 2.9 percent are international students. 10 percent of the 2004 graduating class went on to graduate and professional schools.
Expenses for 2004–05 *Application fee:* $60. *State resident tuition:* $4000 full-time, $170 per credit part-time. *Nonresident tuition:* $8640 full-time, $360 per credit part-time. *Mandatory fees:* $308 full-time, $90.50 per term part-time. Full-time tuition and fees vary according to course load. Part-time tuition and fees vary according to course load.
Financial Aid Forms of aid include need-based and non-need-based scholarships and part-time jobs. The average aided 2004–05 undergraduate received an aid package worth an estimated $5132. The application deadline for financial aid is continuous.
Freshman Admission CSI requires a high school transcript, a minimum 2.0 high school GPA, and TOEFL scores for international

students. An essay, recommendations, an interview, SAT or ACT scores, and SAT Subject Test scores are required for some. The application deadline for regular admission is rolling.

Transfer Admission　The application deadline for admission is rolling.

Entrance Difficulty　CSI has an open admission policy for Associate degree programs. It assesses its entrance difficulty as minimally difficult for transfers.

For Further Information　Contact Ms. Mary-Beth Riley, Director of Admissions and Recruitment, College of Staten Island of the City University of New York, 2800 Victory Boulevard, Building 2A Room 404, Staten Island, NY 10314. *Telephone:* 718-982-2011. *Fax:* 718-982-2500. *E-mail:* recruitment@mail.csi.cuny.edu. *Web site:* http://www.csi.cuny.edu/.

COLUMBIA COLLEGE

New York, New York

Columbia is a coed, private, four-year college of Columbia University, founded in 1754, offering degrees at the bachelor's level. It has a 35-acre campus in New York.

Academic Information　The faculty has 704 full-time members. The student-faculty ratio is 6:1. The library holds 7 million titles and 66,000 serial subscriptions. Special programs include services for learning-disabled students, an honors program, study abroad, advanced placement credit, ESL programs, double majors, independent study, self-designed majors, summer session for credit, internships, and arrangement for off-campus study with Howard University, The Juilliard School. The most frequently chosen baccalaureate fields are English, social sciences and history, visual/performing arts.

Student Body Statistics　The student body is made up of 4,115 undergraduates (1,011 freshmen). 50 percent are women and 50 percent are men. Students come from 54 states and territories and 72 other countries. 26 percent are from New York. 5.6 percent are international students. 80 percent of the 2004 graduating class went on to graduate and professional schools.

Expenses for 2004–05　*Application fee:* $65. *Comprehensive fee:* $40,538 includes full-time tuition ($30,260), mandatory fees ($1212), and college room and board ($9066). *College room only:* $5290.

Financial Aid　Forms of aid include need-based scholarships and part-time jobs. The average aided 2004–05 undergraduate received an aid package worth an estimated $27,749. The application deadline for financial aid is February 10.

Freshman Admission　Columbia requires an essay, a high school transcript, 3 recommendations, SAT or ACT scores, SAT Subject Test scores, and TOEFL scores for international students. The application deadline for regular admission is January 2 and for early decision it is November 1.

Transfer Admission　The application deadline for admission is March 15.

Entrance Difficulty　Columbia assesses its entrance difficulty level as most difficult. For the fall 2004 freshman class, 11 percent of the applicants were accepted.

For Further Information　Contact Ms. Jessica Marinaccio, Director of Undergraduate Admissions, Columbia College, 212 Hamilton Hall MC 2807, 1130 Amsterdam Avenue, New York, NY 10027. *Telephone:* 212-854-2522. *Fax:* 212-854-1209. *E-mail:* ugrad-admiss@columbia.edu. *Web site:* http://www.college.columbia.edu/.

COLUMBIA UNIVERSITY, BARNARD COLLEGE

See Barnard College.

COLUMBIA UNIVERSITY, COLUMBIA COLLEGE

See Columbia College.

COLUMBIA UNIVERSITY, SCHOOL OF GENERAL STUDIES

New York, New York

School of General Studies is a coed, private, four-year college of Columbia University, founded in 1754, offering degrees at the bachelor's level and postbachelor's certificates. It has a 36-acre campus in New York.

Academic Information　The faculty has 632 members (100% full-time), 100% with terminal degrees. The student-faculty ratio is 7:1. The library holds 6 million titles and 59,400 serial subscriptions. Special programs include academic remediation, services for learning-disabled students, an honors program, study abroad, advanced placement credit, accelerated degree programs, ESL programs, double majors, self-designed majors, summer session for credit, part-time degree programs (daytime, evenings, summer), adult/continuing education programs, internships, and arrangement for off-campus study.

Student Body Statistics　The student body totals 1,571, of whom 1,142 are undergraduates. 51 percent are women and 49 percent are men. Students come from 36 states and territories. 62 percent are from New York.

Expenses for 2005–06　*Application fee:* $50. *Tuition:* $30,900 full-time, $1030 per credit part-time. Full-time tuition varies according to course load. Part-time tuition varies according to course load.

Financial Aid　Forms of aid include need-based and non-need-based scholarships and part-time jobs. The priority application deadline for financial aid is July 1.

Freshman Admission　School of General Studies requires an essay, a high school transcript, recommendations, General Studies Admissions Exam, and TOEFL scores for international students. An interview and SAT or ACT scores are required for some. The application deadline for regular admission is July 1.

Transfer Admission　The application deadline for admission is July 1.

Entrance Difficulty　School of General Studies assesses its entrance difficulty level as most difficult. For the fall 2004 freshman class, 50 percent of the applicants were accepted.

For Further Information　Contact Mr. Carlos A. Porro, Director of Admissions, Columbia University, School of General Studies, Mail Code 4101, Lewisohn Hall, 2970 Broadway, New York, NY 10027-9829. *Telephone:* 212-854-2772 or 800-895-1169 (toll-free out-of-state). *Fax:* 212-854-6316. *E-mail:* gsdegree@columbia.edu. *Web site:* http://www.gs.columbia.edu/.

COLUMBIA UNIVERSITY, THE FU FOUNDATION SCHOOL OF ENGINEERING AND APPLIED SCIENCE

New York, New York

Columbia SEAS is a coed, private unit of Columbia University, founded in 1864, offering degrees at the bachelor's, master's, and doctoral levels.

Academic Information　The faculty has 137 full-time members. The undergraduate student-faculty ratio is 10:1. The library holds 7 million titles and 66,000 serial subscriptions. Special programs include services for learning-disabled students, an honors program, study abroad, advanced placement credit, ESL programs, double majors, independent study, summer session for credit, adult/continuing education programs, and internships. The most frequently chosen baccalaureate fields are engineering/engineering technologies, computer/information sciences, social sciences and history.

Student Body Statistics   The student body is made up of 1,387 undergraduates (320 freshmen). 26 percent are women and 74 percent are men. Students come from 44 states and territories and 59 other countries. 30 percent are from New York. 11.2 percent are international students.

Expenses for 2004–05   *Application fee:* $65. *Comprehensive fee:* $40,538 includes full-time tuition ($30,260), mandatory fees ($1212), and college room and board ($9066). *College room only:* $5290. Room and board charges vary according to board plan.

Financial Aid   Forms of aid include need-based scholarships and part-time jobs. The average aided 2004–05 undergraduate received an aid package worth an estimated $26,036. The application deadline for financial aid is February 10.

Freshman Admission   Columbia SEAS requires an essay, a high school transcript, 3 recommendations, SAT or ACT scores, SAT Subject Test scores, and TOEFL scores for international students. An interview is recommended. The application deadline for regular admission is January 2 and for early decision it is November 1.

Transfer Admission   The application deadline for admission is March 15.

Entrance Difficulty   Columbia SEAS assesses its entrance difficulty level as most difficult. For the fall 2004 freshman class, 28 percent of the applicants were accepted.

For Further Information   Contact Ms. Jessica Marinaccio, Director of Undergraduate Admissions, Columbia University, The Fu Foundation School of Engineering and Applied Science, 212 Hamilton Hall MC 2807, 1130 Amsterdam Avenue, New York, NY 10027. *Telephone:* 212-854-2522. *Fax:* 212-854-1209. *E-mail:* ugrad-admiss@columbia.edu. *Web site:* http://www.engineering.columbia.edu/.

CONCORDIA COLLEGE

Bronxville, New York

Concordia is a coed, private, Lutheran, four-year college of Concordia University System, founded in 1881, offering degrees at the associate and bachelor's levels. It has a 33-acre campus in Bronxville near New York City.

Academic Information   The faculty has 78 members (28% full-time), 44% with terminal degrees. The student-faculty ratio is 16:1. The library holds 71,500 titles, 467 serial subscriptions, and 7,660 audiovisual materials. Special programs include academic remediation, services for learning-disabled students, an honors program, study abroad, advanced placement credit, accelerated degree programs, ESL programs, double majors, independent study, distance learning, self-designed majors, part-time degree programs (daytime, evenings), adult/continuing education programs, internships, and arrangement for off-campus study with Concordia University System.

Student Body Statistics   The student body is made up of 655 undergraduates (143 freshmen). 57 percent are women and 43 percent are men. Students come from 34 states and territories and 29 other countries. 76 percent are from New York. 8.7 percent are international students. 25 percent of the 2004 graduating class went on to graduate and professional schools.

Expenses for 2004–05   *Application fee:* $30. *Comprehensive fee:* $26,300 includes full-time tuition ($18,700) and college room and board ($7600). *College room only:* $4050. Room and board charges vary according to board plan. *Part-time tuition:* $504 per credit hour. Part-time tuition varies according to course load.

Financial Aid   Forms of aid include need-based and non-need-based scholarships and part-time jobs. The application deadline for financial aid is continuous.

Freshman Admission   Concordia requires an essay, a high school transcript, 1 recommendation, SAT or ACT scores, and TOEFL scores for international students. A minimum 2.5 high school GPA is recommended. An interview is required for some. The application deadline for regular admission is March 15 and for early action it is November 15.

Transfer Admission   The application deadline for admission is July 15.

Entrance Difficulty   Concordia assesses its entrance difficulty level as moderately difficult. For the fall 2004 freshman class, 75 percent of the applicants were accepted.

For Further Information   Contact Ms. Donna J. Hoyt, Director of Admission, Concordia College, Bronxville, NY 10708. *Telephone:* 914-337-9300 Ext. 2149 or 800-YES-COLLEGE (toll-free). *Fax:* 914-395-4636. *E-mail:* admission@concordia-ny.edu. *Web site:* http://www.concordia-ny.edu/.

See page 106 for a narrative description.

COOPER UNION FOR THE ADVANCEMENT OF SCIENCE AND ART

New York, New York

Cooper Union is a coed, private, four-year college, founded in 1859, offering degrees at the bachelor's level (also offers master's program primarily made up of currently-enrolled students).

Expenses for 2004–05   *Application fee:* $50. *Comprehensive fee:* $14,400 includes full-time tuition ($0), mandatory fees ($1400), and college room and board ($13,000). *College room only:* $9000. All students are awarded full-tuition scholarships. Living expenses are subsidized by college-administered financial aid.

For Further Information   Contact Mr. Richard Bory, Dean of Admissions and Records and Registrar, Cooper Union for the Advancement of Science and Art, 30 Cooper Square, New York, NY 10003. *Telephone:* 212-353-4120. *Fax:* 212-353-4342. *E-mail:* admission@cooper.edu. *Web site:* http://www.cooper.edu/.

CORNELL UNIVERSITY

Ithaca, New York

Cornell is a coed, private university, founded in 1865, offering degrees at the bachelor's, master's, doctoral, and first professional levels. It has a 745-acre campus in Ithaca near Syracuse.

Academic Information   The faculty has 1,826 members (91% full-time), 90% with terminal degrees. The undergraduate student-faculty ratio is 9:1. The library holds 7 million titles, 64,760 serial subscriptions, and 427,798 audiovisual materials. Special programs include academic remediation, services for learning-disabled students, an honors program, cooperative (work-study) education, study abroad, advanced placement credit, accelerated degree programs, ESL programs, double majors, independent study, distance learning, self-designed majors, summer session for credit, internships, and arrangement for off-campus study with Ithaca College, Wells College. The most frequently chosen baccalaureate fields are business/marketing, engineering/engineering technologies, social sciences and history.

Student Body Statistics   The student body totals 19,518, of whom 13,625 are undergraduates (3,054 freshmen). 50 percent are women and 50 percent are men. Students come from 55 states and territories and 109 other countries. 40 percent are from New York. 6.9 percent are international students. 32 percent of the 2004 graduating class went on to graduate and professional schools.

Expenses for 2004–05   *Application fee:* $65. *Comprehensive fee:* $40,049 includes full-time tuition ($30,000), mandatory fees ($167), and college room and board ($9882). *College room only:* $5875. Room and board charges vary according to board plan and housing facility.

Financial Aid   Forms of aid include need-based scholarships and part-time jobs. The average aided 2004–05 undergraduate received an aid package worth an estimated $25,400. The application deadline for financial aid is February 11.

Freshman Admission   Cornell requires an essay, a high school transcript, 1 recommendation, SAT and SAT Subject Test or ACT scores, and TOEFL scores for international students. An interview is required for some. The application deadline for regular admission is January 1 and for early decision it is November 10.

Transfer Admission   The application deadline for admission is March 15.
Entrance Difficulty   Cornell assesses its entrance difficulty level as most difficult. For the fall 2004 freshman class, 29 percent of the applicants were accepted.

For Further Information   Contact Mr. Jason Locke, Director of Undergraduate Admissions, Cornell University, 410 Thurston Avenue, Ithaca, NY 14850. *Telephone:* 607-255-3316. *Fax:* 607-255-0659. *E-mail:* admissions@cornell.edu. *Web site:* http://www.cornell.edu/.

CROUSE HOSPITAL SCHOOL OF NURSING
Syracuse, New York

Crouse Hospital School of Nursing is a coed, private, two-year college, founded in 1913, offering degrees at the associate level.

Academic Information   The faculty has 25 members (64% full-time). The student-faculty ratio is 9:1. Special programs include part-time degree programs (evenings).
Student Body Statistics   The student body is made up of 252 undergraduates (19 freshmen). 88 percent are women and 12 percent are men. Students come from 4 states and territories. 98 percent are from New York.
Expenses for 2005–06   *Application fee:* $30. *Tuition:* $7352 full-time, $225 per credit hour part-time. *Mandatory fees:* $360 full-time, $130 per term part-time. *College room only:* $1750.
Financial Aid   Forms of aid include need-based scholarships and part-time jobs. The priority application deadline for financial aid is April 15.
Freshman Admission   Crouse Hospital School of Nursing requires an essay, a high school transcript, a minimum 2.5 high school GPA, 3 recommendations, and an interview. SAT or ACT scores are recommended. SAT or ACT scores are required for some. The application deadline for regular admission is February 1.
Transfer Admission   The application deadline for admission is February 1.

For Further Information   Contact Ms. Karen Van Sise, Enrollment Management Supervisor, Crouse Hospital School of Nursing, 736 Irving Avenue, Syracuse, NY 13210. *Telephone:* 315-470-7481. *Fax:* 315-470-7925. *Web site:* http://www.crouse.org/nursing/.

THE CULINARY INSTITUTE OF AMERICA
Hyde Park, New York

The CIA is a coed, private, four-year college, founded in 1946, offering degrees at the associate and bachelor's levels. It has a 150-acre campus in Hyde Park.

Academic Information   The faculty has 139 members (88% full-time). The student-faculty ratio is 18:1. The library holds 69,000 titles, 300 serial subscriptions, and 4,195 audiovisual materials. Special programs include academic remediation, services for learning-disabled students, cooperative (work-study) education, distance learning, adult/continuing education programs, internships, and arrangement for off-campus study with The Associated Colleges of the Mid-Hudson Valley. The most frequently chosen baccalaureate field is personal/miscellaneous services.
Student Body Statistics   The student body is made up of 2,409 undergraduates (618 freshmen). 36 percent are women and 64 percent are men. Students come from 53 states and territories and 25 other countries. 24 percent are from New York. 6.1 percent are international students.
Expenses for 2004–05   *Application fee:* $30. *Comprehensive fee:* $25,305 includes full-time tuition ($18,620), mandatory fees ($175), and college room and board ($6510). Full-time tuition and fees vary according to degree level.
Financial Aid   Forms of aid include need-based and non-need-based scholarships and part-time jobs. The average aided 2003–04 undergraduate received an aid package worth $10,663. The application deadline for financial aid is February 15.

Freshman Admission   The CIA requires an essay, a high school transcript, 2 recommendations, and TOEFL scores for international students. SAT or ACT scores are recommended. An interview and an Affidavit of Support are required for some. The application deadline for regular admission is rolling.
Entrance Difficulty   The CIA has an open admission policy.

For Further Information   Contact Ms. Rachel Birchwood, Director of Admissions, The Culinary Institute of America, 1946 Campus Drive, Hudson Hall, Hyde Park, NY 12538. *Telephone:* 800-CULINARY or 800-CULINARY (toll-free). *Fax:* 845-451-1068. *E-mail:* admissions@culinary.edu. *Web site:* http://www.ciachef.edu/.

C.W. POST CAMPUS OF LONG ISLAND UNIVERSITY

See Long Island University, C.W. Post Campus.

DAEMEN COLLEGE
Amherst, New York

Daemen is a coed, private, comprehensive institution, founded in 1947, offering degrees at the bachelor's, master's, and first professional levels and post-master's and postbachelor's certificates. It has a 35-acre campus in Amherst near Buffalo.

Academic Information   The faculty has 215 members (35% full-time), 43% with terminal degrees. The undergraduate student-faculty ratio is 15:1. The library holds 127,232 titles, 889 serial subscriptions, and 10,584 audiovisual materials. Special programs include academic remediation, services for learning-disabled students, an honors program, cooperative (work-study) education, study abroad, advanced placement credit, accelerated degree programs, double majors, independent study, self-designed majors, summer session for credit, part-time degree programs (weekends), adult/continuing education programs, internships, and arrangement for off-campus study with Western New York Consortium. The most frequently chosen baccalaureate fields are education, business/marketing, health professions and related sciences.
Student Body Statistics   The student body totals 2,186, of whom 1,594 are undergraduates (265 freshmen). 77 percent are women and 23 percent are men. Students come from 19 states and territories and 14 other countries. 96 percent are from New York. 1 percent are international students. 19 percent of the 2004 graduating class went on to graduate and professional schools.
Expenses for 2004–05   *Application fee:* $25. *Comprehensive fee:* $23,390 includes full-time tuition ($15,570), mandatory fees ($450), and college room and board ($7370). Room and board charges vary according to board plan and housing facility. *Part-time tuition:* $520 per credit. *Part-time mandatory fees:* $4 per credit, $68 per term. Part-time tuition and fees vary according to course load.
Financial Aid   Forms of aid include need-based and non-need-based scholarships, athletic grants, and part-time jobs. The average aided 2003–04 undergraduate received an aid package worth $13,742. The priority application deadline for financial aid is February 15.
Freshman Admission   Daemen requires a high school transcript, a minimum 2.0 high school GPA, SAT or ACT scores, and TOEFL scores for international students. An essay, 3 recommendations, an interview, and portfolio for art program, supplemental application for physician's assistant program are required for some. The application deadline for regular admission is rolling and for early action it is August 30.
Transfer Admission   The application deadline for admission is rolling.
Entrance Difficulty   Daemen assesses its entrance difficulty level as moderately difficult; very difficult for physical therapy, physician assistant programs. For the fall 2004 freshman class, 73 percent of the applicants were accepted.

For Further Information   Contact Mr. Jason Depoy, Associate Director of Admissions, Daemen College, Amherst, NY 14226-3592. *Telephone:* 716-839-8225 or 800-462-7652 (toll-free). *Fax:* 716-839-8229. *E-mail:* admissions@daemen.edu. *Web site:* http://www.daemen.edu/.

DARKEI NOAM RABBINICAL COLLEGE

Brooklyn, New York

For Information Write to Darkei Noam Rabbinical College, Brooklyn, NY 11210.

DAVIS COLLEGE

Johnson City, New York

Davis College is a coed, private, nondenominational, four-year college, founded in 1900, offering degrees at the associate and bachelor's levels. It has a 22-acre campus in Johnson City near Syracuse.

Expenses for 2004–05 *Application fee:* $25. *Comprehensive fee:* $14,660 includes full-time tuition ($8960), mandatory fees ($700), and college room and board ($5000). Full-time tuition and fees vary according to course load. *Part-time tuition:* $325 per credit. Part-time tuition varies according to class time and course load.

For Further Information Contact Mr. Brian J. Murphy, Director of Admissions, Davis College, PO Box 601, Bible School Park, NY 13737-0601. *Telephone:* 607-729-1581 Ext. 406 or 800-331-4137 Ext. 406 (toll-free). *Fax:* 607-729-2962. *E-mail:* admissions@practical.edu. *Web site:* http://www.davisny.edu/.

DeVRY INSTITUTE OF TECHNOLOGY

Long Island City, New York

DeVry is a coed, proprietary, four-year college of DeVry University, founded in 1998, offering degrees at the associate, bachelor's, and master's levels and postbachelor's certificates. It has a 4-acre campus in Long Island City.

Academic Information The faculty has 83 members (63% full-time). The undergraduate student-faculty ratio is 19:1. The library holds 14,078 titles, 62 serial subscriptions, and 2,057 audiovisual materials. Special programs include academic remediation, cooperative (work-study) education, advanced placement credit, accelerated degree programs, distance learning, summer session for credit, part-time degree programs (daytime, evenings, weekends, summer), and adult/continuing education programs. The most frequently chosen baccalaureate fields are business/marketing, computer/information sciences, engineering/engineering technologies.

Student Body Statistics The student body is made up of 1,453 undergraduates.

Expenses for 2004–05 *Application fee:* $50. *One-time mandatory fee:* $40. *Tuition:* $12,460 full-time, $455 per credit part-time. *Mandatory fees:* $250 full-time, $75 per term part-time. Full-time tuition and fees vary according to course load. Part-time tuition and fees vary according to course load.

Financial Aid Forms of aid include need-based and non-need-based scholarships and part-time jobs. The average aided 2003–04 undergraduate received an aid package worth $10,384. The application deadline for financial aid is continuous.

Freshman Admission DeVry requires a high school transcript, an interview, and TOEFL scores for international students. SAT or ACT scores and CPT are recommended. The application deadline for regular admission is rolling.

Transfer Admission The application deadline for admission is rolling.

Entrance Difficulty DeVry assesses its entrance difficulty level as minimally difficult; moderately difficult for electronics engineering technology program.

For Further Information Contact Ms. Edith Bolanos, New Student Coordinator, DeVry Institute of Technology, 30-20 Thomson Avenue, Long Island City, NY 11101-3051. *Telephone:* 718-361-0004 or 888-71-Devry (toll-free). *Fax:* 718-269-4288. *E-mail:* nyemailleads@ny.devry.edu. *Web site:* http://www.devry.edu/.

DOMINICAN COLLEGE

Orangeburg, New York

Dominican is a coed, private, comprehensive institution, founded in 1952, offering degrees at the associate, bachelor's, and master's levels. It has a 26-acre campus in Orangeburg near New York City.

Academic Information The faculty has 173 members (34% full-time), 25% with terminal degrees. The undergraduate student-faculty ratio is 14:1. The library holds 103,350 titles and 650 serial subscriptions. Special programs include academic remediation, services for learning-disabled students, an honors program, cooperative (work-study) education, advanced placement credit, accelerated degree programs, double majors, independent study, distance learning, summer session for credit, part-time degree programs (daytime, evenings, weekends, summer), adult/continuing education programs, and internships. The most frequently chosen baccalaureate fields are business/marketing, health professions and related sciences, social sciences and history.

Student Body Statistics The student body totals 1,639, of whom 1,535 are undergraduates (236 freshmen). 65 percent are women and 35 percent are men. Students come from 14 states and territories. 79 percent are from New York.

Expenses for 2004–05 *Application fee:* $35. *Comprehensive fee:* $25,720 includes full-time tuition ($16,600), mandatory fees ($650), and college room and board ($8470). *Part-time tuition:* $490 per credit. *Part-time mandatory fees:* $150 per term.

Financial Aid Forms of aid include need-based and non-need-based scholarships, athletic grants, and part-time jobs. The average aided 2004–05 undergraduate received an aid package worth an estimated $13,007. The priority application deadline for financial aid is February 15.

Freshman Admission Dominican requires a high school transcript, SAT or ACT scores, and TOEFL scores for international students. The application deadline for regular admission is rolling.

Transfer Admission The application deadline for admission is rolling.

Entrance Difficulty For the fall 2004 freshman class, 85 percent of the applicants were accepted.

For Further Information Contact Ms. Joyce Elbe, Director of Admissions, Dominican College, Orangeburg, NY 10962-1210. *Telephone:* 845-359-3533 Ext. 15 or 866-432-4636 (toll-free). *Fax:* 845-365-3150. *E-mail:* admissions@dc.edu. *Web site:* http://www.dc.edu/.

DOROTHEA HOPFER SCHOOL OF NURSING AT THE MOUNT VERNON HOSPITAL

Mount Vernon, New York

For Information Write to Dorothea Hopfer School of Nursing at The Mount Vernon Hospital, Mount Vernon, NY 10550.

DOWLING COLLEGE

Oakdale, New York

Dowling is a coed, private, comprehensive institution, founded in 1955, offering degrees at the bachelor's, master's, and doctoral levels and post-master's and postbachelor's certificates. It has a 157-acre campus in Oakdale near New York City.

Academic Information The faculty has 416 members (31% full-time), 42% with terminal degrees. The undergraduate student-faculty ratio is 15:1. The library holds 118,830 titles and 3,131 serial subscriptions. Special programs include academic remediation, services for learning-disabled students, an honors program, cooperative (work-study) education, advanced placement credit, accelerated degree programs, ESL programs, double majors, independent study, self-designed majors, summer session for credit, part-time degree programs, internships, and arrangement for off-campus study with Long Island Regional Advisory Council for Higher Education. The most frequently chosen baccalaureate fields are business/marketing, computer/information sciences, education.

Student Body Statistics   The student body totals 6,092, of whom 3,357 are undergraduates (486 freshmen). 59 percent are women and 41 percent are men. Students come from 28 states and territories and 56 other countries. 91 percent are from New York. 3.8 percent are international students.

Expenses for 2004–05   *Application fee:* $25. *Tuition:* $15,210 full-time, $507 per credit part-time. *Mandatory fees:* $840 full-time, $275 per term part-time. Part-time tuition and fees vary according to course load and degree level. *College room only:* $5512. Room charges vary according to housing facility and location.

Financial Aid   Forms of aid include need-based and non-need-based scholarships, athletic grants, and part-time jobs. The average aided 2004–05 undergraduate received an aid package worth an estimated $13,671. The priority application deadline for financial aid is April 1.

Freshman Admission   Dowling requires a high school transcript and TOEFL scores for international students. SAT or ACT scores are recommended. The application deadline for regular admission is rolling.

Transfer Admission   The application deadline for admission is rolling.

Entrance Difficulty   Dowling assesses its entrance difficulty level as moderately difficult. For the fall 2004 freshman class, 99 percent of the applicants were accepted.

For Further Information   Contact Ms. Bridget Masturzo, Director of Enrollment Services/Recruitment, Dowling College, 150 Idle Hour Boulevard, Oakdale, NY 11769. *Telephone:* 631-244-3101 or 800-DOWLING (toll-free). *Fax:* 631-563-3827. *E-mail:* admissions@dowling.edu. *Web site:* http://www.dowling.edu/.

D'YOUVILLE COLLEGE
Buffalo, New York

SPONSOR
See Front Insert
for Details!

D'Youville is a coed, private, comprehensive institution, founded in 1908, offering degrees at the bachelor's, master's, doctoral, and first professional levels and post-master's and postbachelor's certificates. It has a 7-acre campus in Buffalo.

Academic Information   The faculty has 207 members (51% full-time), 34% with terminal degrees. The undergraduate student-faculty ratio is 13:1. The library holds 122,057 titles, 665 serial subscriptions, and 3,160 audiovisual materials. Special programs include academic remediation, services for learning-disabled students, study abroad, accelerated degree programs, double majors, independent study, distance learning, summer session for credit, part-time degree programs (daytime, evenings, weekends, summer), adult/continuing education programs, internships, and arrangement for off-campus study with Western New York Consortium. The most frequently chosen baccalaureate fields are business/marketing, biological/life sciences, health professions and related sciences.

Student Body Statistics   The student body totals 2,729, of whom 1,225 are undergraduates (228 freshmen). 76 percent are women and 24 percent are men. Students come from 18 states and territories and 28 other countries. 94 percent are from New York. 0.1 percent are international students.

Expenses for 2004–05   *Application fee:* $25. *Comprehensive fee:* $22,230 includes full-time tuition ($14,690), mandatory fees ($200), and college room and board ($7340). Full-time tuition and fees vary according to course level and program. Room and board charges vary according to board plan and housing facility. *Part-time tuition:* $420 per credit. *Part-time mandatory fees:* $100 per term. Part-time tuition and fees vary according to course load.

Financial Aid   Forms of aid include need-based and non-need-based scholarships and part-time jobs. The priority application deadline for financial aid is March 1.

Freshman Admission   D'Youville requires a high school transcript, a minimum 2.0 high school GPA, SAT or ACT scores, and TOEFL scores for international students. An essay, a minimum 3.0 high school GPA, recommendations, and an interview are required for some. The application deadline for regular admission is rolling.

Transfer Admission   The application deadline for admission is rolling.

Entrance Difficulty   D'Youville assesses its entrance difficulty level as moderately difficult; very difficult for physician assistant, physical therapy, information technology. For the fall 2004 freshman class, 72 percent of the applicants were accepted.

SPECIAL MESSAGE TO STUDENTS

Social Life D'Youville College provides more than twenty-five student clubs and organizations, ranging from student government to the ski club. D'Youville is now an NCAA Division III college, offering twelve varsity sports. The proximity to Canada offers students an opportunity to sample the cultural and social life of the country.

Academic Highlights D'Youville's innovative programs keep it in the forefront of education, especially with its new two-degree doctorate programs in chiropractic and physical therapy and the new bachelor's degree in exercise and sports studies. Chiropractic is a seven-year B.S. and D.C. program, and physical therapy is a six-year B.S. and D.P.T. program. The College has many five-year programs that enable students to graduate with both a bachelor's and a master's degree. These programs in information technology (B.S.), international business (M.S.), education, occupational therapy, nursing, international business, and dietetics are innovative, and some are the first of their kind in the United States. These two-degree programs are all direct entry, with no requirement to reapply for upper-division status. The Career Discovery Program is a two-year sequence of courses and activities designed to allow students to explore academic and career options before choosing a major. All of D'Youville's academic programs are direct admission. Many students elect to participate in internships, which often lead to employment offers. Students may be able to lower their tuition and room and board just by applying. D'Youville automatically rewards applicants with academic and achievement scholarships in recognition of their high school accomplishments. The Honor Scholarship offers 50 percent off tuition and 25 percent off room and board. To be eligible, students must have an SAT score of 1100 or better or an ACT score of 24 or better. The Academic Initiative Scholarship offers 25 percent off tuition and 50 percent off room and board. To be eligible, students must have an SAT score of 1000 or better or an ACT score of 21–23 (an 85 average). The Achievement Scholarship offers $1000–$4000. To be eligible, students must have an SAT score of 900–1090 or an ACT score of 19–23 (average 80–84). All scholarships are renewable and not based on financial need. Those who apply and are accepted instantly qualify for one of these scholarships.

Interviews and Campus Visits Although not required, an interview is recommended to enable the student as well as the admission staff to obtain more in-depth information. A strong commitment, coupled with a mature and realistic attitude about one's abilities, help convince the counselor that a candidate would indeed be a capable D'Youville student. Appointments are available daily and on selected Saturdays throughout the year. (The physician assistant program requires an interview.) Throughout the year, special information sessions are held for such programs as occupational therapy, nursing, international business, dietetics, and premed. For information about these sessions, appointments, and campus visits, students should call the Office of Admissions at 716-829-7600 or 800-777-3921 (toll-free), Monday through Friday, 8:30 a.m. to 4:30 p.m. The office is located at 320 Porter Avenue on campus. The nearest commercial airport is Buffalo International.

For Further Information Write to Mr. R. H. Dannecker, Director of Admissions, D'Youville College, 320 Porter Avenue, Buffalo, NY 14201-1084.

See page 108 for a narrative description.

EASTMAN SCHOOL OF MUSIC
See University of Rochester.

ELLIS HOSPITAL SCHOOL OF NURSING
Schenectady, New York

For Information Write to Ellis Hospital School of Nursing, Schenectady, NY 12308.

ELMIRA COLLEGE
Elmira, New York

Elmira is a coed, private, four-year college, founded in 1855, offering degrees at the bachelor's and master's levels (also offers master's degree in education primarily for local students). It has a 42-acre campus in Elmira.

Academic Information The faculty has 97 members (89% full-time), 85% with terminal degrees. The undergraduate student-faculty ratio is 12:1. The library holds 391,038 titles, 859 serial subscriptions, and 4,428 audiovisual materials. Special programs include study abroad, advanced placement credit, accelerated degree programs, ESL programs, double majors, independent study, self-designed majors, summer session for credit, part-time degree programs (daytime, evenings, summer), adult/continuing education programs, internships, and arrangement for off-campus study with members of the May Term Consortium. The most frequently chosen baccalaureate fields are business/marketing, education, psychology.

Student Body Statistics The student body totals 1,853, of whom 1,558 are undergraduates (351 freshmen). 71 percent are women and 29 percent are men. Students come from 35 states and territories and 23 other countries. 52 percent are from New York. 4.5 percent are international students. 41 percent of the 2004 graduating class went on to graduate and professional schools.

Expenses for 2004–05 *Application fee:* $50. *Comprehensive fee:* $35,360 includes full-time tuition ($26,130), mandatory fees ($900), and college room and board ($8330). *Part-time tuition:* $250 per credit.

Financial Aid Forms of aid include need-based and non-need-based scholarships and part-time jobs. The average aided 2004–05 undergraduate received an aid package worth an estimated $21,331. The priority application deadline for financial aid is February 1.

Freshman Admission Elmira requires an essay, a high school transcript, a minimum 2.0 high school GPA, 2 recommendations, SAT or ACT scores, and TOEFL scores for international students. An interview is recommended. An interview is required for some. The application deadline for regular admission is April 15; for early decision plan 1 it is November 15; and for early decision plan 2 it is January 15.

Entrance Difficulty Elmira assesses its entrance difficulty level as moderately difficult; most difficult for accelerated degree program. For the fall 2004 freshman class, 67 percent of the applicants were accepted.

For Further Information Contact Mr. Gary G. Fallis, Dean of Admissions, Elmira College, Office of Admissions, Elmira, NY 14901. *Telephone:* 607-735-1724 or 800-935-6472 (toll-free). *Fax:* 607-735-1718. *E-mail:* admissions@elmira.edu. *Web site:* http://www.elmira.edu/.

See page 110 for a narrative description.

EUGENE LANG COLLEGE, NEW SCHOOL UNIVERSITY
New York, New York

SPONSOR
See Front Insert for Details!

Eugene Lang College is a coed, private, four-year college of New School University, founded in 1978, offering degrees at the bachelor's level. It has a 5-acre campus in New York.

Expenses for 2004–05 *Application fee:* $40. *Comprehensive fee:* $36,280 includes full-time tuition ($25,470) and college room and board ($10,810). *Part-time tuition:* $916 per credit. *Part-time mandatory fees:* $115 per term.

SPECIAL MESSAGE TO STUDENTS

Social Life Social life at the College is reflective of the cultural richness of New York City. The Theresa Lang Student Center provides a central location for student meetings and performances. A special program, Lang in the City, opens up the world of the arts at little or no additional cost to students. Undergraduates publish an award-winning literary magazine and a newspaper, produce several plays a year, and organize lectures and poetry readings. There are social and political groups, such as the Student Union, Latino and African-American organizations, and a volunteer resource center.

Academic Highlights The academic structure at Eugene Lang College is interdisciplinary and emphasizes small seminar classes of no more than 20 students. Students develop a liberal arts program of study around twelve areas of concentration. Internships are also an integral component of the Eugene Lang College education and include placement at schools, media and publishing organizations, nonprofit organizations, and more. Students are encouraged to participate in the internship program as early as their sophomore year. Exchange programs with American and European universities are also options for students.

Interviews and Campus Visits The College's environment is distinctive and challenging, and therefore an interview for admission is highly recommended. Information about Lang College and the student is exchanged through informal conversation directed by the admissions officer. Students should come prepared to discuss their reasons for applying, their particular learning style, and their college expectations. Students are strongly encouraged to sit in on a seminar class and take a campus tour as part of their visit to the College. New York City provides a rich artistic and cultural background for the College. Tours include the College and University facilities as well as historic and artistic sites. Points of interest include the Parsons School of Design building, the Albert List Academic Center, the Orozco Murals (rendered in 1930), Loeb Student Residence Hall, the Theresa Lang Student Center, and the seminar classrooms. New York City architecture and parks are also highlights, especially Washington Square Park and the College's historic Greenwich Village neighborhood. For information about appointments and campus visits, students should call the Office of Admissions at 212-229-5665, Monday through Friday, 9 a.m. to 5 p.m., or e-mail the office using the address in the contact section. The fax number is 212-229-5355. The office is located at 65 West 11th Street, third floor, on campus. The nearest commercial airport is John F. Kennedy International.

For Further Information Write to Nicole Curvin, Director of Admissions, Eugene Lang College, New School University, 65 West 11th Street, Third Floor, New York, NY 10011. *E-mail:* lang@newschool.edu.

See page 112 for a narrative description.

EXCELSIOR COLLEGE
Albany, New York

Excelsior College is a coed, private, comprehensive institution, founded in 1970, offering degrees at the associate, bachelor's, and master's levels and postbachelor's certificates (offers only external degree programs).

Academic Information Special programs include advanced placement credit, accelerated degree programs, independent study, distance learning, self-designed majors, part-time degree programs (daytime, evenings, weekends, summer), external degree programs, and adult/continuing education programs. The most frequently chosen baccalaureate fields are business/marketing, computer/information sciences, liberal arts/general studies.

Student Body Statistics The student body totals 26,395, of whom 26,022 are undergraduates. Students come from 50 states and territories and 51 other countries. 10 percent are from New York. 1.1 percent are international students.

Expenses for 2004–05 *Application fee:* $50. *Tuition:* $240 per credit part-time. *Mandatory fees:* $995 full-time, $495 per year part-time.

Financial Aid Forms of aid include need-based and non-need-based scholarships. The priority application deadline for financial aid is July 1.

Freshman Admission The application deadline for regular admission is rolling.
Transfer Admission The application deadline for admission is rolling.
Entrance Difficulty Excelsior College has an open admission policy except for applicants to nursing program without certain health care experience.

For Further Information Contact Ms. Chari Leader, Vice President for Enrollment Management, Excelsior College, 7 Columbia Circle, Albany, NY 12203-5159. *Telephone:* 518-464-8500 or 888-647-2388 (toll-free). *Fax:* 518-464-8777. *E-mail:* info@excelsior.edu. *Web site:* http://www.excelsior.edu/.

FARMINGDALE STATE UNIVERSITY OF NEW YORK

Farmingdale, New York

Farmingdale State University of New York is a coed, public, four-year college of State University of New York System, founded in 1912, offering degrees at the associate and bachelor's levels. It has a 380-acre campus in Farmingdale near New York City.

Academic Information The faculty has 452 members (35% full-time), 25% with terminal degrees. The student-faculty ratio is 16:1. The library holds 125,000 titles, 800 serial subscriptions, and 1,500 audiovisual materials. Special programs include academic remediation, services for learning-disabled students, study abroad, advanced placement credit, double majors, distance learning, summer session for credit, part-time degree programs (daytime, evenings, weekends, summer), and internships. The most frequently chosen baccalaureate fields are engineering/engineering technologies, communications/communication technologies, trade and industry.
Student Body Statistics The student body is made up of 6,250 undergraduates (899 freshmen). 42 percent are women and 58 percent are men. Students come from 9 states and territories and 13 other countries. 100 percent are from New York. 0.6 percent are international students. 2 percent of the 2004 graduating class went on to graduate and professional schools.
Expenses for 2004–05 *Application fee:* $40. *State resident tuition:* $4350 full-time, $181 per credit part-time. *Nonresident tuition:* $10,300 full-time, $429 per credit part-time. *Mandatory fees:* $861 full-time, $28.85 per credit part-time. *College room and board:* $7680. *College room only:* $4300. Room and board charges vary according to board plan.
Financial Aid Forms of aid include need-based and non-need-based scholarships and part-time jobs. The priority application deadline for financial aid is April 1.
Freshman Admission Farmingdale State University of New York requires a high school transcript, a minimum 2.0 high school GPA, SAT or ACT scores, and TOEFL scores for international students. A portfolio is required for some. The application deadline for regular admission is rolling.
Transfer Admission The application deadline for admission is rolling.
Entrance Difficulty Farmingdale State University of New York assesses its entrance difficulty level as moderately difficult. For the fall 2004 freshman class, 58 percent of the applicants were accepted.

For Further Information Contact Mr. Jim Hall, Director of Admissions, Farmingdale State University of New York, 2350 Broadhollow Road, Farmingdale, NY 11735-1021. *Telephone:* 631-420-2457 or 877-4-FARMINGDALE (toll-free). *Fax:* 631-420-2633. *E-mail:* admissions@farmingdale.edu. *Web site:* http://www.farmingdale.edu/.

FASHION INSTITUTE OF TECHNOLOGY

New York, New York

FIT is a coed, primarily women's, public, comprehensive unit of State University of New York System, founded in 1944, offering degrees at the associate, bachelor's, and master's levels. It has a 5-acre campus in New York.

Academic Information The faculty has 939 members (23% full-time). The undergraduate student-faculty ratio is 17:1. The library holds 176,987 titles, 467 serial subscriptions, and 177,801 audiovisual materials. Special programs include academic remediation, services for learning-disabled students, an honors program, cooperative (work-study) education, study abroad, advanced placement credit, ESL programs, distance learning, summer session for credit, part-time degree programs (evenings, weekends, summer), adult/continuing education programs, and internships. The most frequently chosen baccalaureate fields are business/marketing, architecture, visual/performing arts.
Student Body Statistics The student body totals 10,513, of whom 10,378 are undergraduates (1,055 freshmen). 83 percent are women and 17 percent are men. Students come from 51 states and territories and 60 other countries. 70 percent are from New York. 10.6 percent are international students.
Expenses for 2004–05 *Application fee:* $40. *State resident tuition:* $4350 full-time, $181 per credit part-time. *Nonresident tuition:* $10,300 full-time, $429 per credit part-time. *Mandatory fees:* $370 full-time, $5 per term part-time. Full-time tuition and fees vary according to degree level and program. Part-time tuition and fees vary according to degree level and program. *College room and board:* $7066. *College room only:* $6870. Room and board charges vary according to board plan and housing facility.
Financial Aid Forms of aid include need-based and non-need-based scholarships and part-time jobs. The average aided 2004–05 undergraduate received an aid package worth an estimated $7288.
Freshman Admission FIT requires an essay, a high school transcript, portfolio for art and design programs, and TOEFL scores for international students. SAT or ACT scores are recommended. The application deadline for regular admission is February 15 and for early action it is November 15.
Transfer Admission The application deadline for admission is February 15.
Entrance Difficulty FIT assesses its entrance difficulty level as moderately difficult. For the fall 2004 freshman class, 49 percent of the applicants were accepted.

For Further Information Contact Ms. Dolores Lombardi, Director of Admissions, Fashion Institute of Technology, Seventh Avenue at 27th Street, New York, NY 10001-5992. *Telephone:* 212-217-7675 or 800-GOTOFIT (toll-free out-of-state). *Fax:* 212-217-7481. *E-mail:* fitinfo@fitnyc.edu. *Web site:* http://www.fitnyc.edu/.

See page 114 for a narrative description.

FIVE TOWNS COLLEGE

Dix Hills, New York

Five Towns is a coed, private, comprehensive institution, founded in 1972, offering degrees at the associate, bachelor's, master's, and doctoral levels. It has a 40-acre campus in Dix Hills near New York City.

Academic Information The faculty has 123 members (47% full-time), 23% with terminal degrees. The undergraduate student-faculty ratio is 13:1. The library holds 35,000 titles, 565 serial subscriptions, and 6,500 audiovisual materials. Special programs include academic remediation, services for learning-disabled students, cooperative (work-study) education, advanced placement credit, independent study, distance learning, summer session for credit, part-time degree programs, internships, and arrangement for off-campus study with Long Island Regional Advisory Council for Higher Education. The most frequently chosen baccalaureate fields are business/marketing, education, visual/performing arts.
Student Body Statistics The student body totals 1,162, of whom 1,105 are undergraduates (259 freshmen). 40 percent are women and 60 percent are men. Students come from 10 states and territories. 8 percent of the 2004 graduating class went on to graduate and professional schools.
Expenses for 2005–06 *Application fee:* $25. *Comprehensive fee:* $24,350 includes full-time tuition ($14,100) and college room and board ($10,250). Room and board charges vary according to board plan and location. *Part-time tuition:* $585 per credit.
Financial Aid Forms of aid include need-based and non-need-based scholarships and part-time jobs. The average aided 2004–05 undergraduate

received an aid package worth an estimated $7400. The priority application deadline for financial aid is March 31.

Freshman Admission Five Towns requires an essay, a high school transcript, a minimum 2.3 high school GPA, recommendations, SAT and SAT Subject Test or ACT scores, and TOEFL scores for international students. An interview is required for some. The application deadline for regular admission is rolling.

Transfer Admission The application deadline for admission is rolling.

Entrance Difficulty Five Towns assesses its entrance difficulty level as moderately difficult.

For Further Information Contact Mr. Jerry Cohen, Dean of Enrollment, Five Towns College, 305 North Service Road, Dix Hills, NY 11746-6055. *Telephone:* 631-424-7000 Ext. 2110. *Fax:* 631-656-2172. *Web site:* http://www.fivetowns.edu/.

See page 116 for a narrative description.

FORDHAM UNIVERSITY

New York, New York

SPONSOR
See Front Insert
for Details!

Fordham is a coed, private, Roman Catholic (Jesuit) university, founded in 1841, offering degrees at the bachelor's, master's, doctoral, and first professional levels and post-master's certificates (branch locations at Rose Hill and Lincoln Center). It has an 85-acre campus in New York.

Academic Information The faculty has 1,326 members (49% full-time), 46% with terminal degrees. The undergraduate student-faculty ratio is 11:1. The library holds 2 million titles, 15,943 serial subscriptions, and 20,550 audiovisual materials. Special programs include services for learning-disabled students, an honors program, study abroad, advanced placement credit, accelerated degree programs, ESL programs, double majors, independent study, self-designed majors, summer session for credit, part-time degree programs (evenings, weekends, summer), adult/continuing education programs, internships, and arrangement for off-campus study with University of San Francisco. The most frequently chosen baccalaureate fields are business/marketing, communications/communication technologies, social sciences and history.

Student Body Statistics The student body totals 14,861, of whom 7,394 are undergraduates (1,703 freshmen). 60 percent are women and 40 percent are men. Students come from 53 states and territories and 44 other countries. 57 percent are from New York. 1.3 percent are international students. 25 percent of the 2004 graduating class went on to graduate and professional schools.

Expenses for 2004–05 *Application fee:* $50. *Comprehensive fee:* $37,295 includes full-time tuition ($26,200), mandatory fees ($847), and college room and board ($10,248). *College room only:* $6615. Room and board charges vary according to board plan, housing facility, and location. *Part-time tuition:* $875 per credit. *Part-time mandatory fees:* $40 per term.

Financial Aid Forms of aid include need-based and non-need-based scholarships, athletic grants, and part-time jobs. The average aided 2003–04 undergraduate received an aid package worth $18,363. The priority application deadline for financial aid is February 1.

Freshman Admission Fordham requires an essay, a high school transcript, 1 recommendation, SAT or ACT scores, and TOEFL scores for international students. A minimum 3.0 high school GPA, an interview, and SAT Subject Test scores are recommended. An interview is required for some. The application deadline for regular admission is January 15 and for early action it is November 1.

Transfer Admission The application deadline for admission is July 1.

Entrance Difficulty Fordham assesses its entrance difficulty level as very difficult. For the fall 2004 freshman class, 50 percent of the applicants were accepted.

SPECIAL MESSAGE TO STUDENTS

Social Life Fordham, New York City's Jesuit university, has three residential campuses: green and Gothic Rose Hill, in the North Bronx; Lincoln Center, in the cultural heart of Manhattan; and historic Marymount, in nearby Tarrytown, New York. The University enrolls approximately 8,000 undergraduates and 7,000 students in its graduate and preprofessional schools. Fordham's more than 130 student organizations offer a remarkable range of activities for both residential and commuting students. Fordham athletic teams compete in twenty-two intercollegiate sports and numerous club and intramural sports. Students also benefit from the countless cultural and recreational resources of one of the world's greatest cities.

Academic Highlights Fordham offers more than sixty-five majors in the liberal arts, sciences, and business. The honors programs are coordinated with the comprehensive core curriculum but are distinguished from the core by greater academic intensity. Fordham's GLOBE program allows business students to combine traditional liberal arts and business courses with international and foreign study courses taught by distinguished faculty members from around the world. The study abroad program enables students to extend their collegiate experience to other countries, including Australia, China, England, France, Germany, Ireland, Italy, Spain, and many others. More than 2,600 organizations in the New York metropolitan area offer internships to Fordham students in fields such as business, communications, medicine, law, and education.

Interviews and Campus Visits The interview is an optional part of the admission process. An interview affords the Admission Office the opportunity to assess an applicant's strengths and interests. It also enables a student to raise issues related to both the admission process and the Fordham experience. Availability for interviews is limited, but information sessions are available for all interested students. There are also multiple on-campus events for admitted students. Noteworthy buildings on the Rose Hill campus include Keating Hall, a beautiful Gothic structure that houses Fordham's award-winning 50,000-watt FM radio station. The University church is a New York State landmark with magnificent stained glass windows and the original high altar from St. Patrick's Cathedral. Fordham's new Walsh Library is one of the most technologically advanced college libraries in the country. The centerpiece of the Fordham athletic program is its sports facility, the Vincent T. Lombardi Memorial Center. Set on an open plaza just across the street from Lincoln Center for the Performing Arts, Fordham's Lincoln Center campus is modern and spacious, offering an 850-bed residence hall, which opened in 1993. Marymount College of Fordham University (for women) is the University's fifth undergraduate college, consolidating with Fordham in July 2002. Marymount continues its ninety-year legacy of women's education while enjoying Fordham's wider resources. For information about appointments and campus visits, students should call the Office of Undergraduate Admission at 718-817-4000 or 800-FORDHAM (toll-free), Monday through Friday, 9 a.m. to 5 p.m. The nearest commercial airport is LaGuardia International.

For Further Information Write to John Buckley, Assistant Vice President for Undergraduate Enrollment, Duane Library, Fordham University, New York, NY 10458.

See page 118 for a narrative description.

FRIENDS WORLD COLLEGE

See Long Island University, Friends World Program.

GAMLA COLLEGE

Brooklyn, New York

For Information Write to Gamla College, Brooklyn, NY 11230.

GLOBE INSTITUTE OF TECHNOLOGY

New York, New York

Globe Institute of Technology is a coed, proprietary, four-year college, offering degrees at the associate and bachelor's levels.

Academic Information The faculty has 122 members (19% full-time), 19% with terminal degrees. The student-faculty ratio is 15:1. The library holds 6,678 titles, 1,237 serial subscriptions, and 60 audiovisual materials. Special programs include academic remediation, services for learning-disabled students, advanced placement credit, accelerated degree programs,

ESL programs, part-time degree programs (daytime, evenings), and internships. The most frequently chosen baccalaureate field is computer/information sciences.

Student Body Statistics   The student body is made up of 1,229 undergraduates (538 freshmen). 62 percent are women and 38 percent are men. Students come from 7 states and territories. 89 percent are from New York. 2.2 percent are international students.

Expenses for 2004–05   *Application fee:* $50. *One-time mandatory fee:* $50. *Tuition:* $8950 full-time, $370 per credit part-time. *Mandatory fees:* $136 full-time, $136 per year part-time. *College room only:* $3500.

Financial Aid   Forms of aid include need-based scholarships and part-time jobs. The application deadline for financial aid is continuous.

Freshman Admission   Globe Institute of Technology requires an interview. SAT or ACT scores are recommended.

Entrance Difficulty   Globe Institute of Technology has an open admission policy.

For Further Information   Contact Ms. Tanya Garelik, Admissions Director, Globe Institute of Technology, 291 Broadway, New York, NY 10007. *Telephone:* 212-349-4330 Ext. 117 or 877-394-5623 (toll-free). *Fax:* 212-227-5920. *E-mail:* admissions@globe.edu. *Web site:* http://www.globe.edu/.

HAMILTON COLLEGE
Clinton, New York

Hamilton is a coed, private, four-year college, founded in 1812, offering degrees at the bachelor's level. It has a 1,200-acre campus in Clinton.

Academic Information   The faculty has 205 members (88% full-time), 91% with terminal degrees. The student-faculty ratio is 9:1. The library holds 538,377 titles, 3,585 serial subscriptions, and 52,051 audiovisual materials. Special programs include services for learning-disabled students, study abroad, advanced placement credit, accelerated degree programs, ESL programs, double majors, independent study, self-designed majors, part-time degree programs (daytime), adult/continuing education programs, internships, and arrangement for off-campus study with Colgate University, Syracuse University, Utica College of Syracuse University. The most frequently chosen baccalaureate fields are social sciences and history, English, visual/performing arts.

Student Body Statistics   The student body is made up of 1,792 undergraduates (457 freshmen). 51 percent are women and 49 percent are men. Students come from 41 states and territories and 40 other countries. 38 percent are from New York. 4.8 percent are international students. 20 percent of the 2004 graduating class went on to graduate and professional schools.

Expenses for 2004–05   *Application fee:* $50. *Comprehensive fee:* $39,525 includes full-time tuition ($31,500), mandatory fees ($200), and college room and board ($7825). *College room only:* $4125. Room and board charges vary according to board plan. *Part-time tuition:* $2900 per unit.

Financial Aid   Forms of aid include need-based and non-need-based scholarships and part-time jobs. The average aided 2004–05 undergraduate received an aid package worth an estimated $24,032. The application deadline for financial aid is January 1 with a priority deadline of January 1.

Freshman Admission   Hamilton requires an essay, a high school transcript, 1 recommendation, sample of expository prose, and SAT and SAT Subject Test or ACT scores. An interview and TOEFL scores for international students are recommended. The application deadline for regular admission is January 1 and for early decision it is November 15.

Transfer Admission   The application deadline for admission is March 15.

Entrance Difficulty   Hamilton assesses its entrance difficulty level as very difficult; most difficult for transfers; most difficult for international students needing financial aid. For the fall 2004 freshman class, 34 percent of the applicants were accepted.

For Further Information   Contact Ms. Monica Inzer, Dean of Admission and Financial Aid, Hamilton College, 198 College Hill Road, Clinton, NY 13323. *Telephone:* 315-859-4421 or 800-843-2655 (toll-free). *Fax:* 315-859-4457. *E-mail:* admission@hamilton.edu. *Web site:* http://www.hamilton.edu/.

HARTWICK COLLEGE
Oneonta, New York

Hartwick is a coed, private, four-year college, founded in 1797, offering degrees at the bachelor's level. It has a 425-acre campus in Oneonta near Albany.

Academic Information   The faculty has 154 members (68% full-time), 68% with terminal degrees. The student-faculty ratio is 12:1. The library holds 353,776 titles, 571 serial subscriptions, and 6,171 audiovisual materials. Special programs include services for learning-disabled students, an honors program, study abroad, advanced placement credit, accelerated degree programs, double majors, independent study, self-designed majors, part-time degree programs (daytime, evenings), internships, and arrangement for off-campus study with State University of New York College at Oneonta, American University, Central University of Iowa, Syracuse University, The School for International Training. The most frequently chosen baccalaureate fields are business/marketing, psychology, social sciences and history.

Student Body Statistics   The student body is made up of 1,479 undergraduates (410 freshmen). 57 percent are women and 43 percent are men. Students come from 30 states and territories and 34 other countries. 64 percent are from New York. 3.4 percent are international students.

Expenses for 2005–06   *Application fee:* $35. *Comprehensive fee:* $33,960 includes full-time tuition ($26,480) and college room and board ($7480). *College room only:* $3940. Room and board charges vary according to board plan and housing facility.

Financial Aid   Forms of aid include need-based and non-need-based scholarships, athletic grants, and part-time jobs. The application deadline for financial aid is February 1.

Freshman Admission   Hartwick requires an essay, a high school transcript, 2 recommendations, audition for music program, and TOEFL scores for international students. A minimum 3.0 high school GPA, an interview, and SAT or ACT scores are recommended. The application deadline for regular admission is February 15; for early decision it is January 15; and for early action it is January 1.

Transfer Admission   The application deadline for admission is August 1.

Entrance Difficulty   Hartwick assesses its entrance difficulty level as moderately difficult. For the fall 2004 freshman class, 89 percent of the applicants were accepted.

For Further Information   Contact Ms. Patricia Maben, Director of Admissions, Hartwick College, PO Box 4022, Oneonta, NY 13820-4022. *Telephone:* 607-431-4150 or 888-HARTWICK (toll-free out-of-state). *Fax:* 607-431-4102. *E-mail:* admissions@hartwick.edu. *Web site:* http://www.hartwick.edu/.

See page 120 for a narrative description.

HELENE FULD COLLEGE OF NURSING OF NORTH GENERAL HOSPITAL
New York, New York

For Information   Write to Helene Fuld College of Nursing of North General Hospital, New York, NY 10035-2709.

HILBERT COLLEGE
Hamburg, New York

Hilbert is a coed, private, four-year college, founded in 1957, offering degrees at the associate and bachelor's levels. It has a 40-acre campus in Hamburg near Buffalo.

Academic Information   The faculty has 101 members (43% full-time), 36% with terminal degrees. The student-faculty ratio is 16:1. The library holds 41,322 titles, 12,300 serial subscriptions, and 1,066 audiovisual materials. Special programs include academic remediation, services for learning-disabled students, an honors program, cooperative (work-study) education, advanced placement credit, independent study, summer session for credit, part-time degree programs (daytime, evenings, weekends, summer), and internships. The most frequently chosen baccalaureate fields are business/marketing, law/legal studies, protective services/public administration.

Student Body Statistics The student body is made up of 1,108 undergraduates (161 freshmen). 63 percent are women and 37 percent are men. Students come from 6 states and territories and 2 other countries. 99 percent are from New York. 0.2 percent are international students. 20 percent of the 2004 graduating class went on to graduate and professional schools.

Expenses for 2005–06 *Application fee: $20. Comprehensive fee: $19,680* includes full-time tuition ($13,750), mandatory fees ($550), and college room and board ($5380). *College room only:* $2350. Full-time tuition and fees vary according to course load. Room and board charges vary according to board plan and housing facility. *Part-time tuition:* $322 per credit hour. *Part-time mandatory fees:* $13 per credit hour, $30 per term. Part-time tuition and fees vary according to course load.

Financial Aid Forms of aid include need-based and non-need-based scholarships and part-time jobs. The average aided 2004–05 undergraduate received an aid package worth an estimated $9603. The application deadline for financial aid is May 1 with a priority deadline of March 1.

Freshman Admission Hilbert requires a high school transcript. Recommendations, an interview, and SAT or ACT scores are recommended. An interview is required for some. The application deadline for regular admission is September 1.

Transfer Admission The application deadline for admission is August 1.

Entrance Difficulty Hilbert assesses its entrance difficulty level as minimally difficult. For the fall 2004 freshman class, 93 percent of the applicants were accepted.

For Further Information Contact Mr. Harry Gong, Director of Admissions, Hilbert College, 5200 South Park Avenue, Hamburg, NY 14075-1597. *Telephone:* 716-649-7900 Ext. 244. *Fax:* 716-649-0702. *Web site:* http://www.hilbert.edu/.

See page 122 for a narrative description.

HOBART AND WILLIAM SMITH COLLEGES
Geneva, New York

SPONSOR
See Front Insert
for Details!

HWS is a coed, private, four-year college, founded in 1822, offering degrees at the bachelor's level. It has a 200-acre campus in Geneva near Rochester and Syracuse.

Academic Information The faculty has 185 members (84% full-time), 95% with terminal degrees. The student-faculty ratio is 11:1. The library holds 380,419 titles, 2,469 serial subscriptions, and 10,733 audiovisual materials. Special programs include services for learning-disabled students, an honors program, study abroad, advanced placement credit, accelerated degree programs, ESL programs, double majors, independent study, self-designed majors, adult/continuing education programs, internships, and arrangement for off-campus study with New York State Visiting Student Program. The most frequently chosen baccalaureate fields are English, psychology, social sciences and history.

Student Body Statistics The student body totals 1,847, of whom 1,839 are undergraduates (482 freshmen). 54 percent are women and 46 percent are men. Students come from 44 states and territories and 10 other countries. 47 percent are from New York. 2.1 percent are international students. 30 percent of the 2004 graduating class went on to graduate and professional schools.

Expenses for 2004–05 *Application fee: $45. Comprehensive fee: $38,630* includes full-time tuition ($30,076), mandatory fees ($567), and college room and board ($7987). *College room only:* $4220. Room and board charges vary according to board plan. *Part-time tuition:* $3760 per course.

Financial Aid Forms of aid include need-based and non-need-based scholarships and part-time jobs. The average aided 2004–05 undergraduate received an aid package worth an estimated $23,371. The application deadline for financial aid is March 15 with a priority deadline of February 15.

Freshman Admission HWS requires an essay, a high school transcript, 1 recommendation, SAT or ACT scores, and TOEFL scores for international students. An interview and SAT Subject Test scores are recommended. The application deadline for regular admission is February 1; for early decision plan 1 it is November 15; and for early decision plan 2 it is January 1.

Transfer Admission The application deadline for admission is July 1.

Entrance Difficulty HWS assesses its entrance difficulty level as very difficult. For the fall 2004 freshman class, 63 percent of the applicants were accepted.

SPECIAL MESSAGE TO STUDENTS

Social Life Hobart and William Smith Colleges (HWS) offer a full range of activities in the arts, community service, athletics, clubs, and special interest groups. A wide range of concerts, symposia, films, and lectures are available. The student governments offer their own base of power and opportunities for leadership. Fifteen percent of Hobart students join one of five fraternities. The campus is residential within a small city. Housing on campus is guaranteed for all four years.

Academic Highlights Numerous options are available for off-campus study. HWS offers thirty programs abroad on six continents, in countries such as Australia, China, Ecuador, England, France, India, Israel, Japan, New Zealand, Senegal, Spain, and Vietnam. Programs off campus are also offered in Boston, Los Angeles, New York, and Washington, D.C. Many off-campus programs include internships. The Colleges participate in cooperative programs in engineering and architecture, as well as a 4+1 M.B.A. program, and have an exceptionally strong prelaw and premed advising. In addition to more than twenty-five departmental majors, Hobart and William Smith offer interdisciplinary program majors that focus on cultural climates (African, American, Asian, European, and Latin American studies), political and social concerns (environmental, public policy, and urban studies), gender and orientation issues (women's and lesbian, gay, and bisexual studies), and the arts (theater studies, arts and education, and media and society), as well as other areas.

Interviews and Campus Visits A campus visit is an integral part of the Colleges' admission process. Typically, the visit includes a personal interview or information session and a student-guided tour of the campus. In addition, visitors are encouraged to meet with a member of the faculty or staff and visit a class. The Admissions Office also offers several open house programs and can arrange regional and alumni interviews in many areas of the country. Hobart and William Smith Colleges are located on the north shore of Seneca Lake, the largest of New York's Finger Lakes. This proximity to the lake facilitates crew and sailing activities and provides easy access to the Colleges' 70-foot research and laboratory vessel, the *HWS Explorer.* Interested students may also visit the Colleges' 100-acre nature preserve, where biological fieldwork is conducted. For information about appointments and campus visits, students should call 315-781-3622 or 800-852-2256 (toll-free except AK and HI), Monday through Friday, 8:30 a.m. to 5 p.m.; Saturday, 9 a.m. to noon (September through May); or Monday through Friday, 9 a.m. to 4 p.m. (during the summer). Students can also visit the Colleges' Web site at http://www.hws.edu. The nearest commercial airport is Greater Rochester International.

For Further Information Write to Ms. Mara O'Laughlin, Director of Admissions, Hobart and William Smith Colleges, 639 South Main Street, Geneva, NY 14456. *Web site:* http://www.hws.edu.

HOFSTRA UNIVERSITY
Hempstead, New York

SPONSOR
See Front Insert
for Details!

Hofstra is a coed, private university, founded in 1935, offering degrees at the bachelor's, master's, doctoral, and first professional levels and post-master's and postbachelor's certificates. It has a 240-acre campus in Hempstead near New York City.

Academic Information The faculty has 1,256 members (41% full-time), 57% with terminal degrees. The undergraduate student-faculty ratio is 14:1. The library holds 1 million titles, 8,576 serial subscriptions, and 11,118 audiovisual materials. Special programs include services for learning-disabled students, an honors program, study abroad, advanced placement credit, accelerated degree programs, Freshman Honors College, ESL programs, double majors, independent study, self-designed majors, summer session for credit, part-time degree programs (daytime, evenings, weekends, summer), external degree programs, adult/continuing education programs, and internships. The most frequently chosen baccalaureate fields are business/marketing, education, psychology.

Student Body Statistics   The student body totals 12,999, of whom 9,053 are undergraduates (1,743 freshmen). 54 percent are women and 46 percent are men. Students come from 48 states and territories and 51 other countries. 73 percent are from New York. 1.8 percent are international students.

Expenses for 2004–05   *Application fee:* $40. *Comprehensive fee:* $29,012 includes full-time tuition ($19,010), mandatory fees ($1002), and college room and board ($9000). *College room only:* $5900. Full-time tuition and fees vary according to course load and program. Room and board charges vary according to board plan and housing facility. *Part-time tuition:* $615 per semester hour. *Part-time mandatory fees:* $155 per term. Part-time tuition and fees vary according to course load and program.

Financial Aid   Forms of aid include need-based and non-need-based scholarships, athletic grants, and part-time jobs. The average aided 2004–05 undergraduate received an aid package worth an estimated $11,400. The priority application deadline for financial aid is February 15.

Freshman Admission   Hofstra requires a high school transcript, 1 recommendation, and TOEFL scores for international students. An essay and SAT Subject Test scores are recommended. An interview, proof of degree required for all; TOEFL required for international students, and SAT or ACT scores are required for some. The application deadline for regular admission is rolling and for early action it is November 15.

Entrance Difficulty   Hofstra assesses its entrance difficulty level as moderately difficult; very difficult for Honors College. For the fall 2004 freshman class, 67 percent of the applicants were accepted.

SPECIAL MESSAGE TO STUDENTS

Social Life With more than 120 clubs and organizations on campus, students have many extracurricular activities from which to choose. There are more than 500 concerts and cultural events each year, with many involving well-known talent in addition to Hofstra's drama, music, and dance departments. In addition, scholarly seminars on such topics as the American presidency and great literature are held regularly. Nearly 4,000 of more than 8,100 full-time undergraduate students reside on the picturesque 240-acre campus, including 70 percent of first-time freshmen. About 43 percent of the freshman class come from outside New York State.

Academic Highlights Hofstra students receive a broad-based liberal arts education as the foundation for their academic program in liberal arts or sciences, business, communications, or education or allied human services. Students may choose from about 130 undergraduate programs of study. In addition, Hofstra's Honors College offers a focused, multidisciplinary program for academically accomplished students. For students interested in study-abroad opportunities, Hofstra sponsors a number of programs that include intensive language study and travel experience. The Career Center can assist in arranging internships for students interested in supplementing their education with real-world experience. Many of those internship opportunities are in New York City—just 25 miles away and easily accessible to students by car or railroad.

Interviews and Campus Visits Admission to Hofstra is competitive. Hofstra uses multiple criteria for the admission of freshman candidates. While the interview is not required as part of the application process, it can be quite helpful as an exchange of information about the student and the University. An interview can take place at any point in the admission process, from students who visit late in their junior year to seniors who have been accepted and are seeking specific information prior to making their final college choice. Hofstra also offers an open house in the fall for high school seniors and their parents and in the spring for high school juniors, or students can choose to participate in the Hofstra UpClose Program, which matches a Hofstra student and a high school junior or senior with similar areas of academic interest for a daylong program on campus. The Hofstra University Library contains more than 1.2 million volumes arranged in open stacks to encourage browsing, research, and easy access. Computer access to many databases, CD-ROM, extensive

periodicals, documents, and microfilm augments the collection. The facilities are uniquely advanced. Hofstra ranked fourteenth among the "most connected" campuses in the country in 2004 according to the *Princeton Review*. The Hofstra University Recreation Center and Physical Fitness Center include an indoor circular track, an indoor Olympic-size swimming pool, weight-room, and recreational facilities. For information about appointments and campus visits, students should call the Admissions Office at 800-HOFSTRA (toll-free), Monday through Thursday, 9 a.m. to 8 p.m.; Friday, 9 a.m. to 5 p.m.; and Saturday, 9 a.m. to 2 p.m. The office is located in the Admissions Center on the south campus. The nearest commercial airport is La Guardia.

For Further Information Write to Ms. Gigi Lamens, Vice President for Enrollment Management, 100 Hofstra University, Hempstead, NY 11549.

See page 124 for a narrative description.

HOLY TRINITY ORTHODOX SEMINARY
Jordanville, New York

Holy Trinity Orthodox Seminary is a men's, private, Russian Orthodox, five-year college, founded in 1948, offering degrees at the bachelor's level. It has a 900-acre campus in Jordanville.

Academic Information   The faculty has 18 members (44% full-time), 11% with terminal degrees. The student-faculty ratio is 2:1. The library holds 25,000 titles, 200 serial subscriptions, and 250 audiovisual materials. Special programs include accelerated degree programs, ESL programs, and distance learning. The most frequently chosen baccalaureate field is philosophy, religion, and theology.

Student Body Statistics   The student body is made up of 31 undergraduates (9 freshmen). Students come from 9 states and territories and 11 other countries. 5 percent are from New York. 50 percent are international students. 5 percent of the 2004 graduating class went on to graduate and professional schools.

Expenses for 2004–05   *Application fee:* $0. *Comprehensive fee:* $4025 includes full-time tuition ($2000), mandatory fees ($25), and college room and board ($2000). *Part-time tuition:* $60 per term.

Freshman Admission   Holy Trinity Orthodox Seminary requires an essay, a high school transcript, recommendations, and special examination, proficiency in Russian, Eastern Orthodox baptism. A minimum 3.0 high school GPA is recommended. The application deadline for regular admission is May 1.

Transfer Admission   The application deadline for admission is May 1.

Entrance Difficulty   Holy Trinity Orthodox Seminary assesses its entrance difficulty level as noncompetitive. For the fall 2004 freshman class, 69 percent of the applicants were accepted.

For Further Information   Contact Fr. Vladimir Tsurikov, Assistant Dean, Holy Trinity Orthodox Seminary, PO Box 36, Jordanville, NY 13361. *Telephone:* 315-858-0945. *Fax:* 315-858-0945. *E-mail:* info@ hts.edu. *Web site:* http://www.hts.edu/.

HOUGHTON COLLEGE
Houghton, New York

Houghton is a coed, private, Wesleyan, four-year college, founded in 1883, offering degrees at the associate, bachelor's, and master's levels. It has a 1,300-acre campus in Houghton near Buffalo and Rochester.

Academic Information   The faculty has 101 members (82% full-time), 74% with terminal degrees. The undergraduate student-faculty ratio is 14:1. The library holds 242,866 titles, 4,110 serial subscriptions, and 2,918 audiovisual materials. Special programs include services for learning-disabled students, an honors program, study abroad, advanced placement credit, double majors, independent study, summer session for credit, part-time degree programs (evenings), adult/continuing education programs, internships, and arrangement for off-campus study with members of the Western New York Consortium and the Christian College Consortium. The most frequently chosen baccalaureate fields are business/marketing, education, English.

Student Body Statistics   The student body totals 1,480, of whom 1,468 are undergraduates (326 freshmen). 67 percent are women and 33 percent are men. Students come from 41 states and territories and 21 other countries. 62 percent are from New York. 2.8 percent are international students. 26.7 percent of the 2004 graduating class went on to graduate and professional schools.

Expenses for 2004–05   *Application fee:* $40. *Comprehensive fee:* $24,980 includes full-time tuition ($18,660) and college room and board ($6320). *College room only:* $3160. Full-time tuition varies according to course load, program, and reciprocity agreements. Room and board charges vary according to board plan and housing facility. *Part-time tuition:* $780 per hour.

Financial Aid   Forms of aid include need-based and non-need-based scholarships, athletic grants, and part-time jobs. The average aided 2004–05 undergraduate received an aid package worth an estimated $14,195. The priority application deadline for financial aid is March 1.

Freshman Admission   Houghton requires an essay, a high school transcript, 1 recommendation, an interview, pastoral recommendation, SAT or ACT scores, and TOEFL scores for international students. A minimum 2.5 high school GPA is recommended. The application deadline for regular admission is rolling.

Transfer Admission   The application deadline for admission is rolling.

Entrance Difficulty   Houghton assesses its entrance difficulty level as moderately difficult. For the fall 2004 freshman class, 76 percent of the applicants were accepted.

For Further Information   Contact Mr. Tim Fuller, Vice President for Enrollment, Houghton College, PO Box 128, Houghton, NY 14744. *Telephone:* 585-567-9353 or 800-777-2556 (toll-free). *Fax:* 585-567-9522. *E-mail:* admission@houghton.edu. *Web site:* http://www.houghton.edu/.

HUNTER COLLEGE OF THE CITY UNIVERSITY OF NEW YORK

New York, New York

Hunter College is a coed, public, comprehensive unit of City University of New York System, founded in 1870, offering degrees at the bachelor's and master's levels and post-master's certificates.

Academic Information   The faculty has 1,358 members (47% full-time). The undergraduate student-faculty ratio is 17:1. The library holds 789,718 titles, 4,282 serial subscriptions, and 13,489 audiovisual materials. Special programs include services for learning-disabled students, an honors program, study abroad, advanced placement credit, Freshman Honors College, ESL programs, double majors, independent study, distance learning, self-designed majors, summer session for credit, part-time degree programs (daytime, evenings, weekends, summer), internships, and arrangement for off-campus study with Marymount Manhattan College, New School for Social Research, YIVD Institute, other units of the City University of New York System. The most frequently chosen baccalaureate fields are psychology, social sciences and history, visual/performing arts.

Student Body Statistics   The student body totals 20,243, of whom 15,361 are undergraduates (1,876 freshmen). 69 percent are women and 31 percent are men. Students come from 35 states and territories and 153 other countries. 97 percent are from New York. 6.7 percent are international students.

Expenses for 2004–05   *Application fee:* $50. *State resident tuition:* $4000 full-time, $170 per credit part-time. *Nonresident tuition:* $360 per credit part-time. *Mandatory fees:* $329 full-time, $96 per term part-time. *College room only:* $2600. Room charges vary according to housing facility.

Financial Aid   Forms of aid include need-based and non-need-based scholarships and part-time jobs. The priority application deadline for financial aid is April 1.

Freshman Admission   Hunter College requires a high school transcript, SAT or ACT scores, and TOEFL scores for international students. The application deadline for regular admission is October 1.

Transfer Admission   The application deadline for admission is March 1.

Entrance Difficulty   Hunter College assesses its entrance difficulty level as moderately difficult; minimally difficult for transfers. For the fall 2004 freshman class, 30 percent of the applicants were accepted.

For Further Information   Contact Mr. William Zlata, Director of Admissions, Hunter College of the City University of New York, 695 Park Avenue, New York, NY 10021-5085. *Telephone:* 212-772-4490. *Fax:* 212-650-3472. *Web site:* http://www.hunter.cuny.edu/.

INSTITUTE OF DESIGN AND CONSTRUCTION

Brooklyn, New York

For Information   Write to Institute of Design and Construction, Brooklyn, NY 11201-5317.

IONA COLLEGE

New Rochelle, New York

Iona is a coed, private, comprehensive institution, founded in 1940, affiliated with the Roman Catholic Church, offering degrees at the bachelor's and master's levels and post-master's and postbachelor's certificates. It has a 35-acre campus in New Rochelle near New York City.

Academic Information   The faculty has 370 members (48% full-time). The undergraduate student-faculty ratio is 15:1. The library holds 269,933 titles, 763 serial subscriptions, and 3,018 audiovisual materials. Special programs include services for learning-disabled students, an honors program, study abroad, advanced placement credit, accelerated degree programs, double majors, distance learning, summer session for credit, part-time degree programs (daytime, evenings, weekends, summer), adult/continuing education programs, internships, and arrangement for off-campus study with College of New Rochelle, Concordia College (NY), Marymount College. The most frequently chosen baccalaureate fields are business/marketing, communications/communication technologies, protective services/public administration.

Student Body Statistics   The student body totals 4,329, of whom 3,425 are undergraduates (897 freshmen). 54 percent are women and 46 percent are men. Students come from 37 states and territories and 51 other countries. 82 percent are from New York. 1.7 percent are international students.

Expenses for 2004–05   *Application fee:* $50. *Comprehensive fee:* $29,228 includes full-time tuition ($18,990), mandatory fees ($540), and college room and board ($9698). Full-time tuition and fees vary according to class time. Room and board charges vary according to housing facility. *Part-time tuition:* $630 per credit. *Part-time mandatory fees:* $185 per term. Part-time tuition and fees vary according to class time and course load.

Financial Aid   Forms of aid include need-based and non-need-based scholarships, athletic grants, and part-time jobs. The average aided 2004–05 undergraduate received an aid package worth an estimated $13,197. The priority application deadline for financial aid is April 15.

Freshman Admission   Iona requires a high school transcript, SAT or ACT scores, and TOEFL scores for international students. An essay, a minimum 2.5 high school GPA, recommendations, an interview, and SAT Subject Test scores are recommended. The application deadline for regular admission is February 15 and for early action it is November 15.

Transfer Admission   The application deadline for admission is August 15.

Entrance Difficulty   Iona assesses its entrance difficulty level as moderately difficult. For the fall 2004 freshman class, 60 percent of the applicants were accepted.

For Further Information   Contact Mr. Thomas Weede, Director of Admissions, Iona College, Admissions, 715 North Avenue, New Rochelle, NY 10801. *Telephone:* 914-633-2502 or 800-231-IONA (toll-free in-state). *Fax:* 914-637-2778. *E-mail:* icad@iona.edu. *Web site:* http://www.iona.edu/.

ITHACA COLLEGE

Ithaca, New York

SPONSOR
See Front Insert
for Details!

Ithaca College is a coed, private, comprehensive institution, founded in 1892, offering degrees at the bachelor's and master's levels. It has a 757-acre campus in Ithaca near Syracuse.

Academic Information The faculty has 616 members (72% full-time), 81% with terminal degrees. The undergraduate student-faculty ratio is 12:1. The library holds 376,000 titles, 37,000 serial subscriptions, and 33,000 audiovisual materials. Special programs include services for learning-disabled students, an honors program, study abroad, advanced placement credit, accelerated degree programs, Freshman Honors College, double majors, independent study, self-designed majors, summer session for credit, part-time degree programs (daytime, evenings, summer), adult/continuing education programs, internships, and arrangement for off-campus study with Cornell University, Wells College. The most frequently chosen baccalaureate fields are communications/communication technologies, health professions and related sciences, visual/performing arts.

Student Body Statistics The student body totals 6,337, of whom 6,107 are undergraduates (1,461 freshmen). 57 percent are women and 43 percent are men. Students come from 51 states and territories and 67 other countries. 48 percent are from New York. 3.3 percent are international students. 33 percent of the 2004 graduating class went on to graduate and professional schools.

Expenses for 2004–05 *Application fee:* $55. *Comprehensive fee:* $33,394 includes full-time tuition ($23,690) and college room and board ($9704). *College room only:* $4946. Room and board charges vary according to board plan and housing facility. *Part-time tuition:* $790 per credit hour.

Financial Aid Forms of aid include need-based and non-need-based scholarships and part-time jobs. The average aided 2003–04 undergraduate received an aid package worth $20,902. The priority application deadline for financial aid is February 1.

Freshman Admission Ithaca College requires an essay, a high school transcript, 1 recommendation, SAT or ACT scores, and TOEFL scores for international students. A minimum 3.0 high school GPA and an interview are recommended. Audition is required for some. The application deadline for regular admission is February 1 and for early decision it is November 1.

Transfer Admission The application deadline for admission is February 1.

Entrance Difficulty Ithaca College assesses its entrance difficulty level as moderately difficult; very difficult for film, photography and visual arts, television-radio, physical therapy, theater arts, music programs. For the fall 2004 freshman class, 67 percent of the applicants were accepted.

SPECIAL MESSAGE TO STUDENTS

Social Life Living on campus is part of the educational experience at Ithaca—there are always opportunities to get involved. Students might join the student newspaper, TV or radio stations, one of more than twenty musical ensembles, or any of the more than 130 campus organizations. More than 300 concerts and recitals, dozens of theatrical performances and guest speakers, and a variety of other special events create an atmosphere of cultural and social vitality. Sports events draw spirited crowds: Ithaca has won thirteen national championships and competes in NCAA Division III. Students can also participate in any of several dozen intramural and club sports, ranging from basketball to soccer, softball, skiing, floor hockey, and tennis. Other social events include residential hall activities and dances, open mike, or cabaret night at the Campus Center.

Academic Highlights With more than 100 degree programs in the Schools of Business, Communications, Health Sciences and Human Performance, Humanities and Sciences, and Music and in the College's Division of Interdisciplinary and International Studies, Ithaca offers a professional education within a liberal arts context. Students may choose from such options as the Exploratory Program to help them select a major and a planned studies program to design their own major, enroll in a four-year honors program, or pursue teacher certification in more than a dozen areas. They can spend a semester abroad at Ithaca's London Center or through programs in Australia, Japan, Spain, the Czech Republic, or

elsewhere. Ithaca's internship-based, semester-long program in Washington, D.C., offers exceptional opportunities for hands-on learning in all disciplines; the College's program in Los Angeles for communications students offers similar experiences in the heart of the communication industry. With a student-faculty ratio of 12:1, students are active participants in their education at Ithaca, on campus, and beyond.

Interviews and Campus Visits Prospective students are encouraged to come see for themselves what makes the Ithaca experience special. While an on-campus personal interview is not required, it is recommended for all applicants. Campus tours and interviews are conducted hourly from 9 a.m. to 3 p.m. weekdays and from 9 a.m. to 11 a.m. most Saturdays while the College is in session. Tours and interviews are also available throughout the summer. Tours depart from the Office of Admission in Job Hall. A video is also available online, or the student may request detailed brochures on each of Ithaca's five schools and study-abroad programs. For information or to schedule a tour or an interview, prospective students should contact the Office of Admission at 607-274-3124 or 800-429-4274 (toll-free). The fax number is 607-274-1900. The nearest commercial airport is Tompkins County.

For Further Information Write to the Office of Admission, 100 Job Hall, Ithaca College, Ithaca, NY 14850-7020. *Web site:* http://www.ithaca.edu.

See page 126 for a narrative description.

THE JEWISH THEOLOGICAL SEMINARY

New York, New York

JTS is a coed, private, Jewish university, founded in 1886, offering degrees at the bachelor's, master's, doctoral, and first professional levels (double bachelor's degree with Barnard College, Columbia University, joint bachelor's degree with Columbia University). It has a 1-acre campus in New York.

Academic Information The faculty has 124 members (50% full-time). The undergraduate student-faculty ratio is 5:1. The library holds 380,000 titles and 720 serial subscriptions. Special programs include academic remediation, services for learning-disabled students, an honors program, study abroad, advanced placement credit, Freshman Honors College, double majors, distance learning, self-designed majors, summer session for credit, part-time degree programs, adult/continuing education programs, internships, and arrangement for off-campus study with Barnard College, Columbia University. The most frequently chosen baccalaureate field is philosophy, religion, and theology.

Student Body Statistics The student body totals 669, of whom 198 are undergraduates. Students come from 23 states and territories and 2 other countries. 35 percent are from New York. 60 percent of the 2004 graduating class went on to graduate and professional schools.

Expenses for 2004–05 *Application fee:* $65. *Tuition:* $11,340 full-time, $600 per credit part-time. *Mandatory fees:* $500 full-time, $225 per term part-time. *College room only:* $7706. Room charges vary according to housing facility.

Financial Aid Forms of aid include need-based and non-need-based scholarships. The application deadline for financial aid is March 1.

Freshman Admission JTS requires an essay, a high school transcript, 2 recommendations, SAT and SAT Subject Test or ACT scores, and TOEFL scores for international students. A minimum 3.0 high school GPA and an interview are recommended. The application deadline for regular admission is February 15; for early decision plan 1 it is November 15; and for early decision plan 2 it is January 15.

Transfer Admission The application deadline for admission is May 1.

Entrance Difficulty JTS assesses its entrance difficulty level as very difficult. For the fall 2004 freshman class, 68 percent of the applicants were accepted.

For Further Information Contact The Jewish Theological Seminary, 3080 Broadway, New York, NY 10027. *Telephone:* 212-678-8832. *Fax:* 212-280-6022. *E-mail:* lcadmissions@jtsa.edu. *Web site:* http://www.jtsa.edu/.

JOHN JAY COLLEGE OF CRIMINAL JUSTICE OF THE CITY UNIVERSITY OF NEW YORK

New York, New York

John Jay is a coed, public, comprehensive unit of City University of New York System, founded in 1964, offering degrees at the associate, bachelor's, master's, and doctoral levels and postbachelor's certificates.

Academic Information   The faculty has 913 members (37% full-time). The undergraduate student-faculty ratio is 20:1. The library holds 310,000 titles and 1,325 serial subscriptions. Special programs include academic remediation, services for learning-disabled students, an honors program, cooperative (work-study) education, advanced placement credit, ESL programs, summer session for credit, part-time degree programs (daytime, evenings, weekends, summer), internships, and arrangement for off-campus study with other units of the City University of New York System.
Student Body Statistics   The student body totals 12,984, of whom 11,515 are undergraduates. Students come from 52 states and territories. 13 percent of the 2004 graduating class went on to graduate and professional schools.
Expenses for 2005–06   *Application fee:* $50. *State resident tuition:* $4000 full-time, $170 per credit part-time. *Nonresident tuition:* $8640 full-time, $360 per credit part-time. *Mandatory fees:* $259 full-time, $82.35 per term part-time. Full-time tuition and fees vary according to course level and course load. Part-time tuition and fees vary according to course level and course load.
Financial Aid   Forms of aid include need-based and non-need-based scholarships and part-time jobs. The average aided 2003–04 undergraduate received an aid package worth $5100. The priority application deadline for financial aid is June 1.
Freshman Admission   John Jay requires a high school transcript, a minimum 2.0 high school GPA, SAT or ACT scores, and TOEFL scores for international students. The application deadline for regular admission is March 15.
Transfer Admission   Standardized test scores and a college transcript are required for some. The application deadline for admission is rolling.
Entrance Difficulty   John Jay has an open admission policy for Associate degree programs. It assesses its entrance difficulty as noncompetitive for associate degree programs.

For Further Information   Contact Richard Saulnier, PhD, Dean for Enrollment Services, John Jay College of Criminal Justice of the City University of New York, 445 West 59th Street, Room 4205, New York, NY 10019. *Telephone:* 212-237-8878 or 877-JOHNJAY (toll-free). *Web site:* http://www.jjay.cuny.edu/.

THE JUILLIARD SCHOOL

New York, New York

Juilliard is a coed, private, comprehensive institution, founded in 1905, offering degrees at the bachelor's, master's, and doctoral levels and post-master's and postbachelor's certificates.

Academic Information   The faculty has 270 members (44% full-time). The undergraduate student-faculty ratio is 3:1. The library holds 80,793 titles, 220 serial subscriptions, and 21,867 audiovisual materials. Special programs include study abroad, accelerated degree programs, ESL programs, double majors, adult/continuing education programs, and arrangement for off-campus study with Barnard College, Columbia University. The most frequently chosen baccalaureate field is visual/performing arts.
Student Body Statistics   The student body totals 833, of whom 505 are undergraduates (118 freshmen). 50 percent are women and 50 percent are men. Students come from 41 states and territories and 29 other countries. 19 percent are from New York. 22.8 percent are international students.
Expenses for 2004–05   *Application fee:* $100. *Comprehensive fee:* $32,480 includes full-time tuition ($22,850), mandatory fees ($600), and college room and board ($9030). Room and board charges vary according to housing facility.
Financial Aid   Forms of aid include need-based and non-need-based scholarships and part-time jobs. The average aided 2003–04 undergraduate received an aid package worth $21,298. The application deadline for financial aid is March 1.
Freshman Admission   Juilliard requires an essay, a high school transcript, audition, and TOEFL scores for international students. The application deadline for regular admission is December 1.
Transfer Admission   The application deadline for admission is December 1.
Entrance Difficulty   Juilliard assesses its entrance difficulty level as most difficult. For the fall 2004 freshman class, 7 percent of the applicants were accepted.

For Further Information   Contact Ms. Lee Cioppa, Associate Dean for Admissions, The Juilliard School, 60 Lincoln Center Plaza, New York, NY 10023-6588. *Telephone:* 212-799-5000 Ext. 223. *Fax:* 212-724-0263. *E-mail:* admissions@juilliard.edu. *Web site:* http://www.juilliard.edu/.

KEHILATH YAKOV RABBINICAL SEMINARY

Brooklyn, New York

For Information   Write to Kehilath Yakov Rabbinical Seminary, Brooklyn, NY 11211-7207.

KEUKA COLLEGE

Keuka Park, New York

Keuka is a coed, private, comprehensive institution, founded in 1890, affiliated with the American Baptist Churches in the U.S.A., offering degrees at the bachelor's and master's levels. It has a 173-acre campus in Keuka Park near Rochester.

Academic Information   The faculty has 99 members (55% full-time), 52% with terminal degrees. The undergraduate student-faculty ratio is 13:1. The library holds 117,192 titles and 3,145 audiovisual materials. Special programs include academic remediation, services for learning-disabled students, cooperative (work-study) education, study abroad, advanced placement credit, accelerated degree programs, double majors, independent study, self-designed majors, summer session for credit, part-time degree programs (daytime, evenings), adult/continuing education programs, internships, and arrangement for off-campus study with Rochester Area Colleges. The most frequently chosen baccalaureate fields are business/marketing, education, health professions and related sciences.
Student Body Statistics   The student body is made up of 1,154 undergraduates (252 freshmen). 71 percent are women and 29 percent are men. Students come from 18 states and territories and 2 other countries. 92 percent are from New York. 10 percent of the 2004 graduating class went on to graduate and professional schools.
Expenses for 2004–05   *Application fee:* $30. *Comprehensive fee:* $24,870 includes full-time tuition ($16,820), mandatory fees ($260), and college room and board ($7790). *College room only:* $3700. Full-time tuition and fees vary according to program. Room and board charges vary according to board plan and housing facility. *Part-time tuition:* $525 per credit hour. Part-time tuition varies according to program.
Financial Aid   Forms of aid include need-based and non-need-based scholarships and part-time jobs. The priority application deadline for financial aid is March 15.
Freshman Admission   Keuka requires an essay, a high school transcript, recommendations, SAT or ACT scores, and TOEFL scores for international students. A minimum 2.75 high school GPA and an interview are recommended. An interview is required for some. The application deadline for regular admission is rolling.
Transfer Admission   The application deadline for admission is rolling.

Entrance Difficulty Keuka assesses its entrance difficulty level as moderately difficult. For the fall 2004 freshman class, 85 percent of the applicants were accepted.

For Further Information Contact Ms. Claudine Ninestine, Director of Admissions, Keuka College, Wagner House, Keuka Park, NY 14478. *Telephone:* 315-279-5262 or 800-33-KEUKA (toll-free). *Fax:* 315-279-5386. *E-mail:* admissions@mail.keuka.edu. *Web site:* http://www.keuka.edu/.

THE KING'S COLLEGE
New York, New York

The King's College is a coed, private, four-year college, offering degrees at the associate and bachelor's levels.

Academic Information The faculty has 27 members (48% full-time), 85% with terminal degrees. The student-faculty ratio is 13:1. The library holds 12,000 titles, 75 serial subscriptions, and 300 audiovisual materials. Special programs include academic remediation, study abroad, advanced placement credit, ESL programs, independent study, summer session for credit, internships, and arrangement for off-campus study. The most frequently chosen baccalaureate field is business/marketing.

Student Body Statistics The student body is made up of 263 undergraduates (74 freshmen). 53 percent are women and 47 percent are men. Students come from 29 states and territories and 7 other countries. 38 percent are from New York. 2.7 percent are international students.

Expenses for 2005–06 *Application fee:* $30. *Tuition:* $16,850 full-time, $660 per credit part-time. *Mandatory fees:* $350 full-time, $225 per term part-time. Full-time tuition and fees vary according to course load. Part-time tuition and fees vary according to course load. *College room only:* $7640.

Freshman Admission The King's College requires a high school transcript, an interview, SAT or ACT scores, and TOEFL scores for international students. A minimum 3.0 high school GPA and recommendations are recommended. An essay is required for some. The application deadline for regular admission is February 1 and for early action it is November 15.

Transfer Admission The application deadline for admission is February 1.

Entrance Difficulty The King's College assesses its entrance difficulty level as very difficult; moderately difficult for transfers. For the fall 2004 freshman class, 55 percent of the applicants were accepted.

For Further Information Contact Mr. Brian T. Bell, Vice President of Enrollment Management, The King's College, Empire State Building, 350 Fifth Avenue, Lower Lobby, New York, NY 10118. *Telephone:* 888-969-7200 or 888-969-7200 Ext. 3610 (toll-free). *Fax:* 212-659-3611. *E-mail:* info@tkc.edu. *Web site:* http://www.tkc.edu/.

KOL YAAKOV TORAH CENTER
Monsey, New York

For Information Write to Kol Yaakov Torah Center, Monsey, NY 10952-2954.

LABORATORY INSTITUTE OF MERCHANDISING
New York, New York

LIM is a coed, primarily women's, proprietary, four-year college, founded in 1939, offering degrees at the associate and bachelor's levels.

Academic Information The faculty has 69 members (14% full-time), 13% with terminal degrees. The student-faculty ratio is 9:1. The library holds 10,300 titles, 100 serial subscriptions, and 500 audiovisual materials. Special programs include academic remediation, cooperative (work-study)

education, study abroad, advanced placement credit, accelerated degree programs, summer session for credit, part-time degree programs (daytime, summer), and internships. The most frequently chosen baccalaureate field is business/marketing.

Student Body Statistics The student body is made up of 608 undergraduates (154 freshmen). 97 percent are women and 3 percent are men. Students come from 33 states and territories and 5 other countries. 51 percent are from New York. 0.8 percent are international students.

Expenses for 2005–06 *Application fee:* $40. *Tuition:* $16,600 full-time, $495 per credit part-time. *Mandatory fees:* $450 full-time, $100 per term part-time. *College room only:* $11,000. Room charges vary according to housing facility.

Financial Aid Forms of aid include need-based and non-need-based scholarships and part-time jobs. The average aided 2003–04 undergraduate received an aid package worth $6754. The application deadline for financial aid is continuous.

Freshman Admission LIM requires an essay, a high school transcript, 2 recommendations, an interview, SAT or ACT scores, and TOEFL scores for international students. A minimum 2.5 high school GPA is recommended. The application deadline for regular admission is rolling.

Transfer Admission The application deadline for admission is rolling.

Entrance Difficulty LIM assesses its entrance difficulty level as moderately difficult. For the fall 2004 freshman class, 65 percent of the applicants were accepted.

For Further Information Contact Ms. Kristina Gibson, Director of Admissions, Laboratory Institute of Merchandising, 12 East 53rd Street, New York, NY 10022. *Telephone:* 212-752-1530 Ext. 217 or 800-677-1323 (toll-free). *Fax:* 212-317-8602. *E-mail:* admissions@limcollege.edu. *Web site:* http://www.limcollege.edu/.

LEHMAN COLLEGE OF THE CITY UNIVERSITY OF NEW YORK
Bronx, New York

Lehman is a coed, public, comprehensive unit of City University of New York System, founded in 1931, offering degrees at the bachelor's and master's levels and post-master's certificates. It has a 37-acre campus in Bronx.

Academic Information The faculty has 780 members (43% full-time), 53% with terminal degrees. The undergraduate student-faculty ratio is 14:1. The library holds 541,944 titles and 1,350 serial subscriptions. Special programs include services for learning-disabled students, an honors program, cooperative (work-study) education, study abroad, advanced placement credit, Freshman Honors College, ESL programs, double majors, independent study, distance learning, self-designed majors, summer session for credit, part-time degree programs (daytime, evenings, weekends, summer), adult/continuing education programs, internships, and arrangement for off-campus study with other units of the City University of New York System. The most frequently chosen baccalaureate fields are home economics/vocational home economics, computer/information sciences, social sciences and history.

Student Body Statistics The student body totals 10,281, of whom 8,108 are undergraduates (873 freshmen). 72 percent are women and 28 percent are men. Students come from 5 states and territories and 110 other countries. 100 percent are from New York. 0.3 percent are international students.

Expenses for 2005–06 *Application fee:* $50. *Area resident tuition:* $4000 full-time, $170 per year part-time. *State resident tuition:* $170 per year part-time. *Nonresident tuition:* $8640 full-time, $360 per year part-time. *Mandatory fees:* $270 full-time, $270 per year part-time. Full-time tuition and fees vary according to course load and program. Part-time tuition and fees vary according to course load and program.

Financial Aid Forms of aid include need-based scholarships and part-time jobs. The average aided 2003–04 undergraduate received an aid package worth $3531. The application deadline for financial aid is continuous.

Freshman Admission Lehman requires a high school transcript, a minimum 3.0 high school GPA, SAT or ACT scores, and TOEFL scores for international students. An essay, recommendations, and an interview are required for some. The application deadline for regular admission is rolling.

Transfer Admission The application deadline for admission is rolling.

Entrance Difficulty Lehman assesses its entrance difficulty level as moderately difficult. For the fall 2004 freshman class, 27 percent of the applicants were accepted.

For Further Information Contact Mr. Clarence A. Wilkes, Director of Admissions, Lehman College of the City University of New York, 250 Bedford Park Boulevard West, Bronx, NY 10468. *Telephone:* 718-960-8131 or 877-Lehman1 (toll-free out-of-state). *Fax:* 718-960-8712. *E-mail:* enroll@lehman.cuny.edu. *Web site:* http://www.lehman.cuny.edu/.

LE MOYNE COLLEGE

Syracuse, New York

SPONSOR
See Front Insert for Details!

Le Moyne is a coed, private, Roman Catholic (Jesuit), comprehensive institution, founded in 1946, offering degrees at the bachelor's and master's levels and postbachelor's certificates. It has a 151-acre campus in Syracuse.

Academic Information The faculty has 300 members (51% full-time), 64% with terminal degrees. The undergraduate student-faculty ratio is 13:1. The library holds 256,565 titles, 13,589 serial subscriptions, and 10,935 audiovisual materials. Special programs include academic remediation, services for learning-disabled students, an honors program, study abroad, advanced placement credit, accelerated degree programs, double majors, independent study, summer session for credit, part-time degree programs (daytime, evenings, weekends, summer), adult/continuing education programs, internships, and arrangement for off-campus study with Syracuse Consortium for the Cultural Foundations of Medicine. The most frequently chosen baccalaureate fields are business/marketing, psychology, social sciences and history.

Student Body Statistics The student body totals 3,487, of whom 2,787 are undergraduates (473 freshmen). 63 percent are women and 37 percent are men. Students come from 27 states and territories and 6 other countries. 94 percent are from New York. 0.9 percent are international students. 16 percent of the 2004 graduating class went on to graduate and professional schools.

Expenses for 2004–05 *Application fee:* $35. *Comprehensive fee:* $28,040 includes full-time tuition ($19,640), mandatory fees ($510), and college room and board ($7890). *College room only:* $4990. Room and board charges vary according to board plan and housing facility. *Part-time tuition:* $417 per credit hour. Part-time tuition varies according to class time.

Financial Aid Forms of aid include need-based and non-need-based scholarships, athletic grants, and part-time jobs. The average aided 2003–04 undergraduate received an aid package worth $17,840. The priority application deadline for financial aid is February 1.

Freshman Admission Le Moyne requires an essay, a high school transcript, 2 recommendations, SAT or ACT scores, and TOEFL scores for international students. An interview is recommended. The application deadline for regular admission is February 1 and for early decision it is December 1.

Transfer Admission The application deadline for admission is June 1.

Entrance Difficulty Le Moyne assesses its entrance difficulty level as moderately difficult; very difficult for 3-4 podiatry program, 3-4 optometry program, 3-4 dentistry program. For the fall 2004 freshman class, 74 percent of the applicants were accepted.

SPECIAL MESSAGE TO STUDENTS

Social Life More than 80 percent of Le Moyne students choose to live on campus, including 92 percent of the freshmen. The residential nature of the College fosters a friendly social atmosphere with a wide variety of activities and annual traditions. Students choose from more than seventy clubs and organizations, intramurals, and sixteen men's and women's Division I and Division II varsity teams. The programming board sponsors many cultural and social events like comedians, lecturers, music, movies, and more. The

Multicultural Affairs Committee and El Progreso sponsor events involving African-American and Latino cultures. Off campus, Syracuse, home to more than 20,000 students, offers a year-round calendar of activities geared toward the city's student culture. In addition, students enjoy the many recreational opportunities of scenic central New York, including snowboarding, downhill and cross-country skiing, hiking, bicycling, and swimming—all available within minutes of the campus.

Academic Highlights Le Moyne's Learning Communities facilitate the transition from high school to college by creating supportive learning environments and fostering friendships. The study-abroad program allows students to spend unforgettable semesters in exciting European locations such as Spain, France, and England. Externships let a student shadow alumni who work in the student's area of interest, taking students to places like Washington, D.C., and Albany, New York. Internships with many well-known corporations give Le Moyne students resume-building, real-world experience and credentials. The College also offers a generous academic scholarship program.

Interviews and Campus Visits A campus visit is strongly recommended. Most students who visit wind up applying. Students may choose from personal interviews, campus tours, group information sessions, day visits, and open house programs. Students should contact the Office of Admission at 315-445-4300 or 800-333-4733 (toll-free), from 8:30 a.m. until 4:30 p.m., for more details. The office is located on Salt Springs Road in Syracuse. The nearest commercial airport is Syracuse-Hancock International.

For Further Information Write to Dennis J. Nicholson, Director of Admission, Le Moyne College, Syracuse, NY 13214-1399. *E-mail:* admission@lemoyne.edu. *Web site:* http://www.lemoyne.edu.

See page 128 for a narrative description.

LIST COLLEGE OF JEWISH STUDIES

See The Jewish Theological Seminary.

LONG ISLAND COLLEGE HOSPITAL SCHOOL OF NURSING

Brooklyn, New York

For Information Write to Long Island College Hospital School of Nursing, Brooklyn, NY 11201-5940.

LONG ISLAND UNIVERSITY, BRENTWOOD CAMPUS

Brentwood, New York

Long Island University, Brentwood Campus is a coed, private, upper-level unit of Long Island University, founded in 1959, offering degrees at the bachelor's and master's levels and post-master's certificates. It has a 172-acre campus in Brentwood.

Academic Information The faculty has 110 members (18% full-time), 86% with terminal degrees. The undergraduate student-faculty ratio is 7:1. The library holds 55,000 titles, 285 serial subscriptions, and 12 audiovisual materials. Special programs include services for learning-disabled students, an honors program, advanced placement credit, independent study, summer session for credit, part-time degree programs (daytime, evenings, weekends, summer), and internships.

Student Body Statistics The student body totals 1,115, of whom 62 are undergraduates. 68 percent are women and 32 percent are men. Students come from 1 state or territory. 99 percent are from New York.

Expenses for 2004–05 *Tuition:* $20,870 full-time, $651 per credit part-time. *Mandatory fees:* $930 full-time, $200 per term part-time. Part-time tuition and fees vary according to course load.

Financial Aid Forms of aid include need-based scholarships. The application deadline for financial aid is continuous.

Transfer Admission   Long Island University, Brentwood Campus requires a minimum 2.0 college GPA. A minimum 2.5 college GPA is required for some. The application deadline for admission is September 14.

For Further Information   Contact Mr. John P. Metcalfe, Director of Admissions, Long Island University, Brentwood Campus, 100 Second Avenue, Brentwood, NY 11717. *Telephone:* 631-273-5112 Ext. 26. *Fax:* 631-952-0809. *E-mail:* information@brentwood.liu.edu. *Web site:* http://www.liu.edu/.

LONG ISLAND UNIVERSITY, BROOKLYN CAMPUS

Brooklyn, New York

Brooklyn Campus is a coed, private unit of Long Island University, founded in 1926, offering degrees at the associate, bachelor's, master's, doctoral, and first professional levels and post-master's, first professional, and postbachelor's certificates. It has a 10-acre campus in Brooklyn.

Academic Information   The faculty has 320 full-time members. The undergraduate student-faculty ratio is 17:1. Special programs include academic remediation, services for learning-disabled students, an honors program, cooperative (work-study) education, advanced placement credit, ESL programs, double majors, independent study, self-designed majors, summer session for credit, part-time degree programs (daytime, evenings, weekends, summer), adult/continuing education programs, and internships. The most frequently chosen baccalaureate fields are business/marketing, communications/communication technologies, health professions and related sciences.

Student Body Statistics   The student body totals 8,003, of whom 5,363 are undergraduates (994 freshmen). 72 percent are women and 28 percent are men. Students come from 36 states and territories. 92 percent are from New York. 1.8 percent are international students.

Expenses for 2004–05   *Application fee:* $30. *Comprehensive fee:* $29,272 includes full-time tuition ($20,832), mandatory fees ($1090), and college room and board ($7350). *College room only:* $4420. Full-time tuition and fees vary according to program. Room and board charges vary according to board plan. *Part-time tuition:* $651 per credit. *Part-time mandatory fees:* $264 per term. Part-time tuition and fees vary according to course load and program.

Financial Aid   Forms of aid include need-based and non-need-based scholarships, athletic grants, and part-time jobs. The application deadline for financial aid is continuous.

Freshman Admission   Brooklyn Campus requires a high school transcript, a minimum 2.0 high school GPA, and TOEFL scores for international students. An essay and a minimum 2.5 high school GPA are recommended. A minimum 3.0 high school GPA, 2 recommendations, an interview, and SAT or ACT scores are required for some. The application deadline for regular admission is rolling.

Transfer Admission   The application deadline for admission is rolling.

Entrance Difficulty   Brooklyn Campus assesses its entrance difficulty level as minimally difficult. For the fall 2004 freshman class, 67 percent of the applicants were accepted.

For Further Information   Contact Ms. Kristin Cohen, Dean of Admission and Enrollment Management, Long Island University, Brooklyn Campus, 1 University Plaza, Brooklyn, NY 11201. *Telephone:* 718-488-1011 or 800-LIU-PLAN (toll-free). *Fax:* 718-797-2399. *E-mail:* admissions@brooklyn.liu.edu. *Web site:* http://www.liu.edu/.

LONG ISLAND UNIVERSITY, C.W. POST CAMPUS

Brookville, New York

C.W. Post Campus is a coed, private, comprehensive unit of Long Island University, founded in 1954, offering degrees at the bachelor's, master's, and doctoral levels and post-master's and postbachelor's certificates. It has a 308-acre campus in Brookville near New York City.

Academic Information   The faculty has 1,018 members (32% full-time). The undergraduate student-faculty ratio is 15:1. Special programs include academic remediation, services for learning-disabled students, an honors program, cooperative (work-study) education, study abroad, advanced placement credit, accelerated degree programs, ESL programs, double majors, independent study, self-designed majors, summer session for credit, part-time degree programs (daytime, evenings, weekends, summer), adult/continuing education programs, internships, and arrangement for off-campus study. The most frequently chosen baccalaureate fields are business/marketing, education, visual/performing arts.

Student Body Statistics   The student body totals 8,421, of whom 4,897 are undergraduates (984 freshmen). 63 percent are women and 37 percent are men. Students come from 30 states and territories. 92 percent are from New York. 2.8 percent are international students. 31 percent of the 2004 graduating class went on to graduate and professional schools.

Expenses for 2004–05   *Application fee:* $30. *Comprehensive fee:* $30,200 includes full-time tuition ($20,870), mandatory fees ($1090), and college room and board ($8240). *College room only:* $5460. Full-time tuition and fees vary according to program. Room and board charges vary according to board plan. *Part-time tuition:* $651 per credit. Part-time tuition varies according to course load and program.

Financial Aid   Forms of aid include need-based and non-need-based scholarships, athletic grants, and part-time jobs. The application deadline for financial aid is March 1.

Freshman Admission   C.W. Post Campus requires a high school transcript, a minimum 2.5 high school GPA, SAT or ACT scores, and TOEFL scores for international students. An essay is recommended. The application deadline for regular admission is rolling.

Entrance Difficulty   C.W. Post Campus assesses its entrance difficulty level as moderately difficult; minimally difficult for Higher Education Opportunity Program, General Studies Program. For the fall 2004 freshman class, 75 percent of the applicants were accepted.

For Further Information   Contact Mr. Gary Bergman, Associate Provost for Enrollment Services, Long Island University, C.W. Post Campus, 720 Northern Boulevard, Brookville, NY 11548-1300. *Telephone:* 516-299-2900 or 800-LIU-PLAN (toll-free). *Fax:* 516-299-2137. *E-mail:* enroll@cwpost.liu.edu. *Web site:* http://www.liu.edu/.

LONG ISLAND UNIVERSITY, FRIENDS WORLD PROGRAM

Southampton, New York

Friends World is a coed, private, four-year college of Long Island University, founded in 1965, offering degrees at the bachelor's level. It has a 110-acre campus in Southampton.

Academic Information   The student-faculty ratio is 10:1. The library holds 115,380 titles, 665 serial subscriptions, and 886 audiovisual materials. Special programs include study abroad, advanced placement credit, independent study, self-designed majors, external degree programs, internships, and arrangement for off-campus study with Long Island University (C.W. Post campus, Brooklyn campus). The most frequently chosen baccalaureate field is interdisciplinary studies.

Student Body Statistics   The student body is made up of 195 undergraduates (29 freshmen). 69 percent are women and 31 percent are men. Students come from 29 states and territories and 5 other countries. 20 percent are from New York. 10 percent of the 2004 graduating class went on to graduate and professional schools.

Expenses for 2004–05   *Application fee:* $30. *Comprehensive fee:* $32,870 includes full-time tuition ($20,870), mandatory fees ($6000), and college room and board ($6000). Full-time tuition and fees vary according to location. Room and board charges vary according to board plan, housing facility, and location. *Part-time tuition:* $651 per credit. Part-time tuition varies according to course load.

Freshman Admission   Friends World requires an essay, a high school transcript, an interview, and TOEFL scores for international students. A minimum 3.0 high school GPA is recommended. The application deadline for regular admission is rolling.

Transfer Admission   The application deadline for admission is rolling.

Entrance Difficulty Friends World has an open admission policy except for the Comparative Religion and Culture program.

For Further Information Contact Ms. Joyce Tuttle, Director of Student Services, Friends World Program, Long Island University, Friends World Program, Friends World Program, 239 Montauk Highway, Southampton, NY 11968. *Telephone:* 631-287-8465, 631-287-8474 (toll-free in-state), or 800-287-8093 (toll-free out-of-state). *Fax:* 631-287-8093. *E-mail:* fw@liu.edu. *Web site:* http://www.southampton.liu.edu/fw/.

MACHZIKEI HADATH RABBINICAL COLLEGE

Brooklyn, New York

For Information Write to Machzikei Hadath Rabbinical College, Brooklyn, NY 11204-1805.

MANHATTAN COLLEGE

Riverdale, New York

SPONSOR
See Front Insert
for Details!

Manhattan is a coed, private, comprehensive institution, founded in 1853, affiliated with the Roman Catholic Church, offering degrees at the bachelor's and master's levels and post-master's certificates. It has a 31-acre campus in Riverdale near New York City.

Academic Information The faculty has 282 members (59% full-time), 68% with terminal degrees. The undergraduate student-faculty ratio is 14:1. The library holds 211,376 titles, 1,190 serial subscriptions, and 1,122 audiovisual materials. Special programs include academic remediation, services for learning-disabled students, an honors program, cooperative (work-study) education, study abroad, advanced placement credit, accelerated degree programs, ESL programs, double majors, independent study, summer session for credit, part-time degree programs (daytime, evenings, summer), adult/continuing education programs, internships, and arrangement for off-campus study with College of Mount Saint Vincent. The most frequently chosen baccalaureate fields are business/marketing, education, engineering/engineering technologies.
Student Body Statistics The student body totals 3,301, of whom 2,905 are undergraduates (656 freshmen). 50 percent are women and 50 percent are men. Students come from 42 states and territories and 27 other countries. 72 percent are from New York. 1.5 percent are international students. 38 percent of the 2004 graduating class went on to graduate and professional schools.
Expenses for 2005–06 *Application fee:* $40. *Comprehensive fee:* $29,625 includes full-time tuition ($19,400), mandatory fees ($1200), and college room and board ($9025). Full-time tuition and fees vary according to program. Room and board charges vary according to board plan. *Part-time tuition:* $550 per credit.
Financial Aid Forms of aid include need-based and non-need-based scholarships, athletic grants, and part-time jobs. The average aided 2003–04 undergraduate received an aid package worth $16,455. The priority application deadline for financial aid is March 1.
Freshman Admission Manhattan requires an essay, a high school transcript, a minimum 2.5 high school GPA, 1 recommendation, SAT or ACT scores, and TOEFL scores for international students. A minimum 3.0 high school GPA and an interview are recommended. An interview is required for some. The application deadline for regular admission is March 1 and for early decision it is November 15.
Transfer Admission The application deadline for admission is July 1.
Entrance Difficulty Manhattan assesses its entrance difficulty level as moderately difficult; very difficult for engineering programs. For the fall 2004 freshman class, 53 percent of the applicants were accepted.

SPECIAL MESSAGE TO STUDENTS

Social Life Manhattan College offers more than seventy cocurricular (academic) and extracurricular (social) clubs and organizations. The athletic program offers nineteen Division I varsity sports and extensive club and intramural programs. The Student Government is a very active and integral part of the College, and members of the Student Government are full voting members of the College Senate. Manhattan College is composed of 70 percent resident students and 30 percent commuter students. It is under the sponsorship of the Christian Brothers.

Academic Highlights Career Services and Cooperative Education enrich the academic environment by offering direct career experience in professional work environments. Students earn substantial salaries and establish contacts and confidence in the career world. IBM, Grumman, CIBA, Arthur Anderson, Turner Construction, and Cornell Medical Center are just a few companies that have hired Manhattan College co-op students. Manhattan College sponsors its own study-abroad programs in France and Belgium and is also associated with the Institute of European Studies, which has campuses in Austria, France, Germany, Great Britain, Italy, Japan, Mexico, Singapore, and Spain.

Interviews and Campus Visits A formal interview is strongly encouraged as part of the admission process because it often enables the Admissions Committee to better understand a prospective student's high school records and learn other information not always readily apparent from the application itself. In the fall, there are Saturday information sessions from 10 a.m. to 1 p.m. Tours of the campus are available every hour from 10 a.m. to 3:30 p.m., Monday through Friday. A tour offers valuable insights into the classrooms, laboratory facilities, dormitories, faculty, and students. The multimillion-dollar Research and Learning Center provides research facilities in computer graphics, robotics, lasers, solid-state technology, and drafting. The science labs offer students state-of-the-art equipment for advanced research and experiment opportunities. Draddy Gymnasium is a multipurpose indoor facility housing a six-lane, 200-meter track; three full-size basketball courts; tennis and volleyball courts; a weight room; and an indoor batting cage. Horan Hall Dormitory is the newest addition to the College campus. Opened in 1990, it houses 750 students. In September 2002, a renovated O'Malley Library opened. This new facility provides 45,000 square feet and is the predominant meeting and information center for the college community. For information about appointments and campus visits, students should call the Admission Office at 718-862-7200 or 800-MC2XCEL (toll-free), Monday through Friday, 9 a.m. to 4:30 p.m. The office is located in the O'Malley Library. The nearest commercial airport is La Guardia.

For Further Information Write to Mr. William J. Bisset Jr., Assistant Vice President for Enrollment Management, Admission Office, Manhattan College, Riverdale, NY 10471.

See page 130 for a narrative description.

MANHATTAN SCHOOL OF MUSIC
New York, New York

MSM is a coed, private, comprehensive institution, founded in 1917, offering degrees at the bachelor's, master's, and doctoral levels and post-master's and postbachelor's certificates. It has a 1-acre campus in New York.

Academic Information The faculty has 380 members (20% full-time), 24% with terminal degrees. The undergraduate student-faculty ratio is 7:1. The library holds 107,000 titles, 110 serial subscriptions, and 24,000 audiovisual materials. Special programs include academic remediation, services for learning-disabled students, advanced placement credit, ESL programs, and arrangement for off-campus study with Barnard College. The most frequently chosen baccalaureate field is visual/performing arts.
Student Body Statistics The student body totals 875, of whom 408 are undergraduates (103 freshmen). 48 percent are women and 52 percent are men. Students come from 35 states and territories and 37 other countries. 33 percent are from New York. 20.1 percent are international students. 60 percent of the 2004 graduating class went on to graduate and professional schools.

Expenses for 2005–06 *Application fee:* $100. *Comprehensive fee:* $40,785 includes full-time tuition ($26,000), mandatory fees ($2285), and college room and board ($12,500). *College room only:* $8050. Full-time tuition and fees vary according to course load. Room and board charges vary according to board plan. *Part-time tuition:* $1100 per credit. Part-time tuition varies according to course load.

Financial Aid Forms of aid include need-based and non-need-based scholarships and part-time jobs. The average aided 2003–04 undergraduate received an aid package worth $12,710. The priority application deadline for financial aid is March 1.

Freshman Admission MSM requires an essay, a high school transcript, a minimum 2.8 high school GPA, 1 recommendation, audition, and TOEFL scores for international students. A minimum 3.0 high school GPA, an interview, and SAT or ACT scores are recommended. The application deadline for regular admission is December 1.

Transfer Admission The application deadline for admission is December 1.

Entrance Difficulty MSM assesses its entrance difficulty level as very difficult. For the fall 2004 freshman class, 40 percent of the applicants were accepted.

For Further Information Contact Mrs. Amy Anderson, Director of Admission and Financial Aid, Manhattan School of Music, 120 Claremont Avenue, New York, NY 10027. *Telephone:* 212-749-2802 Ext. 4501. *Fax:* 212-749-3025. *E-mail:* admission@msmnyc.edu. *Web site:* http://www.msmnyc.edu/.

MANHATTANVILLE COLLEGE

Purchase, New York

SPONSOR
See Front Insert for Details!

Manhattanville is a coed, private, comprehensive institution, founded in 1841, offering degrees at the bachelor's and master's levels. It has a 100-acre campus in Purchase near New York City.

Academic Information The faculty has 343 members (26% full-time), 25% with terminal degrees. The undergraduate student-faculty ratio is 12:1. The library holds 292,846 titles, 18,930 serial subscriptions, and 3,957 audiovisual materials. Special programs include academic remediation, services for learning-disabled students, an honors program, study abroad, advanced placement credit, accelerated degree programs, Freshman Honors College, ESL programs, double majors, independent study, distance learning, self-designed majors, summer session for credit, part-time degree programs (daytime, evenings, summer), adult/continuing education programs, internships, and arrangement for off-campus study with Purchase College, State University of New York, Mills College, American University (Washington Semester), New York State Visiting Student Program. The most frequently chosen baccalaureate fields are business/marketing, psychology, social sciences and history.

Student Body Statistics The student body totals 2,608, of whom 1,719 are undergraduates (440 freshmen). 69 percent are women and 31 percent are men. Students come from 35 states and territories and 49 other countries. 72 percent are from New York. 8.4 percent are international students. 29 percent of the 2004 graduating class went on to graduate and professional schools.

Expenses for 2004–05 *Application fee:* $50. *Comprehensive fee:* $34,700 includes full-time tuition ($23,620), mandatory fees ($950), and college room and board ($10,130). *College room only:* $6020. Room and board charges vary according to board plan. *Part-time tuition:* $540 per credit. *Part-time mandatory fees:* $35 per term. Part-time tuition and fees vary according to program.

Financial Aid Forms of aid include need-based and non-need-based scholarships and part-time jobs. The priority application deadline for financial aid is March 1.

Freshman Admission Manhattanville requires an essay, a high school transcript, a minimum 2.0 high school GPA, 2 recommendations, SAT or ACT scores, and TOEFL scores for international students. A minimum 3.0 high school GPA and an interview are recommended. SAT scores, ACT scores, SAT and SAT Subject Test or ACT scores, and SAT Subject Test scores are required for some. The application deadline for regular admission is March 1 and for early decision it is December 1.

Transfer Admission The application deadline for admission is March 1.

Entrance Difficulty Manhattanville assesses its entrance difficulty level as moderately difficult. For the fall 2004 freshman class, 56 percent of the applicants were accepted.

SPECIAL MESSAGE TO STUDENTS

Social Life Student activities include an active student government; more than fifty clubs; fourteen varsity sports; a student-run newspaper, yearbook, and literary magazine; and television and radio stations. Strong community service activities, such as Midnight Runs, are popular among the students. The College's mission is to educate ethically and socially responsible leaders for the global community.

Academic Highlights Manhattanville College combines rigorous liberal arts studies and the portfolio system with interdisciplinary internships and study-abroad opportunities. Students work one-on-one with an adviser throughout their college career as they expand and complete their portfolios. Manhattanville College is well known for its school of education (offering a five-year B.A./M.A.T.) as well as studies in international management, psychology, and math and computer science.

Interviews and Campus Visits Students may visit the campus Monday through Friday, 9 a.m. to 5 p.m. Tours are given at 10:30 a.m. and 2:30 p.m. daily, with interviews scheduled around those times. Saturday tours and interviews during the late fall and early spring are also available from 10 a.m. to 3 p.m. Students who have applied or who have been accepted may spend a day attending classes or stay overnight with a current student. Prior arrangements need to be made for these visits. For information or appointments, students should call the Admissions Office at 800-32-VILLE (toll-free). The nearest commercial airport is Westchester County.

For Further Information Write to Mr. Barry W. Ward, Vice President for Enrollment Management and Student Development, Manhattanville College, 2900 Purchase Street, Purchase, NY 10577. *E-mail:* admissions@mville.com. *Web site:* www.manhattanville.edu.

MANNES COLLEGE THE NEW SCHOOL FOR MUSIC

New York, New York

Mannes is a coed, private, comprehensive unit of New School University, founded in 1916, offering degrees at the bachelor's and master's levels and postbachelor's certificates.

For Further Information Contact Ms. Allison Scola, Director of Enrollment, Mannes College The New School For Music, 150 West 85th Street, New York, NY 10024-4402. *Telephone:* 212-580-0210 Ext. 247 or 800-292-3040 (toll-free). *Fax:* 212-580-1738. *E-mail:* mannesadmissions@newschool.edu. *Web site:* http://www.mannes.edu/.

MARIA COLLEGE

Albany, New York

Maria is a coed, private, two-year college, founded in 1958, offering degrees at the associate level. It has a 9-acre campus in Albany.

Academic Information The faculty has 65 members (45% full-time), 17% with terminal degrees. The student-faculty ratio is 10:1. The library holds 56,746 titles, 160 serial subscriptions, and 375 audiovisual materials. Special programs include academic remediation, services for learning-disabled students, advanced placement credit, independent study, summer session for credit, part-time degree programs (daytime, evenings, weekends, summer), adult/continuing education programs, and arrangement for off-campus study with members of the Hudson-Mohawk Association of Colleges and Universities.

Student Body Statistics The student body is made up of 788 undergraduates (84 freshmen). 87 percent are women and 13 percent are men. Students come from 5 states and territories and 4 other countries. 98 percent are from New York. 0.5 percent are international students. 18 percent of the 2004 graduating class went on to four-year colleges.

Expenses for 2004–05 *Application fee:* $35. *Tuition:* $7100 full-time, $260 per credit part-time. *Mandatory fees:* $160 full-time, $40 per term part-time. Full-time tuition and fees vary according to program. Part-time tuition and fees vary according to program.

Financial Aid Forms of aid include need-based scholarships and part-time jobs. The application deadline for financial aid is continuous.

Freshman Admission Maria requires an essay, a high school transcript, a minimum 2.0 high school GPA, 1 recommendation, an interview, SAT or ACT scores, and TOEFL scores for international students. The application deadline for regular admission is August 26.

Transfer Admission The application deadline for admission is August 26.

Entrance Difficulty Maria assesses its entrance difficulty level as minimally difficult. For the fall 2004 freshman class, 72 percent of the applicants were accepted.

For Further Information Contact Ms. Laurie A. Gilmore, Director of Admissions, Maria College, 700 New Scotland Avenue, Albany, NY 12208. *Telephone:* 518-438-3111 Ext. 217. *Fax:* 518-453-1366. *E-mail:* admissions@mariacollege.edu. *Web site:* http://www.mariacollege.edu/.

MARIST COLLEGE
Poughkeepsie, New York

Marist is a coed, private, comprehensive institution, founded in 1929, offering degrees at the bachelor's and master's levels. It has a 150-acre campus in Poughkeepsie near Albany and New York City.

Academic Information The faculty has 596 members (33% full-time). The undergraduate student-faculty ratio is 15:1. The library holds 176,347 titles, 13,826 serial subscriptions, and 4,940 audiovisual materials. Special programs include academic remediation, services for learning-disabled students, an honors program, cooperative (work-study) education, study abroad, advanced placement credit, accelerated degree programs, ESL programs, double majors, independent study, distance learning, summer session for credit, part-time degree programs (daytime, evenings, weekends, summer), adult/continuing education programs, internships, and arrangement for off-campus study with Associated Colleges of the Mid-Hudson Area. The most frequently chosen baccalaureate fields are business/marketing, communications/communication technologies, education.

Student Body Statistics The student body totals 5,646, of whom 4,800 are undergraduates (955 freshmen). 57 percent are women and 43 percent are men. Students come from 37 states and territories and 19 other countries. 61 percent are from New York. 0.2 percent are international students. 25 percent of the 2004 graduating class went on to graduate and professional schools.

Expenses for 2005–06 *Application fee:* $40. *One-time mandatory fee:* $25. *Comprehensive fee:* $30,233 includes full-time tuition ($20,535), mandatory fees ($480), and college room and board ($9218). *College room only:* $5890. Room and board charges vary according to board plan and housing facility. *Part-time tuition:* $463 per credit. *Part-time mandatory fees:* $65 per term.

Financial Aid Forms of aid include need-based and non-need-based scholarships, athletic grants, and part-time jobs. The average aided 2004–05 undergraduate received an aid package worth an estimated $12,685. The application deadline for financial aid is May 1 with a priority deadline of February 15.

Freshman Admission Marist requires an essay, a high school transcript, 2 recommendations, SAT or ACT scores, and TOEFL scores for international students. The application deadline for regular admission is February 15 and for early action it is December 1.

Transfer Admission The application deadline for admission is June 1.

Entrance Difficulty Marist assesses its entrance difficulty level as moderately difficult; very difficult for computer science, biology, chemistry,

environmental science, psychology, business programs. For the fall 2004 freshman class, 49 percent of the applicants were accepted.

For Further Information Contact Mr. Jay Murray, Director of Admissions, Marist College, 3399 North Road, Poughkeepsie, NY 12601. *Telephone:* 845-575-3226 or 800-436-5483 (toll-free). *Fax:* 845-471-6213. *E-mail:* admissions@marist.edu. *Web site:* http://www.marist.edu/.

MARYMOUNT COLLEGE OF FORDHAM UNIVERSITY
Tarrytown, New York

Marymount is a women's, private, four-year college of Fordham University, founded in 1907, offering degrees at the associate and bachelor's levels. It has a 25-acre campus in Tarrytown near New York City.

Academic Information The faculty has 170 members (31% full-time), 46% with terminal degrees. The student-faculty ratio is 9:1. Special programs include academic remediation, services for learning-disabled students, an honors program, study abroad, advanced placement credit, ESL programs, double majors, independent study, self-designed majors, summer session for credit, part-time degree programs (evenings, weekends), adult/continuing education programs, internships, and arrangement for off-campus study with Touro College; New York Medical College. The most frequently chosen baccalaureate fields are business/marketing, education, visual/performing arts.

Student Body Statistics The student body is made up of 1,036 undergraduates (255 freshmen). Students come from 33 states and territories and 12 other countries. 74 percent are from New York. 1.8 percent are international students. 30 percent of the 2004 graduating class went on to graduate and professional schools.

Expenses for 2004–05 *Application fee:* $30. *Comprehensive fee:* $29,462 includes full-time tuition ($19,100), mandatory fees ($602), and college room and board ($9760). Full-time tuition and fees vary according to student level. Room and board charges vary according to board plan and housing facility. *Part-time tuition:* $635 per credit hour. *Part-time mandatory fees:* $301 per term. Part-time tuition and fees vary according to class time.

Financial Aid Forms of aid include need-based and non-need-based scholarships and part-time jobs. The average aided 2003–04 undergraduate received an aid package worth $15,968. The priority application deadline for financial aid is March 1.

Freshman Admission Marymount requires a high school transcript, a minimum 2.0 high school GPA, SAT or ACT scores, and TOEFL scores for international students. An essay, a minimum 3.0 high school GPA, 1 recommendation, and an interview are recommended. The application deadline for regular admission is August 31 and for early action it is November 1.

Transfer Admission The application deadline for admission is rolling.

Entrance Difficulty Marymount assesses its entrance difficulty level as moderately difficult. For the fall 2004 freshman class, 78 percent of the applicants were accepted.

For Further Information Contact Ms. Dorrie Voulgaris, Associate Director of Admissions, Marymount College of Fordham University, 100 Marymount Avenue, Tarrytown, NY 10591-3796. *Telephone:* 914-332-8295 or 800-724-4312 (toll-free). *Fax:* 914-332-7442. *E-mail:* mcenroll@fordham.edu. *Web site:* http://www.fordham.edu.

MARYMOUNT MANHATTAN COLLEGE
New York, New York

Marymount Manhattan is a coed, private, four-year college, founded in 1936, offering degrees at the bachelor's level. It has a 3-acre campus in New York.

Academic Information The faculty has 316 members (26% full-time), 45% with terminal degrees. The student-faculty ratio is 12:1. The library holds 102,000 titles, 600 serial subscriptions, and 13,285 audiovisual materials. Special programs include academic remediation, services for learning-disabled students, an honors program, study abroad, advanced placement credit, accelerated degree programs, ESL programs, double majors, independent study, summer session for credit, part-time degree programs (daytime, evenings, weekends, summer), adult/continuing education programs, internships, and arrangement for off-campus study with Hunter College of the City University of New York. The most frequently chosen baccalaureate fields are communications/communication technologies, business/marketing, visual/performing arts.

Student Body Statistics   The student body is made up of 2,077 undergraduates (454 freshmen). 78 percent are women and 22 percent are men. Students come from 47 states and territories and 36 other countries. 68 percent are from New York. 3.2 percent are international students. 33 percent of the 2004 graduating class went on to graduate and professional schools.

Expenses for 2004–05   *Application fee:* $60. *Comprehensive fee:* $29,718 includes full-time tuition ($16,606), mandatory fees ($746), and college room and board ($12,366). *College room only:* $9066. Full-time tuition and fees vary according to course load. Room and board charges vary according to board plan and housing facility. *Part-time tuition:* $490 per credit. *Part-time mandatory fees:* $325 per term. Part-time tuition and fees vary according to course load.

Financial Aid   Forms of aid include need-based and non-need-based scholarships and part-time jobs. The priority application deadline for financial aid is March 15.

Freshman Admission   Marymount Manhattan requires an essay, a high school transcript, a minimum 2 high school GPA, 2 recommendations, SAT or ACT scores, and TOEFL scores for international students. An interview is recommended. Audition for dance and theater programs is required for some. The application deadline for regular admission is rolling and for early decision it is November 1.

Transfer Admission   The application deadline for admission is rolling.

Entrance Difficulty   Marymount Manhattan assesses its entrance difficulty level as moderately difficult. For the fall 2004 freshman class, 80 percent of the applicants were accepted.

For Further Information   Contact Mr. Thomas Friebel, Associate Vice President for Enrollment Services, Marymount Manhattan College, 221 East 71st Street, New York, NY 10021. *Telephone:* 212-517-0430 or 800-MARYMOUNT (toll-free out-of-state). *Fax:* 212-517-0448. *E-mail:* admissions@mmm.edu. *Web site:* http://www.mmm.edu/.

See page 132 for a narrative description.

MEDAILLE COLLEGE
Buffalo, New York

Medaille is a coed, private, comprehensive institution, founded in 1875, offering degrees at the associate, bachelor's, and master's levels. It has a 13-acre campus in Buffalo.

Academic Information   The faculty has 297 members (26% full-time), 22% with terminal degrees. The undergraduate student-faculty ratio is 15:1. The library holds 56,854 titles, 238 serial subscriptions, and 2,423 audiovisual materials. Special programs include academic remediation, services for learning-disabled students, an honors program, advanced placement credit, accelerated degree programs, double majors, independent study, self-designed majors, summer session for credit, part-time degree programs (daytime, evenings, weekends, summer), adult/continuing education programs, internships, and arrangement for off-campus study with 16 members of the Western New York Consortium. The most frequently chosen baccalaureate fields are business/marketing, education, liberal arts/general studies.

Student Body Statistics   The student body totals 2,526, of whom 1,708 are undergraduates (307 freshmen). 63 percent are women and 37 percent are men. Students come from 1 state or territory and 2 other countries. 0.4 percent are international students. 20 percent of the 2004 graduating class went on to graduate and professional schools.

Expenses for 2004–05   *Application fee:* $25. *Comprehensive fee:* $21,120 includes full-time tuition ($14,010), mandatory fees ($310), and college room and board ($6800). Full-time tuition and fees vary according to location. Room and board charges vary according to housing facility.

Part-time tuition: $467 per credit hour. *Part-time mandatory fees:* $90 per term. Part-time tuition and fees vary according to course load.

Financial Aid   Forms of aid include need-based and non-need-based scholarships and part-time jobs. The average aided 2003–04 undergraduate received an aid package worth $10,000. The priority application deadline for financial aid is April 1.

Freshman Admission   Medaille requires a high school transcript, an interview, SAT or ACT scores, and TOEFL scores for international students. An essay, a minimum 2.0 high school GPA, 1 recommendation, and SAT scores are recommended. An essay and 2.5 high school GPA for veterinary technology and elementary teacher education majors are required for some. The application deadline for regular admission is August 1.

Transfer Admission   The application deadline for admission is rolling.

Entrance Difficulty   Medaille assesses its entrance difficulty level as moderately difficult; minimally difficult for transfers. For the fall 2004 freshman class, 94 percent of the applicants were accepted.

For Further Information   Contact Medaille College, Medaille College, Office of Admissions, Buffalo, NY 14214. *Telephone:* 716-884-3281 Ext. 203 or 800-292-1582 (toll-free in-state). *Fax:* 716-884-0291. *E-mail:* gflorczak@medaille.edu. *Web site:* http://www.medaille.edu/.

MEDGAR EVERS COLLEGE OF THE CITY UNIVERSITY OF NEW YORK
Brooklyn, New York

Medgar Evers College of the City University of New York is a coed, public, four-year college of City University of New York System, founded in 1969, offering degrees at the associate and bachelor's levels. It has a 1-acre campus in Brooklyn.

Academic Information   The faculty has 339 members (44% full-time). The student-faculty ratio is 17:1. The library holds 111,000 titles, 24,410 serial subscriptions, and 20,000 audiovisual materials. Special programs include academic remediation, services for learning-disabled students, an honors program, cooperative (work-study) education, study abroad, advanced placement credit, ESL programs, independent study, summer session for credit, part-time degree programs (daytime, evenings, weekends, summer), external degree programs, adult/continuing education programs, internships, and arrangement for off-campus study with other units of the City University of New York System. The most frequently chosen baccalaureate fields are business/marketing, education, psychology.

Student Body Statistics   The student body is made up of 5,098 undergraduates (724 freshmen). 77 percent are women and 23 percent are men. Students come from 3 states and territories and 50 other countries. 99 percent are from New York. 4.5 percent are international students.

Expenses for 2004–05   *Application fee:* $60. *State resident tuition:* $4000 full-time, $170 per credit part-time. *Nonresident tuition:* $8640 full-time, $360 per credit part-time. *Mandatory fees:* $230 full-time, $78.35 per term part-time.

Financial Aid   Forms of aid include need-based and non-need-based scholarships and part-time jobs. The priority application deadline for financial aid is April 1.

Freshman Admission   Medgar Evers College of the City University of New York requires a high school transcript, GED, and TOEFL scores for international students. SAT and SAT Subject Test or ACT scores are required for some. The application deadline for regular admission is rolling.

Transfer Admission   The application deadline for admission is rolling.

Entrance Difficulty   Medgar Evers College of the City University of New York has an open admission policy except for nursing program. It assesses its entrance difficulty as moderately difficult for nursing program.

For Further Information   Contact Mr. Warren Heusner, Director of Admissions, Medgar Evers College of the City University of New York, 1665 Bedford Avenue, Brooklyn, NY 11225. *Telephone:* 718-270-6025. *Fax:* 718-270-6198. *E-mail:* enroll@mec.cuny.edu. *Web site:* http://www.mec.cuny.edu/.

MEMORIAL HOSPITAL SCHOOL OF NURSING

Albany, New York

For Information   Write to Memorial Hospital School of Nursing, Albany, NY 12204.

MERCY COLLEGE

Dobbs Ferry, New York

Mercy is a coed, private, comprehensive institution, founded in 1951, offering degrees at the associate, bachelor's, and master's levels. It has a 60-acre campus in Dobbs Ferry near New York City.

Academic Information   The faculty has 989 members (24% full-time). The undergraduate student-faculty ratio is 17:1. The library holds 322,610 titles and 1,765 serial subscriptions. Special programs include academic remediation, services for learning-disabled students, an honors program, cooperative (work-study) education, study abroad, advanced placement credit, accelerated degree programs, ESL programs, double majors, independent study, distance learning, self-designed majors, summer session for credit, part-time degree programs (daytime, evenings, weekends, summer), adult/continuing education programs, internships, and arrangement for off-campus study with Westchester Conservatory of Music, New York Medical College.

Student Body Statistics   The student body totals 10,395, of whom 6,208 are undergraduates (693 freshmen). 35 percent are women and 65 percent are men. Students come from 6 states and territories and 49 other countries. 2 percent are international students.

Expenses for 2004–05   *Application fee:* $35. *Comprehensive fee:* $19,800 includes full-time tuition ($11,230), mandatory fees ($144), and college room and board ($8426). *Part-time tuition:* $472 per credit. *Part-time mandatory fees:* $6 per credit.

Financial Aid   Forms of aid include need-based and non-need-based scholarships, athletic grants, and part-time jobs. The priority application deadline for financial aid is May 1.

Freshman Admission   Mercy requires a high school transcript and 1 recommendation. An interview, SAT scores, and TOEFL scores for international students are recommended. The application deadline for regular admission is rolling.

Transfer Admission   The application deadline for admission is rolling.

Entrance Difficulty   Mercy has an open admission policy. It assesses its entrance difficulty as noncompetitive for transfers.

For Further Information   Contact Mrs. Sharon Handelson, Director of Admissions and Recruitment, Mercy College, 555 Broadway, Dobbs Ferry, NY 10522-1189. *Telephone:* 914-674-7462 or 800-MERCY-NY (toll-free). *Fax:* 914-674-7382. *E-mail:* admissions@mercy.edu. *Web site:* http://www.mercy.edu/.

MESIVTA OF EASTERN PARKWAY RABBINICAL SEMINARY

Brooklyn, New York

For Information   Write to Mesivta of Eastern Parkway Rabbinical Seminary, Brooklyn, NY 11218-5559.

MESIVTA TIFERETH JERUSALEM OF AMERICA

New York, New York

For Information   Write to Mesivta Tifereth Jerusalem of America, New York, NY 10002-6301.

MESIVTA TORAH VODAATH RABBINICAL SEMINARY

Brooklyn, New York

For Information   Write to Mesivta Torah Vodaath Rabbinical Seminary, Brooklyn, NY 11218-5299.

METROPOLITAN COLLEGE OF NEW YORK

New York, New York

Metropolitan College of New York is a coed, primarily women's, private, comprehensive institution, founded in 1964, offering degrees at the associate, bachelor's, and master's levels.

Academic Information   The faculty has 277 members (14% full-time). The undergraduate student-faculty ratio is 16:1. The library holds 26,800 titles, 3,414 serial subscriptions, and 45 audiovisual materials. Special programs include academic remediation, services for learning-disabled students, cooperative (work-study) education, study abroad, accelerated degree programs, ESL programs, summer session for credit, adult/continuing education programs, and internships. The most frequently chosen baccalaureate fields are business/marketing, home economics/vocational home economics.

Student Body Statistics   The student body totals 1,591, of whom 1,273 are undergraduates. 79 percent are women and 21 percent are men. Students come from 5 states and territories. 98 percent are from New York. 0.2 percent are international students.

Expenses for 2005–06   *Application fee:* $30. *Tuition:* $13,824 full-time, $432 per credit part-time. *Mandatory fees:* $300 full-time. Full-time tuition and fees vary according to program. Part-time tuition varies according to program.

Financial Aid   Forms of aid include need-based and non-need-based scholarships and part-time jobs. The application deadline for financial aid is continuous.

Freshman Admission   Metropolitan College of New York requires an essay, a high school transcript, 2 recommendations, an interview, TOEFL scores for international students, and TABE. A minimum 3.0 high school GPA, SAT scores, and SAT or ACT scores are recommended. College entrance exam and TABE are required for some. The application deadline for regular admission is August 15.

Transfer Admission   The application deadline for admission is August 15.

Entrance Difficulty   Metropolitan College of New York assesses its entrance difficulty level as moderately difficult. For the fall 2004 freshman class, 92 percent of the applicants were accepted.

For Further Information   Contact Ms. Sabrina Badal, Director of Admissions, Metropolitan College of New York, 75 Varick Street, 12th Floor, New York, NY 10013. *Telephone:* 212-343-1234 Ext. 2711 or 800-33-THINK Ext. 5001 (toll-free in-state). *Fax:* 212-343-8470. *Web site:* http://www.metropolitan.edu/.

MIRRER YESHIVA

Brooklyn, New York

For Information   Write to Mirrer Yeshiva, Brooklyn, NY 11223-2010.

MOLLOY COLLEGE

Rockville Centre, New York

SPONSOR
See Front Insert for Details!

Molloy College is a coed, private, comprehensive institution, founded in 1955, offering degrees at the associate, bachelor's, and master's levels and post-master's certificates. It has a 30-acre campus in Rockville Centre near New York City.

Academic Information   The faculty has 357 members (39% full-time), 34% with terminal degrees. The undergraduate student-faculty ratio is 10:1. The library holds 135,000 titles and 9,675 audiovisual materials. Special programs include academic remediation, services for learning-disabled students, an honors program, cooperative (work-study) education, study abroad, advanced placement credit, ESL programs, double majors, self-designed majors, summer session for credit, part-time degree programs (daytime, evenings, weekends, summer), adult/continuing education programs, and internships.

Student Body Statistics   The student body totals 3,352, of whom 2,512 are undergraduates (326 freshmen). 77 percent are women and 23 percent are men. Students come from 4 states and territories and 9 other countries. 0.1 percent are international students.

Expenses for 2004–05   *Application fee:* $30. *Tuition:* $15,150 full-time, $505 per credit part-time. *Mandatory fees:* $700 full-time.

Financial Aid   Forms of aid include need-based and non-need-based scholarships, athletic grants, and part-time jobs. The average aided 2003–04 undergraduate received an aid package worth $9362. The priority application deadline for financial aid is May 1.

Freshman Admission   Molloy College requires an essay, a high school transcript, SAT or ACT scores, and TOEFL scores for international students. An interview is recommended. 1 recommendation is required for some. The application deadline for regular admission is rolling and for early decision it is November 1.

Transfer Admission   The application deadline for admission is rolling.

Entrance Difficulty   Molloy College assesses its entrance difficulty level as moderately difficult. For the fall 2004 freshman class, 70 percent of the applicants were accepted.

SPECIAL MESSAGE TO STUDENTS

Social Life Molloy College is a comprehensive, private commuter college in the Dominican tradition. Many students actively participate in clubs and organizations, such as student government and dance, cheerleading, and glee clubs. A great many students also participate in athletic programs, including baseball, basketball, cross-country, the equestrian team, lacrosse, soccer, softball, tennis, and volleyball.

Academic Highlights In a tradition of academic excellence, Molloy College offers more than thirty programs of study. Merit scholarships are available to students based upon academic averages and SAT scores. The College's Freshman Honors program challenges academically talented students. With a student-faculty ratio of 9:1, Molloy's smaller classes foster an interactive learning environment and provide opportunities for individualized attention. Students needing academic assistance may visit the writing lab and participate in tutoring. The internship program at Molloy College offers students the opportunity for on-the-job experience, along with the classroom exposure so essential to the fully educated person. Internships are available and suggested for most majors.

Interviews and Campus Visits Campus interviews are recommended but not required. Students are encouraged to meet with a counselor to ask any questions that they may have. Applicants are also encouraged to visit the campus for a tour either during an open house or on an individual basis. Students who are visiting the campus should see the library, the academic computing lab, the nursing lab, the cablevision studio, and the education resource center. All of these areas provide a sense of the academic life at Molloy. Students are also invited to visit the campus student center, the bookstore, the cafeteria, the student lounge, and Hayes Theatre. These areas give students a taste of Molloy's social life. For information about appointments and campus visits, students should call the Admissions Office at 888-4-MOLLOY (toll-free), Monday through Thursday, 8:30 a.m. to 7 p.m., or Friday, 8:30 a.m. to 5 p.m. The office is located in the Wilbur Arts Center on campus. The nearest commercial airport is John F. Kennedy International.

For Further Information Write to Molloy College, 1000 Hempstead Avenue, P.O. Box 5002, Rockville Centre, NY 11570.

See page 134 for a narrative description.

MONROE COLLEGE
Bronx, New York

Monroe College is a coed, proprietary, primarily two-year college, founded in 1933, offering degrees at the associate and bachelor's levels.

Academic Information   The faculty has 201 members (33% full-time), 18% with terminal degrees. The student-faculty ratio is 21:1. The library holds 28,000 titles and 301 serial subscriptions. Special programs include academic remediation, cooperative (work-study) education, ESL programs, summer session for credit, part-time degree programs (daytime, evenings, weekends, summer), adult/continuing education programs, and internships. The most frequently chosen baccalaureate fields are business/marketing, computer/information sciences.

Student Body Statistics   The student body is made up of 4,284 undergraduates (966 freshmen). 72 percent are women and 28 percent are men. Students come from 7 states and territories and 8 other countries. 99 percent are from New York. 1.1 percent are international students. 26 percent of the 2004 graduating class went on to four-year colleges.

Expenses for 2004–05   *Application fee:* $35. *Comprehensive fee:* $23,370 includes full-time tuition ($8760), mandatory fees ($600), and college room and board ($14,010). Full-time tuition and fees vary according to course load. Room and board charges vary according to housing facility. *Part-time tuition:* $365 per credit. *Part-time mandatory fees:* $150 per term.

Financial Aid   Forms of aid include need-based scholarships and part-time jobs. The application deadline for financial aid is continuous.

Freshman Admission   Monroe College requires a high school transcript, an interview, and TOEFL scores for international students. The application deadline for regular admission is August 26.

Transfer Admission   The application deadline for admission is August 26.

Entrance Difficulty   Monroe College assesses its entrance difficulty level as moderately difficult. For the fall 2004 freshman class, 76 percent of the applicants were accepted.

For Further Information   Contact Mr. Brad Allison, Director of Admissions, Monroe College, Monroe College Way, 2501 Jerome Avenue, Bronx, NY 10468. *Telephone:* 718-933-6700 Ext. 240 or 800-55MONROE (toll-free). *Web site:* http://www.monroecollege.edu/.

MONROE COLLEGE
New Rochelle, New York

Monroe College is a coed, proprietary, primarily two-year college, founded in 1983, offering degrees at the associate and bachelor's levels. It is located in New Rochelle near New York City.

Academic Information   The faculty has 201 members (33% full-time), 18% with terminal degrees. The student-faculty ratio is 20:1. The library holds 8,400 titles and 211 serial subscriptions. Special programs include academic remediation, cooperative (work-study) education, ESL programs, summer session for credit, part-time degree programs (daytime, evenings, weekends, summer), external degree programs, adult/continuing education programs, and internships. The most frequently chosen baccalaureate fields are business/marketing, computer/information sciences.

Student Body Statistics   The student body is made up of 1,570 undergraduates (441 freshmen). 69 percent are women and 31 percent are men. Students come from 9 states and territories and 10 other countries. 98 percent are from New York. 13 percent are international students. 26 percent of the 2004 graduating class went on to four-year colleges.

Expenses for 2004–05   *Application fee:* $35. *Comprehensive fee:* $23,370 includes full-time tuition ($8760), mandatory fees ($600), and college room and board ($14,010). Room and board charges vary according to board plan. *Part-time tuition:* $1095 per course. *Part-time mandatory fees:* $150 per term.

Financial Aid   Forms of aid include need-based scholarships and part-time jobs. The application deadline for financial aid is continuous.

Freshman Admission   Monroe College requires a high school transcript, an interview, and TOEFL scores for international students. The application deadline for regular admission is August 26.

Transfer Admission   The application deadline for admission is August 26.

Entrance Difficulty   Monroe College assesses its entrance difficulty level as moderately difficult. For the fall 2004 freshman class, 73 percent of the applicants were accepted.

For Further Information   Contact Ms. Lisa Scorca, High School Admissions, Monroe College, 434 Main Street, New Rochelle, NY 10801. *Telephone:* 914-654-3200 or 800-55MONROE (toll-free). *Fax:* 914-632-5462. *E-mail:* ejerome@monroecollege.edu. *Web site:* http://www.monroecollege.edu/.

MOUNT SAINT MARY COLLEGE

Newburgh, New York

SPONSOR
See Front Insert for Details!

Mount Saint Mary is a coed, private, comprehensive institution, founded in 1960, offering degrees at the bachelor's and master's levels. It has a 72-acre campus in Newburgh near New York City.

Academic Information   The faculty has 249 members (27% full-time), 37% with terminal degrees. The undergraduate student-faculty ratio is 16:1. The library holds 113,676 titles, 870 serial subscriptions, and 21,297 audiovisual materials. Special programs include academic remediation, an honors program, cooperative (work-study) education, study abroad, advanced placement credit, accelerated degree programs, Freshman Honors College, double majors, independent study, distance learning, self-designed majors, summer session for credit, part-time degree programs (daytime, evenings, weekends, summer), adult/continuing education programs, internships, and arrangement for off-campus study with Associated Colleges of the Mid-Hudson Area. The most frequently chosen baccalaureate fields are business/marketing, English, social sciences and history.

Student Body Statistics   The student body totals 2,621, of whom 2,099 are undergraduates (422 freshmen). 73 percent are women and 27 percent are men. Students come from 15 states and territories and 1 other country. 89 percent are from New York. 18 percent of the 2004 graduating class went on to graduate and professional schools.

Expenses for 2004–05   *Application fee:* $35. *Comprehensive fee:* $23,330 includes full-time tuition ($15,180), mandatory fees ($510), and college room and board ($7640). *College room only:* $4300. Full-time tuition and fees vary according to degree level. Room and board charges vary according to board plan, gender, housing facility, location, and student level. *Part-time tuition:* $506 per credit hour. *Part-time mandatory fees:* $35 per term. Part-time tuition and fees vary according to degree level.

Financial Aid   Forms of aid include need-based and non-need-based scholarships and part-time jobs. The average aided 2004–05 undergraduate received an aid package worth an estimated $11,273. The priority application deadline for financial aid is February 15.

Freshman Admission   Mount Saint Mary requires a high school transcript, SAT or ACT scores, and TOEFL scores for international students. An essay, a minimum 3.0 high school GPA, 3 recommendations, and an interview are recommended. An essay, 3 recommendations, and an interview are required for some. The application deadline for regular admission is rolling.

Transfer Admission   The application deadline for admission is rolling.

Entrance Difficulty   Mount Saint Mary assesses its entrance difficulty level as moderately difficult; very difficult for nursing program. For the fall 2004 freshman class, 79 percent of the applicants were accepted.

SPECIAL MESSAGE TO STUDENTS

Social Life The Mount is a friendly place with an active campus life as well as much to experience off campus. Student government coordinates many activities, such as movie nights, student productions, dinner dances, coffeehouses, lectures, and trips to New York City. The College also has many clubs, including a Gaelic Society, a Black Student Union, and a Latino Student Union, which sponsor events for the entire campus community. Students get involved in community service through organizations such as Habitat for Humanity. Students enjoy intramural sports and the facilities of the Kaplan Recreation Center, including a pool, a track, and exercise rooms. The Mount competes in eleven sports in Division III of the NCAA.

Academic Highlights Mount Saint Mary College offers more than fifty academic programs that help students learn to think, communicate, and value life. Cooperative Education opportunities and internships help students focus on career options. Many students study abroad, expanding their outlook. The College has many honor societies, and tutoring is available to students who want to improve their performance. Professors are accessible and ready to help students achieve their goals. Students may access the Internet in the academic computing lab and around the campus via wireless academic network. Curtin Memorial Library is a technologically advanced research resource that is staffed with helpful librarians. Academic halls feature smart classrooms, with theater-quality video and sound, which that enable professors to create exciting presentations, incorporating video, CDs, and the Internet.

Interviews and Campus Visits The Mount encourages on-campus interviews. Campus visits give students a sense of the atmosphere in which they will live and learn. They give students a chance to meet Mount students and faculty members, sit in on classes, and check out facilities. The Admissions Office conducts open houses throughout the year. Mount Saint Mary College is an independent, liberal arts, coed college with 2,500 students. It is located on 70 acres overlooking the Hudson River in a residential area of Newburgh, New York, about midway between New York City and Albany. For information about appointments and campus visits, students should call the Office of Admissions at 845-569-3248 or 888-YES-MSMC (toll-free). The nearest commercial airport is Stewart International.

For Further Information Write to Mount Saint Mary College, 330 Powell Avenue, Newburgh, NY 12550-3598. *E-mail:* mtstmary@msmc.edu. *Web site:* http://www.msmc.edu.

NAZARETH COLLEGE OF ROCHESTER

Rochester, New York

Nazareth College is a coed, private, comprehensive institution, founded in 1924, offering degrees at the bachelor's and master's levels and post-master's certificates. It has a 150-acre campus in Rochester.

Academic Information   The faculty has 294 members (46% full-time), 54% with terminal degrees. The undergraduate student-faculty ratio is 13:1. The library holds 162,593 titles, 1,888 serial subscriptions, and 12,236 audiovisual materials. Special programs include academic remediation, services for learning-disabled students, an honors program, cooperative (work-study) education, study abroad, advanced placement credit, double majors, independent study, summer session for credit, part-time degree programs (daytime, evenings, summer), adult/continuing education programs, internships, and arrangement for off-campus study with 14 members of the Rochester Area Colleges. The most frequently chosen baccalaureate fields are business/marketing, health professions and related sciences, psychology.

Student Body Statistics   The student body totals 3,140, of whom 2,035 are undergraduates (449 freshmen). 77 percent are women and 23 percent are men. Students come from 23 states and territories. 94 percent are from New York. 0.1 percent are international students. 38.5 percent of the 2004 graduating class went on to graduate and professional schools.

Expenses for 2005–06   *Application fee:* $40. *Comprehensive fee:* $26,616 includes full-time tuition ($18,040), mandatory fees ($736), and college room and board ($7840). *College room only:* $4420. Room and board charges vary according to board plan and housing facility. *Part-time tuition:* $439 per credit hour. *Part-time mandatory fees:* $516 per year.

Financial Aid   Forms of aid include need-based and non-need-based scholarships and part-time jobs. The average aided 2004–05 undergraduate received an aid package worth an estimated $14,497. The priority application deadline for financial aid is February 15.

Freshman Admission   Nazareth College requires an essay, a high school transcript, 1 recommendation, SAT or ACT scores, and TOEFL scores for international students. 2 recommendations and an interview are recommended. Audition/portfolio review is required for some. The application deadline for regular admission is February 15; for early decision it is November 15; and for early action it is December 15.

Transfer Admission   The application deadline for admission is March 15.

Entrance Difficulty   Nazareth College assesses its entrance difficulty level as moderately difficult; very difficult for physical therapy program. For the fall 2004 freshman class, 81 percent of the applicants were accepted.

For Further Information   Contact Mr. Thomas K. DaRin, Vice President for Enrollment Management, Nazareth College of Rochester, 4245 East Avenue, Rochester, NY 14618-3790. *Telephone:* 585-389-2860 or 800-462-3944 (toll-free in-state). *Fax:* 585-389-2826. *E-mail:* admissions@naz.edu. *Web site:* http://www.naz.edu/.

See page 136 for a narrative description.

NEW SCHOOL BACHELOR'S PROGRAM, NEW SCHOOL UNIVERSITY

New York, New York

The New School is a coed, private, upper-level unit of New School University, founded in 1919, offering degrees at the bachelor's, master's, and doctoral levels.

For Further Information   Contact Ms. Gerianne Brusati, Director of Educational Advising and Admissions, New School Bachelor's Program, New School University, 66 West 12th Street, New York, NY 10011-8603. *Telephone:* 212-229-5630. *Fax:* 212-989-3887. *E-mail:* admissions@dialnsa.edu. *Web site:* http://www.nsu.newschool.edu/.

NEW SCHOOL UNIVERSITY, EUGENE LANG COLLEGE

See Eugene Lang College, New School University.

NEW SCHOOL UNIVERSITY, MANNES COLLEGE OF MUSIC

See Mannes College The New School For Music.

NEW SCHOOL UNIVERSITY, PARSONS SCHOOL OF DESIGN

See Parsons School of Design, New School University.

NEW YORK CITY COLLEGE OF TECHNOLOGY OF THE CITY UNIVERSITY OF NEW YORK

Brooklyn, New York

For Information   Write to New York City College of Technology of the City University of New York, Brooklyn, NY 11201-2983.

THE NEW YORK COLLEGE FOR WHOLISTIC HEALTH EDUCATION & RESEARCH

See New York College of Health Professions.

NEW YORK COLLEGE OF HEALTH PROFESSIONS

Syosset, New York

New York College is a coed, private, primarily two-year college, founded in 1981, offering degrees at the associate, incidental bachelor's, and master's levels. It is located in Syosset near New York City.

Expenses for 2004–05   *Application fee:* $85. *Tuition:* $9900 full-time, $275 per credit part-time. *Mandatory fees:* $400 full-time.

For Further Information   Contact Dr. Mary Rodas, Director of Admissions, New York College of Health Professions, 6801 Jericho Turnpike, Syosset, NY 11791. *Telephone:* 800-922-7337 Ext. 354 or 800-922-7337 Ext. 351 (toll-free). *Fax:* 516-364-0989. *E-mail:* admission@nycollege.edu. *Web site:* http://www.nycollege.edu/.

See page 138 for a narrative description.

NEW YORK INSTITUTE OF TECHNOLOGY

Old Westbury, New York

NYIT is a coed, private university, founded in 1955, offering degrees at the associate, bachelor's, master's, doctoral, and first professional levels and post-master's and postbachelor's certificates. It has a 1,050-acre campus in Old Westbury near New York City.

Academic Information   The faculty has 866 members (25% full-time). The undergraduate student-faculty ratio is 16:1. The library holds 208,620 titles, 14,857 serial subscriptions, and 49,239 audiovisual materials. Special programs include academic remediation, services for learning-disabled students, an honors program, cooperative (work-study) education, study abroad, advanced placement credit, accelerated degree programs, ESL programs, double majors, independent study, distance learning, self-designed majors, summer session for credit, part-time degree programs (daytime, evenings, weekends, summer), external degree programs, adult/continuing education programs, internships, and arrangement for off-campus study with New York State Teachers' Centers. The most frequently chosen baccalaureate fields are architecture, business/marketing, communications/communication technologies.

Student Body Statistics   The student body totals 9,387, of whom 5,602 are undergraduates (874 freshmen). 39 percent are women and 61 percent are men. Students come from 48 states and territories and 82 other countries. 81 percent are from New York. 6 percent are international students. 48 percent of the 2004 graduating class went on to graduate and professional schools.

Expenses for 2004–05   *Application fee:* $50. *Comprehensive fee:* $25,970 includes full-time tuition ($17,840), mandatory fees ($350), and college room and board ($7780). *College room only:* $4080. Full-time tuition and fees vary according to course load and program. Room and board charges vary according to board plan, housing facility, and location. *Part-time tuition:* $594 per credit. *Part-time mandatory fees:* $150 per term. Part-time tuition and fees vary according to course load.

Financial Aid   Forms of aid include need-based and non-need-based scholarships, athletic grants, and part-time jobs. The average aided 2003–04 undergraduate received an aid package worth $10,846. The priority application deadline for financial aid is February 1.

Freshman Admission   NYIT requires an essay, a high school transcript, SAT or ACT scores, and TOEFL scores for international students. A minimum X high school GPA, recommendations, an interview, and proof of volunteer or work experience required for physical therapy, physician assistant and occupational therapy programs; portfolio for fine arts programs are required for some. The application deadline for regular admission is rolling.

Transfer Admission   The application deadline for admission is rolling.

Entrance Difficulty   NYIT assesses its entrance difficulty level as moderately difficult; very difficult for BS/DO, honors, occupational therapy, physical therapy, physician assistant programs. For the fall 2004 freshman class, 67 percent of the applicants were accepted.

For Further Information   Contact Ms. Doreen Meyer, Director of Financial Aid, New York Institute of Technology, PO Box 8000, Old Westbury, NY 11568. *Telephone:* 516-686-7871 or 800-345-NYIT (toll-free). *Fax:* 516-686-7613. *E-mail:* admissions@nyit.edu. *Web site:* http://www.nyit.edu/.

NEW YORK SCHOOL OF INTERIOR DESIGN
New York, New York

NYSID is a coed, primarily women's, private, comprehensive institution, founded in 1916, offering degrees at the associate, bachelor's, and master's levels. It has a 1-acre campus in New York.

Academic Information   The faculty has 79 members (3% full-time), 33% with terminal degrees. The undergraduate student-faculty ratio is 10:1. The library holds 12,000 titles, 110 serial subscriptions, and 100 audiovisual materials. Special programs include services for learning-disabled students, study abroad, advanced placement credit, ESL programs, independent study, summer session for credit, part-time degree programs (daytime, evenings, weekends, summer), and internships. The most frequently chosen baccalaureate field is visual/performing arts.
Student Body Statistics   The student body totals 784, of whom 769 are undergraduates (100 freshmen). 91 percent are women and 9 percent are men. Students come from 17 states and territories and 25 other countries. 83 percent are from New York. 12.2 percent are international students.
Expenses for 2005–06   *Application fee:* $50. *Tuition:* $18,880 full-time, $590 per credit part-time. *Mandatory fees:* $170 full-time, $85 per term part-time. Full-time tuition and fees vary according to course load. Part-time tuition and fees vary according to course load.
Financial Aid   Forms of aid include need-based scholarships and part-time jobs. The average aided 2004–05 undergraduate received an aid package worth an estimated $8500. The priority application deadline for financial aid is May 1.
Freshman Admission   NYSID requires an essay, a high school transcript, a minimum 2.8 high school GPA, 2 recommendations, a portfolio, SAT or ACT scores, and TOEFL scores for international students. The application deadline for regular admission is rolling.
Transfer Admission   The application deadline for admission is rolling.
Entrance Difficulty   NYSID assesses its entrance difficulty level as moderately difficult. For the fall 2004 freshman class, 66 percent of the applicants were accepted.

SPECIAL MESSAGE TO STUDENTS

Social Life The student chapter of the American Society of Interior Designers (ASID) is open to degree candidates. The chapter sponsors extracurricular seminars that encourage professional networking, and many feature lectures by well-known designers. In addition, social events, such as the student auction, and trips to sites of historical interest are sponsored by ASID.

Academic Highlights Juried student work is featured in the annual student exhibition of thesis projects, now in its fifty-sixth year. Architectural and design professionals attend this event. Many courses integrate the wealth of New York's resources into the curriculum, with visits to showrooms, museums, studios, and landmark buildings, for example.

Interviews and Campus Visits Visits and interviews are recommended. They provide one-on-one opportunities to meet faculty and staff members and current students. Free open-house lectures are held throughout the year. These interior design seminars offer insights into the profession and answer questions about the design field and training requirements. The School maintains two galleries, which feature special exhibitions, lectures, and symposia related to architecture and design. For information about appointments and campus visits, students should call the Office of Admissions at 212-472-1500 Ext. 204 or 800-336-9743 (toll-free), Monday

through Friday, 9 a.m. to 5 p.m. The fax number is 212-472-1867. The office is located at 170 East 70th Street on campus. The nearest commercial airport is John F. Kennedy International.

For Further Information Write to Mr. David Sprouls, Director of Admissions, New York School of Interior Design, 170 East 70th Street, New York, NY 10021-5110.

See page 140 for a narrative description.

NEW YORK STATE COLLEGE OF CERAMICS
See Alfred University.

NEW YORK UNIVERSITY
New York, New York

NYU is a coed, private university, founded in 1831, offering degrees at the associate, bachelor's, master's, doctoral, and first professional levels and post-master's, first professional, and postbachelor's certificates.

Academic Information   The faculty has 4,167 members (46% full-time), 85% with terminal degrees. The undergraduate student-faculty ratio is 12:1. The library holds 5 million titles, 48,958 serial subscriptions, and 1 million audiovisual materials. Special programs include services for learning-disabled students, an honors program, cooperative (work-study) education, study abroad, advanced placement credit, accelerated degree programs, Freshman Honors College, ESL programs, double majors, independent study, distance learning, self-designed majors, summer session for credit, part-time degree programs (daytime, evenings, weekends, summer), adult/continuing education programs, internships, and arrangement for off-campus study with Spelman College, Morehouse College, Bennett College, Tougaloo College; American University. The most frequently chosen baccalaureate fields are social sciences and history, business/marketing, visual/performing arts.
Student Body Statistics   The student body totals 39,408, of whom 20,212 are undergraduates (4,603 freshmen). 61 percent are women and 39 percent are men. Students come from 52 states and territories and 91 other countries. 42 percent are from New York. 3.8 percent are international students. 18 percent of the 2004 graduating class went on to graduate and professional schools.
Expenses for 2004–05   *Application fee:* $65. *Comprehensive fee:* $41,484 includes full-time tuition ($28,328), mandatory fees ($1766), and college room and board ($11,390). Full-time tuition and fees vary according to program. Room and board charges vary according to board plan and housing facility. *Part-time tuition:* $835 per credit. *Part-time mandatory fees:* $52 per credit, $262 per term. Part-time tuition and fees vary according to program.
Financial Aid   Forms of aid include need-based and non-need-based scholarships and part-time jobs. The average aided 2004–05 undergraduate received an aid package worth an estimated $18,692. The priority application deadline for financial aid is February 15.
Freshman Admission   NYU requires an essay, a high school transcript, a minimum 3.0 high school GPA, 2 recommendations, SAT or ACT scores, and TOEFL scores for international students. SAT Subject Test scores are recommended. An interview, audition, portfolio, and SAT Subject Test scores are required for some. The application deadline for regular admission is January 15 and for early decision it is November 1.
Transfer Admission   The application deadline for admission is April 1.
Entrance Difficulty   NYU assesses its entrance difficulty level as most difficult; very difficult for transfers. For the fall 2004 freshman class, 35 percent of the applicants were accepted.

For Further Information   Contact Ms. Barbara Hall, Associate Provost for Admissions and Financial Aid, New York University, 22 Washington Square North, New York, NY 10011. *Telephone:* 212-998-4500. *Fax:* 212-995-4902. *Web site:* http://www.nyu.edu/.

NIAGARA UNIVERSITY
Niagara Falls, New York

SPONSOR
See Front Insert for Details!

NU is a coed, private, comprehensive institution, founded in 1856, affiliated with the Roman Catholic Church, offering degrees at the associate, bachelor's, and master's levels and post-master's certificates. It has a 160-acre campus in Niagara Falls near Buffalo and Toronto.

Academic Information   The faculty has 327 members (40% full-time). The undergraduate student-faculty ratio is 17:1. The library holds 279,793 titles and 8,600 serial subscriptions. Special programs include academic remediation, services for learning-disabled students, an honors program, cooperative (work-study) education, study abroad, advanced placement credit, accelerated degree programs, Freshman Honors College, ESL programs, double majors, summer session for credit, part-time degree programs (daytime, evenings, summer), adult/continuing education programs, internships, and arrangement for off-campus study with members of the New York State Visiting Student Program, the Western New York Consortium. The most frequently chosen baccalaureate fields are business/marketing, education, social sciences and history.

Student Body Statistics   The student body totals 3,807, of whom 2,943 are undergraduates (738 freshmen). 61 percent are women and 39 percent are men. Students come from 31 states and territories and 16 other countries. 93 percent are from New York. 5.1 percent are international students. 25 percent of the 2004 graduating class went on to graduate and professional schools.

Expenses for 2004–05   *Application fee:* $30. *Comprehensive fee:* $26,470 includes full-time tuition ($17,700), mandatory fees ($720), and college room and board ($8050). *Part-time tuition:* $590 per credit hour. *Part-time mandatory fees:* $20 per term.

Financial Aid   Forms of aid include need-based and non-need-based scholarships, athletic grants, and part-time jobs. The average aided 2004–05 undergraduate received an aid package worth an estimated $17,851. The priority application deadline for financial aid is February 15.

Freshman Admission   NU requires a high school transcript, SAT or ACT scores, and TOEFL scores for international students. A minimum 3.0 high school GPA, 3 recommendations, and an interview are recommended. The application deadline for regular admission is August 1.

Transfer Admission   The application deadline for admission is August 15.

Entrance Difficulty   NU assesses its entrance difficulty level as moderately difficult; minimally difficult for Higher Education Opportunity Program. For the fall 2004 freshman class, 80 percent of the applicants were accepted.

SPECIAL MESSAGE TO STUDENTS

Social Life When it comes to student activities, Niagara University (NU) has something for everyone. With more than seventy different clubs and organizations, students can involve themselves in their current interests, or they can try new activities such as martial arts, student government, yearbook, or any of the other social, cultural, academic, and athletic clubs and organizations NU has to offer. Students can also enjoy using the Kiernan Athletic and Recreation Center as well as the Dwyer Ice Hockey Arena, visit the Castellani Art Museum, or see one of NU's acclaimed theater productions. The University is located 90 minutes from Toronto and 30 minutes from Buffalo, allowing NU students to experience a variety of other cultural, social, and professional sports activities.

Academic Highlights Niagara offers several special academic opportunities. The honors program is designed to recognize and support talented and motivated students. Study abroad, internship, and cooperative education programs provide students with the opportunity to learn about their major field beyond the classroom setting. For those students who are undecided about their major, NU offers the Academic Exploration Program. In addition, a variety of academic and personal services are available, such as the Learning Center, with free tutoring, and the Career Development Office.

Interviews and Campus Visits A visit to NU is strongly recommended. Each prospective student has the opportunity to tour the campus with a Niagara student and to meet with an admission counselor to discuss any concerns he or she has regarding admission, academics, or student life.

During a campus visit, students may also sit in on a class or stay overnight in one of the residence halls, speak with students and faculty members, and meet with a financial aid staff member. By visiting campus, each student can experience firsthand the many benefits of a Niagara education. Prospective students and their families are invited to take a student-guided tour of campus. Questions about student life and activities, student services, and academic facilities can be answered. The tour includes visits to the Student Center, Computer Center, Castellani Art Museum, Alumni Chapel, dining facilities, post office, residence halls, library, communications building, science building, and Kiernan Athletic and Recreation Center. For information about appointments and campus visits, students should call the Office of Admission at 716-286-8700 or 800-462-2111 (toll-free), Monday through Friday, 9 a.m. to 5 p.m., or on selected Saturday mornings, 10 a.m. to noon. The fax number is 716-286-8710. The office is located at 643 Bailo Hall on campus. The nearest commercial airport is Buffalo International.

For Further Information Write to Mr. Mike Konopski, Director of Admission, Office of Admission, Niagara University, 643 Bailo Hall, Niagara University, NY 14109-2011. *E-mail:* admissions@niagara.edu. *Web site:* http://www.niagara.edu.

See page 142 for a narrative description.

NYACK COLLEGE
Nyack, New York

Nyack is a coed, private, comprehensive institution, founded in 1882, affiliated with The Christian and Missionary Alliance, offering degrees at the associate, bachelor's, master's, and first professional levels. It has a 102-acre campus in Nyack near New York City.

Academic Information   The faculty has 288 members (37% full-time), 50% with terminal degrees. The library holds 127,271 titles, 958 serial subscriptions, and 4,739 audiovisual materials. Special programs include academic remediation, an honors program, study abroad, advanced placement credit, accelerated degree programs, ESL programs, double majors, independent study, distance learning, summer session for credit, part-time degree programs (daytime, evenings, weekends, summer), adult/continuing education programs, internships, and arrangement for off-campus study with Council for Christian Colleges and Universities. The most frequently chosen baccalaureate fields are business/marketing, education, liberal arts/general studies.

Student Body Statistics   The student body totals 2,908, of whom 2,056 are undergraduates (277 freshmen). 60 percent are women and 40 percent are men. Students come from 41 states and territories and 30 other countries. 68 percent are from New York. 5.1 percent are international students.

Expenses for 2005–06   *Application fee:* $25. *Comprehensive fee:* $23,150 includes full-time tuition ($14,750), mandatory fees ($800), and college room and board ($7600). Full-time tuition and fees vary according to location and program. Room and board charges vary according to board plan and housing facility. *Part-time tuition:* $600 per credit. *Part-time mandatory fees:* $200 per term. Part-time tuition and fees vary according to course load, location, and program.

Financial Aid   Forms of aid include need-based and non-need-based scholarships, athletic grants, and part-time jobs. The average aided 2003–04 undergraduate received an aid package worth $13,207. The priority application deadline for financial aid is March 1.

Freshman Admission   Nyack requires an essay, a high school transcript, 1 recommendation, and TOEFL scores for international students. An interview, evidence of faith commitment, and SAT or ACT scores are required for some. The application deadline for regular admission is rolling.

Transfer Admission   The application deadline for admission is rolling.

Entrance Difficulty   Nyack assesses its entrance difficulty level as moderately difficult.

For Further Information   Contact Ms. Bethany Ilsley, Director of Admissions, Nyack College, 1 South Boulevard, Nyack, NY 10960-3698. *Telephone:* 845-358-1710 Ext. 350 or 800-33-NYACK (toll-free). *Fax:* 845-353-1297. *E-mail:* admissions@nyack.edu. *Web site:* http://www.nyack.edu.

OHR HAMEIR THEOLOGICAL SEMINARY

Peekskill, New York

For Information Write to Ohr Hameir Theological Seminary, Peekskill, NY 10566.

OHR SOMAYACH/JOSEPH TANENBAUM EDUCATIONAL CENTER

Monsey, New York

Ohr Somayach/Joseph Tanenbaum Educational Center is a men's, private, Jewish, five-year college, founded in 1979, offering degrees at the bachelor's and first professional levels. It has a 7-acre campus in Monsey near New York City.

Academic Information The faculty has 18 members (44% full-time). The library holds 2,300 titles. Special programs include academic remediation, services for learning-disabled students, an honors program, summer session for credit, part-time degree programs (daytime, evenings, weekends, summer), adult/continuing education programs, and internships. The most frequently chosen baccalaureate field is philosophy, religion, and theology.
Student Body Statistics The student body totals 110, of whom 98 are undergraduates (21 freshmen). Students come from 10 states and territories and 8 other countries. 62 percent are from New York. 40.8 percent are international students. 92 percent of the 2004 graduating class went on to graduate and professional schools.
Expenses for 2004–05 *Tuition:* $10,500 full-time.
Financial Aid The priority application deadline for financial aid is July 31.
Freshman Admission Ohr Somayach/Joseph Tanenbaum Educational Center requires recommendations and an interview. A high school transcript is recommended. An essay is required for some. The application deadline for regular admission is rolling.
Transfer Admission The application deadline for admission is rolling.
Entrance Difficulty Ohr Somayach/Joseph Tanenbaum Educational Center assesses its entrance difficulty level as moderately difficult. For the fall 2004 freshman class, 65 percent of the applicants were accepted.

For Further Information Contact Rabbi Avrohom Braun, Dean of Students, Ohr Somayach/Joseph Tanenbaum Educational Center, PO Box 334, Monsey, NY 10952-0334. *Telephone:* 914-425-1370 Ext. 22. *Web site:* http://www.ohrsomayach.edu/.

PACE UNIVERSITY

New York, New York

Pace U is a coed, private university, founded in 1906, offering degrees at the associate, bachelor's, master's, doctoral, and first professional levels and post-master's, first professional, and postbachelor's certificates.

Academic Information The faculty has 1,219 members (38% full-time), 53% with terminal degrees. The undergraduate student-faculty ratio is 15:1. The library holds 813,997 titles and 1,729 serial subscriptions. Special programs include academic remediation, an honors program, cooperative (work-study) education, study abroad, advanced placement credit, accelerated degree programs, Freshman Honors College, ESL programs, double majors, independent study, distance learning, summer session for credit, part-time degree programs (daytime, evenings, summer), adult/continuing education programs, and internships. The most frequently chosen baccalaureate fields are business/marketing, communications/ communication technologies, computer/information sciences.
Student Body Statistics The student body totals 13,670, of whom 8,668 are undergraduates (1,462 freshmen). 61 percent are women and 39 percent are men. Students come from 41 states and territories and 28 other countries. 77 percent are from New York. 4.1 percent are international students.

Expenses for 2004–05 *Application fee:* $45. *Comprehensive fee:* $31,112 includes full-time tuition ($22,100), mandatory fees ($612), and college room and board ($8400). Full-time tuition and fees vary according to student level. Room and board charges vary according to board plan and housing facility. *Part-time tuition:* $634 per credit. *Part-time mandatory fees:* $160 per term. Part-time tuition and fees vary according to course load.
Financial Aid Forms of aid include need-based and non-need-based scholarships, athletic grants, and part-time jobs. The average aided 2003–04 undergraduate received an aid package worth $12,919. The priority application deadline for financial aid is February 15.
Freshman Admission Pace U requires an essay, a high school transcript, 2 recommendations, SAT or ACT scores, and TOEFL scores for international students. A minimum 3.0 high school GPA and an interview are recommended. The application deadline for regular admission is rolling and for early action it is November 1.
Transfer Admission The application deadline for admission is rolling.
Entrance Difficulty Pace U assesses its entrance difficulty level as moderately difficult. For the fall 2004 freshman class, 70 percent of the applicants were accepted.

For Further Information Contact Ms. Joanna Broda, Director of Admission, NY and Westchester, Pace University, One Pace Plaza, New York, NY 10038. *Telephone:* 212-346-1781 or 800-874-7223 (toll-free). *Fax:* 212-346-1040. *E-mail:* infoctr@pace.edu. *Web site:* http://www.pace.edu/.

PARSONS SCHOOL OF DESIGN, NEW SCHOOL UNIVERSITY

New York, New York

Parsons is a coed, private, comprehensive unit of New School University, founded in 1896, offering degrees at the associate, bachelor's, and master's levels. It has a 2-acre campus in New York.

For Further Information Contact Ms. Heather Ward, Director of Admissions, Parsons School of Design, New School University, 66 Fifth Avenue, New York, NY 10011-8878. *Telephone:* 212-229-8910 or 877-528-3321 (toll-free). *Fax:* 212-229-5166. *E-mail:* customer@ newschool.edu. *Web site:* http://www.parsons.edu/.

PAUL SMITH'S COLLEGE OF ARTS AND SCIENCES

Paul Smiths, New York

Paul Smith's is a coed, private, four-year college, founded in 1937, offering degrees at the associate and bachelor's levels. It has a 14,200-acre campus in Paul Smiths.

Academic Information The faculty has 65 members (98% full-time), 18% with terminal degrees. The student-faculty ratio is 14:1. The library holds 56,000 titles and 504 serial subscriptions. Special programs include academic remediation, services for learning-disabled students, an honors program, cooperative (work-study) education, study abroad, advanced placement credit, ESL programs, double majors, self-designed majors, summer session for credit, adult/continuing education programs, and internships. The most frequently chosen baccalaureate fields are natural resources/environmental science, business/marketing, personal/miscellaneous services.
Student Body Statistics The student body is made up of 816 undergraduates (242 freshmen). 31 percent are women and 69 percent are men. Students come from 29 states and territories and 11 other countries. 60 percent are from New York. 0.5 percent are international students.
Expenses for 2005–06 *Application fee:* $30. *Comprehensive fee:* $24,170 includes full-time tuition ($16,100), mandatory fees ($1010), and college room and board ($7060). *College room only:* $3530. Full-time tuition and fees vary according to program. Room and board charges vary according to board plan. *Part-time tuition:* $505 per credit hour. Part-time tuition varies according to course load and program.

Financial Aid Forms of aid include need-based scholarships and part-time jobs. The average aided 2003–04 undergraduate received an aid package worth $5300. The priority application deadline for financial aid is March 3.

Freshman Admission Paul Smith's requires an essay, a high school transcript, 1 recommendation, SAT or ACT scores, and TOEFL scores for international students. An interview is required for some. The application deadline for regular admission is rolling.

Transfer Admission The application deadline for admission is rolling.

Entrance Difficulty Paul Smith's assesses its entrance difficulty level as minimally difficult. For the fall 2004 freshman class, 81 percent of the applicants were accepted.

For Further Information Contact Melik Houry, Vice President of Enrollment, Paul Smith's College of Arts and Sciences, PO Box 265, Paul Smiths, NY 12970-0265. *Telephone:* 518-327-6227 or 800-421-2605 (toll-free). *Fax:* 518-327-6016. *Web site:* http://www.paulsmiths.edu/.

PHILLIPS BETH ISRAEL SCHOOL OF NURSING

New York, New York

Phillips Beth Israel School of Nursing is a coed, primarily women's, private, two-year college, founded in 1904, offering degrees at the associate level.

Academic Information The faculty has 18 members (56% full-time), 44% with terminal degrees. The student-faculty ratio is 8:1. The library holds 600 serial subscriptions. Special programs include advanced placement credit, part-time degree programs (daytime, evenings, weekends), and arrangement for off-campus study with Pace University.

Student Body Statistics The student body is made up of 175 undergraduates (7 freshmen). 75 percent are women and 25 percent are men. Students come from 8 states and territories and 5 other countries. 90 percent are from New York. 4 percent are international students. 10 percent of the 2004 graduating class went on to four-year colleges.

Expenses for 2005–06 *Application fee:* $35. *Tuition:* $11,890 full-time, $290 per credit part-time. *Mandatory fees:* $2095 full-time. Full-time tuition and fees vary according to course level.

Financial Aid Forms of aid include need-based scholarships. The application deadline for financial aid is June 1.

Freshman Admission Phillips Beth Israel School of Nursing requires an essay, a high school transcript, a minimum 2.5 high school GPA, 2 recommendations, an interview, TOEFL scores for international students, and nursing exam. SAT scores are recommended. The application deadline for regular admission is April 1.

Transfer Admission The application deadline for admission is April 1.

Entrance Difficulty Phillips Beth Israel School of Nursing assesses its entrance difficulty level as moderately difficult. For the fall 2004 freshman class, 12 percent of the applicants were accepted.

For Further Information Contact Mrs. Bernice Pass-Stern, Assistant Dean, Phillips Beth Israel School of Nursing, 310 East 22nd Street, 9th Floor, New York, NY 10010-5702. *Telephone:* 212-614-6176. *Fax:* 212-614-6109. *E-mail:* bstern@bethisraelny.org. *Web site:* http://www.futurenursebi.org.

PLATTSBURGH STATE UNIVERSITY OF NEW YORK

See State University of New York at Plattsburgh.

POLYTECHNIC UNIVERSITY, BROOKLYN CAMPUS

Brooklyn, New York

Polytechnic is a coed, private university, founded in 1854, offering degrees at the bachelor's, master's, and doctoral levels and postbachelor's certificates. It has a 3-acre campus in Brooklyn.

Academic Information The faculty has 277 members (47% full-time), 49% with terminal degrees. The undergraduate student-faculty ratio is 12:1. The library holds 150,000 titles, 1,621 serial subscriptions, and 337 audiovisual materials. Special programs include academic remediation, an honors program, cooperative (work-study) education, advanced placement credit, accelerated degree programs, ESL programs, double majors, summer session for credit, part-time degree programs (daytime, evenings, summer), and internships. The most frequently chosen baccalaureate fields are computer/information sciences, engineering/engineering technologies, mathematics.

Student Body Statistics The student body totals 2,819, of whom 1,543 are undergraduates (329 freshmen). 19 percent are women and 81 percent are men. Students come from 18 states and territories and 44 other countries. 96 percent are from New York. 7.6 percent are international students. 19.4 percent of the 2004 graduating class went on to graduate and professional schools.

Expenses for 2004–05 *Application fee:* $50. *Comprehensive fee:* $35,170 includes full-time tuition ($26,200), mandatory fees ($970), and college room and board ($8000). *College room only:* $6500. Full-time tuition and fees vary according to course load. Room and board charges vary according to housing facility. *Part-time tuition:* $835 per credit. *Part-time mandatory fees:* $300 per term. Part-time tuition and fees vary according to course load.

Financial Aid Forms of aid include need-based and non-need-based scholarships and part-time jobs. The average aided 2004–05 undergraduate received an aid package worth an estimated $20,475. The application deadline for financial aid is continuous.

Freshman Admission Polytechnic requires an essay, a high school transcript, 2 recommendations, SAT or ACT scores, and TOEFL scores for international students. An interview and SAT Subject Test scores are recommended. The application deadline for regular admission is February 1.

Transfer Admission The application deadline for admission is rolling.

Entrance Difficulty Polytechnic assesses its entrance difficulty level as very difficult. For the fall 2004 freshman class, 69 percent of the applicants were accepted.

For Further Information Contact Jonathan D. Wexler, Dean of Undergraduate Admissions, Polytechnic University, Brooklyn Campus, Six Metrotech Center, Brooklyn, NY 11201-2990. *Telephone:* 718-260-3100 or 800-POLYTECH (toll-free). *Fax:* 718-260-3446. *E-mail:* admitme@poly.edu. *Web site:* http://www.poly.edu/.

PRATT INSTITUTE

Brooklyn, New York

Pratt is a coed, private, comprehensive institution, founded in 1887, offering degrees at the associate, bachelor's, master's, and first professional levels. It has a 25-acre campus in Brooklyn.

Academic Information The faculty has 834 members (13% full-time), 9% with terminal degrees. The undergraduate student-faculty ratio is 11:1. The library holds 172,000 titles, 540 serial subscriptions, and 2,851 audiovisual materials. Special programs include services for learning-disabled students, study abroad, advanced placement credit, ESL programs, independent study, summer session for credit, part-time degree programs (daytime, evenings, summer), internships, and arrangement for off-campus study with members of the New York State Visiting Student Program, the Consortium of East Coast Art Schools. The most frequently chosen baccalaureate fields are architecture, education, visual/performing arts.

Student Body Statistics The student body totals 4,540, of whom 3,068 are undergraduates (610 freshmen). 57 percent are women and 43 percent are men. Students come from 46 states and territories and 38 other countries. 53 percent are from New York. 9.3 percent are international students.

Expenses for 2005–06   *Application fee:* $40. *Comprehensive fee:* $36,156 includes full-time tuition ($26,500), mandatory fees ($1080), and college room and board ($8576). *College room only:* $5376. Room and board charges vary according to board plan, housing facility, and student level. *Part-time tuition:* $860 per credit.

Financial Aid   Forms of aid include need-based and non-need-based scholarships and part-time jobs. The average aided 2003–04 undergraduate received an aid package worth $14,605. The priority application deadline for financial aid is February 1.

Freshman Admission   Pratt requires an essay, a high school transcript, 1 recommendation, and SAT or ACT scores. A minimum 3.38 high school GPA is recommended. An interview, a portfolio, and SAT Subject Test scores are required for some. The application deadline for regular admission is February 1 and for early decision it is November 15.

Transfer Admission   The application deadline for admission is February 11.

Entrance Difficulty   Pratt assesses its entrance difficulty level as very difficult; most difficult for transfers; most difficult for fashion, computer graphics. For the fall 2004 freshman class, 50 percent of the applicants were accepted.

For Further Information   Contact Mrs. Micah Moody, Visit Coordinator, Pratt Institute, DeKalb Hall, 200 Willoughby Avenue, Brooklyn, NY 11205-3899. *Telephone:* 718-636-3669 Ext. 3743 or 800-331-0834 (toll-free). *Fax:* 718-636-3670. *E-mail:* admissions@pratt.edu. *Web site:* http://www.pratt.edu/.

See page 144 for a narrative description.

PURCHASE COLLEGE, STATE UNIVERSITY OF NEW YORK

Purchase, New York

Purchase is a coed, public, comprehensive unit of State University of New York System, founded in 1967, offering degrees at the bachelor's and master's levels and post-master's certificates. It has a 500-acre campus in Purchase near New York City.

Academic Information   The faculty has 332 members (41% full-time). The undergraduate student-faculty ratio is 17:1. The library holds 281,686 titles, 1,990 serial subscriptions, and 15,578 audiovisual materials. Special programs include academic remediation, study abroad, advanced placement credit, ESL programs, double majors, independent study, distance learning, self-designed majors, summer session for credit, part-time degree programs, adult/continuing education programs, internships, and arrangement for off-campus study with Manhattanville College. The most frequently chosen baccalaureate fields are liberal arts/general studies, social sciences and history, visual/performing arts.

Student Body Statistics   The student body totals 3,832, of whom 3,709 are undergraduates (628 freshmen). 56 percent are women and 44 percent are men. Students come from 44 states and territories and 24 other countries. 83 percent are from New York. 1.5 percent are international students.

Expenses for 2005–06   *Application fee:* $50. *State resident tuition:* $4350 full-time. *Nonresident tuition:* $10,610 full-time. *Mandatory fees:* $1473 full-time. *College room and board:* $7212. *College room only:* $5378. Room and board charges vary according to board plan and housing facility.

Financial Aid   Forms of aid include need-based and non-need-based scholarships and part-time jobs. The priority application deadline for financial aid is March 15.

Freshman Admission   Purchase requires a high school transcript, a minimum 3.0 high school GPA, SAT or ACT scores, and TOEFL scores for international students. An essay, 1 recommendation, an interview, and audition, portfolio are required for some. The application deadline for regular admission is rolling and for early decision it is November 1.

Transfer Admission   The application deadline for admission is rolling.

Entrance Difficulty   Purchase assesses its entrance difficulty level as moderately difficult. For the fall 2004 freshman class, 29 percent of the applicants were accepted.

SPECIAL MESSAGE TO STUDENTS

Social Life Social life at Purchase centers on an extensive cultural calendar of regularly scheduled theater, music, and dance performances; lectures; films; gallery exhibits; and other events. With nationally recognized conservatories in music, dance, theater arts, and film; a school of art and design; and highly praised programs and faculty members in the liberal arts and sciences, the calendar is just as often filled with events presented by students and faculty members as it is with appearances by outside professionals. More than half of the students live on campus, many in learning communities that connect academic and cocurricular activities. There are more than thirty-five student organizations that are active on campus, ranging from the academic to the social and athletic. The Ultimate Frisbee team is annually ranked as one of the best in the country. There is also a men's basketball team. Conveniently, the College is only 35 minutes from New York City.

Academic Highlights Purchase is nationally known for its professional conservatory training in the School of the Arts. The programs are dramatic writing, acting, theater design, film, dance, music, and visual arts. Purchase actors appear in major motion pictures, in Broadway productions, and on television. There are Purchase dancers in nearly every major dance company in the United States, and musicians at Purchase hold positions with major orchestras and chamber groups throughout the world. Purchase's jazz program is one of the most distinctive in the area. Art and design alumni are exhibited nationally and internationally. In liberal arts, the Schools of Humanities and Natural and Social Sciences are highly regarded for their emphasis on small class size and close student-faculty contact as well as such new and expanding programs as creative writing and new media. All degree programs culminate in a senior project—a summative research or creative work. The majors are all oriented towards the senior project from the freshman year, which stresses writing, cultural thinking, and research skills. In recent years, selectivity has increased across all academic programs. There is also a new general education program and freshman experience, which includes residential learning communities and freshman-interest groups. There are opportunities for internships, study abroad, and independent study. Purchase has one of the highest levels of student satisfaction with the faculty in the entire State University of New York System, and its faculty members were ranked highest in their peer group in a recent national survey.

Interviews and Campus Visits Students are encouraged to visit the campus for information sessions and tours, which occur twice a week throughout the academic year and during the summer session. Students who apply for admission to the arts majors of theater design and film are interviewed as a standard part of the admission process. Acting, dance, and music applicants must audition. A slide portfolio of work or a faculty review of work is required of all visual arts applicants. Students who apply for admission to all other programs may be requested to come to campus for an interview after an initial academic review is completed. The original campus design, based on a master plan by Edward Larrabee Barnes, was carried out by some of the most distinguished contemporary architects in the world today. Purchase is especially known for its outstanding academic facilities, which include, among others, the largest public visual arts teaching facility in the nation, one of the largest performing arts centers north of New York City, the eighth-largest university museum in the United States, one of the only facilities in the world built specifically for dance education, and a natural science building with fifteen teaching laboratories and sophisticated research equipment that is readily accessible to the students. The centrally clustered academic and residential core is surrounded by 500 acres of undeveloped forest, fields, and wetlands. For information about appointments and campus visits, students should contact the Office of Admission by visiting their Web site at http://www.purchase.edu or by calling 914-251-6300, Monday through Friday, 8:30 a.m. to 5 p.m. The nearest commercial airport is Westchester County.

For Further Information Write to Ms. Betsy Immergut, Director of Admissions, Purchase College, State University of New York, 735 Anderson Hill Road, Purchase, NY 10577-1400. *E-mail:* admissn@purchase.edu. *Web site:* http://www.purchase.edu.

QUEENS COLLEGE OF THE CITY UNIVERSITY OF NEW YORK

Flushing, New York

SPONSOR
See Front Insert
for Details!

Queens College is a coed, public, comprehensive unit of City University of New York System, founded in 1937, offering degrees at the bachelor's and master's levels and post-master's and postbachelor's certificates. It has a 77-acre campus in Flushing.

Academic Information   The faculty has 1,180 members (46% full-time), 59% with terminal degrees. The undergraduate student-faculty ratio is 17:1. The library holds 985,550 titles, 2,756 serial subscriptions, and 30,505 audiovisual materials. Special programs include services for learning-disabled students, an honors program, cooperative (work-study) education, study abroad, advanced placement credit, accelerated degree programs, Freshman Honors College, ESL programs, double majors, independent study, self-designed majors, summer session for credit, part-time degree programs (daytime, evenings, weekends, summer), adult/continuing education programs, internships, and arrangement for off-campus study with other units of the City University of New York System. The most frequently chosen baccalaureate fields are business/marketing, social sciences and history, visual/performing arts.

Student Body Statistics   The student body totals 17,395, of whom 12,628 are undergraduates (1,384 freshmen). 62 percent are women and 38 percent are men. Students come from 15 states and territories and 130 other countries. 99 percent are from New York. 5.5 percent are international students. 23 percent of the 2004 graduating class went on to graduate and professional schools.

Expenses for 2004–05   *Application fee:* $65. *State resident tuition:* $4000 full-time, $170 per credit part-time. *Nonresident tuition:* $8640 full-time, $360 per credit part-time. *Mandatory fees:* $361 full-time, $112.10 per term part-time. Full-time tuition and fees vary according to program. Part-time tuition and fees vary according to course load and program.

Financial Aid   Forms of aid include need-based and non-need-based scholarships, athletic grants, and part-time jobs. The average aided 2003–04 undergraduate received an aid package worth $5000. The priority application deadline for financial aid is March 1.

Freshman Admission   Queens College requires a high school transcript, a minimum 3.0 high school GPA, SAT scores, and TOEFL scores for international students. SAT Subject Test scores are recommended. The application deadline for regular admission is January 1.

Transfer Admission   The application deadline for admission is February 1.

Entrance Difficulty   Queens College assesses its entrance difficulty level as very difficult; moderately difficult for transfers; most difficult for Queens College Scholars Program, honors programs. For the fall 2004 freshman class, 42 percent of the applicants were accepted.

SPECIAL MESSAGE TO STUDENTS

Social Life Students come from 140 nations, giving the campus an unusually rich flavor. There are more than 100 clubs, from the Accounting Honors Society and Alliance of Latin American Students to clubs for theater, fencing, environmental science, and salsa. Queens participates in Division II sports, sponsoring fifteen men's and women's teams, and has some of the finest athletic facilities in the metropolitan area. Ongoing events include concerts, theater and dance performances, and readings by authors such as Toni Morrison, Frank McCourt, and Norman Mailer. The College is home to the Godwin-Ternbach Museum, the only comprehensive museum in the borough of Queens.

Academic Highlights The wide range of majors and interdisciplinary studies, combined with the award-winning Freshman Year Initiative Program, encourages students to explore their interests to the fullest. The Bachelor of Business Administration degree—with majors in finance, international business, and actuarial studies—provides a solid business education. The business and liberal arts program, designed by leading corporate executives, allows students to study the theory and practice of business in a liberal arts context. The College participates in the CUNY Honors Program, which

includes mentors, internships, study-abroad programs, full tuition and fees, a grant of $7500 over four years, and a laptop computer.

Interviews and Campus Visits Campus tours are offered in the fall and spring semesters. Although interviews are not required, students may meet with a counselor to discuss their goals. Appointments with advisers for prehealth (medical, dental, and veterinary), prelaw, and honors programs may be arranged through the admissions office. Located on the highest spot in Queens, the 77-acre campus is lined with trees surrounding grassy open spaces and a traditional quad. The completely renovated Powdermaker Hall, the major classroom building, features throughout it state-of-the-art technology. The College is also expanding its wireless capability, opening new dining areas, and updating the spacious student union. Notable facilities include the 2,200-seat Colden Center for the Performing Arts; the Aaron Copland School of Music building, with thirty-five practice rooms and the acoustically perfect LeFrak Hall; the Institute for Low-Temperature Physics; and the Speech and Hearing Center. Rosenthal Library has more than 780,000 volumes and is home to the Louis Armstrong Archives, a vast personal collection of Armstrong's photographs, papers, recordings, and memorabilia. The nearest commercial airport is La Guardia.

For Further Information Write to Director of Admissions, Queens College of the City University of New York, 65–30 Kissena Boulevard, Flushing, NY 11367-1597. *Web site:* http://www.qc.cuny.edu.

RABBINICAL ACADEMY MESIVTA RABBI CHAIM BERLIN

Brooklyn, New York

For Information   Write to Rabbinical Academy Mesivta Rabbi Chaim Berlin, Brooklyn, NY 11230-4715.

RABBINICAL COLLEGE BETH SHRAGA

Monsey, New York

For Information   Write to Rabbinical College Beth Shraga, Monsey, NY 10952-3035.

RABBINICAL COLLEGE BOBOVER YESHIVA B'NEI ZION

Brooklyn, New York

For Information   Write to Rabbinical College Bobover Yeshiva B'nei Zion, Brooklyn, NY 11219.

RABBINICAL COLLEGE CH'SAN SOFER

Brooklyn, New York

For Information   Write to Rabbinical College Ch'san Sofer, Brooklyn, NY 11204.

RABBINICAL COLLEGE OF LONG ISLAND

Long Beach, New York

For Information   Write to Rabbinical College of Long Island, Long Beach, NY 11561-3305.

RABBINICAL COLLEGE OF OHR SHIMON YISROEL

Brooklyn, New York

For Information Write to Rabbinical College of Ohr Shimon Yisroel, Brooklyn, NY 11211.

RABBINICAL SEMINARY ADAS YEREIM

Brooklyn, New York

For Information Write to Rabbinical Seminary Adas Yereim, Brooklyn, NY 11211-7206.

RABBINICAL SEMINARY M'KOR CHAIM

Brooklyn, New York

For Information Write to Rabbinical Seminary M'kor Chaim, Brooklyn, NY 11219.

RABBINICAL SEMINARY OF AMERICA

Flushing, New York

For Information Write to Rabbinical Seminary of America, Flushing, NY 11367.

REGENTS COLLEGE

See Excelsior College.

RENSSELAER POLYTECHNIC INSTITUTE

Troy, New York

SPONSOR
See Front Insert
for Details!

Rensselaer is a coed, private university, founded in 1824, offering degrees at the bachelor's, master's, and doctoral levels. It has a 260-acre campus in Troy near Albany.

Academic Information The faculty has 492 members (82% full-time), 96% with terminal degrees. The undergraduate student-faculty ratio is 14:1. The library holds 309,171 titles, 10,210 serial subscriptions, and 91,435 audiovisual materials. Special programs include services for learning-disabled students, an honors program, cooperative (work-study) education, study abroad, advanced placement credit, accelerated degree programs, ESL programs, double majors, independent study, distance learning, self-designed majors, summer session for credit, part-time degree programs (daytime, evenings, summer), adult/continuing education programs, internships, and arrangement for off-campus study with Williams College, Harvey Mudd College. The most frequently chosen baccalaureate fields are computer/information sciences, business/marketing, engineering/engineering technologies.

Student Body Statistics The student body totals 7,521, of whom 4,929 are undergraduates (1,079 freshmen). 25 percent are women and 75 percent are men. Students come from 51 states and territories and 37 other countries. 51 percent are from New York. 4.2 percent are international students. 21 percent of the 2004 graduating class went on to graduate and professional schools.

Expenses for 2004–05 *Application fee:* $70. *Comprehensive fee:* $38,869 includes full-time tuition ($28,950), mandatory fees ($836), and college room and board ($9083). *College room only:* $5101. Room and board charges vary according to board plan, housing facility, and location. *Part-time tuition:* $905 per credit hour.

Financial Aid Forms of aid include need-based and non-need-based scholarships, athletic grants, and part-time jobs. The average aided 2004–05 undergraduate received an aid package worth an estimated $24,862. The priority application deadline for financial aid is February 15.

Freshman Admission Rensselaer requires an essay, a high school transcript, 1 recommendation, SAT or ACT scores, and TOEFL scores for international students. Portfolio for Electronic Arts is required; portfolio for Architecture highly recommended. and is required for some. The application deadline for regular admission is January 1 and for early decision it is November 15.

Transfer Admission The application deadline for admission is July 1.

Entrance Difficulty Rensselaer assesses its entrance difficulty level as very difficult. For the fall 2004 freshman class, 75 percent of the applicants were accepted.

SPECIAL MESSAGE TO STUDENTS

Social Life With a campus teeming with life and activity—140 clubs, twenty-three NCAA intercollegiate teams, the fall 2004 opening of the new Center for Biotechnology and Interdisciplinary Studies facility, and the construction of the Experimental Media and Performing Arts Center (EMPAC) and new athletic venues—Rensselaer offers its students one of the most innovative, educational experiences anywhere. Outside the classroom, students manage the $8.5 million budget for the Rensselaer Union; operate WRPI radio; produce the weekly newspaper, *The Polytechnic*; and participate in clubs and intramural sports ranging from archery and ballroom dancing to wrestling and water polo.

Academic Highlights A pioneer in interactive learning, Rensselaer provides students with a hands-on practical education, enhanced by research and technology to optimize individual and team-based learning. Rensselaer offers academic programs in architecture, engineering, the humanities and social science, information technology, management, science, and additional programs that cut across the academic disciplines and encourage students to learn at the intersection of technology and arts or the life sciences and engineering. Opportunities abound for students to participate in basic and applied research and in co-op, study abroad, and internship programs. Many students have developed marketable products and services while attending Rensselaer and have established businesses in Rensselaer's incubator and eventually moved them into the Rensselaer Technology Park. Students who earn Rensselaer degrees are valued for their creativity, their leadership, and their ability to tackle complexity on a global scale.

Interviews and Campus Visits A campus visit is highly recommended as the best way to see all that Rensselaer has to offer. Typical visits include a student-guided tour and an information session that highlights Rensselaer's outstanding programs, faculty members, and research opportunities, while providing an overview of academic, research, and recreational facilities. Campus visits are available Monday through Friday, and Saturdays during the academic year, September through April, excluding holidays. The Admissions Office is closed on Sundays. The Admissions Office can arrange for prospective students to attend classes and meet with faculty members or coaches with a minimum of two weeks' advance notice. Information about admissions and requirements is available at http://www.rpi.edu, by contacting admissions@rpi.edu, or by calling 518-276-6216, Monday through Friday, 8:30 a.m. to 5 p.m. Rensselaer is located 8 miles from Albany International Airport and is a short drive from the Amtrak rail station at Rensselaer, New York. The nearest commercial airport is Albany International.

For Further Information Write to Rensselaer Admissions, Undergraduate Programs, 110 8th Street, Troy, NY 12180-3590.

ROBERTS WESLEYAN COLLEGE

Rochester, New York

Roberts Wesleyan is a coed, private, comprehensive institution, founded in 1866, affiliated with the Free Methodist Church of North America, offering degrees at the associate, bachelor's, and master's levels. It has a 75-acre campus in Rochester.

Academic Information The faculty has 196 members (46% full-time). The undergraduate student-faculty ratio is 17:1. The library holds 123,434 titles, 1,057 serial subscriptions, and 3,895 audiovisual materials. Special programs include academic remediation, services for learning-disabled students, an honors program, cooperative (work-study) education, study abroad, advanced placement credit, Freshman Honors College, ESL programs, double majors, independent study, summer session for credit, adult/continuing education programs, internships, and arrangement for off-campus study with Rochester Area Colleges, Council of Christian Colleges and Universities. The most frequently chosen baccalaureate fields are business/marketing, education, health professions and related sciences.

Student Body Statistics The student body totals 1,926, of whom 1,376 are undergraduates (258 freshmen). 67 percent are women and 33 percent are men. Students come from 24 states and territories and 19 other countries. 82 percent are from New York. 3.2 percent are international students. 24 percent of the 2004 graduating class went on to graduate and professional schools.

Expenses for 2005–06 *Application fee:* $35. *Comprehensive fee:* $24,352 includes full-time tuition ($18,350), mandatory fees ($974), and college room and board ($5028). *College room only:* $2026. Room and board charges vary according to board plan. *Part-time tuition:* $402 per credit. Part-time tuition varies according to course load.

Financial Aid Forms of aid include need-based and non-need-based scholarships, athletic grants, and part-time jobs. The average aided 2003–04 undergraduate received an aid package worth $14,700. The priority application deadline for financial aid is March 15.

Freshman Admission Roberts Wesleyan requires an essay, a high school transcript, 2 recommendations, SAT or ACT scores, and TOEFL scores for international students. A minimum 2.5 high school GPA and an interview are recommended. The application deadline for regular admission is February 1.

Transfer Admission The application deadline for admission is rolling.

Entrance Difficulty Roberts Wesleyan assesses its entrance difficulty level as moderately difficult. For the fall 2004 freshman class, 82 percent of the applicants were accepted.

For Further Information Contact Ms. Linda Kurtz Hoffman, Vice President for Admissions and Marketing, Roberts Wesleyan College, 2301 Westside Drive, Rochester, NY 14624. *Telephone:* 585-594-6400 or 800-777-4RWC (toll-free). *Fax:* 585-594-6371. *E-mail:* admissions@roberts.edu. *Web site:* http://www.roberts.edu/.

ROCHESTER INSTITUTE OF TECHNOLOGY
Rochester, New York

SPONSOR
See Front Insert
for Details!

RIT is a coed, private, comprehensive institution, founded in 1829, offering degrees at the associate, bachelor's, master's, and doctoral levels and post-master's and postbachelor's certificates. It has a 1,300-acre campus in Rochester near Buffalo.

Academic Information The faculty has 1,218 members (60% full-time), 81% with terminal degrees. The undergraduate student-faculty ratio is 14:1. The library holds 408,000 titles, 2,800 serial subscriptions, and 47,600 audiovisual materials. Special programs include services for learning-disabled students, an honors program, cooperative (work-study) education, study abroad, advanced placement credit, accelerated degree programs, ESL programs, independent study, distance learning, self-designed majors, summer session for credit, part-time degree programs (daytime, evenings, weekends, summer), adult/continuing education programs, internships, and arrangement for off-campus study with members of the Rochester Area Colleges. The most frequently chosen baccalaureate fields are engineering/engineering technologies, computer/information sciences, visual/performing arts.

Student Body Statistics The student body totals 14,552, of whom 12,304 are undergraduates (2,259 freshmen). 29 percent are women and 71 percent are men. Students come from 50 states and territories and 90 other countries. 55 percent are from New York. 4.3 percent are international students. 10 percent of the 2004 graduating class went on to graduate and professional schools.

Expenses for 2004–05 *Application fee:* $50. *Comprehensive fee:* $30,549 includes full-time tuition ($22,056), mandatory fees ($357), and college room and board ($8136). *College room only:* $4653. Full-time tuition and fees vary according to course load, program, and student level. Room and board charges vary according to board plan and housing facility. *Part-time tuition:* $491 per credit hour. *Part-time mandatory fees:* $29 per term. Part-time tuition and fees vary according to course load, program, and student level.

Financial Aid Forms of aid include need-based and non-need-based scholarships and part-time jobs. The average aided 2003–04 undergraduate received an aid package worth $16,300. The priority application deadline for financial aid is March 1.

Freshman Admission RIT requires an essay, a high school transcript, SAT or ACT scores, and TOEFL scores for international students. A minimum 3.0 high school GPA, 1 recommendation, and an interview are recommended. A portfolio is required for some. The application deadline for regular admission is March 15 and for early decision it is December 1.

Entrance Difficulty RIT assesses its entrance difficulty level as moderately difficult; very difficult for imaging science, physician assistant, film and video programs. For the fall 2004 freshman class, 67 percent of the applicants were accepted.

SPECIAL MESSAGE TO STUDENTS

Social Life Because the student body of Rochester Institute of Technology (RIT) is so diverse, there are many different activities, clubs, organizations, and sports in which students may participate. There are seventeen fraternities and seven sororities, representing approximately 5 percent of the student population. A radio station and a biweekly student magazine allow those interested in media to gain experience on campus. A number of special interest clubs and career organizations are also available, and RIT offers twenty-three varsity sports. Approximately 65 percent of RIT's full-time students live on campus in residence halls or apartments.

Academic Highlights Cooperative education (co-op) allows students to alternate periods of classroom study with full-time paid employment. The most obvious benefit of this program is the valuable work experience that helps students gain higher-level positions while earning money. About 60 percent of RIT students take a permanent position with a co-op employer after graduation. The Cooperative Education and Career Services Office carries job listings for both co-op and permanent positions and brings more than 500 employers to campus to interview students. The office also holds seminars on resume writing and interviewing skills.

Interviews and Campus Visits Students are encouraged (although not required) to visit the RIT campus and have an interview. Those who do can discuss career goals and find out more about their program of interest. The visit also gives students the opportunity to see the facilities and equipment RIT students use. Students are also encouraged to visit their department of interest. Students interested in sports may visit the athletic facilities. The Bevier Art Gallery is also an interesting spot for any visitor. The gallery displays the work of RIT students and faculty members in the College of Imaging Arts and Sciences. For information about appointments and campus visits, students should call the Office of Undergraduate Admissions at 585-475-6631, Monday through Friday, 8:30 a.m. to 4:30 p.m. The office is located in the Bausch & Lomb Building on campus. Those interested in arranging a visit to the National Technical Institute for the Deaf should call 585-475-6700 (V/TTY). The nearest commercial airport is Greater Rochester International.

For Further Information Write to the Office of Undergraduate Admissions, Rochester Institute of Technology, 60 Lomb Memorial Drive, Rochester, NY 14623-5604. *Web site:* http://www.rit.edu/admissions.

RUSSELL SAGE COLLEGE
Troy, New York

Russell Sage is a women's, private, four-year college of The Sage Colleges, founded in 1916, offering degrees at the bachelor's level. It has an 8-acre campus in Troy.

Academic Information The faculty has 121 members (52% full-time), 56% with terminal degrees. The student-faculty ratio is 11:1. The library holds 337,694 titles, 19,416 serial subscriptions, and 31,928 audiovisual materials. Special programs include academic remediation, services for learning-disabled students, an honors program, cooperative (work-study) education, study abroad, advanced placement credit, accelerated degree programs, Freshman Honors College, ESL programs, double majors, independent study, self-designed majors, summer session for credit, part-time degree programs (evenings, weekends, summer), adult/continuing education programs, internships, and arrangement for off-campus study with Hudson-Mohawk Association of Colleges and Universities. The most frequently chosen baccalaureate fields are education, health professions and related sciences, psychology.

Student Body Statistics   The student body is made up of 837 undergraduates (138 freshmen). Students come from 15 states and territories and 3 other countries. 91 percent are from New York. 0.4 percent are international students. 42 percent of the 2004 graduating class went on to graduate and professional schools.

Expenses for 2004–05   *Application fee:* $30. *Comprehensive fee:* $29,320 includes full-time tuition ($21,500), mandatory fees ($770), and college room and board ($7050). *College room only:* $3350. *Part-time tuition:* $715 per credit hour.

Financial Aid   Forms of aid include need-based and non-need-based scholarships and part-time jobs. The priority application deadline for financial aid is March 1.

Freshman Admission   Russell Sage requires an essay, a high school transcript, a minimum 2.0 high school GPA, 2 recommendations, SAT or ACT scores, and TOEFL scores for international students. An interview is recommended. The application deadline for regular admission is August 1 and for early decision it is December 1.

Transfer Admission   The application deadline for admission is rolling.

Entrance Difficulty   Russell Sage assesses its entrance difficulty level as moderately difficult; very difficult for 3-2 engineering, physical therapy programs; 3-3 law program; pre-medicine, science programs. For the fall 2004 freshman class, 83 percent of the applicants were accepted.

For Further Information   Contact Ms. Beth Robertson, Director of Undergraduate Admission, Russell Sage College, 45 Ferry Street, Troy, NY 12180. *Telephone:* 518-244-2018, 888-VERY-SAGE (toll-free in-state), or 888-VERY SAGE (toll-free out-of-state). *Fax:* 518-244-6880. *E-mail:* rscadm@sage.edu. *Web site:* http://www.sage.edu/RSC/.

SAGE COLLEGE OF ALBANY
Albany, New York

Sage College of Albany is a coed, private, four-year college of The Sage Colleges, founded in 1957, offering degrees at the associate and bachelor's levels. It has a 15-acre campus in Albany.

Academic Information   The faculty has 77 members (53% full-time), 49% with terminal degrees. The student-faculty ratio is 11:1. The library holds 337,694 titles, 19,416 serial subscriptions, and 31,928 audiovisual materials. Special programs include academic remediation, services for learning-disabled students, an honors program, cooperative (work-study) education, advanced placement credit, Freshman Honors College, ESL programs, independent study, self-designed majors, summer session for credit, part-time degree programs (daytime, evenings, weekends, summer), external degree programs, adult/continuing education programs, internships, and arrangement for off-campus study with members of the Hudson-Mohawk Association of Colleges and Universities. The most frequently chosen baccalaureate fields are business/marketing, protective services/public administration, psychology.

Student Body Statistics   The student body is made up of 1,051 undergraduates (94 freshmen). 71 percent are women and 29 percent are men. Students come from 9 states and territories and 2 other countries. 98 percent are from New York. 0.2 percent are international students.

Expenses for 2004–05   *Application fee:* $30. *Comprehensive fee:* $23,170 includes full-time tuition ($15,250), mandatory fees ($770), and college room and board ($7150). *College room only:* $3450. Room and board charges vary according to board plan and location. *Part-time tuition:* $510 per credit hour.

Financial Aid   Forms of aid include need-based scholarships, athletic grants, and part-time jobs. The priority application deadline for financial aid is March 1.

Freshman Admission   Sage College of Albany requires a high school transcript, 1 recommendation, portfolio for fine arts program, SAT or ACT scores, and TOEFL scores for international students. An essay and an interview are recommended. The application deadline for regular admission is August 1.

Transfer Admission   The application deadline for admission is August 1.

Entrance Difficulty   Sage College of Albany assesses its entrance difficulty level as minimally difficult; moderately difficult for legal studies, computer science, fine arts, humanities programs. For the fall 2004 freshman class, 58 percent of the applicants were accepted.

For Further Information   Contact Ms. Elizabeth Robertson, Director of Undergraduate Admission, Sage College of Albany, 140 New Scotland Avenue, Albany, NY 12208. *Telephone:* 518-292-1730 or 888-VERY-SAGE (toll-free). *Fax:* 518-292-1912. *E-mail:* scaadm@sage.edu. *Web site:* http://www.sage.edu/SCA/.

ST. BONAVENTURE UNIVERSITY
St. Bonaventure, New York

SPONSOR
See Front Insert for Details!

St. Bonaventure is a coed, private, comprehensive institution, founded in 1858, affiliated with the Roman Catholic Church, offering degrees at the bachelor's and master's levels and post-master's and postbachelor's certificates. It has a 600-acre campus in St. Bonaventure.

Academic Information   The faculty has 229 members (68% full-time). The undergraduate student-faculty ratio is 14:1. The library holds 287,622 titles, 1,584 serial subscriptions, and 8,891 audiovisual materials. Special programs include services for learning-disabled students, an honors program, study abroad, advanced placement credit, Freshman Honors College, double majors, independent study, self-designed majors, summer session for credit, part-time degree programs (daytime), internships, and arrangement for off-campus study with American University. The most frequently chosen baccalaureate fields are business/marketing, communications/communication technologies, education.

Student Body Statistics   The student body totals 2,806, of whom 2,291 are undergraduates (596 freshmen). 51 percent are women and 49 percent are men. Students come from 36 states and territories. 75 percent are from New York. 0.3 percent are international students.

Expenses for 2004–05   *Application fee:* $30. *Comprehensive fee:* $26,395 includes full-time tuition ($18,650), mandatory fees ($835), and college room and board ($6910). *College room only:* $3530. Room and board charges vary according to board plan and housing facility.

Financial Aid   Forms of aid include need-based and non-need-based scholarships, athletic grants, and part-time jobs. The average aided 2004–05 undergraduate received an aid package worth an estimated $15,422. The priority application deadline for financial aid is February 1.

Freshman Admission   St. Bonaventure requires a high school transcript, 1 recommendation, and SAT or ACT scores. An essay, a minimum 3.0 high school GPA, 3 recommendations, and an interview are recommended. An essay and SAT or ACT scores are required for some. The application deadline for regular admission is April 15.

Transfer Admission   The application deadline for admission is August 15.

Entrance Difficulty   St. Bonaventure assesses its entrance difficulty level as moderately difficult; minimally difficult for Higher Education Opportunity Program. For the fall 2004 freshman class, 87 percent of the applicants were accepted.

SPECIAL MESSAGE TO STUDENTS

Social Life Everything students need is right outside their door. A 77-acre recreational field and the Reilly Center, a multipurpose recreational facility with a competition-size swimming pool and weight room, are augmented by a new $6.2 million recreation center in the center of the campus, a nine-hole campus golf course, and a major ski resort just 25 minutes away. The Regina A. Quick Center for the Arts provides students with theater, band, choir, and visual arts facilities. Award-winning student media, a lively intramurals program, and a multitude of volunteer ministry opportunities round out campus social life.

Academic Highlights At St. Bonaventure, an education is one of academic, social, physical, and spiritual growth. In four years, students develop more than their intellectual capacity—they develop character as they realize their goals in a supportive environment. Students have access to a dynamic teaching and learning center and career services office, as well as a broadcast journalism laboratory with state-of-the-art equipment and a vibrant field-based teacher education program. Students who seek additional challenges and rewards may elect to participate in the honors program.

Interviews and Campus Visits All students should arrange a campus visit, during which they can speak with an admissions representative, tour the campus with a current student, meet with a professor, or sit in on a class. The University community is friendly, and mutual respect and joy set the tone for life on the 500-acre residential campus. The John Templeton Foundation lists St. Bonaventure on its Honor Roll of Colleges that Build Character, and *U.S. News & World Report* repeatedly ranks St. Bonaventure in its top tier of regional colleges. To arrange a visit, students should call 800-462-5050 (toll-free) from 8:30 a.m. to 5 p.m weekdays. Interviews and tours are available Monday through Friday and on selected Saturdays and holidays. The nearest commercial airport is Greater Buffalo International.

For Further Information Write to Mr. James DiRisio, Director of Admissions, St. Bonaventure University, P.O. Box D, St. Bonaventure, NY 14778. *E-mail:* admissions@sbu.edu. *Web site:* http://www.sbu.edu.

See page 146 for a narrative description.

ST. ELIZABETH COLLEGE OF NURSING
Utica, New York

For Information Write to St. Elizabeth College of Nursing, Utica, NY 13501.

ST. FRANCIS COLLEGE
Brooklyn Heights, New York

St. Francis is a coed, private, Roman Catholic, four-year college, founded in 1884, offering degrees at the associate and bachelor's levels. It has a 1-acre campus in Brooklyn Heights near New York City.

Academic Information The faculty has 211 members (33% full-time), 31% with terminal degrees. The student-faculty ratio is 18:1. The library holds 120,000 titles, 571 serial subscriptions, and 2,150 audiovisual materials. Special programs include academic remediation, an honors program, cooperative (work-study) education, study abroad, advanced placement credit, accelerated degree programs, ESL programs, double majors, independent study, self-designed majors, summer session for credit, part-time degree programs (daytime, evenings, summer), external degree programs, adult/continuing education programs, and internships. The most frequently chosen baccalaureate fields are business/marketing, liberal arts/general studies, social sciences and history.

Student Body Statistics The student body is made up of 2,326 undergraduates (489 freshmen). 56 percent are women and 44 percent are men. Students come from 4 states and territories and 54 other countries. 99 percent are from New York. 11.1 percent are international students. 29 percent of the 2004 graduating class went on to graduate and professional schools.

Expenses for 2004–05 *Application fee:* $35. *One-time mandatory fee:* $25. *Comprehensive fee:* $19,785 includes full-time tuition ($11,420), mandatory fees ($365), and college room and board ($8000). *College room only:* $6500. Full-time tuition and fees vary according to course level, course load, degree level, program, and student level. *Part-time tuition:* $395 per credit. *Part-time mandatory fees:* $70 per term. Part-time tuition and fees vary according to course level, course load, degree level, program, and student level.

Financial Aid Forms of aid include need-based and non-need-based scholarships and part-time jobs. The average aided 2004–05 undergraduate received an aid package worth an estimated $6373. The priority application deadline for financial aid is February 15.

Freshman Admission St. Francis requires an essay, a high school transcript, a minimum 2.0 high school GPA, 1 recommendation, SAT scores, and TOEFL scores for international students. An interview is recommended. The application deadline for regular admission is rolling.

Transfer Admission The application deadline for admission is rolling.

Entrance Difficulty St. Francis assesses its entrance difficulty level as moderately difficult. For the fall 2004 freshman class, 88 percent of the applicants were accepted.

For Further Information Contact Br. George Larkin, OSF, Dean of Admissions, St. Francis College, Brooklyn Heights, NY 11201. *Telephone:* 718-489-5200. *Fax:* 718-802-0453. *E-mail:* admissions@stfranciscollege.edu. *Web site:* http://www.stfranciscollege.edu/.

ST. JOHN FISHER COLLEGE
Rochester, New York

St. John Fisher is a coed, private, comprehensive institution, founded in 1948, affiliated with the Roman Catholic Church, offering degrees at the bachelor's and master's levels and postbachelor's certificates. It has a 136-acre campus in Rochester.

Academic Information The faculty has 355 members (37% full-time). The undergraduate student-faculty ratio is 14:1. The library holds 190,903 titles, 8,964 serial subscriptions, and 29,700 audiovisual materials. Special programs include academic remediation, services for learning-disabled students, an honors program, study abroad, advanced placement credit, accelerated degree programs, double majors, independent study, self-designed majors, summer session for credit, part-time degree programs (daytime, evenings, weekends, summer), adult/continuing education programs, internships, and arrangement for off-campus study with members of the Rochester Area Colleges. The most frequently chosen baccalaureate fields are business/marketing, education, social sciences and history.

Student Body Statistics The student body totals 3,376, of whom 2,605 are undergraduates (531 freshmen). 58 percent are women and 42 percent are men. Students come from 17 states and territories and 6 other countries. 98 percent are from New York. 0.2 percent are international students. 25 percent of the 2004 graduating class went on to graduate and professional schools.

Expenses for 2004–05 *Application fee:* $25. *One-time mandatory fee:* $300. *Comprehensive fee:* $26,350 includes full-time tuition ($18,200), mandatory fees ($250), and college room and board ($7900). *College room only:* $5100. Room and board charges vary according to board plan. *Part-time tuition:* $500 per credit hour. *Part-time mandatory fees:* $25 per term. Part-time tuition and fees vary according to course load.

Financial Aid Forms of aid include need-based and non-need-based scholarships and part-time jobs. The average aided 2004–05 undergraduate received an aid package worth an estimated $14,981. The priority application deadline for financial aid is February 15.

Freshman Admission St. John Fisher requires a high school transcript, a minimum 2.0 high school GPA, 1 recommendation, SAT or ACT scores, and TOEFL scores for international students. An interview is recommended. The application deadline for regular admission is rolling and for early decision it is December 1.

Transfer Admission The application deadline for admission is rolling.

Entrance Difficulty St. John Fisher assesses its entrance difficulty level as moderately difficult. For the fall 2004 freshman class, 70 percent of the applicants were accepted.

For Further Information Contact Mrs. Stacy A. Ledermann, Director of Freshmen Admissions, St. John Fisher College, 3690 East Avenue, Rochester, NY 14618. *Telephone:* 585-385-8064 or 800-444-4640 (toll-free). *Fax:* 585-385-8386. *E-mail:* admissions@sjfc.edu. *Web site:* http://www.sjfc.edu/.

See page 148 for a narrative description.

ST. JOHN'S UNIVERSITY

Jamaica, New York

St. John's is a coed, private university, founded in 1870, affiliated with the Roman Catholic Church, offering degrees at the associate, bachelor's, master's, doctoral, and first professional levels and post-master's and postbachelor's certificates. It has a 98-acre campus in Jamaica near New York City.

Academic Information The faculty has 1,378 members (42% full-time), 56% with terminal degrees. The undergraduate student-faculty ratio is 18:1. The library holds 14 million titles, 19,249 serial subscriptions, and 22,918 audiovisual materials. Special programs include services for learning-disabled students, an honors program, study abroad, advanced placement credit, accelerated degree programs, ESL programs, double majors, independent study, distance learning, summer session for credit, part-time degree programs (daytime, evenings, weekends, summer), adult/continuing education programs, internships, and arrangement for off-campus study with American Academy McAllister Institute of Funeral Service. The most frequently chosen baccalaureate fields are business/marketing, computer/information sciences, education.

Student Body Statistics The student body totals 19,813, of whom 14,848 are undergraduates (3,005 freshmen). 58 percent are women and 42 percent are men. Students come from 45 states and territories and 98 other countries. 90 percent are from New York. 3.3 percent are international students. 27 percent of the 2004 graduating class went on to graduate and professional schools.

Expenses for 2005–06 *Application fee:* $30. *Comprehensive fee:* $34,280 includes full-time tuition ($22,800), mandatory fees ($480), and college room and board ($11,000). *College room only:* $6900. Full-time tuition and fees vary according to class time, course level, course load, program, and student level. Room and board charges vary according to board plan and housing facility. *Part-time tuition:* $760 per credit. *Part-time mandatory fees:* $165 per term. Part-time tuition and fees vary according to class time, course level, course load, program, and student level.

Financial Aid Forms of aid include need-based and non-need-based scholarships, athletic grants, and part-time jobs.

Freshman Admission St. John's requires a high school transcript and SAT or ACT scores. An interview is recommended. A minimum X high school GPA is required for some. The application deadline for regular admission is rolling.

Transfer Admission The application deadline for admission is rolling.

Entrance Difficulty St. John's assesses its entrance difficulty level as moderately difficult. For the fall 2004 freshman class, 62 percent of the applicants were accepted.

SPECIAL MESSAGE TO STUDENTS

Social Life St. John's University offers world-class academic programs, high-tech resources, and vibrant student activities on a traditional residential campus in exciting New York City. For more than 130 years, St. John's has prepared young men and women for personal and professional success. Students can choose from more than 180 student clubs, including academic and honor societies, cultural and religious groups, fraternities and sororities, performing arts, ROTC, and intramural and varsity sports. Students also enjoy St. John's Big East Division 1 athletic facilities. The 105-acre Queens campus features ultramodern suite-style residence halls equipped with cable television, telephones, and Internet access. Housing is also available at the Staten Island and Manhattan campuses.

Academic Highlights St. John's offers more than 100 academic majors in the liberal arts and sciences, business, education, preprofessional programs, and pharmacy and allied health. All students take the Discover New York course, which uses the city as a living textbook, and a Scientific Inquiry course, which introduces all students to scientific reasoning. There is an active study-abroad program offering opportunities to earn college credit in countries such as Hungary, Ireland, Italy, and Japan, among others. Academic Service-Learning allows students to earn class credit while volunteering in the community.

Interviews and Campus Visits The Office of International Admission invites interested students to visit the St. John's campus. On-campus interviews and tours allow students to gain general information, ask specific questions, and experience the campus environment. The 105-acre Queens campus features broad lawns, tree-lined paths, and beautiful facilities, including the 1.7-million-volume University Library, an ultramodern residential village, a University Center, handsome classroom and science facilities, and outstanding athletic facilities. The 17-acre Staten Island campus includes Loretto Memorial Library, apartment-style student residences, and a mix of traditional and contemporary buildings. The prize-winning Manhattan campus is close to the Financial District, Battery Park City, and TriBeCa. For information about campus visits, students should contact the Office of International Admission (Telephone: 718-990-1601; e-mail: intlhelp@stjohns.edu). The nearest commercial airport is La Guardia.

For Further Information Write to Mr. Wayne James, Executive Director of International and Graduate Admission, St. John's University, 8000 Utopia Parkway, Queens, NY 11439.

ST. JOSEPH'S COLLEGE, NEW YORK

Brooklyn, New York

St. Joseph's is a coed, private, four-year college, founded in 1916, offering degrees at the bachelor's and master's levels.

Academic Information The faculty has 137 members (38% full-time). The undergraduate student-faculty ratio is 12:1. The library holds 100,000 titles, 432 serial subscriptions, and 4,482 audiovisual materials. Special programs include an honors program, advanced placement credit, independent study, distance learning, summer session for credit, part-time degree programs (daytime, evenings, weekends, summer), adult/continuing education programs, and internships. The most frequently chosen baccalaureate fields are education, business/marketing, health professions and related sciences.

Student Body Statistics The student body totals 1,313, of whom 1,148 are undergraduates (152 freshmen). 75 percent are women and 25 percent are men. Students come from 4 states and territories and 8 other countries. 99 percent are from New York. 0.7 percent are international students. 40 percent of the 2004 graduating class went on to graduate and professional schools.

Expenses for 2004–05 *Application fee:* $25. *Tuition:* $11,078 full-time, $357 per credit part-time. *Mandatory fees:* $352 full-time, $11 per credit part-time, $30 per term part-time.

Financial Aid Forms of aid include need-based and non-need-based scholarships and part-time jobs. The average aided 2004–05 undergraduate received an aid package worth an estimated $11,000. The priority application deadline for financial aid is February 25.

Freshman Admission St. Joseph's requires a high school transcript, a minimum 3.0 high school GPA, SAT or ACT scores, and TOEFL scores for international students. An essay and 2 recommendations are recommended. An interview is required for some. The application deadline for regular admission is August 15.

Transfer Admission The application deadline for admission is August 15.

Entrance Difficulty St. Joseph's assesses its entrance difficulty level as moderately difficult. For the fall 2004 freshman class, 71 percent of the applicants were accepted.

SPECIAL MESSAGE TO STUDENTS

Social Life At St. Joseph's College (SJC), students can explore all of their interests. The campus community is alive with theater, music, social activities, and countless opportunities to build enduring friendships. There are clubs to meet every interest—political affairs, Asian awareness, science, drama, dance, even Japanese animation—and if a student's ideal club isn't available, there is always the opportunity to start one. For those whose passion is athletics, SJC offers programs that emphasize personal as well as team growth and excitement. Students can join a women's basketball, softball, or volleyball team as well as a men's basketball team. Future plans include men's and women's cross-country and tennis teams along with a men's volleyball team.

Academic Highlights St. Joseph's College encourages all its students to attain their highest academic potential through participating in small class sizes, securing internships, conducting research, and mastering the core curriculum that is ideal for entering virtually any career. The Dillon Child Study Center, a laboratory preschool, provides an on-campus practicum experience for students in the teacher education program while other hands-on internships prepare students for the working world that lies ahead. Senior research projects foster independent thinking and personal growth while preprofessional programs, such as premed and prelaw, provide the firm foundation for continuing professional careers. In addition, to meet the ever-changing needs of their students, SJC has implemented generous financial aid packages that include scholarships, grants, work-study opportunities, and loans.

Interviews and Campus Visits St. Joseph's College is located in historic Clinton Hill, one of the most successfully revitalized neighborhoods. Nestled among scenic brownstones, elegant gardens, lively cafes, bookstores, and restaurants, St. Joseph's is the center stage for a college career. SJC encourages those who are interested to visit the campus and take a guided tour of the various facilities and buildings. Most notable are the state-of-the-art biology and chemistry labs, enhanced computer centers, a research library with more than 200,000 volumes, and the Dillon Child Study Center, home to the nationally renowned education program. Interviews are not required but can be arranged if a prospective student is planning to visit the College. For more information on campus visits, students should call the Admissions Office at 718-636-6868, Monday through Friday, 9 a.m. to 5 p.m. (during the academic year), or Monday through Thursday, 9 a.m. to 4 p.m. (during the summer). The office is located at 245 Clinton Avenue on campus. The nearest commercial airport is John F. Kennedy International.

For Further Information Write to Ms. Theresa LaRocca Meyer, Director of Admissions, St. Joseph's College, Brooklyn Campus, 245 Clinton Avenue, Brooklyn, NY 11205-3688. *E-mail:* brooklynas@sjcny.edu.

See page 150 for a narrative description.

ST. JOSEPH'S COLLEGE, SUFFOLK CAMPUS
Patchogue, New York

St. Joseph's College, Suffolk Campus is a coed, private, comprehensive institution, founded in 1916, offering degrees at the bachelor's and master's levels (master's degree in education only). It has a 28-acre campus in Patchogue near New York City.

Academic Information The faculty has 386 members (30% full-time), 23% with terminal degrees. The undergraduate student-faculty ratio is 16:1. The library holds 82,600 titles, 323 serial subscriptions, and 1,331 audiovisual materials. Special programs include services for learning-disabled students, an honors program, cooperative (work-study) education, study abroad, advanced placement credit, double majors, independent study, distance learning, summer session for credit, part-time degree programs (daytime, evenings, weekends, summer), adult/continuing education programs, internships, and arrangement for off-campus study with Long Island Regional Advisory Council for Higher Education. The most frequently chosen baccalaureate fields are business/marketing, education, health professions and related sciences.
Student Body Statistics The student body totals 4,005, of whom 3,789 are undergraduates (459 freshmen). 75 percent are women and 25 percent are men. Students come from 4 states and territories and 6 other countries. 100 percent are from New York. 0.2 percent are international students. 53 percent of the 2004 graduating class went on to graduate and professional schools.
Expenses for 2005–06 *Application fee:* $25. *Tuition:* $11,612 full-time, $376 per credit part-time. *Mandatory fees:* $342 full-time, $11 per credit part-time, $104 per term part-time. Part-time tuition and fees vary according to course load.
Financial Aid Forms of aid include need-based and non-need-based scholarships and part-time jobs. The average aided 2004–05 undergraduate received an aid package worth an estimated $8228. The priority application deadline for financial aid is February 25.

Freshman Admission St. Joseph's College, Suffolk Campus requires a high school transcript, a minimum 3.0 high school GPA, SAT or ACT scores, and TOEFL scores for international students. An essay and an interview are recommended. 2 recommendations are required for some. The application deadline for regular admission is rolling.
Transfer Admission The application deadline for admission is rolling.
Entrance Difficulty St. Joseph's College, Suffolk Campus assesses its entrance difficulty level as moderately difficult. For the fall 2004 freshman class, 80 percent of the applicants were accepted.

For Further Information Contact Mrs. Marion E. Salgado, Director of Admissions, St. Joseph's College, Suffolk Campus, 155 West Roe Boulevard, Patchogue, NY 11772. *Telephone:* 631-447-3219 or 866-AT ST JOE (toll-free in-state). *Fax:* 631-447-1734. *E-mail:* admissions_patchogue@sjcny.edu. *Web site:* http://www.sjcny.edu/.

SAINT JOSEPH'S HOSPITAL HEALTH CENTER SCHOOL OF NURSING
Syracuse, New York

Saint Joseph's Hospital Health Center School of Nursing is a coed, primarily women's, private, two-year college, offering degrees at the associate level.

Expenses for 2004–05 *Application fee:* $30. *Tuition:* $6500 full-time, $245 per credit hour part-time. *Mandatory fees:* $1300 full-time, $680 per term part-time. *College room only:* $3100.

For Further Information Contact Ms. JoAnne Kiggins, Admission and Recruitment Coordinator, Saint Joseph's Hospital Health Center School of Nursing, 206 Prospect Avenue, Syracuse, NY 13203. *Telephone:* 315-448-5040. *Fax:* 315-448-5745. *Web site:* http://www.sjhsyr.org/nursing/.

ST. LAWRENCE UNIVERSITY
Canton, New York

St. Lawrence is a coed, private, comprehensive institution, founded in 1856, offering degrees at the bachelor's and master's levels and post-master's certificates. It has a 1,000-acre campus in Canton near Ottawa.

Academic Information The faculty has 206 members (80% full-time), 84% with terminal degrees. The undergraduate student-faculty ratio is 11:1. The library holds 555,364 titles, 1,961 serial subscriptions, and 5,281 audiovisual materials. Special programs include services for learning-disabled students, study abroad, advanced placement credit, double majors, independent study, self-designed majors, summer session for credit, part-time degree programs (daytime, evenings, summer), internships, and arrangement for off-campus study with Clarkson University, State University of New York College of Technology at Canton, State University of New York College at Potsdam, Fisk University, American University . The most frequently chosen baccalaureate fields are English, social sciences and history, visual/performing arts.
Student Body Statistics The student body totals 2,277, of whom 2,133 are undergraduates (566 freshmen). 52 percent are women and 48 percent are men. Students come from 41 states and territories and 21 other countries. 50 percent are from New York. 3.9 percent are international students. 20 percent of the 2004 graduating class went on to graduate and professional schools.
Expenses for 2004–05 *Application fee:* $50. *Comprehensive fee:* $38,235 includes full-time tuition ($30,270), mandatory fees ($210), and college room and board ($7755). *College room only:* $4170. Room and board charges vary according to board plan. *Part-time tuition:* $3785 per course.
Financial Aid Forms of aid include need-based and non-need-based scholarships, athletic grants, and part-time jobs. The average aided 2003–04 undergraduate received an aid package worth $26,013. The application deadline for financial aid is February 15.
Freshman Admission St. Lawrence requires an essay, a high school transcript, 2 recommendations, and TOEFL scores for international

students. A minimum 2.0 high school GPA and an interview are recommended. The application deadline for regular admission is February 15; for early decision plan 1 it is November 15; and for early decision plan 2 it is January 15.

Transfer Admission   The application deadline for admission is April 1.

Entrance Difficulty   St. Lawrence assesses its entrance difficulty level as very difficult. For the fall 2004 freshman class, 61 percent of the applicants were accepted.

For Further Information   Contact Ms. Terry Cowdrey, Dean of Admissions and Financial Aid, St. Lawrence University, Payson Hall, Canton, NY 13617-1455. *Telephone:* 315-229-5261 or 800-285-1856 (toll-free). *Fax:* 315-229-5818. *E-mail:* admissions@stlawu.edu. *Web site:* http://www.stlawu.edu/.

ST. THOMAS AQUINAS COLLEGE
Sparkill, New York

St. Thomas Aquinas College is a coed, private, comprehensive institution, founded in 1952, offering degrees at the associate, bachelor's, and master's levels and postbachelor's certificates. It has a 46-acre campus in Sparkill near New York City.

Academic Information   The faculty has 164 members (39% full-time), 45% with terminal degrees. The undergraduate student-faculty ratio is 16:1. The library holds 96,444 titles, 1,090 serial subscriptions, and 3,084 audiovisual materials. Special programs include academic remediation, services for learning-disabled students, an honors program, study abroad, advanced placement credit, accelerated degree programs, Freshman Honors College, double majors, independent study, summer session for credit, part-time degree programs (daytime, evenings, summer), adult/continuing education programs, internships, and arrangement for off-campus study with Barry University, Aquinas College, Dominican College of San Rafael. The most frequently chosen baccalaureate fields are business/marketing, education, social sciences and history.

Student Body Statistics   The student body totals 2,336, of whom 2,120 are undergraduates (352 freshmen). 56 percent are women and 44 percent are men. Students come from 17 states and territories and 10 other countries. 73 percent are from New York. 1.1 percent are international students. 40 percent of the 2004 graduating class went on to graduate and professional schools.

Expenses for 2005–06   *Application fee:* $30. *Comprehensive fee:* $25,450 includes full-time tuition ($16,200), mandatory fees ($400), and college room and board ($8850). *College room only:* $4780. *Part-time tuition:* $540 per credit. *Part-time mandatory fees:* $100 per term.

Financial Aid   Forms of aid include need-based and non-need-based scholarships and part-time jobs. The priority application deadline for financial aid is February 15.

Freshman Admission   St. Thomas Aquinas College requires a high school transcript, a minimum 2.0 high school GPA, SAT or ACT scores, and TOEFL scores for international students. An essay and an interview are recommended. 3 recommendations are required for some. The application deadline for regular admission is rolling; for early decision it is December 1; and for early action it is December 15.

Transfer Admission   The application deadline for admission is rolling.

Entrance Difficulty   St. Thomas Aquinas College assesses its entrance difficulty level as moderately difficult. For the fall 2004 freshman class, 82 percent of the applicants were accepted.

For Further Information   Contact Mr. John Edel, Dean of Enrollment Management, St. Thomas Aquinas College, 125 Route 340, Sparkill, NY 10976. *Telephone:* 845-398-4100 or 800-999-STAC (toll-free). *Web site:* http://www.stac.edu/.

SAINT VINCENT CATHOLIC MEDICAL CENTERS SCHOOL OF NURSING
Fresh Meadows, New York

Saint Vincent Catholic Medical Centers School of Nursing is a coed, private, two-year college, founded in 1969, offering degrees at the associate level. It has a 2-acre campus in Fresh Meadows.

Expenses for 2004–05   *Application fee:* $20. *Tuition:* $205 per credit part-time.

For Further Information   Contact Nancy Wolinski, Chairperson of Admissions, Saint Vincent Catholic Medical Centers School of Nursing, 175-05 Horace Harding Expressway, Fresh Meadows, NY 11365. *Telephone:* 718-357-0500 Ext. 131. *Fax:* 718-357-4683. *Web site:* http://www.svcmcny.org/.

SAMARITAN HOSPITAL SCHOOL OF NURSING
Troy, New York

For Information   Write to Samaritan Hospital School of Nursing, Troy, NY 12180.

SARAH LAWRENCE COLLEGE
Bronxville, New York

Sarah Lawrence is a coed, private, comprehensive institution, founded in 1926, offering degrees at the bachelor's and master's levels. It has a 40-acre campus in Bronxville near New York City.

Academic Information   The faculty has 213 members (84% full-time). The undergraduate student-faculty ratio is 6:1. The library holds 193,581 titles, 1,260 serial subscriptions, and 8,674 audiovisual materials. Special programs include services for learning-disabled students, study abroad, advanced placement credit, double majors, independent study, self-designed majors, part-time degree programs (daytime, evenings, summer), adult/continuing education programs, internships, and arrangement for off-campus study with Reed College, Eugene Lang College, New School University. The most frequently chosen baccalaureate field is liberal arts/general studies.

Student Body Statistics   The student body totals 1,574, of whom 1,260 are undergraduates (329 freshmen). 73 percent are women and 27 percent are men. 24 percent are from New York. 1.8 percent are international students. 30 percent of the 2004 graduating class went on to graduate and professional schools.

Expenses for 2004–05   *Application fee:* $60. *Comprehensive fee:* $43,854 includes full-time tuition ($31,680), mandatory fees ($736), and college room and board ($11,438). *College room only:* $7238. Full-time tuition and fees vary according to course load. Room and board charges vary according to board plan. *Part-time tuition:* $1056 per credit. *Part-time mandatory fees:* $368 per term. Part-time tuition and fees vary according to course load.

Financial Aid   Forms of aid include need-based scholarships and part-time jobs. The average aided 2004–05 undergraduate received an aid package worth an estimated $28,686. The application deadline for financial aid is February 1.

Freshman Admission   Sarah Lawrence requires an essay, a high school transcript, 3 recommendations, and TOEFL scores for international students. A minimum 3.0 high school GPA and an interview are recommended. The application deadline for regular admission is January 1; for early decision plan 1 it is November 15; and for early decision plan 2 it is January 1.

Transfer Admission   The application deadline for admission is March 1.

Entrance Difficulty   Sarah Lawrence assesses its entrance difficulty level as very difficult. For the fall 2004 freshman class, 44 percent of the applicants were accepted.

For Further Information   Contact Ms. Thyra L. Briggs, Dean of Admission, Sarah Lawrence College, 1 Mead Way, Bronxville, NY 10708-5999. *Telephone:* 914-395-2510 or 800-888-2858 (toll-free). *Fax:* 914-395-2515. *E-mail:* slcadmit@slc.edu. *Web site:* http://www.sarahlawrence.edu/.

SCHOOL OF VISUAL ARTS
New York, New York

SVA is a coed, proprietary, comprehensive institution, founded in 1947, offering degrees at the bachelor's and master's levels. It has a 1-acre campus in New York.

Academic Information The faculty has 848 members (17% full-time), 27% with terminal degrees. The undergraduate student-faculty ratio is 8:1. The library holds 71,490 titles, 340 serial subscriptions, and 158,000 audiovisual materials. Special programs include academic remediation, services for learning-disabled students, an honors program, study abroad, advanced placement credit, Freshman Honors College, ESL programs, independent study, summer session for credit, part-time degree programs (daytime, evenings, weekends, summer), and internships. The most frequently chosen baccalaureate field is visual/performing arts.

Student Body Statistics The student body totals 3,442, of whom 3,050 are undergraduates (489 freshmen). 52 percent are women and 48 percent are men. Students come from 45 states and territories and 42 other countries. 61 percent are from New York. 12.9 percent are international students. 6 percent of the 2004 graduating class went on to graduate and professional schools.

Expenses for 2004–05 *Application fee:* $50. *Comprehensive fee:* $30,870 includes full-time tuition ($19,120), mandatory fees ($500), and college room and board ($11,250). *College room only:* $7000. Room and board charges vary according to board plan, gender, housing facility, and location. *Part-time tuition:* $640 per credit.

Financial Aid Forms of aid include need-based and non-need-based scholarships and part-time jobs. The application deadline for financial aid is February 12 with a priority deadline of February 1.

Freshman Admission SVA requires an essay, a high school transcript, a minimum 2.5 high school GPA, a portfolio, SAT or ACT scores, and TOEFL scores for international students. An interview is recommended. 1 recommendation is required for some. The application deadline for regular admission is rolling and for early decision it is December 1.

Transfer Admission The application deadline for admission is rolling.

Entrance Difficulty SVA assesses its entrance difficulty level as moderately difficult. For the fall 2004 freshman class, 68 percent of the applicants were accepted.

For Further Information Contact Mr. Richard M. Longo, Executive Director of Admissions, School of Visual Arts, 209 East 23rd Street, New York, NY 10010. *Telephone:* 212-592-2100 Ext. 2182 or 800-436-4204 (toll-free). *Fax:* 212-592-2116. *E-mail:* admissions@sva.edu. *Web site:* http://www.schoolofvisualarts.edu/.

SH'OR YOSHUV RABBINICAL COLLEGE
Lawrence, New York

For Information Write to Sh'or Yoshuv Rabbinical College, Lawrence, NY 11559-1714.

SIENA COLLEGE
Loudonville, New York

Siena is a coed, private, Roman Catholic, four-year college, founded in 1937, offering degrees at the bachelor's level. It has a 163-acre campus in Loudonville.

Academic Information The faculty has 323 members (54% full-time), 69% with terminal degrees. The student-faculty ratio is 14:1. The library holds 326,332 titles, 5,275 serial subscriptions, and 5,410 audiovisual materials. Special programs include academic remediation, services for learning-disabled students, an honors program, study abroad, advanced placement credit, accelerated degree programs, double majors, independent study, distance learning, summer session for credit, part-time degree programs (daytime, evenings, weekends, summer), adult/continuing education programs, internships, and arrangement for off-campus study with members of the Hudson-Mohawk Association of Colleges and Universities. The most frequently chosen baccalaureate fields are business/marketing, psychology, social sciences and history.

Student Body Statistics The student body is made up of 3,338 undergraduates (716 freshmen). 57 percent are women and 43 percent are men. Students come from 30 states and territories and 7 other countries. 89 percent are from New York. 0.4 percent are international students.

Expenses for 2004–05 *Application fee:* $40. *Comprehensive fee:* $26,705 includes full-time tuition ($18,590), mandatory fees ($540), and college room and board ($7575). *College room only:* $4750. Room and board charges vary according to board plan and housing facility. *Part-time tuition:* $370 per credit hour. *Part-time mandatory fees:* $25 per term.

Financial Aid Forms of aid include need-based and non-need-based scholarships, athletic grants, and part-time jobs. The priority application deadline for financial aid is February 1.

Freshman Admission Siena requires an essay, a high school transcript, 1 recommendation, SAT or ACT scores, and TOEFL scores for international students. An interview is recommended. An interview is required for some. The application deadline for regular admission is March 1; for early decision it is December 1; and for early action it is December 1.

Transfer Admission The application deadline for admission is June 1.

Entrance Difficulty Siena assesses its entrance difficulty level as moderately difficult; most difficult for Siena/Albany Medical College Program. For the fall 2004 freshman class, 60 percent of the applicants were accepted.

SPECIAL MESSAGE TO STUDENTS

Social Life Siena's students are distinguished by their involvement in campus life and the community. Siena fields eighteen Division I varsity men's and women's athletic teams, which are enthusiastically supported by the whole student body. More than 75 percent of Siena students participate in intramural or club athletics, ranging from softball to Tae Kwon Do. Siena's Franciscan Center for Service and Advocacy assists students in reaching out to a wide variety of community service organizations, such as the St. Francis Inn, Habitat for Humanity, and Foster Grandparents. Many students get involved in Siena's excellent theatrical productions, work at the campus radio station, or run for Student Government offices. Being only a few miles from the capital city of Albany gives Siena students access to many cultural and recreational opportunities. Siena is also close to skiing and hiking areas in Vermont and the Adirondacks.

Academic Highlights Siena's faculty members focus their time and attention on teaching their students; classes are all taught by professors, and classes typically have 15 to 20 students. Siena's students identify their close relationships with faculty members as one of the most valuable parts of their college experience. All students follow a core liberal arts curriculum, which equips them for future study and careers. Siena offers a wealth of internship opportunities in state legislature and government, financial institutions, and health-care, research, and communications fields. Study abroad is also popular. Students study and travel all over the world, and the College runs internship/study programs in England, Ireland, France, Italy, Spain, and Australia. Students interested in American government can participate in the Washington semester, interning in the nation's capital and attending classes at American University. Siena offers excellent guidance for students considering medicine, law, and education as well as career counseling and assistance to all its students.

Interviews and Campus Visits A visit and an interview are strongly recommended. An interview at the Admissions Office provides students and their parents with an opportunity to ask questions about the College and admissions process and allows the admissions committee a chance to learn about an applicant in person. A tour with a Siena student ambassador includes visits to classrooms, the library, labs, the chapel, the athletic facility, and residence halls. Siena hosts open houses and Shadow Days, when visitors spend the day attending classes with a Siena student. For information about appointments and campus visits, students should contact the Admissions Office at 518-783-2423 or 888-AT SIENA (toll-free), Monday through Friday, 9 a.m. to 3 p.m., or on most Saturday mornings when school is in session. The nearest commercial airport is Albany International.

For Further Information Write to the Admissions Office, Siena College, 515 Loudon Road, Loudonville, NY 12211.

See page 152 for a narrative description.

SKIDMORE COLLEGE
Saratoga Springs, New York

Skidmore is a coed, private, comprehensive institution, founded in 1903, offering degrees at the bachelor's and master's levels. It has an 800-acre campus in Saratoga Springs near Albany.

Academic Information The faculty has 328 members (71% full-time), 66% with terminal degrees. The undergraduate student-faculty ratio is 9:1. The library holds 352,802 titles, 984 serial subscriptions, and 140,927 audiovisual materials. Special programs include an honors program, study abroad, advanced placement credit, accelerated degree programs, double majors, independent study, distance learning, self-designed majors, summer session for credit, external degree programs, adult/continuing education programs, internships, and arrangement for off-campus study with members of the Hudson-Mohawk Association of Colleges and Universities. The most frequently chosen baccalaureate fields are social sciences and history, business/marketing, visual/performing arts.

Student Body Statistics The student body totals 2,691, of whom 2,637 are undergraduates (676 freshmen). 59 percent are women and 41 percent are men. Students come from 41 states and territories and 28 other countries. 30 percent are from New York. 1.4 percent are international students. 13 percent of the 2004 graduating class went on to graduate and professional schools.

Expenses for 2004–05 *Application fee:* $60. *Comprehensive fee:* $39,818 includes full-time tuition ($30,800), mandatory fees ($308), and college room and board ($8710). *College room only:* $4860. Full-time tuition and fees vary according to course load. Room and board charges vary according to board plan and housing facility. *Part-time tuition:* $1030 per credit hour. *Part-time mandatory fees:* $25 per term. Part-time tuition and fees vary according to course load.

Financial Aid Forms of aid include need-based and non-need-based scholarships and part-time jobs. The average aided 2004–05 undergraduate received an aid package worth an estimated $25,312. The application deadline for financial aid is January 15.

Freshman Admission Skidmore requires an essay, a high school transcript, 2 recommendations, SAT or ACT scores, and TOEFL scores for international students. An interview is recommended. The application deadline for regular admission is January 15; for early decision plan 1 it is November 15; and for early decision plan 2 it is January 15.

Transfer Admission The application deadline for admission is April 1.

Entrance Difficulty Skidmore assesses its entrance difficulty level as very difficult. For the fall 2004 freshman class, 48 percent of the applicants were accepted.

For Further Information Contact Mary Lou W. Bates, Director of Admissions and Financial Aid, Skidmore College, 815 North Broadway, Saratoga Springs, NY 12866-1632. *Telephone:* 518-580-5570 or 800-867-6007 (toll-free). *Fax:* 518-580-5584. *E-mail:* admissions@skidmore.edu. *Web site:* http://www.skidmore.edu/.

STATE UNIVERSITY OF NEW YORK AT ALBANY

See University at Albany, State University of New York.

STATE UNIVERSITY OF NEW YORK AT BINGHAMTON
Binghamton, New York

Binghamton University is a coed, public unit of State University of New York System, founded in 1946, offering degrees at the bachelor's, master's, and doctoral levels and post-master's certificates. It has an 887-acre campus in Binghamton.

Academic Information The faculty has 719 members (71% full-time). The undergraduate student-faculty ratio is 22:1. The library holds 2 million titles, 8,915 serial subscriptions, and 122,518 audiovisual materials. Special programs include academic remediation, services for learning-disabled students, an honors program, study abroad, advanced placement credit, accelerated degree programs, ESL programs, double majors, independent study, distance learning, self-designed majors, summer session for credit, part-time degree programs (daytime, evenings, summer), adult/continuing education programs, internships, and arrangement for off-campus study with National Student Exchange, New York State Visiting Student Program. The most frequently chosen baccalaureate fields are business/marketing, psychology, social sciences and history.

Student Body Statistics The student body totals 13,860, of whom 11,034 are undergraduates (2,160 freshmen). 49 percent are women and 51 percent are men. Students come from 39 states and territories and 67 other countries. 94 percent are from New York. 4 percent are international students. 38 percent of the 2004 graduating class went on to graduate and professional schools.

Expenses for 2004–05 *Application fee:* $40. *State resident tuition:* $4350 full-time, $181 per credit hour part-time. *Nonresident tuition:* $10,610 full-time, $442 per credit hour part-time. *Mandatory fees:* $1406 full-time. *College room and board:* $7710. *College room only:* $4736. Room and board charges vary according to board plan and housing facility.

Financial Aid Forms of aid include need-based and non-need-based scholarships, athletic grants, and part-time jobs. The average aided 2004–05 undergraduate received an aid package worth an estimated $11,089. The priority application deadline for financial aid is March 1.

Freshman Admission Binghamton University requires an essay, a high school transcript, SAT or ACT scores, and TOEFL scores for international students. 1 recommendation and portfolio, audition are required for some. The application deadline for regular admission is rolling and for early action it is November 15.

Transfer Admission The application deadline for admission is rolling.

Entrance Difficulty Binghamton University assesses its entrance difficulty level as very difficult; moderately difficult for transfers. For the fall 2004 freshman class, 44 percent of the applicants were accepted.

For Further Information Contact Ms. Cheryl S. Brown, Director of Admissions, State University of New York at Binghamton, PO Box 6001, Binghamton, NY 13902-6001. *Telephone:* 607-777-2171. *Fax:* 607-777-4445. *E-mail:* admit@binghamton.edu. *Web site:* http://www.binghamton.edu/.

STATE UNIVERSITY OF NEW YORK AT BUFFALO
Buffalo, New York

UB is a coed, public unit of State University of New York System, founded in 1846, offering degrees at the bachelor's, master's, doctoral, and first professional levels and post-master's and first professional certificates. It has a 1,350-acre campus in Buffalo.

Academic Information The faculty has 1,746 members (65% full-time). The undergraduate student-faculty ratio is 15:1. The library holds 3 million titles, 34,126 serial subscriptions, and 188,300 audiovisual materials. Special programs include academic remediation, services for learning-disabled students, an honors program, cooperative (work-study) education, study abroad, advanced placement credit, accelerated degree programs, Freshman Honors College, ESL programs, double majors, independent study, distance learning, self-designed majors, summer session for credit, part-time degree programs (daytime, evenings, summer), adult/continuing education programs, internships, and arrangement for off-campus study with all institutions in the western New York area, Association of Colleges and Universities of the State of New York. The most frequently chosen baccalaureate fields are business/marketing, engineering/engineering technologies, social sciences and history.

Student Body Statistics The student body totals 27,276, of whom 17,838 are undergraduates (3,183 freshmen). 46 percent are women and 54 percent are men. Students come from 40 states and territories and 78 other countries. 98 percent are from New York. 6.2 percent are international students. 36 percent of the 2004 graduating class went on to graduate and professional schools.

Expenses for 2004–05 *Application fee:* $40. *State resident tuition:* $4350 full-time, $181 per credit hour part-time. *Nonresident tuition:* $10,610 full-time, $442 per credit hour part-time. *Mandatory fees:* $1616 full-time, $72 per credit hour part-time. Part-time tuition and fees vary according to course load. *College room and board:* $7226. *College room only:* $4336. Room and board charges vary according to board plan and housing facility.

Financial Aid Forms of aid include need-based and non-need-based scholarships, athletic grants, and part-time jobs. The average aided 2004–05 undergraduate received an aid package worth an estimated $7132. The priority application deadline for financial aid is March 1.

Freshman Admission UB requires a high school transcript, SAT or ACT scores, and TOEFL scores for international students. Recommendations and portfolio, audition are required for some. The application deadline for regular admission is rolling and for early decision it is November 1.

Transfer Admission The application deadline for admission is rolling.

Entrance Difficulty UB assesses its entrance difficulty level as moderately difficult. For the fall 2004 freshman class, 56 percent of the applicants were accepted.

For Further Information Contact Ms. Patricia Armstrong, Director of Admissions, State University of New York at Buffalo, Capen Hall, Room 15, North Campus, Buffalo, NY 14260-1660. *Telephone:* 716-645-6900 or 888-UB-ADMIT (toll-free). *Fax:* 716-645-6411. *E-mail:* ub-admissions@buffalo.edu. *Web site:* http://www.buffalo.edu/.

STATE UNIVERSITY OF NEW YORK AT FARMINGDALE

See Farmingdale State University of New York.

STATE UNIVERSITY OF NEW YORK AT NEW PALTZ

New Paltz, New York

SUNY New Paltz is a coed, public, comprehensive unit of State University of New York System, founded in 1828, offering degrees at the bachelor's and master's levels and post-master's certificates. It has a 216-acre campus in New Paltz.

Academic Information The faculty has 686 members (43% full-time), 36% with terminal degrees. The undergraduate student-faculty ratio is 16:1. The library holds 525,296 titles, 1,253 serial subscriptions, and 1,564 audiovisual materials. Special programs include academic remediation, services for learning-disabled students, an honors program, cooperative (work-study) education, study abroad, advanced placement credit, ESL programs, double majors, independent study, distance learning, self-designed majors, summer session for credit, part-time degree programs (daytime, evenings, weekends, summer), adult/continuing education programs, internships, and arrangement for off-campus study with Associated Colleges of the Mid-Hudson Area. The most frequently chosen baccalaureate fields are business/marketing, education, visual/performing arts.

Student Body Statistics The student body totals 7,603, of whom 6,191 are undergraduates (813 freshmen). 67 percent are women and 33 percent are men. Students come from 23 states and territories and 40 other countries. 97 percent are from New York. 2.3 percent are international students. 29 percent of the 2004 graduating class went on to graduate and professional schools.

Expenses for 2004–05 *Application fee:* $40. *State resident tuition:* $4350 full-time, $181 per credit part-time. *Nonresident tuition:* $10,300 full-time, $429 per credit part-time. *Mandatory fees:* $870 full-time, $25.70 per credit part-time, $125 per term part-time. *College room and board:* $6860. *College room only:* $4240. Room and board charges vary according to board plan.

Financial Aid Forms of aid include need-based and non-need-based scholarships and part-time jobs. The average aided 2003–04 undergraduate received an aid package worth $2446.

Freshman Admission SUNY New Paltz requires a high school transcript, SAT or ACT scores, and TOEFL scores for international

students. A minimum 3.0 high school GPA is recommended. An essay, recommendations, an interview, and portfolio for art program, audition for music and theater programs are required for some. The application deadline for regular admission is March 31 and for early action it is November 15.

Transfer Admission The application deadline for admission is May 1.

Entrance Difficulty SUNY New Paltz assesses its entrance difficulty level as moderately difficult. For the fall 2004 freshman class, 40 percent of the applicants were accepted.

For Further Information Contact Ms. Kimberly A. Lavoie, Director of Freshmen and International Admissions, State University of New York at New Paltz, 75 South Manheim Boulevard, Suite 1, New Paltz, NY 12561-2499. *Telephone:* 845-257-3210 or 888-639-7589 (toll-free in-state). *Fax:* 845-257-3209. *E-mail:* admissions@newpaltz.edu. *Web site:* http://www.newpaltz.edu/.

STATE UNIVERSITY OF NEW YORK AT OSWEGO

Oswego, New York

SPONSOR
See Front Insert
for Details!

Oswego State University is a coed, public, comprehensive unit of State University of New York System, founded in 1861, offering degrees at the bachelor's and master's levels and post-master's certificates. It has a 696-acre campus in Oswego near Syracuse.

Academic Information The faculty has 467 members (67% full-time), 59% with terminal degrees. The undergraduate student-faculty ratio is 19:1. The library holds 477,930 titles, 959 serial subscriptions, and 32,179 audiovisual materials. Special programs include services for learning-disabled students, an honors program, cooperative (work-study) education, study abroad, advanced placement credit, accelerated degree programs, Freshman Honors College, ESL programs, double majors, independent study, distance learning, self-designed majors, summer session for credit, part-time degree programs (daytime, evenings), adult/continuing education programs, internships, and arrangement for off-campus study with Bryant and Stratton North Campus, Finger Lakes Community College, Jefferson-Lewis Board of Cooperative Educational Services, Onondage-Cortland-Madison Board of Cooperative Educational Services. The most frequently chosen baccalaureate fields are business/marketing, communications/communication technologies, education.

Student Body Statistics The student body totals 8,289, of whom 7,059 are undergraduates (1,377 freshmen). 54 percent are women and 46 percent are men. Students come from 28 states and territories and 19 other countries. 98 percent are from New York. 0.9 percent are international students. 12 percent of the 2004 graduating class went on to graduate and professional schools.

Expenses for 2004–05 *Application fee:* $40. *State resident tuition:* $4350 full-time, $181 per credit hour part-time. *Nonresident tuition:* $10,160 full-time, $429 per credit hour part-time. *Mandatory fees:* $888 full-time, $34.14 per credit hour part-time. Part-time tuition and fees vary according to class time and location. *College room and board:* $7890. *College room only:* $4790. Room and board charges vary according to board plan, housing facility, and location.

Financial Aid Forms of aid include need-based and non-need-based scholarships and part-time jobs. The average aided 2004–05 undergraduate received an aid package worth an estimated $8625. The priority application deadline for financial aid is April 1.

Freshman Admission Oswego State University requires a high school transcript, SAT or ACT scores, and TOEFL scores for international students. An essay and an interview are recommended. Recommendations are required for some. The application deadline for regular admission is rolling and for early decision it is November 15.

Transfer Admission The application deadline for admission is rolling.

Entrance Difficulty Oswego State University assesses its entrance difficulty level as moderately difficult. For the fall 2004 freshman class, 57 percent of the applicants were accepted.

SPECIAL MESSAGE TO STUDENTS

Social Life Social opportunities abound at Oswego. More than 125 clubs and organizations, twenty-three intercollegiate athletic teams, and numerous performing arts groups exist to meet the needs and interests of students beyond the classroom. The Student Association serves as the student governing body with representation for students living on and off campus. The Oswego student body is a diverse group. Students consider the campus to be a very friendly place, providing excellent opportunities for students to develop lasting friendships.

Academic Highlights Oswego State offers opportunities to study off campus through a variety of overseas academic programs and numerous internships. Oswego's overseas program, one of the largest in the SUNY system, includes study in Australia, Brazil, China, Cuba, Czech Republic, England, France, Germany, Hungary, Ireland, Italy, Japan, Mexico, New Zealand, Puerto Rico, Russia, and Spain. Students can also choose from more than 300 additional programs available through other colleges or universities within SUNY. Each year, more than 1,000 interns work with campus organizations, nonprofit agencies, small businesses, and large corporations. Semester study programs in Albany, New York, and Washington, D.C., provide students with outstanding internship experiences in state and federal government.

Interviews and Campus Visits A visit to the Oswego campus is recommended. A conversation with a member of the admission committee provides an important opportunity for information exchange. During the academic year and summer sessions, visitors can take a student-guided campus tour, speak with a financial aid counselor, or meet with a faculty member. Group programs for applicants and their families are scheduled on selected days throughout the year. Applicants are invited to explore the College's impressive facilities, including Penfield Library and its extensive collections; language, science, and computer labs; 600-acre Rice Creek Biological Field Station; and Lanigan Hall, housing state-of-the-art broadcasting facilities for communications. Visitors may dine on campus or spend time touring the historic and recreational sights located near Oswego's lakeside campus and in the surrounding area. To schedule an appointment, visitors should go to http://www.oswego.edu/visit or call the Office of Admissions during business hours at 315-312-2250. The office is located at 211 Culkin Hall on campus. The college is located between Route 104 and Lake Ontario, 65 miles east of Rochester and 35 miles northwest of Syracuse. The nearest commercial airport is Syracuse-Hancock International.

For Further Information Write to Dr. Joseph F. Grant Jr., Vice President for Student Affairs and Enrollment, State University of New York at Oswego, 211 Culkin Hall, Oswego, NY 13126. *E-mail:* admiss@oswego.edu. *Web site:* http://www.oswego.edu.

STATE UNIVERSITY OF NEW YORK AT PLATTSBURGH

Plattsburgh, New York

Plattsburgh State University is a coed, public, comprehensive unit of State University of New York System, founded in 1889, offering degrees at the bachelor's and master's levels and post-master's certificates. It has a 265-acre campus in Plattsburgh near Montreal.

Academic Information The faculty has 446 members (57% full-time), 54% with terminal degrees. The undergraduate student-faculty ratio is 17:1. The library holds 378,020 titles, 1,412 serial subscriptions, and 36,749 audiovisual materials. Special programs include academic remediation, services for learning-disabled students, an honors program, cooperative (work-study) education, study abroad, advanced placement credit, accelerated degree programs, ESL programs, double majors, independent study, distance learning, self-designed majors, summer session for credit, part-time degree programs (daytime, evenings, summer), adult/continuing education programs, internships, and arrangement for off-campus study with National Student Exchange, Clinton Community College, State University of New York Empire State College, Adirondack Community College. The most frequently chosen baccalaureate fields are business/marketing, education, social sciences and history.

Student Body Statistics The student body totals 5,909, of whom 5,275 are undergraduates (863 freshmen). 58 percent are women and 42 percent are men. Students come from 26 states and territories and 49 other countries. 96 percent are from New York. 6.1 percent are international students.

Expenses for 2004–05 *Application fee:* $40. *State resident tuition:* $4350 full-time, $181 per credit hour part-time. *Nonresident tuition:* $10,610 full-time, $442 per credit hour part-time. *Mandatory fees:* $918 full-time, $37.50 per credit hour part-time. Part-time tuition and fees vary according to course load. *College room and board:* $6712. *College room only:* $4200. Room and board charges vary according to board plan.

Financial Aid Forms of aid include need-based and non-need-based scholarships and part-time jobs. The average aided 2004–05 undergraduate received an aid package worth an estimated $9139. The priority application deadline for financial aid is March 1.

Freshman Admission Plattsburgh State University requires a high school transcript, a minimum 2.5 high school GPA, SAT or ACT scores, and TOEFL scores for international students. An essay, a minimum 3.4 high school GPA, recommendations, and an interview are recommended. The application deadline for regular admission is August 1 and for early decision it is November 15.

Transfer Admission The application deadline for admission is rolling.

Entrance Difficulty Plattsburgh State University assesses its entrance difficulty level as moderately difficult; very difficult for accounting, communication disorder sciences, education, engineering, nursing, social work programs. For the fall 2004 freshman class, 59 percent of the applicants were accepted.

For Further Information Contact Mr. Richard Higgins, Director of Admissions, State University of New York at Plattsburgh, 101 Broad Street, Plattsburgh, NY 12901-2681. *Telephone:* 518-564-2040 or 888-673-0012 (toll-free in-state). *Fax:* 518-564-2045. *E-mail:* admissions@plattsburgh.edu. *Web site:* http://www.plattsburgh.edu/.

STATE UNIVERSITY OF NEW YORK AT STONY BROOK

See Stony Brook University, State University of New York.

STATE UNIVERSITY OF NEW YORK COLLEGE AT BROCKPORT

Brockport, New York

SUNY Brockport is a coed, public, comprehensive unit of State University of New York System, founded in 1867, offering degrees at the bachelor's and master's levels and post-master's and postbachelor's certificates. It has a 435-acre campus in Brockport near Rochester.

Academic Information The faculty has 565 members (53% full-time), 90% with terminal degrees. The undergraduate student-faculty ratio is 18:1. The library holds 584,687 titles, 1,800 serial subscriptions, and 8,228 audiovisual materials. Special programs include academic remediation, services for learning-disabled students, an honors program, cooperative (work-study) education, study abroad, advanced placement credit, accelerated degree programs, Freshman Honors College, double majors, independent study, distance learning, self-designed majors, summer session for credit, part-time degree programs (daytime, evenings, weekends, summer), internships, and arrangement for off-campus study with Rochester Area Colleges, New York State Visiting Student Program. The most frequently chosen baccalaureate fields are business/marketing, health professions and related sciences, protective services/public administration.

Student Body Statistics The student body totals 8,595, of whom 6,980 are undergraduates (1,055 freshmen). 57 percent are women and 43 percent are men. Students come from 35 states and territories and 26 other countries. 98 percent are from New York. 1.1 percent are international students. 25 percent of the 2004 graduating class went on to graduate and professional schools.

Expenses for 2004–05 *Application fee:* $40. *State resident tuition:* $4350 full-time, $181 per credit hour part-time. *Nonresident tuition:* $10,300 full-time, $429 per credit hour part-time. *Mandatory fees:* $913 full-time, $37.85 per credit hour part-time. Part-time tuition and fees vary according to course load. *College room and board:* $7226. *College room only:* $4500. Room and board charges vary according to board plan and housing facility.
Financial Aid Forms of aid include need-based and non-need-based scholarships and part-time jobs. The average aided 2003–04 undergraduate received an aid package worth $7019. The priority application deadline for financial aid is March 15.
Freshman Admission SUNY Brockport requires a high school transcript, SAT or ACT scores, and TOEFL scores for international students. A minimum 2.6 high school GPA and recommendations are recommended. An essay, recommendations, and an interview are required for some. The application deadline for regular admission is rolling.
Transfer Admission The application deadline for admission is August 1.
Entrance Difficulty SUNY Brockport assesses its entrance difficulty level as moderately difficult; very difficult for education. For the fall 2004 freshman class, 50 percent of the applicants were accepted.

For Further Information Contact Mr. Bernard S. Valento, Director of Undergraduate Admissions, State University of New York College at Brockport, 350 New Campus Drive, Brockport, NY 14420-2997. *Telephone:* 585-395-2751. *Fax:* 585-395-5452. *E-mail:* admit@brockport.edu. *Web site:* http://www.brockport.edu/.

STATE UNIVERSITY OF NEW YORK COLLEGE AT BUFFALO

See Buffalo State College, State University of New York.

STATE UNIVERSITY OF NEW YORK COLLEGE AT CORTLAND

Cortland, New York

SUNY Cortland is a coed, public, comprehensive unit of State University of New York System, founded in 1868, offering degrees at the bachelor's and master's levels and post-master's and postbachelor's certificates. It has a 191-acre campus in Cortland near Syracuse.

Academic Information The faculty has 512 members (52% full-time), 50% with terminal degrees. The undergraduate student-faculty ratio is 16:1. The library holds 82,257 titles. Special programs include academic remediation, services for learning-disabled students, an honors program, cooperative (work-study) education, study abroad, advanced placement credit, double majors, independent study, distance learning, self-designed majors, summer session for credit, part-time degree programs, adult/continuing education programs, internships, and arrangement for off-campus study with other units of the State University of New York System. The most frequently chosen baccalaureate fields are education, communications/communication technologies, social sciences and history.
Student Body Statistics The student body totals 7,331, of whom 5,950 are undergraduates (1,086 freshmen). 58 percent are women and 42 percent are men. Students come from 26 states and territories. 98 percent are from New York. 0.3 percent are international students.
Expenses for 2004–05 *Application fee:* $40. *State resident tuition:* $4350 full-time, $181 per credit part-time. *Nonresident tuition:* $10,300 full-time, $442 per credit part-time. *Mandatory fees:* $950 full-time. *College room and board:* $7290. *College room only:* $4228. Room and board charges vary according to board plan and housing facility.
Financial Aid Forms of aid include need-based and non-need-based scholarships and part-time jobs. The application deadline for financial aid is March 31.

Freshman Admission SUNY Cortland requires an essay, a high school transcript, a minimum 2.3 high school GPA, 1 recommendation, SAT or ACT scores, and TOEFL scores for international students. A minimum 3.0 high school GPA, 3 recommendations, and an interview are recommended. The application deadline for regular admission is rolling and for early decision it is November 15.
Entrance Difficulty SUNY Cortland assesses its entrance difficulty level as moderately difficult. For the fall 2004 freshman class, 47 percent of the applicants were accepted.

For Further Information Contact Mr. Mark Yacavone, Interim Director of Admission, State University of New York College at Cortland, PO Box 2000, Cortland, NY 13045. *Telephone:* 607-753-4711. *Fax:* 607-753-5998. *E-mail:* admssn_info@snycorva.cortland.edu. *Web site:* http://www.cortland.edu/.

STATE UNIVERSITY OF NEW YORK COLLEGE AT GENESEO

Geneseo, New York

Geneseo College is a coed, public, comprehensive unit of State University of New York System, founded in 1871, offering degrees at the bachelor's and master's levels. It has a 220-acre campus in Geneseo near Rochester.

Academic Information The faculty has 345 members (71% full-time), 68% with terminal degrees. The undergraduate student-faculty ratio is 19:1. The library holds 576,700 titles, 1,758 serial subscriptions, and 15,248 audiovisual materials. Special programs include services for learning-disabled students, an honors program, study abroad, advanced placement credit, ESL programs, double majors, independent study, summer session for credit, part-time degree programs (daytime, evenings, summer), internships, and arrangement for off-campus study with Rochester Area Colleges. The most frequently chosen baccalaureate fields are business/marketing, education, social sciences and history.
Student Body Statistics The student body totals 5,573, of whom 5,375 are undergraduates (1,030 freshmen). 61 percent are women and 39 percent are men. Students come from 23 states and territories and 34 other countries. 99 percent are from New York. 2.3 percent are international students. 27 percent of the 2004 graduating class went on to graduate and professional schools.
Expenses for 2004–05 *Application fee:* $40. *State resident tuition:* $4350 full-time, $181 per credit hour part-time. *Nonresident tuition:* $10,610 full-time, $429 per credit hour part-time. *Mandatory fees:* $1085 full-time, $44.20 per credit hour part-time. Part-time tuition and fees vary according to course load. *College room and board:* $6820. Room and board charges vary according to board plan and housing facility.
Financial Aid Forms of aid include need-based and non-need-based scholarships and part-time jobs. The average aided 2004–05 undergraduate received an aid package worth an estimated $9123. The priority application deadline for financial aid is February 15.
Freshman Admission Geneseo College requires an essay, a high school transcript, SAT or ACT scores, and TOEFL scores for international students. Recommendations and an interview are recommended. The application deadline for regular admission is January 15 and for early decision it is November 15.
Transfer Admission The application deadline for admission is January 15.
Entrance Difficulty Geneseo College assesses its entrance difficulty level as very difficult. For the fall 2004 freshman class, 44 percent of the applicants were accepted.

For Further Information Contact Kris Shay, Director of Admissions, State University of New York College at Geneseo, 1 College Circle, Geneseo, NY 14454-1401. *Telephone:* 585-245-5571 or 866-245-5211 (toll-free). *Fax:* 585-245-5550. *E-mail:* admissions@geneseo.edu. *Web site:* http://www.geneseo.edu/.

STATE UNIVERSITY OF NEW YORK COLLEGE AT OLD WESTBURY

Old Westbury, New York

SPONSOR
See Front Insert for Details!

SUNY/Old Westbury is a coed, public, comprehensive unit of State University of New York System, founded in 1965, offering degrees at the bachelor's and master's levels. It has a 605-acre campus in Old Westbury near New York City.

Academic Information   The faculty has 233 members (55% full-time), 55% with terminal degrees. The undergraduate student-faculty ratio is 18:1. The library holds 196,000 titles, 803 serial subscriptions, and 2,057 audiovisual materials. Special programs include academic remediation, services for learning-disabled students, an honors program, study abroad, advanced placement credit, ESL programs, double majors, independent study, distance learning, summer session for credit, part-time degree programs (daytime, evenings, summer), internships, and arrangement for off-campus study with other units of the State University of New York System, Long Island University, C.W. Post Campus, New York Institute of Technology. The most frequently chosen baccalaureate fields are business/marketing, education, social sciences and history.

Student Body Statistics   The student body totals 3,359, of whom 3,340 are undergraduates (390 freshmen). 60 percent are women and 40 percent are men. Students come from 5 states and territories and 27 other countries. 99 percent are from New York. 2.1 percent are international students.

Expenses for 2004–05   *Application fee:* $40. *State resident tuition:* $4350 full-time, $181 per credit part-time. *Nonresident tuition:* $10,610 full-time, $429 per credit part-time. *Mandatory fees:* $722 full-time, $113.50 per term part-time. Part-time tuition and fees vary according to course load. *College room and board:* $7914. *College room only:* $5624. Room and board charges vary according to board plan and housing facility.

Financial Aid   Forms of aid include need-based and non-need-based scholarships and part-time jobs. The priority application deadline for financial aid is April 14.

Freshman Admission   SUNY/Old Westbury requires an essay, a high school transcript, SAT or ACT scores, and TOEFL scores for international students. An essay, 2 recommendations, and an interview are required for some. The application deadline for regular admission is rolling and for early decision it is November 1.

Transfer Admission   The application deadline for admission is December 15.

Entrance Difficulty   SUNY/Old Westbury assesses its entrance difficulty level as moderately difficult. For the fall 2004 freshman class, 52 percent of the applicants were accepted.

SPECIAL MESSAGE TO STUDENTS

Social Life It doesn't take long before students find that Old Westbury is a place where academic and personal growth go hand in hand. To achieve that growth, many Old Westbury students seek activities outside the classroom in fifty student organizations, intramural sports, fraternities, and sororities. or they benefit from such regular features on campus as guest lecturers, musical performances, film series, and student, faculty, and professional art exhibitions.

Academic Highlights Through a School of Business, School of Education, and nine individual academic departments, Old Westbury offers forty-five undergraduate degree programs, enabling students to earn Bachelor of Arts, Bachelor of Science, and Bachelor of Professional Studies degrees. From liberal arts programs that provide a solid basis for future growth—such as English language, humanities, and languages and American studies—to professional programs whose graduates go on to successful careers as accountants, journalists, criminal scientists, psychologists, and teachers, Old Westbury offers it all in a small college environment where student-teacher interaction comes first.

Interviews and Campus Visits Although an interview may not be required to complete the admission process, it is suggested that prospective students consider meeting with an admission counselor to discuss specific concerns and program objectives. The College invites prospective students

to visit the campus and talk with faculty members. Applicants should tour the College's excellent, modern facilities, especially the library, the student union, and Wallace Art Gallery. The Clark Physical Education and Recreation Center offers indoor and outdoor sports, including swimming, tennis, basketball, volleyball, racquetball, and squash. The Natural Science Building provides state-of-the-art laboratories and scientific equipment. For information about appointments and campus visits, students should call the Admissions Office at 516-876-3073, Monday through Friday, 9 a.m. to 5 p.m. The office is located in the Campus Center, Room I-202, on campus. The nearest commercial airport is La Guardia.

For Further Information Write to the Vice President of Enrollment Services, State University of New York College at Old Westbury, Box 307, Old Westbury, NY 11568-0307.

STATE UNIVERSITY OF NEW YORK COLLEGE AT ONEONTA

Oneonta, New York

Oneonta is a coed, public, comprehensive unit of State University of New York System, founded in 1889, offering degrees at the bachelor's and master's levels and post-master's certificates. It has a 250-acre campus in Oneonta.

Academic Information   The faculty has 440 members (57% full-time), 52% with terminal degrees. The undergraduate student-faculty ratio is 18:1. The library holds 552,389 titles, 18,506 serial subscriptions, and 30,320 audiovisual materials. Special programs include academic remediation, services for learning-disabled students, an honors program, study abroad, advanced placement credit, ESL programs, double majors, independent study, distance learning, summer session for credit, part-time degree programs (daytime, evenings, summer), adult/continuing education programs, internships, and arrangement for off-campus study with Hartwick College. The most frequently chosen baccalaureate fields are education, home economics/vocational home economics, visual/performing arts.

Student Body Statistics   The student body totals 5,806, of whom 5,605 are undergraduates (1,057 freshmen). 58 percent are women and 42 percent are men. Students come from 18 states and territories and 17 other countries. 98 percent are from New York. 1.3 percent are international students. 47 percent of the 2004 graduating class went on to graduate and professional schools.

Expenses for 2005–06   *Application fee:* $40. *State resident tuition:* $4350 full-time, $181 per semester hour part-time. *Nonresident tuition:* $10,610 full-time, $442 per semester hour part-time. *Mandatory fees:* $997 full-time, $32.35 per semester hour part-time. Part-time tuition and fees vary according to course load. *College room and board:* $7230. *College room only:* $4230. Room and board charges vary according to board plan and housing facility.

Financial Aid   Forms of aid include need-based and non-need-based scholarships, athletic grants, and part-time jobs. The average aided 2004–05 undergraduate received an aid package worth an estimated $9068. The priority application deadline for financial aid is March 15.

Freshman Admission   Oneonta requires an essay, a high school transcript, SAT or ACT scores, and TOEFL scores for international students. A minimum 3.0 high school GPA and 3 recommendations are recommended. The application deadline for regular admission is rolling and for early action it is November 1.

Transfer Admission   The application deadline for admission is rolling.

Entrance Difficulty   Oneonta assesses its entrance difficulty level as very difficult; moderately difficult for transfers. For the fall 2004 freshman class, 45 percent of the applicants were accepted.

For Further Information   Contact Ms. Karen A. Brown, Director of Admissions, State University of New York College at Oneonta, Alumni Hall 116, Oneonta, NY 13820-4015. *Telephone:* 607-436-2524 or 800-SUNY-123 (toll-free). *Fax:* 607-436-3074. *E-mail:* admissions@oneonta.edu. *Web site:* http://www.oneonta.edu/.

STATE UNIVERSITY OF NEW YORK COLLEGE AT POTSDAM

Potsdam, New York

SUNY Potsdam is a coed, public, comprehensive unit of State University of New York System, founded in 1816, offering degrees at the bachelor's and master's levels. It has a 240-acre campus in Potsdam.

Academic Information   The faculty has 327 members (72% full-time), 69% with terminal degrees. The undergraduate student-faculty ratio is 15:1. The library holds 408,755 titles, 933 serial subscriptions, and 15,570 audiovisual materials. Special programs include services for learning-disabled students, an honors program, study abroad, advanced placement credit, double majors, independent study, distance learning, self-designed majors, summer session for credit, part-time degree programs (daytime, weekends, summer), adult/continuing education programs, internships, and arrangement for off-campus study with Associated Colleges of the St. Lawrence Valley, National Student Exchange. The most frequently chosen baccalaureate fields are English, psychology, social sciences and history.

Student Body Statistics   The student body totals 4,311, of whom 3,539 are undergraduates (753 freshmen). 59 percent are women and 41 percent are men. Students come from 23 states and territories and 25 other countries. 98 percent are from New York. 3.1 percent are international students. 20.2 percent of the 2004 graduating class went on to graduate and professional schools.

Expenses for 2004–05   *Application fee:* $40. *State resident tuition:* $4350 full-time, $181 per credit hour part-time. *Nonresident tuition:* $10,610 full-time, $442 per credit hour part-time. *Mandatory fees:* $900 full-time, $41.80 per credit hour part-time. *College room and board:* $7270. *College room only:* $4220. Room and board charges vary according to board plan and housing facility.

Financial Aid   Forms of aid include need-based and non-need-based scholarships and part-time jobs. The average aided 2004–05 undergraduate received an aid package worth an estimated $11,330. The application deadline for financial aid is May 1 with a priority deadline of March 1.

Freshman Admission   SUNY Potsdam requires a high school transcript, a minimum 3.0 high school GPA, SAT and SAT Subject Test or ACT scores, and TOEFL scores for international students. An interview is recommended. An essay, recommendations, and audition for music program are required for some. The application deadline for regular admission is rolling.

Entrance Difficulty   SUNY Potsdam assesses its entrance difficulty level as moderately difficult. For the fall 2004 freshman class, 72 percent of the applicants were accepted.

For Further Information   Contact Mr. Thomas Nesbitt, Director of Admissions, State University of New York College at Potsdam, 44 Pierrepont Avenue, Potsdam, NY 13676. *Telephone:* 315-267-2180 or 877-POTSDAM (toll-free). *Fax:* 315-267-2163. *E-mail:* admissions@potsdam.edu. *Web site:* http://www.potsdam.edu/.

STATE UNIVERSITY OF NEW YORK COLLEGE AT PURCHASE

See Purchase College, State University of New York.

STATE UNIVERSITY OF NEW YORK COLLEGE OF AGRICULTURE AND TECHNOLOGY AT COBLESKILL

Cobleskill, New York

SUNY Cobleskill is a coed, public, four-year college of State University of New York System, founded in 1916, offering degrees at the associate and bachelor's levels. It has a 750-acre campus in Cobleskill.

Academic Information   The faculty has 146 members (73% full-time), 27% with terminal degrees. The student-faculty ratio is 21:1. The library holds 76,919 titles, 327 serial subscriptions, and 12,601 audiovisual materials. Special programs include academic remediation, services for learning-disabled students, an honors program, study abroad, advanced placement credit, Freshman Honors College, ESL programs, distance learning, summer session for credit, part-time degree programs (daytime, evenings, weekends, summer), adult/continuing education programs, internships, and arrangement for off-campus study with other units of the State University of New York System. The most frequently chosen baccalaureate fields are agriculture, computer/information sciences.

Student Body Statistics   The student body is made up of 2,510 undergraduates (979 freshmen). 46 percent are women and 54 percent are men. Students come from 16 states and territories and 8 other countries. 92 percent are from New York. 2.9 percent are international students.

Expenses for 2005–06   *Application fee:* $40. *State resident tuition:* $4350 full-time. *Nonresident tuition:* $10,610 full-time. *Mandatory fees:* $995 full-time. Full-time tuition and fees vary according to course level and degree level. *College room and board:* $7270. *College room only:* $4300. Room and board charges vary according to board plan and housing facility.

Financial Aid   Forms of aid include need-based scholarships and part-time jobs. The average aided 2004–05 undergraduate received an aid package worth an estimated $5640. The application deadline for financial aid is March 15.

Freshman Admission   SUNY Cobleskill requires a high school transcript and a minimum 2.0 high school GPA. SAT or ACT scores are recommended. An interview and SAT or ACT scores are required for some. The application deadline for regular admission is rolling.

Transfer Admission   The application deadline for admission is rolling.

Entrance Difficulty   SUNY Cobleskill assesses its entrance difficulty level as moderately difficult. For the fall 2004 freshman class, 92 percent of the applicants were accepted.

For Further Information   Contact Mr. Jim Murray, Director of Admissions and Marketing (Interim), State University of New York College of Agriculture and Technology at Cobleskill, Office of Admissions, Cobleskill, NY 12043. *Telephone:* 518-255-5525 or 800-295-8988 (toll-free). *Fax:* 518-255-6769. *E-mail:* admissions@cobleskill.edu. *Web site:* http://www.cobleskill.edu/.

STATE UNIVERSITY OF NEW YORK COLLEGE OF AGRICULTURE AND TECHNOLOGY AT MORRISVILLE

Morrisville, New York

SUNY Morrisville is a coed, public, primarily two-year college of State University of New York System, founded in 1908, offering degrees at the associate and bachelor's levels. It has a 185-acre campus in Morrisville near Syracuse.

Expenses for 2004–05   *Application fee:* $40. *State resident tuition:* $4350 full-time, $140 per credit part-time. *Nonresident tuition:* $7000 full-time, $292 per credit part-time. *Mandatory fees:* $1270 full-time, $15 per term part-time. Full-time tuition and fees vary according to degree level and student level. Part-time tuition and fees vary according to course load. *College room and board:* $6610. *College room only:* $3540. Room and board charges vary according to board plan and housing facility.

For Further Information   Contact Mr. Timothy Williams, Dean of Enrollment Management, State University of New York College of Agriculture and Technology at Morrisville, Box 901, Morrisville, NY 13408. *Telephone:* 315-684-6046 or 800-258-0111 (toll-free in-state). *Fax:* 315-684-6427. *E-mail:* admissions@morrisville.edu. *Web site:* http://www.morrisville.edu/.

STATE UNIVERSITY OF NEW YORK COLLEGE OF ENVIRONMENTAL SCIENCE AND FORESTRY

Syracuse, New York

ESF is a coed, public unit of State University of New York System, founded in 1911, offering degrees at the associate, bachelor's, master's, and doctoral levels. It has a 12-acre campus in Syracuse.

Academic Information   The faculty has 147 members (79% full-time), 87% with terminal degrees. The undergraduate student-faculty ratio is 8:1. The library holds 137,367 titles and 2,000 serial subscriptions. Special programs include academic remediation, services for learning-disabled students, an honors program, cooperative (work-study) education, study abroad, advanced placement credit, accelerated degree programs, Freshman Honors College, ESL programs, double majors, independent study, distance learning, part-time degree programs (daytime, evenings), adult/continuing education programs, internships, and arrangement for off-campus study with Syracuse University. The most frequently chosen baccalaureate fields are biological/life sciences, engineering/engineering technologies, natural resources/environmental science.

Student Body Statistics   The student body totals 2,046, of whom 1,537 are undergraduates (228 freshmen). 38 percent are women and 62 percent are men. Students come from 25 states and territories and 8 other countries. 89 percent are from New York. 0.9 percent are international students. 20 percent of the 2004 graduating class went on to graduate and professional schools.

Expenses for 2004–05   *Application fee:* $40. *State resident tuition:* $4350 full-time, $181 per credit hour part-time. *Nonresident tuition:* $10,610 full-time, $442 per credit hour part-time. *Mandatory fees:* $641 full-time, $16.10 per credit hour part-time, $19.10 per year part-time. Full-time tuition and fees vary according to location. Part-time tuition and fees vary according to course load and location. *College room and board:* $9790. *College room only:* $4890. Room and board charges vary according to board plan, housing facility, and location.

Financial Aid   Forms of aid include need-based and non-need-based scholarships and part-time jobs. The average aided 2004–05 undergraduate received an aid package worth an estimated $8300. The priority application deadline for financial aid is March 1.

Freshman Admission   ESF requires an essay, a high school transcript, a minimum 3.3 high school GPA, supplemental application, SAT or ACT scores, and TOEFL scores for international students. 3 recommendations and an interview are recommended. The application deadline for regular admission is rolling and for early action it is November 15.

Transfer Admission   The application deadline for admission is rolling.

Entrance Difficulty   ESF assesses its entrance difficulty level as moderately difficult. For the fall 2004 freshman class, 64 percent of the applicants were accepted.

For Further Information   Contact Ms. Susan Sanford, Director of Admissions, State University of New York College of Environmental Science and Forestry, Office of Undergraduate Admissions, 106 Bray Hall, 1 Forestry Lane, Syracuse, NY 13210-2779. *Telephone:* 315-470-6600 or 800-777-7373 (toll-free). *Fax:* 315-470-6933. *E-mail:* esfinfo@esf.edu. *Web site:* http://www.esf.edu/.

STATE UNIVERSITY OF NEW YORK COLLEGE OF TECHNOLOGY AT ALFRED

Alfred, New York

Alfred State College is a coed, public, primarily two-year college of State University of New York System, founded in 1908, offering degrees at the associate and bachelor's levels. It has a 175-acre campus in Alfred.

Academic Information   The faculty has 191 members (77% full-time), 14% with terminal degrees. The student-faculty ratio is 19:1. The library holds 71,243 titles, 594 serial subscriptions, and 8,148 audiovisual materials. Special programs include academic remediation, services for learning-disabled students, an honors program, cooperative (work-study) education, study abroad, advanced placement credit, independent study, distance learning, self-designed majors, summer session for credit, part-time degree programs (daytime, evenings, summer), external degree programs, adult/continuing education programs, internships, and arrangement for off-campus study with Alfred University.

Student Body Statistics   The student body is made up of 3,500 undergraduates. Students come from 29 states and territories. 99 percent are from New York. 83 percent of the 2004 graduating class went on to four-year colleges.

Expenses for 2005–06   *Application fee:* $40. *State resident tuition:* $4350 full-time. *Nonresident tuition:* $7210 full-time. *Mandatory fees:* $930 full-time. Full-time tuition and fees vary according to degree level. *College room and board:* $6700. *College room only:* $3770. Room and board charges vary according to board plan and housing facility.

Financial Aid   Forms of aid include need-based scholarships and part-time jobs. The priority application deadline for financial aid is February 15.

Freshman Admission   Alfred State College requires a high school transcript and TOEFL scores for international students. An essay, recommendations, an interview, and SAT or ACT scores are recommended. A minimum 2.0 high school GPA is required for some. The application deadline for regular admission is rolling.

Transfer Admission   The application deadline for admission is rolling.

Entrance Difficulty   Alfred State College assesses its entrance difficulty level as moderately difficult. For the fall 2004 freshman class, 67 percent of the applicants were accepted.

For Further Information   Contact Ms. Deborah J. Goodrich, Director of Admissions, State University of New York College of Technology at Alfred, Huntington Administration Building, 10 Upper College Drive, Alfred, NY 14802. *Telephone:* 607-587-4215 or 800-4-ALFRED (toll-free). *Fax:* 607-587-4299. *E-mail:* admissions@alfredstate.edu. *Web site:* http://www.alfredstate.edu/.

STATE UNIVERSITY OF NEW YORK COLLEGE OF TECHNOLOGY AT CANTON

Canton, New York

SUNY Canton is a coed, public, primarily two-year college of State University of New York System, founded in 1906, offering degrees at the associate and bachelor's levels. It has a 555-acre campus in Canton.

Academic Information   The faculty has 131 members (62% full-time), 14% with terminal degrees. The student-faculty ratio is 23:1. The library holds 64,912 titles, 303 serial subscriptions, and 1,569 audiovisual materials. Special programs include academic remediation, services for learning-disabled students, advanced placement credit, independent study, distance learning, self-designed majors, summer session for credit, part-time degree programs (daytime, evenings, weekends, summer), adult/continuing education programs, internships, and arrangement for off-campus study with the Associated Colleges of the St. Lawrence Valley. The most frequently chosen baccalaureate fields are health professions and related sciences, protective services/public administration.

Student Body Statistics   The student body is made up of 2,518 undergraduates (857 freshmen). 53 percent are women and 47 percent are men. Students come from 15 states and territories and 5 other countries. 97 percent are from New York. 0.5 percent are international students.

Expenses for 2005–06   *Application fee:* $40. *One-time mandatory fee:* $20. *State resident tuition:* $4350 full-time, $181 per credit hour part-time. *Nonresident tuition:* $10,610 full-time, $442 per credit hour part-time. *Mandatory fees:* $1065 full-time, $39.30 per credit hour part-time, $5. Full-time tuition and fees vary according to degree level, location, and program. Part-time tuition and fees vary according to degree level, location, and program. *College room and board:* $7350. *College room only:* $4220. Room and board charges vary according to housing facility.

Financial Aid   Forms of aid include need-based and non-need-based scholarships and part-time jobs. The priority application deadline for financial aid is March 15.

Freshman Admission   SUNY Canton requires a high school transcript and TOEFL scores for international students. A minimum 2.0 high school GPA is recommended. An interview is required for some. The application deadline for regular admission is rolling.

Transfer Admission   The application deadline for admission is rolling.

Entrance Difficulty   SUNY Canton assesses its entrance difficulty level as minimally difficult; very difficult for nursing, veterinary science, engineering science, physical therapy assistant, occupational therapy assistant, liberal arts programs. For the fall 2004 freshman class, 83 percent of the applicants were accepted.

For Further Information   Contact Ms. Jodi L. Revill, Director of Admissions, State University of New York College of Technology at Canton, 34 Cornell Drive, Canton, NY 13617. *Telephone:* 315-386-7123 or 800-388-7123 (toll-free). *Fax:* 315-386-7929. *E-mail:* admissions@canton.edu. *Web site:* http://www.canton.edu/.

STATE UNIVERSITY OF NEW YORK COLLEGE OF TECHNOLOGY AT DELHI
Delhi, New York

State University of New York College of Technology at Delhi is a coed, public, primarily two-year college of State University of New York System, founded in 1913, offering degrees at the associate and bachelor's levels. It has a 405-acre campus in Delhi.

Academic Information   The faculty has 130 members (75% full-time). The student-faculty ratio is 17:1. The library holds 47,909 titles and 384 serial subscriptions. Special programs include academic remediation, services for learning-disabled students, an honors program, advanced placement credit, ESL programs, distance learning, self-designed majors, summer session for credit, part-time degree programs (daytime, evenings, weekends, summer), adult/continuing education programs, and internships.

Student Body Statistics   The student body is made up of 2,170 undergraduates (1,065 freshmen). 43 percent are women and 57 percent are men. Students come from 7 states and territories and 3 other countries. 98 percent are from New York. 2.4 percent are international students. 81 percent of the 2004 graduating class went on to four-year colleges.

Expenses for 2004–05   *Application fee:* $30. *State resident tuition:* $4350 full-time. *Nonresident tuition:* $10,300 full-time. *Mandatory fees:* $1115 full-time. *College room and board:* $6830.

Financial Aid   Forms of aid include need-based scholarships and part-time jobs. The priority application deadline for financial aid is February 15.

Freshman Admission   State University of New York College of Technology at Delhi requires a high school transcript and TOEFL scores for international students. A minimum 2.0 high school GPA is required for some. The application deadline for regular admission is rolling.

Transfer Admission   The application deadline for admission is rolling.

Entrance Difficulty   State University of New York College of Technology at Delhi assesses its entrance difficulty level as moderately difficult. For the fall 2004 freshman class, 61 percent of the applicants were accepted.

For Further Information   Contact Mr. Larry Barrett, Dean of Enroll-ment, State University of New York College of Technology at Delhi, 2 Main Street, Delhi, NY 13753. *Telephone:* 607-746-4000 Ext. 4856 or 800-96-DELHI (toll-free). *Fax:* 607-746-4104. *E-mail:* enroll@delhi.edu. *Web site:* http://www.delhi.edu/.

STATE UNIVERSITY OF NEW YORK DOWNSTATE MEDICAL CENTER
Brooklyn, New York

State University of New York Downstate Medical Center is a coed, public, upper-level unit of State University of New York System, founded in 1858, offering degrees at the bachelor's, master's, doctoral, and first professional levels and post-master's and postbachelor's certificates.

Academic Information   The library holds 357,209 titles, 2,104 serial subscriptions, and 812 audiovisual materials. Special programs include services for learning-disabled students, advanced placement credit, accelerated degree programs, independent study, summer session for credit, part-time degree programs (daytime, evenings), adult/continuing education programs, internships, and arrangement for off-campus study. The most frequently chosen baccalaureate field is health professions and related sciences.

Student Body Statistics   The student body totals 1,569, of whom 354 are undergraduates. 84 percent are women and 16 percent are men. 98 percent are from New York. 1.4 percent are international students.

Expenses for 2004–05   *Application fee:* $30. *State resident tuition:* $4350 full-time, $181 per credit part-time. *Nonresident tuition:* $10,610 full-time, $442 per credit part-time. *Mandatory fees:* $2603 full-time. Full-time tuition and fees vary according to degree level and program. Part-time tuition varies according to degree level and program.

Financial Aid   Forms of aid include need-based scholarships and part-time jobs. The application deadline for financial aid is February 15.

Transfer Admission   State University of New York Downstate Medical Center requires a college transcript and a minimum 2.5 college GPA. The application deadline for admission is May 1.

Entrance Difficulty   State University of New York Downstate Medical Center assesses its entrance difficulty level as moderately difficult.

For Further Information   Contact Mr. Tom Sabia, Assistant Dean of Admissions, State University of New York Downstate Medical Center, 450 Clarkson Avenue, Box 60, Brooklyn, NY 11203. *Telephone:* 718-270-2446. *Fax:* 718-270-7592. *Web site:* http://www.downstate.edu/.

STATE UNIVERSITY OF NEW YORK EMPIRE STATE COLLEGE
Saratoga Springs, New York

Empire State College is a coed, public, comprehensive unit of State University of New York System, founded in 1971, offering degrees at the associate, bachelor's, and master's levels (branch locations at 7 regional centers with 35 auxiliary units).

Academic Information   The faculty has 768 members (20% full-time). The undergraduate student-faculty ratio is 11:1. The library holds 11,000 titles and 10,000 serial subscriptions. Special programs include services for learning-disabled students, cooperative (work-study) education, study abroad, advanced placement credit, independent study, distance learning, self-designed majors, part-time degree programs (daytime, evenings, weekends, summer), external degree programs, adult/continuing education programs, and arrangement for off-campus study with New York State Visiting Student Program.

Student Body Statistics   The student body totals 9,750, of whom 9,327 are undergraduates. 58 percent are women and 42 percent are men. Students come from 52 states and territories and 24 other countries. 85 percent are from New York. 6.3 percent are international students.

Expenses for 2004–05   *Application fee:* $0. *State resident tuition:* $4350 full-time, $181 per credit part-time. *Nonresident tuition:* $10,300 full-time, $429 per credit part-time. *Mandatory fees:* $205 full-time, $4.60 per credit part-time, $75 per term part-time.

Freshman Admission   Empire State College requires an essay and possession of high school diploma or its equivalent. An interview is required for some. The application deadline for regular admission is rolling.

Transfer Admission   The application deadline for admission is rolling.

Entrance Difficulty   Empire State College assesses its entrance difficulty level as minimally difficult. For the fall 2004 freshman class, 43 percent of the applicants were accepted.

For Further Information   Contact Ms. Jennifer Riley, Assistant Director of Admissions, State University of New York Empire State College, One Union Avenue, Saratoga Springs, NY 12866. *Telephone:* 518-587-2100 Ext. 214 or 800-847-3000 (toll-free out-of-state). *Fax:* 518-580-0105. *E-mail:* admissions@esc.edu. *Web site:* http://www.esc.edu/.

STATE UNIVERSITY OF NEW YORK, FREDONIA

Fredonia, New York

SUNY Fredonia is a coed, public, comprehensive unit of State University of New York System, founded in 1826, offering degrees at the bachelor's and master's levels. It has a 266-acre campus in Fredonia near Buffalo.

Academic Information   The faculty has 440 members (57% full-time), 53% with terminal degrees. The undergraduate student-faculty ratio is 18:1. The library holds 396,000 titles, 2,270 serial subscriptions, and 17,607 audiovisual materials. Special programs include services for learning-disabled students, an honors program, study abroad, advanced placement credit, accelerated degree programs, double majors, independent study, distance learning, self-designed majors, summer session for credit, part-time degree programs (daytime, evenings, summer), adult/continuing education programs, internships, and arrangement for off-campus study with Western New York Consortium. The most frequently chosen baccalaureate fields are business/marketing, education, visual/performing arts.

Student Body Statistics   The student body totals 5,359, of whom 4,954 are undergraduates (1,140 freshmen). 57 percent are women and 43 percent are men. Students come from 27 states and territories and 9 other countries. 98 percent are from New York. 1.2 percent are international students. 26 percent of the 2004 graduating class went on to graduate and professional schools.

Expenses for 2005–06   *Application fee:* $40. *State resident tuition:* $4350 full-time, $181 per credit hour part-time. *Nonresident tuition:* $10,300 full-time, $429 per credit hour part-time. *Mandatory fees:* $1041 full-time, $43 per credit hour part-time. *College room and board:* $6940. *College room only:* $4350. Room and board charges vary according to board plan and housing facility.

Financial Aid   Forms of aid include need-based and non-need-based scholarships and part-time jobs. The average aided 2004–05 undergraduate received an aid package worth an estimated $6542. The priority application deadline for financial aid is February 1.

Freshman Admission   SUNY Fredonia requires a high school transcript, a minimum 2.5 high school GPA, SAT or ACT scores, and TOEFL scores for international students. Recommendations are recommended. An essay, an interview, and audition for music and theater programs, portfolio for art and media arts program are required for some. The application deadline for regular admission is rolling and for early decision it is November 1.

Transfer Admission   The application deadline for admission is rolling.

Entrance Difficulty   SUNY Fredonia assesses its entrance difficulty level as moderately difficult; very difficult for music, education, sound recording technology, recombinant gene technology programs. For the fall 2004 freshman class, 56 percent of the applicants were accepted.

For Further Information   Contact Mr. Daniel Tramuta, Director of Admissions, State University of New York, Fredonia, Fredonia, NY 14063-1136. *Telephone:* 716-673-3251 or 800-252-1212 (toll-free). *Fax:* 716-673-3249. *E-mail:* admissions.office@fredonia.edu. *Web site:* http://www.fredonia.edu/.

STATE UNIVERSITY OF NEW YORK HEALTH SCIENCE CENTER AT BROOKLYN

See State University of New York Downstate Medical Center.

STATE UNIVERSITY OF NEW YORK INSTITUTE OF TECHNOLOGY

Utica, New York

SUNY Utica/Rome is a coed, public, comprehensive unit of State University of New York System, founded in 1966, offering degrees at the bachelor's and master's levels and post-master's certificates. It has an 850-acre campus in Utica.

Academic Information   The faculty has 178 members (55% full-time). The undergraduate student-faculty ratio is 18:1. The library holds 193,682 titles, 1,090 serial subscriptions, and 11,818 audiovisual materials. Special programs include academic remediation, services for learning-disabled students, advanced placement credit, accelerated degree programs, ESL programs, double majors, independent study, distance learning, summer session for credit, part-time degree programs (daytime, evenings, weekends, summer), adult/continuing education programs, and internships. The most frequently chosen baccalaureate fields are business/marketing, computer/information sciences, engineering/engineering technologies.

Student Body Statistics   The student body totals 2,432, of whom 1,876 are undergraduates (81 freshmen). 50 percent are women and 50 percent are men. Students come from 10 states and territories and 14 other countries. 99 percent are from New York. 1 percent are international students. 5 percent of the 2004 graduating class went on to graduate and professional schools.

Expenses for 2005–06   *Application fee:* $30. *State resident tuition:* $4350 full-time, $181 per credit hour part-time. *Nonresident tuition:* $10,610 full-time, $442 per credit hour part-time. *Mandatory fees:* $894 full-time, $53 per credit hour part-time. *College room and board:* $7160.

Financial Aid   Forms of aid include need-based and non-need-based scholarships and part-time jobs. The average aided 2003–04 undergraduate received an aid package worth $7608. The application deadline for financial aid is continuous.

Freshman Admission   SUNY Utica/Rome requires TOEFL scores for international students. The application deadline for regular admission is rolling.

Transfer Admission   The application deadline for admission is rolling.

Entrance Difficulty   SUNY Utica/Rome assesses its entrance difficulty level as minimally difficult. For the fall 2004 freshman class, 22 percent of the applicants were accepted.

For Further Information   Contact Ms. Marybeth Lyons, Director of Admissions, State University of New York Institute of Technology, PO Box 3050, Utica, NY 13504-3050. *Telephone:* 315-792-7500 or 800-SUNYTEC (toll-free). *Fax:* 315-792-7837. *E-mail:* admissions@sunyit. edu. *Web site:* http://www.sunyit.edu/.

See page 154 for a narrative description.

STATE UNIVERSITY OF NEW YORK MARITIME COLLEGE

Throggs Neck, New York

Maritime College is a coed, primarily men's, public, comprehensive unit of State University of New York System, founded in 1874, offering degrees at the associate, bachelor's, and master's levels. It has a 56-acre campus in Throggs Neck.

For Further Information   Contact Ms. Deirdre Whitman, Vice President of Enrollment and Campus Life, State University of New York Maritime College, 6 Pennyfield Avenue, Throggs Neck, NY 10465. *Telephone:* 718-409-7220, 800-654-1874 (toll-free in-state), or 800-642-1874 (toll-free out-of-state). *Fax:* 718-409-7465. *E-mail:* admissions@sunymaritime.edu. *Web site:* http://www.sunymaritime. edu/.

STATE UNIVERSITY OF NEW YORK UPSTATE MEDICAL UNIVERSITY

Syracuse, New York

State University of New York Upstate Medical University is a coed, public, upper-level unit of State University of New York System, founded in 1950, offering degrees at the bachelor's, master's, doctoral, and first professional levels and post-master's certificates. It has a 25-acre campus in Syracuse.

Academic Information The faculty has 695 members (69% full-time). The undergraduate student-faculty ratio is 10:1. The library holds 132,500 titles, 1,800 serial subscriptions, and 29,515 audiovisual materials. Special programs include services for learning-disabled students, advanced placement credit, summer session for credit, part-time degree programs (daytime, evenings, summer), internships, and arrangement for off-campus study. The most frequently chosen baccalaureate field is health professions and related sciences.

Student Body Statistics The student body totals 1,180, of whom 258 are undergraduates (138 in entering class). 73 percent are women and 27 percent are men. Students come from 7 states and territories and 9 other countries. 97 percent are from New York. 3.8 percent are international students.

Expenses for 2004–05 *Application fee:* $30. *State resident tuition:* $8700 full-time, $181 per credit hour part-time. *Nonresident tuition:* $21,220 full-time, $442 per credit hour part-time. *Mandatory fees:* $466 full-time. *College room only:* $3586.

Financial Aid Forms of aid include need-based and non-need-based scholarships and part-time jobs. The average aided 2003–04 undergraduate received an aid package worth $18,332. The application deadline for financial aid is April 1 with a priority deadline of March 1.

Transfer Admission State University of New York Upstate Medical University requires a minimum 2.0 college GPA and a college transcript. Standardized test scores are recommended. The application deadline for admission is rolling.

Entrance Difficulty State University of New York Upstate Medical University assesses its entrance difficulty level as moderately difficult; very difficult for out-of-state applicants; most difficult for physical therapy, cardiovascular perfusion programs.

For Further Information Contact Ms. Donna L. Vavonese, Associate Director of Admissions, State University of New York Upstate Medical University, Weiskotten Hall, 766 Irving Avenue, Syracuse, NY 13210. *Telephone:* 315-464-4816 or 800-736-2171 (toll-free). *Fax:* 315-464-8867. *E-mail:* stuadmis@upstate.edu. *Web site:* http://www.upstate.edu/.

STERN COLLEGE FOR WOMEN

See Yeshiva University.

STONY BROOK UNIVERSITY, STATE UNIVERSITY OF NEW YORK

Stony Brook, New York

Stony Brook is a coed, public unit of State University of New York System, founded in 1957, offering degrees at the bachelor's, master's, doctoral, and first professional levels and post-master's, first professional, and postbachelor's certificates. It has a 1,100-acre campus in Stony Brook near New York City.

Academic Information The faculty has 1,338 members (65% full-time), 95% with terminal degrees. The undergraduate student-faculty ratio is 14:1. The library holds 2 million titles, 29,091 serial subscriptions, and 37,441 audiovisual materials. Special programs include academic remediation, services for learning-disabled students, an honors program, study abroad, advanced placement credit, Freshman Honors College, ESL programs, double majors, independent study, distance learning, self-designed majors, summer session for credit, part-time degree programs

(daytime, evenings, summer), adult/continuing education programs, internships, and arrangement for off-campus study with 17 members of the Long Island Regional Advisory Council for Higher Education and The National Student Exchange. The most frequently chosen baccalaureate fields are health professions and related sciences, computer/information sciences, social sciences and history.

Student Body Statistics The student body totals 21,685, of whom 13,858 are undergraduates (2,139 freshmen). 49 percent are women and 51 percent are men. Students come from 42 states and territories and 72 other countries. 98 percent are from New York. 4.6 percent are international students. 47 percent of the 2004 graduating class went on to graduate and professional schools.

Expenses for 2004–05 *Application fee:* $40. *State resident tuition:* $4350 full-time, $181 per credit part-time. *Nonresident tuition:* $10,610 full-time, $442 per credit part-time. *Mandatory fees:* $1039 full-time, $50.20 per credit part-time. *College room and board:* $7730. Room and board charges vary according to board plan and housing facility.

Financial Aid Forms of aid include need-based and non-need-based scholarships, athletic grants, and part-time jobs. The average aided 2003–04 undergraduate received an aid package worth $8555. The priority application deadline for financial aid is March 1.

Freshman Admission Stony Brook requires an essay, a high school transcript, a minimum 3.0 high school GPA, SAT or ACT scores, and TOEFL scores for international students. 2 recommendations, an interview, and SAT Subject Test scores are recommended. Audition is required for some. The application deadline for regular admission is March 1 and for early action it is November 15.

Transfer Admission The application deadline for admission is April 15.

Entrance Difficulty Stony Brook assesses its entrance difficulty level as very difficult. For the fall 2004 freshman class, 49 percent of the applicants were accepted.

For Further Information Contact Ms. Judith Burke-Berhanan, Acting Dean of Admissions and Enrollment Services, Stony Brook University, State University of New York, Stony Brook, NY 11794. *Telephone:* 631-632-6868 or 800-872-7869 (toll-free out-of-state). *Fax:* 631-632-9898. *E-mail:* ugadmissions@notes.cc.sunysb.edu. *Web site:* http://www.sunysb.edu/.

SWEDISH INSTITUTE, COLLEGE OF HEALTH SCIENCES

New York, New York

For Information Write to Swedish Institute, College of Health Sciences, New York, NY 10001-6700.

SYRACUSE UNIVERSITY

Syracuse, New York

SU is a coed, private university, founded in 1870, offering degrees at the bachelor's, master's, doctoral, and first professional levels and post-master's certificates. It has a 200-acre campus in Syracuse.

Academic Information The faculty has 1,406 members (63% full-time). The undergraduate student-faculty ratio is 12:1. The library holds 3 million titles, 15,154 serial subscriptions, and 1 million audiovisual materials. Special programs include services for learning-disabled students, an honors program, cooperative (work-study) education, study abroad, advanced placement credit, accelerated degree programs, ESL programs, double majors, independent study, distance learning, self-designed majors, summer session for credit, part-time degree programs (daytime, evenings, weekends, summer), external degree programs, adult/continuing education programs, internships, and arrangement for off-campus study with State University of New York College of Environmental Science and Forestry. The most frequently chosen baccalaureate fields are business/marketing, social sciences and history, visual/performing arts.

Student Body Statistics The student body totals 16,753, of whom 10,750 are undergraduates (2,671 freshmen). 56 percent are women and 44 percent are men. Students come from 52 states and territories and 59 other countries. 40 percent are from New York. 2.7 percent are international students. 20 percent of the 2004 graduating class went on to graduate and professional schools.

Expenses for 2004–05   *Application fee:* $60. *Comprehensive fee:* $36,704 includes full-time tuition ($25,720), mandatory fees ($1014), and college room and board ($9970). *College room only:* $5400. Room and board charges vary according to board plan and housing facility. *Part-time tuition:* $1120 per credit hour.

Financial Aid   Forms of aid include need-based and non-need-based scholarships, athletic grants, and part-time jobs. The average aided 2004–05 undergraduate received an aid package worth an estimated $18,822. The priority application deadline for financial aid is February 1.

Freshman Admission   SU requires an essay, a high school transcript, 2 recommendations, an interview, SAT or ACT scores, and TOEFL scores for international students. Audition for drama and music programs, portfolio for art and architecture programs is required for some. The application deadline for regular admission is January 1 and for early decision it is November 15.

Transfer Admission   The application deadline for admission is January 1.

Entrance Difficulty   SU assesses its entrance difficulty level as very difficult. For the fall 2004 freshman class, 59 percent of the applicants were accepted.

For Further Information   Contact Ms. Susan E. Donovan, Dean of Admissions, Syracuse University, 201 Tolley Administration Building, Syracuse, NY 13244-1100. *Telephone:* 315-443-3611. *E-mail:* orange@syr.edu. *Web site:* http://www.syracuse.edu/.

SYRACUSE UNIVERSITY, UTICA COLLEGE

See Utica College.

TALMUDICAL INSTITUTE OF UPSTATE NEW YORK

Rochester, New York

For Information   Write to Talmudical Institute of Upstate New York, Rochester, NY 14607-3046.

TALMUDICAL SEMINARY OHOLEI TORAH

Brooklyn, New York

For Information   Write to Talmudical Seminary Oholei Torah, Brooklyn, NY 11213-3310.

TORAH TEMIMAH TALMUDICAL SEMINARY

Brooklyn, New York

For Information   Write to Torah Temimah Talmudical Seminary, Brooklyn, NY 11218-5913.

TOURO COLLEGE

New York, New York

For Information   Write to Touro College, New York, NY 10010.

TROCAIRE COLLEGE

Buffalo, New York

For Information   Write to Trocaire College, Buffalo, NY 14220-2094.

UNION COLLEGE

Schenectady, New York

Union College is a coed, private, four-year college, founded in 1795, offering degrees at the bachelor's level. It has a 100-acre campus in Schenectady.

Academic Information   The faculty has 221 members (83% full-time), 90% with terminal degrees. The student-faculty ratio is 11:1. The library holds 571,508 titles, 3,485 serial subscriptions, and 9,044 audiovisual materials. Special programs include an honors program, cooperative (work-study) education, study abroad, advanced placement credit, accelerated degree programs, double majors, independent study, self-designed majors, summer session for credit, part-time degree programs (daytime, evenings, summer), internships, and arrangement for off-campus study with Hudson-Mohawk Association of Colleges and Universities. The most frequently chosen baccalaureate fields are engineering/engineering technologies, biological/life sciences, social sciences and history.

Student Body Statistics   The student body is made up of 2,192 undergraduates (552 freshmen). 45 percent are women and 55 percent are men. Students come from 36 states and territories and 18 other countries. 1.8 percent are international students. 31 percent of the 2004 graduating class went on to graduate and professional schools.

Expenses for 2004–05   *Application fee:* $50. *Comprehensive fee:* $38,703.

Financial Aid   Forms of aid include need-based and non-need-based scholarships and part-time jobs. The average aided 2003–04 undergraduate received an aid package worth $24,227. The application deadline for financial aid is February 1.

Freshman Admission   Union College requires an essay, a high school transcript, 2 recommendations, SAT or ACT scores, TOEFL scores for international students, and or 2 SAT II Subject Tests. An interview is recommended. SAT Subject Test scores are required for some. The application deadline for regular admission is January 15; for early decision plan 1 it is November 15; and for early decision plan 2 it is January 15.

Transfer Admission   The application deadline for admission is May 1.

Entrance Difficulty   Union College assesses its entrance difficulty level as very difficult; most difficult for 8-year medical education, 6-year law and public policy programs. For the fall 2004 freshman class, 49 percent of the applicants were accepted.

For Further Information   Contact Ms. Dianne Crozier, Director of Admissions, Union College, Grant Hall, Union College, 807 Union Street, Schenectady, NY 12308. *Telephone:* 518-388-6112 or 888-843-6688 (toll-free in-state). *Fax:* 518-388-6986. *E-mail:* admissions@union.edu. *Web site:* http://www.union.edu/.

UNITED STATES MERCHANT MARINE ACADEMY

Kings Point, New York

United States Merchant Marine Academy is a coed, public, four-year college, founded in 1943, offering degrees at the bachelor's level. It has an 82-acre campus in Kings Point near New York City.

Academic Information   The faculty has 95 members (89% full-time). The student-faculty ratio is 11:1. The library holds 185,000 titles, 950 serial subscriptions, and 3,389 audiovisual materials. Special programs include an honors program and internships. The most frequently chosen baccalaureate field is engineering/engineering technologies.

Student Body Statistics   The student body is made up of 1,007 undergraduates (284 freshmen). 14 percent are women and 86 percent are men. Students come from 49 states and territories and 3 other countries. 14 percent are from New York. 2 percent of the 2004 graduating class went on to graduate and professional schools.

Expenses for 2004–05   *Application fee:* $0. Tuition, room and board, and medical and dental care are provided by the U.S. government. Each midshipman receives a monthly salary while assigned aboard ship for training. Entering freshmen are required to deposit $6250 to defray the initial cost of computer equipment and activities fees.

Freshman Admission   United States Merchant Marine Academy requires an essay, a high school transcript, 3 recommendations, SAT or

ACT scores, and TOEFL scores for international students. An interview is recommended. The application deadline for regular admission is March 1 and for early decision it is November 1.

Transfer Admission The application deadline for admission is March 1.

Entrance Difficulty United States Merchant Marine Academy assesses its entrance difficulty level as very difficult. For the fall 2004 freshman class, 16 percent of the applicants were accepted.

For Further Information Contact Capt. Robert Johnson, Director of Admissions and Financial Aid, United States Merchant Marine Academy, 300 Steamboat Road, Kings Point, NY 11024-1699. *Telephone:* 516-773-5391 or 866-546-4778 (toll-free). *Fax:* 516-773-5390. *E-mail:* admissions@usmma.edu. *Web site:* http://www.usmma.edu/.

UNITED STATES MILITARY ACADEMY

West Point, New York

SPONSOR
See Front Insert
for Details!

West Point is a coed, primarily men's, public, four-year college, founded in 1802, offering degrees at the bachelor's level. It has a 16,080-acre campus in West Point near New York City.

Academic Information The faculty has 589 members (100% full-time), 52% with terminal degrees. The student-faculty ratio is 7:1. The library holds 457,340 titles, 2,220 serial subscriptions, and 8,000 audiovisual materials. Special programs include academic remediation, advanced placement credit, double majors, summer session for credit, and arrangement for off-campus study with United States Naval Academy, United States Air Force Academy, United States Coast Guard Academy. The most frequently chosen baccalaureate fields are engineering/engineering technologies, physical sciences, social sciences and history.

Student Body Statistics The student body is made up of 4,183 undergraduates (1,156 freshmen). 15 percent are women and 85 percent are men. Students come from 53 states and territories and 25 other countries. 8 percent are from New York. 1.1 percent are international students. 2 percent of the 2004 graduating class went on to graduate and professional schools.

Expenses for 2004–05 *Application fee:* $0. Tuition, room and board, and medical and dental care are provided by the U.S. government. Each cadet receives a salary from which to pay for personal computer, uniforms, activities, books, services, and personal expenses. Entering freshmen are required to pay a $2400 deposit to defray the initial cost of uniforms, books, supplies, equipment and fees.

Freshman Admission West Point requires an essay, a high school transcript, 4 recommendations, medical examination, authorized nomination, and SAT or ACT scores. An interview is recommended. The application deadline for regular admission is February 28.

Transfer Admission The application deadline for admission is February 28.

Entrance Difficulty West Point assesses its entrance difficulty level as most difficult. For the fall 2004 freshman class, 10 percent of the applicants were accepted.

SPECIAL MESSAGE TO STUDENTS

Social Life Students come from neighboring campuses for frequent dances, and each class has a formal banquet and dance on special weekends. Internationally acclaimed symphony orchestras, ballets, Broadway musicals, plays, and rock performers appear at West Point's Eisenhower Hall. There are more than 100 extracurricular activities, clubs, and organizations, such as the Cadet Glee Club, the rugby team, team handball, crew, and women's lacrosse teams. West Point's mission is to educate, train, and inspire the Corps of Cadets so that each graduate is a commissioned leader of character committed to the values of duty, honor, and country; professional growth throughout a career as an officer in the U.S. Army; and a lifetime of selfless service to the nation. Leadership development opportunities are numerous at West Point. Cadets may be responsible for organizing a plebe (freshman) hop, teaching a first-aid class, or leading a platoon of enlisted soldiers in the active Army. These experiences build a leadership foundation

that is essential when cadets are commissioned second lieutenants upon graduation. The U.S. Military Academy is located 50 miles north of New York City in the picturesque Hudson Valley area. The short travel distance to New York City gives cadets opportunities to attend Broadway shows, museums, sporting events, and other attractions.

Academic Highlights The academic, physical development, and military training programs form the three major aspects of the West Point forty-seven-month leader-development experience. Classes are small with only 12 to 18 cadets. There are currently forty-two majors. Faculty members conduct research with academic departments through the Operations Research Cell, the Photonics Research Center, the Office of Artificial Intelligence and Analysis, and other special department agencies. Cadets may choose one of more than 150 individual academic or military development programs during the summer preceding their junior and senior years. Some cadets do research in technical laboratories in the United States, take immersion-language training in other countries, serve medical internships at Walter Reed Medical Center, or study at other civilian and military institutions. Cadets may also take positions with federal and Department of Defense agencies. Cadets also compete for Rhodes, Olmsted, Gates Cambridge, George Mitchell, Hertz, National Science Foundation, Rotary Foundation, Truman, East-West Center, and Marshall scholarships.

Interviews and Campus Visits West Point candidates are urged to visit the Academy. A candidate orientation gives students an excellent opportunity to view the Academy with a cadet escort and talk to admissions personnel. Admissions interviews are conducted by West Point field representatives who are near a candidate's home. Those interviews are important because they provide additional information for the Admissions Committee during candidate evaluation. West Point candidates are also urged to read as much as possible about West Point and consider their career goals in order to be certain the Academy and the U.S. Army provide the career avenues they desire. Talking to cadets is important in order to gain a fuller understanding of life at West Point. As the nation's oldest service academy, West Point is easily recognized from televised news clips of the Corps of Cadets on parade. West Point is a favorite attraction for more than 2 million visitors annually. The imposing Cadet Chapel, overlooking the Plain, is one of the most picturesque settings in New York's Hudson Valley. The Visitors' Center is normally the first stop for tourists, with the West Point Museum just a few steps away at Pershing Center. The West Point Museum is the oldest of the U.S. Army museums, having opened to the public in 1854. Its collections encompass the military history of the Western world. In the fall, Michie Stadium attracts capacity crowds for Army football and a day at West Point. For information about appointments and campus visits, students should call the Admissions Office at 850-938-4041, Monday through Friday, 7:45 a.m. to 4:30 p.m. The office is located at 606 Thayer Road on campus. The nearest commercial airport is Stewart International.

For Further Information Write to Director of Admissions, United States Military Academy, 646 Swift Road, West Point, NY 10996. *E-mail:* admissions@www.usma.edu. *Web site:* http://admissions.usma.edu.

UNITED TALMUDICAL SEMINARY

Brooklyn, New York

For Information Write to United Talmudical Seminary, Brooklyn, NY 11211-7900.

UNIVERSITY AT ALBANY, STATE UNIVERSITY OF NEW YORK

Albany, New York

University at Albany is a coed, public unit of State University of New York System, founded in 1844, offering degrees at the bachelor's, master's, and doctoral levels and post-master's certificates. It has a 560-acre campus in Albany.

Academic Information   The faculty has 1,121 members (53% full-time). The undergraduate student-faculty ratio is 19:1. The library holds 2 million titles, 39,240 serial subscriptions, and 10,115 audiovisual materials. Special programs include services for learning-disabled students, an honors program, study abroad, advanced placement credit, Freshman Honors College, ESL programs, double majors, independent study, self-designed majors, summer session for credit, internships, and arrangement for off-campus study with New York State Visiting Student Program, Hudson-Mohawk Association of Colleges and Universities. The most frequently chosen baccalaureate fields are business/marketing, psychology, social sciences and history.

Student Body Statistics   The student body totals 16,293, of whom 11,388 are undergraduates (2,020 freshmen). 51 percent are women and 49 percent are men. Students come from 38 states and territories and 51 other countries. 95 percent are from New York. 1.9 percent are international students. 45 percent of the 2004 graduating class went on to graduate and professional schools.

Expenses for 2004–05   *Application fee:* $40. *State resident tuition:* $4350 full-time, $181 per credit part-time. *Nonresident tuition:* $10,610 full-time, $442 per credit part-time. *Mandatory fees:* $1460 full-time. Part-time tuition varies according to course load. *College room and board:* $7540. *College room only:* $4560. Room and board charges vary according to board plan and housing facility.

Financial Aid   Forms of aid include need-based and non-need-based scholarships, athletic grants, and part-time jobs. The application deadline for financial aid is April 15.

Freshman Admission   University at Albany requires a high school transcript, SAT or ACT scores, and TOEFL scores for international students. An essay and recommendations are recommended. Portfolio, audition is required for some. The application deadline for regular admission is March 1 and for early action it is December 1.

Transfer Admission   The application deadline for admission is July 1.

Entrance Difficulty   University at Albany assesses its entrance difficulty level as moderately difficult. For the fall 2004 freshman class, 56 percent of the applicants were accepted.

For Further Information   Contact Mr. Robert Andrea, Director of Undergraduate Admissions, University at Albany, State University of New York, 1400 Washington Avenue, University Administration Building 101, Albany, NY 12222. *Telephone:* 518-442-5435 or 800-293-7869 (toll-free in-state). *E-mail:* ugadmissions@albany.edu. *Web site:* http://www.albany.edu/.

UNIVERSITY AT BUFFALO, THE STATE UNIVERSITY OF NEW YORK

See State University of New York at Buffalo.

UNIVERSITY OF ROCHESTER

Rochester, New York

University of Rochester is a coed, private university, founded in 1850, offering degrees at the bachelor's, master's, doctoral, and first professional levels and post-master's, first professional, and postbachelor's certificates. It has a 534-acre campus in Rochester.

Academic Information   The faculty has 623 members (82% full-time), 75% with terminal degrees. The undergraduate student-faculty ratio is 9:1. The library holds 3 million titles, 11,254 serial subscriptions, and 78,600 audiovisual materials. Special programs include services for learning-disabled students, an honors program, study abroad, advanced placement credit, ESL programs, double majors, independent study, self-designed majors, summer session for credit, part-time degree programs, internships, and arrangement for off-campus study with Rochester Area Colleges. The most frequently chosen baccalaureate fields are biological/life sciences, psychology, social sciences and history.

Student Body Statistics   The student body totals 8,365, of whom 4,535 are undergraduates (1,084 freshmen). 48 percent are women and 52 percent are men. Students come from 52 states and territories and 36 other countries. 3.5 percent are international students. 37 percent of the 2004 graduating class went on to graduate and professional schools.

Expenses for 2004–05   *Application fee:* $50. *Comprehensive fee:* $38,547 includes full-time tuition ($28,250), mandatory fees ($732), and college room and board ($9565). *College room only:* $5460. Room and board charges vary according to board plan. *Part-time tuition:* $494 per credit hour. Part-time tuition varies according to course load.

Financial Aid   Forms of aid include need-based and non-need-based scholarships and part-time jobs. The average aided 2003–04 undergraduate received an aid package worth $22,342. The priority application deadline for financial aid is February 1.

Freshman Admission   University of Rochester requires an essay, a high school transcript, 1 recommendation, SAT or ACT scores, and TOEFL scores for international students. 2 recommendations, an interview, and SAT Subject Test scores are recommended. Audition, portfolio is required for some. The application deadline for regular admission is January 20; for early decision plan 1 it is November 1; and for early decision plan 2 it is January 20.

Transfer Admission   The application deadline for admission is rolling.

Entrance Difficulty   University of Rochester assesses its entrance difficulty level as very difficult. For the fall 2004 freshman class, 48 percent of the applicants were accepted.

For Further Information   Contact Mr. Gregory MacDonald, Director of Admissions, University of Rochester, PO Box 270251, 300 Wilson Boulevard, Rochester, NY 14627-0251. *Telephone:* 585-275-3221 or 888-822-2256 (toll-free). *Fax:* 585-461-4595. *E-mail:* admit@admissions.rochester.edu. *Web site:* http://www.rochester.edu/.

See page 156 for a narrative description.

U.T.A. MESIVTA OF KIRYAS JOEL

Monroe, New York

For Information   Write to U.T.A. Mesivta of Kiryas Joel, Monroe, NY 10950.

UTICA COLLEGE

Utica, New York

Utica College is a coed, private, comprehensive institution, founded in 1946, offering degrees at the bachelor's, master's, and first professional levels. It has a 128-acre campus in Utica.

Academic Information   The faculty has 243 members (44% full-time), 61% with terminal degrees. The undergraduate student-faculty ratio is 15:1. The library holds 183,559 titles, 1,279 serial subscriptions, and 2,042 audiovisual materials. Special programs include academic remediation, services for learning-disabled students, an honors program, cooperative (work-study) education, study abroad, advanced placement credit, accelerated degree programs, double majors, independent study, distance learning, summer session for credit, part-time degree programs (daytime, evenings, weekends, summer), adult/continuing education programs, internships, and arrangement for off-campus study with members of the New York State Visiting Student Program. The most frequently chosen baccalaureate fields are business/marketing, health professions and related sciences, psychology.

Student Body Statistics   The student body totals 2,652, of whom 2,310 are undergraduates (487 freshmen). 57 percent are women and 43 percent are men. Students come from 37 states and territories and 15 other countries. 89 percent are from New York. 1.5 percent are international students. 29 percent of the 2004 graduating class went on to graduate and professional schools.

Expenses for 2004–05   *Application fee:* $40. *Comprehensive fee:* $29,870 includes full-time tuition ($20,980), mandatory fees ($290), and college room and board ($8600). *College room only:* $4500. Full-time tuition and fees vary according to class time and course load. Room and board charges vary according to board plan and housing facility. *Part-time tuition:* $702 per credit hour. *Part-time mandatory fees:* $45 per term. Part-time tuition and fees vary according to class time, course load, and degree level.

Financial Aid Forms of aid include need-based and non-need-based scholarships and part-time jobs. The priority application deadline for financial aid is February 15.

Freshman Admission Utica College requires an essay, a high school transcript, a minimum 2.0 high school GPA, 1 recommendation, and TOEFL scores for international students. An interview and SAT or ACT scores are recommended. A minimum 3.0 high school GPA and SAT or ACT scores are required for some. The application deadline for regular admission is rolling.

Transfer Admission The application deadline for admission is rolling.

Entrance Difficulty Utica College assesses its entrance difficulty level as moderately difficult; very difficult for PT/OT/Joint Health Professions programs. For the fall 2004 freshman class, 80 percent of the applicants were accepted.

For Further Information Contact Mr. Patrick Quinn, Vice President for Enrollment Management, Utica College, 1600 Burrstone Road, Utica, NY 13502. *Telephone:* 315-792-3006 or 800-782-8884 (toll-free). *Fax:* 315-792-3003. *E-mail:* admiss@utica.edu. *Web site:* http://www.utica.edu/.

See page 158 for a narrative description.

VASSAR COLLEGE
Poughkeepsie, New York

Vassar is a coed, private, four-year college, founded in 1861, offering degrees at the bachelor's and master's levels. It has a 1,000-acre campus in Poughkeepsie near New York City.

Academic Information The faculty has 315 members (85% full-time), 89% with terminal degrees. The undergraduate student-faculty ratio is 9:1. The library holds 878,177 titles, 5,302 serial subscriptions, and 22,345 audiovisual materials. Special programs include services for learning-disabled students, cooperative (work-study) education, study abroad, advanced placement credit, double majors, independent study, self-designed majors, part-time degree programs (daytime, evenings), internships, and arrangement for off-campus study with Howard University, Fisk University, Hampton University, Spelman College, Morehouse College, members of the Twelve College Exchange Program, Bard College. The most frequently chosen baccalaureate fields are social sciences and history, English, visual/performing arts.

Student Body Statistics The student body is made up of 2,475 undergraduates (654 freshmen). 60 percent are women and 40 percent are men. Students come from 53 states and territories and 58 other countries. 27 percent are from New York. 5.1 percent are international students. 20 percent of the 2004 graduating class went on to graduate and professional schools.

Expenses for 2004–05 *Application fee:* $60. *Comprehensive fee:* $39,030 includes full-time tuition ($30,895), mandatory fees ($455), and college room and board ($7680). *College room only:* $4080. Room and board charges vary according to board plan and housing facility. *Part-time tuition:* $3635 per course. *Part-time mandatory fees:* $225 per year. Part-time tuition and fees vary according to course load.

Financial Aid Forms of aid include need-based scholarships and part-time jobs. The average aided 2004–05 undergraduate received an aid package worth an estimated $25,296. The application deadline for financial aid is February 1.

Freshman Admission Vassar requires an essay, a high school transcript, 2 recommendations, SAT and SAT Subject Test or ACT scores, and TOEFL scores for international students. The application deadline for regular admission is January 1; for early decision plan 1 it is November 15; and for early decision plan 2 it is January 1.

Transfer Admission The application deadline for admission is April 1.

Entrance Difficulty Vassar assesses its entrance difficulty level as very difficult; most difficult for transfers. For the fall 2004 freshman class, 29 percent of the applicants were accepted.

For Further Information Contact Dr. David M. Borus, Dean of Admission and Financial Aid, Vassar College, 124 Raymond Avenue, Poughkeepsie, NY 12604. *Telephone:* 845-437-7300 or 800-827-7270 (toll-free). *Fax:* 914-437-7063. *E-mail:* admissions@vassar.edu. *Web site:* http://www.vassar.edu/.

VAUGHN COLLEGE OF AERONAUTICS AND TECHNOLOGY
Flushing, New York

Vaughn College of Aeronautics and Technology is a coed, primarily men's, private, four-year college, founded in 1932, offering degrees at the associate and bachelor's levels. It has a 6-acre campus in Flushing.

Academic Information The faculty has 60 members (87% full-time). The student-faculty ratio is 11:1. The library holds 62,000 titles, 400 serial subscriptions, and 1,849 audiovisual materials. Special programs include academic remediation, services for learning-disabled students, cooperative (work-study) education, advanced placement credit, independent study, distance learning, summer session for credit, part-time degree programs (daytime, evenings, weekends, summer), adult/continuing education programs, and internships.

Student Body Statistics The student body is made up of 1,244 undergraduates (254 freshmen). 11 percent are women and 89 percent are men. Students come from 10 states and territories and 15 other countries. 94 percent are from New York. 3.1 percent are international students. 20 percent of the 2004 graduating class went on to graduate and professional schools.

Expenses for 2005–06 *Application fee:* $40. *Tuition:* $13,400 full-time. *Mandatory fees:* $380 full-time. Full-time tuition and fees vary according to course load, degree level, and program.

Financial Aid Forms of aid include need-based and non-need-based scholarships and part-time jobs. The average aided 2003–04 undergraduate received an aid package worth $10,000. The application deadline for financial aid is continuous.

Freshman Admission Vaughn College of Aeronautics and Technology requires an essay, a high school transcript, SAT or ACT scores, and TOEFL scores for international students. An interview and SAT and SAT Subject Test or ACT scores are recommended. An interview is required for some. The application deadline for regular admission is rolling.

Transfer Admission The application deadline for admission is rolling.

Entrance Difficulty Vaughn College of Aeronautics and Technology has an open admission policy for all Associate degree programs; selective for certain Bachelor's degree programs. It assesses its entrance difficulty as moderately difficult for bachelor of science, aircraft operations programs (flight).

For Further Information Contact Thomas Bracken, Associate Director, Admissions, Vaughn College of Aeronautics and Technology, La Guardia Airport, 86-01 23rd Avenue, Flushing, NY 11369. *Telephone:* 718-429-6600 Ext. 102 or 800-776-2376 Ext. 145 (toll-free in-state). *Fax:* 718-779-2231. *E-mail:* admissions@aero.edu. *Web site:* http://www.vaughn.edu/.

VILLA MARIA COLLEGE OF BUFFALO
Buffalo, New York

Villa is a coed, private, two-year college, founded in 1960, affiliated with the Roman Catholic Church, offering degrees at the associate level. It has a 9-acre campus in Buffalo.

Academic Information The faculty has 67 members (37% full-time), 31% with terminal degrees. The student-faculty ratio is 11:1. The library holds 37,000 titles, 130 serial subscriptions, and 3,500 audiovisual materials. Special programs include academic remediation, services for learning-disabled students, cooperative (work-study) education, study abroad, advanced placement credit, double majors, independent study, summer session for credit, part-time degree programs (daytime, evenings, summer), internships, and arrangement for off-campus study with members of the Western New York Consortium.

Student Body Statistics The student body is made up of 504 undergraduates (149 freshmen). 75 percent are women and 25 percent are men. Students come from 3 states and territories and 5 other countries. 99 percent are from New York. 59 percent of the 2004 graduating class went on to four-year colleges.

Expenses for 2004–05 *Application fee:* $35. *Tuition:* $10,150 full-time, $340 per credit hour part-time. *Mandatory fees:* $400 full-time.
Financial Aid Forms of aid include need-based scholarships and part-time jobs.
Freshman Admission Villa requires an essay, a high school transcript, writing sample, and TOEFL scores for international students. The application deadline for regular admission is rolling.
Transfer Admission The application deadline for admission is rolling.
Entrance Difficulty Villa assesses its entrance difficulty level as minimally difficult; moderately difficult for computer management, health science, physical therapy assistant programs. For the fall 2004 freshman class, 80 percent of the applicants were accepted.

For Further Information Contact Mr. Kevin Donovan, Director of Admissions, Villa Maria College of Buffalo, 240 Pine Ridge Road, Buffalo, NY 14225-3999. *Telephone:* 716-896-0700 Ext. 1802. *Fax:* 716-896-0705. *E-mail:* admissions@villa.edu. *Web site:* http://www.villa.edu/.

WAGNER COLLEGE
Staten Island, New York

Wagner is a coed, private, comprehensive institution, founded in 1883, offering degrees at the bachelor's and master's levels and post-master's certificates. It has a 105-acre campus in Staten Island near New York City.

Academic Information The faculty has 209 members (43% full-time). The undergraduate student-faculty ratio is 17:1. The library holds 310,000 titles, 1,000 serial subscriptions, and 1,616 audiovisual materials. Special programs include services for learning-disabled students, an honors program, study abroad, double majors, summer session for credit, part-time degree programs (daytime, evenings, summer), internships, and arrangement for off-campus study with California Lutheran University.
Student Body Statistics The student body totals 2,259, of whom 1,929 are undergraduates (491 freshmen). 61 percent are women and 39 percent are men. Students come from 38 states and territories and 14 other countries. 49 percent are from New York. 0.2 percent are international students. 28 percent of the 2004 graduating class went on to graduate and professional schools.
Expenses for 2004–05 *Application fee:* $50. *Comprehensive fee:* $31,400 includes full-time tuition ($23,900) and college room and board ($7500). *Part-time tuition:* $800 per credit hour.
Financial Aid Forms of aid include need-based and non-need-based scholarships, athletic grants, and part-time jobs. The average aided 2003–04 undergraduate received an aid package worth $14,768. The priority application deadline for financial aid is February 15.
Freshman Admission Wagner requires an essay, a high school transcript, a minimum 2.7 high school GPA, 2 recommendations, and TOEFL scores for international students. A minimum 3.0 high school GPA and an interview are recommended. An interview is required for some. The application deadline for regular admission is February 15 and for early decision it is January 1.
Transfer Admission The application deadline for admission is May 1.
Entrance Difficulty Wagner assesses its entrance difficulty level as moderately difficult. For the fall 2004 freshman class, 67 percent of the applicants were accepted.

For Further Information Contact Mr. Angelo Araimo, Vice President for Enrollment, Wagner College, One Campus Road, Staten Island, NY 10301. *Telephone:* 718-390-3411 Ext. 3412 or 800-221-1010 (toll-free out-of-state). *Fax:* 718-390-3105. *E-mail:* admissions@wagner.edu. *Web site:* http://www.wagner.edu/.

WEBB INSTITUTE
Glen Cove, New York

Webb is a coed, private, four-year college, founded in 1889, offering degrees at the bachelor's level. It has a 26-acre campus in Glen Cove near New York City.

Academic Information The faculty has 14 members (57% full-time), 64% with terminal degrees. The student-faculty ratio is 7:1. The library holds 53,319 titles, 270 serial subscriptions, and 885 audiovisual materials. Special programs include cooperative (work-study) education, double majors, independent study, internships, and arrangement for off-campus study with Hofstra University. The most frequently chosen baccalaureate field is engineering/engineering technologies.
Student Body Statistics The student body is made up of 76 undergraduates (25 freshmen). 22 percent are women and 78 percent are men. Students come from 19 states and territories. 29 percent are from New York. 31 percent of the 2004 graduating class went on to graduate and professional schools.
Expenses for 2005–06 *Application fee:* $25. *Comprehensive fee:* $7900 includes full-time tuition ($0) and college room and board ($7900). All students are awarded full tuition scholarships.
Financial Aid Forms of aid include need-based scholarships. The average aided 2003–04 undergraduate received an aid package worth $4650. The priority application deadline for financial aid is July 1.
Freshman Admission Webb requires a high school transcript, a minimum 3.5 high school GPA, 2 recommendations, an interview, proof of U.S. citizenship or permanent residency status, SAT scores, SAT Subject Test scores, and SAT II Subject Tests in math and either physics or chemistry. The application deadline for regular admission is February 15 and for early decision it is October 15.
Transfer Admission The application deadline for admission is February 15.
Entrance Difficulty Webb assesses its entrance difficulty level as most difficult. For the fall 2004 freshman class, 32 percent of the applicants were accepted.

For Further Information Contact Mr. William G. Murray, Executive Director of Student Administrative Services, Webb Institute, Crescent Beach Road, Glen Cove, NY 11542-1398. *Telephone:* 516-671-2213. *Fax:* 516-674-9838. *E-mail:* admissions@webb-institute.edu. *Web site:* http://www.webb-institute.edu/.

WELLS COLLEGE
Aurora, New York

SPONSOR See Front Insert for Details!

Wells is a coed, primarily women's, private, four-year college, founded in 1868, offering degrees at the bachelor's level. It has a 365-acre campus in Aurora near Syracuse.

Academic Information The faculty has 65 members (72% full-time), 83% with terminal degrees. The student-faculty ratio is 8:1. The library holds 253,458 titles, 411 serial subscriptions, and 1,016 audiovisual materials. Special programs include services for learning-disabled students, study abroad, advanced placement credit, accelerated degree programs, ESL programs, double majors, independent study, self-designed majors, part-time degree programs (daytime), adult/continuing education programs, internships, and arrangement for off-campus study with members of the Association of Colleges and Universities of the State of New York, Cornell University, American University, Ithaca College. The most frequently chosen baccalaureate fields are psychology, biological/life sciences, social sciences and history.
Student Body Statistics The student body is made up of 390 undergraduates (87 freshmen). 100 percent are women and 100 percent are men. Students come from 31 states and territories and 5 other countries. 70 percent are from New York. 2.4 percent are international students. 17 percent of the 2004 graduating class went on to graduate and professional schools.
Expenses for 2004–05 *Application fee:* $40. *Comprehensive fee:* $21,900 includes full-time tuition ($14,000), mandatory fees ($900), and college room and board ($7000). *College room only:* $3500. *Part-time tuition:* $585 per credit hour. *Part-time mandatory fees:* $100 per credit hour.
Financial Aid Forms of aid include need-based and non-need-based scholarships and part-time jobs. The average aided 2004–05 undergraduate received an aid package worth an estimated $17,045. The priority application deadline for financial aid is February 15.

Freshman Admission Wells requires an essay, a high school transcript, 2 recommendations, SAT or ACT scores, and TOEFL scores for international students. An interview is recommended. The application deadline for regular admission is March 1; for early decision it is December 15; and for early action it is December 15.

Transfer Admission The application deadline for admission is rolling.

Entrance Difficulty Wells assesses its entrance difficulty level as moderately difficult. For the fall 2004 freshman class, 77 percent of the applicants were accepted.

SPECIAL MESSAGE TO STUDENTS

Social Life The Wells experience involves being a part of a learning community in and outside of the classroom. At any given time, the weekly activities calendar lists athletic events, art exhibits, concerts, plays, films, lectures by visiting scholars, poetry readings, and club meetings. Wells has a diverse array of student clubs and organizations; even first-year students can obtain an important position in student government, serve as an editor on a student publication, or have a top role in a theater or dance event. For those whose passion is athletics, Wells offers women's cross-country, field hockey, lacrosse, soccer, softball, swimming, and tennis as well as men's cross-country and men's soccer and swimming at the club level.

Academic Highlights Learning at Wells takes place in small, seminar-style classes that encourage spirited discussions. Students work closely with their professors and are afforded the opportunity to work side by side with them on original research projects. Wells helps students connect what is learned in the classroom to the world by offering an extensive experiential learning program and a diverse off-campus study program. Students can study marine life in Florida, art history at the Louvre, or literature at Oxford University. Wells also offers cross-enrollment with both Cornell University and Ithaca College. The academic program allows students substantial freedom to create individually unique educational experiences. Wells is committed to providing educational access to all talented students and, therefore, offers a wide variety of scholarships, grants, and loans, which help make a high-quality college education affordable.

Interviews and Campus Visits Wells is located in the beautiful village of Aurora on the eastern shore of Cayuga Lake in New York's scenic Finger Lakes region. The Wells College campus has been ranked one of the most beautiful in the country and welcomes visitors. The Admissions Office is open Monday through Friday, 8:30 a.m. to 4:30 p.m. for interviews and campus tours, and the College is happy to include class visits and meetings with faculty members, athletic coaches, and financial aid officers. To make arrangements, students should call the Admissions Office at 800-952-9355. The nearest commercial airport is Ithaca.

For Further Information Write to the Admissions Office, Wells College, 170 Main Street, Aurora, NY 13026. *Web site:* admissions@wells.edu.

See page 160 for a narrative description.

WILLIAM SMITH COLLEGE
See Hobart and William Smith Colleges.

YESHIVA AND KOLEL BAIS MEDRASH ELYON
Monsey, New York

For Information Write to Yeshiva and Kolel Bais Medrash Elyon, Monsey, NY 10952.

YESHIVA AND KOLLEL HARBOTZAS TORAH
Brooklyn, New York

For Information Write to Yeshiva and Kollel Harbotzas Torah, Brooklyn, NY 11230.

YESHIVA COLLEGE
See Yeshiva University.

YESHIVA DERECH CHAIM
Brooklyn, New York

For Information Write to Yeshiva Derech Chaim, Brooklyn, NY 11218.

YESHIVA D'MONSEY RABBINICAL COLLEGE
Monsey, New York

For Information Write to Yeshiva D'Monsey Rabbinical College, Monsey, NY 10952.

YESHIVA GEDOLAH IMREI YOSEF D'SPINKA
Brooklyn, New York

For Information Write to Yeshiva Gedolah Imrei Yosef D'Spinka, Brooklyn, NY 11219.

YESHIVA KARLIN STOLIN RABBINICAL INSTITUTE
Brooklyn, New York

For Information Write to Yeshiva Karlin Stolin Rabbinical Institute, Brooklyn, NY 11204.

YESHIVA OF NITRA RABBINICAL COLLEGE
Mount Kisco, New York

For Information Write to Yeshiva of Nitra Rabbinical College, Mount Kisco, NY 10549.

YESHIVA OF THE TELSHE ALUMNI
Riverdale, New York

For Information Write to Yeshiva of the Telshe Alumni, Riverdale, NY 10471.

YESHIVA SHAAREI TORAH OF ROCKLAND

Suffern, New York

For Information Write to Yeshiva Shaarei Torah of Rockland, Suffern, NY 10901.

YESHIVA SHAAR HATORAH TALMUDIC RESEARCH INSTITUTE

Kew Gardens, New York

For Information Write to Yeshiva Shaar Hatorah Talmudic Research Institute, Kew Gardens, NY 11418-1469.

YESHIVAS NOVOMINSK

Brooklyn, New York

For Information Write to Yeshivas Novominsk, Brooklyn, NY 11219.

YESHIVATH VIZNITZ

Monsey, New York

For Information Write to Yeshivath Viznitz, Monsey, NY 10952.

YESHIVATH ZICHRON MOSHE

South Fallsburg, New York

For Information Write to Yeshivath Zichron Moshe, South Fallsburg, NY 12779.

YESHIVAT MIKDASH MELECH

Brooklyn, New York

For Information Write to Yeshivat Mikdash Melech, Brooklyn, NY 11230-5601.

YESHIVA UNIVERSITY

New York, New York

YU is a coed, private university, founded in 1886, offering degrees at the bachelor's, master's, doctoral, and first professional levels (Yeshiva College and Stern College for Women are coordinate undergraduate colleges of arts and sciences for men and women, respectively. Sy Syms School of Business offers programs at both campuses).

Academic Information The faculty has 235 full-time members. The library holds 995,312 titles and 9,760 serial subscriptions. Special programs include an honors program, study abroad, advanced placement credit, ESL programs, double majors, self-designed majors, summer session for credit, internships, and arrangement for off-campus study with Fashion Institute of Technology (Stern College students only).
Student Body Statistics The student body totals 5,998, of whom 2,819 are undergraduates (755 freshmen). 44 percent are women and 56 percent are men. Students come from 31 states and territories and 30 other countries.

Expenses for 2004–05 *Application fee:* $40. *Comprehensive fee:* $30,980 includes full-time tuition ($23,200), mandatory fees ($450), and college room and board ($7330). *College room only:* $5275.
Financial Aid Forms of aid include need-based and non-need-based scholarships and part-time jobs. The application deadline for financial aid is continuous.
Freshman Admission YU requires an essay, a high school transcript, 2 recommendations, an interview, and SAT or ACT scores. SAT Subject Test scores are recommended. The application deadline for regular admission is February 15.
Transfer Admission The application deadline for admission is February 15.
Entrance Difficulty YU assesses its entrance difficulty level as moderately difficult. For the fall 2004 freshman class, 78 percent of the applicants were accepted.

For Further Information Contact Mr. Michael Kranzler, Director of Undergraduate Admissions, Yeshiva University, 500 West 185th Street, New York, NY 10033-3201. *Telephone:* 212-960-5277. *Fax:* 212-960-0086. *E-mail:* yuadmit@ymail.yu.edu. *Web site:* http://www.yu.edu/.

YORK COLLEGE OF THE CITY UNIVERSITY OF NEW YORK

Jamaica, New York

York is a coed, public, four-year college of City University of New York System, founded in 1967, offering degrees at the bachelor's level. It has a 50-acre campus in Jamaica near New York City.

Academic Information The faculty has 400 members (40% full-time), 54% with terminal degrees. The student-faculty ratio is 15:1. The library holds 179,022 titles and 1,962 serial subscriptions. Special programs include services for learning-disabled students, an honors program, cooperative (work-study) education, advanced placement credit, ESL programs, double majors, independent study, summer session for credit, part-time degree programs (daytime, evenings, weekends, summer), adult/continuing education programs, internships, and arrangement for off-campus study with other units of the City University of New York System.
Student Body Statistics The student body is made up of 5,743 undergraduates (764 freshmen). 69 percent are women and 31 percent are men. Students come from 4 states and territories and 100 other countries. 7.2 percent are international students.
Expenses for 2004–05 *Application fee:* $60. *State resident tuition:* $4000 full-time, $170 per credit part-time. *Nonresident tuition:* $8640 full-time, $360 per credit part-time. *Mandatory fees:* $242 full-time, $63. Part-time tuition and fees vary according to program.
Financial Aid Forms of aid include need-based scholarships and part-time jobs. The application deadline for financial aid is continuous.
Freshman Admission York requires a high school transcript, a minimum 2.0 high school GPA, SAT or ACT scores, and TOEFL scores for international students. A minimum 3.0 high school GPA is recommended. A minimum 2.5 high school GPA is required for some. The application deadline for regular admission is rolling.
Transfer Admission The application deadline for admission is rolling.
Entrance Difficulty York assesses its entrance difficulty level as moderately difficult; minimally difficult for for transfers from another school in the City University of New York System. For the fall 2004 freshman class, 32 percent of the applicants were accepted.

For Further Information Contact Mr. Richard Stuckhardt, Director of Admissions, York College of the City University of New York, 94-20 Guy R. Brewer Boulevard, Jamaica, NY 11451. *Telephone:* 718-262-2165. *Fax:* 718-262-2601. *Web site:* http://www.york.cuny.edu/.

In-Depth Descriptions of Colleges in New York

BERNARD M. BARUCH COLLEGE
OF THE CITY UNIVERSITY OF NEW YORK
NEW YORK, NEW YORK

The College

Baruch College, one of the best academic resources in the New York City area, has earned a reputation for excellence that extends to all parts of the world, attracting students from New York State, neighboring states, and abroad. A senior institution of the City University of New York (CUNY), Baruch offers students a broad array of majors through its three schools: the Zicklin School of Business, the Weissman School of Arts and Sciences, and the School of Public Affairs.

Baruch is accredited by the Middle States Association of Colleges and Schools. All baccalaureate and master's programs in business offered by the Zicklin School of Business are accredited by AACSB International–The Association to Advance Collegiate Schools of Business. In addition to the business accreditation, both the undergraduate and graduate accountancy curriculums have been awarded the accounting accreditation from AACSB International.

The student body is remarkably diverse, reflecting the extraordinary ethnic spectrum of the city. Baruch currently enrolls more than 15,000 students, including 2,500 graduate students. There are more than 100 student clubs and organizations representing a wide range of interests: academic, artistic, cultural, ethnic, professional, and athletic. Intercollegiate sports include, among others, basketball, tennis, and volleyball. The Sidney Mishkin Gallery mounts notable exhibitions of photographs, drawings, prints, and paintings. Several music and theater groups are in residence at the College, including the Alexander String Quartet and the Orpheus Chamber Orchestra. Plays, concerts, dance performances, readings, other events are scheduled throughout the year at the Baruch Performing Arts Center, which draws upon the vast cultural offerings of New York City.

In addition to its extensive array of undergraduate majors, Baruch offers graduate programs leading to the M.B.A., M.P.A., M.S., M.S.Ed., M.S.I.L.R., and Ph.D. An M.B.A. in health care administration is offered jointly with the Mount Sinai School of Medicine; a J.D./M.B.A. is offered jointly with Brooklyn Law School.

U.S. News & World Report ranks Baruch's undergraduate business programs among the top fifty in the nation and fourth in New York State. *U.S. News & World Report* also ranks Baruch the fifth-best public college in New York State, and it named the College's part-time M.B.A. program fourteenth best in the nation.

Location

Situated near the Flatiron District of Manhattan, Baruch is in the heart of one of the world's most dynamic financial and cultural centers, within easy reach of Wall Street, Midtown, and the global headquarters of major companies, firms, and organizations. This prime location offers Baruch students unparalleled access to top career and internship opportunities. The College is convenient to public transportation from other boroughs, surrounding counties, and New Jersey and Connecticut.

Majors and Degrees

The Zicklin School of Business, the largest collegiate business school in the country, awards the Bachelor of Business Administration (B.B.A.) degree with majors in accountancy, computer information systems, economics, finance and investments, industrial/organizational psychology, management, marketing, operations research, and statistics. In addition, a five-year, combined bachelor's and master's program in accounting is offered.

The Weissman School of Arts and Sciences awards the Bachelor of Arts (B.A.) degree in thirteen major fields: actuarial science, business communication, economics, English, history, mathematics, music, philosophy, political science, psychology, sociology, Spanish, and statistics. It also offers interdisciplinary specializations in arts administration, business journalism, and management of musical enterprises. Students can work with faculty advisers to design other specialized programs that combine two or more areas of interest.

The School of Public Affairs offers programs in both public affairs and real estate/metropolitan development, leading to a Bachelor of Science (B.S.) degree.

Academic Programs

Baruch College requires that all students take general liberal arts courses as the necessary preparation and framework within which specialized knowledge can be most effectively used.

Baruch's degree programs in business require 124 credits. Candidates for the B.B.A. are required to take at least half of their credits in the liberal arts and sciences. The business base is made up of 29 required credits, and students must take a minimum of 24 credits in the major field. The degree programs in the arts and sciences and public affairs require 120 credits. Candidates for the B.A. degree are expected to complete the base curriculum (at least 54 credits) in their freshman and sophomore years, select a major field of study by their junior year, and complete at least 90 credits in the arts and sciences. All students must maintain an overall C average or better and a C average or better in their major. Students can design a minor by using their free electives to take 12 credits in a specific discipline or 12 credits of intermediate and advanced courses outside their area of specialization. At least 60 percent of the credits in the major must be taken at Baruch.

College credits may be obtained through the University of the State of New York's Regents College Examinations and the College-Level Examination Program. Business students may obtain up to 6 credits for current business experience related to their major during their senior year.

Entering freshmen may receive a maximum of 16 credits for Advanced Placement (AP) examinations on which appropriate grades have been earned and for work completed in recognized prefreshman programs.

Baruch College participates in the Honors College–University Scholars Program. This is a select group of high-achieving students. These students have available to them the combined resources of the country's largest urban university and the world's most exciting city. Special funding provides a package that includes full-tuition coverage and stipends. A Cultural Passport provides an entrée to the riches of the city, including concerts, theater, museums, and other cultural institutions. University Scholars participate in challenging honors programs through the Honors College Seminar, where they take part in a wide range of activities and common projects with honors college students from other CUNY campuses.

Off-Campus Programs

Students may study abroad for credit for a semester or a year through exchange programs with the University of Paris, Ecole Supérieure de Commerce of Rouen (France), Middlesex University (England), Tel Aviv University (Israel), Mannheim University (Germany), and Universidad Iberoamericana (Mexico).

Academic Facilities

Baruch's Information and Technology Building houses the William and Anita Newman Library, one of the most technologically advanced facilities in New York. The 1,450-seat library provides access to extensive print and electronic information resources, including several hundred online databases, many of which are available to students via remote access from off-campus locations. A Web-based reference service, in which librarians answer questions via a "text chat," is available 24 hours a day, seven days a week. In 2003, the library won the prestigious Excellence in Academic Libraries Award for best college library from the Association of College and Research Libraries. Students and faculty members also have access to the 4.5 million volumes in the CUNY library system.

Also housed in the Information and Technology Building is the Baruch Computing and Technology Center, which provides computer access to 250 students at a time. It is the largest student computing center in New York City.

Baruch's award-winning Computer Center for Visually Impaired People provides access to specialized computer equipment and to data in such forms as Braille, large print, and synthetic speech. Staff members are available to translate class material to Braille. In addition, the center has a Kurzweil Reading Machine.

Baruch's College's seventeen-floor, 800,000-square-foot William and Anita Newman Vertical Campus houses both the Weissman School of Arts and Sciences and the Zicklin School of Business as well as and Student Life and Career Services. Classes are held in state-of-the-art classrooms, computer labs, and research facilities, and students enjoy a three-level sports and recreation center and a state-of-the-art performing arts center.

Costs

For a New York State resident, the current undergraduate tuition for full-time attendance (a minimum of 12 credits or the equivalent) is $2000 per semester; for part-time study, tuition is $170 per credit. For nonresidents, tuition is $360 per credit. In addition, full-time day students pay a $75 activity fee; part-time day students pay a $45.85 activity fee. More information about tuition and fees is available on the Baruch Web site. Tuition and fees are subject to change without notice.

Financial Aid

Financial aid is available for eligible students through various state and federal programs, which include the New York State Tuition Assistance Program (TAP), Federal Pell Grant, Federal Supplemental Educational Opportunity Grant (FSEOG), Federal Perkins Loan, and Federal Work-Study Program. To apply for aid, students must complete the Free Application for Federal Student Aid (FAFSA). Applications are processed as long as funds are available.

Baruch rewards academic excellence with generous scholarships to entering freshmen each year. The Presidential Scholarship, the Isabelle and William Brumman Scholarship, the Joseph Crown Scholarship, the Paul Odess Scholarship award, the Abraham Rosenberg Scholarship, and the Henry and Lucy Moses are the most selective and offer full tuition, fees, and most related expenses for four years. The Baruch Incentive Grant offers awards ranging from $500 to $1000 per year for four years.

Faculty

Baruch faculty members are among the most distinguished and most widely known in their fields. They combine outstanding academic credentials with significant real-world experience. Approximately 500 teach full time, with about 95 percent holding a Ph.D. or other terminal degree. Full-time faculty members teach both entry-level and advanced courses and serve as advisers to student organizations and preprofessional programs.

The Zicklin School of Business recently embarked on the most ambitious hiring program at any business school in the United States, bringing 40 new, highly credentialed faculty members to Baruch over a three-year period.

Student Government

The two student government organizations, which represent the undergraduate and graduate students, oversee the granting of club charters and the allocation of student activity fees and participate in campus educational and community affairs.

Admission Requirements

Freshman applicants are screened initially to select those with a minimum of 3 units of both high school English and math and a minimum of two lab sciences. Students who meet these criteria are admitted based on their overall high school performance and their performance on these index subjects. Alternately, the College admits students with a minimum combined SAT score of 1725. Students with a GED score of at least 300 are considered, provided that they have satisfactorily completed the required high school units of English and math. Freshmen are required to submit SAT scores.

The best preparation for success at Baruch College is a full program of college-preparatory courses in high school completed with high grades. The College strongly recommends a minimum of 4 years of English, 4 years of social studies, 3 years of mathematics, 2 years of a foreign language, 2 years of lab sciences, and 1 year of performing or visual arts. Mathematics courses are especially important for Baruch's degree programs, and elementary algebra and geometry should be completed prior to enrollment. For students interested in majoring in business, mathematics, or science, 4 units of mathematics, including trigonometry and precalculus, are recommended.

Students who have attended a college or postsecondary institution must meet admission requirements based on the number of credits they have completed. Prospective transfer students must have a minimum GPA of 2.75 to be considered for admission to the Zicklin School of Business and a minimum of 2.5 for all other schools.

Application and Information

All freshman applications that are received complete with all official documentation and fees on or before October 15 for spring admission or December 15 for fall admission are processed first. Complete transfer applications received on or before October 15 for February admission or March 1 for September admission are processed first. Any freshman or transfer applications received after the dates indicated above are processed on a space-available basis.

Requests to schedule an appointment with an admissions counselor, to join a campus tour, or for application materials and additional information should be made to:

Office of Undergraduate Admissions
Baruch College of the City University of New York
One Bernard Baruch Way, Box H-0720
New York, New York 10010-5585

Telephone: 646-312-1400
Fax: 646-312-1363
E-mail: admissions@baruch.cuny.edu
World Wide Web: http://www.baruch.cuny.edu

BRIARCLIFFE COLLEGE
BETHPAGE, NEW YORK

The College

Briarcliffe College was established in 1966 to serve the educational needs of Long Island residents. A suburb of New York City, Long Island experienced a rapid growth in population that resulted in a potential labor force that attracted many top corporations. The College has grown from an original enrollment of 18 women to the current coeducational enrollment of more than 3,100 students per year. Day, evening, weekend, and summer classes are offered.

A wide range of student activities is coordinated through the College's division of student affairs. Briarcliffe students have many opportunities to participate in college life through academic, social, service, and athletic programs. Typical events include theater trips, guest speakers, community service and charitable activities, concerts, and dances. Special-interest clubs for law, broadcasting, computers, and other academic areas are active on campus. The athletic department sponsors intercollegiate sports, including men's baseball and ice hockey, women's soccer and softball, and men's and women's basketball, bowling, cross-country, golf, and lacrosse. Scholarships are awarded for men's baseball and ice hockey, women's soccer and softball, and men's and women's basketball, bowling, cross-country, golf, and lacrosse.

A high-technology, small-business incubator is located on the main campus. The incubator provides up to twenty young companies with a supportive environment in which to grow. The companies are able to share resources, access the research and intellectual strengths of Briarcliffe College, and provide internship experiences for students.

Location

Briarcliffe College is located on Long Island, New York, with campuses located in Bethpage and Patchogue. Both campuses reflect the natural beauty of Long Island, including its world-renowned shoreline, yet are close enough to Manhattan to facilitate participation in the rich cultural experience that is New York City. Many students commute by car to Briarcliffe College. Housing is provided for out-of-state or international students. In addition, both the Bethpage and Patchogue campuses are only a short drive away from the major airports in the region. John F. Kennedy International, LaGuardia, and Long Island's Islip-MacArthur airport are all easily accessible from either campus.

Majors and Degrees

Briarcliffe College confers the Bachelor of Business Administration (B.B.A.), Bachelor of Fine Arts (B.F.A.) in graphic design, Bachelor of Technology (B.Tech.), Associate in Applied Science (A.A.S.), and Associate in Occupational Studies (A.O.S.) degrees. In addition, the College offers diploma programs in accounting, computer programming, computer service technology, and word processing secretarial.

Program majors are offered in accounting, business administration, computer applications specialist studies, computer information systems, criminal justice, digital photography, graphic design, networking and computer technology, and office technologies.

The Bachelor of Business Administration degree offers concentrations in information technology, management, and marketing.

Academic Programs

The multilevel structure of the academic programs enables students to enroll immediately in four-year programs or to earn a credential by completing short-term diploma or associate degree programs. Briarcliffe College provides a rich, career-oriented curriculum that prepares students to initiate or advance in their careers.

A minimum of 120 credits is required to earn a bachelor's degree, and 60 credits are required for an associate degree. Diploma programs may be completed in two semesters of full-time study by successfully finishing prescribed course work.

In addition to courses directly related to the major field of study, there is a general education requirement for each degree program. A minimum of 42 general education credits is required for the B.B.A. degree, and a minimum of 21 credits in general education are required for the A.A.S. degree.

The College operates on a traditional two-semester calendar for day classes and innovative evening and weekend schedules that enable students to begin classes at four points during the year to earn semester-hour credits.

Academic Facilities

The main campus building was purchased by the College in 1996. The size of the building makes it possible for Briarcliffe College to house lecture halls, computer labs, an electronics lab, conference rooms, faculty offices, counseling offices, and the College library all under one roof. The main campus is wired with fiber-optic cables and connected to the Internet through cable modems and T-1 lines.

In July 2004, the College's branch campus, which is located in Patchogue, New York, moved to a modern 65,000-square-foot facility. Like the College's main campus at Bethpage, New York, the Patchogue campus contains lecture halls, computer labs, conference rooms, faculty offices, student services offices, and a campus library. In addition, the campus is served with a T-1 line that connects the Patchogue facility to the main college computer network. Computers throughout the College are connected using sophisticated network technology. Briarcliffe College has computer labs that operate on DOS/Windows, Macintosh, and UNIX platforms.

The Briarcliffe College Library supports academic programs with electronic and traditional bibliographic resources. The library is a member of the Long Island Library Resource Council and serves as a New York State Electronic Gateway, enabling students and faculty members to access information and materials from libraries throughout the world. Software used throughout the curriculum is installed in computers available for student use in the library.

Specialized programs in networking technology and telecommunications are supported by an electronics laboratory. Student members of the Briarcliffe Amateur Radio Club (BARC) operate a short-wave radio station.

An art studio provides a setting for students to draw still-life and live models. Design software that students are likely to encounter when they enter the workforce is installed on Mac and PC platforms for use by graphic design and architectural design students.

Costs

The tuition for full-time students during the 2004–05 academic year was $6804 per semester. Full-time tuition charges apply to students enrolled in 12 to 18 credits. Tuition for part-time students was $567 per credit.

Financial Aid

Briarcliffe College offers a wide variety of financial aid programs, including scholarships, grants, loans, and work-study. Need-based and achievement-based awards are available. All applicants for financial aid are expected to complete the Briarcliffe College Financial Aid Application and the Free Application for Federal Student Aid (FAFSA). New York State residents receive an Express Tuition Assistance Program Application (ETA), which must also be completed.

Briarcliffe College directly funds several scholarship programs. In order for students to apply for these scholarships, an application must be completed. Alumni Scholarships may award as much as $12,000 for a bachelor's degree program.

Faculty

The primary responsibility of all faculty members at Briarcliffe College is to provide effective learning experiences for their students. There are 40 full-time and 162 part-time faculty members. Faculty members set aside weekly office hours to meet with students and to provide academic advisement and program guidance.

Student Government

The Student Government Association (SGA), through its elected officers, is the official voice of the student body in campus governance. All matriculated students are voting members of the SGA. The SGA sponsors social, cultural, and athletic activities both on and off campus. The College views extracurricular activities as an important component of each student's education and relies heavily on the SGA to identify and support programs that inspire active participation by a broad cross-section of the College community.

Admission Requirements

Briarcliffe College has established admissions criteria that recognize the diversity of the college-bound population. Regular admission as a matriculating student (one who is taking courses with the intention of earning a degree) requires a high school diploma or the equivalent.

Each applicant to the College is encouraged to meet with one of Briarcliffe's admissions counselors. Previous academic records, scores on standardized testing, and recommendations submitted by the applicant are considered by the Admissions Office in making a determination of acceptance.

Transfer students are welcome at Briarcliffe College. Course work in which the student has earned at least a C grade at an accredited college is considered for transfer. International students should contact the Admissions Office or check the College Web site (listed below) for information on admission and obtaining an I-20A/B form.

Application and Information

Students who are applying for fall semester admission are encouraged to submit their applications before January 1. The College has a rolling admissions policy that permits admissions decisions to be made as applications and supporting documentation are reviewed. Applications for the spring and summer terms should be submitted at least sixty days before classes are scheduled to begin. Late applications are considered on a space-available basis.

Additional information and application materials are available by contacting Briarcliffe College at the following addresses:

Bethpage Campus:

Theresa Donohue, Vice President of Marketing and Admissions
Richard Kleinman, Director of Adult Admissions
Jeff Sacks, Director of National Admissions
Lancene Union, Director of High School Admissions
Briarcliffe College
1055 Stewart Avenue
Bethpage, New York 11714
Telephone: 888-333-1150 (toll-free)
Fax: 516-470-6020
E-mail: info@bcl.edu

Patchogue Campus:

Kathy McDermott, Director of Adult Admissions
Maria Quigley, Director of High School Admissions
Janet Schneider, Director of National Admissions
Briarcliffe College
225 West Main Street
Patchogue, New York 11772
Telephone: 866-235-5207 (toll-free)
Fax: 631-654-5082
E-mail: info@bcl.edu
World Wide Web: http://www.briarcliffe.edu

The picnic area near the main campus building is a popular spot to get together with friends.

CANISIUS COLLEGE
BUFFALO, NEW YORK

The College

Canisius College offers the best in high-quality academic programs and facilities as well as an outstanding faculty members who are leaders in their fields. With more than seventy distinct majors, minors, and special programs and an exciting urban location to support internships and out-of-class experiences, Canisius College prepares students for success. More than 92 percent of recent Canisius graduates are employed in their fields or attending graduate or professional schools. Canisius is a place where leaders are made.

Canisius College offers a state-of-the-art campus with enhanced technology in academic and living facilities. Canisius housing is like a home away from home, not just a temporary living accommodation. Bosch and Frisch Residence Halls, renovated in 1997, and Eastwood Hall, set to open in fall 2005, are the primary residences for first-year students at Canisius. Apartment-style living is available to sophomores, juniors, and seniors in one of the newly built Delevan Townhouses or the College's other town house complexes and apartment buildings. Specialty house options include George Martin Honors Hall, available to students in the All-College Honors Program, and the Intercultural Living Center, a learning community residence for international and U.S. students. Each student gets high-speed Internet access and cable television service in all on-campus housing.

Students have opportunities to develop leadership skills through involvement in student clubs and organizations, research, and service learning. There is something for everyone at Canisius. There are more than 100 student organizations and a wide range of athletic teams from which to choose. The students are not only leaders in the classroom but also on the NCAA Division I athletic field. Most of the sixteen Golden Griffin teams compete in the Metro Atlantic Athletic Conference (MAAC), in which a majority of the champions receive an entry into their respective NCAA tournaments. Since joining the MAAC in 1989, men's basketball, baseball, women's cross-country, men's soccer, and softball have claimed conference titles.

Location

Canisius College's urban setting is a significant advantage for students who are seeking internship, research, and service learning opportunities because of the proximity to a wide range of businesses and organizations.

Canisius is located on 36 acres in a residential neighborhood in north central Buffalo. Buffalo is a great college town that has it all: professional sports teams, a world-renowned art gallery, historic architecture, and scenic parks and waterways all within minutes from campus.

The internationally known Albright-Knox Art Gallery holds one of the world's finest collections of nineteenth- and twentieth-century American and European works of art. Buffalo is also home to the Buffalo Philharmonic Orchestra and the Studio Arena Theatre, which provides a wide variety of theater experiences.

The Metro Rail rapid transit system connects the College with some of Buffalo's most exciting venues, including HSBC Arena, home of the National Hockey League's Buffalo Sabres. The arena also hosts college basketball with Canisius' Golden Griffins as well as major popular and rock music concerts. During the summer, students can catch Buffalo Bisons Triple-A baseball games at Dunn Tire Park. At Ralph Wilson Stadium, in Orchard Park, the Buffalo Bills are a focal point throughout the football season.

The Buffalo Zoo and Delaware Park, a 350-acre park with a lake and a golf course, are located less than a mile from the campus.

Majors and Degrees

The College of Arts and Sciences is the largest and most diverse of Canisius' three academic divisions, with majors in the natural and social sciences, humanities, and preprofessional studies. It also houses the core curriculum, which strengthens fundamental critical thinking, oral, and written communication skills and helps enhance students' understanding of other cultures. The College of Arts and Sciences offers programs leading to the Bachelor of Arts (B.A.) degree in anthropology, art history, biochemistry, communication studies, computer science, criminal justice, digital media arts, economics, English, European studies, history, international relations, mathematics and statistics, modern languages (French, German, and Spanish), music, philosophy, political science, psychology, religious studies and theology, sociology, and urban studies. The Bachelor of Science (B.S.) degree is awarded in bioinformatics, biology, chemistry, clinical laboratory science, computer science, environmental science, and physics.

The Richard J. Wehle School of Business offers a well-rounded business curriculum to complement the liberal arts courses in the major, which gives the student an understanding of the broad and interrelated nature of business issues. There are programs leading to the B.S. degree in accounting, accounting information systems, business economics, entrepreneurship, finance, information systems, international business, management, and marketing.

The School of Education and Human Services offers degrees that lead to teacher certification at the early childhood, childhood, middle childhood or adolescent levels, such as adolescence education, athletic training/sports medicine, childhood education, early childhood education, physical education, and special education. All programs are accredited by the National Accreditation of Teacher Education (NCATE).

Canisius also offers diverse and flexible academic programs such as fashion merchandising (in conjunction with the Fashion Institute of Technology), fine arts, and military science, and certification programs in gerontology and women's studies. Preprofessional programs are available in dentistry, engineering, environmental science, and forestry (in conjunction with the State University of New York (SUNY) College of Environmental Science and Forestry at Syracuse), law, medicine, pharmacy, and veterinary medicine. Canisius also has an early assurance of admission agreement for New York State residents, with the Schools of Medicine and Dental Medicine of SUNY at Buffalo and SUNY Medical School at Syracuse. Seven-year joint-degree programs exist between Canisius and the SUNY Buffalo School of Dental Medicine, the Ohio College of Podiatric Medicine, the New York College of Podiatric Medicine, and the SUNY College of Optometry. Joint-degree programs offered with Lake Erie College of Osteopathic Medicine include a seven-year program in osteopathic medicine and a five-year program in pharmacy. A five-year combined-degree program leads to the B.A. in a major in one of the liberal arts disciplines and a Master of Business Administration degree.

Academic Programs

To earn a bachelor's degree from Canisius College, students must complete forty courses and a minimum of 120 credit hours. Within each curriculum, the courses are distributed into three areas: core curriculum, major field requirements, and free electives. The College requires that students complete a rounded program of humanistic studies embracing literature, the physical and social sciences, oral and written communication, philosophy, history, religious studies, and language.

The All-College Honors Program is available for qualified students. This program includes rigorous exploration of the arts and sciences in an enriched curriculum with close faculty supervision and small classes. Students may also obtain college credit through the Advanced Placement Program of the College Board. Students with scores of 4 or better on Advanced Placement tests are considered for credit and advanced standing.

Off-Campus Programs

Many Canisius students choose to spend a semester or a year studying abroad, improving their fluency in another language and opening the doors to exciting personal and professional opportunities. Canisius administers semester-abroad programs in London, England; Oviedo, Spain; Lille, France; Dortmund, Germany; Morelia, Mexico; and Galway, Ireland. Canisius also works with other U.S. colleges and universities to make it possible for students to spend a semester or a year studying in Italy, Australia, Japan, Canada, and other countries. Some Canisius-sponsored programs also enable students to work as volunteers or interns in countries overseas. The Office of International Student Programs assists students in selecting a study-abroad program, organizes a predeparture orientation, and assists students upon their return to the United States.

Students majoring in international relations and political science may participate in programs in Washington, D.C., or Albany, New York, that have been designed to give students practical experience in their fields.

Academic Facilities

Canisius has invested more than $110 million over the last ten years to create state-of-the-art technology classrooms, residence halls, and cultural and recreational spaces. Technology plays a central role in all aspects of the college experience at Canisius, with ninety technology classrooms and wireless zones in three major academic buildings, the library, and the student center. The 96,000-square-foot Andrew L. Bouwhuis Library houses more than 800,000 books, periodicals, microforms, and other materials. The library also provides online database searching and has a number of computerized reference tools on CD-ROMs.

Instructional computing facilities include 276 Windows and Macintosh computers in general-purpose labs and teaching labs. Another thirty-two computers are located in residence hall computer labs, and thirty-four computers serve as e-mail and Internet stations at various convenient locations on campus. All College-provided computers have Internet access, and laser printers are available at all student-use computer labs.

Costs

For the academic year 2004–05, tuition was $20,910, room and board were $8480, and fees were $901. Books and supplies were estimated to cost $700. An additional $1130 per year was recommended for travel and personal expenses.

Financial Aid

Of the class of 2008, 98 percent receive some form of financial aid, and the average award is $18,948. This aid includes Canisius College scholarships and grants, state grants, state and federal loans, federal grants, and Federal Work-Study Program awards. Applications for financial aid should be completed by February 15. The Free Application for Federal Student Aid (FAFSA) and the TAP application (New York State residents only) must be filed before consideration can be given to applicants.

Faculty

The Canisius College faculty numbers 202 full-time teachers, including Jesuits and lay men and women. More than 92.6 percent hold doctorates or other terminal degrees. The primary emphasis of the faculty members is teaching, and many also serve as academic advisers. The student-faculty ratio is 14:1.

Student Government

The Undergraduate Student Association comprises the entire undergraduate student body and is represented by elected officers who serve on the Student Senate. The senate assists and supervises student activities and advocates on behalf of the students, presenting their views to the College administration. In addition, students serve on many College committees.

Admission Requirements

Students' applications for admission are evaluated on a combination of factors, including a student's academic ability, strength of character, high school record, rank in class, an essay, aptitude tests (SAT or ACT), extracurricular activities, and recommendations. An applicant to the College is encouraged to pursue a challenging college-preparatory program in high school. This program of studies should include a minimum of 16 units of credit in the academic subjects of English, foreign language, mathematics, science, and social studies. Recommendations from teachers or guidance counselors are not required but are encouraged, and they are considered in reviewing applications for admission. Campus interviews are strongly recommended and in some cases may be required.

Transfer students are welcome and are admitted to Canisius in the fall and spring semesters. In addition to meeting the academic standards required of all entering students, transfer students are considered for admission if they have a minimum 2.0 cumulative quality point average when transferring from either a two-year or a four-year accredited institution.

Canisius College does not discriminate on the basis of age, race, religion or creed, color, sex, national or ethnic origin, sexual orientation, marital status, veteran's status, genetic predisposition or carrier status, or disability in administration of its educational policies, employment practices, admissions policies, scholarship and loan programs, and athletic and other school-administered programs.

Application and Information

Students are encouraged to submit their applications for admission in the fall of their senior year in high school. Application forms are available from the Office of Admissions or fee-waived applications can be found on the Web at http://www.canisius.edu/admissions. The completed application form should be presented to the high school guidance counselor, to be forwarded to the director of admissions with an official high school transcript, SAT or ACT scores, and any letters of recommendation. Arrangements for interviews may be made by contacting the Office of Admissions at least one week in advance of the desired date for a visit.

Canisius considers applications under a rolling admission policy. Students applying by November 15 are notified of admission decision by December 15, along with scholarship notification. Students are encouraged to apply no later than March 1 for full and equal consideration.

For application forms and additional information, students should contact:

Admissions Office
Canisius College
2001 Main Street
Buffalo, New York 14208
Telephone: 716-888-2200
             800-843-1517 (toll-free)
Fax: 716-888-3230
E-mail: admissions@canisius.edu
World Wide Web: http://www.canisius.edu

Canisius College is the ideal size for each individual to be an important part of campus life.

CLARKSON UNIVERSITY
POTSDAM, NEW YORK

The University

Clarkson University, founded in 1896, is an independent, comprehensive university offering professional programs in business, engineering, liberal arts, and the sciences, including health sciences. Students benefit from a challenging, collaborative culture that develops the technical expertise, management skills, and versatility required in today's knowledge-based economy.

Clarkson has earned a reputation for developing innovative leaders in technology-based fields. It is also known for having a friendly campus where students enjoy personal attention. A rigorous curriculum emphasizes hands-on team projects and real-world, multidisciplinary challenges that develop skills in collaboration, communication, and creative problem solving. About 25 percent of the 2,700 undergraduates are women. Through a comprehensive Graduate School with 400 students, the University offers twenty-two master's degree and ten doctoral programs.

Many extracurricular activities are available to Clarkson students. Its more than 100 organizations include intercollegiate and intramural athletics, student publications (a newspaper and a yearbook), professional and honorary societies, outing club, pep band, jazz band, orchestra, religious clubs, chess club, amateur radio club, automotive association, and photo, drama, ski, cycle, bridge, rifle, international, outing, and table tennis clubs. The University's recreational facilities include a gymnasium and field house, with racquetball courts, a 3,000-square-foot fitness center, and a swimming pool, and a $13-million student center, including a 3,000-seat hockey arena. An outdoor lodge was completed in 2000.

Location

Potsdam, New York (population 9,500) is located in the St. Lawrence River valley of northern New York in the foothills of the Adirondack Mountains. The home of both Clarkson University and the State University of New York College at Potsdam, which have a combined student population approaching 7,000, the village is a friendly and vibrant college town. Many combined social and cultural activities are scheduled during the year. The major international cities of Montreal, Quebec, and Ottawa, Ontario, are within a 2-hour drive.

Majors and Degrees

The Bachelor of Science degree is offered in aeronautical engineering, applied mathematics and statistics, biology, biomolecular science, business and technology management, chemical engineering, chemistry, civil engineering, computer engineering, computer science, digital arts and sciences, e-business, electrical engineering, engineering and management, environmental engineering, environmental science and policy, financial information and analysis, history, humanities, industrial hygiene–environmental toxicology (environmental and occupational health), information systems and business processes, liberal studies, mathematics, mechanical engineering, physical therapy (prephysical therapy leading to a master's degree), physics, political science, Project Aretè (liberal arts/business), psychology, social sciences, software engineering, and technical communications (telecommunications option). Choices that allow students to begin a general program and choose their major at a later date include business studies, engineering studies, science studies, and university studies. Clarkson offers both an honors program and an accelerated three-year bachelor's degree pro-

gram. Special advising and preprofessional programs are available in dentistry, law, medicine, physical therapy, and veterinary sciences.

Academic Programs

At Clarkson, undergraduates can easily customize their studies according to individual interests and goals. Many of today's most profound advances in knowledge are occurring at the intersections of previously distinct academic disciplines. Building on a tradition of collaboration, the University has developed a growing number of interdisciplinary majors, while promoting opportunities for specialization and customization through double majors, minors, concentrations, and electives. Each student must achieve a cumulative GPA of at least 2.0 to qualify for graduation and must earn at least 120 credit hours.

The innovative programs at Clarkson reflect not only the high quality of faculty members and resources, but also the flexibility and vitality of the highly collaborative academic environment. The curriculum in the interdisciplinary engineering and management program, established in 1954, was the first of its kind to be accredited at any college or university in the nation. Other degree programs that combine disciplines include biomolecular science, digital arts and sciences, environmental science and policy, industrial hygiene–environmental toxicology (environmental and occupational health), Project Aretè (a double major program in business and liberal arts), and software engineering.

Undergraduates in all majors also have opportunities to join multidisciplinary academic teams that compete against intercollegiate peers as they tackle creative problem-solving challenges. Students can choose among fourteen different teams at Clarkson, organized through a program called Student Projects for Engineering Experience and Design (SPEED).

Recent recognition of quality at Clarkson includes the following: winner of the IBM Linux Scholar Challenge, a worldwide open programming project-based competition; winner of the Boeing Outstanding Educator Award for its SPEED program; top fifteen ranking in supply chain management in the 2005 *U.S. News & World Report*'s "Best Business Programs"; and a top 100 ranking for entrepreneurship education in *Entrepreneur* magazine.

Off-Campus Programs

Students benefit from the resources of the Associated Colleges of the St. Lawrence Valley, which comprises Clarkson University, St. Lawrence University, SUNY Canton, and SUNY Potsdam. Benefits for students include opportunities to participate in activities ranging from clubs to concerts, interlibrary exchange, and cross-registration that allows students to pursue two courses per year at other member colleges at no extra cost.

Academic Facilities

The University's 640-acre wooded campus is the site of forty-six buildings that comprise 1,224,583 square feet of assignable space. Eighty-five percent of these buildings have been built since 1970. Dedicated exclusively to instructional programs are 371,114 square feet, including 52,713 square feet of traditional classrooms and 166,334 square feet assigned as laboratory areas. In the Center for Advanced Materials Processing (a New York State Center for Advanced Technology), there are seventy state-of-the-art research labs, including many related to nanotechnology and environmental research. Others include a multidisciplinary engineering and project laboratory for team-based projects, such as the mini-Baja and Formulae SAE racers; a robotics laboratory;

a high-voltage lab; electron microscopy; a Class 10 clean room; a polymer fabrication lab; crystal growth labs; and a structural testing lab. School of Arts and Sciences facilities include a virtual reality laboratory, a molecular design laboratory, a human brain electrophysiology laboratory, and other specialized facilities.

Bertrand H. Snell Hall houses the School of Business and School of Arts and Sciences administrative offices as well as fully networked classrooms and study spaces and collaborative centers for team projects and features wireless network access and video-conferencing capabilities. The facility includes three academic centers, available to all students: the Shipley Center for Leadership and Entrepreneurship, the Center for Global Competitiveness, and the Eastman Kodak Center for Excellence in Communication. The Center for Health Sciences at Clarkson is a regional center of excellence for education, treatment, and research in physical rehabilitation and other health sciences.

Costs

For 2005–06, tuition is $25,185; room (2 persons), $4896; and board (all options), $4449. Fees are $400, and books, supplies, travel, and personal expenses vary but may come to approximately $3000.

Financial Aid

More than 90 percent of the student body receive some form of financial aid. This aid includes Clarkson University scholarships; state scholarships and awards; state and federal student loans; industrial, endowed, organizational, and individual scholarships; federal grants; and Federal Work-Study awards. More than half of the freshmen receive renewable scholarships or grants directly from Clarkson.

Faculty

A full-time faculty of 176 serves both the undergraduate and graduate programs, thus enhancing the opportunities for interchange of knowledge among faculty members and students at all levels. Ninety-six percent have their Ph.D.'s. Courses are taught by faculty members, while graduate students assist in laboratory and recitation situations. The faculty-student ratio is 1:16.

Student Government

The Student Senate and the Interfraternity Council combine to form the student government at Clarkson University. The former supervises all extracurricular activities (except athletics) and has responsibility for the allocation of student activity funds and for other appropriate business. The latter prescribes standards and rules for fraternities. Students are involved in the formation of University policies through membership, with faculty and staff representatives, on all important committees.

Admission Requirements

A thorough preparation in mathematics, science, and English is very important in the academic qualifications of a candidate for admission. Candidates for entrance to the Wallace H. Coulter School of Engineering or the School of Arts and Sciences should have successfully completed secondary school courses in physics and chemistry. All candidates for admission are required to take the SAT I or ACT. SAT II Subject Tests are recommended in Writing, Level I or Level II Mathematics, and either Physics or Chemistry (Physics is preferred). The high school record is the most important factor in an admission decision. International students for whom English is a second language must submit a minimum TOEFL score of 550 (paper-based) or 213 (computer-based). All applicants must include a personal statement of 250 to 500 words describing a special interest, experience, or achievement.

Students achieving scores of 4 or better on the College Board's Advanced Placement examinations are considered for advanced placement and credit in virtually all academic areas. Advanced standing is most common in English, mathematics, and science.

An early decision plan is offered on a "first-choice" basis; this plan does not prohibit the student from making other applications, but it does commit the student to withdraw other applications if accepted at Clarkson. Early admission for students who have completed three years of secondary education is encouraged when the academic record, standardized test scores, and recommendations indicate the student has reached a sufficiently high intellectual and emotional level to perform successfully with other college students.

A personal interview is very helpful to the student in formulating his or her college plans. Interviews on campus should be arranged by letter or telephone at least one week prior to the intended visit. The interview is not required but is strongly recommended, especially for early decision candidates. The admission office is open Monday through Friday, from 9 a.m. to 4 p.m., and Saturday by appointment. The University welcomes visitors to the campus and makes arrangements, as requested, for families to tour and meet with academic and other departments on campus.

Application and Information

Office of Undergraduate Admission
Holcroft House
Clarkson University
P.O. Box 5605
Potsdam, New York 13699-5605
Telephone: 315-268-6479 or 6480
         800-527-6577 (toll-free)
Fax: 315-268-7647
E-mail: admission@clarkson.edu
World Wide Web: http://www.clarkson.edu

Clarkson is a leader in project-based learning, providing students with strong communication skills, leadership ability, and technological skill in their fields.

CONCORDIA COLLEGE
BRONXVILLE, NEW YORK

The College

Founded in 1881, Concordia College is a four-year, coeducational liberal arts institution in suburban Westchester County, New York. The College is affiliated with the Lutheran Church and welcomes students of all faiths from twenty-four states and thirty-six countries. Concordia College is a Christian environment where students from many different cultures live, learn, and work together. As members of a close-knit community, Concordia students are mentored by a dedicated faculty and staff, most of whom live within a 10-minute walk of the campus. Students develop lifelong relationships as they prepare for fulfilling lives and careers. During their time at Concordia, students are encouraged to reach their full academic, spiritual, athletic, and artistic potential.

Concordia is intentionally small, with a population of approximately 700; its students are active and involved. The Student Government Association supports more than twenty clubs and organizations. Opportunities range from student publications to social-concern groups, Bible study to student government, and drama to intramurals. Concordia's talented choirs and ensembles perform on campus and throughout the United States and Europe. The College's eleven varsity teams compete in the NCAA Division II. Teams repeatedly earn national ranking, and outstanding individuals are recruited in the professional drafts.

Concordia's beautiful campus is a pleasing mix of new and newly renovated buildings. A standout facility on campus is the Sommer Center for Worship and the Performing Arts, a 650-seat music center so acoustically well-balanced that artists such as Itzhak Perlman, Yehudi Menuhin, and Harry Connick Jr. have recorded there. Other specialized facilities include the Schoenfeld Campus Center, Scheele Memorial Library, and Meyer Athletic Center, which includes a gymnasium, a weight room, a fitness center, two squash courts, three indoor tennis courts, and five outdoor tennis courts (three composite and two clay). Facilities include baseball, soccer, and softball fields.

Concordia College is accredited by the Commission on Higher Education of the Middle States Association of Colleges and Schools and registered by the New York State Education Department.

Location

Concordia's 33-acre campus is set in the affluent and peaceful village of Bronxville. The village is home to more than 7,000 people, including UN diplomats, investment brokers, and a wide range of professionals. Entertainment, shopping, and employment opportunities are available within this safe and picturesque village. Students also benefit from of the limitless experiences offered in New York City, a 25-minute train ride from Bronxville.

Majors and Degrees

Concordia offers the Bachelor of Arts (B.A.) and the Bachelor of Science (B.S.). The B.A. program includes behavioral science, biology, education (New York State and Lutheran certification), English/communication, and liberal studies with the following fields: art, biblical languages, biology, chemistry, English, history, math, music, philosophy, religion, sociology, or Spanish.

The B.S. program includes business administration and social work.

The College also offers special programs in prelaw, premedicine, and preseminary. Additional specializations include family life ministries, international management, and sports management.

Academic Programs

Concordia College provides students with an excellent education by building each degree program upon a foundation of basic skills, knowledge, and values. To graduate, students must complete the Concordia Distinctive (the College's popular core curriculum), the program of study, and general studies requirements, integrated with field experience and internships in Westchester County and the New York area. This is known as the Concordia Experience.

Concordia operates on a two-semester calendar. A minimum of 122 completed semester hours is required to earn a bachelor's degree.

Assistance is available via peer tutors. The staff of the Writing Center works with students at all levels and offers supplemental instruction to support Concordia's Writing Across the Curriculum Program. Concordia puts great emphasis on critical-thinking and communication skills.

The Career Development Center counsels students in career, vocational, and academic choices. The center coordinates resume and interview preparation, tutorial assistance, and postings for full-time and part-time jobs. Concordia alumni achieve significant roles in society: President of PaineWebber, Superintendent of Schools–San Francisco, star of the *Sopranos* cast, software engineers at PriceWaterhouse, social work manager, and publisher of *Business Week* magazine.

The Concordia Fellows Program (honors) is open via application to all students who demonstrate high academic achievement. Fellows are enriched through a variety of unique academic experiences, seminars, and travel.

The Concordia Connection Program is for students with diagnosed learning differences. Support services are provided to qualified students who meet regular admission requirements but need specific assistance in order to maximize their academic success.

Concordia offers an intensive English as a second language (ESL) program, serving students at a variety of proficiency levels. Concordia also offers an Accelerated Degree Program (ADP) for adult students over age 25 who have previously earned a minimum of 60 college credits. ADP students who meet the program requirements can earn their degree in one year of intensive study.

Off-Campus Programs

Concordia is part of the national Concordia University System, which is made up of ten colleges and universities affiliated with the Lutheran Church–Missouri Synod. Students may enroll for up to one year at any of these sister institutions. Students may also study overseas at Oak Hill College in London and other international sites.

Academic Facilities

In addition to traditional holdings, the Scheele Memorial Library participates in a forty-library online system that gives students access to a multitude of academic resources. The library supports 467 active subscriptions and contains the Media Center, a distance learning classroom, a curriculum materials center, and the Concordia Gallery. New construction of a 19,000-square-foot facility, expected to begin in spring 2005, is planned to showcase sophisticated, computer-based, multimedia instructional space, an expanded art gallery, an auditorium-style classroom, a media-production center, and state-of-the-art computer and information technology installations. The new space is on the second floor of the library, which was designed in 1974 to accommodate a significant addition. The library is being renamed the Krenz Academic Center.

Brunn-Maier Science Hall houses science laboratories, the Writing Center, computer labs (PC and Mac), and the Halter Graphics Laboratory, which is equipped for graphics, desktop publishing, and music composition.

The Sommer Center for Worship and the Performing Arts includes a stunning recital/lecture hall, the College Chapel, and private rehearsal rooms for vocal, instrumental, and organ practice. Schoenfeld Campus Center, the hub of student life, provides a venue for student activities, intramurals, and dramatic performances. Historic Stein Hall houses the Concordia Conservatory, including individual and group studios and a keyboard lab.

Costs

Tuition and fees for the 2004–05 academic year were $18,700. Room and board charges were $7600. Costs are the same for in-state, out-of-state, and transfer students.

Financial Aid

Concordia strives to make a college education affordable to students from all backgrounds through an aggressive financial aid program. Need-based grants and merit-based and church vocation scholarships are available. Merit scholarships are awarded to students with academic, music, athletic, and leadership abilities. More than 90 percent of Concordia students receive financial aid.

A student's financial aid package may include a combination of grants, scholarships, employment, and student loans. To be considered, students must file the Free Application for Federal Student Aid (FAFSA). Concordia's FAFSA code is 002709.

Faculty

Concordia College's faculty members are committed to student success. The 14:1 student-faculty ratio enables students and faculty members to interact on a very personal level. The focus of Concordia faculty members is on teaching; teaching assistants are not utilized. Professors and students conduct research at all levels.

Student Government

All full-time students are members of the Student Government Association (SGA) and elect its representatives each spring. The SGA organizes and supports a host of campus events and provides a voice for all student concerns.

Admission Requirements

Concordia College admits students whose academic preparation, abilities, interests, and character show promise for success in college. Applicants are considered on the basis of academic record, class rank, test scores, essay, and recommendations. Students may apply online. To apply, students should submit a completed application, an official high school transcript, SAT or ACT scores, the School Report Form (part of the application form), letters of recommendation, essay, and a $30 application fee. In addition, transfer students must submit official transcripts from all colleges and universities attended, plus SAT or ACT scores (if they have earned fewer than 28 college credits). Concordia College is part of the Common Application Consortium of Colleges. Applications are available online at http://www.commonapp.org.

Prospective students are encouraged to visit the campus and meet with a faculty member in their area of interest. Open house events are regularly scheduled; Concordia is also happy to arrange individual visits.

Application and Information

Applications are accepted on a rolling basis. However, it is recommended that applications and supporting documents for first-year students be received by March 15 and for transfers by July 15. Applications may be accepted thereafter on a space-available basis.

Requests for information and applications should be addressed to:

Office of Admission
Concordia College
171 White Plains Road
Bronxville, New York 10708
Telephone: 914-337-9300 Ext. 2155
        800-YES-COLLEGE (937-2655; toll-free)
Fax: 914-395-4636
E-mail: admission@concordia-ny.edu
World Wide Web: http//www.concordia-ny.edu

At Concordia College, students from many different cultures live, learn, and work together.

D'YOUVILLE COLLEGE
BUFFALO, NEW YORK

The College

D'Youville College is a private, coeducational, liberal arts and professional college that has offered students an education of high quality since 1908. The College was the first in western New York to offer baccalaureate degrees to women. Its current enrollment is 2,500 men and women. Students may choose from thirty undergraduate and graduate degree programs that are enhanced by a 14:1 student-faculty ratio. The College is committed to helping its students to grow not only in academics but in the social and personal areas of their college experience as well.

The multiple-option Nursing Degree Program is one of the largest four-year private-college nursing programs in the country. Available nursing programs include B.S.N., B.S.N./M.S. (five years), and RN to B.S.N. Ninety-four percent of D'Youville's 2003 graduates are employed in their field or are in graduate school.

Students residing in Marguerite Hall have a scenic view of the Niagara River and Lake Erie, which separate the U.S. and Canadian shorelines. The Koessler Administration Building contains the Offices of Admissions, Financial Aid, the President, Student Accounts, and the Registrar; the Learning Center; and the Kavinoky Theatre. The Student Center, the focal point of leisure and extracurricular activities, has a new gymnasium, a swimming pool, a weight-training room, a dance studio, a general recreation center, a pub, and dining facilities. Student organizations and regularly scheduled activities, including intramural sports, NCAA Division III intercollegiate sports (baseball, basketball, volleyball, golf, cross-country, soccer, and softball), a ski club, the College newspaper, the yearbook, and social organizations, as well as academic programs, all help to make up an active campus life.

Location

D'Youville is situated on Buffalo's residential west side. The College is within minutes of many local attractions, including the downtown shopping center, the Kleinhans Music Hall, the Albright-Knox Art Gallery, two museums, and several theaters that offer stage productions. Seasonal changes in the area offer a variety of recreational opportunities. Buffalo is only 90 miles from Toronto and 25 minutes from Niagara Falls, making it a gateway to recreation areas in western New York and Ontario. Holiday Valley, a skier's paradise, is an hour's drive away. The city is served by the New York State Thruway, Amtrak, Greyhound and Trailways bus lines, and most major airlines.

D'Youville enjoys a diversified interchange with the community due to its affiliations with schools, hospitals, and social agencies in the area. College students in the Buffalo area number more than 60,000.

Majors and Degrees

D'Youville offers the degrees of Bachelor of Arts (B.A.), Bachelor of Science (B.S.), and Bachelor of Science in Nursing (B.S.N.). Majors include accounting, biology, business management, chiropractic, dietetics, education (elementary, secondary, and special), English, exercise and sports studies, global studies, health services, history, information technology, international business, nursing, occupational therapy, philosophy, physical therapy, physician assistant studies, preprofessional studies

(dental, law, medicine, and veterinary studies), psychology, and sociology. Five-year combined bachelor's/master's (B.S./M.S.) programs are offered in dietetics, education, information technology (B.S.)/international business (M.S.), international business, nursing, and occupational therapy. A six-year B.S./D.P.T. program is offered in physical therapy. A seven-year B.S./D.C. program is offered in chiropractic.

Academic Programs

The area of concentration recognizes individual differences and varying interests but still provides sufficient specialization in one discipline to form a foundation for graduate studies and professional careers. Students attending D'Youville are expected to complete the requirements of their chosen concentration while earning a minimum of 120 credit hours. Core requirements include humanities, 24 hours; social science, 12 hours; science, 7 hours; mathematics/computer science, 6 hours; and electives, 9 hours. A cumulative average of at least 2.0 must be maintained to meet graduation requirements. Sixteen credit hours, or five or six courses per semester, are considered a normal workload. Internships to meet specific career goals may be arranged in any major.

The College offers a Career Discovery Program that was purposely designed for the undecided student. This program, which can last for two years, offers credit courses and internships.

The academic year is composed of two semesters, each lasting approximately fifteen weeks. The first semester, including final examinations, ends before the Christmas holidays. During the eight-week summer sessions, programs of selected courses are given at all levels on a daily basis.

Off-Campus Programs

The baccalaureate program in nursing is affiliated with thirteen area hospitals and public health agencies. The education program is affiliated with local elementary, junior high, and secondary schools and with special education centers in the area for purposes of student teaching. The occupational therapy, physical therapy, and physician assistant programs are affiliated with appropriate clinical settings throughout the United States.

Academic Facilities

D'Youville's modern Library Resources Center, which was completed in fall 1999, contains 154,000 volumes, including microtext and software, and subscriptions to 870 periodicals and newspapers. The multimillion-dollar Health Science Building houses laboratories, including those for anatomy, organic chemistry, and gross anatomy; activity and daily living labs for the health professions; and additional laboratories for physics, chemistry, quantitative analysis, and computer science. It also houses classrooms, faculty member offices, and development centers, including one for career development. This is augmented by a new, modern academic center, which opened in fall 2001.

Costs

For 2004–05, tuition was $7345 per semester, and room and board cost $3670 per semester. A general College fee is required and is based on credit hours taken; a Student Association fee of

$40 per semester is applied toward concerts, yearbooks, activities, and guest lectures. A $100 deposit ($150 for dietetics, physician assistant studies, occupational therapy, and physical therapy programs), credited toward tuition, must be submitted by all candidates who accept an offer of admission.

Financial Aid

D'Youville attempts to provide financial aid for students who would not otherwise be able to attend. Determination of aid is based on the Free Application for Federal Student Aid. Aid is available in the form of grants, loans, and employment on campus. In addition, D'Youville offers scholarships for academic achievement to incoming students.

All students may qualify for D'Youville's new Instant Scholarship Program, which offers scholarships with total values up to $45,900. Students who apply, are accepted, and meet the criteria instantly qualify for one of these scholarships, all of which are renewable annually. These scholarships are not based on need. The three scholarship programs are the Honors Scholarship, the Academic Initiative Scholarship, and the Achievement Scholarship. The Honors Scholarship requires a minimum SAT I score of 1100 or an ACT score of at least 24 and awards 50 percent of tuition and 25 percent of room and board costs. The Academic Initiative Scholarship requires SAT I scores of at least 1000 or ACT scores of 21 to 23 and an academic average of at least 85. It awards 25 percent of tuition and 50 percent of room and board costs. The Achievement Scholarship criteria include SAT I scores of 900 to 1090 or ACT scores of 19 to 23 and an academic average of 80 to 84. This scholarship awards $1000–$4000.

Faculty

The ratio of faculty members to students is 1:14. All members of the full-time instructional staff hold a doctorate or another advanced degree. Faculty members act as advisers and are available for consultation with students.

Student Government

The Student Association (SA), a representative form of student self-government, seeks to inspire in its members dedication to the intellectual, social, and moral ideals of the College and works closely with the administration and faculty. All students of D'Youville are considered members of the SA and may be elected to the executive council and the student senate. There are seventeen academic and social clubs affiliated with the SA.

Admission Requirements

An applicant must be a high school graduate or have a high school equivalency diploma before matriculating. The applicant should have a college-preparatory background, including required English and history courses and a sequence in either mathematics or science. Scores on the SAT I or the ACT are also required for admission. High school advanced placement credit is acceptable and transferable. The admission decision is based on high school grade point average, rank in class, and scores on the SAT I or ACT. Students who have difficulty meeting normal admission standards may be admitted with a reduced academic load.

The College Learning Center offers academic assistance to students whose education has been interrupted or has not prepared them adequately for college courses. The Tutor Bank, a system of peer tutoring, offers the assistance of qualified students to those who need help in specific academic disciplines.

Application and Information

D'Youville admits students on a rolling admission basis; therefore, applications are reviewed as they are received by the admissions office. Transfer students who have a quality point average of at least 2.0 are encouraged to apply by December 1 for the spring semester and by July 1 for the fall semester. A brochure listing course offerings and giving details about costs and room and board is available upon request.

R. H. Dannecker
Director of Admissions
D'Youville College
One D'Youville Square
320 Porter Avenue
Buffalo, New York 14201-1084
Telephone: 716-829-7600
          800-777-3921 (toll-free)
E-mail: admissions@dyc.edu
World Wide Web: http://www.dyc.edu

ELMIRA COLLEGE
ELMIRA, NEW YORK

The College

Elmira College is a small, independent college that is recognized for its emphasis on education of high quality in the liberal arts and preprofessional preparation. One of the oldest colleges in the United States, Elmira was founded in 1855. The College has always produced graduates interested in both community service and successful careers. Friendliness, personal attention, strong college spirit, and support for learning beyond the classroom help to make Elmira a special place. Elmira College is one of only 270 colleges in the nation to be granted a chapter of the prestigious Phi Beta Kappa honor society.

The full-time undergraduate enrollment is about 1,200 men and women. The students at Elmira represent more than thirty-five states, primarily those in the Northeast, with the highest representation coming from New York, New Jersey, Massachusetts, Connecticut, Maine, and Pennsylvania. International students from twenty-three countries were enrolled in September 2003. Ninety-five percent of the full-time undergraduates live in College residence halls, and dormitory rooms are equipped to provide direct access to the Internet. Wireless access is also available in the 1855 Room, a popular student location.

The intercollegiate sports program includes men's and women's basketball, golf, ice hockey, lacrosse, soccer, and tennis and women's cheerleading, field hockey, softball, and volleyball. An intramural program is also available. Emerson Hall houses the student fitness center, a pool, and a gym capable of seating 1,000, as well as the Gibson Theatre, which has a state-of-the-art sound and lighting system. Professional societies; clubs; music, dance, and drama groups; a student-operated FM radio station; and the student newspaper, yearbook, and literary magazine also provide numerous opportunities for extracurricular activity.

Location

Elmira College is located in the city of Elmira, which has a population of 35,000, in the Finger Lakes region of New York. The campus is a 10-minute walk from downtown Elmira. The relationship between the College and the local community is excellent, and numerous community activities and facilities are open to students, including the Elmira Symphony and Choral Society, the Elmira Little Theatre, clubs and civic groups, museums, movies, and a performing arts center. Excellent recreational areas are available in upstate New York and nearby Pennsylvania.

Majors and Degrees

Elmira College offers programs leading to the bachelor's degree in more than thirty-five majors, including accounting, American studies, art, art education, biochemistry, biology, business administration, chemistry, classical studies, criminal justice, economics, elementary education, English literature, environmental studies, fine arts, French, history, human services, individualized studies, international business, international studies, mathematics, medical technology, music, nursing, philosophy and religion, political science, psychology, public affairs, social studies, sociology and anthropology, Spanish, speech and hearing, and theater. Secondary teaching certification is offered in several areas. A 3-2 program in chemical engineering with Clarkson University is available, and 4-1 M.B.A. programs are available at Alfred University, Clarkson University, and Union College.

Preprofessional preparation is offered in education, medical technology, nursing, and speech pathology and audiology. Faculty advisers assist those who seek preparation for graduate study in dentistry, law, or medicine in choosing appropriate course work. More than 50 percent of Elmira graduates pursue graduate study.

Academic Programs

The College's calendar is composed of two 12-week terms followed by a six-week spring term. Students enroll for four subjects during the twelve-week terms, completing the first term by mid-December and the second during the first week of April. The six-week term, from mid-April through May, may be devoted to a particular project involving travel, internship, research, or independent study. Students are required to participate in internships in order to gain practical and meaningful experience related to their program of study. Credit is awarded for these projects.

Special opportunities for outstanding students include participation in thirteen national honorary societies on campus and a chance to assist faculty members in teaching and research. The College also offers an accelerated three-year graduation option for outstanding students, and an Advanced Placement Program is available.

Army and Air Force ROTC are available.

Off-Campus Programs

Through the Junior Year Abroad programs, students may study in the United Kingdom, France, Spain, and Japan, as well as in other countries throughout Europe and Asia. Elmira students may study at the Washington Center for Learning Alternatives. Students from Elmira may spend the third term studying marine biology or doing sociological research on the island of San Salvador in the Bahamas. Education majors may work as student teachers in the Bahamas and in England.

Academic Facilities

The Elmira campus offers exceptional academic facilities in a beautiful setting. The modern Gannett-Tripp Library houses more than 391,000 volumes, receives 2,500 periodicals, and includes a special Mark Twain collection room and photography and audiovisual facilities.

The College Computer Center offers PC and Apple Macintosh microcomputers for student use.

A Center for Mark Twain Studies has been established at Quarry Farm, the author's summer home, which is located a few miles from campus. The College also operates a Speech and Hearing Clinic on campus, which serves the public and provides valuable internship experience for students. Excellent facilities for drama and music are available.

Costs

Tuition for 2004–05 was $26,130, room was $4950, board was $3380, and fees were $900.

Financial Aid

Financial aid is available for both freshmen and transfer students. Awards are based upon the Free Application for Federal Student Aid (FAFSA) as well as the student's academic potential. Types of aid include grants, scholarships, federal loans, Elmira College loans, and work opportunities. In addition, superior students may qualify for non-need Elmira College Honors Scholarships, which are available to both freshmen and transfer students and range from $4000 to full tuition per year. For 2004–05, the average freshman aid package (including all types of aid) amounted to more than $21,000. About 80 percent of the full-time undergraduates receive financial aid.

Faculty

Members of the faculty are chosen for their ability in and dedication to teaching. All full-time faculty members serve as advisers, and the faculty approves all academic programs. Currently, the full-time faculty consists of 11 full professors, 25 associate professors, 32 assistant professors, and 10 instructors. Ninety-eight percent of the faculty hold the Ph.D. or highest degree necessary to teach in their field.

Student Government

Student government, an important part of the educational system at Elmira College, prepares students for active and responsible citizenship in society. Student government organizations include the Student Senate, the Judicial Board, and the Student Activities Board.

Admission Requirements

The Office of Admissions at Elmira College uses a rolling admission system. Each applicant is evaluated individually on the basis of his or her total application, including academic record, rank in class, SAT or ACT scores, essay, activities, references, and goals. The College strongly advises a personal interview. The recommendations of teachers and guidance counselors are also important. Special consideration is given to applicants from distant states and other countries, applicants with special skills, and applicants who are prepared to become actively involved in designing their own programs.

Elmira has early decision and early admission programs.

Application and Information

For further information, applicants should contact:

Dean of Admissions
Elmira College
Elmira, New York 14901
Telephone: 800-935-6472 (toll-free)
E-mail: admissions@elmira.edu
World Wide Web: http://www.elmira.edu

The Mark Twain Study is one of the most famous literary landmarks in America.

EUGENE LANG COLLEGE, NEW SCHOOL UNIVERSITY

NEW YORK, NEW YORK

The College

Eugene Lang College is the distinctive liberal arts division of New School University, formerly known as the New School for Social Research. It is a major urban university with a tradition of innovative learning. The College offers all the benefits of a small and supportive college as well as the full range of opportunities found in a university setting.

Lang students are encouraged to participate in the creation and direction of their education. The desire to explore and the freedom to imagine shared by students and faculty members contribute to a distinctive academic community.

Eugene Lang College students currently come from forty-five states and thirteen countries. The ratio of men to women is approximately 2:3. About 45 percent of the College's 887 students come from outside the New York metropolitan area; 4 percent hold foreign citizenship and 23 percent are members of minority groups. The student body is composed of both residential and day students. The university operates residence halls within walking distance of classes; incoming freshmen and transfer students are given housing priority within these facilities, and housing is guaranteed for the first year for new students. Great diversity in interests and aspirations is found among the students. Through the Office of Student Services, students produce a student newspaper and an award-winning literary magazine. They organize and participate in dramatic, musical, and artistic events through the "Lang in the City Program," as well as numerous political, social, and cultural organizations at the university and throughout New York City.

The New School for Social Research was founded in 1919 by such notable scholars and intellectuals as John Dewey, Alvin Johnson, and Thorstein Veblen. It has long been a home for leading artists, educators, and public figures. For example, the university was the first institution of higher learning to offer college-level courses in such "new" fields as black culture and race, taught by W. E. B. DuBois, and psychoanalysis, taught by Freud's disciple Sandor Ferenczi. Among the world-famous artists and performers who have taught at the New School are Martha Graham, Aaron Copland, and Thomas Hart Benton. Today, such noted scholars as Robert Heilbroner, Eric Hobsbawm, Jerome Bruner, and Rayna Rapp are among the hundreds of university faculty members accessible to Lang College students.

The other divisions of the university include the Adult Division, which offers more than 2,000 credit and noncredit courses to students each semester; the Graduate Faculty of Political and Social Science (founded in 1933 as the University in Exile), which grants M.A. and Ph.D. degrees; the Robert J. Milano Graduate School of Management and Urban Policy, which awards the M.A. and M.S. degrees; Parsons School of Design, one of the oldest and most influential art schools in the country; and Mannes College of Music, a renowned classical conservatory. The total university enrollment in 2004–05 was approximately 7,500 degree-seeking students.

Location

The university is located in New York City's Greenwich Village, which historically has been a center for intellectual and artistic life. This slower-paced, more personal New York City neighborhood of town houses and tree-lined streets offers students a friendly and stimulating environment. Over and above the resources of Greenwich Village, New York City offers virtually unlimited cultural, artistic, recreational, and intellectual resources that make it one of the world's great cities.

Majors and Degrees

Eugene Lang College awards the Bachelor of Arts degree. Students are encouraged to design their own program of study, which includes an area of concentration, in consultation with their faculty adviser. Lang offers twelve areas of concentration: arts in context; cultural studies and media; dance; education studies; literature; philosophy; psychology; religious studies; science, technology, and society; social and historical inquiry; theater; urban studies; and writing. A student's concentration consists of eight to ten courses (32–40 credits) leading to relatively advanced and specialized knowledge of an area of study. In addition, students are encouraged to pursue an internship, where appropriate.

Students may also apply to a five-year B.A./B.F.A. program in conjunction with Parsons School of Design or in jazz studies at New School University, and advanced students may apply to the five-year B.A./M.A. programs offered in conjunction with the university's graduate divisions.

Academic Programs

When planning a program of study, Eugene Lang College students are encouraged to reflect on what their education means to them. Their program should parallel their own academic and personal development. By actively participating in the process of their education, students gain the knowledge to make informed choices about the direction of their studies with the help of their advisers and peers.

Small seminar classes serve as the focus of the academic program at the College. The maximum class size is 20 students. Classes are in-depth, interdisciplinary inquiries into topics or issues selected each semester by the College's outstanding faculty. Most importantly, the classes engage participants in the study of primary texts, rather than textbooks, and emphasize dialogue between teacher and student as a mode of learning. Here, not only is intellectual curiosity fostered by the small classes, but a genuine sense of community develops as well.

Although the College does not emphasize course requirements outside the area of concentration, freshmen are required to take one writing course and three other seminars of their choice in each of their first two semesters at the College. Upper-level students create their programs by selecting seminars from the College's curriculum, or they may combine offerings of the College with courses and workshops given by the New School's Adult Division, Graduate Faculty of Political and Social Science, Robert J. Milano Graduate School of Management and Urban Policy, and Parsons School of Design.

The College operates on a semester calendar; the first semester runs from September through mid-December and the second, from late January through mid-May. Students generally earn 16 credits per semester; a minimum of 120 credits is required for graduation.

Off-Campus Programs

Eugene Lang College recognizes the immense value of work undertaken beyond the classroom. The College arranges appropriate projects—internships with private and nonprofit organizations—which serve to strengthen the connection between theoretical work in the classroom and practical work on the job.

Sophomores and juniors have the option of spending a year on a sponsored exchange with Sarah Lawrence College and the University of Amsterdam. Other exchanges, both American and abroad, are available.

Academic Facilities

Eugene Lang College is located on 11th Street between Fifth and Sixth Avenues in Greenwich Village. The university includes twelve academic buildings, including a student center, a Computer Instruction Center with more than seventy-five IBM personal computers and Macintosh systems, a 500-seat auditorium, art galleries, studios for the fine arts, classrooms, a writing center, and faculty offices. Lang College students have full and easy access to the Raymond Fogelman Library and the Adam and Sophie Gimbel Design Library. In addition, the university participates in the South Manhattan Library Consortium. Together, the libraries in the consortium house approximately 3 million volumes covering all the traditional liberal arts disciplines and the fine arts.

Costs

Tuition and fees for the 2004–05 academic year were $24,920. Room and board cost approximately $10,000, depending upon the specific meal plan and dormitory accommodations chosen. University fees were $100 per year.

Financial Aid

Students are encouraged to apply for aid by filing the Free Application for Federal Student Aid (FAFSA) and requesting that a copy of the need analysis report be sent to the New School (FAFSA code number 002780). Qualified College students are eligible for all federal and state financial aid programs in addition to university gift aid. University aid is awarded on the basis of need and merit and is part of a package consisting of both gift aid (grants and/or scholarships) and a self-help component (loans and Federal Work-Study awards). Aid is renewable each year as long as need continues and students maintain satisfactory academic standing at the College. Special attention is given to continuing students who have done exceptionally well.

Faculty

At Eugene Lang College, the faculty-student ratio is 1:10. Class size ranges from 10 to 20 students. Faculty members are graduates of outstanding colleges and universities and represent a wide variety of academic disciplines; 95 percent hold Ph.D.'s. College faculty members also serve as academic advisers, who are selected carefully in order to ensure the thoughtful supervision of students' programs and academic progress.

Well-known faculty members from other divisions of the university teach at the College on a regular basis. In addition, every semester, the College hosts distinguished scholars and writers as visiting faculty and guest lecturers who further enrich the academic program of the College and the university.

Student Government

There is a student union at the College, which is an organized vehicle for student expression and action as well as a means of funding student projects and events. Students are encouraged to express their views and concerns about academic policies and community life through regular student-faculty member meetings.

Admission Requirements

Eugene Lang College welcomes admission applications from students of diverse racial, ethnic, religious, and political backgrounds whose past performance and academic and personal promise make them likely to gain from and give much to the College community. The College seeks students who combine inquisitiveness and seriousness of purpose with the ability to engage in a distinctive, rigorous liberal arts program. Each applicant to the College is judged individually; the Admissions Committee, which renders all admission decisions, considers both academic qualifications and the personal, creative, and intellectual qualities of each applicant. A strong academic background, including a college-preparatory program, is recommended. An applicant's transcript; teacher and counselor recommendations; SAT, ACT, or SAT Subject Test scores; and personal essays are all taken into consideration. In addition, an interview, a tour of university facilities, and a visit to Lang College seminars are optional but highly recommended.

High school students for whom the College is their first choice are strongly encouraged to apply as early decision candidates and are notified early of an admission decision. Early entrance is an option for qualified high school juniors who wish to enter college prior to high school graduation. Candidates for early entrance must submit two teacher recommendations.

Students who have successfully completed one full year or more at another accredited institution may apply as transfer candidates. If accepted, transfer students may enter upper-level seminars and pursue advanced work. International students may apply for admission as freshmen or transfers by submitting a regular application to the College. If English is spoken as a second language, TOEFL scores are required. The New York Connection Program invites students from other colleges to Eugene Lang for a semester and incorporates an internship into their studies.

Students interested in applying for the combined B.A./B.F.A. degree program in fine arts or jazz studies are encouraged to apply for admission as freshmen to these special five-year programs. In addition to the admission requirements outlined above, a home exam and a portfolio are required for fine arts, and an audition is required for jazz studies.

Application and Information

Freshmen, transfers, and visiting students may apply for either the September (fall) or January (spring) semester. To apply for admission to the College, students must request an application packet and submit the required credentials and a $40 application fee by the appropriate deadline. (The application fee may be waived in accordance with the College Board's Fee Waiver Service.) For the semester beginning in January, the required credentials must be submitted by November 15, with notification by December 15. For the September semester, early decision candidates must submit the required credentials by November 15, with notification by December 15; for freshman candidates applying for general admission and freshmen early entrants, the deadline is February 1, with notification by April 1; for transfers and visiting students, the deadline is rolling to May 15, with notification rolling until July 1.

For further information, students should contact:

Terence Peavy
Director of Admissions
Eugene Lang College, New School University
65 West 11th Street, Third Floor
New York, New York 10011
Telephone: 212-229-5665
Fax: 212-229-5355
E-mail: lang@newschool.edu
World Wide Web: http://www.lang.edu

FASHION INSTITUTE OF TECHNOLOGY
NEW YORK, NEW YORK

The Institute

Today, to know the Fashion Institute of Technology (FIT) only by name is not to know it very well at all. The name reflects back sixty years to the college's origins, when it was devoted exclusively to educating students for careers in the apparel industry. But the name no longer tells the whole story.

A "fashion college" that offers programs in interior design, jewelry design, advertising and marketing communications, and even toy design, as well as a "community college" that offers bachelor's and master's degree programs in addition to the traditional two-year associate degree, FIT is an educational institution like no other.

FIT is rooted in industry and the world of work. Industry visits by students and lectures by many different leaders in the field provide a cooperative and creative bridge between the classroom and the world of work. Although the college is now associated with many industries and professions, FIT's commitment to career education is still its hallmark and a source of pride to an institution whose industry connection is an integral part of its history. FIT counts among its alumni such luminaries as Calvin Klein and Norma Kamali, as well as successful and talented professionals in advertising, packaging, television, the design fields, merchandising, manufacturing, public relations, retailing, and more.

Founded in 1944, FIT is a college of art and design, business, and technology of the State University of New York. Seventeen majors offered through the School of Art and Design and ten through the School of Business and Technology lead to the A.A.S., B.F.A., or B.S. degrees. The School of Graduate Studies offers programs leading to the Master of Arts or Master of Professional Studies degree. FIT is an accredited institutional member of the Middle States Association of Colleges and Schools, the National Association of Schools of Art and Design, and the Foundation for Interior Design Education Research. The nine-building campus includes classrooms, studios, and labs that reflect the most advanced education and industrial practices. FIT recently opened a new dining center, featuring a wide variety of food stations and freshly prepared entrées. Below this facility is the college bookstore, Barnes & Noble at FIT. The Conference Center at FIT features the John E. Reeves Great Hall, a space suitable for conferences, fashion shows, lectures, and other events. FIT serves more than 6,500 full-time and 4,000 part-time students, who come not only from within commuting distances but also from around the nation and all over the world. Three dormitories serve approximately 1,250 students and offer a variety of accommodations. A fourth residence hall is scheduled to open in fall 2006. Student participation in campus life is encouraged through more than sixty campus clubs, numerous organizations, and several athletic teams.

With a consistent job placement rate of nearly 90 percent, FIT graduates are well prepared to meet employers' needs. Working with both undergraduates and graduates, placement counselors develop job opportunities for full-time, part-time, freelance, and summer employment.

Location

FIT's urban campus is situated amidst the culture and excitement of New York City. FIT's location in the heart of Manhattan on Seventh Avenue at 27th Street—where the worlds of fashion, art, design, communications, and marketing converge—permits an exceptional two-way flow between the college and the industries and professions it serves. Students are encouraged to participate in the cultural activities of New York, where opera, dance, theater, and the visual arts are readily accessible. All of FIT's programs and departments take full advantage of New York's special offerings.

Majors and Degrees

The college offers a two-year program leading to the Associate in Applied Science (A.A.S.) degree and upper-division programs leading to the Bachelor of Fine Arts (B.F.A.) or Bachelor of Science (B.S.) degree. Associate-level art and design majors are offered in accessories design, communication design, display and exhibit design, fash-

ion design, fine arts (with a career-exploration component), illustration, interior design, jewelry design, menswear, photography, and textile/surface design. In the business area, A.A.S. majors are offered in advertising and marketing communications, fashion merchandising management, patternmaking technology, production management: fashion and related industries, and textile development and marketing. Bachelor of Fine Arts degrees are awarded in accessories design and fabrication, advertising design, computer animation and interactive media, fabric styling, fashion design, fine arts, graphic design, illustration, interior design, packaging design, restoration, textile/surface design, and toy design. (Transfer students wishing to enter B.F.A. programs may have to complete the one-year A.A.S. program described below prior to entry into the upper division.) The Bachelor of Science degree is offered in advertising and marketing communications, cosmetics and fragrance marketing, direct marketing, fashion merchandising management, home products development, international trade and marketing for the fashion industries, production management: fashion and related industries, product management: textiles, and textile development and marketing. The B.S. program is open to students who hold an associate degree from the college or an equivalent degree from another accredited institution. Graduates of other accredited institutions of higher learning or transfer students who have a minimum of 30 transferable credits and can satisfy the liberal arts requirements may enter one-year A.A.S. programs in accessories design, advertising and marketing communications, communication design, fashion design, fashion merchandising management, jewelry design, textile development and marketing, and textile/surface design.

Academic Programs

Programs are designed to prepare students for creative and/or business careers in the fashion and related professions and industries. To qualify for the A.A.S., a student must be in degree status, satisfactorily complete the credit hours prescribed for a given major with approximately one third of all required credits in the liberal arts, achieve a minimum GPA of 2.0, and receive the recommendation of the faculty. To qualify for the B.S. or B.F.A., a student must be in degree status, satisfactorily complete the credit and course requirements prescribed by the major, and receive the recommendation of the faculty. A minimum of 60 approved credits is required; at least half of the credits required in the major area must be earned in residence at the upper-division level. If the student has an appropriate Fashion Institute of Technology associate degree, a minimum of 30 approved credits must be earned in residence at the upper-division level. Most majors offer internship programs in their courses of study.

Precollege programs (Saturday/Sunday Live) are available during the fall, spring, and summer. More than forty-five classes offer high school and middle school students the chance to learn in a studio environment, to explore the business and technological sides of the fashion industry, and to discover natural talents and creative abilities. Classes are taught by a faculty of artists, designers, and other professionals. High school credit may be earned at the discretion of each student's high school.

Off-Campus Programs

FIT's International Programs in Fashion Design and Fashion Merchandising Management/Florence and New York provide international experience for students interested in careers in the global fashion industry. Offered to full-time, matriculated FIT students as two distinct programs leading to the A.A.S. and B.F.A. degrees, the curricula are taught in both New York City and Florence, Italy, with students completing a year of study in each city.

Textile/surface design majors may apply for a semester abroad at the Winchester School of Art or Chelsea College of Art and Design near London, the Nova Scotia College of Art and Design in Halifax, or Shenkar College of Textiles and Fashions in Israel. Fashion merchandising management majors may apply for semester-abroad study in merchandising at RMIT in Australia, Manchester Metropolitan University or University of Westminster in England, American University of Rome, CSIS Program in Florence, or Hong Kong Polytechnic University. Seventh-semester advertising design students may study at the London College of Printing's School of Graphic Design, Chelsea College of Art and Design, or Nottingham Trent University in England; seventh-semester students may also study international trade and marketing at the American University in Rome or Middlesex University in London. Advertising and marketing communications students may study for a semester at American University in Rome; CSIS Program in Florence; Institute Commercial de Nancy or Université de Paris, La Sorbonne, in France; or Middlesex University in England. Selected upper-division students majoring in fashion design may study for one semester at Nottingham Trent University or Central St. Martins in England; at Esmod École Privée de Modélists-Stylistes in France; at RMIT in Australia; or at Hong Kong Polytechnic University. Graphic design students may study for a semester at Chelsea College of Art and Design, London College of Printing, or Nottingham Trent University. Brief off-campus courses are offered for credit during summer semesters and include fabric styling in Italy, fashion merchandising in London, fashion in France and Italy, international buying and marketing in Europe, and illustration in Italy.

Academic Facilities

A modern campus with outstanding facilities for studying all aspects of a dynamic industry, FIT comprises an entire city block in Manhattan's Chelsea neighborhood. The Fred P. Pomerantz Art and Design Center offers up-to-date facilities for design studies: photography studios with color and black-and-white darkrooms, painting rooms, a sculpture studio, a printmaking room, a graphics laboratory, display and exhibit design rooms, life-sketching rooms, and a model-making workshop. The Shirley Goodman Resource Center houses the Museum at FIT and the Library/Media Services, with references for history, sociology, technology, art, and literature; international journals and periodicals; sketchbooks and records donated by designers, manufacturers, and merchants; slides, tapes, and periodicals; and a voluminous clipping file. The Gladys Marcus Library houses more than 290,000 volumes, including books, periodicals, and nonprint materials. FIT also has many computer labs for student use. The Instructional Media Services Department provides audiovisual and TV support and a complete in-house TV studio. The Museum at FIT is the repository for one of the world's largest collections of fashion and textiles (with an emphasis on twentieth-century apparel), and is used by students, designers, and historians for research and inspiration. The museum's galleries provide a showcase for a wide spectrum of exhibitions relevant to fashion and its satellite industries. The annual student art and design exhibition is shown here, as are other student projects. Student work is also displayed throughout the campus. Fashion shows featuring the work of graduating B.F.A. students occur each academic year.

The Design/Research Lighting Laboratory, an educational and professional development facility for interior design and other academic disciplines, features more than 400 commercially available lighting fixtures controlled by a computer. The Peter G. Scotese Computer-Aided Design and Communications Facility provides art and design students with the opportunity to explore technology and its integration into the design of textiles, toys, interiors, fashion, and advertising as well as photography and computer graphics. Also located on the campus is the Annette Green/Fragrance Foundation Laboratory, an environment for the study of fragrance development.

Costs

An unusual program of sponsorship, shared by the city and State of New York, makes a comparatively low tuition rate possible. The 2004–05 tuition per semester for New York State residents was $1450 for associate-level programs and $2175 for baccalaureate programs; for out-of-state residents, it was $4350 for associate-level programs and $5150 for baccalaureate programs. Dormitory and meal plan fees were $3175 per semester. Student fees were $145, books and supplies were $700, and personal expenses were about $500. Costs are subject to change.

Financial Aid

The Fashion Institute of Technology attempts to remove financial barriers to college entrance by providing scholarships, grants, loans, and work-study employment for students in financial need. Sixty-five per-cent of full-time, undergraduate, degree-seeking students who applied for financial aid in fall 2005 received some type of financial aid. The college directly administers its own institutional grants and scholarships, which are provided by the Educational Foundation for the Fashion Industries. College-administered federal funding includes Federal Pell Grants, Federal Supplemental Educational Opportunity Grants, Federal Perkins Loans, Federal Work-Study Program awards, and the Federal Family Educational Loan Program, which includes student and parent loans. New York State residents who meet state guidelines for eligibility may also receive TAP and/or Educational Opportunity Program grants. The college tries to meet students' needs by awarding a financial aid package from institutional scholarships and federal grants, loans, and Federal Work-Study Program awards. Financial aid applicants must file the Free Application for Federal Student Aid (FAFSA), on which they apply for the Federal Pell Grant, and should also apply to all available outside sources of aid. Other documentation must be requested from the Financial Aid Office. Applications for financial aid should be completed prior to February 15 for fall admission or prior to November 1 for spring admission.

Faculty

Those who do, teach at FIT. Members of the FIT faculty have considerable experience and are at the forefront of their various fields and industries.

Student Government

The Student Council, the governing body of the Student Association, gives all students the privileges and responsibilities of citizens in a self-governing college community. Many faculty committees include student representatives, and the president of the student government sits on FIT's Board of Trustees.

Admission Requirements

Applicants for admission must be candidates for or hold either a high school diploma or the General Educational Development certificate. Candidates are judged on class rank, grades in college-preparatory course work, and the student essay. Letters of recommendation from teachers and counselors are considered but not required. A portfolio evaluation is required for art and design majors only. Specific portfolio requirements are explained on FIT's Web site.

Transfer students from regionally accredited colleges must submit official transcripts for credit evaluation. Students can qualify for one-year A.A.S. programs if they hold a baccalaureate degree or if they have a minimum of 30 transferable credits from an accredited college, including a minimum of 24 credits that are equivalent to FIT's liberal arts requirements.

Students seeking admission to one of the upper-division majors leading to the Bachelor of Fine Arts or Bachelor of Science degree must hold an Associate in Applied Science degree from FIT or an equivalent degree from an accredited and approved college. They must also meet the appropriate prerequisites as required by the major and have completed FIT's liberal arts requirements. Further requirements may include an individual interview with a departmental committee, review of academic standing, and portfolio review for all applicants to B.F.A. programs. Any student who applies for transfer to FIT from a four-year program must have completed a minimum of 60 credits, including the requisite art or technical courses and the liberal arts requirements.

Application and Information

Candidates who have graduated from a New York State high school should obtain applications from their high school guidance office. Candidates from out-of-state high schools should obtain applications from FIT's Web site or by writing to the Office of Admissions.

Office of Admissions
Fashion Institute of Technology
Seventh Avenue at 27th Street
New York, New York 10001-5992
Telephone: 212-217-7675
            800-GO-TO-FIT (toll-free)
E-mail: fitinfo@fitnyc.edu
World Wide Web: http://www.fitnyc.edu

FIVE TOWNS COLLEGE
DIX HILLS, NEW YORK

The College

Located on Long Island's North Shore, Five Towns College offers students the opportunity to study in a suburban environment that is close to New York City. Founded in 1972, Five Towns College is an independent, nonsectarian, coeducational institution that places its emphasis on the student as an individual. Many students are drawn to the College because of its strong reputation in music, media, and the performing arts. The College offers associate, bachelor's, master's, and doctoral degrees. The College also offers programs leading to the Master of Music (M.M.) degree in jazz/commercial music and in music education as well as a master's in elementary education (M.S.Ed.) and a doctorate in musical arts (D.M.A.).

From as far away as England and Japan and from as close as Long Island and New York City, the 1,000 full-time students reflect a rich cultural diversity. The College's enrollment is 55 percent men and 45 percent women, with a minority population of approximately 34 percent. The College's music programs are contemporary jazz in nature, although classical musicians are also part of this creative community. The most popular programs are audio recording technology, broadcasting, journalism, music performance, music business, music and elementary teacher education, theater, and film/video production.

Coeducational living accommodations are available on campus. The Five Towns College Living/Learning Center is a brand-new complex containing modern dormitories. Each residence hall contains single- and double-occupancy rooms equipped with private bathrooms, broadband Internet access, cable television, and other amenities.

Location

The College's beautiful 40-acre campus, located in the wooded countryside of Dix Hills, New York, provides students with a parklike refuge where they can pursue their studies. Just off campus is Long Island's bustling Route 110 corridor, the home of numerous national and multinational corporations. New York City, with everything from Lincoln Center to Broadway, is just a train ride away and provides students with some of the best cultural advantages in the world.

Closer to campus, the many communities of Long Island abound with cultural and recreational opportunities. The College is located within the historic town of Huntington, which is home to the Cinema Arts Center, InterMedia Arts Center, Hecksher Museum, Vanderbilt Museum, numerous restaurants, coffeehouses, and quaint shops. The nearby shores of Jones Beach State Park and the Fire Island National Seashore are world renowned for their white, sandy beaches.

Majors and Degrees

The College offers the Associate in Arts (A.A.) degree in liberal arts, with concentrations in literature and theater arts; the Associate in Science (A.S.) degree in business administration; the Associate in Applied Science (A.A.S.) degree in business management and in jazz commercial music, with concentrations in audio recording technology, broadcasting, computer business applications, marketing/retailing, music business, and video arts; the Bachelor of Music (Mus.B.) degree in music education and in jazz/commercial music, with concentrations in audio recording technology, composition/songwriting, music business, musical theater, performance, and video music; the Bachelor of Fine Arts (B.F.A.) degree in theater, with concentrations in acting and mu-

sical theater; the Bachelor of Professional Studies (B.P.S.) degree in business management, with concentrations in audio recording technology, music business, and video arts; and the Bachelor of Science (B.S.) in childhood education, with concentrations in an elective program, music, and theater. A Bachelor of Science (B.S.) in mass communication features broadcasting and journalism concentrations.

Academic Programs

The following describes some of the more popular programs at Five Towns College. For a complete description of the College's academic program, students should visit the Five Towns College Web site at the address listed below.

The music education program is designed for students interested in a career as a teacher of music in a public or private school. The undergraduate program leads to New York State provisional certification, while the graduate program leads to permanent certification. The course work provides professional training and includes a student-teaching experience. Music students are required to complete at least 40 credits, achieve a GPA of at least 3.0, and pass a piano qualifying examination before being admitted to this program. The audio recording technology concentration is designed to provide students with the tools needed to succeed as professional studio engineers and producers in the music industry. The music business concentration is designed for students interested in a career in entertainment-related business fields. The course work includes the technical, legal, production, management, and merchandising aspects of the music business. The composition/songwriting concentration provides intensive instruction in a core of technical studies in harmony, orchestration, counterpoint, MIDI, songwriting, form and analysis, arranging, and composition for those who intend to pursue careers as composers, arrangers, and songwriters. The performance concentration includes a common core of technical studies and a foundation of specialized courses, such as music history, harmony, counterpoint, improvisation, ensemble performance, and private instruction. The video music concentration includes professional training in music scoring and compositional techniques and in the artistic and technical skills required for the creation of synchronized music. The theater arts program is designed for students interested in careers as actors, entertainers, scenic designers, directors, stage managers, and lighting or sound directors. The film/video concentration includes extensive technical preparation in videography, filmmaking, linear and nonlinear editing, storyboarding, scriptwriting, producing, and directing for filmmakers and videographers. Elementary education students are prepared as teachers for grades 1–6, while those interested in journalism and broadcasting are prepared for careers in radio, television, newspaper, and editorial writing.

To earn a bachelor's degree, students must accumulate between 120 and 128 credits, depending upon the program of study, with a proper distribution of courses and a GPA of at least 2.0. To earn an associate degree, students must accumulate between 60 and 64 credits.

Off-Campus Programs

Off-campus internship opportunities are available to Five Towns College students who have fulfilled the necessary prerequisites, including a cumulative grade point average of at least 2.5., with a 3.0 in their major. In recent semesters, students have interned for major corporations such as MTV, Atlantic Records, Polygram

Records, CBS, ABC, EMI Records, MCA Records, SONY Records, The Power Station, Pyramid Recording Studios, Channel 12 News, and many others.

Academic Facilities

Five Towns College occupies a multiwinged facility that comprises approximately 120,000 square feet and includes a 500-seat auditorium, production studios, athletic and dining facilities, classrooms, PC and Mac computer labs, and a student center. T-3 lines connect the College's completely fiber-optic computer network to the Internet. All students have access to this network and are provided with an e-mail account.

The Five Towns College Library has more than 35,000 print and nonprint materials. These include nearly 30,000 books and print items, 464 periodical subscriptions, and approximately 5,000 records, 2,500 videos and DVDs, and more than 2,000 CDs. Through its membership in the Long Island Library Resource Council (LILRC), students have access to other libraries around the country.

The Technical Wing at Five Towns College consists of eleven studio/control rooms. These facilities house the College's state-of-the-art 72-channel SL9000J audio board, 48-track SSL and 24-track digital recording studios and the Electronic Music-MIDI Studio. The Film/Video Studio utilizes Beta Sp, SVHS video formats, and the 16mm film format. Nonlinear edit suites utilize the Media 100 XS and XR operating systems on Macintosh G4 platforms. Students utilize these facilities to develop their skills while creating professional quality productions, both in the studio and on location, under the supervision of industry professionals. Student productions include CDs, music videos, documentaries, sitcoms, public service announcements, commercials, and talk shows, among many others.

The Dix Hills Center for Performing Arts at Five Towns College is an acoustically "perfect" venue, with digital lighting systems, digital sound reinforcement for concert production, and a Barco 6300 digital projection system for multimedia productions. The professional stage is 60 feet wide, with a proscenium opening of 16 feet and 32 feet of fly space. Students utilize this facility to produce live concerts, plays, musicals, and other performances and special presentations.

Costs

The tuition for 2004–05 was $13,200 per year. Miscellaneous fees cost approximately $400, and books cost about $700. Private instruction fees for performing music students are $675 per semester.

Financial Aid

The annual tuition at Five Towns College is among the lowest of all the private colleges in the region. Nevertheless, approximately 68 percent of all students receive some form of financial assistance. Need-based and/or merit-based grants, scholarships, loans, and work-study programs are available to qualified recipients, including transfer students. Prospective students are urged to contact the Financial Aid Office as early as possible.

Faculty

The College's growing faculty consists of 125 full- and part-time members. The student-faculty ratio is 13:1. While the faculty is more strongly committed to teaching than to research, many members continue to be active in their respective areas of expertise.

Student Government

The Student Council (SC) serves as the representative governance body for all students. The SC consists of an elected president and vice president and 9 elected at-large representatives who select from among themselves a secretary and a treasurer.

The Student Council charters clubs and organizations, allocates student activity fees, and recommends policies that affect student life. There is also a Dormitory Council.

Admission Requirements

The College encourages applications from students who will engage themselves in its creative community and who will contribute to the academic debate with honor and integrity. Students seeking a seat in the entering class of students should have attained a minimum high school grade point average of 78 percent. The SAT I or ACT exam is required for all freshmen. Transfer students must also submit official transcripts of all college-level work attempted. International students from non-English-speaking countries must submit a TOEFL score of at least 500 or its equivalent. Students may be admitted for deferred entrance or with advanced standing. The College does not accept students on an early admissions basis, although early decision is available. Candidates for admission must submit a completed Application for Undergraduate Admission, official high school transcripts, at least two letters of recommendation, and a personal statement. International students must submit additional information and should contact the Foreign Student Advisor.

Application and Information

Admission into any music program is contingent upon passing an audition demonstrating skill in performance on a major instrument or vocally. Music students must also take written and aural examinations in harmony, sight singing, and ear training in order to demonstrate talent, well-developed musicianship, and artistic sensibilities. Admission into any theater program is also contingent upon passing an audition. In some cases, the Admissions Committee may request an on-campus interview with an applicant. Music, theater, and film/video students are encouraged to submit a portfolio tape or reel, if available.

Except for applicants applying on an early decision basis, new students are accepted on a rolling basis, with decisions for the fall and spring semesters mailed starting February 15 and October 15, respectively. There is an application fee of $35.

For further information, students should contact:

Director of Admissions
Five Towns College
305 North Service Road
Dix Hills, New York 11746-5871
Telephone: 631-424-7000 Ext. 2110
Fax: 631-656-2172
E-mail: admissions@ftc.edu
World Wide Web: http://www.ftc.edu

Five Towns College Studio A.

FORDHAM UNIVERSITY
NEW YORK, NEW YORK

The University

Fordham, New York City's Jesuit University, offers a distinctive educational experience that is rooted in the 450-year-old Jesuit tradition of intellectual rigor and personal respect for the individual. The University enrolls approximately 15,000 students, of whom 8,000 are undergraduates.

Fordham has five undergraduate colleges and six graduate schools. In addition to its full-time undergraduate programs, the University offers part-time undergraduate study at Fordham College of Liberal Studies and during two summer sessions.

Fordham College at Rose Hill and the College of Business Administration, located on the Rose Hill campus, are adjacent to the New York Botanical Garden and the Bronx Zoo. Rose Hill is a self-contained 85-acre campus with residential facilities for more than 3,000 students and ample parking for commuters. It is easily accessible by public and private transportation. Fordham also provides an intercampus van service to transport students to and from Manhattan. Fordham College at Lincoln Center is located in midtown Manhattan, overlooking the famous Lincoln Center for the Performing Arts complex. The Lincoln Center campus has a new 850-bed apartment-style residence called McMahon Hall, and is accessible via the West Side Highway and major subway lines.

In July 2002, Fordham added a third residential campus when Marymount College in Tarrytown, New York, consolidated with Fordham to form a new undergraduate college for women. Located in the historic village of Tarrytown and overlooking the Hudson River, the beautiful 25-acre Marymount campus of Fordham University is located just 25 miles north of New York City. Fordham and Marymount have enjoyed a relationship since 1975 when Marymount campus became home to Fordham's Graduate School of Education and Graduate School of Social Service.

The University has an extensive athletics program consisting of twenty-two varsity sports and numerous club and intramural sports. The newly renovated Murphy Field is the heart of intramural and recreational sports at Fordham, hosting softball, soccer, and flag football games. The Vincent T. Lombardi Memorial Center provides sports facilities to the campus for basketball, squash, swimming and diving, tennis, track, and water polo.

Location

As New York City's Jesuit University, Fordham can offer its students the unparalleled cultural, recreational, and academic advantages of one of the world's great cities. More than 2,600 corporations and organizations offer valuable work experience to Fordham interns. The University also provides unusual opportunities for participating in activities of direct service to the city, ranging from small-group community projects to large government-sponsored projects.

Majors and Degrees

Fordham University offers undergraduates more than sixty-five majors. Fordham College at Rose Hill offers programs of study leading to the B.A. or B.S. in African and African-American studies, anthropology, art history, biological sciences, chemistry, classical civilization, classical languages (Latin and Greek),

communication and media studies, comparative literature, computer and information sciences, economics, English, fine arts, French language and literature, French studies, general science, German, German studies, history, information systems, international political economy, Italian, Italian studies, Latin American and Latino studies, mathematics, mathematics/economics, medieval studies, Middle East studies, music, philosophy, physics, political science, psychology, religious studies, Russian and East European studies, sociology, Spanish language and literature, Spanish studies, theology, urban studies, and women's studies.

Also at the Rose Hill campus, the College of Business Administration offers programs leading to the B.S. in accounting (public or management), business administration, and management of information and communication systems, with areas of concentration in business economics, finance, human resource management, information and communications systems, management systems, and marketing. The G.L.O.B.E. Program provides business students with an international study option that incorporates course offerings from both Fordham College at Rose Hill and the College of Business Administration.

Special programs at Rose Hill include a cooperative engineering program, double major or individualized majors, interdisciplinary studies, the B.S./M.B.A. program, and honors programs. Preprofessional programs are offered in architecture, dentistry, law, medicine, and veterinary medicine, and a program for teacher certification is offered in elementary and secondary education.

Fordham College at Lincoln Center offers the B.A. in African and African American studies, anthropology, art history, classical civilization, classical languages (Latin and Greek), communication and media studies, comparative literature, computer science, economics, English, French language and literature, French studies, history, information systems, international/intercultural studies, Italian, Italian studies, Latin American and Latino studies, mathematics, mathematics/economics, medieval studies, Middle East studies, natural science, philosophy, political science, psychology, religious studies, social science, social work, sociology, Spanish language and literature, Spanish studies, theater, theology, urban studies, visual arts, and women's studies. Special programs at Fordham College at Lincoln Center include extensive offerings in the performing arts (including a B.F.A. in dance with the Alvin Ailey Dance Company), a cooperative engineering program, creative writing, double major or individualized majors, independent study, and interdisciplinary studies. Preprofessional studies are offered in dentistry, health, and law. A teacher certification program is offered in elementary and secondary education.

Academic Programs

Students in all the undergraduate colleges pursue a common core curriculum designed to provide them with the breadth of knowledge that marks the educated person. Drawn from nine disciplines, the core includes the study of philosophy, English composition and literature, history, theology, mathematical reasoning, natural science, social sciences, the fine arts, and foreign language. Business students benefit from the common core as well as from additional business core courses.

Off-Campus Programs

Fordham participates in an exchange program with other major U.S. universities and in special programs that provide opportunities to study abroad at universities in Australia, China, El Salvador, England, Ireland, Italy, Korea, Mexico, Spain, and many other countries. More than 250 Fordham students study abroad each year. Fordham also offers international community-service trips through its global outreach program.

Academic Facilities

The outstanding libraries on the two campuses have combined holdings of more than 1.8 million volumes and 14,000 periodicals. On the Rose Hill campus, the William D. Walsh Family Library, which serves the entire Fordham community, has seating for more than 1,500 and a state-of-the-art Electronic Information Center, as well as media production laboratories, studios, and auditoriums. Students also have access to the vast library facilities of New York City, neighboring universities, and the various specialized collections maintained by numerous local museums and other institutions. Among laboratory facilities utilized by undergraduates are Mulcahy Hall (chemistry), Larkin Hall (biology), and Freeman Hall (physics and biology). The University has more than forty buildings that provide ample space for classrooms, science laboratories, theaters, and athletic facilities.

Costs

At the Rose Hill and Lincoln Center campuses, undergraduate costs for the 2004–05 academic year were $26,200 for tuition and fees and averaged $10,000 for room and board. Residence halls are available at each campus. Chemistry, physics, and biology fees were approximately $50 per laboratory course. Nominally priced meals are available in cafeterias on each campus. Such incidentals as transportation and laundry vary in cost. There is no difference in fees for out-of-state students.

Financial Aid

More than 75 percent of the entering students enroll with aid Fordham as well as from outside sources. Among the n. aid programs are the Federal Pell Grants, Federal Sup ntal Educational Opportunity Grants, Federal Perkins Loans, grants sponsored by both the government and the Universi d University grants-in-aid. Outside sources of aid include sta holarships (more than 20,000 are awarded to students ente colleges in New York State each year), the New York State Tuition Assistance Program (TAP), privately sponsored scho hips, state government loan programs, and deferred-payme programs. The University also offers academic scholars ranging from $7500 to the full cost of tuition and room.

Applicants for must submit the Free Application for Federal Student Aid (F A) and the College Scholarship Service (CSS) PROFILE. Inq s should be directed to Fordham's Office of Undergradua Admission or Office of Student Financial Services.

Faculty

The University has a full-time faculty of 625 and a student-faculty ratio of 11:1. Most members of the undergraduate faculty also teach at the graduate level, and 97 percent of the full-time faculty members hold doctoral or other terminal degrees.

Student Government

The traditional student governing body at Fordham has been the United Student Government, composed of undergraduates attending the University.

Admission Requirements

Admission is based on academic performance, class rank (if available), secondary school recommendation, and SAT I or ACT scores. Extracurricular activities and essays are also factors in the evaluation process. Religious preference, physical handicap, race, or ethnic origin are not considered. Out-of-state students are encouraged to apply. More than 70 percent of the students accepted for the freshman class ranked in the top fifth of their secondary school class. The average combined SAT I score for students entering in fall 2004 was approximately 1240. Recommended are 22 high school units, including 4 in English, 3 in mathematics, 3 in science, 2 in social studies, 2 in foreign language, 2 in history, and 6 electives. For regular admission, the SAT I or the ACT should be taken no later than the January preceding entrance. Candidates for early action should complete the examinations by October of their senior year. The University participates in the College Board's Advanced Placement Program. Personal interviews are not required but may be arranged by contacting the Office of Undergraduate Admission.

Application and Information

Application may be made for either September or January enrollment. The application deadline is February 1 for fall admission. The completed application, the secondary school report, the results of the SAT I or ACT, all financial aid forms, and an application fee of $50 (check or money order made payable to Fordham University) should be submitted by this date. Students are notified beginning April 1. Candidates for early action should apply by November 1 and receive notification by December 25. Transfer students must apply by December 1 for spring admission or by July 1 for fall admission.

For additional details and application forms, students should contact:

Fordham University
Office of Undergraduate Admission
Thebaud Hall
441 East Fordham Road
New York, New York 10458-9993

Telephone: 800-FORDHAM (367-3426) (toll-free)
E-mail: enroll@fordham.edu
World Wide Web: http://www.fordham.edu

The William D. Walsh Family Library at Fordham University.

HARTWICK COLLEGE
ONEONTA, NEW YORK

HARTWICK
est. 1797

The College

Hartwick College, a private college located in the northern foothills of the Catskill Mountain region of New York State, was founded in 1797 as the first Lutheran seminary in America. Hartwick became a four-year coeducational liberal arts and sciences college under its current charter in 1928 and separated from the Lutheran Church in 1968. The current enrollment is 1,450 students (42 percent men and 58 percent women).

Approximately 60 percent of Hartwick's students come from New York State, and about 40 percent come from elsewhere in the Northeast or from outside the Northeast. The student body represents thirty-six states and thirty countries. The majority of students live on campus and eat together in the College Commons. Residence halls are coeducational by floor or wing. As an alternative to downtown living, the College has twenty self-contained town houses on campus that house 80 students. Each two-story unit has one double and two single bedrooms, two baths, a living room, a study area, and a kitchen. About 100 students live in the five fraternity and four sorority houses. Other off-campus housing includes facilities at the Pine Lake Environmental Campus.

There are approximately sixty student clubs and organizations on campus. A variety of social and cultural events, including special weekends, are offered throughout the academic year.

More than three quarters of the students participate in recreational, intramural, or intercollegiate sports. Hartwick is well known for its NCAA Division I men's soccer program, and its NCAA Division I women's water polo team is the premier team in the East. Women's track and field and field hockey and men's and women's basketball, lacrosse, and swimming are also successful programs among the College's twenty-four intercollegiate sports.

The Career Services Office begins working with first-year students in developing career goals and helps students find internships (most often for academic credit) related to their academic and career interests throughout their time at Hartwick. The office also coordinates MetroLink, an award-winning program that connects students with Hartwick alumni and parents for shadow experiences and career networking. MetroLink is conducted in New York City, Boston, and Washington, D.C.

Hartwick continues to provide every student with a powerful notebook computer, printer, and software that is ready to link to Hartwick's campus network. Technology is integrated into the daily life of the College—in the classroom, library, and residence halls.

Location

The city of Oneonta, with a population of 14,000, is a college town. Hartwick College and the State University of New York College at Oneonta are located in the city. Students have access to the libraries on both campuses, and cross-registration for courses is also possible. Hartwick College is an integral part of the Oneonta community, and many area residents share in campus activities. Oneonta has a variety of shops, restaurants, and theaters. Many cultural and recreational resources exist in the city and throughout the area, including the Catskill Symphony Orchestra, the Catskill Choral Society, the Orpheus Theatre, several ski centers, city and state parks, golf courses, tennis courts, and lakes. Oneonta is also home to the National Soccer Hall of Fame and is near Cooperstown, the site of the National Baseball Hall of Fame.

Majors and Degrees

Hartwick students may select courses from thirty majors and forty minors offered by nineteen departments. They may pursue independent study or create an individual student program, or they may take advantage of numerous special study options on and off campus available through Hartwick and cooperating educational insti-

tutions. Hartwick awards the B.S. degree in accounting, biochemistry, chemistry, computer science, environmental chemistry, information science, medical technology, music education, and nursing. It awards the B.A. degree in anthropology, art, art history, biology, chemistry, economics, English, French, geological and environmental sciences, German, history, management, mathematics, music, philosophy, physics, political science, psychology, religious studies, sociology, Spanish, and theater arts. An accelerated B.A./B.S. option is available.

Twenty-two teacher certification programs are offered in adolescence, childhood, and middle childhood education in English languages, mathematics, science, social studies, and K–12 music. Preprofessional programs in engineering are offered in cooperation with Clarkson University and with Columbia University School of Engineering and Applied Science. Hartwick also participates in a cooperative 4+1 M.B.A./M.S. program with Clarkson University, a 3+3 cooperative program with Albany Law School, a collaborative agreement in physical and occupational therapy with Sage Graduate School, and a Partnership for Nursing Opportunities Program with Bassett Healthcare. Nursing students, upon graduation, are qualified to take the New York State Board Examination for licensure as registered professional nurses. Students graduating with a medical technology major are qualified to take the National Registry Examination for the professional certification MT (ASCP).

Academic Programs

Hartwick's distinctive Liberal Arts in Practice approach connects liberal arts education with practical experiences. Hartwick breaks down the boundaries that separate the classroom from the world, so students learn by going out into the real world and bringing the real world back to the classroom. A Hartwick education is not about memorizing facts: it's about creating knowledge and developing skills that last a lifetime. A Hartwick education happens in small classes taught by professors who make teaching their first priority. Hartwick's learning-by-doing approach has proven highly successful in producing engaged citizens and successful professionals who can apply their knowledge to practical problems. Independent study, internships, study abroad, and research are integral parts of the curriculum.

The College's calendar consists of two 15-week terms and one 4-week term in January. Hartwick's January Term allows students to participate in an internship, travel abroad, or take one intensive course during the month.

Hartwick College grants credit for College Board Advanced Placement test scores of 4 or higher in biology, chemistry, economics (micro or macro), and psychology. Credit is granted for AP test scores of 3 or higher in all other subject areas. AP scores must be submitted to the College Registrar's Office for credit. Advanced placement for credit is also offered through the College-Level Examination Program (CLEP) to students who have acquired mastery of a subject in ways other than the traditional classroom experience.

Off-Campus Programs

Hartwick has recently been ranked among the top twenty liberal arts colleges in the nation for the percentage of students who engage in study-abroad programs. Hartwick offers numerous opportunities for off-campus study. Some of the programs in which students participated in January Term 2005 included Culture, History, and Ecology of South Africa; Plants and People of Thailand; Art in Italy; Imagined Communities in France; Literary Ireland; Golden Prague; German Term in Vienna; Enchanted Spain; Island Biogeography in the Bahamas; Transcultural Nursing in Jamaica; 21st Century Puerto Rico; Transnational Solidarity in Mexico; and Geology and Natural History of Hawaii.

Academic Facilities

Hartwick's Science Center recently received a $12-million renovation and addition that provide shared spaces for cross-disciplinary teaching and student/faculty research. The facility includes new classrooms and laboratories, a tissue-culture lab, a greenhouse, an herbarium, a cold room, a biotechnology "clean lab," a science communications center and graphics imaging lab, a nursing lab and resource room, and a dark room. Clark Hall is home to English, the Writing Center, foreign languages, psychology, education, and the Technology Services Center. Yager Hall houses the College's 300,000-volume library; the Sondhi Limthongkul Center for Independence, which coordinates Hartwick's study-abroad and off-campus programs; the Yager Museum; the College's archives; classrooms; a computing lab; and laboratory and office space. The Yager Collection contains more than 6,000 American Indian artifacts, covering a period of 10,000 years. It is one of the largest and most important collections of its kind in New York State. Arnold and Bresee Halls contain classrooms, faculty and administrative offices, and a black box theater. The Anderson Center for the Arts is a contemporary building that houses the fine and performing arts. The center includes studios and classrooms, soundproof practice rooms, a theater, and the Foreman Gallery. The Binder Physical Education Center provides facilities for recreation; physical education classes; intramural, club, and intercollegiate sports; a fitness center; a strength-training facility; and the Moyer Pool. The Pine Lake Environmental Campus, a 920-acre site 8 miles from the main campus, offers student housing and serves as an important resource for environmental study and recreation. The Ernest B. Wright 16-inch Telescope and Observatory is located at the top of Hartwick's multitiered campus.

Costs

Tuition and fees and for 2004–05 were $28,105, room was $3840, and board was $3440. The estimated cost of books, personal expenses, and transportation is $1400.

Financial Aid

Hartwick College grants financial aid on the basis of both academic merit and financial need. A large number of scholarships based on merit are awarded annually to prospective students, including transfers, and are based upon outstanding academic achievement and leadership in high school and/or college. The average amount of a financial aid award to first-year students is approximately $17,000. Approximately 78 percent of Hartwick students receive some form of aid.

Students requesting financial aid must file a Hartwick College financial aid application with the College and submit the Free Application for Federal Student Aid (FAFSA). The deadline is February 15. All forms should be mailed by early January. Some work opportunities are also available for students not receiving financial aid.

Faculty

Hartwick has 144 faculty members (101 are full-time). The Hartwick faculty is a teaching faculty, with principal responsibilities and commitments to students in the classroom. Faculty members serve as student advisers, share committee assignments with students and staff members, and act as advisers to student organizations. The student-faculty ratio is 12:1. Ninety-four percent of the faculty members hold the Ph.D. or other terminal degrees.

Student Government

The Student Senate serves as the central voice of the student body and carries out executive and legislative functions of the Hartwick College student government. Students share responsibilities with faculty members, administrators, and trustees on a number of committees established by the faculty and Board of Trustees, as well as on the Judicial Board and the College Traffic Court.

Admission Requirements

Hartwick College seeks secondary school graduates who demonstrate academic competence and show evidence of being able to benefit from, and take full advantage of, the living and learning experience at Hartwick. Applicants are evaluated not only on class rank and test scores but also on personal qualities, activities, special talents, and recommendations. Applicants are required to submit a secondary school transcript, an essay, and one recommendation. Transfer students must submit official transcripts of work at other institutions, a secondary school transcript, and a letter of recommendation from an official of the college previously attended. On-campus interviews and scores on the SAT or ACT are strongly recommended for all applicants but are not required.

Application and Information

Applications for regular admission must be filed by February 15 in the year of expected college entrance in the fall. Requests for an early decision may be made by November 15 for early decision I and January 15 for early decision II of the year of entrance. Admission decisions for early decision are made within three weeks after the early decision application deadline. Regular decision candidates are notified on or about March 15. A nonrefundable fee of $35 must accompany the application. The College accepts the Common Application and online applications (on the College's Web site).

Prospective students may obtain application forms and additional information by contacting:

Office of Admissions
Hartwick College
Oneonta, New York 13820
Telephone: 607-431-4150
        888-HARTWICK (toll-free)
E-mail: admissions@hartwick.edu
World Wide Web: http://www.hartwick.edu

A view of the campus at Hartwick College.

HILBERT COLLEGE
HAMBURG, NEW YORK

The College

Since its founding in 1957, Hilbert College has provided challenging academic programs and close personal attention to its students. The College is an independent, Catholic, four-year institution that grants degrees on both the baccalaureate and associate levels. There is a strong commitment to the philosophy of a liberal arts education being the cornerstone of any Hilbert graduate's success. In harmony with its Franciscan Spirit, the College provides individual counseling and support services for students whose diversified needs are best met in this small-college setting. Hilbert's campus consists of nine buildings: Bogel Hall, which is the academic building; the Francis J. and Marie McGrath Library; the Campus Center; three on-campus residence halls; one traditional-style and two apartment-style facilities; a grounds and maintenance building; the Hafner Recreation Center; and Franciscan Hall, which is the student services and administration building. Hilbert is also home to the Institute for Law and Justice, a local, regional, and national resource for law enforcement, crime prevention, and community well-being.

Hilbert College has a student body of approximately 1,100 students. There is an on-campus residential population of 160 students; Hilbert College offers students both a traditional-style residence hall, and four new apartment-style facilities. All students are offered myriad social activities ranging from academic and student clubs to NCAA Division III athletics. Student government takes an active role in the planning and operation of most campus events. Hilbert also offers a select comprehensive Leadership Development Program as well as an Honors Program.

The College's Division III athletics program offers intercollegiate competition in men's baseball, basketball, cross-country, golf, soccer, and volleyball. Women's sports include basketball, cross-country, soccer, softball, and volleyball. Hilbert College competes as a member of the Allegheny Mountain Collegiate Conference. In addition, cheerleading, lacrosse, bowling, and hockey all compete as club-level sports.

Location

Hilbert College's nearly 50-acre campus is located in the town of Hamburg in western New York State on the shore of Lake Erie. The campus is approximately 15 miles south of Buffalo, a city of 350,000 people. Hilbert's proximity to Buffalo makes many cultural and recreational resources easily accessible to its students. Downtown attractions include Kleinhans Music Hall, Studio Arena Theatre, the Albright-Knox Art Gallery, the Museum of Science, and the Buffalo Zoo. The historic Shea's Theatre is also located downtown and is Buffalo's home to many concerts, operas, and Broadway shows. Niagara Falls, one of the nation's greatest natural attractions, is just a 35-minute drive from the campus. Buffalo also provides professional sports in football, hockey, lacrosse, and triple-A baseball. Hamburg also is located a short distance from several cross-country and downhill ski resorts.

Majors and Degrees

Hilbert College offers programs of study leading to a Bachelor of Arts (B.A.) degree in communication studies, English, liberal studies (law and government), and psychology. The Bachelor of

Science (B.S.) degree is offered in accounting, business administration, criminal justice, economic crime investigation, human services, paralegal studies, and rehabilitation studies. The College also offers associate degree programs (A.A. and A.A.S.) in accounting, banking, business administration, criminal justice, human services, liberal arts, management information systems, and paralegal studies.

Academic Programs

The Bachelor of Arts and Bachelor of Science degrees are granted upon completion of 120 credit hours.

The Associate in Arts, the Associate in Applied Science, and the Associate in Science degrees are all granted upon successful completion of 60 credit hours.

Common to all programs is the completion of the Liberal Learning Core Curriculum. All students must fulfill the following graduation requirements: advanced communication skills, intercultural awareness, responsible local and global citizenship, an array of inquiry strategies, advanced research skills, the capacity for integrative learning, and a commitment to lifelong learning. The purpose of the Liberal Learning Core Curriculum is to provide students with a cumulative, holistic liberal arts education to complement and strengthen their professional training. The curriculum is designed to develop habits of critical examination, methods of critical investigation, and ethical perspectives that enable students to make sound judgments and increase their capacity for leading fuller lives. By studying the various liberal arts disciplines, students should achieve a greater awareness of their cultural and social identity while cultivating the intellectual skills and competence that allow them to perform successfully in their chosen careers.

Hilbert has developed a series of transfer articulation agreements with most two-year colleges in New York State. These agreements allow two-year college graduates to move directly into related four-year programs at Hilbert College as full juniors and with no course duplication. In addition, Hilbert is accredited by the Commission on Higher Education of the Middle States Association of Colleges and Schools. Therefore, its credits are readily transferable nationwide to other four-year colleges and universities.

Academic Facilities

Bogel Hall, the academic building, contains the Palisano Lecture Hall, faculty offices, two computer labs, a hands-on economic crime investigation computer lab, the Academic Services Center, the chapel, and most classroom space.

McGrath Library, an expansive building consisting of a two-level core housing the library collection, a seminar wing, and a conference wing, maintains a collection approaching 40,000 volumes, more than 340 periodicals, and a large selection of microforms and audio and video materials. The first floor houses the reference, index, and periodical collections. Computer workstations with the library catalog and numerous full-text databases, which enormously supplement the periodical collection, are also available on this floor. The circulating book collection begins on this level and continues in the stacks located on the second floor. The second level primarily houses the McGrath Library Law Collection in support of the paralegal studies and law and government programs on the campus. This collection ranks as one of the largest academic law collections open to the public in western New York State. The library's seminar wing has video-equipped classrooms and a legal research lab. Ample study space is available throughout the library with both private carrels and group-study tables available for student use.

Costs

For 2004–05, tuition and fees were $14,300, and room and board were $5505. The approximate cost for books and supplies is $700 and for travel and miscellaneous expenses, $1000.

Financial Aid

Ninety-two percent of the members of the current freshman class receive financial aid. Financial aid packages consist of loans, scholarships, grants, and jobs. Most awards are provided on the basis of need, as established by the Free Application for Federal Student Aid (FAFSA), and as funds are available. There are several merit-based scholarships for academic and leadership talents as well as transfer articulation and minority scholarships.

Faculty

Hilbert has a faculty of 87 men and women. Sixty-four percent of the faculty members hold doctoral or terminal degrees; 36 percent hold master's degrees. The student-faculty ratio is 14:1, with an average class size of 25.

Student Government

The largest student organization on campus is the Student Government Association (SGA). Headed by student-elected officers, this representative organization acts on the behalf of the entire student body. The SGA administers student funds to sponsor on-campus activities and events that range from intimate concerts to larger campuswide festivities. The SGA is composed of two bodies, the association and the student senate. The association comprises elected students who represent the needs of different classes, residents, and commuters. The student senate is a smaller group that consists of student government–elected officers and individual class representatives. The senate is responsible for the disbursement of funds to student-run clubs and organizations.

Admission Requirements

Hilbert College is open to men and women regardless of faith, race, age, physical handicap, or national origin. All students have an equal opportunity to pursue their educational goals through programs available at the College.

The College considers for admission to regular degree study those applicants who have been awarded a high school diploma or a New York State High School Equivalency Diploma.

Application and Information

The closing date for the receipt of applications is September 1. Admission decisions are made on a rolling basis.

For a catalog or an application, students should contact:

Office of Admissions
Hilbert College
5200 South Park Avenue
Hamburg, New York 14075
Telephone: 716-649-7900
          800-649-8003 (toll-free)
E-mail: admissions@hilbert.edu
World Wide Web: http://www.hilbert.edu

Franciscan Hall, the Student Services Center.

HOFSTRA UNIVERSITY
HEMPSTEAD, NEW YORK

The University

Hofstra University is an independent, dynamic, private University offering more than 130 undergraduate and 140 graduate programs in liberal arts and sciences, business, communications, education and allied human services, law, and honors studies. With a student-faculty ratio of 14:1, professors teach small classes that emphasize interaction, critical thinking, and development of judgment. At Hofstra, students have the resources they need—high-speed, readily available access to the Internet, excellent library resources, and state-of-the-art classrooms and learning and laboratory facilities. With a diverse mix of students, Hofstra University's vibrant campus hosts a wide selection of cultural, social, and athletic activities, providing students with the full college experience.

Undergraduate students attending Hofstra come from forty-seven states and seventy-eight countries. The freshman class numbers almost 1,900. The total enrollment at Hofstra is approximately 13,400; there are almost 8,400 full-time undergraduates and 1,000 part-time undergraduates.

Six separate undergraduate colleges at Hofstra ensure that students have a broad array of academic offerings from which to choose. Major University divisions are the Hofstra College of Liberal Arts and Sciences, the School of Communication, the Zarb School of Business, the School of Education and Allied Human Services, the Honors College, New College, the School of Law, the School for University Studies, the Saturday College, and the University College for Continuing Education. Residential facilities accommodate more than 4,000 students in thirty-seven modern on-campus residence halls. As a result of the Program for the Higher Education of the Disabled, Hofstra is 100 percent accessible to persons with disabilities. Necessary services are provided for wheelchair-bound and other disabled students who meet all academic requirements for admission.

A dynamic student life permeates campus with more than 130 clubs and organizations, thirty local and national fraternities and sororities, eighteen NCAA Division I athletic teams for men and women, and more than 500 cultural events on campus each year. With NCAA Division I athletic programs, Hofstra has a 15,000-seat stadium, a 5,000-seat arena, a 1,600-seat field turf soccer stadium, a physical fitness center, a swim center with an Olympic-size swimming pool and high-dive area, a softball stadium, a recreation center offering a multipurpose gymnasium, an indoor track, a fully equipped weight room, spacious locker rooms, a cardio area, and mirrored aerobics/martial arts room. Extensive recreational and intramural sports are also available.

Location

A nationally accredited arboretum, Hofstra's picturesque campus covers 240 acres and is situated just 25 miles east of New York City. It is easily accessible by car and railroad. The location also gives students easy access to the incredible cultural resources of New York City as well as the corporate headquarters of some of the world's leading companies, where many students find internships that lead to careers. The surrounding Long Island area offers recreation of all kinds and includes boating facilities, beaches, golf courses, and theaters. Long Island's Nassau Coliseum, featuring NHL's Islanders and numerous concerts and cultural events each year, is just steps away from Hofstra's campus.

Majors and Degrees

The Bachelor of Arts (B.A.) is awarded in adolescence education (dual enrollment required), Africana studies, American studies, anthropology, art education, art history, Asian studies, audio/radio, biology, broadcast journalism, chemistry, classics, comparative literature, computer science, computer science and mathematics, creative studies, dance, drama, early childhood education (dual enrollment required), economics, elementary bilingual education, elementary education (dual enrollment required), engineering science, English, film studies and production, fine arts, French, geography, geology, German, Hebrew, history, humanities, Ibero-American studies, interdisciplinary studies, Italian, Jewish studies, labor studies, Latin American and Caribbean studies, liberal arts, mass media studies, mathematics, music, music education, natural science, philosophy, physics, political science, psychology, public relations, Russian, social science, sociology, Spanish, speech communication and rhetorical studies, speech communication and education, speech-language hearing sciences, University Without Walls, and video/television. The Bachelor of Business Administration (B.B.A.) is awarded in accounting, business, business computer information systems, business education, entrepreneurship, finance, international business, legal studies in business, management, and marketing. The Bachelor of Science (B.S.) is offered in applied physics, athletic training, biochemistry, biology, chemistry, community health, computer engineering, computer science, computer science and mathematics, economics, electrical engineering, environmental resources, exercise specialist studies, fine arts, geology, health education, industrial engineering, mathematics, mechanical engineering, music, physician assistant studies, professional studies (Saturday College), school health education, University Without Walls, video/television, video/television and business, and video/television and film. The Bachelor of Science in Education (B.S.Ed.) is offered with specializations in fine arts, music, and physical education. The Bachelor of Engineering (B.E.) is offered in engineering science with specializations in biomedical engineering, civil engineering, and environmental engineering. The Bachelor of Fine Arts (B.F.A.) is awarded in theater arts.

Academic Programs

Requirements for graduation vary among schools and majors. A liberal arts core curriculum is an integral part of all areas of concentration. The baccalaureate degree requires completion of at least 128 credits. The University calendar is organized on a traditional semester system, including two 6-week summer sessions. Some divisions offer part-time programs during the day and evening and on weekends.

Hofstra University Honors College (HUHC) provides a rich academic and social experience for students who show both the potential and the desire to excel. HUHC takes full advantage of one of Hofstra's most outstanding qualities—the wealth of opportunities associated with large universities combined with the personality and individual attention of a small college. Honors students can elect to study in any of the University's more than 130 undergraduate programs; these students are involved in all fields of advanced study, including premedicine, prelaw, engineering, business, communications and media arts, humanities, and social sciences.

Off-Campus Programs

Hofstra sponsors study-abroad programs during various sessions in such places as China, England, France, Germany, Italy, South Korea, the Netherlands, Spain, Jamaica, the West Indies, Singapore, Belgium, Australia, Austria, Ukraine, Russia, Taiwan, and Japan. Students wishing to pursue such study should consult the Study Abroad Office and may wish to also consult with the Advisement Office. Other overseas courses are organized by faculty members as part of credit-bearing courses. Recent courses have been held in Greece, Mexico, Egypt; and China.

Academic Facilities

Hofstra's fully computerized library has seating for almost 1,200 students and contains more than 1.6 million volumes and volume equivalents as well as special units for periodicals, reserve books, documents, curriculum materials, special collections, and microfilm. Hofstra University's Student Computing Services provides students with a multitude of resources and learning opportunities. The Hofstra computer network provides individual accounts for all students for Internet, e-mail, and about 200 networked software programs. Almost 1,500 PC, Macintosh, and UNIX workstations are available to students in the various labs and classrooms on campus. The labs are staffed, and one computer lab is open 24 hours a day, seven days a week. All campus workstations have high-speed Internet access. All resident students are provided with Internet and e-mail access from their dorm rooms. Other facilities include an art gallery, an arboretum, a museum, bird sanctuary, writing center, career center, cultural center, language lab, technology lab, seven theaters, dance studios and performing arts classrooms, a rooftop observatory with powerful telescopes, and several computer labs for student use. The state-of-the-art facilities in Hofstra's School of Communication house a 24-hour student-operated radio station, one of the largest noncommercial broadcast facilities in the Northeast; audio production studios; a film/video screening room; and film editing rooms. The innovative new School of Education and Allied Health Services building is a completely wireless environment featuring assessment centers for child observation and mock counseling and a child-care institute.

Costs

Tuition and fees totaled about $20,010 for the 2004–05 college year. Room and board averaged $9000. Off-campus housing is also available.

Financial Aid

Hofstra University awards both merit-based and need-based awards to incoming students. Seventy-six percent of full-time undergraduates receive aid. The average award for new freshmen is $10,939, and almost 1,000 freshmen received merit-based scholarships from the University, ranging from $4000 to full-tuition scholarships. A package of assistance may include grants, loans, or work-study programs. Hofstra encourages all students to apply for financial assistance using the FAFSA. Priority consideration for assistance is given to those students who file the FAFSA by February 15.

Faculty

Hofstra has 1,325 faculty members, including 524 full-time members; 90 percent of the full-time faculty members hold the highest degree in their field. The faculty members are dedicated to excellence in teaching, scholarship, and research, and many have been recognized with the nation's highest academic honors, including membership in the National Academy of Science, MacArthur and Guggenheim Fellowships, Emmy Awards, and Pulitzer Prizes. The student-faculty ratio is 14:1. The average class size is 22. All classes are taught by faculty members who make it a point to be accessible to their students outside the classroom; no courses are taught by graduate assistants.

Student Government

The chief instrument of government is the Student Government Association, which supervises and coordinates all student activities and serves as a liaison with the faculty and administration. The Student Government Association sends representatives to the committees of the University Senate. The Judiciary Board has responsibility for promoting justice in the conduct of student affairs.

Admission Requirements

Hofstra is a selective institution that seeks to enroll those students who demonstrate the academic ability, intellectual curiosity, and motivation to succeed and to contribute to the campus community. Careful consideration is given to a student's high school record, SAT or ACT scores, letters of recommendation, extracurricular involvement, and a personal essay. Typical applicants rank in the top third of their graduating class and present 16 academic units, including 4 of English, 3 of history and social studies, 2 of foreign language, 3 of mathematics, and 3 of science. Prospective engineering majors need at least 4 years of mathematics, 1 year of chemistry, and 1 year of physics. All freshman candidates must submit SAT or ACT scores. Campus visits are strongly recommended for applicants. Hofstra accepts applications from freshmen, transfers, and international students.

The University has an early action plan for students whose first choice is Hofstra. The completed application must be submitted by November 15. Students applying for regular decision are considered on a rolling basis. For those students interested in consideration for scholarship or placement in housing, there is a priority deadline of December 15.

Freshman applicants must submit the application, a $40 application fee, their high school transcript, SAT or ACT scores, and a guidance counselor's recommendation. Hofstra accepts applications via mail or online and participates in the Common Application.

Application and Information

Peter Farrell, Dean of Admissions
Hofstra University
Hempstead, New York 11549
Telephone: 516-463-6700
            800-HOFSTRA (toll-free)
Fax: 516-463-5100
World Wide Web: http://www.hofstra.edu

ITHACA COLLEGE
ITHACA, NEW YORK

The College

Coeducational and nonsectarian since its founding in 1892, Ithaca College enrolls approximately 6,350 students. The College community is a diverse one; virtually every state is represented in the student population, as are sixty-nine other countries. Students come to Ithaca College to get active, hands-on learning that brings together the best of liberal arts and professional studies. The program is offered in five schools—the School of Humanities and Sciences (2,500 students), School of Business (600 students), Roy H. Park School of Communications (1,200 students), School of Health Sciences and Human Performance (1,200 students), and School of Music (500 students)—and the Division of Interdisciplinary and International Studies (100). There are approximately 250 graduate students.

Freshmen and most upperclassmen (with some exceptions) are expected to live on campus. There are fifty-one residence halls, which range from garden apartments to fourteen-story towers. Extracurricular life abounds at Ithaca. There are approximately 150 student organizations, a strong Division III intercollegiate athletic program (twenty-five teams), extensive intramural and club sports programs, and dramatic and musical ensembles. A wide range of services are available, beginning with summer orientation for new students and including career planning and placement assistance, a counseling center, and a health center that is staffed by 4 physicians as well as numerous physician assistants and nurses.

According to College surveys completed in the past three years, 97 percent of first-year graduates are employed and/or are full-time graduate students.

Location

Ithaca College is in Ithaca, New York. Approximately 90,000 people live in the surrounding county, more than a quarter of whom are Ithaca College or Cornell University students. The city combines the cultural and commercial features of a diverse, multicultural, mostly youthful population with the spectacular scenery of central New York's Finger Lakes.

Majors and Degrees

Ithaca awards the Bachelor of Arts, Bachelor of Science, Bachelor of Fine Arts, Bachelor of Music, and the Master of Music, Master of Business Administration, and Master of Science degrees in the more than 100 degree programs offered through its five schools and its Division of Interdisciplinary and International Studies.

The School of Business offers a B.S. in business administration, with concentrations in corporate accounting, finance, international business, management, and marketing as well as a B.S./M.B.A. degree in accounting for those pursuing CPA licensure. In addition, the School of Business also offers a one-year M.B.A. program.

The Roy H. Park School of Communications offers the B.A. in journalism. Also offered are the B.S. in cinema and photography; organizational communication, learning, and design; integrated marketing communications; and television-radio and the B.F.A. in film, photography, and visual arts.

Through the School of Health Sciences and Human Performance, students can earn a B.A. degree in health policy studies or sport studies or a B.S. degree in athletic training/exercise science, clinical exercise science, community health education, exercise science, health education*, health and physical education*, health sciences, leisure services, outdoor adventure leadership, physical education*, speech-language pathology and audiology, sport management, sport media, and therapeutic recreation. They may also enroll in the five-year B.S./M.S. clinical science/physical therapy or occupational science/occupational therapy programs.

The School of Humanities and Sciences offers the B.A. in anthropology, art, art education*, art history, biochemistry, biology*, chemistry*, computer science, drama, economics, English*, environmental studies, French*, German area studies*, history, Italian studies, mathematics*, mathematics–computer science*, mathematics-economics, mathematics-physics, philosophy, philosophy-religion, physics*, planned studies, politics, psychology, social studies*, sociology, Spanish*, speech communication, and writing; the B.S. is offered in applied economics, applied psychology, chemistry*, computer information systems, computer science, mathematics–computer science*, planned studies, and theater arts management; the B.F.A. is offered in acting, art, musical theater, and theatrical production arts.

The * indicates areas that lead to teacher certification.

Students in the School of Music can earn the B.A. in music and the B.M. in composition, jazz studies, music education, music in combination with an outside field, performance, performance/music education, sound recording technology, and theory.

Special programs offered by Ithaca include the Exploratory Program for undecided majors; accelerated programs with the Pennsylvania College of Optometry and the State University of New York College of Optometry; 3-2 programs in chemistry-engineering and in physics-engineering, offered in cooperation with Cornell University, Rensselaer Polytechnic Institute, and other schools; and M.B.A. 4+1 programs offered with Clarkson University, the Rochester Institute of Technology, and Thunderbird, the Garvin School of International Management.

The Division of Interdisciplinary and International Studies offers the B.A. in culture and communication, gerontology, and legal studies; the B.S. is also offered in gerontology.

Academic Programs

Undergraduate programs of study address two primary issues: the need for rigorous academic preparation in highly specialized professional fields and the need for students to prepare for the complex demands of society by acquiring an intellectual breadth that extends beyond their chosen profession. Each degree offered requires a minimum of 120 credit hours and a specified number of liberal arts credits. Minors, academic concentrations, and numerous teacher certification programs are available. Exceptionally qualified applicants to the School of Humanities and Sciences will be invited to apply to the honors program, an intensive four-year program of interdisciplinary seminars. The Writing Center offers assistance to students at any stage of the writing process, and Information Technology Services aids students in the use of personal and College computers. The Center for the Study of Culture, Race, and Ethnicity serves as a multidisciplinary clearinghouse for studying the experiences of groups that traditionally have been marginalized, underrepresented, or misrepresented in the United States as well as in college curricula. The Gerontology Institute provides opportunities for students to work with the elderly in a variety of community settings. The Center for Teacher Education serves to coordinate the courses of study leading to a teaching certificate.

ROTC programs are offered in conjunction with Cornell University.

The academic year comprises two 15-week semesters, from late August to mid-December and from mid-January to mid-May.

Off-Campus Programs

The College maintains a center in London, England, and offers courses in the liberal arts, business, communications, music, and theater arts. Study-abroad options include Ithaca's new Walkabout Down Under in Australia and programs in the Czech Republic, Ireland, Japan, Singapore, and Spain or in nearly fifty countries through affiliate arrangements with the Center for Cross-Cultural Study, the Institute for the International Education of Students, the Institute for American Universities, and the School for International Training. Selected juniors and seniors in communications may study at the Ithaca College James B. Pendleton Center in Los Angeles, which offers outstanding internship opportunities. Students from all disciplines may participate in an internship semester in Washington, D.C.

Academic Facilities

All academic facilities have been constructed since 1960; the most recent buildings include a health sciences facility, a 69,000-square-foot addition to the music building, and a fitness center. The Roy H. Park School of Communications contains television and radio studios, a film and photography complex, and a variety of digital laboratories. The College's two science buildings house state-of-the-art physics, biology, chemistry, mathematics, computer, and psychology laboratories. Additional campus facilities include theaters, auditoriums, concert halls, an observatory, and research laboratories. Computing facilities include hundreds of computers in labs and classrooms across campus, allowing easy access to e-mail and the Internet. The library contains approximately 400,000 materials in various formats.

Costs

For 2004–05, tuition was $23,690, room was $4960, board was $4758, and the health and accident insurance fee was $350.

Financial Aid

Financial aid totaling more than $111 million from all sources is extended to approximately 80 percent of Ithaca students. To apply for financial aid, students should check the proper space on the College's admission application, and if seeking federal aid, submit the Free Application for Federal Student Aid (FAFSA) by February 1 with the U.S. Department of Education at the address indicated on the form. Early decision candidates should follow the time line outlined under the Application and Information section below. All accepted applicants are considered for merit aid in recognition of their academic and personal achievement. Federal aid programs include Stafford, Perkins, and PLUS loans; work-study funds; Pell grants, and Supplemental Educational Opportunity Grants.

Faculty

There are 453 full-time and 180 part-time faculty members; the overall student-faculty ratio is 12:1. Ninety percent of the full-time faculty members have a Ph.D. or a terminal degree in their field. While the faculty is principally devoted to teaching at all levels, there is also significant publishing and research in various disciplines. Faculty members serve as academic advisers to students and are active in the community.

Student Government

The student government is composed of the student congress, all-College committee representatives, executive officers and assistants, and the student government executive board. Students administer a budget of approximately $400,000. The student congress includes representatives from each residence hall and school as well as students who live off campus. There is a student member of the Ithaca College Board of Trustees, and the student government appoints representatives to several standing all-College committees, including the Academic Policies Committee. The College encourages and expects student participation in governance.

Admission Requirements

Admission is based on the high school record, personal recommendations, SAT or ACT scores, and, for some programs, auditions or portfolios. Campus visits are recommended but not required. Admission is selective and competitive; individual talents and circumstances are always given serious consideration. Transfer students must also submit official transcripts from each college or university they have attended. Applicants whose native language is not English must take the Test of English as a Foreign Language. Typically, there are about 11,100 applicants for 1,475 places in the freshman class.

Application and Information

For freshman regular decision, prospective students should apply early in their senior year and no later than March 1; applicants are notified of a decision on a rolling basis no later than April 15 and must confirm their enrollment by May 1. Freshman applicants seeking institutional and federal aid should file the FAFSA by February 1 with the federal processor.

For freshman early decision, which is binding, students should apply by November 1; applicants are notified by December 15 and must confirm their enrollment by February 1. Early decision applicants seeking institutional and federal financial aid should submit the Financial Aid Profile, available from the College Scholarship Service, by November 1 and the FAFSA by February 1.

Students who want to transfer into Ithaca College should apply by March 1 for fall admission and by December 1 for spring admission. Applicants seeking institutional and federal financial aid should file the FAFSA by February 1.

All applicants must submit a $55 application fee. Ithaca's application for admission is available on the College's Web site at http://www.ithaca.edu/admission.

For additional information and application forms, students should contact:

Paula J. Mitchell
Director of Admission
Office of Admission
Ithaca College
100 Job Hall
Ithaca, New York 14850-7020
Telephone: 607-274-3124
　　　　　800-429-4274 (toll-free)
Fax: 607-274-1900
E-mail: admission@ithaca.edu
World Wide Web: http://www.ithaca.edu

The Ithaca College campus.

LE MOYNE COLLEGE
SYRACUSE, NEW YORK

The College

Le Moyne College is a four-year, coeducational Jesuit college of approximately 2,500 undergraduate students that uniquely balances a comprehensive liberal arts education with preparation for specific career paths or graduate study. Founded by the Society of Jesus in 1946, Le Moyne is the second-youngest of the twenty-eight Jesuit colleges and universities in the United States. Its emphasis is on the education of the whole person and on the search for meaning and value as integral parts of an intellectual life. Le Moyne's personal approach to education is reflected in the quality of contact between students and faculty members. A wide range of student-directed activities, athletics, clubs, and service organizations complement the academic experience. Intramural sports are very popular with Le Moyne students; nearly 85 percent of the students participate. Le Moyne also has sixteen NCAA intercollegiate teams (eight for men and eight for women). Athletic facilities include soccer/lacrosse, softball, and baseball fields; tennis, basketball, and racquetball courts; a weight-training and fitness center; practice fields; and two gymnasiums. A recreation center houses an Olympic-size indoor swimming pool, jogging track, indoor tennis and volleyball courts, and additional basketball, racquetball, and fitness areas. More than 80 percent of students live in residence halls, apartments, and town houses on campus. The Residence Hall Councils and the Le Moyne Student Programming Board organize a variety of campus activities, including concerts, dances, a weekly film series, student talent programs, and special lectures as well as off-campus trips and skiing excursions.

Location

Le Moyne's 150-acre, tree-lined campus is located in a residential setting 10 minutes from downtown Syracuse, the heart of New York State, whose metropolitan population is about 700,000. Syracuse is convenient to most major cities throughout the Northeast, New England, and Canada and offers a wide array of shopping centers and restaurants, many near Le Moyne. Syracuse offers year-round entertainment in the form of rock concerts at Landmark Theatre; professional baseball, hockey, and lacrosse; Bristol Omnitheatre; the Syracuse Symphony Orchestra; Syracuse Stage; Everson Museum of Art; and the Armory Square district downtown, offering one-of-a-kind eateries, pubs, and coffeehouses in addition to a wide variety of social and cultural events. All are easily accessible via the excellent public transportation service, which schedules regular stops on Le Moyne's campus. Just a few miles outside the city are the rolling hills, picturesque lakes, and miles of open country for which central New York is renowned. An extensive network of state and county parks, recreational areas, and other facilities offer an abundance of recreational opportunities, including swimming, boating, hiking, downhill and cross-country skiing, snowboarding, and golf.

Majors and Degrees

Le Moyne College awards the Bachelor of Arts degree in biology, communication, communication/advertising, communication/print journalism, communication/public relations, communication/television and radio, criminology and crime and justice studies, economics, English, English/creative writing, English/drama, English/literature, French, history, mathematics, mathematics/actuarial science, mathematics/operations research, mathematics/pure mathematics, mathematics/statistics, peace and global studies/general studies, peace and global studies/Latin American studies, philosophy, physics, political science, psychology, religious studies, sociology, sociology/anthropology, sociology/criminology and criminal justice, sociology/human services, sociology/research and theory, Spanish, and theater arts. The Bachelor of Science degree is awarded in accounting, biochemistry, biology, biology/physician assistant studies, business administration, business/applied management analysis, business/finance, business/information systems, business/leadership, business/marketing, chemistry, economics, industrial relations and human resource management, information systems, multiple science, nursing, physics, physics/pre-engineering, and psychology.

Students may minor in anthropology, Catholic studies, classic humanities, fine arts, Japanese, Latin, music, urban studies, or women's studies as well as in any of the major fields of study offered. Preprofessional programs are offered in dentistry, law, medicine, optometry, and veterinary science. Students may prepare for teaching careers through certification programs in adolescent education, dual adolescent/special education, dual childhood/special education, middle childhood specialist studies, and TESOL.

Formal accelerated 3-4 programs are offered in dentistry, optometry, and podiatry in cooperation with SUNY at Buffalo School of Dental Medicine, Pennsylvania College of Optometry, and the New York College of Podiatric Medicine. Predental students may also participate in an early assurance program with SUNY at Buffalo School of Dental Medicine. Cooperative 3-2 dual-degree programs in engineering are available with Clarkson University, Manhattan College, and University of Detroit Mercy. A 2-2 program in environmental science and forestry is available in cooperation with SUNY College of Environmental Science and Forestry in Syracuse.

SUNY Upstate Medical University in Syracuse offers students pursuing careers in the health-related professions an accelerated 3-3 doctoral-level transfer program in physical therapy as well as two-year cooperative transfer programs in cytotechnology, medical technology, and respiratory care. Premedical students at Le Moyne are also offered the opportunity to participate in a medical school early assurance program. An early assurance program for premedical students is also available through SUNY at Buffalo School of Medicine.

Academic Programs

While each major department has its own sequence requirements for the minimum 120 credit hours needed for the Le Moyne degree, the College is convinced that there is a fundamental intellectual discipline that should characterize the graduate of a superior liberal arts college. Le Moyne's core curriculum provides this foundation by including studies of English language and literature, foreign language, philosophy, history, religious studies, natural sciences, mathematics, and social sciences.

For exceptional students, Le Moyne offers an integral honors program that includes an interdisciplinary humanities sequence as well as departmental honors courses. Le Moyne also offers a part-time course of study during evening hours through its Center for Continuous Education.

Le Moyne students may enroll in Army and Air Force ROTC programs at Syracuse University.

Off-Campus Programs

The study-abroad program allows students to spend semesters in Australia, China, Dominican Republic, Japan, and exciting European locations such as England, France, Ireland, Italy, Scotland, and Spain. Le Moyne is a participant in the sixty-member New York State Visiting Student Program. For career preparation, Le Moyne's strong emphasis on internships has been a continuing and expanding source of resume-building and real-world experiences for students from several different majors, all of whom have gained invaluable credentials to take to their first interviews. In addition, science interns have been given extraordinary access to research opportunities with some of the leading labs and companies. Externships allow students to observe alumni working in a particular area of interest. This program has taken students to places such as the White House and Capitol Building in Washington, D.C.; New York State's seat of government in Albany; and hospitals, Fortune 500 companies, and a wide array of small businesses. In addition, many student-teaching opportunities exist. In every education class, from freshman through senior years, students are required to spend time in a classroom.

Academic Facilities

Le Moyne students benefit from an ongoing commitment to technological excellence. The College's thirty-four buildings are equipped with accounting, biology, chemistry, computer science, physics, psychology, and statistics laboratories. The W. Carroll Coyne Center for the Performing Arts houses generous production, performance, and classroom space; the latest light and sound technology; scene and costume shops; an aerobics and dance studio; and rehearsal rooms for instrumental and choral music. Academic facilities also include an extensively renovated color television studio; a radio/recording studio; a receiver-antenna satellite dish; transmission and scanning electron microscopes; a nuclear magnetic resonance spectrometer; a gas chromatograph/mass spectrophotometer; a 230,000-volume, open-stack library; and extensive on-site computer facilities. A fiber-optic network enables students to access the library system, the campus network, and the Internet from several computer labs around campus or from their personal computers in their rooms. All classrooms have been converted to smart classrooms, with multimedia capabilities that expand and enrich the learning process. Le Moyne students have access to other libraries through the Central New York Library Resources Council, and the campus Academic Support Center is available to students for instructional support.

Costs

For 2004–05, Le Moyne's tuition was $19,640. Room and board charges were $7530. Additional fees amounted to approximately $500, and books and supplies cost approximately $600.

Financial Aid

Financial aid is offered to a large percentage of Le Moyne's students through scholarships, grants, loans, and work-study assignments. Le Moyne offers a generous program of merit-based academic and athletic scholarships as well as financial aid based on a student's need and academic promise. Federal funds are available through the Federal Pell Grant, Federal Work-Study, Federal Supplemental Educational Opportunity Grant, and Federal Perkins Loan programs. A student's eligibility for need-based financial aid is determined from both the Free Application for Federal Student Aid (FAFSA) and the Le Moyne Financial Aid Application Form. It is recommended that these forms be mailed by February 1.

Faculty

The Le Moyne full-time faculty numbers 152 men and women; 91 percent have earned the highest degree in their fields. With an average class size of 20 students, a student-faculty ratio of 13:1, and private offices for all full-time faculty members, the College promotes a personal as well as academic relationship between students and faculty members. All classroom instruction is done by faculty members, and they are happy to assist and encourage students who wish to pursue undergraduate research through tutorials or senior research projects. These projects are carried out in an atmosphere free of competition from graduate students for books, laboratories, or professors' time. Le Moyne emphasizes advising and academic counseling for students throughout their four years.

Student Government

The College encourages student leadership in all activities. Positions of leadership are open to students in all class years. Students are represented by a Student Senate and have formal representation through the senate on most College-wide committees involved in decision making and policy formation.

Admission Requirements

Le Moyne seeks qualified students who are well prepared for serious academic study. Secondary school preparation must have included at least 17 college-preparatory high school units, 4 of which must be in English, 4 in social studies, 3–4 in mathematics, 3–4 in foreign language, and 3–4 in science. It is also recommended that prospective science and mathematics majors complete 4 units of mathematics and science. The SAT or ACT is required and should be taken by December or January of the senior year in high school. Campus visits are strongly recommended, as the admission process is a personal one. As bases for selection, academic achievement and secondary school recommendations are of primary importance; SAT or ACT scores are important as they relate to the record of achievement and to recommendations. Out-of-state students are encouraged to apply.

Application and Information

The Admission Committee reviews applications and mails decisions on a rolling admission cycle beginning January 1. The priority deadline for applications is February 1; all students who wish to be considered for academic merit scholarships should have a completed application on file in the Office of Admission before this date. Students who wish to be considered under the early-decision program must have a completed application submitted by December 1. Early-decision applicants are notified by December 15. Transfer students are encouraged to apply before June 1 for the fall semester and December 1 for the spring semester. A two-day orientation program takes place in midsummer.

Dennis J. Nicholson
Director of Admission
Le Moyne College
Syracuse, New York 13214-1399
Telephone: 315-445-4300
         800-333-4733 (toll-free)
E-mail: admission@lemoyne.edu
World Wide Web: http://www.lemoyne.edu

Grewen Hall, the oldest building on campus, overlooks Le Moyne's beautiful 150-acre campus.

MANHATTAN COLLEGE
RIVERDALE, NEW YORK

The College

Currently celebrating 150 years of excellence in Lasallian education, Manhattan College was founded by the Brothers of the Christian Schools in 1853 and chartered by the state of New York in 1863. The College has an enrollment of more than 3,200, of whom 2,500 are undergraduates. Approximately 72 percent of Manhattan's students come from New York State; 28 percent represent thirty-nine other states and the remainder represent fifty other countries. Approximately 1,500 housing units are available, consisting of on-campus residence halls and off-campus apartments. Seventy percent of the students reside on campus. Manhattan offers seventy extracurricular organizations and five student publications and fields twenty varsity and club sports teams. Of Manhattan's 40,000 living alumni, more than 18,000 work in the New York City area. Manhattan graduates are prominent leaders in business, government, education, the arts, the sciences, and engineering.

Location

The main campus of the College is located 10 miles north of midtown Manhattan in the suburban Riverdale section of the Bronx, about a mile from Westchester County. Riverdale is an upper-middle-class community, the home of many New York business, political, and education leaders. The area offers the calm and quiet of a residential, suburban setting as well as easy access to the many advantages of New York City. The College is easily accessible by subway, bus, or highway.

Majors and Degrees

The liberal arts curriculum of the School of Arts provides programs that lead to a Bachelor of Arts or Bachelor of Science with majors in the humanities and the social sciences, including communications, economics, English, fine arts, government, history, modern foreign languages, philosophy, psychology, religious studies, and sociology. Interdisciplinary majors include international studies, peace studies, and urban affairs. In the School of Science, programs lead to a Bachelor of Science or Bachelor of Arts with majors in biochemistry, biology, chemistry, computer science, mathematics, and physics.

The School of Engineering has a day session with programs leading to a Bachelor of Science in chemical, civil, computer, electrical, environmental, and mechanical engineering.

The School of Business has programs leading to a Bachelor of Science in Business Administration with majors in accounting, computer information systems, economics, finance, global business, managerial sciences, and marketing.

The School of Education offers a curriculum leading to a Bachelor of Arts for teachers of English, foreign languages, and social studies and to a Bachelor of Science for teachers of biology, chemistry, computer science, general science, mathematics, physics, and special education. The physical education curriculum leads to a Bachelor of Science in physical education in one of three concentrations: teaching, pre–physical therapy, or sports medicine. The health education curriculum leads to a Bachelor of Science in health education or community health. Curricula in radiological and health sciences lead to a Bachelor of Science in radiation therapy or nuclear medicine technology.

Academic Programs

The core curriculum shared by the School of Arts and the School of Science studies some of the vital works of humankind, explores new ideas, examines the meaning of scientific experimentation, and encourages a student to develop his or her thinking and leadership abilities. The major programs offer advanced work in specific humanistic and scientific disciplines and opportunities to work on research projects in collaboration with faculty scholars.

In the School of Engineering, all engineering students follow a common core curriculum during the first two years and choose a major at the beginning of the junior year. Each curriculum includes a generous selection of courses in basic sciences, the engineering sciences, humanistic studies, and mathematics.

The School of Business prepares students for positions of executive responsibility in business, government, and nonprofit organizations. The business curriculum is based on a strong commitment to liberal education and is well balanced between professional business courses, humanities, sciences, and social sciences. This is a reflection of the School's belief that executives should be broadly educated and should involve themselves, as well as their organizations, in efforts to solve social problems.

The School of Education prepares students for teaching, counseling, and health professions. Students complete the College's core curriculum in liberal arts and sciences and then complete a major in various programs in the School's three departments: Education, Physical Education and Human Performance, and Radiological and Health Professions. All programs include internships/practicums in schools, hospitals, or other institutions. Graduates of the School's teacher-preparation programs receive New York State provisional teaching certification. The School also offers a five-year B.A./M.S. program in elementary or secondary education and special education.

Off-Campus Programs

Students in the liberal arts curricula who have demonstrated superior achievement in their first two years are encouraged to spend their junior year studying abroad. Manhattan College offers study-abroad programs; arrangements can be made to a country of choice. Students in the School of Business may participate in the International Field Studies Seminar. As participants in the seminar, students spend time in another country studying the effect of that environment on international firms. Career services and co-op education integrate classroom theory with the practical experience of a job in industry, business, the social services, the arts, or government. Portions of the education courses are conducted in New York City schools, in order that student teachers may gain experience in urban education at an early stage. Manhattan College and the neighboring College of Mount Saint Vincent collaborate in an exchange of students and facilities to provide more extensive opportunities for academic development.

Academic Facilities

There are more than forty scientific and engineering laboratories at Manhattan, including the Research and Learning Center, as well as a modern language laboratory and a computer information systems laboratory. Manhattan's new O'Malley

Library is a state-of-the-art facility featuring modern accomodations for study and research. It is connected to the renovated and updated Cardinal Hayes Pavilion, formerly the Cardinal Hayes Library. The library combines Hayes' traditional neo-Georgian accents with strong contemporary lines. The five-story addition to the original building doubles the original square footage and connects the current library to the upper campus. Students and faculty members are able to enter directly from a brick walkway that starts at the Quadrangle.

Costs

For 2004–05, the tuition for all curricula was $18,600 per year. A fee that varies among programs was added. Room and board came to $8100 per year for the nineteen meals/week plan.

Financial Aid

Manhattan grants or administers financial assistance in the form of tuition awards to students on the basis of need and/or ability. Need is evaluated through the FAFSA. In addition to a general scholarship fund, Manhattan offers endowed scholarships, special-category scholarships and grants, student athletic grants, Federal Pell Grants, Federal Supplemental Educational Opportunity Grants, student loans, Federal Work-Study Program awards, and New York State financial assistance. A total of 1,650 students receive financial aid from Manhattan College, and approximately 87 percent receive financial aid from government or private agencies.

Faculty

Manhattan's faculty has 190 full-time and 82 part-time teachers. The faculty-student ratio is approximately 1:13. Nearly 95 percent of the faculty members hold doctorates. The maximum teaching load on the undergraduate level is 12 credit hours per semester. Faculty members serve on the College Senate, the Council for Faculty Affairs, and numerous faculty and campus committees. In addition, they are available to students for informal guidance and counseling and also serve as official moderators of many campus organizations.

Student Government

The Manhattan Student Government is composed of students elected annually by their peers to fill posts outlined in the Student Government Constitution. The Student Government allocates funds to all student organizations. Members of the Student Government are also full voting members of the College Senate.

Admission Requirements

Manhattan has a long-standing policy of nondiscrimination. No applicant is refused admission because of race, color, religion, age, national origin, sex, or handicap. All applicants must present an academic diploma from an accredited high school and must offer a minimum of 16 credits in academic subjects. Liberal arts candidates must be proficient in at least one foreign language. At the discretion of the Committee on Admissions, quantitative requirements may be modified for applicants with especially strong records who show promise of doing well in college. In the selection process, attention is given to scholastic ability as indicated by grades and rank in class, as well as to standardized test scores and recommendations from principals and counselors. All candidates must submit either SAT I or ACT results. An interview with a member of the admission staff is recommended. Applicants may submit scores on the General Educational Development test in lieu of a formal high school diploma. However, all such applicants must submit the results of the appropriate College Board tests. Manhattan College offers early acceptance for high school seniors, admission to advanced standing, advanced placement, and credit by examination. Junior college or other transfer students are welcome. Manhattan College requires applicants whose native language is not English to take the Test of English as a Foreign Language (TOEFL) as well as the SAT I. The average SAT I scores of entering freshmen in 2004 were 563 in mathematics and 547 in the verbal portion.

Application and Information

Application forms are furnished by the Admission Office on request. The Common Application Form, which is available in many high school guidance offices, may also be used. After supplying the information required, students must send the application for admission to the Admission Office at Manhattan College. The high school report and the student evaluation and transcript must be submitted by the high school guidance counselor. This should be done after six terms of high school or right after the seventh term. There is a rolling admissions policy and a March 1 deadline for financial aid applications. A nonrefundable application fee of $40 is required.

William J. Bisset
Assistant Vice President for Enrollment Management
Manhattan College
Riverdale, New York 10471
Telephone: 718-862-7200
          800-MC2-XCEL (toll-free)
E-mail: admit@manhattan.edu

Students entering the Quadrangle of the Manhattan College campus.

MARYMOUNT MANHATTAN COLLEGE

NEW YORK, NEW YORK

The College

Marymount Manhattan College (MMC) is an urban, independent undergraduate liberal arts college. The mission of the College is to educate a socially and economically diverse population by fostering intellectual achievement and personal growth and by providing opportunities for career development. Inherent in this mission is the intent to develop an awareness of social, political, cultural, and ethical issues in the belief that this awareness will lead to concern for, participation in, and the improvement of society. To accomplish this mission, the College offers a strong program in the arts and sciences to students of all ages as well as substantial preprofessional preparation. Central to these efforts is the particular attention given to the individual student. Marymount Manhattan College also seeks to be a resource and learning center for the metropolitan community.

The social and extracurricular life of the student body of approximately 2,100 students centers on a number of clubs and organizations sponsored through the Student Affairs Office, including the International Students Club, Amnesty International, the French Club, softball and soccer clubs, the Nature/Science Club, the student newspaper and magazine, Student Government, the student volunteer organization, and the Student Development Committee. Students attend musical events, and MMC's own off-Broadway theater, the only one on the Upper East Side of Manhattan, offers students an opportunity to participate in student productions.

The Residence Life Office at Marymount Manhattan College is committed to providing residents with numerous opportunities and experiences that foster intellectual achievement and social and personal growth. Students are encouraged to become involved in the many activities that are sponsored by Residence Life and are assisted with assuming responsibility for their own lives and living environment. The College provides housing for approximately 650 students at three locations. The buildings offer suite-style, traditional dormitories, or apartment-style living, with classrooms, lounges, a laundry room, and rehearsal space. Additional off-campus facilities are obtained as needed.

The Office of Academic and Career Advisement serves the entire College community by providing an integrated program of academic and career counseling. The office helps students by offering internship opportunities and workshops in job placement, resume writing, and graduate school preparation. For the past five years, 90 percent of biology majors who apply are accepted to advanced professional schools, including Mt. Sinai School of Medicine and Cornell Medical College. Other College services include personal and financial aid counseling and campus ministry.

Location

Marymount Manhattan College is centrally located on Manhattan's Upper East Side at 221 East 71st Street between Second and Third avenues. Within walking distance of the campus are the Frick, Metropolitan, Whitney, and Guggenheim museums; the Asian Society, French Institute, and National Audubon Society; Central Park; New York Hospital and Sloan-Kettering Research Center; and public libraries. All forms of public transportation are easily accessible. Within minutes of the College are shops, restaurants, and movie theaters. This location gives students the opportunity to take advantage of New York City's rich culture and to explore a variety of neighborhoods.

Majors and Degrees

Marymount Manhattan College offers programs leading to the Bachelor of Arts, Bachelor of Science, and Bachelor of Fine Arts degrees. Majors are offered in accounting, acting, art, biology, business management, communication arts, dance (B.A. and B.F.A.), English, history, humanities, international studies, political science, psychology, sociology, speech-language pathology and audiology, and theater arts (B.A. and B.F.A.). Some of the minors offered are business, business communications, creative writing, education, French, media studies, religious studies, Spanish, and writing. Certificate programs are offered in substance abuse counseling, business management, computer information management, gerontology, industrial organizational psychology, and teacher certification.

Academic Programs

Marymount Manhattan College has designed its programs to enable students to meet the challenges of contemporary society. MMC is committed to the belief that a liberal arts education provides students with the ability and the flexibility to manage change and with broad understanding and the communication and problem-solving skills that are essential for success in any career and in life. To accomplish its goals, the College offers a liberal arts education, integrated with preprofessional training opportunities and individualized attention. The curricula are organized into five divisions: humanities, fine and performing arts, sciences, social sciences, and business management. Also offered are special-interest sequences that complement the student's major and minor with added concentration in such areas as prelaw, premedicine, social work, marketing, international business, finance and investments, and creative writing. The College's small size provides students with an individually planned academic career, reflects students' academic needs and interests, and supports their career goals.

Candidates for the Bachelor of Arts, Bachelor of Science, and Bachelor of Fine Arts degrees must complete 120 credits. To qualify for a degree, a student must maintain an overall scholastic average of at least 2.0. Requirements for certificate programs vary.

The College recognizes various types of nontraditional credit, including credit for acceptable scores on the Advanced Placement (AP), College-Level Examination Program (CLEP), and New York State College Proficiency Examination (CPE) tests and credit for life experience.

MMC encourages its students to participate in internship programs in New York City that range from work at hospitals, financial institutions, magazines, publishing houses, and off-Broadway theaters to HBO and CBS.

Off-Campus Programs

The College's Academic Year Abroad offers an opportunity for students to broaden their educational experience and to gain cultural perspectives through study at other colleges in the Americas and overseas. Students may spend one or both semesters of their junior year in this program. MMC summer sessions and January intersessions also offer students opportunities in travel/study-abroad courses in Egypt, France, Great Britain, Eastern Europe, Ireland, Russia, and Spain.

Academic Facilities

The Thomas J. Shanahan Library at MMC is a library/learning center. It contains more than 100,000 volumes in open stacks and maintains an extensive periodical collection. The media center, on the main library floor, houses nonprint materials, microfiche, microfilm, filmstrips, slides, tapes, videotapes, and records. Through the library's affiliation with the New York Metropolitan Reference and Research Library Agency, MMC faculty members and students have access to the materials of the member libraries.

The library also participates in the Online Computer Library Center (OCLC), a computerized database of the holdings of some 4,000 libraries that is currently being used for cataloging and reference purposes.

The modern 250-seat Theresa Lang Theatre is equipped with an orchestra pit capable of accommodating 40 musicians. The theater has a special acoustical design, a sprung dance floor, a full technical balcony with equipment for lighting and sound, thirty-five counterweighted-line sets in the fly system, dressing rooms with showers, and a scene shop. Students benefit from exposure to the numerous professional dance, opera, and theatrical groups that perform at the College.

Recently, two completely remodeled laboratory facilities were opened to strengthen education in two areas in which MMC has always excelled—science and communication arts.

MMC's science facilities in biology, chemistry, and physics underwent a total reconstruction valued at close to $1 million, thanks to the generosity of the Samuel Freeman Charitable Trust and the Ira De Camp Foundation. The Samuel Freeman Science Center opens many new doors of opportunity to students who are biology/premedicine majors or who are interested in pursuing careers in other science or health-related fields.

The College's Theresa Lang Center for Producing features the latest in digital computer technology and is one of the most advanced facilities of its kind in New York City. With digital multimedia capability, a decor inspired by top television postproduction houses, and access to the public library's B. Altman Advanced Learning Superblock, the center further enhances students' skills in traditional video and television production and allows them to develop, design, and evaluate cutting-edge multimedia projects. In conjunction with the Communication Arts Department, the College offers students the Media Library, where many videos and screening computers are available to students.

The Writing Center at MMC provides a range of services and activities, including career-based courses, personal critiques and one-on-one assistance, lectures, workshops, and special events such as the Best-Selling Author Series and Annual Writers' Conference, as well as a minor in creative writing. This enables students to be a part of the highly respected New York City writing community.

Costs

For the 2004–05 academic year, full-time tuition was $16,606 plus required fees of $806. The fee for a space in a residence provided by the College was approximately $9100 per year. There is also a mandatory meal plan for resident students at $1600 per year. For part-time students, tuition was $490 per credit. Additional fees are applicable for various laboratory and studio classes.

Financial Aid

The College administers a variety of financial aid programs, including scholarships sponsored by the College. Some of the awards are based on academic achievement; others are based on financial need. Students are also eligible for aid through a wide variety of state and federal programs. In addition, a number of jobs are available for students on campus, and the Offices of Financial Aid and Academic and Career Advisement can help students locate part-time off-campus jobs to help finance their education. More than 80 percent of MMC students receive some form of financial assistance. Therefore, limited finances alone need not prevent any student from attending the College. The suggested deadlines for applying for financial aid are February 15 for the fall semester and November 15 for the spring semester.

Faculty

Marymount Manhattan College's student-faculty ratio is 18:1. In addition to the staff of the advisement office, faculty members act as advisors to students. Full-time faculty members teach in all sessions and divisions (days, evenings, and weekends). Part-time instructors, who are drawn from the wealth of experienced teaching professionals in New York City, supplement the full-time faculty.

Student Government

The Student Government Association responds to three areas of concern at MMC. The association primarily serves the needs of its constituents by managing the student government budget, planning and publicizing events, and establishing organizations that reflect the interests of the students. In addition, the association assists faculty and administrative groups and committees in their policy and procedural tasks and communicates the results of committee work to the student body. Finally, the Student Government Association provides special representatives for students' rights and freedoms through established and clearly defined channels of authority.

Admission Requirements

Marymount Manhattan College seeks candidates with qualities that indicate potential for success in higher education and the ability to contribute to the College community. Admission is based on a combination of factors: the student's academic program, including scholastic average and rank in class; two recommendations from teachers, counselors, or employers; an essay; and activities. SAT I scores are required for general admission.

Each year the College enrolls an increasing number of transfer students. Transfer students may receive up to 90 credits for course work completed in an accredited postsecondary institution with a grade of C- or better. Transcripts are evaluated on a course-by-course basis.

Prior to registering, all new students are required to take placement examinations in the basic subject areas of English composition, reading, algebra, and mathematics.

Application and Information

The admissions application must be received by February 1 for MMC scholarship consideration. Students may apply online. For application forms and for more information about Marymount Manhattan College, students should contact:

Office of Admissions
Marymount Manhattan College
221 East 71st Street
New York, New York 10021
Telephone: 212-517-0430
          800-MARYMOUNT (toll-free)
E-mail: admissions@mmm.edu
World Wide Web: http://www.mmm.edu

Marymount Manhattan College, in the heart of Manhattan.

MOLLOY COLLEGE
ROCKVILLE CENTRE, NEW YORK

The College

In 1955, 44 students became part of an exciting new tradition in higher education on Long Island. As the first freshman class of Molloy College, these young students made a commitment to academic excellence. So did the College, which had a distinguished faculty of 15 and a library containing 5,000 books.

Today, Molloy College has become one of the most respected four-year private coeducational institutions of higher learning in the area. It provides academic programs in both day and evening divisions. The Molloy population consists of recent high school graduates, transfer students, and graduate students whose average age is 24. Molloy College is accredited by the Board of Regents of the University of the State of New York and the Middle States Association of Colleges and Schools, and its programs in nursing and social work are accredited by the National League for Nursing Accrediting Commission and the Council on Social Work Education.

Despite its growth over the years, Molloy College retains an intimate and personal atmosphere. It encourages the 3,000 students to develop close working relationships with the faculty. The student body represents many ethnic and socioeconomic groups; to meet their varied needs, the College offers thirty-three undergraduate majors and programs.

The key word at the College is involvement. Student-run clubs and organizations offer a variety of planned activities. Student publications, which include the yearbook, a literary magazine, a newspaper, and a weekly newsletter, provide an outlet for students who want to share their literary and journalistic talents.

Molloy College offers opportunities for students to exercise their leadership abilities, contribute their special talents, utilize their initiative, and expand their social horizons through the variety of activities made conveniently available to them. Athletics, an integral part of student life, are represented at Molloy College on the varsity level by women's basketball, cross-country, lacrosse, soccer, softball, tennis, and volleyball. These teams compete in the NCAA, the ECAC, and the NYCAC. The equestrian team holds membership in the Intercollegiate Horse Show Association. Men's baseball, basketball, cross-country, lacrosse, and soccer are played at Division II level.

Student services include the Counseling and Career Services, the Campus Ministry, the Siena Women's Center, health services, and referrals for off-campus housing.

On the graduate level, Molloy College offers a Master of Science degree in nursing and education and post-master's certification in nursing. M.B.A. programs are available in both business and accounting.

Location

Located on a 30-acre campus in Rockville Centre, Long Island, Molloy College is close to metropolitan New York and all its diverse and rich resources. The College is easily accessible from all parts of Nassau, Suffolk, and Queens counties.

Majors and Degrees

Molloy College offers the A.A. degree in liberal arts; the A.A.S. degree in health information technology, nuclear medicine technology, and respiratory care; and B.A. or B.S. degrees in accounting, art, biology, business management, communications, computer information systems, computer science, criminal justice, English, environmental studies, history, interdisciplinary studies, international peace and justice studies, mathematics, music, music therapy, nursing, philosophy, political science, psychology, social work, sociology, Spanish, speech-language pathology and audiology, and theology. Teacher certification programs are available in childhood (1–6), adolescence (7–12), and special education.

Special advisement is offered for students interested in predental, prelaw, premedical, or preveterinary programs.

The internship program at the College offers students the opportunity for on-the-job experience along with the classroom exposure so essential to the completely educated person. Internships are available in accounting, art, business management, communications, computer science, criminal justice, English, history, IPJ studies, mathematics, music therapy, political science, psychology, social work, and sociology.

Academic Programs

Molloy College, dedicated to the total development of the student, offers a strong liberal arts core curriculum as an integral part of all major fields of study. A minimum of 128 credits is required for a baccalaureate degree. Double majors can be chosen, and numerous minors are available.

Advanced placement credit is granted for a score of 3 or better on the AP exam. CLEP and CPE credit is also given. Qualified full-time students may participate in the Army ROTC program at Hofstra University or St. John's University on a cross-enrolled basis. Molloy students may also elect Air Force ROTC on a cross-enrolled basis with New York Institute of Technology.

Molloy has a 4-1-4 academic calendar.

Academic Facilities

Molloy's James Edward Tobin Library has 133,500 books, 700 periodical subscriptions, 13,500 bound periodicals, 2,950 microfilms, 1,200 microfiches, four OCLC computer terminals, and twelve microcomputers for student research. The Media Center houses 500 pieces of hardware, 9,700 pieces of software, and 2,700 videocassettes and DVDs.

The College computer labs house 260 microcomputers. In addition, many academic departments have their own computer labs. For example, the International Business Center has sixteen state-of-the-art microcomputers with Internet and e-mail accessibility, DVD drives, and zip drives for students to communicate internationally.

The Wilbur Arts Center features numerous art studios, music studios, a cable television studio, and the Lucille B. Hays Theatre.

Kellenberg Hall houses six science labs, a language lab, and the education resource center. Casey Hall houses two nursing labs and the behavioral sciences research facility.

Costs

For 2003–04, tuition and fees were $15,150. The cost per credit for part-time students was $505.

Financial Aid

More than 85 percent of the student body of Molloy College is awarded financial aid in the form of scholarships, grants, loans, and Federal Work-Study Program employment. Financial aid awards are based on academic achievement and financial need. Completion of the Molloy College Application for Financial Aid/Scholarship and the Free Application for Federal Student Aid (FAFSA) is required. No-need scholarships and grants are also available. Students who have attained a 95 percent or better high school average and a minimum combined score of 1250 on the SAT I are considered for the Molloy Scholars' Program, which awards full tuition scholarships. Partial scholarships are available under Dominican Scholarships, Encarnacion Amor Verde Scholarship, Girl Scout Gold Award, and the Fine and Performing Arts Scholarships. The Transfer Scholarship Program grants partial tuition scholarships to students transferring into Molloy College with at least a 3.0 cumulative average. Athletic grants (Division II only) are awarded to full-time students based on athletic ability in baseball, basketball, cross-country, equestrian, lacrosse, soccer, softball, tennis, and volleyball. The Community Service Award is awarded to full-time freshmen demonstrating a commitment to their community and their school.

Faculty

The 307 full-time and part-time faculty members at Molloy are dedicated as much to the students as to their respective fields. The 10:1 student-faculty ratio allows for small classes where students can receive the individual attention they deserve.

In addition to their teaching responsibilities, faculty members advise students in their fields to help them select courses that both satisfy major course requirements and lead to the attainment of career goals.

Student Government

Every member of the Molloy College student body belongs to the Molloy Student Association, whose elected leaders form the Molloy Student Government. This group of students provides the leadership necessary to keep extracurricular life at Molloy College alive, productive, and practical.

Admission Requirements

Recommended admission qualifications include graduation from a four-year public or private high school or equivalent (GED test) with a minimum of 18.5 units, including 4 in English, 4 in social studies, 3 in a foreign language, 3 in mathematics, and 3 in science. Nursing applicants must have taken courses in biology and chemistry. Mathematics applicants must have taken 4 units of math and 3 of science (including chemistry or physics). Biology applicants must have credits in biology, chemistry, and physics and 4 units of math. A portfolio is required of art applicants, and music students must audition. Social work applicants must file a special application with the director of the social work program.

The admissions committee bases its selection of candidates on the secondary school record, SAT or ACT scores, class rank, and the school's recommendation. A particular talent or ability can be important. Character and personality, extracurricular participation, and alumni relationships are all considered. On-campus interviews are recommended but not required.

The St. Thomas Aquinas Program, which houses both HEOP and the Albertus Magnus Program, may be options for students not normally eligible for admission.

An early admission plan is available.

Application and Information

To apply to Molloy College, students should submit the following credentials to the Admissions Office: a completed application for admission, a nonrefundable $30 application fee, an official high school transcript or GED score report, official results of the SAT or ACT, and official college transcripts (transfer students only).

The College uses a rolling admission system. Students are advised of an admission decision within a few weeks after the application filing process is complete.

For further information, prospective students should contact:

Director of Admissions
Molloy College
1000 Hempstead Avenue
P.O. Box 5002
Rockville Centre, New York 11570
Telephone: 888-4-MOLLOY (toll-free)
World Wide Web: http://www.molloy.edu

An aerial view of Molloy College.

NAZARETH COLLEGE OF ROCHESTER

ROCHESTER, NEW YORK

The College

Nazareth College is an independent, coeducational, comprehensive college that offers career programs solidly based in the liberal arts. Its suburban campus is located in Pittsford in western upstate New York, approximately 7 miles from the city of Rochester. Founded in 1924, the College has conferred more than 12,000 baccalaureate and master's degrees. Of the more than 3,200 men and women enrolled at Nazareth, more than 2,000 are undergraduates.

Twenty-two buildings of traditional and contemporary design are conveniently situated on the College's 150-acre parklike campus. The Otto A. Shults Community Center, housing a 20,000-square-foot gymnasium, the student union, a multifaith religious center, a 25-meter swimming pool, the newly expanded fitness center, and student personnel offices, is the hub of on-campus student life. The resident students, constituting two-thirds of the undergraduate population, are housed in eleven separate residence halls. As an alternative to traditional campus housing, foreign language majors may live in La Maison Française, which is maintained by the language department. The Casa Italiana, Casa Hispana, and German Cultural Center serve as facilities for social, cultural, and academic programs reflecting Italian, Spanish, and German heritages, respectively.

Intercollegiate and intramural athletics are fully represented in the areas of men's and women's basketball, equestrian, lacrosse, soccer, swimming and diving, tennis, and track and field and cross-country, and volleyball; women's field hockey; and a variety of other NCAA-recognized sports programs.

Location

Rochester, a city of more than 300,000 people, is the third-largest city in New York State and the site of cultural, educational, and industrial centers. Located on the shore of Lake Ontario, the city is noted for the Eastman Theatre, the Strasenburg Planetarium, and the International Museum of Photography at the George Eastman House. Rochester is the world headquarters of Eastman Kodak and Bausch & Lomb and the site of a major Xerox facility. It is only 20 minutes from beautiful mountains, lakes, and recreational areas, where students can enjoy various outdoor activities, including skiing, hiking, water sports, and camping. The city supports professional sports teams in baseball, hockey, lacrosse, and soccer.

Majors and Degrees

Nazareth College awards the Bachelor of Music degree and Bachelor of Arts and Bachelor of Science degrees in accounting, American studies, applied music, art (studio), art education, art history, biochemistry, biology, business administration, business education, chemistry, economics, English, environmental science, fine arts, foreign languages (French, German, Italian, and Spanish), history, information technology, international studies, management science, mathematics, music, music education, music theater, music theory, music therapy, nursing, philoso-

phy, physical therapy, political science, psychology, religious studies, social science, social work, sociology, speech pathology, and theater arts.

Preprofessional programs are available in dentistry, law, and medicine. Teacher certification (grades 1–9 and 7–12) is offered with many majors. Certification in learning disabilities is available through an undergraduate program in inclusive education. Certification for birth–12 is offered in art education, music education, and speech pathology (communication sciences and disorders).

Academic Programs

To qualify for a degree, a candidate must fulfill the core curriculum requirements of the College as well as those of the major department or area of concentration. The candidate must also earn a minimum of 120 semester credits and satisfy a comprehensive test requirement in the major field during the senior year.

Off-Campus Programs

Nazareth College offers Junior Year Abroad programs in affiliation with the Université de Haute Bretagne in Rennes, France; the Institute of Spanish Students in Valencia, Spain; and the Universita degli G. D'Annunzio in Pescara, Italy. Students need not be language majors to take advantage of this exceptional program. Language students taking German or Japanese have the opportunity to study at the Studienforum in Berlin and Osaka University in Japan, respectively.

Nazareth College is a member of the Rochester Area Colleges, a consortium that includes Rochester Institute of Technology, the State University of New York College at Geneseo, and the University of Rochester, among others. Through this consortium, Nazareth College students can cross-register for credit in up to two courses per semester at any of the member institutions on a space-available basis.

Academic Facilities

Most of Nazareth's classrooms, laboratories, and studios are in Smyth Hall and the award-winning Arts Center, which houses art, music, and theater facilities as well as a 1,200-seat auditorium within its three wings. Carroll Hall houses speech pathology, physical therapy, counseling, and health services. Lorette Wilmot Library houses 238,863 volumes and has extensive resources in such areas as women's studies, education, minority issues, and religions in America. The library subscribes to approximately 3,300 periodicals and other serials. The building has seating for 450 students and includes a large number of individual carrels. The library also has a fine collection of lecture tapes and a growing collection of musical and spoken-word disks and tapes. The Rare Book Room is distinguished by special collections of works by Maurice Baring, Hilaire Belloc, Gilbert Keith Chesterton, and the Sitwells. The library is currently enlarging its resources and services in the nonprint media. In addition, the College's membership in the regional consortium and the Online Computer Library Center provides students with access to the resources of 1,300 other academic and research libraries.

Costs

Total costs for 2004–05 were $26,300. This included $18,040 for tuition, $7700 for room and board, and $560 for the required fees. The total does not include books, personal expenses, or transportation (if applicable). All fees are subject to change; up-to-date information can be obtained from the Admissions Office.

Financial Aid

Nazareth College endeavors to meet financial need as demonstrated on the Free Application for Federal Student Aid (FAFSA). The FAFSA should be submitted by February 15 of the year in which the student intends to enroll. The CSS PROFILE is required of early decision applicants only and should be submitted by November 15. Financial assistance is available through grants, loans, employment, and scholarships. Sources of aid include the Federal Pell Grant, New York Tuition Assistance, Federal Perkins Loan, and Federal Work-Study programs; the New York State Higher Education Services Corporation; and Nazareth College merit scholarships and grants.

Faculty

The full-time faculty members in the various academic departments hold advanced degrees from more than 100 institutions throughout the United States and abroad. Nintey-two percent of the faculty members hold the highest degree offered in their field of study. The student-faculty ratio of approximately 13:1 and an average class size of 22 ensure that students receive the individual attention that only a small college can offer.

Student Government

The Undergraduate Association of Nazareth College is the vehicle through which students can express the need for and initiate change within the College community. It is also responsible for the disbursement of funds, generated from the undergraduate activities fee, to various activities and social/cultural clubs.

Admission Requirements

Nazareth College welcomes applicants of all ages and educational backgrounds. Students of any race, color, sex, or national or ethnic origin are admitted to all of the rights, privileges, programs, and activities generally accorded or made available to students at the College. Nazareth College does not discriminate on the basis of race, color, sex, or national or ethnic origin in the administration of its educational policies, scholarship and loan programs, and sports and other school-administered programs.

Recommended academic preparation includes courses in English, college-preparatory mathematics, social studies, a foreign language, and science. Although the Admissions Committee gives primary consideration to academic achievement and potential for collegiate success, it also considers talent in art, drama, or music and involvement in cocurricular activities. A personal interview, although not required, is recommended, as it allows the applicant to view the campus and facilities, talk with students and faculty members, and meet with an admissions counselor.

Nazareth College is pleased to consider applications from students in good standing at accredited two- and four-year colleges and universities. A minimum GPA of 2.5 or better is expected. Transfer applicants who hold, or will hold prior to registration, the Associate in Arts (A.A.) or the Associate in Science (A.S.) degree from a fully accredited college may transfer a maximum of 60 semester hours of credit and enter with full junior status. Transfer applicants who hold, or will hold prior to registration, the Associate in Applied Science (A.A.S.) degree or the Associate of Occupational Studies (A.O.S.) degree from a fully accredited college or institute will have these credits evaluated on a course-by-course basis. Careful advisement on tailoring programs for holders of these degrees is offered by Nazareth College.

Application and Information

Regular decision applicants for the fall semester should submit the application form, transcripts, standardized test scores, an essay, recommendations, and a $40 application fee by February 15 (November 15 for early decision and December 15 for early action). Notification for regular decision begins February 15 (December 15 for early decision and January 15 for early action). For more information regarding the different application options, students should contact the Admissions Office.

For an application packet or information about a campus tour and interview, applicants should contact:

Vice President for Enrollment Management
Nazareth College
4245 East Avenue
Rochester, New York 14618-3790
Telephone: 585-389-2860
               800-462-3944 (toll-free)

THE NEW YORK COLLEGE OF HEALTH PROFESSIONS
School of Massage Therapy
SYOSSET AND BROOKLYN, NEW YORK

New York
COLLEGE
of Health Professions

The College and Its Mission

New York College of Health Professions, a private nonprofit institution, is one of the nation's premier centers of holistic medicine. The College educates students, treats patients, and conducts innovative research. Founded in 1981, New York College is firmly rooted in the principles of holistic health care as well as the blending of Western and Eastern practices, or integrative medicine.

New York College offers accredited degree programs in the field of complementary medicine. Undergraduate programs include an associate degree in massage therapy and a bachelor's degree in advanced Asian bodywork. Graduate programs include combined bachelor's and master's degrees in acupuncture or oriental medicine (the combined study of acupuncture and herbs). All programs lead to New York State licensing and/or national certification.

The College also offers a 495-clock-hour continuing education program in holistic nursing for RNs and a selection of other continuing education courses and workshops for both health-care professionals and the general public. In 2003, New York College was awarded a grant from New York State to train all the RNs at Bellevue Hospital in New York City in an Introduction to Holistic Nursing course.

New York College is chartered by the Board of Regents of the University of the State of New York, and all programs are registered by the New York State Education Department. The acupuncture and Oriental medicine programs are accredited by the Accrediting Commission for Acupuncture and Oriental Medicine (ACAOM). The Oriental medicine program is also approved by the California Acupuncture Board. The College is approved as a provider of Continuing Education by the New York State Nurses Association Council on Continuing Education and the National Certification Board for Therapeutic Massage and Bodywork. The College is a member of numerous professional organizations related to the fields of Oriental medicine and massage therapy. There are an on-site café and a bookstore at the Syosset campus.

Academic Programs

The massage therapy program at New York College began in 1981 and was the School's first educational program. It has since become nationally recognized and was cited for academic excellence in 1997 by the National Certification Board for Therapeutic Massage and Bodywork. In 1996, New York College became the first college in the United States to award an associate degree in massage therapy. The program exceeds national certification and state licensing requirements. In August 2003, first-time candidates from New York College had an 88 percent pass rate on the New York State Massage Therapy Licensing Examination.

The benefits of massage therapy have become widely recognized. Documentation on the effects of massage shows that it improves circulation and lymph drainage and can help treat sports injuries and alleviate stress, headaches, and other aches and pains. When practiced in conjunction with Western medical treatment, massage can also be used to treat arthritis, hypertension, diabetes, asthma, bronchitis, and neuromuscular diseases, among others. Massage therapy most commonly falls into two categories: Western (Swedish), which focuses on the musculoskeletal system and is based on standard Western anatomy and physiology, and Eastern, or Oriental, which is based on the movement of energy through various channels in the body. At New York College, students learn both of these modalities as well as the specific techniques for sports massage, chair massage, shiatsu, reflexology, and more.

New York College's massage therapy program is a 72-credit program. Upon completion, graduates receive an Associate of Occupational Studies (A.O.S.) degree in massage therapy. They are eligible to sit for the New York State Licensing Exam in Massage Therapy, the National Certification Exam for Therapeutic Massage and Body-

work, and the NCCAOM National Certification Exam for Oriental Bodywork Therapy. Course work for the massage therapy program includes in-depth study of both Western and Eastern health sciences, Western and Oriental bodywork techniques, and tai chi chuan, qi gong, or yoga. Courses are also offered in ethics, professional development, and business practice. The culmination of the program is the intensive clinical internship that students undergo in the College's on-site teaching clinic.

New York College operates on a fifteen-week trimester system. New students are admitted to the College for the September, January, and May trimesters. Ten-week, second-cycle trimester admissions may be added when there is sufficient demand. The program can be completed in twenty months, twenty-four months, or thirty-six months on a part-time basis.

Off-Campus Programs

New York College offers study abroad at its Luo Yang Medical Center facility in the People's Republic of China. Programs range from three-week immersion programs to a full trimester in China. Students study in the hospitals of Luo Yang as well as attend lectures at the medical center. The clinic rotations give students the opportunity to observe and participate in patient treatments. The courses taken in China are those required by the student's curriculum, and the classes and clinic time count toward their required credits. Currently, only students in the School of Massage Therapy are eligible to study at the College's facility in China.

Costs

Tuition is based on a per-credit charge of $275 and is paid each semester. The application fee is $85, and required fees total approximately $110 per semester. Students should expect to incur an additional $1500 in expenses for texts and supplies.

Financial Aid

New York College is an eligible institution approved by the United States Department of Education and the New York State Education Department to participate in the following programs: Federal Pell Grant, Federal Supplemental Educational Opportunity Grant (FSEOG), Tuition Assistance Program (TAP), Aid for Part-Time Study, Federal Work-Study Program, Veterans Administration, Vocational Rehabilitation, Federal Stafford Student Loan, Federal PLUS loan, and alternative financing. For additional information, students should contact the College's Office of Financial Aid (800-922-7337 Ext. 244).

Faculty

New York College has a total of 90 faculty members, 15 of whom are full-time. The faculty-student ratio is 1:16 for technique classes, 1:45 for didactic classes, and up to 1:6 for clinical internships.

Student Body Profile

Total current enrollment at New York College is more than 800 students, most of whom are in the massage therapy program. New York College does not have student housing; therefore, most students are from the local area, with the majority coming from Long Island, Brooklyn, and Queens. However, the College attracts a percentage of both international and out-of-state students.

Facilities and Resources

The main campus of the College in Syosset occupies 70,000 square feet in a modern facility on three levels. Within the facility are the administrative offices, classrooms for all College educational programs, a physical arts deck, the Integrative Health Center, Academic Health Care Clinics, the Herbal Dispensary, the James and Lenore Jacobson Library, the café, the bookstore, and student and faculty lounges. Classrooms are designed and used specifically for lecture or technique work and contain the most recent instructional materials. The physical arts deck for the practice of tai chi, hatha yoga, and qi gong is specifically designed with space, light, and quiet.

The James and Lenore Jacobson Library contains the most extensive collection of materials about holistic medicine available on Long Island. The library houses a collection of books and journals specializing in Oriental medicine, complementary and alternative therapies, acupuncture, herbs, massage therapy, and holistic nursing. The library belongs to a consortium of special and medical libraries that provide interloans of additional books and journal articles. Several networked workstations provide access to the computerized book collection catalog and magazine subject index, various software and CD-ROM programs, the Internet, and various online professional databases.

The Academic Health Care Teaching Clinics are an integral part of a student's educational experience. The clinics provide affordable holistic health care to members of the community, treating more than 30,000 patients annually. Supervised student treatments include Swedish massage, Amma massage, acupuncture, herbal consultations, and holistic nursing.

In January 2004, New York College opened a center in Brooklyn, New York, and began conducting classes in all degree programs. Located in a private wing of the Brooklyn Hospital Center, Caledonian Campus, this additional location is convenient and easily reached by subway or bus for students from the outer boroughs of New York City as well as Manhattan. This facility has both didactic and technique classrooms, a solarium for physical arts, administration and faculty offices, a student lounge for studying, and a student locker room. It is located close to the Brooklyn Public Library and to stores and restaurants. The College offers day, evening, and weekend classes in Brooklyn.

The College has been a pioneer in the field of holistic health care since its inception. The Integrative Health Center is the professional family clinic of the College and offers the skills and services of licensed holistic practitioners to patients of all ages. For more than twenty-five years, this fully integrated clinic has provided patients with minimally invasive therapies, including acupuncture; herbal medicine; many modalities of massage therapy such as Swedish, sports, Amma, shiatsu, reflexology, and pregnancy massage; and chiropractic and holistic nursing. Special patient programs exist for smoking cessation, weight loss, and cancer support.

The Dean of Students is responsible for special-needs students, academic progress advisement, the organization of study groups, and tutoring services. New York College's Career Services Office offers graduates assistance with job placement. Currently, the College lists more than 300 employment and rental opportunities for its licensed graduates. Sponsorship opportunities for graduates waiting to sit for licensure are also available.

Location

The main campus of New York College is located in Syosset, on the North Shore of Long Island, approximately 30 miles from Manhattan. Its proximity to all major parkways and railroad service provides easy access to one of the world's most exciting cities, while capturing the serenity, beauty, and open space of the suburbs. Long Island stretches for 110 miles and is a wealth of natural, cultural, and historic treasures. Some of the world's most beautiful sandy beaches surround the island—from the popular Jones Beach to the chic Hamptons to the barrier isle of Fire Island with its pristine beaches and absence of automobiles. The island's fifteen state parks also offer an abundance of recreational opportunities and even include a polo field. There are nearly 100 museums on the island.

New York College operates a center in Brooklyn, located at the Brooklyn Hospital Center, Caledonian Campus, at 100 Parkside Avenue. This facility is located directly across the street from Prospect Park and is reached easily by bus or subway from all of the boroughs of New York City, including Manhattan.

New York College owns the Luo Yang Medical Center in the People's Republic of China. Situated in the ancient capital of China, the 35-acre site is surrounded by historic and important attractions. Modern buildings are fully equipped with Western fixtures.

Admission Requirements

New York College is deeply committed to recruiting the most highly qualified and motivated candidates for admission. The College is particularly proud of its diverse population that is made up of students from a variety of cultural backgrounds, who possess many unique gifts and strengths. New York College students contribute to the friendly and supportive atmosphere at the College.

Applicants who have graduated from high school must have achieved a minimum GPA of 2.0 or have equivalent qualifications. Students may earn their GED certificate while enrolled in a massage therapy degree program by successfully completing 24 credits of specified credit courses in six subject areas. Candidates must be at least 17 years of age and, in accordance with New York State guidelines, must hold U.S. citizenship, be an alien lawfully admitted for permanent residence in the U.S., or hold a valid visa. The College is authorized under federal law to enroll nonimmigrant alien students.

Candidates must complete and submit an application along with an $85 application fee and arrange for the submission of an official high school transcript (or proof of equivalency) and official transcripts from all previously attended higher educational institutions. Candidates are notified promptly of the receipt of their application and advised which, if any, of the required documents have not been received by the Admissions Department. An admissions interview is required. The College offers on-the-spot enrollment: a student can be interviewed and conditionally admitted and enrolled in one visit.

Application and Information

New students are admitted to New York College for the September, January, and May trimesters. Additional second-cycle trimesters may be added if there is sufficient demand. It is recommended that applications be submitted three to four months prior to the desired entrance date.

Admissions Department
The New York College of Health Professions
6801 Jericho Turnpike
Syosset, New York 11791

Telephone: 800-9-CAREER Ext. 351 (toll-free)
Fax: 516-364-0989
E-mail: admissions@nycollege.edu
World Wide Web: http://www.nycollege.edu

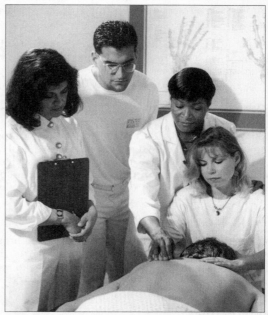

The Academic Health Care Clinics are an integral part of a student's education.

NEW YORK SCHOOL OF INTERIOR DESIGN
NEW YORK, NEW YORK

The School

The New York School of Interior Design (NYSID) is an independent, coeducational, nonprofit college accredited by NASAD. It was established in 1916 by architect Sherrill Whiton and chartered by the Board of Regents of the University of the State of New York in 1924. Throughout its history, the School has devoted all of its resources to a single field of study—interior design—and has played a significant role in the development of the interior design profession. Enrollment is approximately 750.

NYSID continually updates its curriculum to reflect the many changes taking place in interior design. Today's students learn not only the colors and materials appropriate to period residential interiors, but also how to design hospitals and restaurants and offices with barrier-free access. Whether learning the importance of historic preservation or the latest programs in computer-aided design, NYSID students learn a wide range of skills and techniques taught by faculty members who work in the field. The area's professional design studios, art and antique shops, showrooms, and museums are all an exciting part of the college's "campus."

The atmosphere of the college is cosmopolitan, not only because of its excellent location but also because it attracts students from all areas of the United States and abroad. International students make up approximately 10 percent of the student population. Students also transfer from other colleges in order to obtain a more professional, career-directed education.

Because of its select faculty and established reputation, the School continues to maintain a close relationship with the interior design industry. This provides an excellent means for students to develop associations that offer opportunities to move into the profession after completing their degree program at NYSID.

In addition to the three programs in interior design listed below, NYSID also offers a postprofessional Master of Fine Arts (M.F.A.) degree in interior design.

Location

The New York School of Interior Design is located on Manhattan's upper East Side, where many of the major interior design studios are located. Many of the world's most important museums, galleries, and showrooms are close by, most within walking distance. The city is world-renowned for its cultural activities, architecture, historic districts, and cosmopolitan urban experience. The college can be reached easily by bus, subway, train, and car.

Majors and Degrees

The New York School of Interior Design offers three programs in interior design: a four-year Bachelor of Fine Arts (B.F.A.) degree accredited by FIDER, a two-year Associate in Applied Science (A.A.S.) degree, and a 24-credit nondegree Basic Interior Design Program.

Academic Programs

The New York School of Interior Design is a single-major college. It devotes all of its resources to providing a comprehensive education in interior design, and the carefully organized curriculum is constantly evaluated by professionals in the field. The various academic programs compose an integrated curriculum covering interior design concepts; history of art, architecture, interiors, and furniture; technical and communication skills, materials and methods, philosophy and theory; and professional design procedures and design problem solving.

The Basic Interior Design Program consists of a 24-credit required sequence of foundation courses in which all students enroll. These courses provide a general, cultural, and professional introduction to the field of interior design. Although completion of the Basic Interior Design Program may be the major goal for some, for most students it serves as the foundation for matriculation into the degree programs.

The A.A.S. degree program provides the minimum educational requirement to become a certified interior designer in New York State. The 66-credit program includes professional, design, and liberal arts courses.

The 132-credit Bachelor of Fine Arts degree program provides the education that, with practical experience, enables the graduate to take qualifying exams for interior design certification in many states and to join national and local professional associations. Studies focus on the development of a broad array of technical skills, conceptual analysis, creative problem solving, and relevant cultural developments. Students are required to take 32 credits of liberal arts courses in addition to 100 credits of professional design-related courses.

The program planning is flexible and permits students to take courses on a full-time or part-time basis during the day, evening, and on Saturday. The School maintains an active job placement service. Students may be placed in a wide variety of positions that reflect the full spectrum of job opportunities in the interior design profession.

Academic Facilities

The NYSID campus occupies two buildings on Manhattan's Upper East Side. The college has a first-rate physical plant with light-filled studios; a unique lighting laboratory; a centralized computer facility for computer-aided design (CAD); a large atelier for independent work furnished with drafting tables, computers, and a materials collection for use in projects; a lecture hall and seminar rooms; a well-stocked bookstore; and a handsome auditorium. The library contains more than 12,000 volumes devoted to design, 100 periodical subscriptions, a product literature collection, and a select collection of 35 mm slides illustrating the history of interior design and decorative arts.

Costs

Tuition for 2005–06 is $590 per credit, plus an $85 registration/technology fee each semester. Typical expenses for the first year are $18,880 for tuition and $170 in registration fees.

Financial Aid

The New York School of Interior Design makes every effort to provide assistance to students with financial need. Several institutional scholarships are available for students who meet the criteria. Students are encouraged to apply for the New York State Tuition Assistance Program (TAP—for New York State residents only), the Federal Pell Grant, and Federal Education Loans. The college also participates in the Federal College Work-Study Program, which offers opportunities for on-campus employment.

Faculty

The college's programs are supported by an excellent and dedicated faculty of 85. In addition to teaching, faculty members have active professional careers in interior design, architecture, lighting design, fine arts, furniture and fabric design, history, psychology, decorative arts, law, and appraising.

Student Government

The college has an active student chapter of the American Society of Interior Designers (ASID). ASID organizes lectures, tours, workshops, and other events throughout the school year, providing an inside view of the interior design industry.

Admission Requirements

All applicants must submit an application, an official secondary school transcript, SAT I or ACT scores, and two letters of recommendation. Applicants to degree programs must meet the visual requirements by providing a portfolio or sketchbook described in the catalog; transfer students must also submit college transcripts.

Interviews are recommended for all applicants.

International applicants should contact the college's International Student Adviser for assistance in applying.

Application and Information

Admission decisions are made on a rolling basis. However, for processing purposes, it is recommended that the Admissions Office receive an application for fall admission by March 1. An application for spring admission should be received by November 1. Applicants are notified of the Admission Committee's decision by mail shortly after all required documents have been received and visual requirements fulfilled.

Inquiries and applications should be directed to:

Director of Admissions
New York School of Interior Design
170 East 70th Street
New York, New York 10021-5110
Telephone: 212-472-1500 Ext. 204
          800-33NYSID (toll-free)
Fax: 212-472-1867
E-mail: admissions@nysid.edu
World Wide Web: http://www.nysid.edu

The campus of the New York School of Interior Design is centered on its building at 170 East 70th Street in the Upper East Side Historic District.

NIAGARA UNIVERSITY
NIAGARA UNIVERSITY, NEW YORK

The University

Niagara University (NU), founded in 1856, is a private, independent university rooted in a Catholic and Vincentian tradition. The suburban 160-acre campus combines the old and new; both ivy-covered buildings and modern architectural structures are among its thirty-three buildings. The University is easily accessible from every major city in the eastern and midwestern United States via the New York State Thruway, Buffalo International Airport, and rail and bus service.

There are 2,700 undergraduate and more than 800 graduate students enrolled at Niagara. A large percentage of these students take advantage of the more than seventy extracurricular and cocurricular activities offered. Volunteer work in the community is popular among the students and enhances community relations. Students work with numerous organizations including: Habitat for Humanity, Big Brothers/Big Sisters, Maranatha (a shelter for homeless men), and the Skating Association for the Blind and Handicapped. University teams compete on the Division I level and are members of the NCAA, the Eastern College Athletic Conference, and the Metro Atlantic Athletic Conference. Intercollegiate sports include baseball, basketball, cross-country, golf, ice hockey, lacrosse, soccer, softball, swimming and diving, tennis, and volleyball. Club sports include hockey, lacrosse, martial arts, and rugby. The Kiernan Center offers a variety of sports and recreational facilities, including a multipurpose gymnasium, a swimming and diving pool, an indoor track, racquetball courts, free-weight and Nautilus rooms, and aerobics rooms. There are several outdoor athletic fields and basketball and tennis courts.

Special student services include the Health Center, which provides inpatient and outpatient care during the day; the Learning Center, which provides free tutoring services; and the Career Development Office, which offers professional and career counseling. Other services include counseling, orientation, academic planning, career planning, and job placement.

Niagara University's housing accommodations include five residence halls, a grouping of four small cottages, and a student apartment complex. Both coed and single-gender accommodations are available.

The University offers graduate studies in business, counseling, criminal justice, and education.

Location

Niagara University is situated on Monteagle Ridge overlooking the gorge of the Niagara River, which connects the two Great Lakes of Erie and Ontario. Niagara's suburban campus setting is just a few miles from the world-famous Niagara Falls. Millions of visitors view the scenic majesty of the Falls every year. NU is located 20 minutes from Buffalo, which offers a variety of cultural events, sports, and entertainment opportunities. Toronto, Canada's largest metropolitan area, is just 90 minutes north of Niagara's campus and offers an even wider variety of experiences for NU students. In addition, the University is minutes away from the quaint village of Lewiston, New York, and the city of Niagara Falls, New York.

Majors and Degrees

The College of Arts and Sciences offers the Bachelor of Arts degree in chemistry, communication studies, English, French, history, international studies, liberal arts, life sciences, mathematics, philosophy, political science, psychology, religious studies, social sciences, sociology, and Spanish. The Bachelor of Science degree is awarded in biochemistry, biology (with a concentration in biotechnology), chemistry (with a concentration in computational chemistry), computer and information sciences, criminal justice and criminology, mathematics, and social work. This division also offers the Bachelor of

Fine Arts degree in theater studies (with concentrations in design technology, general theater, and performance). Preprofessional programs are offered in dentistry, law, medicine, pharmacology, pharmacy studies, veterinary medicine, and Army-ROTC. Pre-engineering is offered as a two-year A.S. degree transfer program. An Associate of Arts degree is available in liberal arts. In addition, Niagara offers an environmental studies concentration to supplement a degree in biology, chemistry, or political science. Enrichment courses in fine arts and languages are also available.

In addition to the programs listed above NU offers a number of joint degree programs. These include a 3+4 program in medicine at the State University of New York at Buffalo, a 3+4 program in medicine at the Lake Erie College of Osteopathic Medicine, a 3+4 program in dentistry at the State University of New York at Buffalo, a 2+3 program in pharmacy at the Lake Erie college of Osteopathic Medicine, and a 2+2 program in engineering with the State University of New York at Buffalo. Qualified premedical Niagara students are eligible to apply for the early assurance program sponsored by the State University of New York at Buffalo.

The College of Business Administration grants a B.B.A. and a combination B.B.A./M.B.A. degree in accounting. This division offers a B.S. degree in commerce with concentrations in economics and finance, general business, human resources, international business, management, marketing, and transportation and logistics. In addition, an A.A.S. degree can be earned in business. Through various innovative programs and courses, such as the cooperative education programs and the small-business institute, students have the opportunity to gain valuable work-related experience.

The College of Education offers bachelor's degree programs leading to New York State initial certification in early childhood (birth–grade 6), childhood (grades 1–6), childhood and middle childhood (grades 1–9), middle childhood and adolescence (grades 5–12), adolescence (grades 7–12), and certification for teaching students with disabilities (grades 1–6 childhood and grades 7–12 adolescence). All education majors pursue an academic concentration to establish expertise in one of the following subject areas: biology, business, chemistry, English, French, mathematics, social studies, and Spanish. Business education is offered only at grades 5–12. The academic concentration in liberal arts can only be pursued in the early childhood and childhood (birth–grade 6) and in the special education and childhood (grades 1–6) dual major programs. Most other states, and Puerto Rico, have reciprocity agreements with New York, meaning that an NU education would qualify education majors to teach in those states as well. In addition, the Canadian province of Ontario recognizes Niagara graduates as qualified for the Letter of Eligibility to teach in that province.

The College of Hospitality and Tourism Management provides a career-oriented curriculum leading to a B.S. degree in two specific areas: hotel and restaurant management (concentrations in hotel and restaurant planning and control, foodservice management, and hotel entrepreneurship) and tourism and recreation management (concentrations in tourism marketing and sports and recreation management). NU offered the world's first bachelor's degree in tourism when it was founded in 1968. NU's hotel and restaurant program, the second oldest in New York State, has the distinction of being the seventh program nationally to be accredited by the Accreditation Commission for Programs in Hospitality Administration by the Council of Hotel, Restaurant, and Institutional Education. The College introduces students to a comprehensive body of knowledge about the hotel, restaurant, tourism, and recreational areas and applies this knowledge to current industry challenges. The College requires that its students accumulate 800 hours of industry-related experience. These and other practical experiences offer NU students the knowledge necessary to advance in the field. Students work with industry leaders in classroom projects, join academic clubs and professional organizations, and participate in special field trips to trade shows and conventions and specially designed study-abroad experiences, making NU a national leader in the area.

For students who are undecided about which major to choose, Niagara University offers an Academic Exploration Program (AEP). AEP provides a structured opportunity for students to participate in a thorough, organized process of selecting a major that meets their academic talents and career goals.

Academic Programs

Niagara University's curricula enable students to pursue their academic preferences and to complete courses that lead to proficiency in other academic areas. Courses that have been considered upper-division courses are available to all students. This provides students with the opportunity to avoid introductory and survey courses and permits motivated students to take advantage of more challenging courses early in their collegiate career. The honors program provides special academic opportunities that stimulate, encourage, and challenge participants. In addition, an accelerated three-year degree program is offered to qualified students.

Students pursuing a bachelor's degree must complete a total of 40 or 42 course units (120 or 126 hours) to meet graduation requirements. Niagara grants credit for successful scores on the Advanced Placement and College-Level Examination Program tests.

Internships, research, independent study, and cooperative education are available in many academic programs. An Army ROTC program is also offered.

The University operates on a two-semester plan (fall and spring). A comprehensive summer session offers a diversity of courses.

NU is fully accredited by the Middle States Association of Colleges and Schools. Its programs in the respective areas are accredited by the National Council for Accreditation of Teacher Education, AACSB International–The Association to Advance Collegiate Schools of Business, the Council on Social Work Education, and the chemistry department has the approval of the American Chemical Society. The travel, hotel, and restaurant administration program is accredited by the Commission for Programs in Hospitality Administration.

Off-Campus Programs

For those students who wish to study abroad, the University offers semester and summer programs in Chile, England, France, Ireland, Mexico, Spain, and Switzerland. Upon request, programs may be offered in other countries. NU is also affiliated with Western New York Consortium. Through this program, students may take courses at other colleges and universities and apply the credits to Niagra's graduation requirements.

Academic Facilities

The University's open-stack library exceeds 250,000 books and has more than 8,600 periodicals in paper and electronic format. In addition, the library holds 76,987 units of microfilm. The library is housed in a modern facility that includes seating for 500 people, including individual study carrels. The library is affiliated with the Online Computer Library Center (OCLC) network.

The prize-winning Dunleavy Hall, outstanding both educationally and architecturally, includes a behavioral science laboratory, a computerized lecture hall, and TV production rooms. The University's facilities also include the Computer Center; DePaul Hall of Science; St. Vincent's Hall; the Kiernan Center, NU's athletic and recreation center; the Leary Theatre; the Castellani Art Museum; Bailo Hall, which houses the Office of Admissions; and the Dwyer Arena, a dual-rink ice hockey complex.

Costs

Tuition for 2004–05 was $17,700. Room and board (with a choice of meal plans) cost an additional $8050 per year. Fees were estimated at $720 per year. Niagara estimates that an additional $2300 per year is adequate for books, laundry, and other essentials, such as travel to and from home.

Financial Aid

Ninety-eight percent of the incoming students who enrolled at NU received a financial aid package averaging $18,190 per year. They receive assistance in the form of merit scholarships, loans, grants, or campus employment. Students seeking financial aid should file the Free Application for Federal Student Aid (FAFSA). New York State residents should also file a Tuition Assistance Program (TAP) application.

Faculty

Niagara University has a dedicated, accessible faculty who genuinely cares about the academic and personal growth of their students. Their commitment to teaching is their primary concern. A student-faculty ratio of 16:1 and an average class size of 25 allow personal attention and classroom interaction.

Student Government

The Student Government represents all parts of the student body equally. It coordinates and legislates all student activities, serving as both liaison to and a participating member of the University as a whole. In addition, students serve on all major departmental committees and on the University Senate, which is the major advisory committee to the president and Board of Trustees.

Admission Requirements

The University welcomes men and women who have demonstrated aptitude and academic achievement at the high school level. Either SAT I or ACT test scores are required. International students are required to submit the results of their TOEFL examination. Interviews are recommended. Transfer students are accepted in any semester. (Transfer credit is evaluated individually by the dean of each division.) Students who complete high school in less than four years are eligible for early admission. Students may also apply under an early action program. Economically and educationally disadvantaged students from New York State are eligible to apply for admission through the Higher Educational Opportunity Program (HEOP).

Application and Information

Niagara operates on a rolling admission basis and adheres to the College Board Candidates Reply Date. A visit to the campus is encouraged, and overnight accommodations in a residence hall are available.

Information on all aspects of the University can be obtained by contacting the Office of Admissions.

Mike Konopski
Director of Admissions
639 Bailo Hall
Niagara University, New York 14109-2011
Telephone: 716-286-8700
          800-462-2111 (toll-free)
Fax: 716-286-8710
E-mail: admissions@niagara.edu
World Wide Web: http://www.niagara.edu

The main campus of Niagara University.

PRATT INSTITUTE
BROOKLYN, NEW YORK

The Institute

Founded in 1887 on its present site in Brooklyn by industrialist and philanthropist Charles Pratt, the Institute educated on nonbaccalaureate levels for its first half-century. As the educational preparation necessary for various professions expanded, Pratt Institute moved with the times. It granted its first baccalaureate degree in 1938 and started its first graduate program in 1950. Pratt continues to add programs at all educational levels, including undergraduate programs in creative writing and critical and visual studies, undergraduate and graduate programs in art history, and graduate programs in art education, arts and cultural management, historic preservation, and design management. Although the characteristics and educational requirements of the professions for which Pratt prepares people have changed over the course of a century, the Institute has succeeded in pursuing its abiding purpose—to blend theoretical learning with professional and humanistic development.

In educating more than four generations of students to be creative, technically skilled, and adaptable professionals as well as responsible citizens, Pratt has gained a national and international reputation that attracts undergraduate and graduate students from more than forty-six states, the District of Columbia, Puerto Rico, the Virgin Islands, and seventy countries. Unlike the typical American college student, most of those who choose Pratt already have career objectives, or at least they know they want to study art, design, architecture, or creative writing.

A short bus or subway ride from the museum, gallery, and design centers of both Manhattan and Brooklyn, Pratt Institute has twenty-four buildings of differing architectural styles spread about a 25-acre campus. Eighteen of the buildings house studios, classrooms, laboratories, administrative offices, auditoria, sports facilities, food services, and student centers. Six buildings are student residences, including the new Stabile Hall freshman residence, which provides studio space on each floor. There are adequate parking facilities for residents and commuters. Student services include career planning and placement, health and counseling, and student development. The more than sixty student organizations include fraternities and sororities, honorary societies, professional societies, and clubs.

Location

Pratt Institute, the country's premier college of art, design, writing, and architecture is located in the Clinton Hill section of Brooklyn, just minutes from downtown Manhattan. The majority of Pratt's freshmen live on the school's 25-acre, tree-lined campus. Pratt offers four-year bachelor's, two-year associate, and combined bachelor's and master's degrees.

Majors and Degrees

Pratt Institute offers the Bachelor of Architecture, Bachelor of Fine Arts, Bachelor of Art, Bachelor of Industrial Design, Bachelor of Professional Studies, Bachelor of Science, Associate of Occupational Studies, and Associate of Applied Science degrees.

The Bachelor of Architecture degree program is a five-year accredited program. For the Bachelor of Fine Arts degree, a candidate may choose to major in art and design education, art history, communications design (advertising, graphic design, illustration), computer graphics, fashion design, fashion merchandising and management, film/video, fine arts (ceramics, drawing, jewelry, painting, printmaking, sculpture), industrial design, interior design, photography, or writing for publication, performance, and media. The Bachelor of Art is in critical and visual studies and art history. In the Bachelor of Professional Studies degree program, the major is in construction management. Students seeking the Bachelor of Science degree can major in construction management. The two-year Associate of Occupational Studies degree is offered in digital design and interactive media, graphic design, and illustration. The Associate of Applied Science is offered in painting/drawing and graphic design/illustration. The two-year A.A.S. degree is transferable to a four-year program.

Students may also earn combined bachelor's/master's degrees. Programs include the B.F.A./M.S. in art history.

Academic Programs

Educating artists and creative professionals to be responsible contributors to society has been the mission of Pratt Institute since it assembled its first group of students in 1887. Within the structure of that professional education, Pratt students are encouraged to acquire the diverse knowledge that is necessary for them to succeed in their chosen fields. In addition to the professional studies, the curriculum in each of Pratt's schools includes a broad range of liberal arts courses. Students from all schools take these courses together and have the opportunity to examine the interrelationships of art, science, technology, and human need.

At the time of graduation, students in the associate degree programs have completed 67 credit hours of course work. In the bachelor's programs, credit-hour requirements range from 132 to 135 credits, depending on the particular program. For the Bachelor of Architecture degree, 175 credits are required.

Pratt's academic calendar consists of two semesters plus optional summer terms that allows students to choose alternative courses or various options usually not offered during the fall or spring semester. Two summer sessions are offered.

Off-Campus Programs

Pratt Institute offers credit for a wide variety of off-campus study programs. The Internship Program offers qualified students challenging on-the-job experience related to their major fields of interest; this extension of the classroom and laboratory into the professional world adds a practical dimension to periods of on-campus study.

International programs, available during all academic sessions, have included art and design offerings in the cities of Copenhagen and Rome and in the countries of England, France, and Italy. Architecture programs have been held in Venice, Italy, and in Finland and Japan. New programs are developed regularly in these and other countries.

Academic Facilities

Founded as the first free library in Brooklyn, the Pratt Institute Library now has more than 208,175 bound volumes, 540 periodical and newspaper subscriptions, 66,000 slides, 190,000 pictures, and 50,000 microforms the largest collection of any independent art school. Through the use of their ID cards, Pratt students also have access to numerous college libraries in the metropolitan area. The Multi-Media Center has been developed to facilitate and improve the educational communication process by providing materials in multimedia formats to support and enrich the Institute's curricula. These include slides, ¾-inch videotapes, 16-mm films, audiocassettes, and other formats appropriate for group use.

Extensive studio and state-of-the-art computer lab facilities are provided for all Pratt students. In the School of Art and Design, these include studio, shop, and technical facilities for work in all media, from the traditional to the most experimental. Graphics labs include color Macintosh IIs, Macintosh SEs, Cubicomps, Targa TIPS PCs with digitizer tablets, ALIAS labs, and a Quantel graphics system. Within the School of Architecture, students benefit not only from the design studios but also from the collective research facilities of the Institute. The School of Architecture uses SKOK CAD, Sun, and IRIS workstations. The School of Liberal Arts and Sciences maintains laboratory facilities for all science courses. Apple, AT&T, IBM, LSI-11, and TI microcomputers; a Burroughs batch-processing system; and an HP 100 computer are available to students in all majors. Pratt also has a DEC VAX 6210 minicomputer for Institute-wide integration of computer graphics and computer-aided design capabilities as well as AT&T 386 PCs and an extensive telecommunications laboratory. Gallery space, both on campus and at Pratt Manhattan, is extensive, showing the work of students, alumni, faculty members, staff members, and other well-known artists, architects, and designers. The Pratt Institute Center for Community and Environmental Development functions as a laboratory for the study of planning and advocacy issues in real-world situations.

Costs

Tuition for the 2005–06 academic year was $26,500. Room charges were $5376 per academic year. A meal plan is available and costs about $3200 per year. The fees were $1080. The estimated cost of books and supplies is $3000 per academic year. Students should allow an additional $650 for transportation and personal expenses.

Financial Aid

Pratt Institute offers a large number of grants, scholarships, loans, and awards on the basis of academic achievement, talent, financial need, or all three. More than 75 percent of Pratt students receive aid in one or more of these kinds of aid. Through funds from the federal and state governments, contributions from Pratt alumni, and industry scholarships, Pratt is able to maintain an effective aid program in a time of escalating costs. Pratt attempts to ensure that no student is prevented by lack of funds from completing his or her education.

Faculty

The faculty at Pratt Institute is exceptional in that a large number of practicing professionals augment the regular full-time faculty. There are 98 full-time and 658 part-time faculty members; there are no graduate teaching assistants. In small classes and studios, students have easy access to professors whose natural environment is the design studio, the architectural office, or the industrial research department.

Student Government

The Student Government Association (SGA) maintains primary responsibility for all student interests and involvement at Pratt. The SGA structure includes the Executive Committee, Senate, Finance Committee, Buildings and Grounds Committee, Academic and Administrative Affairs Committee, and Program Board. Student representatives serve on the Board of Trustees and on its various committees. All undergraduate students are encouraged to become involved in the SGA, whose main functions are allocating and administering funds collected through the student activities fee, scheduling student activities, and representing the student viewpoint to the rest of the Pratt community.

Admission Requirements

Pratt Institute attracts and enrolls highly motivated and talented students from diverse backgrounds. Applications are welcome from all qualified students, regardless of age, sex, race, color, religion, national origin, or handicap. Admission standards at Pratt are high. One of the major components for admission consideration in art, design, or architecture is the evaluation of a student's art portfolio by means of an interview, attendance at a Portfolio Day, or through the submission of work samples on slides.

All applicants must submit transcripts and letters of recommendation from any high schools and colleges attended. Additional professional requirements are specific to each school or major. Instructions can be found at http://www.pratt.edu/admiss/apply.

The admission committee bases its decisions on careful reviews of all credentials submitted by applicants in relation to the requirements of the program to which students seek admission. The SAT I or ACT and a strong college-preparatory background are required of all applicants for four-year programs. In certain cases an extraordinary talent may offset a low grade or a test score.

Application and Information

Pratt has three admissions deadlines: November 15 for early action and January 1 and February 1 for regular admissions. To receive full consideration, students must submit applications by February 1 for anticipated entrance in the fall semester and by October 15 for anticipated entrance in the spring semester.

For more information about Pratt Institute, students should contact:

Office of Admissions
Pratt Institute
200 Willoughby Avenue
Brooklyn, New York 11205
Telephone: 718-636-3514
              800-331-0834 (toll-free)
E-mail: admissions@pratt.edu
World Wide Web: http://www.pratt.edu

ST. BONAVENTURE UNIVERSITY

ST. BONAVENTURE, NEW YORK

The University

St. Bonaventure University provides a values-based, Franciscan liberal arts education with individual attention from professors, a beautiful residential setting, and a friendly, close-knit atmosphere. Of the 2,800 students enrolled, 2,200 are undergraduates. More than 74 percent of the undergraduates are full-time residents. Complementing St. Bonaventure's traditions are innovative degree programs, computerized career placement aids, comprehensive student life activities, and modern academic facilities. Among major campus events during the academic year are concerts and coffeehouse acts, indoor and outdoor recreational programs, current and classic film offerings, and dramatic and musical plays. Aspiring writers and broadcasters from all academic majors—Bonaventure has produced 5 Pulitzer Prize winners—find challenging and plentiful opportunities working with one of the four University media: WSBU-88.3 FM-The Buzz, the nationally ranked campus radio station; *The Bona Venture*, the award-winning weekly newspaper; *The Bonadieu*, the yearbook; and *The Laurel*, the nation's oldest student literary publication, which marked its 100th anniversary in 1999. Other organizations on campus include academic fraternities, academic honor societies, a variety of club and intramural sports, and arts organizations that include choral, instrumental, dance, and drama ensembles. The Thomas Merton Ministry Center is open 24 hours a day and aims to foster a community of friendship and mutual service. Many students take the opportunity to serve as Bona Buddies to area children or senior citizens; help with the national award–winning soup kitchen The Warming House, which is the oldest student-run soup kitchen in the nation; or volunteer in other service organizations. Volunteer opportunities expanded with the opening of St. Bonaventure's Franciscan Center for Social Concern, which offers immersion experiences and service opportunities with the poor.

St. Bonaventure University students enjoy two athletic facilities: the new $6.2-million Richter Center, which is open 24 hours a day, features three basketball courts, a running/walking track, racquetball/squash/wallyball courts, an aerobics room, a recreational area for roller hockey, a weight room, a cardiovascular fitness room, locker rooms, an equipment check-out, a reception area, a juice bar, and a climbing wall; and the Reilly Center, housing a 6,000-seat sports arena, swimming pool, and weight room. Also available are outdoor tennis and basketball courts and a nine-hole golf course. NCAA Division I athletics for men are baseball, basketball, cross-country, golf, soccer, swimming, and tennis. Division I competition for women includes basketball, cross-country, lacrosse, soccer, softball, swimming, and tennis.

In addition to its undergraduate programs, St. Bonaventure offers the Master of Arts degree in English, Franciscan studies, and theology. A Master of Science is offered in professional leadership, while a Master of Science in Education program includes adolescence education, advanced inclusive processes, advanced teacher education, counselor education, educational administration, health education, literacy, and supervision and curriculum. A Master of Business Administration degree program is available with concentrations in accounting/finance, general business, international business, and management/marketing, and a Master of Arts degree in integrated marketing communications was added in 2003.

Location

St. Bonaventure is located on Route 417 between Olean, a city of approximately 17,000 residents, and Allegany, a village with about 2,000 residents. Shops, restaurants, and movie theaters are all within walking distance. The campus is spread over 500 acres in a valley surrounded by the Allegheny Mountains. The free Bona Bus connects the campus with Olean and Allegany, carrying students to and from the area attractions. The region around St. Bonaventure provides a beautiful setting for many outdoor activities. A ski resort, ice rink, and snow-tubing resort attract students, and nearby Allegany State Park offers excellent facilities for swimming, boating, and hiking. St. Bonaventure is accessible by car, bus, and commercial air transportation, with Buffalo/Niagara International the nearest airport.

Majors and Degrees

St. Bonaventure University grants the Bachelor of Arts degree with majors in classical languages, English, history, interdisciplinary studies, journalism and mass communication, modern languages (French and Spanish), music, philosophy, political science, psychology, social sciences, sociology, theology, and visual arts. The Bachelor of Science is granted with majors in biochemistry, biology, chemistry, computer science, economics, elementary/special education (dual certification), environmental science, interdisciplinary studies, mathematics, physical education, physics, and psychology. The Bachelor of Business Administration is granted with majors in accounting, finance, management sciences, and marketing. Popular five-year programs are also available in business, English, physics, and psychology. Certification programs in business, education, and Franciscan and theological studies are also offered.

Academic Programs

Students in all majors begin their intellectual journey in Clare College, St. Bonaventure's nationally acclaimed core curriculum, which offers a values-based education grounded in the vision of St. Francis and St. Bonaventure. Composed of 49 credits, it begins with "The Intellectual Journey" and continues through courses in composition and critical thinking and various core areas, followed by a capstone University forum.

A candidate for a bachelor's degree must complete at least 120 credit hours, with a cumulative index of 2.0 or better in the major field and the overall program. A pass/fail grade option, available to all upperclass students, may be elected for one course per semester, but not for courses in a student's major field.

Advanced credit is granted for grades of C or better on either the College Proficiency Examination or the College-Level Examination Program (CLEP) tests. Advanced placement is granted on the basis of scores obtained on the College Board's Advanced Placement (AP) examinations.

Men and women may also elect to participate in the University's Army ROTC program, which earned the MacArthur Award as best small unit in the nation in 1998.

Off-Campus Programs

Through St. Bonaventure's membership in the College Consortium for International Studies (CCIS), St. Bonaventure students have access to six continents. More than sixty semester-long international study programs, including St. Bonaventure–sponsored study in Spain, Ireland, and Australia, are available to students in good academic standing in their junior year. Faculty-directed, short-term opportunities include a three-week intersession in China, the Francis E. Kelly Oxford summer program, and a three-week travel study program to Mexico. For further information, students should contact the Office of International Studies. Fieldwork or internships are available in several major programs.

Academic Facilities

Friedsam Memorial Library houses more than 250,000 volumes and includes a trilevel resource center with a curriculum center, the University archives, and digital media and conferencing centers, as well as world-class special collections. An automated online card catalog greatly improves research capabilities.

DeLaRoche Hall, which is planned to soon undergo an $8.5-million upgrade, houses equipment for instruction and research in a variety of fields, including chemistry, geology, mathematics, microbiology, physics, and psychology. Research facilities include an atomic absorption spectrophotometer, a tissue-culture laboratory, a greenhouse, a radioactivity laboratory, equipment for research in the growth of microorganisms, and an extensive mammal collection.

The John J. Murphy Professional Building provides the most up-to-date equipment for the School of Business and the School of Journalism and Mass Communication. The Bob Koop Broadcast Journalism Laboratory features a television studio with an anchor desk, digital and videotape editing bays, while the building also houses offices, classrooms, and a 432-seat auditorium. A fiber-optic network connects microcomputers in academic and administrative areas. There are seven labs for student use containing more than 100 DOS and Macintosh systems. St. Bonaventure students also have access to the Internet via every residence hall.

An annex to Plassmann Hall houses computer-adaptable education classrooms, seminar rooms, and offices for the education faculty. An observatory allows students access to three compact telescopes, two 8-inch Celestron telescopes, and one 11-inch Schmidt-Cassegrain telescope, along with a heated classroom.

The Regina A. Quick Center for the Arts provides acoustically designed classroom space for music courses and painting and drawing studios for students enrolled in visual arts classes. The center also includes a musical instrument digital interface lab, a 325-seat theater, and an atrium that is often used for poetry readings and impromptu musical performances.

The F. Donald Kenney Museum and Art Study Wing, dedicated in 2001, includes four climate-controlled galleries offering nationally acclaimed traveling exhibits, works from the University's permanent collections, and student exhibits.

In 1999, St. Bonaventure completed the most comprehensive renovation project in its history, comprising $5 million in renovations to its residence halls and academic facilities and an additional $2 million to fund new apartment housing for 96 students.

Costs

For 2004–05, the annual costs were $18,650 for tuition and $835 for fees. Room and meal plans averaged $6850 per year.

Financial Aid

Students who qualify for financial aid normally receive a package consisting of a combination of scholarships, grants, loans, and work-study awards. Athletic Grants-in-Aid are available for men in baseball, basketball, golf, soccer, swimming, and tennis and for women in basketball, lacrosse, soccer, softball, swimming, and tennis. Music scholarships are also available. Students must file the Free Application for Federal Student Aid (FAFSA) in order to be considered for financial assistance. For more complete details, a student should contact the director of financial aid at the University.

Faculty

Like the student body, the 160 full-time and 67 part-time faculty members at St. Bonaventure come from a wide range of geographic, ethnic, and religious backgrounds. The student-faculty ratio of 15:1 allows faculty members the time to help each student to understand different modes of thinking, develop as a person, and lay a foundation for lifelong learning. Eighty-four percent of the faculty members hold the terminal degree in their field. Friars, many of whom teach, add to the unique atmosphere of St. Bonaventure.

Student Government

Life at St. Bonaventure is centered on the residence halls, and the foundation of student government begins in the dormitories with the Residence Hall Councils. The elected council members determine the norms by which the residents are guided in their daily lives. The Student Government, whose members are elected from the student body, serves as the general student-governing unit, and its members serve on every major University board and committee.

Admission Requirements

St. Bonaventure University welcomes applications for admission from all serious candidates from a variety of backgrounds. St. Bonaventure University provides equal opportunity without regard to race, creed, color, gender, age, national or ethnic origin, marital status, veteran status, or disability in admission, employment, and in all of its educational programs and activities. Applicants, who are welcome to apply online, must show evidence of academic achievement to be selected for admission. The criteria used in making admission decisions, in order of importance, are quality of the high school curriculum, grade point average in college-preparatory courses, ACT (preferred) or SAT I scores, class rank, recommendations from high school teachers and counselors, and extracurricular activities.

Application and Information

For more information about St. Bonaventure University, prospective students should contact:

Director of Admissions
St. Bonaventure University
P.O. Box D
St. Bonaventure, New York 14778
Telephone: 716-375-2400
             800-462-5050 (toll-free)
E-mail: admissions@sbu.edu
World Wide Web: http://www.sbu.edu

Built in 1928 and renovated in 1999, Devereux Hall is an example of the beautiful Florentine architecture found at St. Bonaventure University.

ST. JOHN FISHER COLLEGE
ROCHESTER, NEW YORK

The College

Founded in 1948 by the Basilian fathers, St. John Fisher College is dedicated to serving the individual needs of its students. Originally a Catholic college for men, Fisher is now an independent, coeducational college with 58 percent women and 55 percent resident students. The College offers twenty-eight undergraduate programs in business, the humanities, nursing, sciences, and social sciences and is accredited by the Middle States Association of Colleges and Schools. The College also offers twelve graduate programs leading to the Master of Business Administration, the Master of Science, and the Master of Science in Education.

Fisher's unique First-Year Program reaches beyond the transition to college to focus on developing responsible campus citizens with independent learning skills, who fully explore educational and career aspirations. The Learning Community Program gives first-year students the opportunity to take courses in clusters that focus on a central theme. Through this approach to learning, students and faculty members examine a complex topic from multiple perspectives and discover connections among various disciplines. Fisher's Learning Communities also enable students to learn cooperatively and develop close working relationships with other students and faculty members.

Fisher offers a full range of extracurricular activities designed to cater to the diverse interests of the nearly 2,400 full-time and 900 part-time students. Such activities include a student newspaper, a campus radio station, a complete intramural program, and more than fifty student organizations. In addition, the Student Activities Board sponsors appearances by on-campus lecturers and entertainers.

Fisher is a member of NCAA Division III, ECAC, the NYS Women's Collegiate Athletic Association, and the Empire 8. Men's intercollegiate sports are baseball, basketball, football, golf, lacrosse, soccer, and tennis. Women's intercollegiate sports are basketball, cheerleading, lacrosse, soccer, softball, tennis, and volleyball. Club sports include ice hockey and men's and women's rugby. The Student Life Center, which is the hub of the athletic activities, includes courts for basketball, racquetball, squash, tennis, and volleyball; a sauna; a whirlpool; a lounge; an exercise area; and game rooms. Growney Stadium, complete with 2,100 bleacher seats and a press box, is equipped with an all-weather synthetic playing field to allow for all-season and nighttime play. Other on-campus athletics facilities include a nine-hole golf course, a softball field, a baseball complex, four outdoor tennis courts, and two grass practice fields. In the summer, Fisher is proud to host the Buffalo Bills training camp on campus.

Location

Located on 140 parklike acres, Fisher offers a balance of city activity and suburban tranquility. Just 10 minutes from the Fisher campus, Rochester, the "World's Image Center," offers many cultural attractions, including the Eastman Theater, the Rochester Philharmonic Orchestra, the International Museum of Photography at George Eastman House, the Rochester Museum and Science Center, and the Strasenburgh Planetarium. Home to a number of Fortune 500 companies, such as Eastman Kodak Company, Xerox Corporation, and Bausch and Lomb, the city of Rochester offers Fisher students opportunities for internships and employment after graduation.

Majors and Degrees

St. John Fisher College offers courses leading to the Bachelor of Arts and Bachelor of Science degrees. Undergraduate majors are offered in accounting, American studies, anthropology, applied information technology, biology, chemistry, childhood education, communication/journalism, computer science, economics, English, French, history, interdisciplinary studies, international studies, management, math-

ematical sciences and technology integration, mathematics, nursing, philosophy, physics, political science, psychology, religious studies, sociology, Spanish, special education, and sport studies. The areas of concentration available in the management major include finance, general business management, human resource management, and marketing.

Fisher offers a fast track to the B.S./M.S. in advanced practice nursing. The College also offers a cooperative 3+4 program with the Pennsylvania College of Optometry and a cooperative engineering program with the University of Detroit Mercy, Clarkson University, Manhattan College, Columbia University, and the University at Buffalo, The State University of New York.

Academic Programs

The bachelor's degree is conferred upon those who complete a minimum of 120 semester hours of credit with a cumulative GPA of at least 2.0. Thirty hours of credit and half of the requirements for the major must be earned at St. John Fisher College. Graduates of the accounting program are eligible to sit for the CPA and CMA examinations.

Off-Campus Programs

Fisher offers a multitude of special programs that are designed to complement its academic programs. Students in various disciplines can take advantage of an internship program, Albany and Washington Semesters, and cross-registration with fourteen member colleges of the Rochester Area College Consortium. Study-abroad opportunities throughout the world are also available to students.

Academic Facilities

Over the last five years, most of the academic and athletic facilities on campus have been upgraded and enhanced. Classrooms have been modernized and outfitted with state-of-the-art media facilities. Laboratory space has been upgraded with state-of-the-market educational technology. The Golisano Academic Gateway, complete with the Frontier Cyber Café and the learning resource center, opened in January 2001. The residence halls have been renovated, giving all students access to the Internet and cable TV in their rooms. The Ralph C. Wilson, Jr. Building opened in September 2003, expanding classroom capacity by 20 percent and providing additional faculty offices, seminar rooms, and meeting spaces.

The Charles J. Lavery Library is well positioned to meet the information needs of twenty-first-century students. A healthy blend of traditional and electronic resources, covering a broad range of subjects, is available to both the novice and experienced researcher. The library's Web-based catalog is supplemented by more than 90 electronic databases, and Internet access adds a whole new realm of information sources. Traditional resources in Lavery Library include 190,000 volumes, approximately 30,000 multimedia items, 1,000 print periodical subscriptions, and access to 8,000 electronic periodical titles. The library is open 95 hours per week for the convenience of students and provides a variety of study venues. Fisher's Career Services Department is also housed in the library.

Costs

Tuition for 2004–05 was $18,200. Room and board were $7900 with a fourteen-meal plan and a room in one of Fisher's residence halls.

Financial Aid

Committed to helping students meet the cost of their education, Fisher works to assess each individual's financial need. Financial aid is provided through scholarships, grants, loans, and work-study arrangements and is awarded by Fisher, the state, and the federal government. In 2004–05, the average financial aid package for Fisher students was $15,600.

St. John Fisher College offers a generous academic scholarship program that is based on high school average, class rank, and SAT or ACT results. Students eligible for academic scholarships are automatically notified by the Office of Undergraduate Admissions. Scholarship award amounts are $2500 to $10,000 per year. The College also offers an honors program and a science scholars program. The award in each of these programs is $2500, in addition to an academic scholarship.

Nine years ago, the College introduced the Service Scholars Program. This program is designed to recognize and reward high school seniors who demonstrate an ongoing interest in serving the needs of others through a commitment to community service. Scholarship awards equal one third of the total yearly cost of tuition, fees, room, and board for four years. In 2002, the Service Scholars Program won the President's Community Volunteer Award—the highest national honor for volunteering. The College was honored, along with 19 other winners from across the country, at a White House ceremony. Fisher was the only college or university and the only organization in New York State to be honored that year.

In 1998, the College announced the creation of the Fannie and Sam Constantino First Generation Scholarship Program, designed to provide financial assistance to students whose parents did not attend a postsecondary institution—much like the pioneer classes of St. John Fisher College. Recipients receive annual scholarships ranging from $5000 to one third of the total yearly cost of Fisher's tuition, fees, room, and board for four years.

Faculty

Fisher's 132 full-time faculty members are dedicated to helping students, both in and out of the classroom, as they strive to achieve their goals. Eighty-three percent of full-time faculty members hold doctoral or terminal degrees. The student-teacher ratio of 10:1 offers a personal approach to education; 75 percent of all classes have fewer than 30 students. Fisher's Office of Academic Affairs and an outstanding faculty share responsibility for academic advising, helping students to explore the twenty-eight majors that are available to them.

Student Government

Student leadership skills are developed through the Student Government Association, which is responsible for the social, cultural, and judicial areas of student life. Resident students elect a Resident Student Association, while commuting students elect a Commuter Council to represent them in planning special activities. The Student Activities Board is responsible for social activities and cultural events throughout the academic year.

Admission Requirements

Admission to St. John Fisher College is based primarily on the following: high school record, scores on standardized tests (SAT/ACT), extracurricular activities and/or work experience, and the high school's evaluation of the candidate. Interviews are also considered and strongly encouraged.

A candidate for admission to the freshman class must be a graduate of an approved secondary school and present a minimum of 16 units of college-preparatory course work in English, foreign languages, mathematics, and natural and social sciences. An applicant should present a secondary school average of 85 percent or above in these academic subjects.

Fisher welcomes qualified transfer students from two- and four-year colleges for both the fall and spring terms. To be considered for admission, transfer students must have a cumulative grade point average of 2.0 or better. If the student has obtained an A.A., A.S., or A.A.S. degree, 60 to 66 credit hours are transferred. All transfer applicants should consult the Undergraduate Bulletin for details.

The College has various special admission programs, including early decision, abbreviated procedures for veterans and other military personnel, and admission for nondegree and part-time study.

The College offers the New York State Higher Education Opportunity Program (NYS HEOP) for students who need special academic and financial assistance. The program provides academic support services, counseling, and financial aid for qualified students to help them achieve academic success.

Fisher grants college credit for satisfactory grades on the Advanced Placement test, the New York College Proficiency Examination, and the College-Level Examination Program (CLEP). Only students who receive a 3 or better in all AP subjects and a 4 or better on the AP science and language exams are granted Advanced Placement credit. CLEP scoring guidelines are available through the Office of Undergraduate Admissions. Credit is only granted for subject-specific CLEP exams. Fisher recognizes the International Baccalaureate Organization. Equivalent College credit is granted for those students who complete the International Baccalaureate (I.B.) curriculum and exams according to policies developed by individual departments.

Application and Information

Applications are accepted on a rolling basis. Early-decision applications are due December 1. The priority deadline for freshman applications is March 1. A personal interview is not ordinarily required for admission; however, all applicants are encouraged to visit the College. Interviews and campus tours are available weekdays from 8:30 a.m. to 4:30 p.m. and on specified Saturdays from 9 a.m. to noon.

For additional information or an application, students should contact:

Office of Undergraduate Admissions
St. John Fisher College
3690 East Avenue
Rochester, New York 14618
Telephone: 585-385-8064
　　　　　 800-444-4640 (toll-free)
Fax: 585-385-8386
E-mail: admissions@sjfc.edu
World Wide Web: http://www.sjfc.edu

Kearney Hall, Fisher's main administration building.

ST. JOSEPH'S COLLEGE
BROOKLYN AND PATCHOGUE, NEW YORK

The College

St. Joseph's College, founded in 1916, is a private, coeducational institution specializing in the liberal arts and preprofessional programs. The College maintains separate campuses in Brooklyn and Patchogue, New York, and enrolls a total of 4,294 students in its School of Arts and Sciences and School of Adult and Professional Education.

The College seeks to create a free atmosphere in which students and faculty members together can investigate the major areas of human knowledge as the basis for a more effective participation in today's world. In support of this philosophy, the College pursues a number of specific objectives, including providing an atmosphere for open dialogue, individual attention, and innovative teaching; inspiring in students a spirit of inquiry and the joy of learning as an ongoing part of their lives; and preparing students for their lifework by providing the necessary professional and preprofessional training.

In conjunction with Polytechnic University, St. Joseph's offers rooms at Polytechnic's new residence hall, located near St. Joseph's Brooklyn campus. St. Joseph's College offers numerous extracurricular and cocurricular activities designed to help its students grow personally as well as academically. Each campus offers more than twenty clubs and activities, including intercollegiate basketball, women's softball, and volleyball. The Patchogue campus also offers men's soccer, a women's swim team, and a coed equestrian team. The social life is maintained through these clubs, which sponsor numerous dances, barbecues, intramural sports, screenings of current films, and vacation trips each year. Since all students live in the vicinity of their respective campuses, they often organize informal social events among themselves.

The ultramodern, 48,250-square-foot John A. Danzi Athletic Center houses a competition-sized basketball court, an elevated jogging and walking track, seating for 1,500 spectators, a 25-yard pool, and an aerobic and fitness center.

Location

The Brooklyn campus in the historic Clinton Hill section of Brooklyn is easily accessible by public transit lines and automobile. The convenient location, where undergraduates can enjoy the freedom of campus life while profiting from the many cultural advantages of the New York City area, attracts students from every part of the metropolitan region. The College is in the center of one of the nation's most diversified academic communities, with six colleges and universities within a 2-mile radius. St. Joseph's offers its students easy access to the other colleges and such cultural facilities as the Brooklyn Academy of Music, the Brooklyn Public Library, and the Brooklyn Museum.

The Patchogue campus, located on the beautiful south shore of Long Island, is easily accessible to its students from both Nassau and Suffolk Counties. Situated on the western rim of the Great Patchogue Lake, the 28-acre campus features comfortable classrooms and administrative and student facilities, surrounded by athletic fields and spacious lawns. The College and its students have established close ties with the neighboring communities and with the village of Patchogue itself.

Majors and Degrees

The Brooklyn campus offers four-year programs leading to B.A. and B.S. degrees, with majors in accounting, biology, business administration, chemistry, child study (a sequence in special education is optional), computer information systems, English, history, human relations, mathematics, psychology, social science (including economics, political science, and sociology), Spanish, and speech communication. Certificate programs are available in criminology/criminal justice, gerontology, information technology applications, leadership and supervision, management, and marketing, advertising, and public relations.

Through a partnership between St. Joseph's College and Polytechnic University, students at St. Joseph's now have the opportunity to earn a bachelor's degree in the field of their choice and a master's degree in computer science in a combined B.A./B.S. plus M.S. program. The bachelor's degree is issued from St. Joseph's, and the master's degree is issued from Polytechnic University.

The Brooklyn campus also offers an accelerated biomedical program in cooperation with the New York College of Podiatric Medicine (NYCPM). After two years at St. Joseph's, students spend four years at the NYCPM. At the end of the six years, students receive a B.S. in biology as well as the D.P.M. from NYCPM.

The Patchogue campus offers four-year programs leading to the B.A. degree, with majors in child study (including special education), English, history, human relations, mathematics, psychology, social sciences, and speech communication. The B.S. degree is available in accounting, biology, business administration, mathematics, mathematics/computers, and recreation. Certificate programs, which are registered with the New York State Education Department, are offered in applied sociology, criminology/criminal justice, gerontology, human resources, information technology applications, leadership and supervision, management, and marketing, advertising, and public relations.

Both campuses offer preprofessional programs in law, teaching, and numerous health fields, including dentistry, medicine, and optometry.

The School of Adult and Professional Education at each campus is designed especially for adults with nontraditional academic backgrounds or with professional training and experience. Bachelor of Science degrees are offered in community health, general studies, health administration, organizational management, and nursing.

Academic Programs

The School of Arts and Sciences at each campus operates on the semester system, and there are limited course offerings during the summer and in January. Since students are expected to attain breadth and balance in their academic studies, a core curriculum is an integral part of the 128 credits required for graduation. However, a wide range of choices to satisfy the core curriculum requirements allows students to tailor their academic program in accordance with their personal and professional needs.

The College recognizes the Advanced Placement (AP) Program and offers credit and placement for scores of 3, 4, or 5 on the AP test. In each case, the score is reviewed by the registrar and/or department chairperson to determine credit and placement. Depending on the specific area covered by a College-Level Examination Program (CLEP) test, credit may be granted.

The School of Adult and Professional Education on each campus operates on numerous schedules. Courses are offered during the day, evenings, or weekends to best meet the needs of working students who are pursuing a degree. Some courses meet for a semester, some in six- or twelve-week sessions. An extensive summer program is offered.

Academic Facilities

The Brooklyn campus is composed of eight buildings. The Dillon Child Study Center, a laboratory preschool enrolling approximately a hundred 3-, 4-, and 5-year-olds, is used by child study students as a teaching and observation resource. McEntegart Hall, a modern five-level structure, houses the 122,563-volume library, audiovisual resource center, curriculum library, archives, and computer labs. Other academic facilities include fully equipped biology, chemistry, computer, physics, and psychology research laboratories.

At the Patchogue campus, the main building houses administrative and faculty offices; laboratories for biology, chemistry, physics, and psychology; the computer center; art and music studios; the Local History Center; and the Office of Counseling. A library building, with a capacity of 120,000 volumes, houses a curriculum library, seminar rooms, administrative offices, and two classrooms. The Clare Rose Playhouse, situated on the northeast corner of the campus, is an educational and cultural learning facility where students and local communities can explore the various aspects of theater from production to performance.

The College has constructed a high-speed fiber-optic intracampus network that connects all offices, institutional facilities, computer laboratories, and libraries on the Brooklyn and Patchogue campuses. Direct Internet access is available to all students and faculty and staff members through the College's server. The integrated online library system enables students to locate and check out books at either campus and also provides links to online databases and other electronic information sources.

Costs

In Brooklyn, the annual full-time undergraduate tuition for 2004–05 was $11,078. The cost for nonmatriculated or part-time students was $357 per credit. In Patchogue, the annual full-time undergraduate tuition for 2004–05 was $11,600. The cost for nonmatriculated or part-time students was $376 per credit. Mandatory fees were $322.

Financial Aid

Scholarships and grants-in-aid are available at St. Joseph's College. Students wishing to apply for either form of assistance must file the Free Application for Federal Student Aid (FAFSA), an institutional aid form, and a state aid form. After a student has been accepted to the College and all financial aid forms are properly processed, the Financial Aid Office will prepare packages of aid that usually consist of federal, state, and College funds. St. Joseph's is fully approved for veterans. Campus work-study programs are also available.

Faculty

The College's 16:1 student-faculty ratio ensures very close relationships between students and their professors. Faculty members serve as academic advisers, are active on student affairs committees, and act as moderators to student organizations.

Student Government

Student government on each campus is active in many facets of academic and student life and organizes social events such as mixers, film festivals, lectures, and off-campus trips.

Admission Requirements

St. Joseph's College seeks a diverse student body and welcomes applications from high school students, transfer students, and others who may have a nontraditional academic background. The College offers programs to serve all of these groups.

Students who wish to enter as freshmen are expected to have completed at least 18 units of college-preparatory work by the end of their senior year. This should include the following distribution: 4 years of English, 2 years of foreign language, 3 years of mathematics, 2 years of science, and 4 years of social studies. Applicants interested in accounting, allied health fields, biology, business administration, chemistry, or mathematics should have more extensive backgrounds in mathematics and science. The College will also consider students who have received a general equivalency diploma.

The School of Arts and Sciences requires the submission of official results from the SAT I.

St. Joseph's College will accept a block transfer of credits from students holding an A.A. or A.S. degree in certain majors from an accredited junior or community college. All other transfers are considered on an individual basis.

The Division of General Studies has more flexible admission requirements, reflecting its enrollment of adults with nontraditional academic backgrounds and work experience.

Application and Information

Admission is offered on a rolling basis. Applications and supporting documents should be submitted to the appropriate address below, along with a nonrefundable application fee of $25. Each application is reviewed very carefully, and a decision is usually sent within one month after receiving all necessary credentials. For more information, students can access the school's Web site.

Director of Admissions
St. Joseph's College
245 Clinton Avenue
Brooklyn, New York 11205
Telephone: 718-636-6868

Director of Admissions
St. Joseph's College
155 West Roe Boulevard
Patchogue, New York 11772
World Wide Web: http://www.sjcny.edu

Both campuses of St. Joseph's College provide up-to-date science, computer, and psychology laboratories.

SIENA COLLEGE
LOUDONVILLE, NEW YORK

The College

Siena College is a four-year, coeducational, independent liberal arts college with a Franciscan and Catholic tradition. It is a community of 2,900 full-time students that offers undergraduate degrees in business, liberal arts, and sciences. Student-focused professors are at the heart of a supportive and challenging learning community that prepares students for careers and an active role in their communities. Founded by the Franciscan Friars in 1937, Siena provides a personal, values-oriented education—one student at a time. It welcomes all races and creeds and prides itself on the care and concern for the intellectual, personal, and social growth of all students.

Approximately 80 percent of the College's students live on campus in numerous housing options. Siena offers traditional residence halls, suites, and town-house units. When Siena students are not in class, they have plenty to do. More than sixty clubs and organizations are active each year. The Franciscan Center for Service and Advocacy is the College's primary vehicle for service with and among the poor and marginalized and offers service to Habitat for Humanity, soup kitchens, and teaching in religious education programs. More than 75 percent of the student body is involved in some type of athletic program. The College offers eighteen Division I intercollegiate sports, club teams, and intramurals. Siena also provides numerous student support services, including counseling, tutoring, health services, peer counseling, and a career center. Popular activities include the Stage III Theatre, the student newspaper, the radio station, the yearbook, the Rugby Club, the Black and Latino Student Union, and Model United Nations.

Siena provides additional learning and cultural experiences outside of its academic programs to both its students and the wider community. Examples of these efforts to offer programs on topics of current interest include the Martin Luther King Jr. Lecture Series, the Niebuhr Institute of Religion and Culture, and the Sister Thea Bowman Center for Women.

Siena has developed a number of cooperative and special programs. In addition to the college-wide honors program, Siena offers a premed program with Albany Medical College; a five-year M.B.A. program with Clarkson University, Union University, and Pace University; a seven-year accelerated predental program with Boston University; a 3-2 engineering program in cooperation with Clarkson University, Catholic University, Rensselaer Polytechnic Institute, Manhattan College, SUNY Binghamton, and Western New England College; and the Washington Semester at American University.

Location

Siena's 155-acre campus is located in Loudonville, a residential community 2 miles north of Albany, the New York State capital. With eighteen colleges in the area, there is a wide variety of activities off campus. The Pepsi Arena hosts performances by major concert artists and professional sporting events. Within 50 miles are the Adirondacks, Berkshires, and the Catskill mountains, providing outdoor recreation throughout the year.

Montreal, New York City, and Boston are less than 3 hours away. With all of the professional, cultural, and recreational opportunities the Capital Region offers, many Siena graduates choose to begin their careers here.

Majors and Degrees

The College offers bachelor's degrees in the following areas: accounting, American studies, biochemistry, biology, chemistry, classics, computer science, creative arts, economics, English, environmental studies, finance, French, history, marketing and management, mathematics, philosophy, physics, political science, psychology, religious studies, social work, sociology, and Spanish. Current certificate programs are available in business, computer science, environmental studies, foreign language, informational systems, international studies, peace studies, and theater.

Academic Programs

A strong liberal arts core forms the basis for all of Siena's programs. All students take courses within a broad core requirement: 30 hours in the humanities and social sciences (including a 6-credit freshman foundations course), 9 hours in mathematics and science (with 3 of these in a natural science), and 3 hours in creative arts. Students must also maintain a minimum cumulative index of 2.0 and earn at least a C in every major field concentration course. Within the major, students must take a minimum of 30 credits, with no more than 39 credits counting toward the degree requirements. A total of 120 hours is required to qualify for a bachelor's degree.

Students may get credit for prior work by taking standardized college proficiency exams with the approval of the head of the department in the discipline to be examined. A total of 18 credits may be obtained this way. Siena offers honors courses in English, history, philosophy, and political science. ROTC affiliation is available at Siena in a U.S. Army unit, and an Air Force ROTC unit is available at a nearby college through cross-registration.

Off-Campus Programs

Siena students have the opportunity to spend a semester or a year studying abroad. Programs directly affiliated with the College include Siena at Regent's College, London; the Siena in London Internship Experience; the Siena semester at the Centre d'Etudes Franco-Americain de Management in Lyon, France; and the Center for Cross-Cultural Studies in Seville, Spain. In addition, programs are available for all majors everywhere on the globe. International study is typically pursued during the junior year.

Locally, internships are available through government, business, and nonprofit organizations on a two- or three-day-a-week basis, enabling students to continue with their course work at the same time. Many students are offered jobs by their internship organization upon graduation.

In addition, through the Hudson Mohawk Association of Colleges and Universities (which comprises the eighteen colleges in the area), cross-registration is possible at such institutions as Union College, Skidmore College, Rensselaer Polytechnic Institute, and the University at Albany.

Academic Facilities

The Standish Library collection of more than 321,000 volumes consists of books, journals, microforms, compact discs, video-cassettes, and a growing number of electronic information sources. More than 6,000 volumes are added annually, and 1,600 serial subscriptions are currently maintained, with electronic access to thousands of additional journals. In 2004, Siena completed the renovation of Siena Hall. The new Siena Hall is a high-technology teaching and learning center. It is also home to Siena's Hickey Financial Technology Center. The Hickey Center provides Siena's students the opportunity to trade stocks, bonds, cash, and currency in a virtual environment and provides students with access to leading sources of financial data.

All academic and residential buildings are interconnected with a high-speed Ethernet network connected via fiber optics. This network backbone runs at 10 and 100 Mbps. Every student residence space includes a 10 Mbps connection point to access the College's network and the Internet. The network includes more than 2,500 ports. The computer facilities are accessible 24 hours a day, seven days a week. Numerous computers are available throughout the campus for student use.

The Marcelle Athletic Complex features a natatorium, a field house with an elevated running track, racquetball and squash courts, an aerobics/dance studio, and an area with exercise and other weight-training equipment.

Costs

Tuition at Siena remains reasonable, helping the College to provide an education of fine quality at moderate cost. For 2005–06, tuition is $20,100; room, $4985; and board, $3000. There are lab fees for accounting, natural sciences, languages, and some fine arts and psychology courses. Miscellaneous fees may account for about $640 per year.

Financial Aid

Federal programs that Siena students may qualify for include Federal Pell Grants, Federal Supplemental Educational Opportunity Grants, Federal Perkins Loans, Federal Stafford Student Loans, and Federal PLUS loans. Residents of New York State may receive Tuition Assistance Program and Aid for Part-time Work-Study awards. Financial need is determined by the Free Application for Federal Student Aid and, where applicable, the state version of the supplemental Financial Aid Form. Aid is usually awarded in a package combining scholarships or grants, loans, and a job. Students who remain in good academic standing have their aid renewed.

Faculty

Siena's faculty members are committed to teaching. Student concerns and development are at the heart of the curriculum. Eighty-three percent of the 171 full-time faculty members have terminal degrees. The student-faculty ratio of 14:1 helps to develop interaction with students, as does the fact that Siena professors teach labs. Students are assigned a faculty adviser to help in the planning of their course of study.

Student Government

The Student Senate oversees student involvement in academic and social life and interprets students' attitudes, opinions, and rights for the faculty and administration. It charters all student organizations and provides funds for many through fees collected by the College. The governing board is made up of officers and representatives of all four classes and of the commuting students. Elections are held in April for the following year, except for freshmen, who are elected in September.

Admission Requirements

Siena seeks bright, articulate people who will blossom in the caring atmosphere that the College provides. Academic standards are demanding without being threatening. Seventy percent of incoming freshmen have combined SAT scores (math and verbal) ranging from 1050 to 1200. The high school curriculum, activities, recommendations, and campus visit all affect the final decision. Students seeking degrees in the science or business division should be well versed in mathematics. Those interested in American studies, English, history, or philosophy are likely to find a working knowledge of a foreign language very helpful.

Application and Information

The preferred deadline for the submission of a regular application is March 1 of a student's senior year in high school. Decisions are sent starting in mid-March. Siena also offers an early decision and an early action program. Early applications should be submitted before December 1. Candidates are notified by January 1. Presidential Scholar candidates must apply by January 15.

Transfer students must apply by December 1 for the spring semester or by June 1 for the fall semester. Generally, transfers are expected to have a cumulative average of at least 2.5. A minimum of 30 semester hours and half of the credits for the major must be earned at Siena. A maximum of 66 credits may be transferred from accredited two-year institutions. Credit is given only for courses that are similar in content, level, and scope to those at Siena.

For more information, students should contact:

Admissions Office
Siena College
515 Loudon Road
Loudonville, New York 12211
Telephone: 518-783-2423
          888-AT-SIENA (toll-free)
E-mail: admit@siena.edu
World Wide Web: http://www.siena.edu

STATE UNIVERSITY OF NEW YORK INSTITUTE OF TECHNOLOGY AT UTICA/ROME

UTICA, NEW YORK

The Institute

As a unique member of the State University of New York family, SUNY Institute of Technology (SUNYIT) is the ideal choice for focused students interested in technology and professional studies. SUNYIT's broad curriculum also embraces the humanities, communications, math, and science. Students enjoy close contact with faculty members in small classes, most with fewer than 20 students.

Founded as an upper-division and graduate institution in 1966, SUNYIT now offers eleven bachelor's degree programs for freshmen, twenty bachelor's degree programs for transfer students, and eleven graduate degrees, including the Master of Business Administration in technology management.

SUNY Institute of Technology enrolled 2,057 undergraduate and 624 graduate students on both a full-time and part-time basis in 2003–04. The men-women ratio was approximately 1:1. Eleven and a half percent of the students were members of minority groups; 4 percent were international students.

In addition to its academic facilities, SUNYIT provides student services through the Campus Life, Career Services, Health, and Counseling Center Offices. Townhouse-style residence halls provide on-campus housing to 584 students. The Campus Center provides health, physical education, and recreation facilities as well as a dining hall and student services offices. In addition to providing a wide variety of intramural sports for students, SUNYIT has competitive intercollegiate teams in men's and women's basketball, bowling, and soccer; men's baseball, golf, and lacrosse; and women's softball, cross-country, and volleyball.

Location

SUNYIT is located in Utica, New York. The city of Utica, which has a population of 60,000, is situated in the geographic center of New York State, approximately 220 miles from New York City and 190 miles from Buffalo on the New York State Thruway. Utica, a cultural and recreational center for this area of New York State, has a variety of recreational and educational opportunities. Museums, theaters, restaurants, and professional sports events are available either within walking distance of the campus or a short bus ride away. As a natural gateway to the Adirondack Mountains, Utica provides its residents with access to hiking, boating, skiing, and other outdoor activities. Served by buses, Amtrak, and airlines, the city is easily reached from locations throughout the eastern United States.

Majors and Degrees

SUNYIT awards the following baccalaureate degrees: Bachelor of Professional Studies (B.P.S.), Bachelor of Science (B.S.), Bachelor of Arts (B.A.), and Bachelor of Business Administration (B.B.A.).

Academic majors available to freshmen and transfer students include accounting, applied mathematics, business/public management, computer and information science, computer engineering technology, computer information systems, finance, health-information management, health-services management, industrial engineering technology, and mechanical engineering technology. Additional academic majors available to transfer students are civil engineering technology, electrical engineering, electrical engineering technology, general studies, nursing, professional and technical communication, psychology, sociology, and telecommunications.

A number of options and concentrations within specific curricula are also available, as well as minors in accounting; anthropology; computer science; economics; finance; gerontology; health-services management; manufacturing/quality assurance technology; mathematics; physics; professional and technical communication; psychology; science, technology, and society; and sociology.

Academic Programs

SUNYIT's mission is to provide professionally oriented education in a variety of academic areas. The academic year is divided into two semesters and runs from September through May. Summer and Winterm sessions are also available.

Baccalaureate degree requirements vary from program to program but usually consist of a combination of specific major courses and liberal arts studies. Specializations and other options exist within the Schools of Arts and Sciences, Information Systems and Engineering Technology, Nursing and Health Systems, and Management. Specializations are developed through the use of electives and individual advisement.

Off-Campus Programs

Internship and cooperative education experiences are integral to effective career planning and job search strategies. These experiences can influence career plans by providing an opportunity for occupational exploration, developing marketable career-related skills and characteristics, and establishing a network of contacts that can provide relevant and timely information critical to the career decision-making process. In addition, employers are increasingly using internships and cooperative education programs as training opportunities leading to full-time permanent employment. All students, regardless of major, are encouraged to consider gaining experience in their chosen field that complements classroom learning. For additional information, students should contact the academic department or the Office of Career Services.

Academic Facilities

SUNYIT's academic facilities are located on its scenic 850-acre campus just north of the city of Utica and are easily accessible by municipal bus service. The campus consists of four building complexes, a facilities building, and residence halls. SUNYIT's newest addition is the Peter J. Cayan Library, a $14-million dollar project comprising 68,000 square feet of space, group and individual study rooms, and an advanced computerized library instruction room. Dedicated in May 2003, the state-of-the-art building houses library resources that include more than 194,000 bound volumes, 65,583 microforms, and an extensive collection of professional journals, newspapers, and other national publications. In addition, the library is a federal depository for government documents. Full-text databases and databases in FirstSearch are provided; all workstations have high-speed Internet access.

Kunsela Hall contains administrative offices, classrooms, and laboratories for the telecommunications, electrical engineering, electrical engineering technology, and computer science programs. Donovan Hall, the academic complex, houses classrooms, faculty offices, and laboratory facilities for all other programs, including business, industrial engineering technology, mechanical engineering technology, health-services management, nursing, and arts and sciences. A comprehensive student center contains a gymnasium, a swimming pool, recreational facilities, a cafeteria, a bookstore, student services offices, and meeting rooms for clubs, special activities, and student government.

Costs

Costs for the 2003–04 academic year included state resident tuition and fees of $5154 and out-of-state tuition and fees of $11,104. Room and board costs were $6800, and personal expenses, books, supplies, and travel cost approximately $2730. The total expenses were about $14,684 for New York State residents and $20,634 for out-of-state students. Costs may be subject to change.

Financial Aid

A wide variety of financial aid is available to students at SUNYIT. All financial aid is awarded on the basis of need, as determined by an assessment of the Free Application for Federal Student Aid. At present, approximately 85 percent of the students receive financial assistance. The forms of financial aid available include Tuition Assistance Program awards (for New York State residents only), Federal Supplemental Educational Opportunity Grants, Federal Pell Grants, Federal Work-Study Program employment, Federal Perkins Loans, federal Nursing Student Loans, Federal Direct Student Loans, a variety of state-sponsored loans, and a broad range of private scholarships and grants. Students with a GPA of 3.25 or better or a high school average of 90 are automatically considered for merit scholarships at the time of their application.

Faculty

SUNYIT faculty members come from all over the world and are committed to teaching, research, and service to the community. Among the faculty members are a Distinguished Service Professor, a Fulbright Scholar, and numerous recipients of the Chancellor's Award for Excellence in Teaching. Eighty percent of SUNYIT's full-time faculty members have doctoral or terminal degrees. The faculty members are fully engaged in academic orientation and advisement, individualized instruction, cooperative faculty-student efforts in research projects, and concern for students as individuals. In the classroom, the average student-faculty ratio is 18:1.

Student Government

All full-time undergraduates are members of the SUNYIT Student Association. Its primary functions are to develop and monitor the student-activity-fee budget, to approve and oversee all student organizations, to debate issues of concern to students and take action as needed, and to develop programs of interest to all students. Student government consists of a 7-person executive committee and 11 senators. Students are encouraged to take an active role in the governance process, and many opportunities for involvement, in addition to those listed above, are available for interested students.

Admission Requirements

Admission to SUNYIT as a freshman is competitive and selective. In order to be considered, students should have a minimum of a B+ average in a college-preparatory program, with approximate scores of at least 1140 on the SAT I or 25 on the ACT. In addition to the admission application, test scores, and high school transcripts, a supplemental application, and an essay are required as part of the process. Students who have completed Adavanced Placement course work in high school with a score of 3, 4, or 5 are considered for transfer credit.

Admission to SUNYIT as a transfer student is also competitive. Most programs require a minimum GPA of 2.5 for guaranteed admission. Transfer students below a 2.5 GPA but above a 2.0 GPA may be required to participate in an interview. Transfer students are required to furnish an official transcript from all previous colleges they attended.

Most programs are competitive, requiring a minimum GPA of 2.5 for guaranteed admission. Students with a cumulative GPA of at least 3.25 are automatically considered for merit and residential scholarships; no separate application is required.

Application and Information

Freshman applications are reviewed beginning January 15 and are considered on a rolling admissions basis thereafter. Freshman applicants may also apply for admission through the Early Decision program. Early Decision applicants must apply by November 15. A supplemental application, including an essay, is required for consideration.

Transfer applications are accepted on a rolling admissions basis. Prospective students are urged to apply early.

Students who wish to apply should obtain a copy of the State University of New York application booklet from a two-year college, a local high school, or the Admissions Office. In addition, students may apply online through the SUNYIT Web site listed below. Application forms for international students may also be obtained through the Admissions Office.

SUNY Institute of Technology adheres to the principle that all persons should have equal opportunity and access to its educational facilities without regard to race, creed, sex, or national origin.

Official transcripts from all previously attended high schools and colleges should be sent to the Director of Admissions. All communications and requests for additional information should also be directed to:

Director of Admissions
SUNY Institute of Technology
P.O. Box 3050
Utica, New York 13504-3050
Telephone: 315-792-7500
          866-2SUNYIT (toll-free)
Fax: 315-792-7837
E-mail: admissions@sunyit.edu
World Wide Web: http://www.sunyit.edu

Townhouse-style residence halls afford students the opportunity to live and learn in a convenient, safe, and comfortable environment.

UNIVERSITY OF ROCHESTER
ROCHESTER, NEW YORK

The University

Founded in 1850, Rochester is one of the leading private universities in the country, one of sixty-three members of the prestigious Association of American Universities, and one of eight members of the University Athletic Association, which is made up of national research institutions with similar academic and athletic philosophies. Including the University's Eastman School of Music, the University has a full-time enrollment of 4,348 undergraduates and 2,325 graduate students. Rochester's personal scale and the breadth of its research and academic programs permit both attention to the individual and unusual flexibility in planning undergraduate studies. Along with the distinctive Rochester Curriculum to help make the most of the undergraduate years, students in the college (arts, sciences, and engineering) also find ready resources through the Eastman School of Music, the Simon Graduate School of Business Administration, the Warner Graduate School of Education and Human Development, the School of Medicine and Dentistry, and the School of Nursing. Special opportunities include the Take Five program, which allows selected undergraduates a tuition-free fifth year of courses; Rochester Early Medical Scholars (REMS), an eight-year combined B.A. or B.S./M.D. program; study abroad; Quest courses; seven certificate programs; Senior Scholars Program; and employment opportunities that include a national summer jobs program and paid internship experiences.

Located on a bend in the Genesee River, the River Campus is home to most undergraduates, who live in a variety of residence halls, fraternity houses, and special interest housing. Most of the original buildings have been recently renovated, and all residence halls are fully wired for computer access and cable television. Among the facilities are Wilson Commons, the student union; the multipurpose Robert B. Goergen Athletic Center; the Computer Studies Building; and Gleason Hall (Business School). Students participate in more than 200 student organizations, including twenty-two varsity teams, thirty-six intramural and club sports, eighteen fraternities and ten sororities, performing arts groups, musical ensembles, a radio station, and a newspaper.

Location

With Lake Ontario on its northern border and the scenic Finger Lakes to the south, the Rochester area of more than a million people is located in an attractive setting that has been rated among the most livable in the United States. It offers a wide range of cultural and recreational opportunities through its museums, parks, orchestras, planetarium, theater companies, and professional sports teams.

Majors and Degrees

The University of Rochester offers a Bachelor of Arts program through the college, with majors in African and African-American studies, American Sign Language, anthropology, art history, biology, brain and cognitive sciences, chemistry, classics, comparative literature, computer science, economics, English, environmental studies, film and media studies, French, geological sciences, German, health and society, history, interdepartmental studies, Japanese, linguistics, mathematics, mathematics/statistics, music, philosophy, physics, physics and astronomy, political science, psychology, religion, Russian, Russian studies, Spanish, statistics, studio arts, and women's studies. Bachelor of Science programs are offered in the college, with majors in applied mathematics, biological sciences (biochemistry, cell and developmental biology, ecology and evolutionary biology, microbiology, molecular genetics, or neuroscience), brain and cognitive sciences, chemistry, computer science, environmental science, geological sciences, geomechanics, physics, and physics and astronomy. The college also offers certificate programs in actuarial studies, Asian studies, biotechnology, international relations, management studies, mathematical modeling in

political science and economics, and Polish and Central European studies. The School of Engineering and Applied Sciences—part of the college—offers Bachelor of Science programs in biomedical, chemical, electrical and computer, and mechanical engineering; geomechanics; optics; and engineering and applied science, an interdepartmental program with specializations in a variety of areas. A B.A. program in engineering science is also offered. In addition to the college's B.A. in music, a Bachelor of Music degree is offered through the Eastman School, with majors in applied music, composition, jazz studies and contemporary media, music education, musical arts, and music theory. A B.S. degree is offered through the School of Nursing for those who already have their RN certification.

Additional opportunities include a 3-2 program offered through the William E. Simon Graduate School of Business Administration, in which students earn both a B.A. or B.S. from the college and an M.B.A. from the Simon School in five years; 3-2 B.S./M.S. programs in biological sciences—biomedical engineering, chemical engineering, electrical and computer engineering, mechanical engineering, neuroscience, and optics; a program leading to a B.A. or B.S. and a master's in public health; a 3-2 program leading to a B.A. in music and an M.A. in music education; and a 3-2 program leading to a B.A. or B.S. in an undergraduate major and an M.S. in human development from the Warner School. Transfer students can pursue a 3-2 program that combines a B.A. and a B.S. in an engineering concentration.

Academic Programs

The University's calendar includes two regular semesters. To receive a bachelor's degree, students should maintain a minimum average of C and complete thirty-two courses (thirty-two to thirty-six for the Bachelor of Science).

The distinctive Rochester Curriculum allows students to select their major from one of the three branches of learning (the humanities, the natural sciences, and the social sciences). In each of the two branches outside their major, students choose a "cluster" of three courses that allows them to dig deeply in an area that particularly interests them. For most students, there are no other distribution requirements, except a freshman-year writing class.

The Take Five program offers selected students the opportunity to take a tuition-free fifth year in order to pursue their varied interests.

The Quest program offers first-year students the advantages of small classes, student/teacher collaboration, and original research. As a result, Quest courses teach students how to learn, both as undergraduates and beyond.

Students may arrange independent study courses or pursue research in most departments. Those whose interests may not be fully realized through a traditional major, double major, or major/minor, may work with faculty advisers to design an interdepartmental concentration.

Undergraduates from any academic discipline may devote their senior year to a self-designed creative project in the form of scholarly research, a scientific experiment, or a literary or artistic work through the Senior Scholars Program.

Undergraduates enrolled in the college may take private instruction at the Eastman School of Music. A double-degree program leading to the Bachelor of Music degree from Eastman and a bachelor's degree from the college is also available.

The Rochester Early Medical Scholars program is an eight-year B.A. or B.S./M.D. program for exceptionally talented undergraduates. Students enrolled in this program enter the University of Rochester with assurance of admission to the University's medical school upon successful completion of their undergraduate degree program.

The University's research centers include the Frederick Douglass Institute for African and African-American Studies, the Susan B. Anthony Institute for Gender and Women's Studies, the Center for Future Health, the Center for Judaic Studies, the W. Allen Wallis Institute of Political Economy, the Center for Visual Science, the Sign Language Research Center, the Skalny Center for Polish and Central European Studies, the Center for Optics Manufacturing, the Center for Electronic Imaging Systems, and the Center for Biomedical Ultrasound.

Off-Campus Programs

Rochester offers full-year and semester-long study-abroad opportunities, as well as special summer and winter trips, through fifty different study-abroad programs. Semester and full-year destinations include Argentina, Australia, Austria, Belgium, Chile, China, Czech Republic, Egypt, England, France, Germany, Ghana, Hungary, Ireland, Israel, Italy, Japan, Jordan, Mexico, Netherlands, New Zealand, Peru, Poland, Russia, Senegal, Spain, Sweden, and Taiwan. International internships are offered in Berlin, Bonn, Brussels, London, Madrid, and Paris.

Academic Facilities

As one of the smallest of the 151 American universities classified by the Carnegie Foundation for the Advancement of Teaching as offering an extensive range of doctoral programs, Rochester offers an environment that combines the vast learning resources of a national university with the intensive personalized attention of a private college. Research opportunities for undergraduates are available in every field. Major research facilities include a comprehensive Medical Center; an extensive on-campus computer system; direct access to the CYBER 205 Supercomputer in Princeton, New Jersey; fifteen electron microscopes; a 12-trillion watt, 24-beam laser fusion laboratory; and a 3-million-volume library system, including the Eastman School's Sibley Music Library, the largest collection of any music school in the Western Hemisphere. The University is widely known as the nation's premier institution for the study of optics and is home to the Omega, the world's most powerful ultraviolet laser.

Costs

In 2004–05, tuition and fees cost $28,982; room and board averaged $9845; and books, transportation, and other expenses averaged $1750. Part-time study is offered on a per-course basis.

Financial Aid

The University offers a strong program of financial assistance, including academic merit scholarships, grants, loans, tuition payment plans, and part-time jobs. Applicants for financial aid should submit the CSS PROFILE application and the Free Application for Federal Student Aid (FAFSA). Special awards include full-tuition Renaissance Scholarships, Bausch & Lomb Honorary Science Scholarships, the Frederick Douglass and Susan B. Anthony Scholarships in Humanities and Social Sciences, Kodak Young Leaders Scholarships, Xerox Scholarships for Innovation and Information Technology, International Baccalaureate Scholarships, Rush Rhees Scholarships, FIRST Scholarships, National Merit Scholarships, National Achievement Scholarships, Urban League Scholarships, AHORA Scholarships, and other merit-based awards. The University also awards grants to children of alumni, room and board grants to selected Naval ROTC scholars, and Phi Theta Kappa Scholarships for transfer students. Special applications are not required for merit scholarship consideration.

Faculty

Students work closely with a stimulating faculty of internationally renowned scholars, all of whom engage both in advanced research and in teaching at the undergraduate level. The University's faculty is held in particularly high regard by colleagues at sister institutions, and many of its departments are widely recognized as among the best in the country.

Student Government

All undergraduates are members of the Students' Association, which has an annually elected president and a student Senate; there is also a Judicial Council, whose members are appointed by the Senate. The Students' Association in the college strives to coordinate student activities; protect academic freedom; improve students' cultural, social, and physical welfare; develop educational standards and facilities; and provide a forum for the expression of student views and interests.

Admission Requirements

The University of Rochester seeks to admit students who will take advantage of its resources, be strongly motivated to do their best, and contribute to the life of the University community. An applicant's character, extracurricular activities, job experience, academic accomplishments, and career goals are considered. More than half of last year's enrolled students ranked in the top tenth of their secondary school classes. The middle 50 percent of enrolled freshmen scored between 1230 and 1410 on the SAT and between 27 and 32 on the ACT.

The recommended application filing date for freshman applicants is January 20 for fall admission and October 1 for spring admission. An early decision plan is available. Transfer students are welcome for entrance in the fall and spring semesters, and applications are reviewed on a rolling basis. The University accepts the Common Application in lieu of its own school application. An electronic online application is available from the University's Web site. Applicants for freshman admission are required to submit scores from either the SAT or the ACT. SAT Subject Test results are reviewed, but not required. Candidates for admission from lower-income groups are encouraged to investigate the Higher Education Opportunity Program (New York State residents only), which provides supportive services and financial aid.

The University of Rochester values diversity and is committed to equal opportunity for all persons regardless of age, color, disability, ethnicity, marital status, national origin, race, religion, sex, sexual orientation, or veteran status. Further, the University complies with all applicable nondiscrimination laws in the administration of its policies, programs, and activities.

Application and Information

To obtain application forms and further information on admission and financial aid, students should contact:

Director of Admissions
University of Rochester
P.O. Box 270251
Rochester, New York 14627-0251
Telephone: 585-275-3221
          888-822-2256 (toll-free)
World Wide Web: http://www.enrollment.rochester.edu/admissions

Director of Admissions
Eastman School of Music
Rochester, New York 14604
Telephone: 585-274-1060
World Wide Web: http://www.rochester.edu/eastman

Rush Rhees Library on the University of Rochester's Eastman Quadrangle.

UTICA COLLEGE
UTICA, NEW YORK

The College

Founded by Syracuse University in 1946, Utica College (UC) is known for its excellent academic programs, outstanding faculty members, personal attention, and diversity among students. The hallmarks of Utica College's academic programs are the integration of liberal and professional studies and a strong emphasis on internships, research, and other experiential learning opportunities, but UC is best known for the close, personal relationship students have with both faculty and staff members. Approximately 2,650 undergraduate and graduate students attend UC, including men and women from a wide variety of socioeconomic and cultural backgrounds as well as older students, veterans, and students with disabilities. While most students come from New York, New England, and the Middle Atlantic States, students are drawn to UC from all parts of the United States, and there is a growing international student population.

Academic programs of note include biology, economic crime investigation, management, the health sciences, public relations and journalism, and English. Utica College also offers a robust study-abroad program as well as an honors program. Thanks to a unique relationship with its founding college, Utica College also offers the Syracuse University undergraduate degree.

Utica College is located on a modern, 128-acre campus on the southwestern edge of Utica, New York. Its facilities include an academic complex where most classes are held, the Frank E. Gannett Memorial Library, six residence halls, an athletic center, a 1,200 seat stadium, and numerous athletic fields. A seventh residence hall, Bell Hall, is scheduled to open in August 2005.

More than half of UC's students live on campus in residence halls that feature a variety of housing options, modern amenities, and lounges for studying or relaxing with friends. Freshmen primarily live in North and South Halls, which offer mostly double-occupancy rooms. Campus dining services provide a wide variety of options, including American and international cuisines, vegetarian meals, a large salad bar, and lighter fare such as burgers and pizza. Whether students live on or off campus, they can take advantage of more than eighty student organizations—all devoted to such interests as community service, fraternities and sororities, music, theater, and politics as well as major-related clubs that provide opportunities for students to organize career-related events. Students can write for the student newspaper, work at the College's radio station, submit entries for the College's literary magazine, or work on the yearbook. Events throughout the year give students opportunities to enjoy lectures, concerts, poetry readings, art exhibits, plays, and nationally recognized speakers.

Utica College offers nineteen NCAA Division III varsity sports, including men's baseball, basketball, football, ice hockey, lacrosse, soccer, swimming and diving, and tennis; women's basketball, field hockey, ice hockey, lacrosse, soccer, softball, swimming and diving, tennis, volleyball, and water polo; and coed golf. UC also offers club sports and a wide variety of intramural opportunities. Utica College is a member of the Empire 8 Athletic Conference, the Eastern College Athletic Conference, and the New York State Women's Collegiate Athletic Association. Nearly 25 percent of all UC students participate in at least one Division III intercollegiate sport, and more than 60 percent are active in intramural or nonvarsity club sports.

Athletic facilities include a 1,200-seat multisport stadium with a state-of-the-art Field Turf synthetic grass playing surface; the Clark Athletic Center, which contains a large gymnasium, racquetball courts, a swimming pool, saunas, a free-weight room, and a fully equipped fitness room; and numerous outdoor fields and courts. Ice hockey games are played at the downtown Utica Memorial Auditorium, which features pro-style hockey locker rooms and training facilities.

Graduate degrees are available in business administration, economic crime management, education, liberal studies, occupational therapy, and physical therapy.

Location

The city of Utica, with a population of 300,000, is located in the heart of the historic Mohawk Valley. Just 90 miles west of Albany and 50 miles east of Syracuse, Utica has a thriving arts community, beautiful parks, and expanding shopping centers featuring national retailers. There are also numerous recreational facilities, including a municipal ski slope and a world-class golf course less than a mile from the Utica College campus. Other nearby recreational opportunities include tennis, swimming, boating, fishing, hiking, and camping.

Majors and Degrees

Utica College offers undergraduate degree programs in accounting, accounting-CPA, biology, business economics, chemistry, communication arts, computer science, criminal justice, criminal justice-economic crime investigation, economics, English, government and politics, health studies, health studies–human behavior, health studies–management, history, international studies, journalism studies, liberal studies, management, mathematics, nursing, occupational therapy, philosophy, physical therapy, physics, psychology, psychology–child life, public relations, public relations/journalism studies, sociology and anthropology, and therapeutic recreation.

Students interested in occupational therapy or physical therapy complete three years in the health-studies program and then immediately enter UC's graduate programs, earning both their bachelor's and their master's degree in six years.

Students may minor in anthropology, chemistry, communication arts, computer science, economics, English language, film studies, French, gender studies, geoscience, gerontology, government, history, human rights advocacy, literature, management, mathematics, philosophy, psychology, recreation leadership, sociology, Spanish, theater, and writing.

Preprofessional programs include dentistry, law, medicine, optometry, podiatry, and veterinary medicine. Special programs are available in teacher education, gerontology, engineering, and joint health professions.

Academic Programs

Students may choose from thirty undergraduate majors and twenty-four minors in a wide variety of fields as well as accelerated programs, independent study, cooperative education, field placements, and internships. Utica College also offers a rapidly growing education program; students wishing to pursue a career in teaching choose either a liberal arts major (to teach elementary education) or a major in their intended field (to teach at the secondary level).

For those students who are undecided, the Academic Support Services Center provides academic advising and career counseling, and Career Services offers students opportunities to explore career options.

To earn a bachelor's degree, students must complete a minimum of 120 to 128 credits, satisfy major and major-related requirements, and complete any special program requirements. In addition, all Utica College students, regardless of their major, must complete a liberal arts core program as part of the degree requirements.

Utica College operates on a semester system, with the fall term beginning in late August and ending shortly before Christmas, and the spring term beginning in late January and ending in early May. Summer and winter sessions offer students opportunities to accelerate their studies or take classes for which they have no time during the regular academic year.

First-Year Seminar offers freshmen and transfer students opportunities to earn academic credit while learning how to make the transition to college. Utica College offers the Higher Education Opportunity Program (HEOP), the Collegiate Science and Technology Entry Program (CSTEP), and a Summer Institute, which serves as an academic bridge between high school and college.

Off-Campus Programs

Studying abroad gives students opportunities to widen their global perspectives. Utica College is proud to participate in exchange programs with universities in Spain, Italy, Poland, Finland, Hungary, Peru, Scotland, and Wales. Students may also study at American College in Dublin in Ireland. UC students are also eligible to participate in Syracuse University's Division of International Programs Abroad. This arrangement allows students to study in Madrid, Strasbourg, Florence, London, and Hong Kong.

Students are encouraged to complete internships and field placements to gain professional experience with businesses and organizations while they are earning college credit. Utica College's cooperative education program allows students to earn money while gaining professional experience.

Academic Facilities

The Frank E. Gannett Memorial Library collection includes 200,000 volumes, 1,200 serial subscriptions, hundreds of online journals, and a microform collection of more than 60,000 journals, newspapers, and books. The library is fully automated and shares a local system with Mid-York Library System. It also is a member of OCLC, a bibliographic database through which it is possible to locate and borrow interlibrary loan items from local, regional, national, and international libraries. Located on the lower level of the library are the Media Center, computer labs, the Edith Langley Barrett Fine Arts Gallery, and a large concourse—the site of special events, such as musical recitals, receptions, and guest lectures.

Classes, laboratories, and faculty offices are primarily located in an academic complex composed of four buildings: Hubbard Hall, White Hall, Gordon Science Center, and the Faculty Center. Other offices are located in DePerno Hall.

Utica College maintains eight academic computer laboratories with both IBM-compatible and Macintosh computers, including two portable wireless laptop laboratories. Students have additional Internet access in the Pioneer Café and in all student residence hall rooms. Other resources include the Academic Support Services Center, the Math/Science Center, and the Writing Center.

Costs

For 2004–05, tuition was $20,980. Room and board costs were $8600. Student activity and technology fees cost $290. Books and supplies average $800 per year.

Financial Aid

The College is recognized as a best buy in education and works to control costs and keep its education affordable. The average financial aid package for 2004–05 freshmen was $21,902. About two thirds of that aid came from grants and a third from loans and/or jobs. Approximately 90 percent of the freshmen received a financial aid package. At the same time, UC awarded numerous merit scholarships to students with outstanding grades and test scores.

Almost every federal and state financial aid program is available through Utica College. Students apply for institutional and governmental financial aid by filing the required financial aid forms by February 15. In addition, UC offers three different deferred-payment programs that spread payments over the academic year.

Faculty

Utica College's faculty is a diverse group of academicians who can best be described as energetic, accomplished, and devoted to their students. The vast majority—96 percent—have earned their Ph.D. or other terminal degree, and while many are involved in research, the primary focus of faculty members is teaching. The typical class size is 20 students, the student-faculty ratio is 18:1, and all faculty members are involved in assisting students with their academic planning.

Student Government

One of Utica College's strongest traditions is student participation in the College's governance structure. Students may serve on a number of student governing bodies, and students also serve on all standing committees of the College.

Admission Requirements

Utica College admits students who can best benefit from the educational opportunities the College offers. The Admission Committee gives each application individual attention, and the potential for a student's success at UC is measured primarily by an evaluation of past academic performance, scholastic ability, and personal characteristics. Freshman applicants must have completed 16 academic units, including 4 years of English. Students should follow a college-preparatory program, including 3 units of mathematics, 3 units of science, 2 units of foreign language, and 3 units of social studies.

Application and Information

Students may apply for fall, spring, or summer admission. Materials required include a completed Utica College application form, official high school or college transcripts, and a $40 application fee. Utica College prefers, but does not require, SAT or ACT scores, with the exception of the programs listed below. A personal interview for all applications is strongly suggested.

Occupational therapy, physical therapy, nursing, HEOP, and joint health professions program applicants must submit SAT or ACT scores, a preferred letter of clinical recommendation if applicable, and a personal statement. International students must complete the international student application form. The application fee is waived for students who apply to HEOP or CSTEP. The College conducts a rolling admissions program, except for those applying for occupational therapy, physical therapy, the joint health professions program, or for academic achievement awards, for which the application deadline is January 15, or for the nursing program, for which the preferred application deadline is February 1. The priority application deadline for HEOP is March 1. In addition, a tuition deposit of $100 is required by April 1 to secure a place in this program. Additional admissions information can be found online at http://www.utica.edu/enrollment/admission/international.htm or http://www.utica.edu/enrollment/admission/transfer/htm or http://www.utica.edu/academic/honorsprogram.htm.

Inquiries should be sent to:

Director of Admissions
Utica College
1600 Burrstone Road
Utica, New York 13502-4892
Telephone: 315-792-3006
          800-782-8884 (toll-free)
E-mail: admiss@utica.edu
World Wide Web: http://www.utica.edu

The Addison Miller White Hall Plaza.

WELLS COLLEGE
AURORA, NEW YORK

The College

Wells College is consistently ranked among the nation's top liberal arts colleges that offer high-quality education at an affordable price and have one of the most beautiful campuses in the United States. The College was established in 1868 by Henry Wells, who also founded the Wells Fargo and American Express companies. Wells recently shifted its women's college mission to co-education and now enrolls both women and men.

At Wells, professors are dedicated to teaching, and because of the intimate nature of the campus community (the student body is 450), they get to know their students as individuals in and outside the classroom. Students frequently collaborate with their professors on original research and creative projects. At most other schools, these opportunities are only available to graduate students. Because faculty members at Wells know their students so well, they are especially effective advisers and mentors. Students have a competitive edge entering careers and top graduate and professional schools.

Another aspect of the Wells tradition is hands-on learning. In addition to dynamic classroom teaching, Wells students have a variety of other experiential opportunities: internships, service, study abroad, and off-campus study. Professors encourage students to apply theory in practical settings and to discover what they want to do in life through involvement.

Women who are interested in athletics may participate on intercollegiate teams in field hockey, lacrosse, soccer, softball, swimming, and tennis. Men may participate in cross-country, soccer, and swimming. There are also a number of intramural opportunities, including basketball, soccer, swimming, tennis, and volleyball. Athletic facilities include indoor and outdoor tennis courts, a gymnasium, a weight room, a nine-hole golf course, and a campus boathouse and dock used in teaching sailing, canoeing, and lifeguarding.

Wells has a full range of active student organizations, including a literary magazine and newspaper, music and drama groups, environmental and political organizations, and abundant opportunities for community service, among others. A busy calendar of cultural events, symposia, and lectures enhances the academic and social life of the College.

Location

Wells is located in the village of Aurora on the eastern shore of Cayuga Lake—part of New York's scenic Finger Lakes region. The area is well known for its high concentration of prestigious colleges and universities, including Cornell University, Ithaca College, Hobart and William Smith Colleges, Colgate University, Hamilton College, and Syracuse University. Aurora is 25 miles from Ithaca and 60 miles from both Rochester and Syracuse. Students have abundant opportunities for outdoor recreation and sports, including sailing, swimming, horseback riding, skiing, and hiking.

Majors and Degrees

Wells offers majors and concentrations in African-American studies, American studies, anthropology/cross-cultural sociology, art history, biochemistry and molecular biology, biology, chemistry, computer science, creative writing, economics, English, environmental studies, French, government and politics, history, human nature and values, international studies, literature, management, mathematics, music, physics, psychology, religion, sociology, Spanish, studio art, theater and dance, and women's studies. Students also have the option of a self-designed major. In addition, they can choose minors from a list of more than thirty programs.

The College has preprofessional programs in dentistry, engineering, law, medicine, teaching, and veterinary medicine. Wells has a cross-registration agreement with nearby Cornell University and affiliations with Cornell's engineering and veterinary medicine schools.

Wells awards the Bachelor of Arts degree and has a number of programs through which students can earn their bachelor's degree at Wells and a graduate or professional degree from an affiliated university. Participating schools are Clarkson University, Columbia University, and Cornell University (engineering); the University of Rochester (business, community health, education); and Cornell (veterinary medicine).

Academic Programs

All Wells students benefit from an academic environment similar to honors programs available to only a small number of students at other schools. The College has a tradition of preparing students for leadership in their chosen fields, and the breadth of knowledge they gain and the range of life experiences they encounter enable them to achieve their career goals and establish a foundation for a rich and fulfilling life.

All students entering Wells to pursue a four-year course of study leading to a bachelor's degree are required to take Approaches to Liberal Arts (WLLS 101) and the First-Year Seminar (WLLS 102). Distribution requirements are: foreign language (two courses or exemption by exam); formal reasoning (one course); arts and humanities (three courses); natural and social sciences (three courses; and physical education (four courses). Team sports and dance technique can partially satisfy requirements.

Approximately sixteen courses must be taken in the student's major, and at least six must be taken at Wells. Eighteen credit hours must be taken at the 300 level or above. A senior project or thesis and a comprehensive evaluation are required for graduation.

A student must successfully complete 120 semester hours (60 of which must be taken at Wells and through affiliated programs, such as study abroad) to be recommended by the faculty for a degree. To learn more about the academic program and requirements for transfer students, prospective students should visit the Wells College Web site.

Off-Campus Programs

Students can spend January term, a semester, or even a year in another college or university abroad or in the United States. Typically, Wells students choose to study off campus for a semester during the junior year, but many different possibilities are available depending on a student's academic program and interests.

The College offers affiliated study-abroad experiences in Denmark, The Dominican Republic, France, Germany, Great Britain, Ireland, Italy, Japan, Mexico, Senegal, Spain, and Sweden. Currently, the three most popular programs are study abroad in Florence, Italy; Paris, France; and Seville, Spain. These off-campus study experiences are flexible as well as financially and academically accessible. After at least one semester at Wells, a student's financial aid applies to one semester of off-campus study.

Wells provides off-campus study options in the United States through its affiliations with American University, serving a wide range of academic and internship interests in Washington, D.C.; the Salt Center, offering documentary field studies in Portland, Maine; and the Public Leadership Education Network (PLEN), providing leadership development through seminars and internships in Washington, D.C. As part of the PLEN affiliation, students can spend a semester studying at the London School of Economics and Political Science and hold an internship in the British government. Through the School for Field Studies, Wells offers semester-long study-abroad experiences in Africa, Australia, the Caribbean, and other locations. The College also offers credit-bearing courses during the January term that take students to a single destination in the U.S. or abroad for intensive study that requires travel in a region or country with a faculty member.

Academic Facilities

From the contemporary elegance of Weld House to the nineteenth-century Glen Park mansion, the former home of College founder Henry Wells, the residence halls encompass enough variety to satisfy every taste. Students eat their meals together in the majestic Tudor-style dining hall in Main Building.

The Louis Jefferson Long Library has received numerous awards for its architectural design. Facilities include an online computer center, individual study carrels, seminar and group-study rooms, and an art gallery. There are department libraries in art, economics, English, mathematics, music, philosophy, and the sciences located across the campus.

The Barler Hall of Music houses a recital hall with superb acoustics, vocal and instrumental practice rooms, a music library, and a listening laboratory. Facilities for printmaking, painting, ceramics, sculpture, and photography are located in the Campbell Arts Building. The Cleveland Hall of Languages contains state-of-the-art equipment for learning foreign languages. The Zabriskie Science Building houses laboratories for chemistry, biology, and physics as well as a computer laboratory, library, darkroom, and greenhouse. Morgan Hall houses the Book Arts Center and the Wells College Press. Macmillan Hall has classrooms, faculty and administrative offices, several computer laboratories, and department libraries. The east wing of Macmillan contains the Margaret Phipps Auditorium, a theater facility used for teaching, concerts, lectures, and dramatic productions.

Costs

Wells has a long-term commitment to providing talented students with access to the best education, which requires offering excellence at an affordable price. Wells is ranked among the best liberal arts colleges in the nation, yet the cost of a Wells education is, in many cases, about half the price charged by other comparable schools.

Wells students today still benefit from a 30 percent tuition reduction policy that brought the College national acclaim several years ago. The cost of a Wells education for the 2004–05 year was $14,000 for tuition, $7000 for room and board, and $700 for fees.

Financial Aid

Approximately 90 percent of Wells students receive financial aid packaged in the form of grants, scholarships, loans, and work-study opportunities. The College works closely with students and their families to design a financial aid package that meets their needs and their budgets.

Award determinations are made on a rolling basis following acceptance. College financial aid is complex; however, Wells College's well-informed financial aid and admissions professionals are always pleased to answer questions and discuss methods of financing higher education with prospective students.

Faculty

At Wells, learning takes place in small, seminar-style classes where students are partners with faculty members in the learning process. Starting immediately in their first semester, students take classes with scholars who are recognized experts in their fields—not teaching assistants.

All Wells professors hold terminal degrees in their areas of expertise. They have been educated at the world's leading research universities, including Harvard, Yale, Columbia, Cornell, Brown, and Stanford. What students discover in Wells' classes is the importance of exploring ideas with others.

Wells is student centered, and academic programs focus on collaborative learning and teaching that meets the needs of students' different learning styles. As one would expect at a nationally recognized liberal arts college, professors are also engaged in research and a full range of scholarly activities. Their books are published by leading academic presses, their articles appear in top journals, and they are a presence at national and international conferences. Due to close faculty-student interaction, students have numerous opportunities to collaborate with faculty members on research, publications, and presentations.

Student Government

The student body is self-governing through the Collegiate Association. The three main governing bodies of the association are the Student-Faculty Administration Board, the Collegiate Council, and the Community Court. Students serve on faculty committees that make decisions concerning administrative and curricular matters.

Leadership development is an inherent part of the Wells experience, and students are encouraged to take an active role in student government and in the life of the campus community.

Admission Requirements

Wells admits students on the basis of the strength of their academic preparation. A student is expected to possess intellectual curiosity, motivation, and maturity to profit from the experience. In all cases, the College seeks students who have followed a solid college-preparatory program throughout high school.

Wells seeks students from varied backgrounds with diverse interests and talents in order to promote a stimulating learning community. Every admissions decision is made on an individual basis.

Wells students share an enthusiasm for academic pursuits and a serious intent to use their education in the future to enhance both their lives and the communities in which they choose to live.

Application and Information

Applications should be received early in the senior year of high school and not later than March 1 of the year in which entrance is desired. Applications from early decision and early action candidates must be received by December 15.

Transfer applications are reviewed on a rolling basis. Transfer students are eligible for merit scholarships and financial aid.

A campus visit is highly recommended for prospective students. For more information about Wells College or to schedule a campus visit, students should contact:

Admissions Office
Wells College
Aurora, New York 13026
Telephone: 800-952-9355 (toll-free)
E-mail: admissions@wells.edu
World Wide Web: http://www.wells.edu

Students enjoy a close-knit college environment at Wells.

Profiles and In-Depth Descriptions of Other Colleges to Consider

Arizona

PRESCOTT COLLEGE
Prescott, Arizona

Prescott College is a coed, private, comprehensive institution, founded in 1966, offering degrees at the bachelor's and master's levels.

Academic Information   The faculty has 70 members (84% full-time), 49% with terminal degrees. The undergraduate student-faculty ratio is 12:1. The library holds 23,899 titles, 270 serial subscriptions, and 1,151 audiovisual materials. Special programs include services for learning-disabled students, advanced placement credit, double majors, independent study, self-designed majors, summer session for credit, external degree programs, adult/continuing education programs, internships, and arrangement for off-campus study with Four Corners School of Outdoor Education, Grand Canyon Field Institute. The most frequently chosen baccalaureate fields are education, natural resources/environmental science, psychology.

Student Body Statistics   The student body totals 1,036, of whom 805 are undergraduates (41 freshmen). 60 percent are women and 40 percent are men. Students come from 44 states and territories and 1 other country. 13 percent are from Arizona. 0.1 percent are international students.

Expenses for 2005–06   *Application fee:* $25. *Tuition:* $17,280 full-time, $480 per credit hour part-time. *Mandatory fees:* $170 full-time, $85 per term part-time.

Financial Aid   Forms of aid include need-based scholarships and part-time jobs. The application deadline for financial aid is continuous.

Freshman Admission   Prescott College requires an essay, a high school transcript, 2 recommendations, and TOEFL scores for international students. An interview is required for some. The application deadline for regular admission is February 1.

Transfer Admission   The application deadline for admission is February 1.

Entrance Difficulty   Prescott College assesses its entrance difficulty level as moderately difficult. For the fall 2004 freshman class, 84 percent of the applicants were accepted.

For Further Information   Contact Mr. Timothy Robison, Director of RDP Admissions, Prescott College, 220 Grove Avenue, Prescott, AZ 86301. *Telephone:* 800-628-6364 Ext. 2103, 800-628-6364 (toll-free in-state), or 800-628-6364-2100 (toll-free out-of-state). *Fax:* 928-776-5242. *E-mail:* admissions@prescott.edu. *Web site:* http://www.prescott.edu/.

See page 182 for a narrative description.

Connecticut

MITCHELL COLLEGE
New London, Connecticut

Mitchell is a coed, private, four-year college, founded in 1938, offering degrees at the associate and bachelor's levels. It has a 67-acre campus in New London near Hartford and Providence.

Academic Information   The faculty has 71 members (37% full-time), 30% with terminal degrees. The student-faculty ratio is 12:1. The library holds 80,000 titles, 120 serial subscriptions, and 300 audiovisual materials. Special programs include services for learning-disabled students, cooperative (work-study) education, advanced placement credit, ESL programs, double majors, summer session for credit, part-time degree programs (daytime, summer), adult/continuing education programs, and internships. The most frequently chosen baccalaureate fields are liberal arts/general studies, law/legal studies, psychology.

Student Body Statistics   The student body is made up of 555 undergraduates (191 freshmen). 52 percent are women and 48 percent are men. Students come from 22 states and territories and 5 other countries. 58 percent are from Connecticut. 1.8 percent are international students.

Expenses for 2005–06   *Application fee:* $30. *Comprehensive fee:* $30,035 includes full-time tuition ($19,405), mandatory fees ($1300), and college room and board ($9330). *College room only:* $4850. *Part-time tuition:* $275 per credit hour. *Part-time mandatory fees:* $35 per term.

Financial Aid   Forms of aid include need-based scholarships, athletic grants, and part-time jobs. The average aided 2004–05 undergraduate received an aid package worth an estimated $16,357. The priority application deadline for financial aid is April 1.

Freshman Admission   Mitchell requires an essay, a high school transcript, a minimum 2.0 high school GPA, recommendations, and SAT or ACT scores. An interview is recommended. The application deadline for regular admission is rolling and for early decision it is November 15.

Transfer Admission   The application deadline for admission is rolling.

Entrance Difficulty   Mitchell assesses its entrance difficulty level as minimally difficult; moderately difficult for transfers. For the fall 2004 freshman class, 58 percent of the applicants were accepted.

For Further Information   Contact Ms. Kimberly Hodges, Associate Director of Enrollment Management and Marketing, Mitchell College, 437 Pequot Avenue, New London, CT 06320. *Telephone:* 860-701-5038 or 800-443-2811 (toll-free). *Fax:* 860-444-1209. *E-mail:* admissions@mitchell.edu. *Web site:* http://www.mitchell.edu/.

See page 176 for a narrative description.

POST UNIVERSITY
Waterbury, Connecticut

Post University is a coed, private, four-year college, founded in 1890, offering degrees at the associate and bachelor's levels and postbachelor's certificates. It has a 70-acre campus in Waterbury near Hartford.

Academic Information   The faculty has 127 members (24% full-time), 16% with terminal degrees. The student-faculty ratio is 14:1. The library holds 85,000 titles, 500 serial subscriptions, and 1,027 audiovisual materials. Special programs include academic remediation, services for learning-disabled students, cooperative (work-study) education, study abroad, advanced placement credit, accelerated degree programs, ESL programs, double majors, independent study, distance learning, summer session for credit, part-time degree programs (daytime, evenings, weekends, summer), adult/continuing education programs, and internships. The most frequently chosen baccalaureate fields are business/marketing, liberal arts/general studies, protective services/public administration.

Student Body Statistics   The student body is made up of 1,198 undergraduates (221 freshmen). 62 percent are women and 38 percent are men. Students come from 13 states and territories and 15 other countries. 79 percent are from Connecticut. 5 percent are international students. 25 percent of the 2004 graduating class went on to graduate and professional schools.

Expenses for 2004–05   *Application fee:* $40. *Comprehensive fee:* $26,750 includes full-time tuition ($18,150), mandatory fees ($650), and college room and board ($7950). *Part-time tuition:* $605 per credit. Part-time tuition varies according to class time and course load.

Financial Aid   Forms of aid include need-based and non-need-based scholarships, athletic grants, and part-time jobs. The average aided 2004–05 undergraduate received an aid package worth an estimated $10,827.

Freshman Admission   Post University requires a high school transcript, 1 recommendation, SAT or ACT scores, and TOEFL scores for international students. An essay and an interview are recommended. The application deadline for regular admission is rolling.

Transfer Admission   The application deadline for admission is rolling.

Entrance Difficulty   Post University assesses its entrance difficulty level as minimally difficult. For the fall 2004 freshman class, 65 percent of the applicants were accepted.

For Further Information   Contact Mr. William Johnson, Senior Assistant Director of Admissions, Post University, PO Box 2540, Waterbury, CT 06723. *Telephone:* 203-596-4510 or 800-345-2562 (toll-free). *Fax:* 203-756-5810. *E-mail:* tpuadmiss@teikyopost.edu. *Web site:* http://teikyopost.edu/.

See page 180 for a narrative description.

QUINNIPIAC UNIVERSITY
Hamden, Connecticut

Quinnipiac is a coed, private, comprehensive institution, founded in 1929, offering degrees at the bachelor's, master's, doctoral, and first professional levels and postbachelor's certificates. It has a 400-acre campus in Hamden near Hartford.

Academic Information   The faculty has 741 members (38% full-time), 29% with terminal degrees. The undergraduate student-faculty ratio is 15:1. The library holds 285,000 titles and 4,400 serial subscriptions. Special programs include services for learning-disabled students, an honors program, study abroad, advanced placement credit, double majors, independent study, distance learning, self-designed majors, summer session for credit, part-time degree programs (daytime, evenings, summer), adult/continuing education programs, and internships. The most frequently chosen baccalaureate fields are business/marketing, communications/communication technologies, health professions and related sciences.

Student Body Statistics   The student body totals 7,220, of whom 5,464 are undergraduates (1,336 freshmen). 61 percent are women and 39 percent are men. Students come from 28 states and territories and 20 other countries. 28 percent are from Connecticut. 1.2 percent are international students. 23 percent of the 2004 graduating class went on to graduate and professional schools.

Expenses for 2005–06   *Application fee:* $45. *Comprehensive fee:* $34,640 includes full-time tuition ($23,360), mandatory fees ($980), and college room and board ($10,300). Room and board charges vary according to housing facility. *Part-time tuition:* $570 per credit. *Part-time mandatory fees:* $30 per credit. Part-time tuition and fees vary according to course load.

Financial Aid   Forms of aid include need-based and non-need-based scholarships, athletic grants, and part-time jobs. The average aided 2004–05 undergraduate received an aid package worth an estimated $13,160. The priority application deadline for financial aid is March 1.

Freshman Admission   Quinnipiac requires an essay, a high school transcript, 1 recommendation, SAT or ACT scores, and TOEFL scores for international students. A minimum 2.5 high school GPA and an interview are recommended. A minimum 3.0 high school GPA is required for some. The application deadline for regular admission is February 1.

Transfer Admission   The application deadline for admission is May 1.

Entrance Difficulty   Quinnipiac assesses its entrance difficulty level as moderately difficult; very difficult for physical therapy, occupational therapy, physician assistant program. For the fall 2004 freshman class, 55 percent of the applicants were accepted.

For Further Information   Contact Ms. Joan Isaac Mohr, Vice President and Dean of Admissions, Quinnipiac University, 275 Mount Carmel Avenue, Hamden, CT 06518-1940. *Telephone:* 203-582-8600 or 800-462-1944 (toll-free out-of-state). *Fax:* 203-582-8906. *E-mail:* admissions@quinnipiac.edu. *Web site:* http://www.quinnipiac.edu/.

See page 184 for a narrative description.

Florida

UNIVERSITY OF WEST FLORIDA
Pensacola, Florida

UWF is a coed, public, comprehensive unit of State University System of Florida, founded in 1963, offering degrees at the associate, bachelor's, master's, and doctoral levels. It has a 1,600-acre campus in Pensacola.

Academic Information   The faculty has 547 members (47% full-time). The undergraduate student-faculty ratio is 20:1. The library holds 414,418 titles, 3,236 serial subscriptions, and 4,303 audiovisual materials. Special programs include services for learning-disabled students, an honors program, cooperative (work-study) education, study abroad, advanced placement credit, ESL programs, independent study, distance learning, summer session for credit, part-time degree programs (daytime, evenings, summer), internships, and arrangement for off-campus study with other members of the State University System of Florida. The most frequently chosen baccalaureate fields are business/marketing, education, protective services/public administration.

Student Body Statistics   The student body totals 9,518, of whom 7,974 are undergraduates (956 freshmen). 59 percent are women and 41 percent are men. Students come from 49 states and territories. 87 percent are from Florida. 0.8 percent are international students.

Expenses for 2004–05   *Application fee:* $30. *State resident tuition:* $2045 full-time, $68.16 per semester hour part-time. *Nonresident tuition:* $14,552 full-time, $485.04 per semester hour part-time. *Mandatory fees:* $994 full-time, $33.15 per semester hour part-time. Full-time tuition and fees vary according to location. Part-time tuition and fees vary according to location. *College room and board:* $6294. Room and board charges vary according to housing facility.

Financial Aid   Forms of aid include need-based and non-need-based scholarships, athletic grants, and part-time jobs. The application deadline for financial aid is continuous.

Freshman Admission   UWF requires a high school transcript, a minimum 2.0 high school GPA, SAT or ACT scores, and TOEFL scores for international students. The application deadline for regular admission is June 30.

Transfer Admission   The application deadline for admission is June 30.

Entrance Difficulty   UWF assesses its entrance difficulty level as moderately difficult; noncompetitive for applicants with associate degrees from Florida public junior colleges. For the fall 2004 freshman class, 66 percent of the applicants were accepted.

For Further Information   Contact Mr. R. Matt Hulett, Director of Admissions, University of West Florida, Admissions, 11000 University Parkway, Pensacola, FL 32514. *Telephone:* 850-474-2230 or 800-263-1074 (toll-free). *Fax:* 850-474-2096. *E-mail:* admissions@uwf.edu. *Web site:* http://uwf.edu/.

See page 188 for a narrative description.

Hawaii

CHAMINADE UNIVERSITY OF HONOLULU
Honolulu, Hawaii

Chaminade University is a coed, private, Roman Catholic, comprehensive institution, founded in 1955, offering degrees at the associate, bachelor's, and master's levels and postbachelor's certificates. It has a 62-acre campus in Honolulu.

Academic Information   The faculty has 136 members (57% full-time), 40% with terminal degrees. The undergraduate student-faculty ratio is

11:1. The library holds 78,000 titles, 6,730 serial subscriptions, and 566 audiovisual materials. Special programs include academic remediation, advanced placement credit, accelerated degree programs, double majors, independent study, distance learning, self-designed majors, summer session for credit, part-time degree programs (daytime, evenings, weekends, summer), adult/continuing education programs, internships, and arrangement for off-campus study with University of Hawaii at Manoa, Brigham Young University, Hawaii Pacific University. The most frequently chosen baccalaureate fields are protective services/public administration, psychology, social sciences and history.

Student Body Statistics The student body totals 1,783, of whom 1,079 are undergraduates (248 freshmen). 69 percent are women and 31 percent are men. Students come from 41 states and territories and 11 other countries. 57 percent are from Hawaii. 2.2 percent are international students.

Expenses for 2005–06 *Application fee:* $50. *Comprehensive fee:* $23,200 includes full-time tuition ($14,330) and college room and board ($8870). *College room only:* $4680. Full-time tuition varies according to course load. Room and board charges vary according to board plan. *Part-time tuition:* $478 per credit. Part-time tuition varies according to course load.

Financial Aid Forms of aid include need-based and non-need-based scholarships, athletic grants, and part-time jobs. The average aided 2004–05 undergraduate received an aid package worth an estimated $12,846. The priority application deadline for financial aid is March 1.

Freshman Admission Chaminade University requires a high school transcript, SAT or ACT scores, and TOEFL scores for international students. A minimum 2.0 high school GPA is recommended. An interview is required for some. The application deadline for regular admission is rolling.

Transfer Admission The application deadline for admission is rolling.

Entrance Difficulty Chaminade University assesses its entrance difficulty level as minimally difficult. For the fall 2004 freshman class, 97 percent of the applicants were accepted.

For Further Information Contact Ao' Lani Lorenzo, Admissions Counselor, Chaminade University of Honolulu, 3140 Waialae Avenue, Honolulu, HI 96816-1578. *Telephone:* 808-735-4735 or 800-735-3733 (toll-free out-of-state). *Fax:* 808-739-4647. *E-mail:* admissions@chaminade.edu. *Web site:* http://www.chaminade.edu/.

See page 172 for a narrative description.

Maryland

BALTIMORE INTERNATIONAL COLLEGE
Baltimore, Maryland

BIC is a coed, private, primarily two-year college, founded in 1972, offering degrees at the associate and bachelor's levels. It has a 6-acre campus in Baltimore near Washington, DC.

Academic Information The faculty has 32 members (41% full-time), 75% with terminal degrees. The student-faculty ratio is 9:1. The library holds 13,000 titles, 200 serial subscriptions, and 1,000 audiovisual materials. Special programs include academic remediation, an honors program, cooperative (work-study) education, study abroad, advanced placement credit, accelerated degree programs, double majors, adult/continuing education programs, internships, and arrangement for off-campus study with Virginia Park Campus, County Cavan, Ireland. The most frequently chosen baccalaureate field is personal/miscellaneous services.

Student Body Statistics The student body is made up of 556 undergraduates (130 freshmen). 55 percent are women and 45 percent are men. Students come from 19 states and territories and 5 other countries. 97 percent are from Maryland. 1.4 percent are international students.

Expenses for 2005–06 *Application fee:* $35. *Comprehensive fee:* $20,313 includes full-time tuition ($14,751), mandatory fees ($107), and college room and board ($5455). *College room only:* $3255. Room and board charges vary according to housing facility.

Financial Aid Forms of aid include need-based scholarships and part-time jobs. The application deadline for financial aid is continuous.

Freshman Admission BIC requires a high school transcript and TOEFL scores for international students. An interview is recommended. An essay and SAT or ACT scores are required for some. The application deadline for regular admission is rolling and for early action it is December 15.

Transfer Admission The application deadline for admission is rolling.

Entrance Difficulty BIC assesses its entrance difficulty level as minimally difficult. For the fall 2004 freshman class, 52 percent of the applicants were accepted.

For Further Information Contact Kristin Ciarlo, Director of Admissions, Baltimore International College, Commerce Exchange, 17 Commerce Street, Baltimore, MD 21202-3230. *Telephone:* 410-752-4710 Ext. 124 or 800-624-9926 Ext. 120 (toll-free out-of-state). *Fax:* 410-752-3730. *E-mail:* admissions@bic.edu. *Web site:* http://www.bic.edu/.

See page 170 for a narrative description.

North Carolina

NORTH CAROLINA AGRICULTURAL AND TECHNICAL STATE UNIVERSITY
Greensboro, North Carolina

North Carolina A&T is a coed, public unit of University of North Carolina System, founded in 1891, offering degrees at the bachelor's, master's, and doctoral levels. It has a 191-acre campus in Greensboro.

Academic Information The faculty has 458 members. The undergraduate student-faculty ratio is 17:1. The library holds 541,403 titles, 31,674 serial subscriptions, and 35,735 audiovisual materials. Special programs include academic remediation, services for learning-disabled students, an honors program, cooperative (work-study) education, study abroad, advanced placement credit, summer session for credit, part-time degree programs (daytime, evenings, summer), adult/continuing education programs, internships, and arrangement for off-campus study with University of North Carolina at Greensboro, Guilford College, Bennett College, High Point University, Greensboro College.

Student Body Statistics The student body totals 9,115, of whom 7,982 are undergraduates (2,043 freshmen). 52 percent are women and 48 percent are men. Students come from 42 states and territories. 80 percent are from North Carolina. 0.8 percent are international students.

Expenses for 2004–05 *Application fee:* $35. *State resident tuition:* $1769 full-time, $361.80 per credit hour part-time. *Nonresident tuition:* $11,211 full-time, $1,542.05 per credit hour part-time. *Mandatory fees:* $1297 full-time. *College room and board:* $5070. *College room only:* $2700.

Financial Aid Forms of aid include need-based and non-need-based scholarships, athletic grants, and part-time jobs. The average aided 2003–04 undergraduate received an aid package worth $5238. The priority application deadline for financial aid is March 15.

Freshman Admission North Carolina A&T requires a high school transcript, a minimum 2.0 high school GPA, and TOEFL scores for international students. SAT or ACT scores are recommended. The application deadline for regular admission is June 1.

Transfer Admission The application deadline for admission is June 1.

Entrance Difficulty   North Carolina A&T assesses its entrance difficulty level as moderately difficult. For the fall 2004 freshman class, 81 percent of the applicants were accepted.

For Further Information   Contact Mr. John Smith, Director of Admissions, North Carolina Agricultural and Technical State University, 1601 East Market Street, Webb Hall, Greensboro, NC 27411. *Telephone:* 336-334-7946 or 800-443-8964 (toll-free in-state). *Fax:* 336-334-7478. *E-mail:* uadmit@ncat.edu. *Web site:* http://www.ncat.edu/.

See page 178 for a narrative description.

Pennsylvania

CHATHAM COLLEGE
Pittsburgh, Pennsylvania

Chatham is a women's, private, comprehensive institution, founded in 1869, offering degrees at the bachelor's, master's, and doctoral levels and post-master's and postbachelor's certificates. It has a 32-acre campus in Pittsburgh.

Academic Information   The faculty has 75 members (93% full-time), 84% with terminal degrees. The undergraduate student-faculty ratio is 13:1. The library holds 95,480 titles, 392 serial subscriptions, and 354 audiovisual materials. Special programs include services for learning-disabled students, cooperative (work-study) education, study abroad, advanced placement credit, accelerated degree programs, ESL programs, double majors, independent study, distance learning, self-designed majors, summer session for credit, part-time degree programs (daytime, evenings, weekends, summer), adult/continuing education programs, internships, and arrangement for off-campus study with members of the Pittsburgh Council on Higher Education. The most frequently chosen baccalaureate fields are biological/life sciences, business/marketing, psychology.

Student Body Statistics   The student body totals 1,249, of whom 665 are undergraduates (91 freshmen). Students come from 34 states and territories and 19 other countries. 79 percent are from Pennsylvania. 6.5 percent are international students. 43 percent of the 2004 graduating class went on to graduate and professional schools.

Expenses for 2004–05   *Application fee:* $35. *Comprehensive fee:* $29,046 includes full-time tuition ($21,780), mandatory fees ($216), and college room and board ($7050). *College room only:* $3690. Room and board charges vary according to board plan and housing facility. *Part-time tuition:* $530 per credit. *Part-time mandatory fees:* $9 per credit. Part-time tuition and fees vary according to course load.

Financial Aid   Forms of aid include need-based and non-need-based scholarships and part-time jobs. The average aided 2004–05 undergraduate received an aid package worth an estimated $22,273. The priority application deadline for financial aid is May 1.

Freshman Admission   Chatham requires an essay, a high school transcript, a minimum 2.5 high school GPA, 1 recommendation, SAT or ACT scores, and TOEFL scores for international students. A minimum 3.0 high school GPA, 3 recommendations, and an interview are recommended. The application deadline for regular admission is rolling.

Transfer Admission   The application deadline for admission is rolling.

Entrance Difficulty   Chatham assesses its entrance difficulty level as moderately difficult. For the fall 2004 freshman class, 62 percent of the applicants were accepted.

For Further Information   Contact Sarah J. Sperry, Director of Undergraduate Admissions, Chatham College, Woodland Road, Pittsburgh, PA 15232. *Telephone:* 412-365-1290 or 800-837-1290 (toll-free). *Fax:* 412-365-1609. *E-mail:* admissions@chatham.edu. *Web site:* http://www.chatham.edu/.

See page 174 for a narrative description.

West Virginia

SHEPHERD UNIVERSITY
Shepherdstown, West Virginia

Shepherd is a coed, public, comprehensive unit of West Virginia Higher Education Policy Commission, founded in 1871, offering degrees at the associate, bachelor's, and master's levels. It has a 320-acre campus in Shepherdstown near Washington, DC.

Academic Information   The faculty has 310 members (38% full-time), 43% with terminal degrees. The undergraduate student-faculty ratio is 21:1. The library holds 183,197 titles, 918 serial subscriptions, and 11,393 audiovisual materials. Special programs include academic remediation, services for learning-disabled students, an honors program, cooperative (work-study) education, study abroad, advanced placement credit, accelerated degree programs, double majors, independent study, summer session for credit, part-time degree programs (daytime, evenings, weekends, summer), adult/continuing education programs, and internships.

Student Body Statistics   The student body totals 5,206, of whom 5,141 are undergraduates (843 freshmen). 57 percent are women and 43 percent are men. Students come from 49 states and territories and 21 other countries. 70 percent are from West Virginia. 0.8 percent are international students. 12 percent of the 2004 graduating class went on to graduate and professional schools.

Expenses for 2004–05   *Application fee:* $35. *State resident tuition:* $3654 full-time. *Nonresident tuition:* $9234 full-time. Full-time tuition varies according to degree level, program, and reciprocity agreements. *College room and board:* $5574. Room and board charges vary according to board plan and housing facility.

Financial Aid   Forms of aid include need-based and non-need-based scholarships, athletic grants, and part-time jobs. The average aided 2004–05 undergraduate received an aid package worth an estimated $7797. The priority application deadline for financial aid is March 1.

Freshman Admission   Shepherd requires a high school transcript, a minimum 2.0 high school GPA, SAT or ACT scores, and TOEFL scores for international students. An essay, a minimum 3.0 high school GPA, and 3 recommendations are recommended. The application deadline for regular admission is rolling and for early action it is November 15.

Transfer Admission   The application deadline for admission is rolling.

Entrance Difficulty   Shepherd assesses its entrance difficulty level as moderately difficult; very difficult for nursing, engineering, education, art, music programs. For the fall 2004 freshman class, 91 percent of the applicants were accepted.

For Further Information   Contact Ms. Kimberly C. Scranage, Director of Admissions, Shepherd University, PO Box 3210, Shepherdstown, WV 25443-3210. *Telephone:* 304-876-5212 or 800-344-5231 (toll-free). *Fax:* 304-876-5165. *E-mail:* admoff@shepherd.edu. *Web site:* http://www.shepherd.edu/.

See page 186 for a narrative description.

WEST VIRGINIA WESLEYAN COLLEGE
Buckhannon, West Virginia

Wesleyan is a coed, private, comprehensive institution, founded in 1890, affiliated with the United Methodist Church, offering degrees at the bachelor's and master's levels. It has an 80-acre campus in Buckhannon.

Academic Information   The faculty has 154 members (54% full-time). The undergraduate student-faculty ratio is 14:1. The library holds 91,061 titles, 2,462 serial subscriptions, and 7,605 audiovisual materials. Special programs include academic remediation, services for learning-disabled students, an honors program, study abroad, advanced placement credit, ESL programs, double majors, independent study, self-designed majors, summer session for credit, part-time degree programs (daytime), adult/continuing education programs, internships, and arrangement for off-campus study with Mountain State Association of Colleges. The most frequently chosen baccalaureate fields are business/marketing, education, social sciences and history.

Student Body Statistics   The student body totals 1,522, of whom 1,486 are undergraduates (350 freshmen). 54 percent are women and 46 percent are men. Students come from 36 states and territories and 14 other countries. 55 percent are from West Virginia. 2.9 percent are international students. 26 percent of the 2004 graduating class went on to graduate and professional schools.

Expenses for 2005–06   *Application fee:* $35. *Comprehensive fee:* $26,750 includes full-time tuition ($20,250), mandatory fees ($1000), and college room and board ($5500). Full-time tuition and fees vary according to course load. Room and board charges vary according to board plan and housing facility. *Part-time tuition:* varies with course load.

Financial Aid   Forms of aid include need-based and non-need-based scholarships, athletic grants, and part-time jobs. The average aided 2004–05 undergraduate received an aid package worth an estimated $20,197. The priority application deadline for financial aid is February 15.

Freshman Admission   Wesleyan requires a high school transcript, SAT or ACT scores, and TOEFL scores for international students. An essay, recommendations, and an interview are recommended. SAT or ACT scores and SAT Subject Test scores are required for some. The application deadline for regular admission is July 1; for early decision it is December 1; and for early action it is October 1.

Transfer Admission   The application deadline for admission is July 1.

Entrance Difficulty   Wesleyan assesses its entrance difficulty level as moderately difficult. For the fall 2004 freshman class, 77 percent of the applicants were accepted.

For Further Information   Contact Mr. Robert N. Skinner II, Director of Admission, West Virginia Wesleyan College, 59 College Avenue, Buckhannon, WV 26201. *Telephone:* 304-473-8510 or 800-722-9933 (toll-free out-of-state). *Fax:* 304-473-8108. *E-mail:* admissions@wvwc.edu. *Web site:* http://www.wvwc.edu/.

See page 190 for a narrative description.

BALTIMORE INTERNATIONAL COLLEGE
School of Culinary Arts
School of Business and Management
BALTIMORE, MARYLAND; VIRGINIA; AND COUNTY CAVAN, IRELAND

The College

The Baltimore International College, a regionally accredited independent college, was founded in 1972 to provide theoretical and technical skills education for individuals seeking careers as hospitality professionals. The College is committed to providing students with the knowledge and ability necessary for employment and success in the hospitality industry.

In 1985, the College was authorized by the state of Maryland to grant associate degrees. As part of the College's continued growth, restaurant and food service management and innkeeping management were added to its curriculum. In 1987, the Virginia Park Campus in Ireland was founded, enabling students to study under European chefs and hoteliers in a European environment. In 1996, the College was granted accreditation by the Commission on Institutions of Higher Education of the Middle States Association of Colleges and Schools. In 1998, the College was authorized by the state of Maryland to grant four-year baccalaureate degrees. In addition to classrooms, offices, and dorms, the College's campus in Baltimore includes a campus bookstore, a student union, a hotel, an inn, two restaurants, parking, student dining facilities, a Career Development Center, and a Learning Resources Center, which includes a library, two academic computer labs, and an art gallery.

Location

The College's main campus, located in downtown Baltimore, is just two blocks from the city's famous Inner Harbor, a location that puts the College in the midst of numerous hotels and restaurants. The city offers year-round cultural and entertainment opportunities, such as theater, opera, the Baltimore Symphony Orchestra, museums, sporting events, and festivals. Other attractions in Baltimore that are within walking distance of the College are the National Aquarium, Harborplace, Oriole Park at Camden Yards, Ravens Stadium, Maryland Science Center, and many historic sites, including Fort McHenry, the neighborhood of Mount Vernon, and the Walters Art Museum. Baltimore also has parks and miles of waterfront for those who enjoy outdoor recreation. Washington, D.C., the nation's capital, is just 30 miles from downtown Baltimore. The city of Baltimore is easily accessed by major highways and bus, rail, and air service. Baltimore/Washington International Airport is a short drive from the campus.

Majors and Degrees

Baltimore International College offers baccalaureate degrees in culinary management, hospitality management, and hospitality management with a concentration in professional marketing. The College also offers associate degrees in food and beverage management, hotel/motel/innkeeping management, professional baking and pastry, professional cooking, and professional cooking and baking. In addition, students can receive professional certificates in culinary arts, professional baking and pastry, professional cooking, professional cooking and baking, and professional marketing.

Academic Programs

The College provides a comprehensive curriculum, which includes an honors study-abroad program at the Baltimore International College, Virginia Park Campus, near Dublin, Ireland.

The College's professional cooking program and the combined programs in professional cooking and baking and baking and pastry operate throughout the calendar year; new classes begin in the spring, summer, and fall. The College's business and management programs accept freshmen in the fall and spring semesters. The culinary arts certificate, which combines cooking and baking, is available through evening classes and begins in the fall and spring semesters.

To earn an associate degree in professional cooking, professional baking and pastry, or professional cooking and baking, the student must complete 62 to 64 credits. To earn an associate degree in food and beverage management or hotel/motel/innkeeping management, the student must complete 54 credits; this program is intended for students who already have a strong academic background. The associate degree program combines technical, hands-on courses with general education courses (such as nutrition, psychology, English, and mathematics) as well as an internship or externship.

The associate degree is offered separately and as part of the 2+2 program at Baltimore International College. In the 2+2 program, students receive their two-year degree and then continue to complete a four-year bachelor's degree in culinary management or hospitality management. Bachelor's degree programs require 125 to 133 credits.

Off-Campus Programs

The Honors Program has been developed for qualified culinary arts and business and management majors. The Honors Program is taught at the College's historic 100-acre Virginia Park Campus in County Cavan, Ireland. Culinary students who are selected for the Honors Program further enhance their skills in and knowledge of European cuisine, baking, pastry, and à la carte service. Business and management students selected for the Honors Program have the opportunity to learn the day-to-day operation of a hotel and restaurant, from reception to housekeeping and from restaurant management to accounting. Students fully enjoy the cross-cultural experience of living in an English-speaking foreign country.

Academic Facilities

The Baltimore campus includes kitchens, storerooms, cooking demonstration theaters, academic classrooms, multipurpose rooms, a library, two computer labs, a student union, and auxiliary services. Public operations that function as in-house training for students include the Mount Vernon Hotel and Bay Atlantic Seafood Restaurant, the Hopkins Inn, and the Bay Atlantic Club Restaurant.

The Virginia Park Campus is located on 100 acres, 50 miles from Dublin, and offers student housing, with laboratory kitchens and lecture facilities. The complex also includes the Park Hotel, with public operations that function as in-house training for students, including the Marquis Dining Room and the Marchioness Ballroom. The Park Hotel has thirty-six guest rooms. All students enjoy unlimited golf and fishing as well as hiking trails.

The College's Career Development Center offers students access to information about careers in food service and hospitality management. The College's Career Development

Services are located in the Career Information Center, where coordinators organize on-campus recruiting and offer workshops and assistance in resume writing and interviewing skills.

The College's Learning Resource Center is a member of an interlibrary loan network that enables users to borrow from public, academic, and private libraries throughout Maryland. The library's current core collection has approximately 13,000 volumes, 200 periodicals, and almost 800 audiovisual selections. The library offers students access to the Internet, a worldwide network of electronic information. In-house services include two computer labs, electronic databases for research, and a photocopier.

The College's art gallery is part of the Learning Resource Center and features a permanent display of edible art. Student participation in all exhibits is encouraged. Culinary competitions are held in the gallery.

The College offers general academic counseling for all students, peer tutoring on request, and a variety of referrals for support services. In addition, Student Services provides many recreation and leisure activities, including the student union, a series of activities sponsored by the College, and information about cultural programs around the city. Student Services also provides ongoing support to the College's alumni through surveys, mailings about the College's growth, and involvement in College-sponsored events such as open houses, resume referrals, and career fairs.

Costs

Tuition for 2004–05 was $7024. Fees range from $150 to $2361, depending on a student's major. Student housing costs range from $3100 to $5196 per semester for dormitory-style housing, which includes a meal plan.

Financial Aid

Students receive financial aid from federal, state, institutional, and private sources and may be employed during their attendance as full-time students. The forms of financial aid available at the College through federal sources include the Federal Pell Grant, the Federal Supplemental Educational Opportunity Grant, the Federal Work-Study Program, the Federal Subsidized and Unsubsidized Stafford Student Loans, PLUS loans, and veterans' educational benefits. Students are encouraged to investigate the scholarship programs in their home state and apply for state scholarships if the grants can be used in Maryland. The College also offers its own series of scholarships and payment options. In 2003–04, College-funded scholarships averaged $3300 per academic year. Students can request a financial aid application from the Student Financial Planning Office. The College employs the Federal Methodology of Need Analysis, approved by the U.S. Department of Education, as a fair and equitable means of determining the family's ability to contribute to the student's educational expenses, as well as eligibility for other financial programs.

Faculty

Baltimore International College faculty members include 29 chefs and academic instructors of high academic distinction. The student-faculty ratio averages 15:1 in culinary labs and 25:1 in academic classes. Each student is assigned to a faculty adviser who oversees the student's progress and answers questions about academic and career concerns. Students are encouraged to discuss program-related issues with the Director of Student Counseling.

Student Government

Many students become junior members of the Greater Baltimore Chapter of the American Culinary Federation. Member-ship is open to all students in good standing. Meetings, which are held monthly, are announced at the College.

Admission Requirements

Creativity and skill of students must be matched by dedication. The College seeks candidates who desire a professional career in the hospitality industry.

Individuals seeking admission to the College must have earned a high school diploma or have passed the GED. Applicants must either pass the College's Admissions Test, take developmental courses during their first semester, or have one of the following: a minimum SAT score of 430 verbal and 420 math, a minimum composite ACT score of 16, minimum CLEP scores in the 50th percentile in math and English composition with essay, a secondary degree, or 16 credit hours at the postsecondary level with a minimum average of C in math and English. Transfer students must submit an official college transcript as well as catalog course descriptions for credits they wish to transfer.

The College affords equally to all students the rights, privileges, programs, activities, scholarships and loan programs, and other programs administered by the College without regard to race, color, creed, sex, age, handicap, or national or ethnic origin.

Application and Information

Applicants are required to submit an application form along with a $35 nonrefundable fee. Requests by the College for additional information must be handled in a timely manner. An admission decision is made as soon as a file is complete. Upon acceptance, applicants are asked to submit a $100 tuition deposit.

For additional information, students should contact:

Office of Admissions
Commerce Exchange
Baltimore International College
17 Commerce Street
Baltimore, Maryland 21202-3230
Telephone: 410-752-4710 Ext. 120
              800-624-9926 Ext. 120 (toll-free)
E-mail: admissions@bic.edu
World Wide Web: http://www.bic.edu

Small classes at Baltimore International College enable students to receive individual instruction that helps them perfect their skills.

CHAMINADE UNIVERSITY OF HONOLULU

HONOLULU, HAWAII

The University

Chaminade University of Honolulu, a private, coeducational institution, was established in 1955 by the Society of Mary (Marianists). Named after Father William Joseph Chaminade, a French Catholic priest who ministered to his people during the late eighteenth and early nineteenth centuries and who founded the Society in 1817, the University today continues the Marianist mission of educating leaders through faith and reason. To achieve this mission, Chaminade forms a community encompassing people from diverse cultural origins, both traditional and nontraditional, who hold a variety of religious beliefs. The University encourages learning through cooperation, self-discipline, caring, and mutual respect while offering individualized attention that promotes personal and intellectual growth. A major goal of the University is to educate and train students for leadership both within Chaminade and in communities beyond the campus. The University advocates a personal concern for social justice, ethics, responsibility, and service to the community and exerts institutional leadership by promoting Chaminade's ideals outside the University community.

At any one time, 2,600 to 2,800 students are enrolled in a range of daytime and evening classes. Of this number, approximately 1,100 are full-time undergraduates, 1,200 are part-time undergraduates enrolled in the evening program, and 500 are graduate students. Nearly 60 percent of the full-time undergraduates are from Hawaii, 24 percent are from the mainland, 13 percent are from U.S. trust territories, and 3 percent are from other countries. Thirty-four states and thirty-one countries are represented in the student body.

Clubs and associations offer all Chaminade students a chance to pursue interests and extend their activities beyond the classroom. Student publications include the *Aulama*, a literary and art magazine; the *Silverword*, the monthly student newspaper; and *Ahinahina*, the Chaminade yearbook. Chaminade also sponsors chapters of Delta Epsilon Sigma, the national scholastic honor society for students at colleges and universities with a Catholic tradition; Phi Alpha Theta, the history national honor society; Delta Mu Delta, a national honor society in business administration; Sigma Tau Delta, the national English honor society; Pi Sigma Alpha, a national honor society in political science, and Alpha Phi Sigma, a national honor society for criminal justice.

Intercollegiate athletic teams are currently sponsored in men's basketball and water polo, women's softball and volleyball, and men's and women's cross-country and tennis. Intramural competitive and noncompetitive sports and recreation programs are open to all students, faculty and staff members, and alumni.

Chaminade University of Honolulu is accredited by the Accrediting Commission for Senior Colleges and Universities of the Western Association of Schools and Colleges. The University also has two sister universities on the mainland: the University of Dayton in Dayton, Ohio, and St. Mary's University in San Antonio, Texas.

Chaminade offers graduate degrees in business administration (M.B.A.), counseling psychology (M.S.C.P.), criminal justice administration (M.S.C.J.A.), education (M.Ed.), pastoral leadership (M.A.P.L.), and public administration (M.P.A.).

Location

Honolulu, a multicultural community, is enriched by a great diversity of ethnic activities and traditions. Chaminade is located on a hillside with a spectacular view sweeping across Waikiki to downtown Honolulu, from Diamond Head to the blue Pacific Ocean. This idyllic site is only minutes from the city, cultural activities, and the beach. The University also operates ten off-campus sites, primarily at military installations on the island of Oahu.

Majors and Degrees

The University offers twenty-one major programs of study at the undergraduate level as well as two associate degree programs. The Bachelor of Arts (B.A.) degree is offered in biology, chemistry, communication, English, historical and political studies, humanities, international studies, management, philosophy, psychology, religious studies, and social studies; the Bachelor of Fine Arts (B.F.A.) degree is offered in interior design; and the Bachelor of Science (B.S.) degree is offered in accounting, behavioral sciences, biology, computer information systems, criminal justice, early childhood education, elementary education, environmental studies, and forensic science. The Associate in Arts (A.A.) degree is offered in management; the Associate in Science (A.S.) degree is offered in computer science and criminal justice.

Preprofessional programs are offered in law, health sciences, nursing, and engineering.

Students may elect to pursue a minor program in most major programs as well as in anthropology, history, physics, political science, sociology, and studio art.

Academic Programs

The core curriculum at Chaminade is in liberal arts. The University is committed to a broad liberal education for its students and believes that such an education provides a basis for long-term personal growth, a foundation for a career that may encounter job changes, and a background that allows students to rise to leadership positions in their chosen fields and communities. Through undergraduate programs based on the liberal arts tradition, Chaminade seeks to heighten cultural awareness. Coupled with understanding diverse methods of inquiry and participation in Chaminade's multicultural interdependent community, cultural awareness prepares all students for lifelong learning—about themselves, each other, and the world in which they live.

Undergraduate study is structured into four parts: practice in basic skills, liberal arts course work that provides a general education, intensive study in a chosen field of concentration (the major), and elective courses outside the major field to complement general and specialized knowledge. All baccalaureate degrees require a minimum of 120 credit hours of course work with a minimum of 45 hours in upper-division courses. Within these guidelines, the student selects a program of study appropriate to personal needs and interests. All appropriate courses at Chaminade require writing assignments from students. Upper-division courses in most fields train students to write in the style and format appropriate to the discipline.

In all fields of study at Chaminade, students are encouraged to apply their academic experience to on-the-job practice for academic credit. Faculty members may ask students to work with a specific organization, or students may develop internship possibilities on their own. Interns usually have at least junior-level standing, but in special cases sophomores are considered. Depending on the organization with which they work, students may or may not receive a salary for their internship experience.

The First Year Experience Seminar supports students in their transition from high school to college. The program provides an orientation to University functions and resources. This course also helps freshmen adjust to the University, gain a better understanding of the learning process and develop critical-thinking skills and provides a support group for students by examining problems that are common to the freshman experience.

Chaminade cooperates with two major programs that enable students to receive college credit prior to admission. These two programs, Advanced Placement and College-Level Examination Program, are sponsored by the College Board.

Off-Campus Programs

In 1990, Chaminade University and its sister universities signed an agreement through which any student at any of the three universities can enroll for their junior year at any of the other campuses. Full credit is given by Chaminade for approved courses taken at either university. Chaminade also encourages students to pursue part of their undergraduate education in another country.

Academic Facilities

Located in Henry Hall, Sullivan Library occupies three floors and houses a collection of approximately 74,000 volumes and 874 periodicals. Special collections include the Oceania Collection, the Catholic Authors Collection, the Julius J. Nodel Judaica Collection, and the David L. Carlson Japan Collection. Services offered include reference consultation, computerized information retrieval, and instruction in library use. Also in Henry Hall, the Computer Center provides students and faculty members with a variety of microcomputers, software programs, and reference materials for instruction, word processing, and programming. The multipurpose Audio Visual Media Resource Center provides instructional media technology support to all divisions of the University, student activities, special programs, and other events. The center is also a resource for films, slides, records, and videotapes.

Costs

Full-time undergraduate tuition for 2005–06 is $7165 per semester. Part-time undergraduate tuition is $478 per semester hour. Housing costs per semester range from $1550 to $3175, depending upon accommodations. Meal plans range from $1580 to $2095 per semester, depending upon the plan chosen. Various other fees for independent/individualized directed studies, parking, labs, and studios are also charged. The tuition charged by Chaminade University does not cover the total cost of instruction for each student. Gifts and grants are used to balance the difference. Tuition and fees must be paid at or prior to the time of registration.

Financial Aid

Those with a high school GPA between 3.5 and 4.0 are eligible for a $6000 yearly scholarship; between 3.0 and 3.49, a $5000 yearly scholarship; between 2.5 and 2.99, a $4500 yearly grant; and between 2.25 to 2.49, a $3000 yearly Father Chaminade Grant. The Hawaii Grant for new full-time day session students from Hawaii is $1500 per semester. Scholarships and grants, available to regular full-time undergraduate students, are renewable for four years and are awarded without regard to financial need. Students may obtain only one of the Chaminade scholarships or grants. When a first member of a family pays full-time day un-

dergraduate tuition, additional members who are concurrently enrolled in the day undergraduate program may receive a tuition discount of 20 percent.

Faculty

The University is dedicated to teaching and to building the leadership skills of its students, and its major strengths lie in its relatively small size and its talented faculty. Classes are small, allowing faculty members to provide a significant amount of individual and small-group attention. Classes are taught by professors or professionals in their fields, not graduate students.

Student Government

The Chaminade University Student Association is the official representative of the student body. Each full-time student of Chaminade becomes a member upon payment of fees. Membership is open to all students at all instructional sites. The Senate, chaired by the student body president and composed of elected representatives, focuses on improving the quality of undergraduate student life and represents the needs, interests, and concerns of its constituents.

The Dean of Students, through the Assistant Dean of Students, initiates all disciplinary action. The committee is composed of administrators, faculty and staff members, and students. Chaminade does not condone activities on campus that violate state or federal regulations, including illegal possession of drugs or the illegal consumption of alcoholic beverages. Students found to be in violation of these regulations are subject to immediate disciplinary action.

Admission Requirements

Applications for admission are reviewed for specific majors or, when applicable, for "undecided" status. Chaminade considers several factors when assessing students' preparation for a selected area of study: grades throughout high school, selection of courses in preparation for college, scores from either the SAT or ACT, and an essay that provides information about the applicant's character and record of leadership and service.

Application and Information

Chaminade University has a rolling admission process. As soon as all required information is received by the Admission Office, the application is reviewed by an application committee. Students are notified of the committee's decision usually within three to four weeks. Applications are accepted throughout the year. A $50 fee is payable upon application. Web site applications are also available for a $25 fee. All students desiring housing must file an application along with a $300 deposit applicable to the total cost per semester. Space and placement are not guaranteed without this deposit. A housing damage deposit of $100 is also required. Evidence of health insurance coverage from a U.S. insurer is required of all dormitory residents and international students.

To ensure full consideration for scholarships or grants, students are urged to complete the appropriate application by April 1. Award notices are mailed by April 30. For more information and application materials, students should contact:

Admission Office
Chaminade University
3140 Waialae Avenue
Honolulu, Hawaii 96816
Telephone: 808-735-4735
                800-735-3733 (toll-free)
Fax: 808-739-4647
E-mail: admissions@chaminade.edu
World Wide Web: http://www.chaminade.edu

CHATHAM COLLEGE
PITTSBURGH, PENNSYLVANIA

The College

Chatham College, founded in 1869, is one of the oldest women's colleges in the United States and is focused on preparing students for the future. A Chatham education emphasizes environmental awareness, global issues, and women's leadership. Chatham empowers women to assume their roles as World Ready Women®, as it has for more than 135 years.

Students' personal, professional, and leadership skills are developed to their fullest potential through Chatham's internship program, study abroad, service learning, leadership training opportunities, and personal development seminars. Chatham students may participate in up to six internships related to their major and career goals before they graduate. Recent examples include World Bank, Pittsburgh Council of International Visitors, PPG Industries, Senator H. J. Heinz III History Center, (affiliated with the Smithsonian Institution), Pittsburgh Children's Hospital, Carnegie Museum, the Pennsylvania Senate, the Washington Center Internship Program, Coro Center for Civic Leadership, WQED, Pittsburgh Zoo and Aquarium, YMCA Legal Resources for Women, Women's Law Project, UPMC Rehabilitation Hospital, UPMC Western Psychiatric Hospital, and numerous sites in Pittsburgh's corporate, nonprofit, government, health-care, and communications communities. Last year, 71 percent of Chatham seniors participated in service learning, more than twice the national average. Overall, the student body completed more than 46,000 hours.

The student body of more than 1,250 represents twenty-five states and eighteen other countries. Members of minority groups and international students represent 20 percent of the student body. Both resident and commuting students participate actively in the numerous professional, academic, social, and special interest organizations at the College. Health services and personal and career counseling services are available on campus. The College offers NCAA Division III intercollegiate competition in basketball, ice hockey, soccer, softball, swimming, tennis, and volleyball and intramural and recreational competition in other sports. There are several student publications, and the College sponsors frequent programs and speakers in the arts, environment, sciences, and public leadership arena.

Chatham offers coeducational graduate programs in biology, business administration, counseling psychology, interior architecture, landscape architecture, landscape studies, organizational and community psychology, physical therapy, physician assistant studies, professional writing, and teaching. An M.B.A. in health care and an M.F.A. in writing are also offered.

Location

Chatham's 32-acre parklike, suburban campus is located in a beautiful, safe neighborhood minutes from downtown Pittsburgh. Steeped in history, the campus features towering trees, wandering paths, and period architecture, including century-old mansions, which serve as fully networked residence halls. Chatham also features a $10-million science complex and a new state-of-the-art athletic facility with an eight-lane competition pool, gymnasium, squash courts, cardio rooms, climbing wall, a running track, and exercise and dance studios.

Pittsburgh is one of the safest and most dynamic cities in the country. The city is headquarters to major businesses and industries in finance, health care, and technology. Students find eclectic city neighborhoods that reflect Pittsburgh's historic qualities yet appeal to a wide audience. Pittsburgh offers numerous arts and entertainment options in the Pittsburgh Symphony; world-renowned opera, ballet, and theater companies; and two established lecture series, featuring some of the world's most prominent figures. Nearby parks and ski areas and the city's three rivers provide ample opportunities for hiking, biking, kayaking, skiing, white-water rafting, and numerous other recreational activities. Pittsburgh is also well known for its three professional sports teams: the NHL Penguins, the MLB Pirates, and the NFL Steelers. Excellent bus, rail, and air connections are available to and from most major cities. For more information, students should visit http://www.pittsburghregion.org.

Majors and Degrees

Chatham College offers the following majors, leading to a Bachelor of Arts or Bachelor of Science degree: accounting, art (design, eco-art, electronic media, photography, studio arts), art history, arts management, biochemistry, biology, bioinformatics, business economics, chemistry, cultural studies, economics, education, English, environmental studies, exercise science, French, global policy studies, health-care studies, history, interior architecture, international business, management, marketing, mathematics, music, physics, political science, professional communication (broadcast journalism, print journalism, professional writing, public relations), psychology, public policy studies, social work, Spanish, theater, and women's studies. Students may choose a traditional major, an interdisciplinary major, a double major, or a self-designed major.

Preprofessional programs are offered in education with teaching certification, law, medicine and health professions, physical therapy, and veterinary medicine. There is also a joint-degree engineering program with Carnegie Mellon University in Pittsburgh. Postbaccalaureate certificate programs are available in accounting, children's and adolescent writing, education for gifted and talented children, English as a second language, horticulture, instructional technology, landscape studies, nonfiction writing, premed, school counseling, and special education. Teacher certification is available through the education program in early childhood, elementary, environmental, school counseling, special education, and secondary education.

Well-qualified students can enroll in the College's Accelerated Master's Program. Through this program, students earn both a bachelor's and master's degree in as few as five years in conjunction with nearly all of the College's graduate programs. Well-qualified Chatham juniors may also apply to the Accelerated Master's Program with the Carnegie Mellon University H. John Heinz III School of Public Policy.

Academic Programs

Chatham's general education curriculum includes six required interdisciplinary courses, plus analytical reasoning, an international or intercultural experience, and wellness courses. Graduation requirements include the general education courses, a major, and the senior tutorial—an original research/capstone project. Students are mentored one-on-one by a faculty member throughout the tutorial process. The project provides an excellent bridge to graduate and professional schools and strong preparation for law and medical schools.

The College's 4-4-1 academic calendar consists of fall and spring terms, plus a three-week "Maymester." Maymester programs include study abroad, concentrated study, experimental projects, travel and field experiences, internships, interdisciplinary study, and student exchanges with other colleges.

The First-Year Student Sequence introduces students to the College community and its culture and provides opportunities to learn about the resources of the urban environment and study issues of concern to women. These courses provide students with the analytical and communication skills essential for successful college performance.

Chatham's Career Services coordinates student internships, placement, workshops, recruitment, and mentor programs as well as health and wellness issues and academic and personal counseling. Its placement rate for students is 92 percent.

The Rachel Carson Institute honors Chatham's 1929 alumna and her commitment to the environment. The institute's focus is on global environmental issues, with a concentration on the impact of environmental degradation on women's health and societal roles and the promotion of women's leadership in the environmental movement.

The Pennsylvania Center for Women, Politics, and Public Policy introduces students to the world of politics, public policy, and civic engagement. It provides opportunities for one-on-one mentoring with local politicians, judges, state-level policy makers, and others. Students may also choose to participate in seminars and internships in Washington, D.C.

Off-Campus Arrangements

Chatham students may register for classes at any of Pittsburgh's eight other colleges and universities, including Carnegie Mellon University and the University of Pittsburgh, both of which are within walking distance of the campus. Chatham Abroad involves a three-week travel experience with faculty members during students' sophomore year and has taken students to Belize, the Galapagos Islands, Morocco, Egypt, Italy, Spain, France, Ireland, England, and Russia for an additional nominal fee. The Internship Program enables students to gain firsthand experience in field placements in a wide variety of agencies, businesses, and professional organizations.

Academic Facilities

All academic buildings have computer classrooms, labs, and smart classrooms connected to both the campus LAN and the Internet via fiber-optic connections. All residence halls have computer labs and high-speed network printers. Central computer equipment supports e-mail, computer-mediated courseware, personal Web pages, and file and print servers. Public computer labs in the residence halls and academic buildings supply high-end personal computer workstations, Macintosh G-5s, laser printers, scanners, and CD-ROM burners.

The modern Jennie King Mellon Library has 90,000 volumes and more than 600 current subscriptions, individual study areas, special seminar rooms, and a 285-seat theater. Chatham participates in campuswide software license agreements that permit students to install select productivity software on their personal machines at no additional cost. Library facilities at neighboring colleges and universities are also available for Chatham students.

The Science Laboratory houses state-of-the-art science laboratories and individual laboratory units. Psychology and language laboratories and audiovisual facilities are also available. The Media Center contains equipment used by students to gain experience with some of the sophisticated technology of audio, visual, and video presentations.

With completion of the new Athletic and Fitness Center, the College converted its old gymnasium into the new Art and Design Center, featuring fine and applied art studios, a computer lab, and classroom space, as well as gallery and student exhibition space.

Costs

For 2004–05, full-time tuition was $21,780 per year and room and board were approximately $7120. The student activity fee was $8 per credit. A one-time deposit of $100 for tuition and $100 for on-campus housing is paid by newly admitted students and is applied to first-semester charges. Regularly enrolled full-time students pay no additional costs for Maymester courses, except for special supplies or travel. Additional fees are required for art supplies and music lessons. Students are required to have health and accident insurance.

Financial Aid

Financial aid is awarded on the basis of an individual's financial need, as determined through the Free Application for Federal Student Aid. The awards combine grants, loans, and employment. The priority financial aid deadline is May 1.

Sources of financial aid include Chatham grants and loans, state grants, Federal Pell Grants, Federal Supplemental Educational Opportunity Grants, federally funded student loans, and jobs provided under the Federal Work-Study Program. Chatham Merit scholarships for entering students are awarded on the basis of high academic achievement and an on-campus interview without regard to need. Scholarships begin at approximately $4000 and are awarded based upon the student's match with Chatham's mission, as well as the academic merits accompanying the student's application for admission. Minna Kaufmann Ruud Scholarships are available for students with exceptional ability in vocal music, based on an on-campus audition. Approximately 90 percent of undergraduate students receive aid administered by the College.

Faculty

The Chatham environment features a student-teacher ratio of 13:1. Faculty members also advise students as they choose from more than thirty-five majors. The low student-teacher ratio ensures close student-faculty relationships and individual consideration of students by the faculty members. Each student is assigned a faculty member, who serves as her adviser through the completion of her degree program. Ninety percent of all faculty members hold doctoral degrees.

Student Government

The Chatham Student Government coordinates student involvement in the affairs of the College, gives voice to student concerns, maintains student participation on College committees, and oversees various student boards and organizations. Chatham students serve as voting members on many of the College's planning and policy committees.

Admission Requirements

The prospective student must demonstrate academic strength, motivation, an enthusiasm for learning, and potential for growth. Evaluation of students is made on the basis of the student's academic record, recommendations, SAT or ACT scores, involvement in activities, essay, and other submitted material. The College seeks to enroll students representing a variety of cultural, geographical, racial, religious, and socioeconomic backgrounds and with diverse talents in both academic and creative areas.

It is strongly recommended that candidates arrange to visit the College for a personal appointment, a tour of the campus with a student guide, observation of one or more classes, and conversations with faculty members, staff members, and students. Early entrance is available for well-qualified and mature students who wish to begin college at the close of their junior year in high school; early entrance candidates are required to come to the College for interviews. The College also welcomes the opportunity to discuss future educational plans with transfer candidates, including junior college and community college graduates, in good academic standing. Chatham grants college course credit for grades of 4 or 5 on the Advanced Placement examinations of the College Board. Certain prerequisites in course offerings may be fulfilled by attaining scores of 3, 4, or 5.

Application and Information

Candidates for admission must file an application with the Admissions Office, together with a nonrefundable processing fee in the amount of $35. Students may also take advantage of the College's free online application on the Web site, listed in this In-Depth Description. Applications are accepted on a rolling basis.

Vice President of Admissions and Financial Aid
Office of Admissions
Chatham College
Pittsburgh, Pennsylvania 15232
Telephone: 412-365-1290
         800-837-1290 (toll-free)
Fax: 412-365-1609
E-mail: admissions@chatham.edu
World Wide Web: http://www.chatham.edu

View of the Chatham College campus.

MITCHELL COLLEGE
NEW LONDON, CONNECTICUT

The College

Mitchell is a private, coeducational four- and two-year residential college. With 850 full-time students and a 12:1 student-faculty ratio, the College provides a supportive student-centered learning environment that addresses the educational needs of all students, including those with learning disabilities. Mitchell is especially proud of its success in working with students who have yet to reach their full academic potential. To that end, the College maintains access for students with varied academic abilities who are highly motivated to succeed.

Mitchell's nationally recognized student support program, C.A.R.E.S. (Careering, Advising, Retaining, Educating, and Supporting), includes extensive hands-on internship experiences; a First-Year Seminar helps students successfully make the transition to college; and career and transfer assistance helps students plan the next step in their learning adventure.

Nearly 90 percent of the full-time students live in three traditional residence halls, each housing 100 students. Each building has three floors with double rooms and common baths. The College also offers four historic Victorian and Colonial waterfront residence halls accommodating between 20 and 30 students each. Other facilities include a fully equipped gymnasium, a fitness center, athletic fields, a sailing dock, and indoor recreation areas.

Nearly all full-time students are of traditional college age, 18 to 22, and come from throughout the country and around the globe. Most students come from New England states, with about 60 percent from Connecticut, 30 percent from other New England states, and the remaining 10 percent from other states. International students and representatives of multicultural groups make up approximately 28 percent of the student population. About 150 part-time students, many of whom are adult commuters, enhance the classroom experience.

Clubs for students interested in biking, business, community service, choir, Hillel, music, the newspaper, the yearbook, skiing, multicultural affairs, psychology, and history bring together students with similar interests. Weekends are filled with guest comedians, bands, formal and casual dances, lectures, and organized trips to Boston and New York City.

Mitchell College is a provisional member of the NCAA Division III and fields ten intercollegiate teams. Men play baseball, basketball, cheerleading, cross-country, golf, lacrosse, sailing, soccer, and tennis; women play basketball, cheerleading, cross-country, golf, sailing, soccer, softball, tennis, and volleyball. The College has a history of athletic excellence, winning many national and New England championships. A full schedule of intramural sports is organized for students of all athletic experience and ability.

Location

New London, Connecticut, where Mitchell College makes its home, is a major center of activity in southeastern Connecticut, a region rich in historic significance. This small but sophisticated city, also home to Connecticut College and the U.S. Coast Guard Academy, is a maritime and resort center located midway between Boston and New York City on the main rail line.

The campus is situated in the city's most scenic residential section. Bordered by a long stretch of sandy beach, the campus consists of 65 acres of gently sloping hillside and forest. Places for shopping, banking, dining, and fun are within easy walking distance or can be accessed by buses that pass the College entrance. Major shopping malls, factory outlets, and fine and casual dining are minutes from the campus. The region is also home to major tourist attractions, such as the U.S.S. Nautilus and Submarine Museum, Mystic Marinelife Aquarium, Mystic Seaport, Olde Mystic Village, Ocean Beach Park, Stonington Vineyards, Foxwoods Resort and Casino, the Mohegan Sun Casino, and the Essex Steam Train.

Majors and Degrees

Baccalaureate degrees are offered in business administration, criminal justice, early childhood education, human development and family studies, liberal and professional studies, psychology, and sport management. Associate degrees are offered in business administration–management, computer information systems, criminal justice, early childhood education, graphic design, human development and family studies, human services, liberal arts, physical education, and sport management.

Students undecided about their academic majors are enrolled in the Discovery Program, which is specially designed to provide special courses, additional advising, and services to explore their full potential and assistance in choosing a major.

Academic Programs

The academic calendar consists of two full semesters that run from September to December and from January to May. A mini-term in January and five summer sessions are also offered.

All students must complete the core curriculum, which consists of expository writing, composition and literature, effective speaking, introduction to computer and information systems, an introductory psychology or sociology course, a mathematics course, a lab science, and either U.S. history I and II or Western civilization I and II.

If a student is having difficulty, it is recognized early. Mitchell grades at five-week intervals rather than just at midterms and finals. If a student is experiencing a problem, faculty members and the student's academic adviser work with the student to get back on course. Mitchell's Tutoring Center provides free, unlimited individualized tutoring by trained professionals (not peer tutors) in every academic discipline. It also offers assistance in improving writing, research, and computer skills as well as test and exam preparation and study skills development. Some of Mitchell's most successful students are regular users of the Tutoring Center, and they attribute much of their success to its programs.

Students with diagnosed learning disabilities may enroll in the College's nationally recognized Learning Resource Center, which provides instruction and support to complement a student's regular academic program. Each student is assigned two learning specialists to work one-on-one with the student and in small-group settings. The program is designed to teach the learning strategies a student needs to gain independence.

Following completion of their associate degree, 90 percent of the student body continue in one of Mitchell's baccalaureate programs or successfully transfer to the four-year college or university of their choice.

Off-Campus Programs

When not in class, Mitchell students gain the skills and experience they need to succeed in their careers and to make a difference in their communities. Nearly all academic programs require or encourage students to participate in volunteer opportunities, internships, or practical experiences as part of their curriculum.

Some of the opportunities include exploring the seacoast with a nationally recognized scientist, teaching at a local elementary school, partnering with a local police officer, helping to negotiate a bill through the state legislature, assisting with advertising campaigns, coaching developmentally challenged athletes and practicing the skills of injury prevention, and sparking the imagination of local school children through storytelling sessions.

Academic Facilities

Mitchell's unique 65-acre waterfront campus includes a 45,000-volume library and two primary classroom buildings. Students have full use of Mitchell's state-of-the-art computing facilities with high-speed, full T-1 Internet access. Open seven days a week and staffed with fully trained help-desk consultants, students may use the computer labs to e-mail, scan images, print documents, and complete academic assignments. This same high-speed network and Internet access is also available in each student's residence hall room. For those who do not own a computer, Mitchell offers a computer purchasing plan and service agreement.

Costs

Tuition, room and board, and fees for the 2004–05 year were $27,710. Additional annual miscellaneous expenses, including books, were estimated at $1500 per year. Students enrolled in the Learning Resource Center paid an additional $6000 per year.

Financial Aid

Mitchell annually awards more than $3 million in financial aid, both in need-based and merit-based scholarships and in grant programs designed to recognize academic, athletic, and leadership abilities. Accepted students may qualify for grants and scholarships that do not need to be repaid. They include the Connecticut Independent College Student Grant Program, Federal Pell Grants, Federal Supplemental Educational Opportunity Grants, and Mitchell Scholarships. Self-help aid in the form of loans is also available. They include Federal Stafford Student Loans (subsidized and unsubsidized), Federal PLUS Loans, and Federal Perkins Loan programs. On-campus job opportunities are plentiful for students regardless of their financial aid status.

Mitchell Valued Potential (MVP) scholarships are awarded based on an individual student's ability to contribute to the College. They may be given to students who demonstrate potential in leadership, volunteerism, and involvement in school activities. Athletic scholarships are available to students who participate in men's and women's baseball, basketball, soccer, and softball; women's volleyball; and men's lacrosse. Various payment plans are available.

Faculty

Twenty-nine full-time and 46 part-time faculty members teach in Mitchell's classrooms. The student-faculty ratio is 12:1.

Student Government

The Student Government Association (SGA) is made up of officers and senators who represent the residents and commuters. It addresses issues with campus administration, organizes community projects, serves as the active voice for the student body, and sponsors at least one campuswide program each semester. The SGA also works in tandem with the Student Activities Office concerning club funding and overall programming.

Student involvement is not only encouraged but also expected of all Mitchell students. An active student leads to a well-rounded person. Students enhance their life with self-discipline skills, demonstrate selfless service, and become happier members of the College family through involvement in student activities, athletics, campus employment, and community service opportunities.

Admission Requirements

Each student is evaluated individually as soon as the completed application, along with the official transcript, is received. Admission is based on academic preparation, scholastic aptitude, personal character, and potential for academic success. Other important factors taken into consideration include the student's motivation, initiative, maturity, seriousness of purpose, and leadership potential. SAT I or ACT test scores are required. A campus visit and admissions interview are required. Open houses are held in October, January, April, and throughout the summer.

Application and Information

Mitchell uses a rolling admission policy. Students can expect to be notified of decisions within weeks of the College's receipt of completed applications and official transcripts sent directly from the students' high schools.

For more information, students should contact:

Kevin Mayne
Vice President for Enrollment Management and Marketing
Mitchell College
437 Pequot Avenue
New London, Connecticut 06320-4498

Telephone: 800-443-2811 (toll-free)
Fax: 860-444-1209
E-mail: admissions@mitchell.edu
World Wide Web: http://www.mitchell.edu

Mitchell College's 65–acre campus is located in New London, Connecticut, where the Thames River meets the Long Island Sound.

NORTH CAROLINA AGRICULTURAL AND TECHNICAL STATE UNIVERSITY

GREENSBORO, NORTH CAROLINA

The University

North Carolina Agricultural and Technical State University was founded in 1891 as one of two land-grant institutions in the state. Originally, it was established to provide postsecondary education and training for black students. Today, the University is a comprehensive institution of higher education with an integrated faculty and student body, and it has been designated a constituent institution of the University of North Carolina, offering degrees at the baccalaureate, master's, and doctoral degree levels. Located on a 191-acre campus, the University has 110 buildings, including single-sex and coeducational residence halls. Of a total of 9,121 undergraduates, 4,383 are men and 4,738 are women. The total population is approximately 10,383.

North Carolina Agricultural and Technical State University (A&T) provides outstanding academic programs through five undergraduate schools, two colleges, and a graduate school.

The mission of the University is to provide an intellectual setting in which students may find a sense of belonging, responsibility, and achievement that prepares them for roles of leadership and service in the communities where they will live and work. In this sense, the University serves as a laboratory for the development of excellence in teaching, research, and public service. As a result, A&T today stands as an example of well-directed higher education for all students.

Student life at the University is active and purposeful. The broad objective of the program provided by Student Development Services is to aid students in attaining the attitudes, understandings, insights, and skills that enable them to be socially competent. The program places special emphasis on campus relationships and experiences that complement formal instruction. Some of the services available are counseling, housing, health, and placement services. There is a University Student Union, and there are special services for international and minority students, veterans, and handicapped students. The University also provides a well-balanced program of activities to foster the moral, spiritual, cultural, and physical development of its students.

Location

Greensboro, North Carolina, is 300 miles south of Washington, D.C., and 349 miles north of Atlanta. It is readily accessible by air, bus, and automobile. The city offers a variety of cultural and recreational activities and facilities. These include sports events, concerts, bowling, boating, fishing, tennis, golf, and other popular forms of recreation. There are major shopping centers, churches, theaters, and medical facilities near the University. The heavy concentration of factories, service industries, government agencies, and shopping centers provides many job opportunities for students who desire part-time employment.

Majors and Degrees

North Carolina Agricultural and Technical State University grants the following degrees: Bachelor of Arts, Bachelor of Science, Bachelor of Fine Arts, Bachelor of Science in Nursing, and Bachelor of Social Work.

The School of Agriculture and Environmental Sciences offers programs in agricultural economics, agricultural economics (agricultural business), agricultural education, agricultural education (agricultural extension), agricultural science–earth and environmental science (earth and environmental science, landscape horticulture design, plant science, soil science), agricultural science–natural resources (plant science), animal science, animal

science (animal industry), child development, child development–early education and family studies B–K (teaching), family and consumer science (fashion merchandising and design), family and consumer science education, food and nutritional sciences, laboratory animal science, and landscape architecture.

In the College of Arts and Sciences, programs are available in applied mathematics, biology, biology–secondary education, broadcast production, chemistry, chemistry–secondary education, criminal justice, electronic/media journalism, English, English–secondary education, history, history–secondary education, journalism and mass communications, liberal studies-African American studies, liberal studies-international studies, liberal studies-dance, mathematics, mathematics–secondary education, media management, music education, music–general, music–performance, physics, physics–secondary education, political science, print journalism, professional theater, psychology, public relations, sociology, social work, Romance languages and literatures-French, Romance languages and literatures-French secondary education, Romance languages and literatures-Spanish, Romance languages and literatures-Spanish secondary education, speech, speech (speech pathology/audiology), visual arts–art education, and visual arts–design.

The School of Business and Economics offers programs in accounting, business administration, business education, business education (administrative systems, vocational business education, vocational business education–data processing), economics, finance, management, management (management information systems), marketing, and transportation.

In the School of Education, programs are available in elementary education, human performance and leisure studies (fitness/wellness management), human performance and leisure studies (teaching), human performance and leisure studies (sports science and fitness management), recreation administration, and special education.

In the College of Engineering, programs are offered in architectural engineering, bioenvironmental engineering, chemical engineering, civil engineering, computer science, electrical engineering, industrial engineering, and mechanical engineering.

The School of Nursing grants the Bachelor of Science in Nursing (B.S.N.) degree.

The School of Technology has programs in computer-aided drafting and design, construction management, electronics technology, electronics technology (computational technology), electronics technology (information technology), graphic communication systems, integrated Internet technologies, manufacturing systems, manufacturing systems (motor sports), occupational safety and health, printing and publishing, technology education (teaching), trade and industrial education (teaching), and training and development for industry.

Academic Programs

Students must complete a minimum of 124 semester hours to earn a bachelor's degree; the exact number varies with the program. Students are also required to demonstrate competence in English and mathematics.

As complements to the academic programs, the University's Army and Air Force ROTC programs and cooperative education program provide excellent opportunities for students to enrich their educational experiences. The ROTC programs are designed to prepare college graduates for military service careers. The cooperative education program provides an opportunity for qualified students to alternate periods of study on campus and meaningful employment off campus in private industrial or business firms or government agencies.

Academic Facilities

The University library has current holdings that include 507,036 book volumes and bound periodicals, as well as 5,446 current serials. As a select depository in North Carolina for U.S. government documents, the library contains a collection of more than 250,000 official publications. Among the library's other holdings are a collection of audiovisuals and 1,038,474 microforms, archives, and special collections in black studies and teacher-education materials. Special services are provided through formal and informal library instruction, interlibrary loans, and photocopying facilities.

The University's educational support centers are the Learning Assistance Center, the Audiovisual Center, the Closed Circuit Television Facility, a 1,000-watt student-operated educational radio station, the Computer Center, the Reading Center, the Language Laboratory, and the Center for Manpower Research and Training. The H. Clinton Taylor Art Gallery and the African Heritage Center are two exceptional art museums on campus. Throughout the year, these museums have on display a number of special exhibits of sculpture, paintings, graphics, and other media.

Costs

In 2004–05, tuition and fees for North Carolina residents were $3066 per year; for nonresidents of the state, they were $12,508. Board and lodging for the academic year were $5,070.

Financial Aid

Through the student financial aid program, the University makes every effort to ensure that no qualified student is denied the opportunity to attend because of a lack of funds. Students who demonstrate financial need and have the potential to achieve academic success at the University may obtain assistance to meet their expenses in accordance with the funds available. Financial aid is awarded without regard to race, religion, color, national origin, or sex. The University provides financial aid for students from four basic sources: grants, scholarships, loans, and employment. To apply for aid, students must submit the Free Application for Federal Student Aid (FAFSA). The priority filing deadline is March 15 for fall semester. North Carolina residents may call 800-443-0835 (toll-free).

Faculty

The University's teaching faculty consists of more than 600 highly qualified members. Approximately 90 percent of them hold the doctoral degree or the first professional degree in their discipline. Faculty members are recruited from many areas and backgrounds, thereby bringing together a diverse cadre of academic professionals from many nations.

Student Government

The Student Government Association (SGA), composed of senators elected from the student body, is primarily a policy-recommending group and represents the views and concerns of the students. The president of SGA reports directly to the vice-chancellor for student affairs. In addition, each student organization is represented by a senator, and these senators sit on the Faculty Senate.

Admission Requirements

Applicants for undergraduate admission are considered individually and in accordance with criteria applied flexibly to ensure that applicants with unusual qualifications are not denied admission. However, admission for out-of-state freshman students is competitive due to an 18 percent out-of-state enrollment cap. Students who are applying for admission as freshmen are expected to have completed a college-preparatory program in high school and taken the SAT or the ACT. General requirements include graduation from an accredited high school with 19 units of credit, with no more than 4 units in vocational subjects and with at least 2 units in physical education; a satisfactory score on the SAT or ACT; and a respectable GPA and/or class rank. The General Educational Development (GED) test score results or a high school equivalency certificate from the state department of education may be submitted in lieu of the high school transcript for applicants receiving equivalency before January 1988.

North Carolina A&T State University welcomes applications from graduates of accredited community, technical, and junior colleges and from students who wish to transfer from other senior colleges.

Application and Information

The suggested application deadline for students who expect to live on campus is February 1; for commuting students, it is June 1. Applications are processed upon the receipt of the completed application form with the application fee of $35, official transcripts, and SAT or ACT scores. Out-of-state admission is limited; therefore, applications for admission should be filed by February 1.

To arrange an interview or a visit to the campus, students should contact:

Office of Admissions
B. C. Webb Hall
North Carolina Agricultural and Technical State University
Greensboro, North Carolina 27411
Telephone: 336-334-7946 or 7947
          800-443-8964 (toll-free in North Carolina)
World Wide Web: http://www.ncat.edu

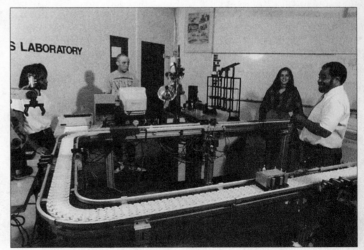

A professor and students in the chemical engineering lab.

POST UNIVERSITY
WATERBURY, CONNECTICUT

The University

Founded in 1890, Post University (formerly Teikyo Post University) is a small, business- and arts and science–focused, private, coeducational, residential institution. The University is accredited by the New England Association of Schools and Colleges. The diversity of the student body makes this University a particularly attractive choice for those seeking a good education and a place to grow and interact with a small yet unique group of people.

The University is dedicated to providing a cohesive global environment in which more than 1,200 students from the United States and sixteen countries learn to become knowledgeable participants in the global marketplace. While engaging in a close and caring university community, students learn to appreciate other attitudes and cultures through classes, course offerings, activities, and one-on-one relationships with faculty members and peers. Approximately half of Post University's students live on campus in one of the six residence halls. International students make up 17 percent of the student body.

The 58-acre campus is a safe, comfortable, and convenient location for learning. The Leever Student Center houses a dining facility, student service offices, and a student lounge. The Post student activities calendar is filled with a variety of options and opportunities. Local civic, religious, and professional organizations bring forums, seminars, lectures, exhibits, shows, and other events to the University. Clubs and activities abound, including Future Business Leaders of America, People Lending a Hand (community service), the Outdoors Club, the Hispanic Awareness Club, and the Campus Activities Team. Day trips are often scheduled to New York City and Boston.

Post students participate in a year-round schedule of intercollegiate and intramural athletic activities. The Post University Eagles are members of the National Collegiate Athletic Association (NCAA) Division II and the Central Atlantic Collegiate Conference (CACC). Men's intercollegiate sports teams include baseball, basketball, cross-country, golf, soccer, and tennis. Women's athletic teams include basketball, cross-country, soccer, softball, and volleyball. The University also sponsors an active, coeducational equestrian team. Intramural sports are diverse, ranging from softball and volleyball to basketball and flag football. Students enjoy the facilities of the Drubner Conference and Fitness Center, including a gymnasium, a swimming pool, tennis and racquetball courts, a fitness club, and weight training rooms. The Drubner Conference and Fitness Center also houses the campus bookstore.

Location

Located midway between New York City and Boston, Post University's 58-acre campus in the hills outside suburban Waterbury, Connecticut, offers a variety of opportunities for social, cultural, and recreational activities with its proximity to the Yale museums and theater and the Connecticut shoreline.

Majors and Degrees

Post offers four undergraduate degrees: the Bachelor of Arts, the Bachelor of Science, the Associate in Arts, and the Associate in Science.

The School of Business and Professional Studies offers the Bachelor of Science degree with majors in accounting, business administration, computer information systems, criminal justice, equine management, international business, legal studies, management, and marketing. The Associate in Science degree is offered with majors in accounting, equine studies, legal studies, management, and marketing. The School of Arts and Sciences offers the Bachelor of Science in biology, environmental science, general studies, and human services and the Bachelor of Arts with majors in English, environmental studies, history, psychology, and sociology; and the Associate in Science with majors in early childhood education, equine studies, and general studies. Advising in course selection for prelaw, premedical, predental, and preveterinary concentrations is also available.

Academic Programs

For the bachelor's degree, students must complete a minimum of 120 credit hours. To receive an associate degree from Post, students must complete a minimum of 60 credit hours.

All programs offer opportunities for internships and cooperative education. For students seeking additional academic challenges, the Post University Honors Program offers the opportunity to pursue independent research and special projects under the guidance of a faculty member.

The University has a two-semester calendar.

Off-Campus Programs

Post University offers students the opportunity to study abroad through a University-sponsored program and/or an approved study/internship-abroad program at another institution. The equine management program offers a study-abroad option in England. Through these programs, students have an opportunity to broaden their perspective and experience. Courses taken abroad are accepted for degree credit at Post University.

To qualify for study abroad, a student must have a cumulative grade point average of 2.5 or better at the time of attendance.

Academic Facilities

All classroom buildings are equipped with the facilities necessary for the applied arts and sciences, business, and liberal arts curricula. The Academic Computer Center houses microcomputers to serve all components of the academic curriculum. The center is open to all students who use the facility for course assignments, simulations, and special projects. The Harold Leever Learning Center provides learning systems structured to meet the needs of individual students. A media-equipped Programmed Auto Learning Systems Laboratory (PALS Lab) is an integral part of this program. The PALS Lab is a unique, self-paced, and widely diverse facility giving instructional support to the center's program by providing supplementary and review materials through the use of audiovisual software, media equipment, and innovative use of computer-assisted instruction. Post's Writing Center is staffed by 5 experienced writing coaches, who work with students at all levels of ability. The Traurig Library and Learning Resource Center has a capacity of more then 45,000 volumes and a growing media collection. As a government document depository, the library houses an extensive government publications collection. University-wide Internet access is available. Students majoring in the equine area use several nearby facilities.

Costs

For 2005–06, full-time resident students pay a comprehensive fee of $28,600, covering tuition, most fees, and room and board. For commuting students, this comprehensive fee is $20,200 per year. Equine and laboratory fees, the $40 application fee, and an estimated $500 per year for books and supplies are not included in this basic comprehensive fee.

Financial Aid

Post offers financial assistance through the Federal Work-Study, Federal Supplemental Educational Opportunity Grant, Federal Stafford Student Loan, and Federal Perkins Loan programs. Aid is awarded upon evidence of financial need, as determined by the Free Application for Federal Student Aid (FAFSA). In addition, the University has its own scholarship and grant-in-aid programs, both academic and athletic, and participates in all state programs that are applicable. In order to apply for financial assistance, a student must apply for admission and be accepted to Post and then submit the FAFSA. An institutional application for financial aid must also be submitted. A student may apply for the Federal Pell Grant by submitting the application directly to the federal government or by submitting the FAFSA.

Faculty

The Post faculty has 34 full-time and 46 part-time members, the majority of whom hold advanced degrees in their respective fields. Faculty members focus on instruction and are involved in all facets of student life. All full-time faculty members serve as academic advisers and maintain weekly office hours for student consultation. The student-faculty ratio is 15:1.

Student Government

Students actively participate in the operation of the University. The Student Government Association (SGA) is the official vehicle for student advocacy at Post University. SGA formulates major recommendations regarding student life on campus, oversees all student organizations, and provides funding for all active clubs. The Campus Activities Team (CAT) plays an active role in programming and calendar planning. Students are represented on many of the University's standing committees.

Admission Requirements

Post University seeks students who are likely to benefit from the University's diverse atmosphere and welcomes applications from individuals interested in pursuing academic studies. A decision with respect to a candidate's admission is made by the Admissions Committee and is based upon careful evaluation of the student's qualifications. A student who wishes to be considered for admission should provide Post with an official copy of the secondary school transcript, a written recommendation from a counselor or teacher, and SAT or ACT scores. If the candidate holds an equivalency diploma (GED), a copy must be submitted in lieu of a secondary school transcript. International students must submit a minimum TOEFL score of 500 in addition to the requirements listed above. Post offers English as a second language to those students who do not meet the minimum TOEFL score requirement. If possible, an interview with an admissions counselor is strongly recommended.

Students interested in transferring to Post must submit transcripts from all colleges previously attended. A CGPA of at least 2.0 (on a 4.0 scale) is required. Credit may be awarded for grades of C or better. Post University accepts a maximum of 90 credits toward the baccalaureate degree and a maximum of 30 credits toward an associate degree. A student may transfer up to 90 credits from accredited four-year colleges or universities; no more than 75 credits may be transferred from a two-year college.

Application and Information

Students should send an application for admission, accompanied by a nonrefundable application fee of $40. Post University accommodates candidates by processing applications on a rolling basis. It is advantageous to file an application as early as possible. This allows the Admissions Committee to give an application the attention it deserves and enables the applicant to prepare for college life. An application is reviewed when all the necessary credentials have been received. Applications are available online at the University's Web site.

Further information may be obtained by contacting:

Office of Admission
Post University
800 Country Club Road
P.O. Box 2540
Waterbury, Connecticut 06723-2540
Telephone: 203-596-4520
　　　　　　 800-345-2562 (toll-free)
Fax: 203-756-5810
E-mail: admissions@post.edu
World Wide Web: http://www.post.edu

The Post University campus is lovely year-round.

PRESCOTT COLLEGE
Resident Degree Program
PRESCOTT, ARIZONA

The College

Prescott College is a small, private, liberal arts college dedicated to environmental protection; social justice; service learning; experiential education; small, innovative classes; a large field-based curriculum; and the integration of the intellectual, emotional, spiritual, and social development of students. Prescott College, founded in 1966, is a small college trying to make a big difference in the world.

At Prescott College, a student's education is as individual as he or she is. The College believes that education should be personalized—a meaningful activity that goes beyond imparting facts. A Prescott College education instills values, critical-thinking skills, and the ability to adapt to the ever-changing internal landscape of ideas and knowledge as well as the ever-changing external landscape of the social and physical ecology of our times.

Prescott College offers bachelor's and master's degrees. A bachelor's degree can be earned via one of two routes: as a full-time resident student or as an adult student with limited residency. These routes are referred to, respectively, as the Resident Degree Program (RDP) and the Adult Degree Program (ADP). The 2002–03 resident degree enrollment was about 450 students. The information provided in this description pertains to the RDP. The Master of Arts degree is a limited-residency, independent, research-based degree program.

Location

Prescott is located in the mountains of central Arizona, surrounded by national forest at an elevation of more than 5,200 feet. The town is at the juncture of three ecosystems: interior chaparral, Ponderosa pines, and Pinon-Juniper. Desert or alpine ecosystems are within a short drive from Prescott.

With four mild seasons, more than a million acres of national forest, and almost 800 miles of trails, Prescott offers diverse outdoor activities, including rock climbing, hiking, mountain biking, horseback riding, and nearby canoeing, rafting, and snow skiing.

The Grand Canyon, the red rocks of Sedona, the old mining town of Jerome, and shopping and cultural events in Flagstaff, Phoenix, and Tucson are all within a few hours' drive. The Four Corners area, The Navajo Nation, Albuquerque, Las Vegas, San Diego, Mexico, Lake Powell, and Denver are all great destinations for weekend trips or extended visits during breaks.

Prescott is also the home of a lively and growing artistic community, with many art fairs and gallery openings. Many people are active in photography, music, weaving, and dance. The Mountain Artists Guild and the Prescott Fine Arts Association make a substantial cultural impact. The Phoenix Symphony, visiting ballet and opera companies, and numerous arts shows also provide regular programs.

Majors and Degrees

Prescott College offers the Bachelor of Arts (B.A.) degree in six general areas: adventure education, arts and letters, cultural and regional studies, education, environmental studies, and human development. Students create competence-based graduation plans in such topics as agroecology, conservation, counseling, ecological design, ecopsychology, education, environmental education, experiential education, field ecology, fine arts, holistic health, human ecology, literature, natural history, peace studies, philosophy, photography, psychology, religion, social and political studies, wilderness leadership, and writing.

Academic Programs

Prescott College is known for its innovative approach to higher education. It offers small classes (a student-faculty ratio of 10:1 in classrooms), extensive field work (a student-faculty ratio of 5:1 in the field), a close community atmosphere, and the opportunity for students to design their own educational paths. The philosophy of experiential education emphasizes the concept that learning is a lifelong process that helps students gain competence, creativity, and self-direction. In cooperation with an outstanding faculty, students are able to work in such special interdisciplinary fields as cultural and regional studies, ecopsychology, education and interpretation, human ecology, outdoor adventure education, social and political studies, and wilderness leadership.

Academic Facilities

Prescott College does not have a sprawling campus with ivy-covered towers. The campus, located near downtown Prescott, is an eclectic mix of buildings that once served other purposes. "Recycling" buildings is one tangible way in which the College demonstrates sustainability and minimizes its footprint upon the environment.

Prescott College's recently completed building, the Crossroad Center, incorporates various recycled or environmentally friendly elements in its design and construction. For example, the bathrooms feature original murals designed by Prescott students. The granite used in the murals was excess material donated to the project by a local enterprise that manufacturers and installs countertops.

Many classes at the College are held in the field. Prescott uses the Southwest for ecological field studies, wilderness pursuits, social observations, artistic endeavors, and therapeutic facilitation. The fragile southwestern desert can convey to students the vulnerability of the Equatorial rain forest and the destructibility of the Siberian tundra. The proximity to the Mexican border provides access to the crucial interactions between developing world politics, economics, and social and environmental issues. Thus, the Southwest provides a unique microcosm of the rapidly changing globe.

The Prescott College Information Commons (library) has a collection of more than 28,000 volumes, 125 microforms, 1,200 audio and videocassettes, and 408 periodical titles, all of which relate specifically to the College's program offerings. The Information Commons is computer-networked with all the regional libraries in the area, including two other college libraries and the public libraries. If students have difficulty locating information from any of these sources, the College librarian borrows books through the interlibrary loan system. Because the College places great emphasis on student services, faculty and staff members work diligently to assist each student in finding all information necessary for his or her pursuit of knowledge.

There are three fully equipped computer labs on campus. All labs are staffed full-time by a competent team of computer professionals and College work-study students. Laser printers are available, and students have access to the Internet for research and e-mail. The largest lab houses IBM-compatible computers. The Geographic Information Science Lab has its own computer lab for conducting research in land-use planning and management. The College also offers a Mac lab for fine arts students who are interested in graphic manipulation and digital imaging.

In addition, the College has a campus in Tucson and three off-campus research stations—Kino Bay, Walnut Creek Station, and Wolfberry Farm. The Tucson campus of Prescott College serves students who are enrolled either in the Adult Degree Program, through which working adults earn a bachelor's degree, or the Master of Arts degree program.

The Kino Bay Center for Cultural and Ecological Studies is Prescott's field station on the Sonoran shores of the Gulf of California, one of the most remote and unexplored seas remaining in the world today. The Kino Bay Center provides educational opportunities for hands-on field study in the areas of marine studies, environmental sciences, resource conservation and management, cultural studies, Latin America studies, adventure education, writing, and Spanish language studies.

Wolfberry Farm is Prescott College's experimental farm dedicated to education, demonstration, and research in agroecology. The 30-acre farm is located 15 miles north of Prescott in Chino Valley, a town with a rich agricultural history. Students address the question: Can agriculture be more ecologically sustainable and economically viable? They experiment with water-saving irrigation technologies, regional and adapted crops, specialty crops, and fertility-generating rotations.

The Walnut Creek Station for Educational Research is run through a collaborative partnership between Prescott College, Yavapai College, Sharlot Hall Museum, Northern Arizona University, and the Prescott National Forest. During the high season, two or three classes per week use the station for courses, including Ecopsychology, Interpreting Nature Through Art and Photography, Geographical Information Systems, Drawing and Painting the Southwestern Landscape, Aboriginal Living Skills, Wildlife Management, Riparian Restoration, and many independent studies.

In addition, the station hosts research projects, such as the Hantavirus Longitudinal Study, which was funded by the Centers for Disease Control; the Arenavirus Distribution Study, funded by the National Institutes of Health; an Arizona Department of Water Resources inventory and monitoring study grant; and the Rattlesnake Radio Telemetry Project.

Costs

Tuition for 2004–05 was $16,320; tuition increases may occur in July of each year.

Financial Aid

The types of financial aid available are Federal Pell Grants, Prescott College grants, Arizona State Student Incentive Grants, Federal Supplemental Educational Opportunity Grants, student employment, Federal Stafford Student Loans, the Arizona Voucher Program, campus employment, and scholarships. More than 67 percent of the students at Prescott College receive financial aid.

Prescott College uses the Free Application for Federal Student Aid (FAFSA) to determine a student's financial need. Students wishing to apply for aid for the fall term should complete the financial aid form by April 15 for priority funding. Aid is awarded on a first-come, first-served basis until all available funds are used. FAFSA forms take four to six weeks to process, so students should submit them early, even if their plans are indefinite. Students who complete forms online may experience a quicker response than those who complete paper applications.

Faculty

Faculty members at Prescott College are devoted solely to the instruction of students. They are not burdened by the traditional "publish or perish" mandate faced by most educators; instead, they direct their energy toward being innovative instructors, positive role models, mentors, advisers, and friends. The College recognizes the importance of individualized attention and small classes. Faculty members are committed to the educational mission of Prescott College and thoroughly enjoy teaching, participating in College social activities, and working with individual students to help them comprehend challenging material. Approximately 60 percent of the 45 full-time RDP faculty members hold doctorates or terminal degrees.

Student Government

Students participate in all levels of governance at Prescott College. Currently, one student is a full voting member of the Board of Trustees. Students are also represented on hiring committees. The Student Union is composed of all full-time students, each of whom has a vote.

Admission Requirements

In evaluating an applicant, the Admissions Committee seeks evidence of preparation for college-level academic work, a strong sense of community, and a desire to become a self-directed learner. The Admissions Committee looks for the ability to plan and make decisions and commitments and carry them out effectively. The applicant's essays, letters of recommendation, and transcripts are the strongest determining factors in the admission decision. Visits to the College and personal interviews are strongly recommended, and, in some cases, they are required. Students who consider applying to Prescott College should first attempt to gain a thorough understanding of the College's educational philosophy and practices.

Prescott College has created a special learning environment that requires motivation, maturity, and a desire to be actively involved in learning.

Application and Information

The Admissions Office strongly encourages applicants to submit all required application materials by the priority filing date. Complete files are then reviewed by the Admissions Committee, and admissions decisions are communicated by the notification date. Files that are received or completed after the priority filing date will still be considered on a rolling basis.

Once students are offered admission to an incoming class, they must submit a tuition deposit prior to the reply date to give evidence of intention to enroll and to reserve a space in that class. Tuition deposits are nonrefundable; applicants are advised to submit them only after determining that they are ready to commit to Prescott College. Tuition deposits received after the reply date are accepted on a first-come, first-served basis until the class has filled. Students whose deposits are received after the class is filled are placed on a wait list.

Applications for fall should be received by March 1; for spring, the priority filing date is November 1. The reply dates (deposit due dates) for fall and spring are, respectively, May 1 and December 1. Applications that are received or completed after the priority filing date are still considered. These applications are reviewed after those that were received and completed by the priority filing date.

For more information, students should contact:

Resident Degree Program–Admissions
Prescott College
220 Grove Avenue
Prescott, Arizona 86301
Telephone: 928-776-5180
          800-628-6364 (toll-free)
E-mail: admissions@prescott.edu
World Wide Web: http://www.prescott.edu

Prescott College students experience active education in a Southwestern classroom.

QUINNIPIAC UNIVERSITY
HAMDEN, CONNECTICUT

The University

Quinnipiac offers four-year and graduate-level degree programs leading to careers in health sciences, business, communications, natural sciences, education, liberal arts, and law. A curriculum that combines a career focus with a globally oriented liberal arts background prepares graduates for the future, whether they start their careers right after commencement or opt to pursue advanced study.

Quinnipiac is coeducational and nonsectarian and currently enrolls 5,091 full-time undergraduates, 1,150 full-time graduates, and 979 part-time students in its undergraduate, graduate, professional, and continuing education programs. Less than 35 percent of the students are residents of Connecticut; the rest represent all regions of the United States and many other countries. The emphasis at Quinnipiac is on community. Students, faculty members, and staff members interact both in and out of the classroom and office. Quinnipiac is big enough to sustain a wide variety of people and programs but small enough to keep students from getting lost in the shuffle. Life on campus emphasizes students' personal, as well as academic, growth. The approximately sixty-five student organizations and extracurricular activities, including intramural and intercollegiate (NCAA Division I) athletics, give students a chance to exercise their talents, their muscles, and their leadership skills. The University has a student newspaper and an FM radio station (WQAQ) and intercollegiate teams in men's baseball, basketball, cross-country, golf, ice hockey, lacrosse, soccer, tennis, and track and in women's basketball, cross-country, field hockey, ice hockey, lacrosse, soccer, softball, tennis, track, and volleyball.

Quinnipiac's 500-acre main campus has fifty buildings. In addition to the academic facilities described in the section on the next page, the University has twenty-five residence halls of different styles, all with functional furnishings and decor. The residence halls house 3,500 men and women, about 70 percent of the undergraduate population. All students have in-room access to e-mail and the campus network. Housing on campus is guaranteed for three years. The Carl Hansen Student Center—containing recreational facilities, meeting rooms, and offices for student organizations—is adjacent to Alumni Hall, a large multipurpose auditorium used for theater productions, concerts, lectures, films, and various University and community events.

Facilities for athletic and fitness activities are found in and around the gymnasium and physical education building. The gymnasium seats 1,500 and includes two regulation-size basketball courts. Also available are a steam room, a sauna, and a 24,000-square-foot recreation/fitness center with a large free-weight room; an exercise machine center; aerobics studios; basketball, volleyball, and tennis courts; and a suspended indoor track. There are also lighted tennis courts, playing fields, and miles of scenic routes for running and biking.

Quinnipiac offers a full range of services to assist students in achieving personal and career goals. Individual career counseling is supplemented by a computerized guidance system that lets students enter information about their interests and skills and receive a printout with current data on professions, jobs, and graduate schools. Quinnipiac also has an active career and internship placement office that serves as a liaison between the corporate community and students, new graduates, and alumni.

Graduate programs lead to the Master of Science degree in advanced accounting, advanced practice or orthopedic physical therapy, computer information systems, interactive communications, journalism, and molecular and cell biology; the Master of Health Science in medical lab sciences, pathologist assistant studies, and physician assistant studies; the Master of Science in Nursing in nurse practitioner studies; the Master of Business Administration; and the Master of Arts in Teaching. A $22-million, on-campus facility houses the Quinnipiac University School of Law and its library. The School offers full-time and part-time programs leading to a J.D. degree or J.D./M.B.A. degree in combination with the School of Business.

Location

Situated at the foot of Sleeping Giant Mountain in the New Haven suburb of Hamden, Quinnipiac provides the best of the country and the city. The University is only 10 minutes from New Haven, 30 minutes from Hartford (the state capital), and less than 2 hours from New York City and Boston. The University shuttle bus provides easy access to area shopping and attractions. Bordering the campus is Sleeping Giant State Park, which also provides a range of recreational activities. In addition to adjacent towns such as Cheshire, Wallingford, and North Haven, a short trip by car or bus puts students in New Haven, where they can visit the acclaimed Yale Center for British Art, attend a performance at the Schubert or Long Wharf Theater, marvel at the dinosaurs in the Peabody Museum of Natural History, or dine in fine restaurants. Quinnipiac's New England location also makes it convenient to enjoy a day in the surf or on the slopes. The beaches on Long Island Sound are easy to reach, and major ski resorts are only an hour's drive from campus.

Majors and Degrees

The School of Health Sciences grants bachelor's degrees in athletic training/sports medicine, biochemistry, biology (with premedical options in chiropractic, dentistry, medicine, podiatry, and veterinary medicine), biomedical science, chemistry, diagnostic imaging, microbiology/molecular biology, nursing, occupational therapy (5½-year entry-level master's), physical therapy (6½-year entry-level doctorate), physician assistant studies (6-year freshman entry-level master's), respiratory care, and veterinary technology.

In the School of Business, bachelor's degree programs are offered in accounting, advertising, computer information systems, entrepreneurship, finance, international business, management, and marketing. The School also offers a five-year combined-degree program in which students may be awarded the B.S. degree in business and a graduate degree in accounting, business administration, or computer information systems (M.S. or M.B.A.).

The College of Liberal Arts offers bachelor's degree programs in computer science, criminal justice, English, gerontology, history, interactive digital design, legal studies (paralegal), liberal studies, mathematics, political science, psychology, social services, sociology, and Spanish. Students can also design their own majors. Certification for teaching elementary, intermediate, and secondary education is offered through a five-year program, resulting in a Master of Arts in Teaching. A bachelor's degree program in psychobiology is interdisciplinary in nature. Students can also continue their study in graduate programs in business, law, journalism, or e-media.

The School of Communications offers undergraduate majors in journalism, media studies, production, and public relations and graduate programs in journalism and e-media for writing and design in the journalistic community.

Academic Programs

All degree programs at Quinnipiac University are offered through one of the five academic schools. The academic year consists of two 15-week fall and spring semesters and two summer sessions. All baccalaureate candidates are required to complete the Core Curriculum, which consists of up to 50 of the 120 semester hours of credit generally needed for graduation at the bachelor's degree level. The Core Curriculum promotes the achievement of college-level competence in English, mathematics, and such specialized areas as foreign language or computer science. It requires study in the artistic tradition, behavioral and social sciences, humanities, and physical and biological sciences.

Advanced placement, credit, or both are given for appropriate scores on Advanced Placement tests and CLEP general and subject examinations as well as for International Baccalaureate higher-level subjects.

Off-Campus Programs

Students in any of the four undergraduate schools can get hands-on experience in their field through off-campus internships. The University is affiliated with outstanding health and scientific institutions—such as Children's Hospital (Boston), Yale–New Haven Hospital, Hartford Hospital, Gaylord Rehabilitation Hospital (Wallingford), and the University of Connecticut Health Center—throughout the state and the nation. Opportunities for internships also exist in industry, large and small businesses, media outlets, and social and governmental agencies. Academic credit is available for internships and affiliations, which are often part of degree requirements.

Academic Facilities

Academic life focuses on the Bernhard Library, which opened in the fall of 2000. This attractive facility provides users with 600 seats, arranged as individual carrels and small rooms for group study and is open until 3 a.m. weekdays during the academic year. More than 150 personal computer workstations, 600 data ports, and a new wireless network are located throughout the library and provide access to automated library systems and extensive Web-based resources. In addition, students use the workstations in the library's Cyber Café for online research and classroom assignments. The library houses an extensive collection of books, periodicals, government documents, films, tapes, and microforms. Members of the Quinnipiac University community may also draw on resources from local and statewide institutions through interlibrary loans and shared electronic resources.

Quinnipiac University is one of the most-wired campuses in the country and this is reflected in its academic facilities and programs. All incoming students must purchase a University-recommended laptop computer for use in the classroom. Students also use their computers for e-mail and course registration; to access online library resources, the Internet, course-related materials, and assignments; and to view their grades.

More specialized student-computing facilities are located in classrooms throughout the campus. Tator Hall has five computer classrooms and four teaching laboratories containing approximately 200 computers. The multimedia and video laboratories in the Ed McMahon Mass Communications Center each have fourteen Apple MacIntosh G5 and G4 workstations. The computer cluster in the Financial Technology Center at Quinnipiac University's School of Business is a high-tech, simulated trading floor providing students with the opportunity to access real-time financial data, conduct interactive trading simulations, and develop financial models in preparation for careers in finance. Other teaching space is also well equipped with technology for teaching. All classrooms have connections to the campus network and Internet, eighty-six have data projectors or large-screen computer monitors, and more than twenty-two have wireless connectivity for student laptops.

The Academic Center houses classrooms, laboratories, and an auditorium lecture hall. The Echlin Health Sciences Center houses physical and occupational therapy, nursing, and related fields of study. Buckman Center is where many of the science labs are located, including those for chemistry, respiratory care, and veterinary technology. A clinical skills lab, for use by nursing students and the physician assistant program, simulates a critical care hospital center. Also in the Center is the Buckman Theatre, which holds plays, concerts, and lectures. The Lender School of Business has local area network classrooms, satellite capabilities, and the Ed McMahon Mass Communications Center, containing a state-of-the-art, fully digital, high-definition TV production studio, print journalism and desktop publishing laboratories, and a news technology center.

Costs

The basic 2004–05 cost was $32,400, of which tuition and fees were $22,500 and room and board were, on average, $9900. Other expenses, typically $1200 per year, include books, laboratory and course fees associated with specific courses, and travel costs.

Financial Aid

Quinnipiac designs financial aid packages to include grants and scholarships that do not have to be repaid, self-help financial aid programs such as federal and University-based work study, and loans. Quinnipiac uses the Free Application for Federal Student Aid (FAFSA) to determine need. Transfer students are eligible for the same need-based financial aid consideration as first-time freshmen. Quinnipiac also offers a number of renewable scholarships to new, full-time freshmen that are awarded partly or entirely on the basis of academic merit.

Faculty

The faculty is characterized by its teaching competence and outstanding academic qualifications. Of the 286 full-time faculty members, 70 percent have earned a Ph.D. or the appropriate terminal degree in their field. The faculty also includes a number of part-time teachers who are practicing professionals and experts in their fields. Classes are taught by these scholars and professionals and not by student instructors, and a low student-faculty ratio promotes close associations among faculty and students.

Student Government

The Student Government is the student legislative body of Quinnipiac. It represents student opinion, promotes student welfare, supervises student organizations, appropriates funds for student groups, and provides voting student representation on the Judicial Board, the College Senate, and the Board of Trustees.

Admission Requirements

Quinnipiac seeks students from a broad range of backgrounds. Candidates are evaluated on the basis of a completed application, as described below. Interviews are not always required, but visits to campus are strongly encouraged. Transfer students are welcome. Quinnipiac sponsors four open house programs during the year and several Saturday morning information sessions followed by a campus tour.

Application and Information

Quinnipiac has a rolling admission policy for its undergraduate programs but recommends that freshman applicants submit their application materials well before the deadline of February 1 and that students applying to the physical and occupational therapy and physician assistant studies programs submit their applications by December 31. Applications can be filed at any time beginning in the senior year of high school. Selection decisions are made as soon as applications are completed. For most programs, a completed application consists of a Quinnipiac application form; a transcript of completed high school courses, including grades for the first quarter of the senior year; a score report for either the SAT I or ACT; a personal statement (essay); and the application fee: $45 for paper or $30 online at the University Web site. Students placed on a waiting list are notified of any openings by June 1. Transfer students are expected to forward a transcript of college course work undertaken. Quinnipiac subscribes to the May 1 Candidates Reply Date Agreement. For information regarding full-time undergraduate study, students should contact:

Office of Undergraduate Admissions
Quinnipiac University
Hamden, Connecticut 06518-1940
Telephone: 203-582-8600
           800-462-1944 (toll-free)
Fax: 203-582-8906
E-mail: admissions@quinnipiac.edu
World Wide Web: http://www.quinnipiac.edu

For information regarding transfer and part-time study:

Office of Transfer and Part-time Admissions
Quinnipiac University
Hamden, Connecticut 06518-1940
Telephone: 203-582-8612
World Wide Web: http://www.quinnipiac.edu

SHEPHERD UNIVERSITY

SHEPHERDSTOWN, WEST VIRGINIA

The University

Shepherd University, founded in 1871, is a very competitive, four-year, state-supported institution offering more than seventy undergraduate fields of study in the liberal arts and sciences, business, and teacher education. Graduate programs are offered in ten fields. Shepherd is the fastest-growing institution in West Virginia. There are 4,800 students on the 323-acre campus; 60 percent come from West Virginia, and the remaining 40 percent represent forty-eight other states and twenty-four countries.

The University prides itself on its friendly and helpful atmosphere and the individual contact the students receive as a result of small classes. On campus there are fifty organizations, ranging from national fraternities and sororities to community service groups, from professional organizations to student government. Students are encouraged to join and interact with all of the groups that interest them.

Shepherd University also offers both men's and women's intercollegiate sports. The men's program consists of baseball, basketball, football, golf, soccer, and tennis. The women's sports program consists of basketball, cheerleading, soccer, softball, tennis, and volleyball. Men and women compete in the NCAA Division II program. An NCLC club lacrosse program is available for both men and women. For students not interested in playing intercollegiate sports, an extensive intramural and recreation program is also available.

Students are housed on campus in twelve residence halls. Seven offer suite arrangements with 4 students sharing two bedrooms, a living room, and bath. Five buildings house students in traditional 2-student dorm rooms. All buildings are coeducational. An apartment complex is being built for upperclass and graduate students.

Location

Shepherd University is located in historic Shepherdstown (founded in 1730), a small community on the banks of the Potomac River with a population of approximately 7,000. Shepherdstown is the oldest town in West Virginia and the site of the launching of the first successful steamboat in 1787 by James Rumsey. Shepherdstown hosted the Syrian-Israeli Peace Talks in January 2000. Other historic landmarks, located within 8 miles of campus, include the Antietam National Battlefield Park, Harpers Ferry National Historical Park, and the Chesapeake and Ohio Canal Historical Park and Trail. The area is rural, and fishing, horseback riding, hunting, snow skiing, and waterskiing are available for recreation. Communication and cooperation between the community and the University are very good, and many cultural events are sponsored jointly.

The University is a 10-minute drive from Martinsburg, West Virginia; 15 minutes from Charles Town and Harpers Ferry, West Virginia; 25 minutes from Hagerstown and Frederick, Maryland; and 70 minutes from Washington, D.C., and Baltimore, Maryland.

Majors and Degrees

Shepherd University offers the Bachelor of Arts, Bachelor of Fine Arts, and Bachelor of Science degrees in accounting, aquatic science, art and art education (graphic design, painting, photography, printmaking, and sculpture), athletic training, biochemistry, biology, broadcasting, business administration, business education, chemistry, Civil War and nineteenth-century American history, communications, computer science, computer programming and information systems, criminal justice, early child-

hood education, economics, elementary education, English, environmental chemistry, environmental engineering, environmental studies, exercise science/fitness, family and consumer sciences, finance, general science, health education, historic preservation, history, literature, management, marketing, mathematics, music and music education (musical theater, performance, piano pedagogy, and theory/composition), networking and data communication, physical education, physics, political science, psychology, recreation and leisure services (commercial and hospitality, sport communications, sport and event management, and therapeutic recreation), sociology, and theater; the Bachelor of Science in Nursing degree in nursing; and the Bachelor of Social Work degree in social work.

Shepherd University offers the Associate of Arts, Associate of Applied Science, and Associate of Science degrees in business, criminal justice, culinary arts, emergency medical services, engineering (2-2 program), fashion merchandising, fire service and safety technology, general studies, graphic design, information technology, nursing, office technology, photography, and studio art.

Preprofessional programs are available in the fields of dentistry, law, medicine, pharmacy, theology, and veterinary science.

An early acceptance to the medical school program with the West Virginia University School of Health Sciences is available to premedical students.

Academic Programs

All candidates for the baccalaureate degree must complete a minimum of 128 semester hours of course work with a minimum 2.0 overall average and a minimum 2.0 average in their major. Students in teacher education must have a minimum 2.5 average in their elementary education or secondary education field. The 128 semester hours include a general studies core, consisting of 19 hours in the humanities, 11 hours in science and mathematics, 15 hours in social sciences, and 2 hours in physical education. To earn the associate degree, students must complete 64 to 73 semester hours, depending on the program of study.

Student internships and practicums are required or recommended in the following areas of study: education, fashion merchandising, graphic design, mass communications, nursing, photography, psychology, recreation and leisure services, and social work. Biology and chemistry majors may utilize such nearby research facilities as the U.S. Fish and Wildlife Service National Education Training Center, the National Cancer Research Center at Fort Dietrick, the National Fisheries Center at Leetown, and the Appalachian Fruit Research Center at Bardane for their directed research projects. CIS majors may do their internships with the IRS National Computer Center, ATF Firearms Identification Center, or the Coast Guard Vessel Identification Center located in Martinsburg. The Washington Gateway and Washington Semester programs provide formal internships in Washington, D.C. Co-op programs may be arranged in most major fields.

Academic Facilities

Academic facilities on the Shepherd University campus include an open-stack library with a collection of 500,000 materials; six academic buildings housing classrooms and laboratories; a Creative Arts Center housing the departments of art, music, and theater; and a comprehensive health, physical education, and athletic complex. The nearby libraries, museums, and cultural and research centers of the Washington, D.C., metropolitan area are also available for research and study.

Costs

For 2004–05, tuition and fees were $3654 per year for West Virginia residents and $9234 per year for out-of-state students. Average room and board charges were $5574 per year. Books and supplies were about $1000 a year. Additional expenses vary, depending on a student's personal tastes, but were estimated to be between $40 and $80 per week.

Financial Aid

The University offers financial aid through the Federal Pell Grant, Federal Supplemental Educational Opportunity Grant, Federal Perkins Loan, Federal Stafford Student Loan, and Federal Work-Study programs. Federally insured student loans (arranged in cooperation with the student's local bank) are also available. The University offers academic, athletic, and talent scholarships based on merit.

Faculty

Of the University's 120 full-time faculty members, 85 percent have earned doctorates or terminal degrees; all other faculty members have completed advanced work beyond the master's level, and many are doctoral candidates. All teaching is done by faculty members. The student-faculty ratio is 19:1. Faculty members serve as advisers to students in their respective disciplines, and they work with and participate in extracurricular organizations and activities on campus.

Student Government

The Shepherd University Student Government Association (SGA) consists of a policy-making body, the Executive Council, composed of the student body president and the cabinet, and an advisory and regulatory body, the Senate, composed of student representatives. Also affiliated with the SGA are 3 students who are elected to serve on the Student Affairs Committee, the central decision-making body on the campus concerned with student-life policies. The SGA sanctions student organizations and activities and controls the student activity fees and their disbursement among the various units of the University. Student representatives are members of all policymaking and program committees on campus.

Admission Requirements

Applicants must be graduates of accredited high schools and have at least 21 academic units of high school credit. Shepherd University requires that the 21 units be in the following areas: English, 4 units (years); mathematics, 3 units (algebra I and II and geometry); science, 3 units (biology, chemistry, and physics); social studies, 3 units (including American history); foreign language, 2 units; physical education, 2 units; and electives, at least 4 units (in such areas as music, art, drama, and computer science). Art applicants must submit a portfolio, and music majors must audition for admission to the program. Teacher education majors must take and pass the PPST examination before enrollment in any Education Department courses.

Applicants wishing full consideration for admission should have at least a 2.0 academic grade point average in high school and a minimum combined SAT score of 910 or a minimum composite ACT score of 19. Students are encouraged to take honors or

Advanced Placement Program courses in high school. College credit is given for most Advanced Placement test scores of 4 and 5 and in some cases for scores of 3. Written recommendations from high school guidance counselors are highly recommended for all freshman applicants. Admission interviews are not required, but campus visits are strongly advised.

Transfer students should have a minimum cumulative grade point average of 2.0 at their previous institution. Shepherd University does not admit transfer students who are on academic probation or suspension at any other institution.

Application and Information

Applications are accepted on a rolling basis; however, there are some academic programs with additional deadlines. A separate departmental application must be filed along with the University application for entrance to the engineering and nursing programs (for fall term only). Early decision applicants are notified of their admission status after November 15 of their senior year in high school. Students applying for regular admission are notified of their admission status on a rolling basis. Students are strongly encouraged to call the admissions office to schedule an admissions interview and a tour of campus.

For information about admission and programs, prospective students should contact:

Office of Admissions
Shepherd University
P.O. Box 3210
Shepherdstown, West Virginia 25443-3210
Telephone: 304-876-5212
            800-344-5231 (toll-free)
Fax: 304-876-5165
E-mail: admoff@shepherd.edu
World Wide Web: http://www.shepherd.edu

McMurran Hall, built in 1859, houses the Office of Admissions.

UNIVERSITY OF WEST FLORIDA

PENSACOLA, FLORIDA

The University

One of the eleven state universities of Florida, the University of West Florida (UWF) enrolls approximately 9,500 students in its Colleges of Arts and Sciences, Business, and Professional Studies. The University of West Florida, which opened in fall 1967, is located on a 1,600-acre nature preserve 10 miles north of downtown Pensacola. The University's facilities, valued at more than $81 million, have been designed to complement the natural beauty of the site.

The University currently enrolls students from forty-seven states and sixty countries. Students and professors enjoy a relationship that is more common at a small, private college. Approximately 940 freshmen began their studies at UWF last year. The middle 50 percent statistics for the class are as follows: high school grade point average ranged from 3.1 to 3.9; SAT I total score ranged from 1020 to 1210; and ACT composite ranged from 21 to 26.

In addition to its undergraduate programs, UWF also offers the master's degree in twenty-nine areas of study and specialist and Ed.D. degrees in education.

UWF operates centers in downtown Pensacola and at Eglin Air Force Base, a branch campus in Fort Walton Beach (in conjunction with a local community college), and a Navy program office at Naval Air Station Pensacola. In addition, UWF owns 152 acres of beachfront property on nearby Santa Rosa Island, adjacent to the Gulf Islands National Seashore. Available for both recreation and research, this property provides special opportunities for students pursuing degrees in marine biology, maritime studies, and coastal zone studies.

The University of West Florida is a member of the NCAA Division II. Men's sports include baseball, basketball, cross-country, golf, soccer, and tennis. Women's sports include basketball, cross-country, golf, soccer, softball, tennis, and volleyball. Students also participate in more than nineteen intramural sports and twenty club sports. The Program Council and the Residence Hall Advisory Council provide activities and events open to the entire campus community. UWF hosts six national sororities and five national fraternities; 110 professional, academic, and religious organizations are open to UWF students.

A natatorium housing an Olympic-size pool adjoins the Field House, center for indoor sports and large-group activities and events. Varsity soccer fields, tennis courts, handball and racquetball courts, jogging trails, picnic areas, and sites for canoeing are available on campus. Varsity baseball and softball fields and a lighted track complete the UWF sports complex. Sailing and waterskiing facilities are nearby, and campus nature trails attract thousands of visitors annually.

Students may choose to live on or off campus. The Office of Housing oversees 1,450 total residence hall spaces that include low-rise residence halls, two- or four-bedroom residence hall apartments that are equipped with modern conveniences, and three new residence halls, one with 300 spaces and the other two with 200 spaces.

There are also various apartment complexes conveniently located just beyond the campus.

Location

Students and visitors alike delight in the beauty of the campus, which is nestled in the rolling hills outside Pensacola, Florida.

Wide verandas, massive moss-draped oaks, and spacious lawns capture the traditional charm and grace of the South, while modern architecture and state-of-the-art facilities blend in naturally among loblolly pines and meandering walkways.

Only minutes from the campus gate are the emerald waters and white beaches of the Gulf of Mexico and the Gulf Islands National Seashore, one of the nation's most beautiful beaches. The Pensacola area attracts vacationers from all around the country to its historic Seville Square, golf tournaments, sailing regattas, restaurants on the bay, and a variety of art and music festivals. WUWF, the University's public radio station, produces a monthly live program, Gulf Coast RadioLive. UWF is 3½ hours from New Orleans, 1 hour from Mobile, 3 hours from Tallahassee, and 5 hours from Atlanta.

Majors and Degrees

The University of West Florida awards the bachelor's degree in forty-four undergraduate programs with many areas of specialization. Undergraduate majors are available in the College of Arts and Sciences in anthropology, art, biology, chemistry, communication arts, computer information systems, computer science, English, environmental studies, fine arts, history, interdisciplinary humanities studies, interdisciplinary information technology, interdisciplinary science, international studies, leisure studies, marine biology, mathematics, medical technology, music, nursing, philosophy, physics, pre-engineering, preprofessional studies, psychology, social sciences (interdisciplinary), studio art, and theater as well as joint computer engineering, electrical engineering, and seven-year predental B.S./D.M.D. programs with the University of Florida.

Undergraduate majors in the College of Business include accounting, economics, finance, management, management information systems, and marketing. The College of Business is accredited by AACSB International–The Association to Advance Collegiate Schools of Business.

The College of Professional Studies, which includes education programs that are accredited by the National Council for Accreditation of Teacher Education (NCATE), offers professional training and majors leading to bachelor's degrees in the following areas: criminal justice; elementary education; engineering technology; health education; health, leisure, and science; legal administration; middle school education; political science; prekindergarten/primary education; prelaw; social work; special education (emotionally handicapped, learning-disabled, mentally handicapped); sports science; and vocational education. There are specialist programs in educational leadership and in curriculum and instruction and a doctoral program in curriculum and instruction.

Academic Programs

A general curriculum is required for entering freshmen and for transfer students without an Associate in Arts degree from a Florida public community college. General studies provide students with a broad foundation in the liberal arts, science, and career and life planning. The academic skills of reading, writing, discourse, critical inquiry, logical thinking, and mathematical reasoning are central elements of the general studies curriculum.

Students of high ability may enter an honors program offering intensive instruction in a more individualized setting. Cooperative education programs are available in nearly every field, allowing UWF students to get a head start on their careers while paying for their education. Army and Air Force ROTC programs and scholarships are also available.

Off-Campus Programs

The Office of International Education and Programs arranges more than twenty study-abroad and student exchange programs on every continent except Antarctica. Participants may study in Austria, Canada, England, Finland, France, Germany, Japan, Mexico, the Netherlands, and Portugal.

Academic Facilities

The main campus consists of more than 100 buildings. One of the most prominent of these is the five-floor John C. Pace Library, which houses a collection of more than 2.3 million bound volumes and micropieces. Interconnected through computer linkages with state and national libraries for research purposes, the UWF library contains one of the finest special collections about the Gulf Coast area. Some of the items in this collection date back to the fourteenth century, and there are also a manuscript letter signed by Thomas Jefferson, books autographed by Albert Einstein, and materials carried aboard the space shuttle by UWF alumni.

Excellent science and technology laboratories for preprofessional majors, extensive video and film equipment, desktop publishing labs, an AP wire service, and an impressive computer science facility also support students' scholarly endeavors. Microcomputers, minicomputers, a diverse inventory of software, a real-time laboratory, modem linkages to residence halls, and 24-hour-a-day access to the computer center all are available to students in every field of study. Other major facilities include a Center for Fine and Performing Arts, a College of Professional Studies Complex, a Student Services Complex, and a Commons.

Expansion and renovation continue to enhance the main campus. The Commons feature a bookstore, post office, and snack bar. An archaeology building and museum opened in 1999. An expansion and renovation of the student sports and recreation facility is in process.

Costs

For fall 2004, tuition was $95.19 per credit for Florida residents and $462.79 per credit for out-of-state students. Room and board cost total $6000. The cost of books was estimated at $800. Transportation and personal expenses vary according to students' individual needs.

Financial Aid

About 60 percent of UWF students receive some form of financial aid and scholarships. UWF is committed to meeting a student's financial need. Aid is awarded on a first-come, first-served basis.

The Scholarship Program for outstanding freshmen allows students to receive early scholarship commitments as soon as they have decided to enroll in UWF. The John C. Pace Jr. scholarships are awarded to meritorious freshmen and transfers with A.A. degrees from Florida's community colleges. Awards are $1000 per year. Special scholarships for National Achievement Scholars and students with talent in the arts are awarded. Non-Florida tuition grants are awarded to outstanding freshmen and transfer students. These awards reduce the amount of out-of-state fees.

Faculty

Faculty members at the University of West Florida include published authors, scientists engaged in a wide range of research projects, and journalists skilled in advertising and filmmaking. Eighty percent of the faculty members hold doctoral degrees from major institutions throughout the United States.

Student Government

The Student Government Association is authorized to represent the student body in all matters concerning student life. The basic purposes of the student government are to provide students with an opportunity to participate in the decision-making process of the University; to review, evaluate, and allocate all student activity and service fee monies as allowed by state law (annually, some $1 million is allocated by students); to consider and make recommendations on all phases of student life; and to serve as the principal forum for discussion of matters of broad concern to the students.

Admission Requirements

The University of West Florida admits freshman applicants based on high school GPA, completion of college-preparatory courses, and test scores (either the ACT or the SAT I is accepted). Special consideration is given to applicants with special talents. College-preparatory courses should include 4 years of English; 3 each of math, social science, and natural science; 2 of the same foreign language; and 4 academic electives.

Transfer applicants with fewer than 60 hours are required to submit SAT I or ACT test scores and official transcripts from both the college(s) and the high school attended. Students transferring with 60 hours or more must submit their college transcript(s) only.

Application and Information

Students are encouraged to apply early in order to allow time for receipt of transcripts and to receive full consideration for financial aid, scholarships, and housing. Admissions decisions are made on a rolling basis. The University encourages visits to its beautiful campus and offers riding tours Monday through Friday at 10 a.m. and 1 p.m. central standard time. Students can visit the University of West Florida's home page via the Internet at the World Wide Web address listed below. Among the available features are the catalog, Saturday Open House dates, applications for admission, and the course guide for the current term. The Lighthouse Information System allows applicants to view their admission and financial aid status via the Internet.

Additional information and application materials may be obtained by writing or calling:

Office of Admissions
University of West Florida
11000 University Parkway
Pensacola, Florida 32514-5750
Telephone: 850-474-2230
          800-263-1074 (toll-free)
E-mail: admissions@uwf.edu
World Wide Web: http://uwf.edu

The UWF Sailing Club goes out for a day of sun and recreation on Pensacola Bay.

WEST VIRGINIA WESLEYAN COLLEGE

BUCKHANNON, WEST VIRGINIA

The College

Founded by the United Methodist Church in 1890, West Virginia Wesleyan is a coeducational, residential, liberal arts college. The College has an enrollment of 1,530 undergraduate students from thirty-five states and twenty-three countries. The average class size is 19 and the student-faculty ratio is 15:1. Nearly 80 percent of the faculty members hold the highest degree in their respective teaching field. Each fall, West Virginia Wesleyan enrolls approximately 425 freshmen and 45 transfers. Forty-five percent of the students originate from West Virginia, and the male-female ratio is 1:1. Approximately 10 percent of the students are minority or international students. Nearly 90 percent of the students live on campus, and housing is guaranteed for all four years of study. Housing options include residence halls, suites, on-campus apartments, and campus-adjacent residence units.

Wesleyan offers a timely and unique technology program where laptops, campuswide Ethernet connections, and a fast, dependable network have given students and faculty members a distinct advantage in learning and teaching. Wesleyan participates in the Dell University Program, which allows students to purchase, immediately own, and keep laptop computers customized exactly to their own specifications. This allows students to communicate with faculty members, do research, complete essays, and e-mail family and friends from the privacy of their residence hall rooms. With more than 2,500 Ethernet connection points, in addition to wireless Internet access, logging on is never a problem.

Wesleyan students are encouraged to pursue international travel and career-related internship opportunities. The international experience is available to students during the fall and spring semesters and during the three-week optional May Term. Wesleyan students also pursue a variety of semester-long internship programs, including the Washington Center for Internships.

Among the many services available to students is an Advising and Career Center that helps students with job placement, class scheduling, selection of a major program of study, internship opportunities, and international travel. The center also provides special tests, such as the LSAT, GRE, or GMAT to prepare graduates for professional schools. A Counseling and Wellness Center allows students to receive personal and educational guidance, as well as health services, through the Health Center. The Student Academic Support Services provides learning resources for all students, as well as specific services for students with diagnosed learning differences.

In addition to a challenging academic curriculum and innovative technology, Wesleyan offers a balanced and comprehensive student life program. Cocurricular activities include seventeen NCAA II sports, intramurals, outdoor recreation adventures, vocal and instrumental musical ensembles, theater arts, dance, community service, religious life programs, and fraternities and sororities. There are more than seventy campus organizations, including a radio station, student newspaper, and yearbook. The Campus Activities Board schedules a variety of cultural and social entertainment every week during the academic year.

Location

Situated in the foothills of the Allegheny Mountains, Wesleyan's 100-acre park-like campus is located in the historic town of Buckhannon, West Virginia. Buckhannon is 2 ¼ hours south of Pittsburgh, Pennsylvania, and 1 ¾ hours north of Charleston, West Virginia. It is easily accessible by interstate highways. Buckhannon has been included in Norman Crampton's book, *The Top 100 Best Small Towns in America*, a Random House publication. Students are drawn to this picturesque and friendly setting and the many restaurants, social events, and outdoor adventures available within a short distance from campus.

Majors and Degrees

The College awards a Master of Business Administration (M.B.A.) degree and has a five-year undergraduate Master of Business Administration (M.B.A.) program in accounting, business administration (M.B.A.), economics, international business, management, and marketing. Wesleyan also offers four undergraduate degrees: the Bachelor of Arts in art (ceramics, painting and drawing, graphic design, and intermedia), arts administration (art, music, and theater arts), chemistry, Christian education and church leadership, communication studies, criminal justice, education (elementary, secondary, and combined elementary/secondary), English (literature, teaching, and writing), environmental science, history, human services, international studies, music (applied and theory), musical theater, philosophy, physics, political science, psychology, public relations, religion, sociology, and theater arts; the Bachelor of Fine Arts in musical theater, theater performance, and technical theater design; the Bachelor of Music Education; the Bachelor of Science in accounting, athletic training, biology, business administration, chemistry, computer information science, computer science, economics, engineering physics, environmental science, finance, international business, management, marketing, mathematics, and physical education (health promotion and fitness management).

Preprofessional programs are offered in dentistry, law, medicine, ministry, optometry, pharmacy, physical therapy, and veterinary medicine. The degrees are determined by the content of the student's program.

Academic Programs

Students are required to complete 120 credit hours of course work to become eligible for graduation. Approximately one third of those hours are taken in a student's major, one third in the general studies curriculum requirement, and one third in electives. The general studies and elective courses are taken to develop and enhance a student's world view. These classes range from contemporary issues to humanities and can be taken along with courses within the individual's major concentration throughout the four years.

Wesleyan operates on a traditional semester system. The optional May Term is a three-week intensive period of study giving students the opportunity to earn 3 credit hours.

The honors program is offered for superior students who meet the specific requirements and are willing to commit themselves to a rigorous and enriching curriculum that affirms the highest ideals of a liberal arts institution. Challenging classes and cultural outings are an integral part of the honors program and are offered throughout the academic year.

Advanced credit is available for students who achieve required scores on Advanced Placement exams, International Baccalaureate exams, and CLEP tests.

New students are assigned a faculty adviser who assists with course selection and student concerns. All first-year students are required to successfully complete the one-hour Freshman Seminar course. This course eases the transition from high school to college by providing faculty advising and student mentoring for the first semester. The program begins at orientation and helps students become acclimated to the Wesleyan community.

Off-Campus Programs

Study abroad is highly encouraged and is an important part of the Wesleyan student's experience. In the past, students have studied in such countries as Australia, Austria, Bulgaria, England, Ireland, Italy, Korea, Spain, and Wales, but there are a number of other countries in which students may study. Internships are required for many majors and highly encouraged for others. They are available locally, as well as in such cities as Pittsburgh, New York City, Washington,

D.C., and other cities around the globe. These off-campus opportunities can be taken for a complete semester or during the May Term.

Academic Facilities

Wesleyan's twenty-three buildings, including ten modern residence hall units, house some of the most impressive facilities in the region. The Annie Merner Pfeiffer Library is a spacious facility housing more than 105,000 volumes, 700 periodicals, and 10,000 media materials. With its wireless environment, more than 220 million additional resources worldwide can be accessed online or through a number of CD-ROM databases. Located in the center of the campus is Wesley Chapel, the largest sanctuary in West Virginia, and the Martin Religious Center. The Benedum Campus and Community Center houses a convenience store, bookstore, swimming pool, the Cat's Claw restaurant, the campus radio station, and student services offices. The Rockefeller Health and Physical Education Center includes a main gymnasium that seats 3,700 spectators, an intramural gymnasium, Nautilus and weight-training rooms, and an indoor Astroturf training and recreational area. Other vital buildings include Christopher Hall of Science, which houses well-equipped laboratories that complement the building's planetarium, herbarium, and greenhouse; the Loar Memorial Building, which includes a 165-seat recital hall and a state-of-the-art computer music lab; Middleton Hall, which houses admission and financial planning offices as well as the Nursing Department; Haymond Hall of Science; and the Lynch-Raine Administration Building.

Costs

The 2004–05 costs at Wesleyan were $19,450 for tuition, $5200 for room and board, and $1000 for fees. Students should allow $700 for books per year. Wesleyan offers an interest-free monthly payment plan during the academic year.

Financial Aid

Wesleyan allocates nearly $15 million each year to help supplement the financial needs of students and their families. Merit scholarships are available for students who demonstrate excellence in the classroom, as well as those who demonstrate talent in the arts and athletics. Scholarship opportunities are available for students who have a strong commitment to community service and for those who have a comprehensive cocurricular resume. A variety of need-based programs are also available, including government grants and loans, institutional grants, and student employment. Students and their parents should file the Free Application for Federal Student Aid by February 15. The institutional code number is 003830.

Faculty

The faculty at Wesleyan has a primary goal of teaching and advising. Nearly 80 percent of the full-time faculty members hold the highest degree in their respective fields. With a 15:1 student-faculty ratio, classes are small, and personal attention is evident in all departments. Not only are faculty members teachers and advisers, but they are also mentors and friends.

Student Government

The Community Council, one of the first college-based community governing bodies in the country, is structured to encourage and promote student participation. The four peer-elected officers are elected by their respective classes or representative student organizations. The Community Council meets weekly, along with faculty members, administration, and staff members, and is recognized as the driving force behind many issues on campus.

Admission Requirements

Wesleyan seeks students who have proven academic credentials, combined with achievements and talents that enhance the quality of life on campus. Students are selected by the Office of Admission on the basis of their high school transcripts, college entrance exam results, letters of recommendation, campus interviews, and other supportive information. All applicants must take the SAT or ACT and submit secondary school transcripts from all schools attended, along with the application for admission. Candidates are considered on an individual basis without regard to race, religion, geographic origin, or handicap. Essays and campus interviews are strongly encouraged and may be required in some instances.

Transfer students from accredited institutions are considered for admission. All official college transcripts must be submitted, along with high school transcripts and college entrance exam results.

Applicants who complete their secondary education through an alternative program (e.g., home schooling) must present evidence that they have been adequately prepared for college work to be considered for admission. SAT or ACT results are also required.

Application and Information

Applicants must submit an application for admission, official transcripts, and ACT or SAT scores. While applying online is free of charge, a $25 nonrefundable fee for paper applications is required. Early decision applicants must have their completed application submitted by December 1. Admission decisions are made on a rolling basis, and students are notified within three weeks of receipt of all required documents. The preferred application deadline for the fall semester is March 1, and December 1 for the spring semester. Applicants who wish to be considered for merit scholarships must apply before March 1. Interviews, campus tours, faculty and staff appointments, and class visits are encouraged and may be arranged through the Office of Admission.

For additional information, students should contact:

Office of Admission
West Virginia Wesleyan College
59 College Avenue
Buckhannon, West Virginia 26201
Telephone: 304-473-8510
　　　　　　800-722-9933 (toll-free)
E-mail: admission@wvwc.edu
World Wide Web: http://www.wvwc.edu

The Benedum Campus and Community Center is the hub of student life—both inside and out.

Indexes

Majors and Degrees

Accounting

Adelphi U, NY	B
Alfred U, NY	B
Berkeley Coll-New York City Campus, NY	A,B
Berkeley Coll-Westchester Campus, NY	A,B
Bernard M. Baruch Coll of the City U of New York, NY	B
Briarcliffe Coll, NY	A,B
Brooklyn Coll of the City U of New York, NY	B
Bryant and Stratton Coll, Amherst Campus, NY	A
Canisius Coll, NY	B
Cazenovia Coll, NY	B
Chaminade U of Honolulu, HI	B
Chatham Coll, PA	B
Clarkson U, NY	B
The Coll of Saint Rose, NY	B
Coll of Staten Island of the City U of New York, NY	B
Cornell U, NY	B
Daemen Coll, NY	B
Dominican Coll, NY	B
Dowling Coll, NY	B
D'Youville Coll, NY	B
Elmira Coll, NY	B
Excelsior Coll, NY	B
Fordham U, NY	B
Globe Inst of Technology, NY	B
Hartwick Coll, NY	B
Hilbert Coll, NY	B
Hofstra U, NY	B
Houghton Coll, NY	B
Hunter Coll of the City U of New York, NY	B
Iona Coll, NY	B
Ithaca Coll, NY	B
Keuka Coll, NY	B
Lehman Coll of the City U of New York, NY	B
Le Moyne Coll, NY	B
Long Island U, Brentwood Campus, NY	B
Long Island U, Brooklyn Campus, NY	B
Long Island U, C.W. Post Campus, NY	B
Manhattan Coll, NY	B
Maria Coll, NY	A
Marist Coll, NY	B
Marymount Coll of Fordham U, NY	B
Marymount Manhattan Coll, NY	B
Medaille Coll, NY	B
Medgar Evers Coll of the City U of New York, NY	B
Mercy Coll, NY	B
Mitchell Coll, CT	A
Molloy Coll, NY	B
Monroe Coll, Bronx, NY	A,B
Monroe Coll, New Rochelle, NY	A,B
Mount Saint Mary Coll, NY	B
Nazareth Coll of Rochester, NY	B
New York Inst of Technology, NY	B
New York U, NY	B
Niagara U, NY	B
North Carolina Ag and Tech State U, NC	B
Nyack Coll, NY	B
Pace U, NY	B
Post U, CT	A,B
Prescott Coll, AZ	B
Queens Coll of the City U of New York, NY	B
Quinnipiac U, CT	B
Roberts Wesleyan Coll, NY	B
Rochester Inst of Technology, NY	B
Sage Coll of Albany, NY	B
St. Bonaventure U, NY	B
St. Francis Coll, NY	B
St. John Fisher Coll, NY	B
St. John's U, NY	A,B
St. Joseph's Coll, New York, NY	B
St. Joseph's Coll, Suffolk Campus, NY	B
St. Thomas Aquinas Coll, NY	B
Shepherd U, WV	B
Siena Coll, NY	B
State U of New York at Binghamton, NY	B
State U of New York at New Paltz, NY	B
State U of New York at Oswego, NY	B
State U of New York at Plattsburgh, NY	B
State U of New York Coll at Brockport, NY	B
State U of New York Coll at Geneseo, NY	B
State U of New York Coll at Old Westbury, NY	B
State U of New York Coll at Oneonta, NY	B
State U of New York Coll of Agriculture and Technology at Cobleskill, NY	A
State U of New York Coll of Technology at Alfred, NY	A
State U of New York Coll of Technology at Canton, NY	A
State U of New York Coll of Technology at Delhi, NY	A
State U of New York, Fredonia, NY	B
State U of New York Inst of Technology, NY	B
Syracuse U, NY	B
U at Albany, State U of New York, NY	B
U of West Florida, FL	B
Utica Coll, NY	B
Wagner Coll, NY	B
West Virginia Wesleyan Coll, WV	B
Yeshiva U, NY	B
York Coll of the City U of New York, NY	B

Accounting and Computer Science

Fordham U, NY	B

Accounting Related

State U of New York at Oswego, NY	B

Accounting Technology and Bookkeeping

Canisius Coll, NY	B
New York Inst of Technology, NY	A
Pace U, NY	B

Acting

Bard Coll, NY	B
Cornell U, NY	B
Ithaca Coll, NY	B
The Juilliard School, NY	B
Long Island U, C.W. Post Campus, NY	B
Marymount Manhattan Coll, NY	B
Sarah Lawrence Coll, NY	B
State U of New York Coll at Brockport, NY	B
Syracuse U, NY	B

Actuarial Science

Bernard M. Baruch Coll of the City U of New York, NY	B
Hofstra U, NY	B
Mercy Coll, NY	B
New York U, NY	B

Queens Coll of the City U of New York, NY	B
Quinnipiac U, CT	B
St. John's U, NY	B
U at Albany, State U of New York, NY	B

Administrative Assistant and Secretarial Science

Briarcliffe Coll, NY	A
Bryant and Stratton Coll, Amherst Campus, NY	A
Concordia Coll, NY	A
Hofstra U, NY	B
New York Inst of Technology, NY	A
North Carolina Ag and Tech State U, NC	B
Villa Maria Coll of Buffalo, NY	A

Adult and Continuing Education

Pratt Inst, NY	B
St. Joseph's Coll, Suffolk Campus, NY	B

Adult Health Nursing

State U of New York at Buffalo, NY	B

Advertising

Bernard M. Baruch Coll of the City U of New York, NY	B
Fashion Inst of Technology, NY	A
Iona Coll, NY	B
Marist Coll, NY	B
New York Inst of Technology, NY	B
Pace U, NY	B
Quinnipiac U, CT	B
Rochester Inst of Technology, NY	B
School of Visual Arts, NY	B
Syracuse U, NY	B

Aeronautical/Aerospace Engineering Technology

New York Inst of Technology, NY	B

Aeronautics/Aviation/Aerospace Science and Technology

Vaughn Coll of Aeronautics and Technology, NY	A

Aerospace, Aeronautical and Astronautical Engineering

Clarkson U, NY	B
Cornell U, NY	B
Dowling Coll, NY	B
Rensselaer Polytechnic Inst, NY	B
Rochester Inst of Technology, NY	B
State U of New York at Buffalo, NY	B
Syracuse U, NY	B
United States Military Academy, NY	B

African-American/Black Studies

City Coll of the City U of New York, NY	B
Colgate U, NY	B
Coll of Staten Island of the City U of New York, NY	B
Columbia Coll, NY	B
Columbia U, School of General Studies, NY	B
Cornell U, NY	B
Fordham U, NY	B
Hobart and William Smith Colls, NY	B
Hunter Coll of the City U of New York, NY	B
Lehman Coll of the City U of New York, NY	B
New York U, NY	B
Sarah Lawrence Coll, NY	B
State U of New York at Binghamton, NY	B

State U of New York at Buffalo, NY	B
State U of New York at New Paltz, NY	B
State U of New York Coll at Brockport, NY	B
State U of New York Coll at Cortland, NY	B
State U of New York Coll at Geneseo, NY	B
State U of New York Coll at Oneonta, NY	B
Stony Brook U, State U of New York, NY	B
Syracuse U, NY	B
U at Albany, State U of New York, NY	B
U of Rochester, NY	B
Wells Coll, NY	B
York Coll of the City U of New York, NY	B

African Studies

Bard Coll, NY	B
Barnard Coll, NY	B
Brooklyn Coll of the City U of New York, NY	B
Colgate U, NY	B
Fordham U, NY	B
Hamilton Coll, NY	B
Hobart and William Smith Colls, NY	B
Hofstra U, NY	B
Queens Coll of the City U of New York, NY	B
St. Lawrence U, NY	B
Sarah Lawrence Coll, NY	B
State U of New York at Binghamton, NY	B
State U of New York Coll at Brockport, NY	B
Vassar Coll, NY	B

Agricultural and Extension Education

Cornell U, NY	B

Agricultural and Horticultural Plant Breeding

Cornell U, NY	B

Agricultural Animal Breeding

Cornell U, NY	B

Agricultural/Biological Engineering and Bioengineering

Cornell U, NY	B
State U of New York Coll of Agriculture and Technology at Cobleskill, NY	A

Agricultural Business and Management

Cornell U, NY	B
North Carolina Ag and Tech State U, NC	B
State U of New York Coll of Agriculture and Technology at Cobleskill, NY	A,B
State U of New York Coll of Technology at Alfred, NY	A

Agricultural Economics

Cornell U, NY	B
North Carolina Ag and Tech State U, NC	B

Agricultural Mechanization

North Carolina Ag and Tech State U, NC	B
State U of New York Coll of Agriculture and Technology at Cobleskill, NY	A,B

A—associate degree; B—bachelor's degree

Agricultural Teacher Education
Cornell U, NY — B
North Carolina Ag and Tech State U, NC — B
State U of New York at Oswego, NY — B

Agriculture
Cornell U, NY — B
North Carolina Ag and Tech State U, NC — B
State U of New York Coll of Agriculture and Technology at Cobleskill, NY — A
State U of New York Coll of Technology at Alfred, NY — A

Agronomy and Crop Science
Cornell U, NY — B
State U of New York Coll of Agriculture and Technology at Cobleskill, NY — A,B

Air Force R.O.T.C./Air Science
Rensselaer Polytechnic Inst, NY — B

Airframe Mechanics and Aircraft Maintenance Technology
Vaughn Coll of Aeronautics and Technology, NY — A,B

Airline Pilot and Flight Crew
Farmingdale State U of New York, NY — B
Vaughn Coll of Aeronautics and Technology, NY — A

American Government and Politics
Bard Coll, NY — B
Cornell U, NY — B

American History
Bard Coll, NY — B
Cornell U, NY — B
Sarah Lawrence Coll, NY — B

American Indian/Native American Studies
Colgate U, NY — B
Cornell U, NY — B

American Literature
Cornell U, NY — B
Sarah Lawrence Coll, NY — B
State U of New York Coll at Brockport, NY — B

American Sign Language (Asl)
Rochester Inst of Technology, NY — A,B
U of Rochester, NY — B

American Studies
Bard Coll, NY — B
Barnard Coll, NY — B
Brooklyn Coll of the City U of New York, NY — B
The Coll of Saint Rose, NY — B
Coll of Staten Island of the City U of New York, NY — B
Columbia Coll, NY — B
Cornell U, NY — B
Dominican Coll, NY — B
Elmira Coll, NY — B
Fordham U, NY — B
Hamilton Coll, NY — B
Hobart and William Smith Colls, NY — B
Hofstra U, NY — B
Lehman Coll of the City U of New York, NY — B
Long Island U, C.W. Post Campus, NY — B
Manhattanville Coll, NY — B
Marist Coll, NY — B
Marymount Coll of Fordham U, NY — B
Nazareth Coll of Rochester, NY — B
Paul Smith's Coll of Arts and Sciences, NY — A
Queens Coll of the City U of New York, NY — B
St. John Fisher Coll, NY — B
Sarah Lawrence Coll, NY — B
Siena Coll, NY — B
State U of New York at Buffalo, NY — B

State U of New York at Oswego, NY — B
State U of New York Coll at Geneseo, NY — B
State U of New York Coll at Old Westbury, NY — B
State U of New York, Fredonia, NY — B
Stony Brook U, State U of New York, NY — B
Syracuse U, NY — B
Union Coll, NY — B
United States Military Academy, NY — B
Vassar Coll, NY — B
Wells Coll, NY — B

Analysis and Functional Analysis
Cornell U, NY — B

Analytical Chemistry
Cornell U, NY — B

Ancient/Classical Greek
Bard Coll, NY — B
Barnard Coll, NY — B
Columbia Coll, NY — B
Hobart and William Smith Colls, NY — B
Hunter Coll of the City U of New York, NY — B
Queens Coll of the City U of New York, NY — B
Vassar Coll, NY — B

Ancient Near Eastern and Biblical Languages
The Jewish Theological Seminary, NY — B

Ancient Studies
Barnard Coll, NY — B
Columbia Coll, NY — B

Animal Genetics
Cornell U, NY — B
Sarah Lawrence Coll, NY — B

Animal Nutrition
Cornell U, NY — B

Animal Physiology
Cornell U, NY — B

Animal Sciences
Cornell U, NY — B
North Carolina Ag and Tech State U, NC — B
State U of New York Coll of Agriculture and Technology at Cobleskill, NY — A
State U of New York Coll of Technology at Alfred, NY — A

Animal Sciences Related
Cornell U, NY — B

Animation, Interactive Technology, Video Graphics and Special Effects
Rochester Inst of Technology, NY — B

Anthropology
Adelphi U, NY — B
Bard Coll, NY — B
Barnard Coll, NY — B
Brooklyn Coll of the City U of New York, NY — B
Buffalo State Coll, State U of New York, NY — B
Canisius Coll, NY — B
City Coll of the City U of New York, NY — B
Colgate U, NY — B
Columbia Coll, NY — B
Columbia U, School of General Studies, NY — B
Cornell U, NY — B
Dowling Coll, NY — B
Elmira Coll, NY — B
Fordham U, NY — B
Hamilton Coll, NY — B
Hartwick Coll, NY — B
Hobart and William Smith Colls, NY — B
Hofstra U, NY — B
Hunter Coll of the City U of New York, NY — B
Ithaca Coll, NY — B

Lehman Coll of the City U of New York, NY — B
Nazareth Coll of Rochester, NY — B
New York U, NY — B
Prescott Coll, AZ — B
Purchase Coll, State U of New York, NY — B
Queens Coll of the City U of New York, NY — B
St. John Fisher Coll, NY — B
St. John's U, NY — B
St. Lawrence U, NY — B
Sarah Lawrence Coll, NY — B
Skidmore Coll, NY — B
State U of New York at Binghamton, NY — B
State U of New York at Buffalo, NY — B
State U of New York at New Paltz, NY — B
State U of New York at Oswego, NY — B
State U of New York at Plattsburgh, NY — B
State U of New York Coll at Brockport, NY — B
State U of New York Coll at Cortland, NY — B
State U of New York Coll at Geneseo, NY — B
State U of New York Coll at Oneonta, NY — B
State U of New York Coll at Potsdam, NY — B
Stony Brook U, State U of New York, NY — B
Syracuse U, NY — B
Union Coll, NY — B
U at Albany, State U of New York, NY — B
U of Rochester, NY — B
U of West Florida, FL — B
Vassar Coll, NY — B
Wagner Coll, NY — B
Wells Coll, NY — B
York Coll of the City U of New York, NY — B

Apparel and Textiles
Cornell U, NY — B
Fashion Inst of Technology, NY — A,B
Syracuse U, NY — B

Applied Art
Alfred U, NY — B
Buffalo State Coll, State U of New York, NY — B
Columbia U, School of General Studies, NY — B
Cornell U, NY — B
Daemen Coll, NY — B
Dowling Coll, NY — B
Pratt Inst, NY — B
Rochester Inst of Technology, NY — A,B
St. Thomas Aquinas Coll, NY — B
School of Visual Arts, NY — B
State U of New York, Fredonia, NY — B
Syracuse U, NY — B

Applied Economics
Cornell U, NY — B
Ithaca Coll, NY — B

Applied Mathematics
Barnard Coll, NY — B
Clarkson U, NY — B
Columbia U, School of General Studies, NY — B
Columbia U, The Fu Foundation School of Engineering and Applied Science, NY — B
Cornell U, NY — B
Farmingdale State U of New York, NY — B
Hofstra U, NY — B
Iona Coll, NY — B
Ithaca Coll, NY — B
Le Moyne Coll, NY — B
Long Island U, C.W. Post Campus, NY — B
Medgar Evers Coll of the City U of New York, NY — B

North Carolina Ag and Tech State U, NC — B
Queens Coll of the City U of New York, NY — B
Quinnipiac U, CT — B
Rensselaer Polytechnic Inst, NY — B
Rochester Inst of Technology, NY — A,B
St. Thomas Aquinas Coll, NY — B
State U of New York at New Paltz, NY — B
State U of New York at Oswego, NY — B
State U of New York Inst of Technology, NY — B
Stony Brook U, State U of New York, NY — B
United States Military Academy, NY — B
U at Albany, State U of New York, NY — B
U of Rochester, NY — B

Arabic
State U of New York at Binghamton, NY — B
United States Military Academy, NY — B

Archeology
Bard Coll, NY — B
Columbia Coll, NY — B
Cornell U, NY — B
Hamilton Coll, NY — B
Hunter Coll of the City U of New York, NY — B
New York U, NY — B
Sarah Lawrence Coll, NY — B
State U of New York Coll at Potsdam, NY — B

Architectural Engineering
North Carolina Ag and Tech State U, NC — B

Architectural Engineering Technology
Farmingdale State U of New York, NY — B
State U of New York Coll of Technology at Alfred, NY — A,B
State U of New York Coll of Technology at Delhi, NY — A

Architectural History and Criticism
Barnard Coll, NY — B
Cornell U, NY — B
Sarah Lawrence Coll, NY — B

Architecture
Barnard Coll, NY — B
City Coll of the City U of New York, NY — B
Coll of Staten Island of the City U of New York, NY — A
Columbia Coll, NY — B
Columbia U, School of General Studies, NY — B
Cornell U, NY — B
Hobart and William Smith Colls, NY — B
New York Inst of Technology, NY — A,B
Pratt Inst, NY — B
Rensselaer Polytechnic Inst, NY — B
State U of New York at Buffalo, NY — B
Syracuse U, NY — B

Architecture Related
Columbia Coll, NY — B
Cornell U, NY — B
New York Inst of Technology, NY — B
Rensselaer Polytechnic Inst, NY — B

Area, Ethnic, Cultural, and Gender Studies Related
Chatham Coll, PA — B
New York U, NY — B
Pratt Inst, NY — B
St. John's U, NY — B
Skidmore Coll, NY — B
Syracuse U, NY — B

Area Studies
Bard Coll, NY — B

Excelsior Coll, NY — B
Marymount Coll of Fordham U, NY — B

Area Studies Related
Barnard Coll, NY — B
Hofstra U, NY — B
St. Francis Coll, NY — B
St. John's U, NY — B

Army R.O.T.C./Military Science
Rensselaer Polytechnic Inst, NY — B
United States Military Academy, NY — B

Art
Alfred U, NY — B
Bard Coll, NY — B
Brooklyn Coll of the City U of New York, NY — B
Buffalo State Coll, State U of New York, NY — B
City Coll of the City U of New York, NY — B
Colgate U, NY — B
Cornell U, NY — B
Daemen Coll, NY — B
Elmira Coll, NY — B
Fashion Inst of Technology, NY — A
Fordham U, NY — B
Hamilton Coll, NY — B
Hartwick Coll, NY — B
Hobart and William Smith Colls, NY — B
Houghton Coll, NY — B
Hunter Coll of the City U of New York, NY — B
Ithaca Coll, NY — B
Lehman Coll of the City U of New York, NY — B
Long Island U, Brooklyn Campus, NY — B
Marist Coll, NY — B
Marymount Coll of Fordham U, NY — B
Marymount Manhattan Coll, NY — B
Medaille Coll, NY — B
Mercy Coll, NY — B
Molloy Coll, NY — B
Nazareth Coll of Rochester, NY — B
New York U, NY — B
Pace U, NY — B
Pratt Inst, NY — B
Prescott Coll, AZ — B
Purchase Coll, State U of New York, NY — B
Queens Coll of the City U of New York, NY — B
Roberts Wesleyan Coll, NY — B
Rochester Inst of Technology, NY — A,B
St. Lawrence U, NY — B
St. Thomas Aquinas Coll, NY — B
Sarah Lawrence Coll, NY — B
School of Visual Arts, NY — B
Shepherd U, WV — B
State U of New York at Binghamton, NY — B
State U of New York at Buffalo, NY — B
State U of New York at New Paltz, NY — B
State U of New York at Oswego, NY — B
State U of New York Coll at Brockport, NY — B
State U of New York Coll at Geneseo, NY — B
State U of New York Coll at Old Westbury, NY — B
State U of New York Coll at Oneonta, NY — B
State U of New York Coll at Potsdam, NY — B
State U of New York Empire State Coll, NY — A,B
State U of New York, Fredonia, NY — B
Syracuse U, NY — B
U at Albany, State U of New York, NY — B
U of West Florida, FL — B
Wagner Coll, NY — B

Wells Coll, NY — B
West Virginia Wesleyan Coll, WV — B
York Coll of the City U of New York, NY — B

Art History, Criticism and Conservation
Adelphi U, NY — B
Bard Coll, NY — B
Barnard Coll, NY — B
Brooklyn Coll of the City U of New York, NY — B
Buffalo State Coll, State U of New York, NY — B
Canisius Coll, NY — B
Chatham Coll, PA — B
City Coll of the City U of New York, NY — B
Colgate U, NY — B
The Coll of New Rochelle, NY — B
Columbia Coll, NY — B
Columbia U, School of General Studies, NY — B
Cornell U, NY — B
Fashion Inst of Technology, NY — B
Fordham U, NY — B
Hamilton Coll, NY — B
Hartwick Coll, NY — B
Hobart and William Smith Colls, NY — B
Hofstra U, NY — B
Hunter Coll of the City U of New York, NY — B
Ithaca Coll, NY — B
Lehman Coll of the City U of New York, NY — B
Long Island U, C.W. Post Campus, NY — B
Manhattanville Coll, NY — B
Marymount Coll of Fordham U, NY — B
Marymount Manhattan Coll, NY — B
Nazareth Coll of Rochester, NY — B
New York U, NY — B
Pace U, NY — B
Pratt Inst, NY — B
Purchase Coll, State U of New York, NY — B
Queens Coll of the City U of New York, NY — B
St. Lawrence U, NY — B
Sarah Lawrence Coll, NY — B
Skidmore Coll, NY — B
State U of New York at Binghamton, NY — B
State U of New York at Buffalo, NY — B
State U of New York at New Paltz, NY — B
State U of New York at Plattsburgh, NY — B
State U of New York Coll at Cortland, NY — B
State U of New York Coll at Geneseo, NY — B
State U of New York Coll at Oneonta, NY — B
State U of New York Coll at Potsdam, NY — B
State U of New York, Fredonia, NY — B
Stony Brook U, State U of New York, NY — B
Syracuse U, NY — B
U at Albany, State U of New York, NY — B
U of Rochester, NY — B
U of West Florida, FL — B
Vassar Coll, NY — B
Wells Coll, NY — B
West Virginia Wesleyan Coll, WV — B

Arts Management
Bernard M. Baruch Coll of the City U of New York, NY — B
Chatham Coll, PA — B
Concordia Coll, NY — B
Ithaca Coll, NY — B
Long Island U, C.W. Post Campus, NY — B

State U of New York, Fredonia, NY — B
Wagner Coll, NY — B

Art Teacher Education
Adelphi U, NY — B
Alfred U, NY — B
Brooklyn Coll of the City U of New York, NY — B
Buffalo State Coll, State U of New York, NY — B
City Coll of the City U of New York, NY — B
The Coll of New Rochelle, NY — B
The Coll of Saint Rose, NY — B
Daemen Coll, NY — B
Dowling Coll, NY — B
Elmira Coll, NY — B
Hofstra U, NY — B
Houghton Coll, NY — B
Ithaca Coll, NY — B
Lehman Coll of the City U of New York, NY — B
Long Island U, Brooklyn Campus, NY — B
Long Island U, C.W. Post Campus, NY — B
Manhattanville Coll, NY — B
Marymount Coll of Fordham U, NY — B
Nazareth Coll of Rochester, NY — B
New York Inst of Technology, NY — B
North Carolina Ag and Tech State U, NC — B
Pratt Inst, NY — B
Queens Coll of the City U of New York, NY — B
Roberts Wesleyan Coll, NY — B
St. Bonaventure U, NY — B
St. John's U, NY — B
St. Thomas Aquinas Coll, NY — B
School of Visual Arts, NY — B
State U of New York at New Paltz, NY — B
Syracuse U, NY — B
U of West Florida, FL — B
West Virginia Wesleyan Coll, WV — B

Art Therapy
The Coll of New Rochelle, NY — B
Long Island U, C.W. Post Campus, NY — B
Marymount Coll of Fordham U, NY — B
Nazareth Coll of Rochester, NY — B
Prescott Coll, AZ — B
Russell Sage Coll, NY — B
St. Thomas Aquinas Coll, NY — B
School of Visual Arts, NY — B

Asian-American Studies
Columbia Coll, NY — B
State U of New York at Binghamton, NY — B

Asian History
Bard Coll, NY — B
Cornell U, NY — B
Sarah Lawrence Coll, NY — B

Asian Studies
Bard Coll, NY — B
Barnard Coll, NY — B
City Coll of the City U of New York, NY — B
Colgate U, NY — B
Cornell U, NY — B
Hamilton Coll, NY — B
Hobart and William Smith Colls, NY — B
Hofstra U, NY — B
Manhattanville Coll, NY — B
St. John's U, NY — B
St. Lawrence U, NY — B
Sarah Lawrence Coll, NY — B
Skidmore Coll, NY — B
State U of New York at Buffalo, NY — B
State U of New York Coll at Brockport, NY — B

State U of New York, Fredonia, NY — B
Wagner Coll, NY — B

U at Albany, State U of New York, NY — B
Vassar Coll, NY — B

Asian Studies (East)
Colgate U, NY — B
Columbia Coll, NY — B
Columbia U, School of General Studies, NY — B
Cornell U, NY — B
Hamilton Coll, NY — B
New York U, NY — B
Queens Coll of the City U of New York, NY — B
St. John's U, NY — B
Sarah Lawrence Coll, NY — B
United States Military Academy, NY — B
U at Albany, State U of New York, NY — B

Asian Studies (South)
Sarah Lawrence Coll, NY — B
Syracuse U, NY — B

Astronomy
Barnard Coll, NY — B
Colgate U, NY — B
Columbia Coll, NY — B
Columbia U, School of General Studies, NY — B
Cornell U, NY — B
Sarah Lawrence Coll, NY — B
State U of New York Coll at Brockport, NY — B
Stony Brook U, State U of New York, NY — B
Vassar Coll, NY — B

Astrophysics
Barnard Coll, NY — B
Colgate U, NY — B
Columbia Coll, NY — B
Cornell U, NY — B

Athletic Training
Alfred U, NY — B
Canisius Coll, NY — B
Dominican Coll, NY — B
Hofstra U, NY — B
Ithaca Coll, NY — B
Long Island U, Brooklyn Campus, NY — B
Marist Coll, NY — B
Mitchell Coll, CT — A
Quinnipiac U, CT — B
Russell Sage Coll, NY — B
State U of New York Coll at Brockport, NY — B
State U of New York Coll at Cortland, NY — B
Stony Brook U, State U of New York, NY — B
West Virginia Wesleyan Coll, WV — B

Atmospheric Sciences and Meteorology
Cornell U, NY — B
State U of New York at Oswego, NY — B
State U of New York Coll at Brockport, NY — B
State U of New York Coll at Oneonta, NY — B
U at Albany, State U of New York, NY — B

Atomic/Molecular Physics
Columbia Coll, NY — B

Audio Engineering
Five Towns Coll, NY — A,B
State U of New York, Fredonia, NY — B

Audiology and Speech-Language Pathology
Adelphi U, NY — B
Brooklyn Coll of the City U of New York, NY — B
Buffalo State Coll, State U of New York, NY — B
The Coll of Saint Rose, NY — B
Elmira Coll, NY — B

A—associate degree; B—bachelor's degree

Hofstra U, NY — B
Hunter Coll of the City U of New York, NY — B
Iona Coll, NY — B
Ithaca Coll, NY — B
Lehman Coll of the City U of New York, NY — B
Long Island U, C.W. Post Campus, NY — B
Marymount Manhattan Coll, NY — B
Mercy Coll, NY — B
Molloy Coll, NY — B
Nazareth Coll of Rochester, NY — B
St. John's U, NY — B
State U of New York at Buffalo, NY — B
State U of New York at New Paltz, NY — B
State U of New York at Plattsburgh, NY — B
State U of New York Coll at Cortland, NY — B
State U of New York Coll at Geneseo, NY — B
State U of New York, Fredonia, NY — B
Syracuse U, NY — B
Yeshiva U, NY — B

Audiovisual Communications Technologies Related
Hofstra U, NY — B

Autobody/Collision and Repair Technology
State U of New York Coll of Technology at Alfred, NY — A

Automobile/Automotive Mechanics Technology
State U of New York Coll of Technology at Alfred, NY — A
State U of New York Coll of Technology at Canton, NY — A

Automotive Engineering Technology
Farmingdale State U of New York, NY — A,B

Aviation/Airway Management
Farmingdale State U of New York, NY — B
Vaughn Coll of Aeronautics and Technology, NY — B

Avionics Maintenance Technology
Vaughn Coll of Aeronautics and Technology, NY — A,B

Baking and Pastry Arts
The Culinary Inst of America, NY — A,B

Banking and Financial Support Services
Globe Inst of Technology, NY — A
Hilbert Coll, NY — A
State U of New York Coll of Technology at Canton, NY — B

Behavioral Sciences
Chaminade U of Honolulu, HI — B
Iona Coll, NY — B
John Jay Coll of Criminal Justice of the City U of New York, NY — B
Marist Coll, NY — B
Mercy Coll, NY — B
St. Joseph's Coll, Suffolk Campus, NY — B
United States Military Academy, NY — B

Biblical Studies
Houghton Coll, NY — A,B
The Jewish Theological Seminary, NY — B
Nyack Coll, NY — B

Bilingual and Multilingual Education
Boricua Coll, NY — B
Brooklyn Coll of the City U of New York, NY — B
Fordham U, NY — B
Hofstra U, NY — B

Long Island U, Brooklyn Campus, NY — B
Mercy Coll, NY — B
Prescott Coll, AZ — B
State U of New York Coll at Old Westbury, NY — B

Bilingual, Multilingual, and Multicultural Education Related
St. John's U, NY — B
State U of New York Coll at Brockport, NY — B

Biochemical Technology
State U of New York at Buffalo, NY — B

Biochemistry
Adelphi U, NY — B
Bard Coll, NY — B
Barnard Coll, NY — B
Canisius Coll, NY — B
Chatham Coll, PA — B
City Coll of the City U of New York, NY — B
Clarkson U, NY — B
Colgate U, NY — B
Coll of Mount Saint Vincent, NY — B
The Coll of Saint Rose, NY — B
Coll of Staten Island of the City U of New York, NY — B
Columbia Coll, NY — B
Cornell U, NY — B
Daemen Coll, NY — B
Elmira Coll, NY — B
Hamilton Coll, NY — B
Hartwick Coll, NY — B
Hobart and William Smith Colls, NY — B
Hofstra U, NY — B
Iona Coll, NY — B
Ithaca Coll, NY — B
Keuka Coll, NY — B
Lehman Coll of the City U of New York, NY — B
Le Moyne Coll, NY — B
Manhattan Coll, NY — B
Manhattanville Coll, NY — B
Marist Coll, NY — B
Nazareth Coll of Rochester, NY — B
New York U, NY — B
Niagara U, NY — B
Pace U, NY — B
Queens Coll of the City U of New York, NY — B
Quinnipiac U, CT — B
Rensselaer Polytechnic Inst, NY — B
Roberts Wesleyan Coll, NY — B
Rochester Inst of Technology, NY — B
Russell Sage Coll, NY — B
St. Bonaventure U, NY — B
St. John Fisher Coll, NY — B
St. Lawrence U, NY — B
Skidmore Coll, NY — B
State U of New York at Binghamton, NY — B
State U of New York at Buffalo, NY — B
State U of New York at New Paltz, NY — B
State U of New York at Plattsburgh, NY — B
State U of New York Coll at Brockport, NY — B
State U of New York Coll at Geneseo, NY — B
State U of New York Coll at Oneonta, NY — B
State U of New York Coll of Environmental Science and Forestry, NY — B
State U of New York, Fredonia, NY — B
Stony Brook U, State U of New York, NY — B
Syracuse U, NY — B
Union Coll, NY — B
U at Albany, State U of New York, NY — B
Vassar Coll, NY — B
Wells Coll, NY — B

Biochemistry/Biophysics and Molecular Biology
Cornell U, NY — B

Bioinformatics
Canisius Coll, NY — B
Chatham Coll, PA — B
Rensselaer Polytechnic Inst, NY — B
Rochester Inst of Technology, NY — B
State U of New York at Buffalo, NY — B

Biological and Biomedical Sciences Related
Cornell U, NY — B
Farmingdale State U of New York, NY — B
Rensselaer Polytechnic Inst, NY — B
Rochester Inst of Technology, NY — B
Skidmore Coll, NY — B

Biological and Physical Sciences
Alfred U, NY — B
Bard Coll, NY — B
Canisius Coll, NY — B
Dowling Coll, NY — B
Fordham U, NY — B
Houghton Coll, NY — B
Le Moyne Coll, NY — B
Long Island U, Brooklyn Campus, NY — B
Marymount Coll of Fordham U, NY — B
Medgar Evers Coll of the City U of New York, NY — A
Mitchell Coll, CT — A
Quinnipiac U, CT — B
Rensselaer Polytechnic Inst, NY — B
Roberts Wesleyan Coll, NY — B
Sarah Lawrence Coll, NY — B
State U of New York Coll of Agriculture and Technology at Cobleskill, NY — A
State U of New York Coll of Environmental Science and Forestry, NY — B
State U of New York Coll of Technology at Alfred, NY — A
State U of New York Coll of Technology at Canton, NY — A
State U of New York Empire State Coll, NY — A,B
State U of New York, Fredonia, NY — B
Union Coll, NY — B
United States Military Academy, NY — B
U of Rochester, NY — B
U of West Florida, FL — B

Biology/Biological Sciences
Adelphi U, NY — B
Alfred U, NY — B
Bard Coll, NY — B
Barnard Coll, NY — B
Brooklyn Coll of the City U of New York, NY — B
Buffalo State Coll, State U of New York, NY — B
Chaminade U of Honolulu, HI — B
Chatham Coll, PA — B
City Coll of the City U of New York, NY — B
Clarkson U, NY — B
Colgate U, NY — B
Coll of Mount Saint Vincent, NY — B
The Coll of New Rochelle, NY — B
The Coll of Saint Rose, NY — B
Coll of Staten Island of the City U of New York, NY — B
Columbia Coll, NY — B
Columbia U, School of General Studies, NY — B
Concordia Coll, NY — B
Cornell U, NY — B
Daemen Coll, NY — B
Dominican Coll, NY — B
Dowling Coll, NY — B
D'Youville Coll, NY — B
Elmira Coll, NY — B
Excelsior Coll, NY — B
Fordham U, NY — B
Hamilton Coll, NY — B
Hartwick Coll, NY — B

Hobart and William Smith Colls, NY — B
Hofstra U, NY — B
Houghton Coll, NY — B
Hunter Coll of the City U of New York, NY — B
Iona Coll, NY — B
Ithaca Coll, NY — B
Keuka Coll, NY — B
Lehman Coll of the City U of New York, NY — B
Le Moyne Coll, NY — B
Long Island U, Brooklyn Campus, NY — B
Long Island U, C.W. Post Campus, NY — B
Manhattan Coll, NY — B
Manhattanville Coll, NY — B
Marist Coll, NY — B
Marymount Coll of Fordham U, NY — B
Marymount Manhattan Coll, NY — B
Medaille Coll, NY — B
Medgar Evers Coll of the City U of New York, NY — B
Mercy Coll, NY — B
Molloy Coll, NY — B
Mount Saint Mary Coll, NY — B
Nazareth Coll of Rochester, NY — B
New York Inst of Technology, NY — B
New York U, NY — B
Niagara U, NY — B
North Carolina Ag and Tech State U, NC — B
Pace U, NY — B
Post U, CT — B
Prescott Coll, AZ — B
Purchase Coll, State U of New York, NY — B
Queens Coll of the City U of New York, NY — B
Quinnipiac U, CT — B
Rensselaer Polytechnic Inst, NY — B
Roberts Wesleyan Coll, NY — B
Rochester Inst of Technology, NY — A,B
Russell Sage Coll, NY — B
St. Bonaventure U, NY — B
St. Francis Coll, NY — B
St. John Fisher Coll, NY — B
St. John's U, NY — B
St. Joseph's Coll, New York, NY — B
St. Joseph's Coll, Suffolk Campus, NY — B
St. Lawrence U, NY — B
St. Thomas Aquinas Coll, NY — B
Sarah Lawrence Coll, NY — B
Shepherd U, WV — B
Siena Coll, NY — B
Skidmore Coll, NY — B
State U of New York at Binghamton, NY — B
State U of New York at Buffalo, NY — B
State U of New York at New Paltz, NY — B
State U of New York at Oswego, NY — B
State U of New York at Plattsburgh, NY — B
State U of New York Coll at Brockport, NY — B
State U of New York Coll at Cortland, NY — B
State U of New York Coll at Geneseo, NY — B
State U of New York Coll at Old Westbury, NY — B
State U of New York Coll at Oneonta, NY — B
State U of New York Coll at Potsdam, NY — B
State U of New York Coll of Environmental Science and Forestry, NY — B
State U of New York, Fredonia, NY — B
Stony Brook U, State U of New York, NY — B
Syracuse U, NY — B
Union Coll, NY — B
United States Military Academy, NY — B

U at Albany, State U of New
York, NY B
U of Rochester, NY B
U of West Florida, FL B
Utica Coll, NY B
Vassar Coll, NY B
Wagner Coll, NY B
Wells Coll, NY B
West Virginia Wesleyan Coll,
WV B
Yeshiva U, NY B
York Coll of the City U of New
York, NY B

Biology/Biotechnology Laboratory Technician
Niagara U, NY B
State U of New York Coll at
Brockport, NY B
State U of New York Coll at
Oneonta, NY B
State U of New York Coll of
Agriculture and Technology at
Cobleskill, NY A
State U of New York Coll of
Technology at Alfred, NY A
State U of New York, Fredonia,
NY B
York Coll of the City U of New
York, NY B

Biology Teacher Education
Brooklyn Coll of the City U of
New York, NY B
City Coll of the City U of New
York, NY B
The Coll of Saint Rose, NY B
Daemen Coll, NY B
Dominican Coll, NY B
Dowling Coll, NY B
Elmira Coll, NY B
Hofstra U, NY B
Hunter Coll of the City U of
New York, NY B
Iona Coll, NY B
Ithaca Coll, NY B
Keuka Coll, NY B
Le Moyne Coll, NY B
Long Island U, C.W. Post
Campus, NY B
Manhattanville Coll, NY B
Marymount Coll of Fordham U,
NY B
Molloy Coll, NY B
Nazareth Coll of Rochester, NY B
New York Inst of Technology, NY B
New York U, NY B
Niagara U, NY B
Pace U, NY B
Roberts Wesleyan Coll, NY B
St. Bonaventure U, NY B
St. Francis Coll, NY B
St. John's U, NY B
State U of New York Coll at
Brockport, NY B
State U of New York Coll at
Cortland, NY B
State U of New York Coll at Old
Westbury, NY B
State U of New York Coll at
Oneonta, NY B
State U of New York Coll at
Potsdam, NY B
State U of New York Coll of
Environmental Science and
Forestry, NY B
Syracuse U, NY B
U at Albany, State U of New
York, NY B
Utica Coll, NY B

Biomathematics and Bioinformatics Related
Cornell U, NY B

Biomedical/Medical Engineering
City Coll of the City U of New
York, NY B
Columbia U, The Fu Foundation
School of Engineering and
Applied Science, NY B
Cornell U, NY B

Hofstra U, NY B
Rensselaer Polytechnic Inst, NY B
Rochester Inst of Technology, NY B
State U of New York at
Binghamton, NY B
Stony Brook U, State U of New
York, NY B
Syracuse U, NY B
U of Rochester, NY B

Biomedical Sciences
Albany Coll of Pharmacy of
Union U, NY B
City Coll of the City U of New
York, NY B
Keuka Coll, NY B
St. Francis Coll, NY B
State U of New York, Fredonia,
NY B

Biomedical Technology
Alfred U, NY B
New York Inst of Technology, NY B

Biometry/Biometrics
Cornell U, NY B

Biophysics
Barnard Coll, NY B
Clarkson U, NY B
Columbia Coll, NY B
Cornell U, NY B
Rensselaer Polytechnic Inst, NY B
St. Bonaventure U, NY B
St. Lawrence U, NY B
State U of New York at Buffalo,
NY B
State U of New York Coll at
Geneseo, NY B

Biopsychology
Barnard Coll, NY B
Columbia Coll, NY B
Cornell U, NY B
Rochester Inst of Technology, NY B
Russell Sage Coll, NY B

Biotechnology
Clarkson U, NY B
Manhattan Coll, NY B
Rochester Inst of Technology, NY B
State U of New York at Buffalo,
NY B
State U of New York Coll at
Brockport, NY B
State U of New York Coll of
Environmental Science and
Forestry, NY B

Biotechnology Research
Hunter Coll of the City U of
New York, NY B

Botany/Plant Biology
Cornell U, NY B
State U of New York Coll of
Environmental Science and
Forestry, NY B

Broadcast Journalism
Brooklyn Coll of the City U of
New York, NY B
Buffalo State Coll, State U of
New York, NY B
The Coll of New Rochelle, NY B
Five Towns Coll, NY A
Fordham U, NY B
Hofstra U, NY B
Ithaca Coll, NY B
Long Island U, C.W. Post
Campus, NY B
Marist Coll, NY B
Quinnipiac U, CT B
State U of New York at New
Paltz, NY B
State U of New York at
Plattsburgh, NY B
State U of New York Coll at
Brockport, NY B
State U of New York, Fredonia,
NY B
Syracuse U, NY B

Business Administration and Management
Adelphi U, NY B
Alfred U, NY B
Baltimore International Coll, MD B
Berkeley Coll-New York City
Campus, NY A,B
Berkeley Coll-Westchester
Campus, NY A,B
Bernard M. Baruch Coll of the
City U of New York, NY B
Boricua Coll, NY B
Briarcliffe Coll, NY A
Buffalo State Coll, State U of
New York, NY B
Canisius Coll, NY B
Cazenovia Coll, NY B
Chaminade U of Honolulu, HI A,B
Chatham Coll, PA B
City Coll of the City U of New
York, NY B
Clarkson U, NY B
Coll of Mount Saint Vincent, NY A,B
The Coll of New Rochelle, NY B
The Coll of Saint Rose, NY B
Concordia Coll, NY A,B
Cornell U, NY B
Daemen Coll, NY B
Dominican Coll, NY B
Dowling Coll, NY B
D'Youville Coll, NY B
Elmira Coll, NY B
Excelsior Coll, NY A,B
Farmingdale State U of New
York, NY A
Five Towns Coll, NY A,B
Fordham U, NY B
Globe Inst of Technology, NY A,B
Hartwick Coll, NY B
Hilbert Coll, NY A,B
Hofstra U, NY B
Houghton Coll, NY B
Iona Coll, NY B
Ithaca Coll, NY B
Keuka Coll, NY B
The King's Coll, NY B
Lehman Coll of the City U of
New York, NY B
Le Moyne Coll, NY B
Long Island U, Brentwood
Campus, NY B
Long Island U, Brooklyn
Campus, NY A,B
Long Island U, C.W. Post
Campus, NY B
Manhattanville Coll, NY A
Maria Coll, NY A
Marist Coll, NY B
Marymount Coll of Fordham U,
NY B
Marymount Manhattan Coll, NY B
Medaille Coll, NY A,B
Medgar Evers Coll of the City U
of New York, NY A,B
Mercy Coll, NY B
Metropolitan Coll of New York,
NY B
Mitchell Coll, CT A,B
Molloy Coll, NY B
Monroe Coll, Bronx, NY A,B
Monroe Coll, New Rochelle, NY A,B
Mount Saint Mary Coll, NY B
Nazareth Coll of Rochester, NY B
New York Inst of Technology, NY A,B
New York U, NY B
Niagara U, NY A,B
North Carolina Ag and Tech
State U, NC B
Nyack Coll, NY A,B
Pace U, NY B
Paul Smith's Coll of Arts and
Sciences, NY A
Post U, CT A,B
Quinnipiac U, CT B
Rensselaer Polytechnic Inst, NY B
Roberts Wesleyan Coll, NY B
Rochester Inst of Technology, NY A,B
Russell Sage Coll, NY B
Sage Coll of Albany, NY A,B
St. Bonaventure U, NY B
St. Francis Coll, NY A,B

St. John Fisher Coll, NY B
St. John's U, NY B
St. Joseph's Coll, New York, NY B
St. Joseph's Coll, Suffolk Campus,
NY B
St. Thomas Aquinas Coll, NY B
Shepherd U, WV A,B
State U of New York at Buffalo,
NY B
State U of New York at New
Paltz, NY B
State U of New York at Oswego,
NY B
State U of New York at
Plattsburgh, NY B
State U of New York Coll at
Brockport, NY B
State U of New York Coll at
Geneseo, NY B
State U of New York Coll at Old
Westbury, NY B
State U of New York Coll at
Potsdam, NY B
State U of New York Coll of
Agriculture and Technology at
Cobleskill, NY A
State U of New York Coll of
Technology at Alfred, NY A
State U of New York Coll of
Technology at Canton, NY A
State U of New York Coll of
Technology at Delhi, NY A
State U of New York Empire
State Coll, NY A,B
State U of New York, Fredonia,
NY B
State U of New York Inst of
Technology, NY B
Stony Brook U, State U of New
York, NY B
Syracuse U, NY B
United States Military Academy,
NY B
U at Albany, State U of New
York, NY B
U of West Florida, FL B
Utica Coll, NY B
Villa Maria Coll of Buffalo, NY A
Wagner Coll, NY B
Wells Coll, NY B
West Virginia Wesleyan Coll,
WV B
Yeshiva U, NY B
York Coll of the City U of New
York, NY B

Business Administration, Management and Operations Related
Briarcliffe Coll, NY A
Bryant and Stratton Coll,
Amherst Campus, NY A
Canisius Coll, NY B
DeVry Inst of Technology, NY B
Post U, CT B

Business Automation/Technology/Data Entry
Pace U, NY A

Business/Commerce
Berkeley Coll-New York City
Campus, NY B
Berkeley Coll-Westchester
Campus, NY B
Coll of Staten Island of the City
U of New York, NY A,B
Cornell U, NY B
Hofstra U, NY B
Ithaca Coll, NY B
Marymount Coll of Fordham U,
NY A
Niagara U, NY B
St. Bonaventure U, NY B
Skidmore Coll, NY B

Business/Corporate Communications
State U of New York Coll of
Agriculture and Technology at
Cobleskill, NY B

A—associate degree; B—bachelor's degree

Business Family and Consumer Sciences/Human Sciences
Cornell U, NY — B

Business, Management, and Marketing Related
Adelphi U, NY — B
Dowling Coll, NY — B
New York U, NY — B
Skidmore Coll, NY — B
Utica Coll, NY — B

Business/Managerial Economics
Bernard M. Baruch Coll of the City U of New York, NY — B
Coll of Mount Saint Vincent, NY — B
Elmira Coll, NY — B
Fordham U, NY — B
Hofstra U, NY — B
Ithaca Coll, NY — B
Marymount Coll of Fordham U, NY — B
Mercy Coll, NY — B
New York U, NY — B
Niagara U, NY — B
Quinnipiac U, CT — B
St. Bonaventure U, NY — B
St. John's U, NY — B
State U of New York at New Paltz, NY — B
State U of New York at Plattsburgh, NY — B
State U of New York Coll at Oneonta, NY — B
State U of New York Coll at Potsdam, NY — B
State U of New York Coll of Technology at Canton, NY — A
U of West Florida, FL — B
Utica Coll, NY — B
West Virginia Wesleyan Coll, WV — B

Business Teacher Education
Alfred U, NY — B
Buffalo State Coll, State U of New York, NY — B
Concordia Coll, NY — B
Dowling Coll, NY — B
D'Youville Coll, NY — B
Hofstra U, NY — B
Lehman Coll of the City U of New York, NY — B
Le Moyne Coll, NY — B
Nazareth Coll of Rochester, NY — B
New York Inst of Technology, NY — B
Niagara U, NY — B
North Carolina Ag and Tech State U, NC — B
Pace U, NY — B
St. Francis Coll, NY — B
Utica Coll, NY — B

Canadian Studies
St. Lawrence U, NY — B
State U of New York at Plattsburgh, NY — B

Cardiovascular Technology
Molloy Coll, NY — A
State U of New York Upstate Medical U, NY — B

Caribbean Studies
Brooklyn Coll of the City U of New York, NY — B
Hofstra U, NY — B

Carpentry
State U of New York Coll of Technology at Alfred, NY — A
State U of New York Coll of Technology at Canton, NY — A
State U of New York Coll of Technology at Delhi, NY — A

Cartography
State U of New York Coll at Oneonta, NY — B

Cell and Molecular Biology
State U of New York Coll at Brockport, NY — B

Cell Biology and Histology
Clarkson U, NY — B
The Coll of Saint Rose, NY — B

Cornell U, NY — B
State U of New York Coll at Brockport, NY — B

Ceramic Arts and Ceramics
Alfred U, NY — B
Hofstra U, NY — B
Nazareth Coll of Rochester, NY — B
Pratt Inst, NY — B
Rochester Inst of Technology, NY — A,B
State U of New York at New Paltz, NY — B
State U of New York Coll at Brockport, NY — B
State U of New York Coll at Potsdam, NY — B
Syracuse U, NY — B
West Virginia Wesleyan Coll, WV — B

Ceramic Sciences and Engineering
Alfred U, NY — B

Chemical Engineering
City Coll of the City U of New York, NY — B
Clarkson U, NY — B
Columbia U, The Fu Foundation School of Engineering and Applied Science, NY — B
Cornell U, NY — B
Excelsior Coll, NY — A,B
Manhattan Coll, NY — B
North Carolina Ag and Tech State U, NC — B
Polytechnic U, Brooklyn Campus, NY — B
Rensselaer Polytechnic Inst, NY — B
State U of New York at Buffalo, NY — B
State U of New York Coll of Environmental Science and Forestry, NY — B
Syracuse U, NY — B
United States Military Academy, NY — B
U of Rochester, NY — B

Chemical Physics
Barnard Coll, NY — B

Chemical Technology
State U of New York Coll of Agriculture and Technology at Cobleskill, NY — A

Chemistry
Adelphi U, NY — B
Alfred U, NY — B
Bard Coll, NY — B
Barnard Coll, NY — B
Brooklyn Coll of the City U of New York, NY — B
Buffalo State Coll, State U of New York, NY — B
Canisius Coll, NY — B
Chatham Coll, PA — B
City Coll of the City U of New York, NY — B
Clarkson U, NY — B
Colgate U, NY — B
Coll of Mount Saint Vincent, NY — B
The Coll of New Rochelle, NY — B
The Coll of Saint Rose, NY — B
Coll of Staten Island of the City U of New York, NY — B
Columbia Coll, NY — B
Columbia U, School of General Studies, NY — B
Cornell U, NY — B
Elmira Coll, NY — B
Excelsior Coll, NY — B
Fordham U, NY — B
Hamilton Coll, NY — B
Hartwick Coll, NY — B
Hobart and William Smith Colls, NY — B
Hofstra U, NY — B
Houghton Coll, NY — B
Hunter Coll of the City U of New York, NY — B
Iona Coll, NY — B
Ithaca Coll, NY — B
Lehman Coll of the City U of New York, NY — B

Le Moyne Coll, NY — B
Long Island U, Brooklyn Campus, NY — B
Long Island U, C.W. Post Campus, NY — B
Manhattan Coll, NY — B
Manhattanville Coll, NY — B
Marist Coll, NY — B
Marymount Coll of Fordham U, NY — B
Mount Saint Mary Coll, NY — B
Nazareth Coll of Rochester, NY — B
New York Inst of Technology, NY — B
New York U, NY — B
Niagara U, NY — B
North Carolina Ag and Tech State U, NC — B
Pace U, NY — B
Polytechnic U, Brooklyn Campus, NY — B
Purchase Coll, State U of New York, NY — B
Queens Coll of the City U of New York, NY — B
Quinnipiac U, CT — B
Rensselaer Polytechnic Inst, NY — B
Roberts Wesleyan Coll, NY — B
Rochester Inst of Technology, NY — A,B
Russell Sage Coll, NY — B
St. Bonaventure U, NY — B
St. Francis Coll, NY — B
St. John Fisher Coll, NY — B
St. John's U, NY — B
St. Joseph's Coll, New York, NY — B
St. Lawrence U, NY — B
Sarah Lawrence Coll, NY — B
Shepherd U, WV — B
Siena Coll, NY — B
Skidmore Coll, NY — B
State U of New York at Binghamton, NY — B
State U of New York at Buffalo, NY — B
State U of New York at New Paltz, NY — B
State U of New York at Oswego, NY — B
State U of New York at Plattsburgh, NY — B
State U of New York Coll at Brockport, NY — B
State U of New York Coll at Cortland, NY — B
State U of New York Coll at Geneseo, NY — B
State U of New York Coll at Old Westbury, NY — B
State U of New York Coll at Oneonta, NY — B
State U of New York Coll at Potsdam, NY — B
State U of New York Coll of Environmental Science and Forestry, NY — B
State U of New York, Fredonia, NY — B
Stony Brook U, State U of New York, NY — B
Syracuse U, NY — B
Union Coll, NY — B
United States Military Academy, NY — B
U at Albany, State U of New York, NY — B
U of Rochester, NY — B
U of West Florida, FL — B
Utica Coll, NY — B
Vassar Coll, NY — B
Wagner Coll, NY — B
Wells Coll, NY — B
West Virginia Wesleyan Coll, WV — B
Yeshiva U, NY — B
York Coll of the City U of New York, NY — B

Chemistry Related
Cornell U, NY — B
Hofstra U, NY — B
Stony Brook U, State U of New York, NY — B

Chemistry Teacher Education
Brooklyn Coll of the City U of New York, NY — B
Chatham Coll, PA — B
City Coll of the City U of New York, NY — B
The Coll of Saint Rose, NY — B
Elmira Coll, NY — B
Hofstra U, NY — B
Ithaca Coll, NY — B
Le Moyne Coll, NY — B
Long Island U, Brooklyn Campus, NY — B
Long Island U, C.W. Post Campus, NY — B
Manhattanville Coll, NY — B
Marymount Coll of Fordham U, NY — B
Nazareth Coll of Rochester, NY — B
New York Inst of Technology, NY — B
New York U, NY — B
Niagara U, NY — B
Pace U, NY — B
Roberts Wesleyan Coll, NY — B
St. Bonaventure U, NY — B
St. Francis Coll, NY — B
St. John's U, NY — B
State U of New York Coll at Brockport, NY — B
State U of New York Coll at Cortland, NY — B
State U of New York Coll at Old Westbury, NY — B
State U of New York Coll at Oneonta, NY — B
State U of New York Coll at Potsdam, NY — B
State U of New York Coll of Environmental Science and Forestry, NY — B
Syracuse U, NY — B
U at Albany, State U of New York, NY — B
Utica Coll, NY — B

Child Care and Support Services Management
Post U, CT — A

Child Care Provision
Mercy Coll, NY — A

Child Development
Mitchell Coll, CT — A,B
North Carolina Ag and Tech State U, NC — B
Quinnipiac U, CT — B
State U of New York at Plattsburgh, NY — B
State U of New York Coll at Oneonta, NY — B
Syracuse U, NY — B

Child Guidance
Pace U, NY — B
St. Joseph's Coll, New York, NY — B

Chinese
Bard Coll, NY — B
Brooklyn Coll of the City U of New York, NY — B
Colgate U, NY — B
Cornell U, NY — B
Hobart and William Smith Colls, NY — B
Hunter Coll of the City U of New York, NY — B
United States Military Academy, NY — B
U at Albany, State U of New York, NY — B

Chinese Studies
Sarah Lawrence Coll, NY — B

Cinematography and Film/Video Production
Bard Coll, NY — B
Brooklyn Coll of the City U of New York, NY — B
City Coll of the City U of New York, NY — B
Coll of Staten Island of the City U of New York, NY — B
Five Towns Coll, NY — A,B

Hofstra U, NY — B
Hunter Coll of the City U of New York, NY — B
Ithaca Coll, NY — B
Long Island U, C.W. Post Campus, NY — B
New York U, NY — B
Pratt Inst, NY — B
Purchase Coll, State U of New York, NY — B
Quinnipiac U, CT — B
Rochester Inst of Technology, NY — A,B
Sarah Lawrence Coll, NY — B
School of Visual Arts, NY — B
Syracuse U, NY — B

City/Urban, Community and Regional Planning
Buffalo State Coll, State U of New York, NY — B
Cornell U, NY — B
New York U, NY — B
Pratt Inst, NY — B
State U of New York at New Paltz, NY — B
State U of New York Coll of Environmental Science and Forestry, NY — B

Civil Engineering
City Coll of the City U of New York, NY — B
Clarkson U, NY — B
Columbia U, The Fu Foundation School of Engineering and Applied Science, NY — B
Cornell U, NY — B
Hofstra U, NY — B
Manhattan Coll, NY — B
North Carolina Ag and Tech State U, NC — B
Polytechnic U, Brooklyn Campus, NY — B
Rensselaer Polytechnic Inst, NY — B
State U of New York at Buffalo, NY — B
Syracuse U, NY — B
United States Military Academy, NY — B

Civil Engineering Technology
Rochester Inst of Technology, NY — B
State U of New York Coll of Technology at Alfred, NY — A
State U of New York Coll of Technology at Canton, NY — A
State U of New York Inst of Technology, NY — B

Classical, Ancient Mediterranean and Near Eastern Studies and Archaeology
Columbia Coll, NY — B

Classics
Hunter Coll of the City U of New York, NY — B

Classics and Classical Languages Related
St. Bonaventure U, NY — B

Classics and Languages, Literatures and Linguistics
Bard Coll, NY — B
Barnard Coll, NY — B
Brooklyn Coll of the City U of New York, NY — B
Colgate U, NY — B
The Coll of New Rochelle, NY — B
Columbia Coll, NY — B
Columbia U, School of General Studies, NY — B
Cornell U, NY — B
Elmira Coll, NY — B
Fordham U, NY — B
Hamilton Coll, NY — B
Hobart and William Smith Colls, NY — B
Hofstra U, NY — B
Hunter Coll of the City U of New York, NY — B
Lehman Coll of the City U of New York, NY — B

Manhattan Coll, NY — B
Manhattanville Coll, NY — B
New York U, NY — B
St. Bonaventure U, NY — B
Sarah Lawrence Coll, NY — B
Siena Coll, NY — B
Skidmore Coll, NY — B
State U of New York at Binghamton, NY — B
State U of New York at Buffalo, NY — B
Syracuse U, NY — B
Union Coll, NY — B
U at Albany, State U of New York, NY — B
U of Rochester, NY — B
Vassar Coll, NY — B
Yeshiva U, NY — B

Clinical Child Psychology
St. John's U, NY — B

Clinical Laboratory Science/ Medical Technology
The Coll of Saint Rose, NY — B
Coll of Staten Island of the City U of New York, NY — B
Elmira Coll, NY — B
Hartwick Coll, NY — B
Houghton Coll, NY — B
Iona Coll, NY — B
Keuka Coll, NY — B
Long Island U, Brooklyn Campus, NY — B
Long Island U, C.W. Post Campus, NY — B
Marist Coll, NY — B
Marymount Coll of Fordham U, NY — B
Mercy Coll, NY — B
Mount Saint Mary Coll, NY — B
Pace U, NY — B
Roberts Wesleyan Coll, NY — B
Rochester Inst of Technology, NY — B
St. Francis Coll, NY — B
St. John's U, NY — B
St. Thomas Aquinas Coll, NY — B
State U of New York at Buffalo, NY — B
State U of New York at Plattsburgh, NY — B
State U of New York Coll at Brockport, NY — B
State U of New York, Fredonia, NY — B
State U of New York Upstate Medical U, NY — B
Stony Brook U, State U of New York, NY — B
U of West Florida, FL — B
York Coll of the City U of New York, NY — B

Clinical/Medical Laboratory Science and Allied Professions Related
Hunter Coll of the City U of New York, NY — B

Clinical/Medical Laboratory Technology
Alfred U, NY — B
Coll of Staten Island of the City U of New York, NY — A
Farmingdale State U of New York, NY — A
Long Island U, C.W. Post Campus, NY — B
Mount Saint Mary Coll, NY — B
St. Thomas Aquinas Coll, NY — B
State U of New York Coll of Agriculture and Technology at Cobleskill, NY — A
State U of New York Coll of Technology at Canton, NY — A

Clothing/Textiles
Marymount Coll of Fordham U, NY — B
North Carolina Ag and Tech State U, NC — B
Syracuse U, NY — B

Cognitive Psychology and Psycholinguistics
State U of New York at Oswego, NY — B
Vassar Coll, NY — B

Cognitive Science
Cornell U, NY — B
State U of New York at Oswego, NY — B
U of Rochester, NY — B

Commercial and Advertising Art
Briarcliffe Coll, NY — A
Bryant and Stratton Coll, Amherst Campus, NY — A
Buffalo State Coll, State U of New York, NY — B
The Coll of Saint Rose, NY — B
Dowling Coll, NY — B
Fashion Inst of Technology, NY — A,B
Fordham U, NY — B
Mercy Coll, NY — B
Mitchell Coll, CT — A
Nazareth Coll of Rochester, NY — B
New York Inst of Technology, NY — B
Pace U, NY — A
Pratt Inst, NY — A,B
Sage Coll of Albany, NY — A
St. John's U, NY — B
St. Thomas Aquinas Coll, NY — B
School of Visual Arts, NY — B
State U of New York at New Paltz, NY — B
State U of New York at Oswego, NY — B
State U of New York, Fredonia, NY — B
Syracuse U, NY — B
Villa Maria Coll of Buffalo, NY — A
West Virginia Wesleyan Coll, WV — B

Commercial Photography
Rochester Inst of Technology, NY — B

Communication and Journalism Related
Alfred U, NY — B
Ithaca Coll, NY — B
Lehman Coll of the City U of New York, NY — B
Pace U, NY — B
Quinnipiac U, CT — B
State U of New York Coll at Brockport, NY — B
State U of New York Inst of Technology, NY — B
Syracuse U, NY — B

Communication and Media Related
Canisius Coll, NY — B
Rochester Inst of Technology, NY — B
State U of New York Coll at Brockport, NY — B

Communication Disorders
The Coll of Saint Rose, NY — B
Pace U, NY — B
Queens Coll of the City U of New York, NY — B
State U of New York at Plattsburgh, NY — B
State U of New York, Fredonia, NY — B

Communication Disorders Sciences and Services Related
Long Island U, Brooklyn Campus, NY — B
Syracuse U, NY — B

Communication/Speech Communication and Rhetoric
Adelphi U, NY — B
Brooklyn Coll of the City U of New York, NY — B
Buffalo State Coll, State U of New York, NY — B
Chatham Coll, PA — B
Clarkson U, NY — B
The Coll of Saint Rose, NY — B
Coll of Staten Island of the City U of New York, NY — B

Cornell U, NY — B
Dowling Coll, NY — B
Hofstra U, NY — B
Iona Coll, NY — B
Keuka Coll, NY — B
Le Moyne Coll, NY — B
Long Island U, Brooklyn Campus, NY — B
Long Island U, C.W. Post Campus, NY — B
Marist Coll, NY — B
Molloy Coll, NY — B
New York U, NY — B
Nyack Coll, NY — B
Pace U, NY — B
Prescott Coll, AZ — B
Purchase Coll, State U of New York, NY — B
Queens Coll of the City U of New York, NY — B
Rensselaer Polytechnic Inst, NY — B
Roberts Wesleyan Coll, NY — B
Sage Coll of Albany, NY — A
St. Francis Coll, NY — B
St. John's U, NY — B
Shepherd U, WV — B
State U of New York at Buffalo, NY — B
State U of New York at Plattsburgh, NY — B
State U of New York Coll at Brockport, NY — B
State U of New York Coll at Cortland, NY — B
State U of New York Coll at Geneseo, NY — B
State U of New York Coll at Old Westbury, NY — B
Syracuse U, NY — B
U of West Florida, FL — B
Utica Coll, NY — B
West Virginia Wesleyan Coll, WV — B

Communications Technologies and Support Services Related
Hofstra U, NY — B

Communications Technology
The Coll of Saint Rose, NY — B

Community Health and Preventive Medicine
Hofstra U, NY — B

Community Health Services Counseling
Long Island U, Brooklyn Campus, NY — B
Marymount Coll of Fordham U, NY — B
U of West Florida, FL — B

Community Organization and Advocacy
Cazenovia Coll, NY — A,B
Cornell U, NY — B
Pace U, NY — B
State U of New York Empire State Coll, NY — A,B

Community Psychology
New York Inst of Technology, NY — B

Comparative Literature
Bard Coll, NY — B
Barnard Coll, NY — B
Brooklyn Coll of the City U of New York, NY — B
Columbia Coll, NY — B
Columbia U, School of General Studies, NY — B
Cornell U, NY — B
Fordham U, NY — B
Hamilton Coll, NY — B
Hobart and William Smith Colls, NY — B
Hofstra U, NY — B
Hunter Coll of the City U of New York, NY — B
New York U, NY — B
Queens Coll of the City U of New York, NY — B
Sarah Lawrence Coll, NY — B

A—associate degree; B—bachelor's degree

State U of New York at
  Binghamton, NY — B
State U of New York at New
  Paltz, NY — B
State U of New York Coll at
  Geneseo, NY — B
Stony Brook U, State U of New
  York, NY — B
U of Rochester, NY — B

Computational Mathematics
Brooklyn Coll of the City U of
  New York, NY — B

**Computer and Information
Sciences**
Adelphi U, NY — B
Alfred U, NY — B
Barnard Coll, NY — B
Brooklyn Coll of the City U of
  New York, NY — B
Bryant and Stratton Coll,
  Amherst Campus, NY — A
Chaminade U of Honolulu, HI — A,B
Chatham Coll, PA — B
Clarkson U, NY — B
The Coll of Saint Rose, NY — B
Coll of Staten Island of the City
  U of New York, NY — B
Cornell U, NY — B
Dominican Coll, NY — B
Dowling Coll, NY — B
Fordham U, NY — B
Globe Inst of Technology, NY — A,B
Hartwick Coll, NY — B
Ithaca Coll, NY — B
Lehman Coll of the City U of
  New York, NY — B
Long Island U, Brooklyn
  Campus, NY — B
Long Island U, C.W. Post
  Campus, NY — B
Marymount Coll of Fordham U,
  NY — B
Medaille Coll, NY — B
Mount Saint Mary Coll, NY — B
New York Inst of Technology, NY — B
New York U, NY — B
Pace U, NY — B
Prescott Coll, AZ — B
Rensselaer Polytechnic Inst, NY — B
Rochester Inst of Technology, NY — B
Sage Coll of Albany, NY — A,B
St. John's U, NY — B
Shepherd U, WV — B
Siena Coll, NY — B
Skidmore Coll, NY — B
State U of New York Coll at Old
  Westbury, NY — B
State U of New York Coll at
  Potsdam, NY — B
State U of New York Coll of
  Technology at Alfred, NY — A,B
State U of New York Inst of
  Technology, NY — B
Syracuse U, NY — B
Union Coll, NY — B
U at Albany, State U of New
  York, NY — B
U of West Florida, FL — B
Utica Coll, NY — B
Vassar Coll, NY — B
West Virginia Wesleyan Coll,
  WV — B

**Computer and Information
Sciences and Support Services
Related**
Coll of Staten Island of the City
  U of New York, NY — B
Dowling Coll, NY — B
Long Island U, C.W. Post
  Campus, NY — B
Roberts Wesleyan Coll, NY — B

**Computer and Information
Systems Security**
Rochester Inst of Technology, NY — B

Computer Engineering
Clarkson U, NY — B
Columbia U, The Fu Foundation
  School of Engineering and
  Applied Science, NY — B
Hofstra U, NY — B

Manhattan Coll, NY — B
Polytechnic U, Brooklyn Campus,
  NY — B
Rensselaer Polytechnic Inst, NY — B
Rochester Inst of Technology, NY — B
State U of New York at
  Binghamton, NY — B
State U of New York at Buffalo,
  NY — B
State U of New York at New
  Paltz, NY — B
Syracuse U, NY — B
United States Military Academy,
  NY — B
U of West Florida, FL — B

Computer Engineering Technology
DeVry Inst of Technology, NY — B
Excelsior Coll, NY — A,B
Farmingdale State U of New
  York, NY — B
Marist Coll, NY — B
Rochester Inst of Technology, NY — B
State U of New York Coll of
  Technology at Alfred, NY — A,B
State U of New York Inst of
  Technology, NY — B

Computer Graphics
Brooklyn Coll of the City U of
  New York, NY — B
Pratt Inst, NY — B
Rochester Inst of Technology, NY — B
School of Visual Arts, NY — B
State U of New York Coll at
  Oneonta, NY — B
State U of New York Coll of
  Technology at Alfred, NY — A
State U of New York, Fredonia,
  NY — B
Syracuse U, NY — B
Vaughn Coll of Aeronautics and
  Technology, NY — A,B

Computer Hardware Engineering
Rochester Inst of Technology, NY — B
State U of New York Coll of
  Technology at Alfred, NY — B
Stony Brook U, State U of New
  York, NY — B

**Computer/Information Technology
Services Administration Related**
Maria Coll, NY — A
Medgar Evers Coll of the City U
  of New York, NY — A
State U of New York Coll of
  Technology at Alfred, NY — B
State U of New York Coll of
  Technology at Canton, NY — A,B
State U of New York Coll of
  Technology at Delhi, NY — B

**Computer Installation and Repair
Technology**
State U of New York Coll of
  Technology at Alfred, NY — A

Computer Management
Five Towns Coll, NY — A
Fordham U, NY — B
Lehman Coll of the City U of
  New York, NY — B
Villa Maria Coll of Buffalo, NY — A
York Coll of the City U of New
  York, NY — B

Computer Programming
Briarcliffe Coll, NY — A
Coll of Staten Island of the City
  U of New York, NY — A
Farmingdale State U of New
  York, NY — A,B
Globe Inst of Technology, NY — B
Medaille Coll, NY — B
New York U, NY — A
State U of New York Coll of
  Agriculture and Technology at
  Cobleskill, NY — A

Computer Programming Related
Farmingdale State U of New
  York, NY — B

**Computer Programming (Specific
Applications)**
Rochester Inst of Technology, NY — B

Computer Science
Bard Coll, NY — B
Canisius Coll, NY — B
City Coll of the City U of New
  York, NY — B
Clarkson U, NY — B
Colgate U, NY — B
Coll of Mount Saint Vincent, NY — B
Columbia Coll, NY — B
Columbia U, School of General
  Studies, NY — B
Columbia U, The Fu Foundation
  School of Engineering and
  Applied Science, NY — B
Cornell U, NY — B
Excelsior Coll, NY — A,B
Farmingdale State U of New
  York, NY — A
Fordham U, NY — B
Hamilton Coll, NY — B
Hartwick Coll, NY — B
Hobart and William Smith Colls,
  NY — B
Hofstra U, NY — B
Houghton Coll, NY — B
Hunter Coll of the City U of
  New York, NY — B
Iona Coll, NY — B
Ithaca Coll, NY — B
Lehman Coll of the City U of
  New York, NY — B
Long Island U, Brooklyn
  Campus, NY — B
Long Island U, C.W. Post
  Campus, NY — B
Manhattan Coll, NY — B
Manhattanville Coll, NY — B
Marist Coll, NY — B
Medgar Evers Coll of the City U
  of New York, NY — A
Mercy Coll, NY — B
Molloy Coll, NY — B
Monroe Coll, Bronx, NY — A
Monroe Coll, New Rochelle, NY — A
Mount Saint Mary Coll, NY — B
New York U, NY — B
Niagara U, NY — B
North Carolina Ag and Tech
  State U, NC — B
Nyack Coll, NY — B
Polytechnic U, Brooklyn Campus,
  NY — B
Queens Coll of the City U of
  New York, NY — B
Quinnipiac U, CT — B
Rensselaer Polytechnic Inst, NY — B
Roberts Wesleyan Coll, NY — B
Rochester Inst of Technology, NY — A,B
St. Bonaventure U, NY — B
St. John Fisher Coll, NY — B
St. Joseph's Coll, Suffolk Campus,
  NY — B
St. Lawrence U, NY — B
Sarah Lawrence Coll, NY — B
State U of New York at
  Binghamton, NY — B
State U of New York at Buffalo,
  NY — B
State U of New York at New
  Paltz, NY — B
State U of New York at Oswego,
  NY — B
State U of New York at
  Plattsburgh, NY — B
State U of New York Coll at
  Brockport, NY — B
State U of New York Coll at
  Geneseo, NY — B
State U of New York Coll at
  Oneonta, NY — B
State U of New York Coll of
  Agriculture and Technology at
  Cobleskill, NY — A
State U of New York Coll of
  Technology at Alfred, NY — A
State U of New York, Fredonia,
  NY — B
State U of New York Inst of
  Technology, NY — B

Stony Brook U, State U of New
  York, NY — B
United States Military Academy,
  NY — B
U at Albany, State U of New
  York, NY — B
U of Rochester, NY — B
Wagner Coll, NY — B
Wells Coll, NY — B
West Virginia Wesleyan Coll,
  WV — B
Yeshiva U, NY — B

Computer Software Engineering
Clarkson U, NY — B
Rochester Inst of Technology, NY — B

Computer Systems Analysis
DeVry Inst of Technology, NY — B
Rochester Inst of Technology, NY — B

**Computer Systems Networking
and Telecommunications**
DeVry Inst of Technology, NY — B
Rochester Inst of Technology, NY — B
Sage Coll of Albany, NY — A,B

Computer Teacher Education
Long Island U, Brooklyn
  Campus, NY — B
Utica Coll, NY — B

Computer/Technical Support
State U of New York Coll of
  Technology at Alfred, NY — B

**Computer Technology/Computer
Systems Technology**
State U of New York Coll of
  Agriculture and Technology at
  Cobleskill, NY — A

**Computer Typography and
Composition Equipment Operation**
State U of New York Coll of
  Technology at Alfred, NY — A

Construction Engineering
Clarkson U, NY — B
State U of New York Coll of
  Environmental Science and
  Forestry, NY — B
State U of New York Coll of
  Technology at Alfred, NY — A,B

**Construction Engineering
Technology**
Coll of Staten Island of the City
  U of New York, NY — A
Farmingdale State U of New
  York, NY — B
State U of New York Coll of
  Technology at Alfred, NY — A
State U of New York Coll of
  Technology at Canton, NY — A
State U of New York Coll of
  Technology at Delhi, NY — A

Construction Management
Farmingdale State U of New
  York, NY — B
North Carolina Ag and Tech
  State U, NC — B
Polytechnic U, Brooklyn Campus,
  NY — B
Pratt Inst, NY — A,B
State U of New York Coll of
  Technology at Delhi, NY — A

Consumer Economics
Cornell U, NY — B

**Consumer Merchandising/Retailing
Management**
Syracuse U, NY — B

Consumer Services and Advocacy
State U of New York Coll at
  Oneonta, NY — B
Syracuse U, NY — B

Corrections
John Jay Coll of Criminal Justice
  of the City U of New York, NY — A,B
State U of New York Coll at
  Brockport, NY — B
State U of New York Coll of
  Technology at Canton, NY — A

Corrections and Criminal Justice Related
John Jay Coll of Criminal Justice of the City U of New York, NY — B
Monroe Coll, New Rochelle, NY — A,B
State U of New York Coll at Brockport, NY — B

Counseling Psychology
Chatham Coll, PA — B

Counselor Education/School Counseling and Guidance
Cornell U, NY — B
St. John's U, NY — B

Court Reporting
State U of New York Coll of Technology at Alfred, NY — A

Crafts, Folk Art and Artisanry
Rochester Inst of Technology, NY — B

Creative Writing
Bard Coll, NY — B
Bernard M. Baruch Coll of the City U of New York, NY — B
Brooklyn Coll of the City U of New York, NY — B
Chatham Coll, PA — B
City Coll of the City U of New York, NY — B
Columbia Coll, NY — B
Cornell U, NY — B
Fordham U, NY — B
Hamilton Coll, NY — B
Hofstra U, NY — B
Houghton Coll, NY — B
Ithaca Coll, NY — B
Lehman Coll of the City U of New York, NY — B
Le Moyne Coll, NY — B
Marymount Coll of Fordham U, NY — B
Medaille Coll, NY — B
Nazareth Coll of Rochester, NY — B
Pratt Inst, NY — B
Purchase Coll, State U of New York, NY — B
St. Lawrence U, NY — B
Sarah Lawrence Coll, NY — B
State U of New York at New Paltz, NY — B
State U of New York at Oswego, NY — B
State U of New York Coll at Brockport, NY — B
Wells Coll, NY — B
West Virginia Wesleyan Coll, WV — B

Criminal Justice/Law Enforcement Administration
Adelphi U, NY — B
Alfred U, NY — B
Buffalo State Coll, State U of New York, NY — B
Canisius Coll, NY — B
The Coll of Saint Rose, NY — B
Elmira Coll, NY — B
Farmingdale State U of New York, NY — A
Fordham U, NY — B
Hilbert Coll, NY — A,B
Iona Coll, NY — B
John Jay Coll of Criminal Justice of the City U of New York, NY — B
Keuka Coll, NY — B
Long Island U, C.W. Post Campus, NY — B
Marist Coll, NY — B
Mercy Coll, NY — B
Mitchell Coll, CT — A,B
Monroe Coll, Bronx, NY — A,B
New York Inst of Technology, NY — B
Niagara U, NY — B
Pace U, NY — B
Post U, CT — B
Roberts Wesleyan Coll, NY — B
Rochester Inst of Technology, NY — B
Russell Sage Coll, NY — B
Sage Coll of Albany, NY — B
St. John's U, NY — A,B

St. Thomas Aquinas Coll, NY — B
State U of New York at Oswego, NY — B
State U of New York Coll at Brockport, NY — B
State U of New York Coll of Technology at Canton, NY — A
State U of New York, Fredonia, NY — B
U at Albany, State U of New York, NY — B
Utica Coll, NY — B
West Virginia Wesleyan Coll, WV — B

Criminal Justice/Police Science
Hilbert Coll, NY — B
John Jay Coll of Criminal Justice of the City U of New York, NY — A,B
Monroe Coll, Bronx, NY — A,B
State U of New York Coll at Brockport, NY — B
State U of New York Coll of Technology at Canton, NY — A,B

Criminal Justice/Safety
Cazenovia Coll, NY — A,B
Long Island U, Brentwood Campus, NY — B
Long Island U, C.W. Post Campus, NY — B
Medaille Coll, NY — B
Molloy Coll, NY — B
Mount Saint Mary Coll, NY — B
Prescott Coll, AZ — B
Quinnipiac U, CT — B
Rochester Inst of Technology, NY — B
St. Francis Coll, NY — A,B
Shepherd U, WV — A
State U of New York Coll at Oneonta, NY — B
State U of New York Coll at Potsdam, NY — B
U of West Florida, FL — B

Criminology
Chaminade U of Honolulu, HI — A,B
Le Moyne Coll, NY — B
Niagara U, NY — B
St. John's U, NY — B
State U of New York at Plattsburgh, NY — B
State U of New York Coll at Brockport, NY — B
State U of New York Coll at Cortland, NY — B
State U of New York Coll at Old Westbury, NY — B

Critical Care Nursing
State U of New York at Buffalo, NY — B

Crop Production
Cornell U, NY — B

Culinary Arts
Baltimore International Coll, MD — A,B
The Culinary Inst of America, NY — A,B
Paul Smith's Coll of Arts and Sciences, NY — A,B
State U of New York Coll of Agriculture and Technology at Cobleskill, NY — A
State U of New York Coll of Technology at Alfred, NY — A
State U of New York Coll of Technology at Delhi, NY — A,B

Culinary Arts Related
The Culinary Inst of America, NY — A,B
New York Inst of Technology, NY — A
Shepherd U, WV — A

Cultural Studies
Bard Coll, NY — B
Houghton Coll, NY — B
The Jewish Theological Seminary, NY — B

Curriculum and Instruction
St. John's U, NY — B

Cytotechnology
The Coll of Saint Rose, NY — B
Long Island U, Brooklyn Campus, NY — B
Long Island U, C.W. Post Campus, NY — B
St. John's U, NY — B
State U of New York Upstate Medical U, NY — B
Stony Brook U, State U of New York, NY — B

Dairy Science
Cornell U, NY — B
State U of New York Coll of Agriculture and Technology at Cobleskill, NY — A,B
State U of New York Coll of Technology at Alfred, NY — A

Dance
Adelphi U, NY — B
Bard Coll, NY — B
Barnard Coll, NY — B
Columbia Coll, NY — B
Columbia U, School of General Studies, NY — B
Cornell U, NY — B
Fordham U, NY — B
Hamilton Coll, NY — B
Hobart and William Smith Colls, NY — B
Hofstra U, NY — B
Hunter Coll of the City U of New York, NY — B
Ithaca Coll, NY — B
The Juilliard School, NY — B
Lehman Coll of the City U of New York, NY — B
Long Island U, Brooklyn Campus, NY — B
Long Island U, C.W. Post Campus, NY — B
Manhattanville Coll, NY — B
Marymount Manhattan Coll, NY — B
New York U, NY — B
Prescott Coll, AZ — B
Purchase Coll, State U of New York, NY — B
Queens Coll of the City U of New York, NY — B
Sarah Lawrence Coll, NY — B
Skidmore Coll, NY — B
State U of New York at Buffalo, NY — B
State U of New York Coll at Brockport, NY — B
State U of New York Coll at Potsdam, NY — B
State U of New York, Fredonia, NY — B
Wells Coll, NY — B

Dance Related
Sarah Lawrence Coll, NY — B

Data Modeling/Warehousing and Database Administration
Rochester Inst of Technology, NY — B

Data Processing and Data Processing Technology
Farmingdale State U of New York, NY — A
Five Towns Coll, NY — A
Long Island U, Brooklyn Campus, NY — B
New York Inst of Technology, NY — A
St. Francis Coll, NY — A
St. John's U, NY — A
State U of New York Coll of Agriculture and Technology at Cobleskill, NY — A
State U of New York Coll of Technology at Alfred, NY — A

Demography and Population
Cornell U, NY — B

Dental Hygiene
Farmingdale State U of New York, NY — A,B
New York U, NY — A,B

Design and Applied Arts Related
Daemen Coll, NY — B
Fashion Inst of Technology, NY — B
New York Inst of Technology, NY — B
Pratt Inst, NY — B

Design and Visual Communications
Buffalo State Coll, State U of New York, NY — B
Cazenovia Coll, NY — B
Cornell U, NY — B
Farmingdale State U of New York, NY — B
Pace U, NY — A
Rochester Inst of Technology, NY — A
Shepherd U, WV — A
Syracuse U, NY — B

Developmental and Child Psychology
Brooklyn Coll of the City U of New York, NY — B
Cornell U, NY — B
Mitchell Coll, CT — A
Quinnipiac U, CT — B
St. Joseph's Coll, New York, NY — B
St. Joseph's Coll, Suffolk Campus, NY — B
Sarah Lawrence Coll, NY — B
Utica Coll, NY — B

Diagnostic Medical Sonography and Ultrasound Technology
New York U, NY — A
Rochester Inst of Technology, NY — B
State U of New York Downstate Medical Center, NY — B

Dietetics
Buffalo State Coll, State U of New York, NY — B
D'Youville Coll, NY — B
Lehman Coll of the City U of New York, NY — B
Marymount Coll of Fordham U, NY — B
North Carolina Ag and Tech State U, NC — B
Rochester Inst of Technology, NY — A,B
State U of New York Coll at Oneonta, NY — B
Syracuse U, NY — B

Digital Communication and Media/Multimedia
Canisius Coll, NY — B
Clarkson U, NY — B
Marist Coll, NY — B
New York U, NY — B

Directing and Theatrical Production
Sarah Lawrence Coll, NY — B

Divinity/Ministry
Roberts Wesleyan Coll, NY — B
St. John's U, NY — B

Drafting and Design Technology
State U of New York Coll of Technology at Alfred, NY — A
State U of New York Coll of Technology at Delhi, NY — A

Dramatic/Theater Arts
Adelphi U, NY — B
Alfred U, NY — B
Bard Coll, NY — B
Barnard Coll, NY — B
Buffalo State Coll, State U of New York, NY — B
Chatham Coll, PA — B
City Coll of the City U of New York, NY — B
Colgate U, NY — B
Coll of Staten Island of the City U of New York, NY — B
Columbia Coll, NY — B
Columbia U, School of General Studies, NY — B
Cornell U, NY — B
Elmira Coll, NY — B
Five Towns Coll, NY — A,B
Fordham U, NY — B

A—associate degree; B—bachelor's degree

Hamilton Coll, NY — B
Hartwick Coll, NY — B
Hobart and William Smith Colls, NY
Hofstra U, NY — B
Hunter Coll of the City U of New York, NY — B
Iona Coll, NY — B
Ithaca Coll, NY — B
Lehman Coll of the City U of New York, NY — B
Le Moyne Coll, NY — B
Long Island U, C.W. Post Campus, NY — B
Marist Coll, NY — B
Marymount Coll of Fordham U, NY
Marymount Manhattan Coll, NY — B
Nazareth Coll of Rochester, NY — B
New York U, NY — B
Niagara U, NY — B
North Carolina Ag and Tech State U, NC — B
Prescott Coll, AZ — B
Purchase Coll, State U of New York, NY
Queens Coll of the City U of New York, NY — B
Russell Sage Coll, NY — B
St. Lawrence U, NY — B
Sarah Lawrence Coll, NY — B
Skidmore Coll, NY — B
State U of New York at Binghamton, NY — B
State U of New York at Buffalo, NY — B
State U of New York at New Paltz, NY — B
State U of New York at Oswego, NY — B
State U of New York at Plattsburgh, NY — B
State U of New York Coll at Brockport, NY — B
State U of New York Coll at Geneseo, NY — B
State U of New York Coll at Oneonta, NY — B
State U of New York Coll at Potsdam, NY — B
State U of New York, Fredonia, NY — B
Stony Brook U, State U of New York, NY — B
Syracuse U, NY — B
U at Albany, State U of New York, NY — B
U of West Florida, FL — B
Vassar Coll, NY — B
Wagner Coll, NY — B
Wells Coll, NY — B
West Virginia Wesleyan Coll, WV — B
Yeshiva U, NY — B
York Coll of the City U of New York, NY — B

Dramatic/Theater Arts and Stagecraft Related
State U of New York at Buffalo, NY — B

Drawing
Bard Coll, NY — B
Buffalo State Coll, State U of New York, NY — B
Nazareth Coll of Rochester, NY — B
Pratt Inst, NY — A,B
Sarah Lawrence Coll, NY — B
School of Visual Arts, NY — B
State U of New York at Binghamton, NY — B
State U of New York at New Paltz, NY — B
State U of New York Coll at Brockport, NY — B
State U of New York, Fredonia, NY — B
West Virginia Wesleyan Coll, WV — B

Early Childhood Education
Brooklyn Coll of the City U of New York, NY — B

Canisius Coll, NY — B
Cazenovia Coll, NY — B
Chaminade U of Honolulu, HI — B
City Coll of the City U of New York, NY — B
Daemen Coll, NY — B
Hofstra U, NY — B
Iona Coll, NY — B
St. Bonaventure U, NY — B
St. John's U, NY — B
St. Joseph's Coll, Suffolk Campus, NY
Sarah Lawrence Coll, NY — B
State U of New York Coll at Brockport, NY — B
State U of New York Coll at Old Westbury, NY — B
State U of New York Coll at Oneonta, NY — B
U of West Florida, FL — B

East Asian Languages
Columbia Coll, NY — B
Cornell U, NY — B

Ecology
Adelphi U, NY — B
Bard Coll, NY — B
Clarkson U, NY — B
Concordia Coll, NY — B
Cornell U, NY — B
Iona Coll, NY — B
Pace U, NY — B
Paul Smith's Coll of Arts and Sciences, NY — A
Prescott Coll, AZ — B
St. John's U, NY — B
Sarah Lawrence Coll, NY — B
Siena Coll, NY — B
State U of New York Coll of Environmental Science and Forestry, NY — B

Econometrics and Quantitative Economics
State U of New York at Oswego, NY — B

Economics
Adelphi U, NY — B
Alfred U, NY — B
Bard Coll, NY — B
Barnard Coll, NY — B
Bernard M. Baruch Coll of the City of New York, NY — B
Brooklyn Coll of the City U of New York, NY — B
Buffalo State Coll, State U of New York, NY — B
Canisius Coll, NY — B
Chatham Coll, PA — B
City Coll of the City U of New York, NY — B
Colgate U, NY — B
Coll of Mount Saint Vincent, NY — B
The Coll of New Rochelle, NY — B
Coll of Staten Island of the City U of New York, NY — B
Columbia Coll, NY — B
Columbia U, School of General Studies, NY — B
Cornell U, NY — B
Dominican Coll, NY — B
Dowling Coll, NY — B
Elmira Coll, NY — B
Excelsior Coll, NY — B
Fordham U, NY — B
Hamilton Coll, NY — B
Hartwick Coll, NY — B
Hobart and William Smith Colls, NY — B
Hofstra U, NY — B
Hunter Coll of the City U of New York, NY — B
Iona Coll, NY — B
Ithaca Coll, NY — B
Lehman Coll of the City U of New York, NY — B
Le Moyne Coll, NY — B
Long Island U, Brooklyn Campus, NY — B
Long Island U, C.W. Post Campus, NY — B
Manhattan Coll, NY — B

Manhattanville Coll, NY — B
Marist Coll, NY — B
Marymount Coll of Fordham U, NY
Nazareth Coll of Rochester, NY — B
New York Inst of Technology, NY — B
New York U, NY — B
Niagara U, NY — B
North Carolina Ag and Tech State U, NC — B
Pace U, NY — B
Purchase Coll, State U of New York, NY — B
Queens Coll of the City U of New York, NY — B
Quinnipiac U, CT — B
Rensselaer Polytechnic Inst, NY — B
Rochester Inst of Technology, NY — B
St. Francis Coll, NY — B
St. John Fisher Coll, NY — B
St. John's U, NY — B
St. Joseph's Coll, Suffolk Campus, NY — B
St. Lawrence U, NY — B
Sarah Lawrence Coll, NY — B
Shepherd U, WV — B
Siena Coll, NY — B
Skidmore Coll, NY — B
State U of New York at Binghamton, NY — B
State U of New York at Buffalo, NY — B
State U of New York at New Paltz, NY — B
State U of New York at Oswego, NY — B
State U of New York at Plattsburgh, NY — B
State U of New York Coll at Brockport, NY — B
State U of New York Coll at Cortland, NY — B
State U of New York Coll at Geneseo, NY — B
State U of New York Coll at Oneonta, NY — B
State U of New York Coll at Potsdam, NY — B
State U of New York Empire State Coll, NY — A,B
State U of New York, Fredonia, NY — B
Stony Brook U, State U of New York, NY — B
Syracuse U, NY — B
Union Coll, NY — B
United States Military Academy, NY — B
U at Albany, State U of New York, NY — B
U of Rochester, NY — B
Utica Coll, NY — B
Vassar Coll, NY — B
Wells Coll, NY — B
West Virginia Wesleyan Coll, WV — B
Yeshiva U, NY — B
York Coll of the City U of New York, NY — B

Economics Related
Barnard Coll, NY — B
State U of New York at Buffalo, NY — B

Education
Adelphi U, NY — B
Bernard M. Baruch Coll of the City U of New York, NY — B
Brooklyn Coll of the City U of New York, NY — B
City Coll of the City U of New York, NY — B
Colgate U, NY — B
Coll of Mount Saint Vincent, NY — B
The Coll of New Rochelle, NY — B
Concordia Coll, NY — B
Cornell U, NY — B
Dominican Coll, NY — B
Dowling Coll, NY — B
D'Youville Coll, NY — B
Elmira Coll, NY — B
Fordham U, NY — B

Hofstra U, NY — B
Iona Coll, NY — B
The King's Coll, NY — B
Long Island U, Brooklyn Campus, NY — B
Long Island U, C.W. Post Campus, NY — B
Manhattan Coll, NY — B
Manhattanville Coll, NY — B
Marymount Coll of Fordham U, NY — B
Medaille Coll, NY — B
Medgar Evers Coll of the City U of New York, NY — A,B
Mercy Coll, NY — B
Molloy Coll, NY — B
Mount Saint Mary Coll, NY — B
Nazareth Coll of Rochester, NY — B
New York Inst of Technology, NY — B
New York U, NY — B
Niagara U, NY — B
North Carolina Ag and Tech State U, NC — B
Prescott Coll, AZ — B
Quinnipiac U, CT — B
Roberts Wesleyan Coll, NY — B
St. Joseph's Coll, New York, NY — B
St. Joseph's Coll, Suffolk Campus, NY — B
St. Thomas Aquinas Coll, NY — B
Sarah Lawrence Coll, NY — B
State U of New York at New Paltz, NY — B
State U of New York at Oswego, NY — B
State U of New York at Plattsburgh, NY — B
State U of New York Coll at Brockport, NY — B
State U of New York Coll at Geneseo, NY — B
State U of New York Coll at Oneonta, NY — B
State U of New York Empire State Coll, NY — A,B
State U of New York, Fredonia, NY — B
Villa Maria Coll of Buffalo, NY — A
Wagner Coll, NY — B
Wells Coll, NY — B
West Virginia Wesleyan Coll, WV — B
Yeshiva U, NY — B

Educational Administration and Supervision Related
Cazenovia Coll, NY — B

Educational/Instructional Media Design
Ithaca Coll, NY — B

Educational Leadership and Administration
Cornell U, NY — B
St. John's U, NY — B

Educational Psychology
Cornell U, NY — B

Educational Statistics and Research Methods
Cornell U, NY — B

Education (K–12)
Columbia Coll, NY — B
D'Youville Coll, NY — B
Ithaca Coll, NY — B
Mount Saint Mary Coll, NY — B
Syracuse U, NY — B
West Virginia Wesleyan Coll, WV — B

Education (Multiple Levels)
Iona Coll, NY — B
Ithaca Coll, NY — B
Manhattan Coll, NY — B

Education Related
Long Island U, Brooklyn Campus, NY — B
Pace U, NY — B
State U of New York Coll at Potsdam, NY — B
Syracuse U, NY — B

Peterson's Colleges in New York 2006
www.petersons.com
203

Education (Specific Subject Areas) Related
Hofstra U, NY — B
Syracuse U, NY — B

Electrical and Electronic Engineering Technologies Related
New York Inst of Technology, NY — A,B

Electrical and Power Transmission Installation
State U of New York Coll of Technology at Delhi, NY — A

Electrical, Electronic and Communications Engineering Technology
Briarcliffe Coll, NY — A
Bryant and Stratton Coll, Amherst Campus, NY — A
Buffalo State Coll, State U of New York, NY — B
DeVry Inst of Technology, NY — A,B
Excelsior Coll, NY — A,B
Farmingdale State U of New York, NY — B
New York Inst of Technology, NY — B
Rochester Inst of Technology, NY — A,B
Shepherd U, WV — A
State U of New York Coll of Technology at Alfred, NY — A,B
State U of New York Coll of Technology at Canton, NY — A
State U of New York Inst of Technology, NY — B

Electrical, Electronics and Communications Engineering
Alfred U, NY — B
City Coll of the City U of New York, NY — B
Clarkson U, NY — B
Columbia U, The Fu Foundation School of Engineering and Applied Science, NY — B
Cornell U, NY — B
Hofstra U, NY — B
Manhattan Coll, NY — B
New York Inst of Technology, NY — B
North Carolina Ag and Tech State U, NC — B
Polytechnic U, Brooklyn Campus, NY — B
Rensselaer Polytechnic Inst, NY — B
Rochester Inst of Technology, NY — B
State U of New York at Binghamton, NY — B
State U of New York at Buffalo, NY — B
State U of New York at New Paltz, NY — B
Stony Brook U, State U of New York, NY — B
Syracuse U, NY — B
Union Coll, NY — B
United States Military Academy, NY — B
U of Rochester, NY — B
U of West Florida, FL — B

Electrical/Electronics Equipment Installation and Repair
State U of New York Coll of Technology at Alfred, NY — A

Electromechanical Technology
Buffalo State Coll, State U of New York, NY — B
Excelsior Coll, NY — A,B
Rochester Inst of Technology, NY — B
Shepherd U, WV — A
State U of New York Coll of Technology at Alfred, NY — A,B

Elementary Education
Alfred U, NY — B
Boricua Coll, NY — B
Brooklyn Coll of the City U of New York, NY — B
Buffalo State Coll, State U of New York, NY — B
Chaminade U of Honolulu, HI — B
Chatham Coll, PA — B

City Coll of the City U of New York, NY — B
Coll of Mount Saint Vincent, NY — B
The Coll of New Rochelle, NY — B
The Coll of Saint Rose, NY — B
Concordia Coll, NY — B
Daemen Coll, NY — B
Dominican Coll, NY — B
Dowling Coll, NY — B
D'Youville Coll, NY — B
Elmira Coll, NY — B
Five Towns Coll, NY — B
Fordham U, NY — B
Hofstra U, NY — B
Houghton Coll, NY — B
Hunter Coll of the City U of New York, NY — B
Iona Coll, NY — B
Keuka Coll, NY — B
The King's Coll, NY — B
Le Moyne Coll, NY — B
Long Island U, Brooklyn Campus, NY — B
Long Island U, C.W. Post Campus, NY — B
Manhattan Coll, NY — B
Manhattanville Coll, NY — B
Marist Coll, NY — B
Marymount Coll of Fordham U, NY — B
Medaille Coll, NY — B
Mercy Coll, NY — B
Molloy Coll, NY — B
Mount Saint Mary Coll, NY — B
Nazareth Coll of Rochester, NY — B
New York Inst of Technology, NY — B
New York U, NY — B
Niagara U, NY — B
North Carolina Ag and Tech State U, NC — B
Nyack Coll, NY — B
Pace U, NY — B
Prescott Coll, AZ — B
Queens Coll of the City U of New York, NY — B
Roberts Wesleyan Coll, NY — B
Russell Sage Coll, NY — B
St. Bonaventure U, NY — B
St. John Fisher Coll, NY — B
St. John's U, NY — B
St. Joseph's Coll, Suffolk Campus, NY — B
St. Thomas Aquinas Coll, NY — B
Sarah Lawrence Coll, NY — B
Shepherd U, WV — B
Skidmore Coll, NY — B
State U of New York at New Paltz, NY — B
State U of New York at Oswego, NY — B
State U of New York at Plattsburgh, NY — B
State U of New York Coll at Brockport, NY — B
State U of New York Coll at Cortland, NY — B
State U of New York Coll at Geneseo, NY — B
State U of New York Coll at Old Westbury, NY — B
State U of New York Coll at Oneonta, NY — B
State U of New York Coll at Potsdam, NY — B
State U of New York, Fredonia, NY — B
U of West Florida, FL — B
Utica Coll, NY — B
Wagner Coll, NY — B
Wells Coll, NY — B
West Virginia Wesleyan Coll, WV — B
Yeshiva U, NY — B

Emergency Medical Technology (EMT Paramedic)
Shepherd U, WV — A

Engineering
Buffalo State Coll, State U of New York, NY — B
Chatham Coll, PA — B

Clarkson U, NY — B
Coll of Staten Island of the City U of New York, NY — A,B
Cornell U, NY — B
Manhattan Coll, NY — B
Mitchell Coll, CT — A
Rensselaer Polytechnic Inst, NY — B
Rochester Inst of Technology, NY — B
Russell Sage Coll, NY — B
Stony Brook U, State U of New York, NY — B
United States Military Academy, NY — B
Wells Coll, NY — B

Engineering/Industrial Management
Columbia U, The Fu Foundation School of Engineering and Applied Science, NY — B
Farmingdale State U of New York, NY — B
United States Merchant Marine Academy, NY — B
United States Military Academy, NY — B

Engineering Mechanics
Columbia U, The Fu Foundation School of Engineering and Applied Science, NY — B
West Virginia Wesleyan Coll, WV — B

Engineering Physics
Columbia U, The Fu Foundation School of Engineering and Applied Science, NY — B
Cornell U, NY — B
North Carolina Ag and Tech State U, NC — B
Rensselaer Polytechnic Inst, NY — B
St. Bonaventure U, NY — B
State U of New York at Buffalo, NY — B
State U of New York at New Paltz, NY — B
Syracuse U, NY — B
United States Military Academy, NY — B
West Virginia Wesleyan Coll, WV — B

Engineering Related
Canisius Coll, NY — B
Dowling Coll, NY — B
New York U, NY — B
Rochester Inst of Technology, NY — B
Syracuse U, NY — B

Engineering-Related Technologies
Rochester Inst of Technology, NY — B
United States Merchant Marine Academy, NY — B

Engineering Science
Hofstra U, NY — B
Rensselaer Polytechnic Inst, NY — B
Rochester Inst of Technology, NY — A
St. Thomas Aquinas Coll, NY — B
State U of New York Coll at Oneonta, NY — B
State U of New York Coll of Technology at Alfred, NY — A
State U of New York Coll of Technology at Canton, NY — A
State U of New York Coll of Technology at Delhi, NY — A
U of Rochester, NY — B

Engineering Technologies Related
Shepherd U, WV — A

Engineering Technology
Buffalo State Coll, State U of New York, NY — B
Rochester Inst of Technology, NY — B
Rochester Inst of Technology, NY — A,B
State U of New York Coll of Agriculture and Technology at Cobleskill, NY — A
State U of New York Coll of Technology at Canton, NY — A
State U of New York Coll of Technology at Delhi, NY — A

U of West Florida, FL — B
Vaughn Coll of Aeronautics and Technology, NY — A

English
Adelphi U, NY — B
Alfred U, NY — B
Bard Coll, NY — B
Barnard Coll, NY — B
Bernard M. Baruch Coll of the City U of New York, NY — B
Brooklyn Coll of the City U of New York, NY — B
Buffalo State Coll, State U of New York, NY — B
Canisius Coll, NY — B
Cazenovia Coll, NY — B
Chaminade U of Honolulu, HI — B
Chatham Coll, PA — B
City Coll of the City U of New York, NY — B
Colgate U, NY — B
Coll of Mount Saint Vincent, NY — B
The Coll of New Rochelle, NY — B
The Coll of Saint Rose, NY — B
Coll of Staten Island of the City U of New York, NY — B
Columbia Coll, NY — B
Columbia U, School of General Studies, NY — B
Concordia Coll, NY — B
Cornell U, NY — B
Daemen Coll, NY — B
Dominican Coll, NY — B
Dowling Coll, NY — B
D'Youville Coll, NY — B
Elmira Coll, NY — B
Fordham U, NY — B
Hamilton Coll, NY — B
Hartwick Coll, NY — B
Hilbert Coll, NY — B
Hobart and William Smith Colls, NY — B
Hofstra U, NY — B
Houghton Coll, NY — B
Hunter Coll of the City U of New York, NY — B
Iona Coll, NY — B
Ithaca Coll, NY — B
Keuka Coll, NY — B
Lehman Coll of the City U of New York, NY — B
Le Moyne Coll, NY — B
Long Island U, Brooklyn Campus, NY — B
Long Island U, C.W. Post Campus, NY — B
Manhattan Coll, NY — B
Manhattanville Coll, NY — B
Marist Coll, NY — B
Marymount Coll of Fordham U, NY — B
Marymount Manhattan Coll, NY — B
Medaille Coll, NY — B
Mercy Coll, NY — B
Molloy Coll, NY — B
Mount Saint Mary Coll, NY — B
Nazareth Coll of Rochester, NY — B
New York Inst of Technology, NY — B
New York U, NY — B
Niagara U, NY — B
North Carolina Ag and Tech State U, NC — B
Nyack Coll, NY — B
Pace U, NY — B
Post U, CT — B
Queens Coll of the City U of New York, NY — B
Quinnipiac U, CT — B
Roberts Wesleyan Coll, NY — B
Russell Sage Coll, NY — B
St. Bonaventure U, NY — B
St. Francis Coll, NY — B
St. John Fisher Coll, NY — B
St. John's U, NY — B
St. Joseph's Coll, New York, NY — B
St. Joseph's Coll, Suffolk Campus, NY — B
St. Lawrence U, NY — B
St. Thomas Aquinas Coll, NY — B
Sarah Lawrence Coll, NY — B

A—associate degree; B—bachelor's degree

Shepherd U, WV — B
Siena Coll, NY — B
State U of New York at Binghamton, NY — B
State U of New York at Buffalo, NY — B
State U of New York at New Paltz, NY — B
State U of New York at Oswego, NY — B
State U of New York at Plattsburgh, NY — B
State U of New York Coll at Brockport, NY — B
State U of New York Coll at Cortland, NY — B
State U of New York Coll at Geneseo, NY — B
State U of New York Coll at Oneonta, NY — B
State U of New York Coll at Potsdam, NY — B
State U of New York, Fredonia, NY — B
Stony Brook U, State U of New York, NY — B
Syracuse U, NY — B
Union Coll, NY — B
U at Albany, State U of New York, NY — B
U of Rochester, NY — B
U of West Florida, FL — B
Utica Coll, NY — B
Vassar Coll, NY — B
Wagner Coll, NY — B
Wells Coll, NY — B
West Virginia Wesleyan Coll, WV — B
Yeshiva U, NY — B
York Coll of the City U of New York, NY — B

English as a Second/Foreign Language (Teaching)
Cornell U, NY — B
Mercy Coll, NY — B
Nyack Coll, NY — B
Queens Coll of the City U of New York, NY — B
St. John's U, NY — B

English Language and Literature Related
Sarah Lawrence Coll, NY — B
Skidmore Coll, NY — B

English/Language Arts Teacher Education
Brooklyn Coll of the City U of New York, NY — B
Buffalo State Coll, State U of New York, NY — B
Chatham Coll, PA — B
The Coll of Saint Rose, NY — B
Cornell U, NY — B
Daemen Coll, NY — B
Dominican Coll, NY — B
Dowling Coll, NY — B
Elmira Coll, NY — B
Hofstra U, NY — B
Iona Coll, NY — B
Ithaca Coll, NY — B
Keuka Coll, NY — B
Le Moyne Coll, NY — B
Long Island U, Brooklyn Campus, NY — B
Long Island U, C.W. Post Campus, NY — B
Manhattanville Coll, NY — B
Molloy Coll, NY — B
Nazareth Coll of Rochester, NY — B
New York Inst of Technology, NY — B
New York U, NY — B
Pace U, NY — B
Prescott Coll, AZ — B
Queens Coll of the City U of New York, NY — B
Roberts Wesleyan Coll, NY — B
St. Bonaventure U, NY — B
St. Francis Coll, NY — B
St. John's U, NY — B
State U of New York Coll at Brockport, NY — B

State U of New York Coll at Oneonta, NY — B
State U of New York Coll at Potsdam, NY — B
Syracuse U, NY — B
U at Albany, State U of New York, NY — B
U of West Florida, FL — B
Utica Coll, NY — B
West Virginia Wesleyan Coll, WV — B

English Literature (British and Commonwealth)
Cornell U, NY — B
Hofstra U, NY — B
Hunter Coll of the City U of New York, NY — B
Sarah Lawrence Coll, NY — B
Syracuse U, NY — B

Entomology
Cornell U, NY — B
State U of New York Coll of Environmental Science and Forestry, NY — B

Entrepreneurship
Canisius Coll, NY — B
Fordham U, NY — B
Hofstra U, NY — B
Pace U, NY — B
Rensselaer Polytechnic Inst, NY — B
Syracuse U, NY — B

Environmental Biology
Bard Coll, NY — B
Barnard Coll, NY — B
Colgate U, NY — B
Columbia Coll, NY — B
Marist Coll, NY — B
State U of New York Coll at Brockport, NY — B
State U of New York Coll at Cortland, NY — B
State U of New York Coll of Environmental Science and Forestry, NY — B

Environmental Control Technologies Related
New York Inst of Technology, NY — B

Environmental Design/Architecture
Cornell U, NY — B
Prescott Coll, AZ — B
State U of New York at Buffalo, NY — B
State U of New York Coll of Environmental Science and Forestry, NY — B

Environmental Education
Prescott Coll, AZ — B
State U of New York Coll of Environmental Science and Forestry, NY — B

Environmental Engineering Technology
New York Inst of Technology, NY — A,B

Environmental/Environmental Health Engineering
Clarkson U, NY — B
Columbia U, The Fu Foundation School of Engineering and Applied Science, NY — B
Cornell U, NY — B
Hofstra U, NY — B
Manhattan Coll, NY — B
Rensselaer Polytechnic Inst, NY — B
State U of New York at Buffalo, NY — B
State U of New York Coll of Environmental Science and Forestry, NY — B
Syracuse U, NY — B
United States Military Academy, NY — B

Environmental Health
Clarkson U, NY — B
York Coll of the City U of New York, NY — B

Environmental Science
Barnard Coll, NY — B
Canisius Coll, NY — B
Hofstra U, NY — B
Hunter Coll of the City U of New York, NY — B
Keuka Coll, NY — B
Long Island U, C.W. Post Campus, NY — B
Nazareth Coll of Rochester, NY — B
Post U, CT — B
Queens Coll of the City U of New York, NY — B
Rochester Inst of Technology, NY — B
Skidmore Coll, NY — B
State U of New York Coll at Cortland, NY — B
U at Albany, State U of New York, NY — B
U of Rochester, NY — B
Vassar Coll, NY — B
West Virginia Wesleyan Coll, WV — B

Environmental Studies
Alfred U, NY — B
Bard Coll, NY — B
Barnard Coll, NY — B
Brooklyn Coll of the City U of New York, NY — B
Cazenovia Coll, NY — B
Chaminade U of Honolulu, HI — B
Chatham Coll, PA — B
Clarkson U, NY — B
Colgate U, NY — B
The Coll of New Rochelle, NY — B
The Coll of Saint Rose, NY — B
Columbia Coll, NY — B
Cornell U, NY — B
Elmira Coll, NY — B
Hobart and William Smith Colls, NY — B
Ithaca Coll, NY — B
Long Island U, C.W. Post Campus, NY — B
Marist Coll, NY — B
Medgar Evers Coll of the City U of New York, NY — B
Molloy Coll, NY — B
Nazareth Coll of Rochester, NY — B
Paul Smith's Coll of Arts and Sciences, NY — A,B
Post U, CT — B
Prescott Coll, AZ — B
Purchase Coll, State U of New York, NY — B
Queens Coll of the City U of New York, NY — B
St. Bonaventure U, NY — B
St. John's U, NY — B
St. Lawrence U, NY — B
Sarah Lawrence Coll, NY — B
Shepherd U, WV — B
Skidmore Coll, NY — B
State U of New York at Binghamton, NY — B
State U of New York at New Paltz, NY — B
State U of New York at Plattsburgh, NY — B
State U of New York Coll at Brockport, NY — B
State U of New York Coll at Cortland, NY — B
State U of New York Coll at Oneonta, NY — B
State U of New York Coll at Potsdam, NY — B
State U of New York Coll of Agriculture and Technology at Cobleskill, NY — A,B
State U of New York Coll of Environmental Science and Forestry, NY — B
State U of New York Coll of Technology at Alfred, NY — A
State U of New York Coll of Technology at Canton, NY — A
State U of New York, Fredonia, NY — B
Stony Brook U, State U of New York, NY — B

United States Military Academy, NY — B
U of Rochester, NY — B
U of West Florida, FL — B
Vassar Coll, NY — B
Wells Coll, NY — B

Environmental Toxicology
Cornell U, NY — B

Epidemiology
Cornell U, NY — B

Equestrian Studies
Cazenovia Coll, NY — B
Post U, CT — A,B
State U of New York Coll of Agriculture and Technology at Cobleskill, NY — A

Ethnic, Cultural Minority, and Gender Studies Related
St. Francis Coll, NY — B

European History
Bard Coll, NY — B
Cornell U, NY — B
Sarah Lawrence Coll, NY — B

European Studies
Bard Coll, NY — B
Barnard Coll, NY — B
Canisius Coll, NY — B
Elmira Coll, NY — B
Hobart and William Smith Colls, NY — B
New York U, NY — B
Sarah Lawrence Coll, NY — B
State U of New York Coll at Brockport, NY — B
United States Military Academy, NY — B

European Studies (Central and Eastern)
Bard Coll, NY — B
Fordham U, NY — B
Sarah Lawrence Coll, NY — B
United States Military Academy, NY — B
U at Albany, State U of New York, NY — B

Evolutionary Biology
Cornell U, NY — B

Exercise Physiology
State U of New York Coll at Brockport, NY — B

Experimental Psychology
St. John's U, NY — B

Family and Community Services
State U of New York Coll of Agriculture and Technology at Cobleskill, NY — A
Syracuse U, NY — B

Family and Consumer Sciences/Home Economics Teacher Education
Cornell U, NY — B
Marymount Coll of Fordham U, NY — B
North Carolina Ag and Tech State U, NC — B
Queens Coll of the City U of New York, NY — B
State U of New York Coll at Oneonta, NY — B
Syracuse U, NY — B

Family and Consumer Sciences/Human Sciences
Cornell U, NY — B
Marymount Coll of Fordham U, NY — B
North Carolina Ag and Tech State U, NC — B
Queens Coll of the City U of New York, NY — B
Shepherd U, WV — B
State U of New York Coll at Oneonta, NY — B

Family Practice Nursing/Nurse Practitioner
State U of New York at Buffalo, NY — B

Family Resource Management
Cornell U, NY — B

Family Systems
Syracuse U, NY — B

Farm and Ranch Management
Cornell U, NY — B

Fashion/Apparel Design
Buffalo State Coll, State U of New York, NY — B
Cazenovia Coll, NY — A,B
Cornell U, NY — B
Fashion Inst of Technology, NY — A,B
Marist Coll, NY — B
Marymount Coll of Fordham U, NY — B
Pratt Inst, NY — B
Syracuse U, NY — B

Fashion Merchandising
Berkeley Coll-New York City Campus, NY — A
Berkeley Coll-Westchester Campus, NY — A
Buffalo State Coll, State U of New York, NY — B
Fashion Inst of Technology, NY — B
Laboratory Inst of Merchandising, NY — A,B
Marist Coll, NY — B
Marymount Coll of Fordham U, NY — B
Shepherd U, WV — A
State U of New York Coll at Oneonta, NY — B

Fiber, Textile and Weaving Arts
Cornell U, NY — B
Syracuse U, NY — B

Film/Cinema Studies
Bard Coll, NY — B
Barnard Coll, NY — B
Brooklyn Coll of the City U of New York, NY — B
Columbia Coll, NY — B
Columbia U, School of General Studies, NY — B
Cornell U, NY — B
Fordham U, NY — B
Hofstra U, NY — B
Hunter Coll of the City U of New York, NY — B
Ithaca Coll, NY — B
New York U, NY — B
Prescott Coll, AZ — B
Purchase Coll, State U of New York, NY — B
Queens Coll of the City U of New York, NY — B
Quinnipiac U, CT — B
Sarah Lawrence Coll, NY — B
School of Visual Arts, NY — B
State U of New York at Binghamton, NY — B
State U of New York at Buffalo, NY — B
State U of New York, Fredonia, NY — B
U of Rochester, NY — B
Vassar Coll, NY — B

Film/Video and Photographic Arts Related
Pratt Inst, NY — B

Finance
Adelphi U, NY — B
Bernard M. Baruch Coll of the City U of New York, NY — B
Canisius Coll, NY — B
Clarkson U, NY — B
Cornell U, NY — B
Dominican Coll, NY — B
Dowling Coll, NY — B
Excelsior Coll, NY — B
Fordham U, NY — B
Globe Inst of Technology, NY — B

Hilbert Coll, NY — B
Hofstra U, NY — B
Iona Coll, NY — B
Ithaca Coll, NY — B
The King's Coll, NY — B
Long Island U, Brentwood Campus, NY — B
Long Island U, Brooklyn Campus, NY — B
Long Island U, C.W. Post Campus, NY — B
Manhattan Coll, NY — B
Manhattanville Coll, NY — B
Marymount Coll of Fordham U, NY — B
Mercy Coll, NY — B
New York Inst of Technology, NY — B
New York U, NY — B
Post U, CT — B
Queens Coll of the City U of New York, NY — B
Quinnipiac U, CT — B
Rensselaer Polytechnic Inst, NY — B
Rochester Inst of Technology, NY — B
St. Bonaventure U, NY — B
St. John Fisher Coll, NY — B
St. John's U, NY — B
St. Thomas Aquinas Coll, NY — B
Siena Coll, NY — B
State U of New York at New Paltz, NY — B
State U of New York at Oswego, NY — B
State U of New York Coll at Brockport, NY — B
State U of New York Coll at Old Westbury, NY — B
State U of New York Coll of Technology at Alfred, NY — A
State U of New York, Fredonia, NY — B
State U of New York Inst of Technology, NY — B
Syracuse U, NY — B
U of West Florida, FL — B
Wagner Coll, NY — B
West Virginia Wesleyan Coll, WV — B
Yeshiva U, NY — B

Financial Planning and Services
Medaille Coll, NY — B

Fine Arts Related
Adelphi U, NY — B
Coll of Staten Island of the City U of New York, NY — B
Dowling Coll, NY — B
Long Island U, Brooklyn Campus, NY — B
Long Island U, C.W. Post Campus, NY — B
Pratt Inst, NY — B
St. John's U, NY — B
Skidmore Coll, NY — B
Syracuse U, NY — B

Fine/Studio Arts
Alfred U, NY — B
Bard Coll, NY — B
Brooklyn Coll of the City U of New York, NY — B
Buffalo State Coll, State U of New York, NY — B
Cazenovia Coll, NY — B
Chatham Coll, PA — B
The Coll of New Rochelle, NY — B
The Coll of Saint Rose, NY — B
Cornell U, NY — B
Daemen Coll, NY — B
Dowling Coll, NY — B
Elmira Coll, NY — B
Fordham U, NY — B
Hamilton Coll, NY — B
Hobart and William Smith Colls, NY — B
Hofstra U, NY — B
Hunter Coll of the City U of New York, NY — B
Ithaca Coll, NY — B
Long Island U, C.W. Post Campus, NY — B

Manhattanville Coll, NY — B
Marist Coll, NY — B
Marymount Coll of Fordham U, NY — B
Marymount Manhattan Coll, NY — B
Nazareth Coll of Rochester, NY — B
New York Inst of Technology, NY — B
New York U, NY — B
Pace U, NY — A
Pratt Inst, NY — A,B
Queens Coll of the City U of New York, NY — B
Roberts Wesleyan Coll, NY — B
Rochester Inst of Technology, NY — A,B
Sage Coll of Albany, NY — A
St. John's U, NY — B
St. Thomas Aquinas Coll, NY — B
Sarah Lawrence Coll, NY — B
School of Visual Arts, NY — B
Siena Coll, NY — B
State U of New York at Binghamton, NY — B
State U of New York at Buffalo, NY — B
State U of New York at New Paltz, NY — B
State U of New York at Plattsburgh, NY — B
State U of New York Coll at Brockport, NY — B
State U of New York Coll at Cortland, NY — B
State U of New York Coll at Geneseo, NY — B
State U of New York Coll at Oneonta, NY — B
State U of New York, Fredonia, NY — B
Stony Brook U, State U of New York, NY — B
Syracuse U, NY — B
Union Coll, NY — B
U of Rochester, NY — B
U of West Florida, FL — B
Vassar Coll, NY — B
Wells Coll, NY — B
West Virginia Wesleyan Coll, WV — B

Fire Science
John Jay Coll of Criminal Justice of the City U of New York, NY — B
Mercy Coll, NY — B

Fire Services Administration
John Jay Coll of Criminal Justice of the City U of New York, NY — B

Fish/Game Management
State U of New York Coll of Agriculture and Technology at Cobleskill, NY — A
State U of New York Coll of Environmental Science and Forestry, NY — B

Fishing and Fisheries Sciences and Management
State U of New York Coll of Agriculture and Technology at Cobleskill, NY — B
State U of New York Coll of Environmental Science and Forestry, NY — B

Food Science
Cornell U, NY — B
Marymount Coll of Fordham U, NY — B
North Carolina Ag and Tech State U, NC — B

Food Services Technology
State U of New York Coll of Agriculture and Technology at Cobleskill, NY — A

Foodservice Systems Administration
Cornell U, NY — B
Rochester Inst of Technology, NY — B
State U of New York Coll at Oneonta, NY — B

Foods, Nutrition, and Wellness
Brooklyn Coll of the City U of New York, NY — B
Cornell U, NY — B
Hunter Coll of the City U of New York, NY — B
Ithaca Coll, NY — B
Lehman Coll of the City U of New York, NY — B
Marymount Coll of Fordham U, NY — B
New York U, NY — B
North Carolina Ag and Tech State U, NC — B
State U of New York at Plattsburgh, NY — B
Syracuse U, NY — B

Food Technology and Processing
Cornell U, NY — B

Foreign Languages and Literatures
Dowling Coll, NY — B
Elmira Coll, NY — B
Excelsior Coll, NY — B
Long Island U, Brooklyn Campus, NY — B
Long Island U, C.W. Post Campus, NY — B
Pace U, NY — B
St. Lawrence U, NY — B
Sarah Lawrence Coll, NY — B
Syracuse U, NY — B
Union Coll, NY — B

Foreign Languages Related
The Coll of New Rochelle, NY — B
Hofstra U, NY — B

Foreign Language Teacher Education
Buffalo State Coll, State U of New York, NY — B
Cornell U, NY — B
Elmira Coll, NY — B
Hofstra U, NY — B
Le Moyne Coll, NY — B
Long Island U, C.W. Post Campus, NY — B
Nazareth Coll of Rochester, NY — B
New York U, NY — B
Queens Coll of the City U of New York, NY — B
St. Bonaventure U, NY — B
St. John's U, NY — B
State U of New York Coll at Brockport, NY — B
State U of New York Coll at Old Westbury, NY — B
State U of New York Coll at Potsdam, NY — B
U at Albany, State U of New York, NY — B
U of West Florida, FL — B

Forensic Psychology
John Jay Coll of Criminal Justice of the City U of New York, NY — B

Forensic Science and Technology
Buffalo State Coll, State U of New York, NY — B
Chaminade U of Honolulu, HI — B
John Jay Coll of Criminal Justice of the City U of New York, NY — B
Long Island U, C.W. Post Campus, NY — B

Forest Engineering
State U of New York Coll of Environmental Science and Forestry, NY — B

Forest/Forest Resources Management
State U of New York Coll of Environmental Science and Forestry, NY — B

Forestry
Paul Smith's Coll of Arts and Sciences, NY — A

A—associate degree; B—bachelor's degree

State U of New York Coll of Environmental Science and Forestry, NY — B
State U of New York Coll of Technology at Delhi, NY — A

Forestry Technology
Paul Smith's Coll of Arts and Sciences, NY — A
State U of New York Coll of Technology at Canton, NY — A

Forest Sciences and Biology
Canisius Coll, NY — B

French
Adelphi U, NY — B
Alfred U, NY — B
Bard Coll, NY — B
Barnard Coll, NY — B
Brooklyn Coll of the City U of New York, NY — B
Buffalo State Coll, State U of New York, NY — B
Canisius Coll, NY — B
Chatham Coll, PA — B
City Coll of the City U of New York, NY — B
Colgate U, NY — B
Coll of Mount Saint Vincent, NY — B
The Coll of New Rochelle, NY — B
Columbia Coll, NY — B
Columbia U, School of General Studies, NY — B
Cornell U, NY — B
Daemen Coll, NY — B
Elmira Coll, NY — B
Fordham U, NY — B
Hamilton Coll, NY — B
Hartwick Coll, NY — B
Hobart and William Smith Colls, NY — B
Hofstra U, NY — B
Houghton Coll, NY — B
Hunter Coll of the City U of New York, NY — B
Iona Coll, NY — B
Ithaca Coll, NY — B
Lehman Coll of the City U of New York, NY — B
Le Moyne Coll, NY — B
Long Island U, C.W. Post Campus, NY — B
Manhattan Coll, NY — B
Manhattanville Coll, NY — B
Marist Coll, NY — B
Marymount Coll of Fordham U, NY — B
Mercy Coll, NY — B
Molloy Coll, NY — B
Nazareth Coll of Rochester, NY — B
New York U, NY — B
Niagara U, NY — B
North Carolina Ag and Tech State U, NC — B
Pace U, NY — B
Purchase Coll, State U of New York, NY — B
Queens Coll of the City U of New York, NY — B
St. Bonaventure U, NY — B
St. John Fisher Coll, NY — B
St. John's U, NY — B
St. Lawrence U, NY — B
Sarah Lawrence Coll, NY — B
Siena Coll, NY — B
Skidmore Coll, NY — B
State U of New York at Binghamton, NY — B
State U of New York at Buffalo, NY — B
State U of New York at New Paltz, NY — B
State U of New York at Oswego, NY — B
State U of New York at Plattsburgh, NY — B
State U of New York Coll at Brockport, NY — B
State U of New York Coll at Cortland, NY — B
State U of New York Coll at Geneseo, NY — B

State U of New York Coll at Oneonta, NY — B
State U of New York Coll at Potsdam, NY — B
State U of New York, Fredonia, NY — B
Stony Brook U, State U of New York, NY — B
Syracuse U, NY — B
United States Military Academy, NY — B
U at Albany, State U of New York, NY — B
U of Rochester, NY — B
Vassar Coll, NY — B
Wells Coll, NY — B
Yeshiva U, NY — B
York Coll of the City U of New York, NY — B

French Language Teacher Education
Brooklyn Coll of the City U of New York, NY — B
Daemen Coll, NY — B
Elmira Coll, NY — B
Hofstra U, NY — B
Iona Coll, NY — B
Ithaca Coll, NY — B
Le Moyne Coll, NY — B
Long Island U, C.W. Post Campus, NY — B
Manhattanville Coll, NY — B
Marymount Coll of Fordham U, NY — B
Molloy Coll, NY — B
New York U, NY — B
Niagara U, NY — B
Pace U, NY — B
St. Bonaventure U, NY — B
St. John's U, NY — B
State U of New York Coll at Brockport, NY — B
State U of New York Coll at Cortland, NY — B
State U of New York Coll at Oneonta, NY — B
State U of New York Coll at Potsdam, NY — B
U at Albany, State U of New York, NY — B

French Studies
Barnard Coll, NY — B
Columbia Coll, NY — B
Fordham U, NY — B

Funeral Service and Mortuary Science
St. John's U, NY — B
State U of New York Coll of Technology at Canton, NY — A

Furniture Design and Manufacturing
Rochester Inst of Technology, NY — A,B

Gay/Lesbian Studies
Cornell U, NY — B
Hobart and William Smith Colls, NY — B
Sarah Lawrence Coll, NY — B

General Studies
Alfred U, NY — B
Buffalo State Coll, State U of New York, NY — B
Canisius Coll, NY — B
Chaminade U of Honolulu, HI — A
Long Island U, C.W. Post Campus, NY — B
New York U, NY — A
Nyack Coll, NY — A
Rochester Inst of Technology, NY — A,B
St. Joseph's Coll, New York, NY — A
Shepherd U, WV — A,B
State U of New York Coll of Technology at Delhi, NY — A
State U of New York Inst of Technology, NY — B

Genetics
Cornell U, NY — B
Rochester Inst of Technology, NY — B

Geochemistry
Columbia Coll, NY — B
Cornell U, NY — B
State U of New York at Oswego, NY — B
State U of New York Coll at Cortland, NY — B
State U of New York Coll at Geneseo, NY — B
State U of New York, Fredonia, NY — B

Geography
Barnard Coll, NY — B
Buffalo State Coll, State U of New York, NY — B
City Coll of the City U of New York, NY — B
Colgate U, NY — B
Excelsior Coll, NY — B
Hofstra U, NY — B
Hunter Coll of the City U of New York, NY — B
Lehman Coll of the City U of New York, NY — B
Long Island U, C.W. Post Campus, NY — B
State U of New York at Binghamton, NY — B
State U of New York at Buffalo, NY — B
State U of New York at New Paltz, NY — B
State U of New York at Plattsburgh, NY — B
State U of New York Coll at Cortland, NY — B
State U of New York Coll at Geneseo, NY — B
State U of New York Coll at Oneonta, NY — B
State U of New York Coll at Potsdam, NY — B
Syracuse U, NY — B
United States Military Academy, NY — B
U at Albany, State U of New York, NY — B
Vassar Coll, NY — B

Geography Related
Cornell U, NY — B

Geological and Earth Sciences/ Geosciences Related
Cornell U, NY — B
State U of New York Coll at Brockport, NY — B

Geological/Geophysical Engineering
Cornell U, NY — B
U of Rochester, NY — B

Geology/Earth Science
Alfred U, NY — B
Barnard Coll, NY — B
Brooklyn Coll of the City U of New York, NY — B
Buffalo State Coll, State U of New York, NY — B
City Coll of the City U of New York, NY — B
Colgate U, NY — B
Columbia Coll, NY — B
Columbia U, School of General Studies, NY — B
Cornell U, NY — B
Excelsior Coll, NY — B
Hamilton Coll, NY — B
Hartwick Coll, NY — B
Hobart and William Smith Colls, NY — B
Hofstra U, NY — B
Lehman Coll of the City U of New York, NY — B
Long Island U, C.W. Post Campus, NY — B
Pace U, NY — B
Queens Coll of the City U of New York, NY — B
Rensselaer Polytechnic Inst, NY — B
St. Lawrence U, NY — B
Sarah Lawrence Coll, NY — B
Skidmore Coll, NY — B

Geophysics and Seismology
Cornell U, NY — B
St. Lawrence U, NY — B
State U of New York Coll at Geneseo, NY — B
State U of New York, Fredonia, NY — B

Geotechnical Engineering
Cornell U, NY — B

German
Alfred U, NY — B
Bard Coll, NY — B
Barnard Coll, NY — B
Brooklyn Coll of the City U of New York, NY — B
Colgate U, NY — B
Columbia Coll, NY — B
Columbia U, School of General Studies, NY — B
Cornell U, NY — B
Fordham U, NY — B
Hamilton Coll, NY — B
Hartwick Coll, NY — B
Hofstra U, NY — B
Hunter Coll of the City U of New York, NY — B
Ithaca Coll, NY — B
Long Island U, C.W. Post Campus, NY — B
Nazareth Coll of Rochester, NY — B
New York U, NY — B
Queens Coll of the City U of New York, NY — B
St. John Fisher Coll, NY — B
St. Lawrence U, NY — B
Sarah Lawrence Coll, NY — B
Skidmore Coll, NY — B
State U of New York at Binghamton, NY — B
State U of New York at Buffalo, NY — B
State U of New York at New Paltz, NY — B
State U of New York at Oswego, NY — B
State U of New York Coll at Cortland, NY — B
Stony Brook U, State U of New York, NY — B
Syracuse U, NY — B
United States Military Academy, NY — B
U of Rochester, NY — B
Vassar Coll, NY — B

Germanic Languages
Canisius Coll, NY — B

German Language Teacher Education
Hofstra U, NY — B
Hunter Coll of the City U of New York, NY — B
Ithaca Coll, NY — B
St. Bonaventure U, NY — B

German Studies
Barnard Coll, NY — B
Columbia Coll, NY — B
Cornell U, NY — B
Fordham U, NY — B
Manhattanville Coll, NY — B

Gerontology
Alfred U, NY — B
Ithaca Coll, NY — B
Mercy Coll, NY — B
Nazareth Coll of Rochester, NY — B
Quinnipiac U, CT — B
State U of New York Coll at Oneonta, NY — B
State U of New York, Fredonia, NY — B
Wagner Coll, NY — B
York Coll of the City U of New York, NY — B

Graphic Communications
New York U, NY — B
Rochester Inst of Technology, NY — B

Graphic Design
City Coll of the City U of New York, NY — B
Daemen Coll, NY — B
Pratt Inst, NY — A,B
Rochester Inst of Technology, NY — A,B
St. John's U, NY — B

Hazardous Materials Management and Waste Technology
Rochester Inst of Technology, NY — B

Health and Physical Education
Houghton Coll, NY — B
Ithaca Coll, NY — B
Queens Coll of the City U of New York, NY — B
State U of New York Coll at Brockport, NY — B
State U of New York Coll of Technology at Delhi, NY — A
U of West Florida, FL — B
West Virginia Wesleyan Coll, WV — B

Health and Physical Education Related
Ithaca Coll, NY — B
St. John Fisher Coll, NY — B
State U of New York Coll at Brockport, NY — B

Health/Health Care Administration
Alfred U, NY — B
Dominican Coll, NY — B
D'Youville Coll, NY — B
Iona Coll, NY — B
Ithaca Coll, NY — B
Lehman Coll of the City U of New York, NY — B
Mercy Coll, NY — B
New York U, NY — A,B
St. John's U, NY — B
St. Joseph's Coll, New York, NY — B
St. Joseph's Coll, Suffolk Campus, NY — B
State U of New York Coll at Brockport, NY — B
State U of New York Coll of Technology at Canton, NY — B
State U of New York, Fredonia, NY — B
State U of New York Inst of Technology, NY — B

Health Information/Medical Records Administration
Long Island U, C.W. Post Campus, NY — B
Pace U, NY — B
State U of New York Coll of Technology at Alfred, NY — A

State U of New York Downstate Medical Center, NY — B
State U of New York Inst of Technology, NY — B

Health Information/Medical Records Technology
Molloy Coll, NY — A
New York U, NY — A

Health/Medical Preparatory Programs Related
Fordham U, NY — B
Ithaca Coll, NY — B
Utica Coll, NY — B

Health/Medical Psychology
Iona Coll, NY — B

Health Occupations Teacher Education
New York Inst of Technology, NY — B

Health Professions Related
Albany Coll of Pharmacy of Union U, NY — B
Chatham Coll, PA — B
Dowling Coll, NY — B
D'Youville Coll, NY — B
Hofstra U, NY — B
Long Island U, Brooklyn Campus, NY — B
Long Island U, C.W. Post Campus, NY — B
St. Francis Coll, NY — B
Stony Brook U, State U of New York, NY — B

Health Science
Coll of Mount Saint Vincent, NY — B
Long Island U, Brooklyn Campus, NY — B
State U of New York Coll at Brockport, NY — B
State U of New York Coll at Cortland, NY — B
Syracuse U, NY — B
Villa Maria Coll of Buffalo, NY — A

Health Services/Allied Health/Health Sciences
Daemen Coll, NY — B
D'Youville Coll, NY — B

Health Teacher Education
Brooklyn Coll of the City U of New York, NY — B
Coll of Mount Saint Vincent, NY — B
Hofstra U, NY — B
Hunter Coll of the City U of New York, NY — B
Ithaca Coll, NY — B
Lehman Coll of the City U of New York, NY — B
Long Island U, C.W. Post Campus, NY — B
North Carolina Ag and Tech State U, NC — B
State U of New York at Oswego, NY — B
State U of New York Coll at Brockport, NY — B
State U of New York Coll at Cortland, NY — B
West Virginia Wesleyan Coll, WV — B
York Coll of the City U of New York, NY — B

Heating, Air Conditioning and Refrigeration Technology
State U of New York Coll of Technology at Delhi, NY — A

Heating, Air Conditioning, Ventilation and Refrigeration Maintenance Technology
State U of New York Coll of Technology at Alfred, NY — A
State U of New York Coll of Technology at Canton, NY — A
State U of New York Coll of Technology at Delhi, NY — A

Heavy Equipment Maintenance Technology
State U of New York Coll of Technology at Alfred, NY — A

Hebrew
Bard Coll, NY — B
Brooklyn Coll of the City U of New York, NY — B
Hofstra U, NY — B
Hunter Coll of the City U of New York, NY — B
The Jewish Theological Seminary, NY — B
Lehman Coll of the City U of New York, NY — B
New York U, NY — B
Queens Coll of the City U of New York, NY — B
State U of New York at Binghamton, NY — B
Yeshiva U, NY — B

Hispanic-American, Puerto Rican, and Mexican-American/Chicano Studies
Brooklyn Coll of the City U of New York, NY — B
Columbia Coll, NY — B
Columbia U, School of General Studies, NY — B
Cornell U, NY — B
Fordham U, NY — B
Hofstra U, NY — B
Hunter Coll of the City U of New York, NY — B
Mount Saint Mary Coll, NY — B
State U of New York Coll at Oneonta, NY — B
U at Albany, State U of New York, NY — B

Historic Preservation and Conservation
Cornell U, NY — B

History
Adelphi U, NY — B
Alfred U, NY — B
Bard Coll, NY — B
Barnard Coll, NY — B
Bernard M. Baruch Coll of the City U of New York, NY — B
Brooklyn Coll of the City U of New York, NY — B
Buffalo State Coll, State U of New York, NY — B
Canisius Coll, NY — B
Chaminade U of Honolulu, HI — B
Chatham Coll, PA — B
City Coll of the City U of New York, NY — B
Clarkson U, NY — B
Colgate U, NY — B
Coll of Mount Saint Vincent, NY — B
The Coll of New Rochelle, NY — B
The Coll of Saint Rose, NY — B
Coll of Staten Island of the City U of New York, NY — B
Columbia Coll, NY — B
Columbia U, School of General Studies, NY — B
Concordia Coll, NY — B
Cornell U, NY — B
Daemen Coll, NY — B
Dominican Coll, NY — B
Dowling Coll, NY — B
D'Youville Coll, NY — B
Elmira Coll, NY — B
Excelsior Coll, NY — B
Fordham U, NY — B
Hamilton Coll, NY — B
Hartwick Coll, NY — B
Hobart and William Smith Colls, NY — B
Hofstra U, NY — B
Houghton Coll, NY — B
Hunter Coll of the City U of New York, NY — B
Iona Coll, NY — B
Ithaca Coll, NY — B

The Jewish Theological Seminary, NY — B
Keuka Coll, NY — B
Lehman Coll of the City U of New York, NY — B
Le Moyne Coll, NY — B
Long Island U, Brooklyn Campus, NY — B
Long Island U, C.W. Post Campus, NY — B
Manhattan Coll, NY — B
Manhattanville Coll, NY — B
Marist Coll, NY — B
Marymount Coll of Fordham U, NY — B
Marymount Manhattan Coll, NY — B
Mercy Coll, NY — B
Molloy Coll, NY — B
Mount Saint Mary Coll, NY — B
Nazareth Coll of Rochester, NY — B
New York U, NY — B
Niagara U, NY — B
North Carolina Ag and Tech State U, NC — B
Nyack Coll, NY — B
Pace U, NY — B
Post U, CT — B
Prescott Coll, AZ — B
Purchase Coll, State U of New York, NY — B
Queens Coll of the City U of New York, NY — B
Quinnipiac U, CT — B
Roberts Wesleyan Coll, NY — B
Russell Sage Coll, NY — B
St. Bonaventure U, NY — B
St. Francis Coll, NY — B
St. John Fisher Coll, NY — B
St. John's U, NY — B
St. Joseph's Coll, New York, NY — B
St. Joseph's Coll, Suffolk Campus, NY — B
St. Lawrence U, NY — B
St. Thomas Aquinas Coll, NY — B
Sarah Lawrence Coll, NY — B
Shepherd U, WV — B
Siena Coll, NY — B
Skidmore Coll, NY — B
State U of New York at Binghamton, NY — B
State U of New York at Buffalo, NY — B
State U of New York at New Paltz, NY — B
State U of New York at Oswego, NY — B
State U of New York at Plattsburgh, NY — B
State U of New York Coll at Brockport, NY — B
State U of New York Coll at Cortland, NY — B
State U of New York Coll at Geneseo, NY — B
State U of New York Coll at Oneonta, NY — B
State U of New York Coll at Potsdam, NY — B
State U of New York Empire State Coll, NY — A,B
State U of New York, Fredonia, NY — B
Stony Brook U, State U of New York, NY — B
Syracuse U, NY — B
Union Coll, NY — B
United States Military Academy, NY — B
U at Albany, State U of New York, NY — B
U of Rochester, NY — B
U of West Florida, FL — B
Utica Coll, NY — B
Wagner Coll, NY — B
Wells Coll, NY — B
West Virginia Wesleyan Coll, WV — B
Yeshiva U, NY — B
York Coll of the City U of New York, NY — B

A—associate degree; B—bachelor's degree

History and Philosophy of Science and Technology
Bard Coll, NY — B
Cornell U, NY — B
Sarah Lawrence Coll, NY — B

History of Philosophy
Bard Coll, NY — B

History Related
Bard Coll, NY — B
Cornell U, NY — B
D'Youville Coll, NY — B
Hamilton Coll, NY — B
Sarah Lawrence Coll, NY — B

History Teacher Education
Dominican Coll, NY — B
Elmira Coll, NY — B
Ithaca Coll, NY — B
Nazareth Coll of Rochester, NY — B
State U of New York Coll at
  Brockport, NY — B
Utica Coll, NY — B

Horticultural Science
Cornell U, NY — B
State U of New York Coll of
  Agriculture and Technology at
  Cobleskill, NY — A,B
State U of New York Coll of
  Technology at Delhi, NY — A

Hospital and Health Care Facilities Administration
Coll of Mount Saint Vincent, NY — B
Ithaca Coll, NY — B
Long Island U, C.W. Post
  Campus, NY — B
St. John's U, NY — B

Hospitality Administration
Baltimore International Coll, MD — A
Buffalo State Coll, State U of
  New York, NY — B
Cornell U, NY — B
Monroe Coll, Bronx, NY — A
Monroe Coll, New Rochelle, NY — A
New York U, NY — B
Paul Smith's Coll of Arts and
  Sciences, NY — A
Rochester Inst of Technology, NY — B
St. John's U, NY — B
Syracuse U, NY — B
U of West Florida, FL — B

Hospitality Administration Related
Cornell U, NY — B
Niagara U, NY — B

Hospitality and Recreation Marketing
Rochester Inst of Technology, NY — B
State U of New York Coll of
  Technology at Delhi, NY — A

Hotel/Motel Administration
Baltimore International Coll, MD — A,B
Buffalo State Coll, State U of
  New York, NY — B
Cornell U, NY — B
Keuka Coll, NY — B
New York Inst of Technology, NY — B
New York U, NY — B
Niagara U, NY — B
Pace U, NY — B
Paul Smith's Coll of Arts and
  Sciences, NY — A,B
Rochester Inst of Technology, NY — A,B
St. John's U, NY — B
State U of New York at
  Plattsburgh, NY — B
State U of New York Coll of
  Agriculture and Technology at
  Cobleskill, NY — A
State U of New York Coll of
  Technology at Delhi, NY — A,B

Housing and Human Environments
Cornell U, NY — B
Syracuse U, NY — B

Human Development and Family Studies
Cornell U, NY — B
Mitchell Coll, CT — A,B
Prescott Coll, AZ — B

Sarah Lawrence Coll, NY — B
State U of New York at Oswego,
  NY — B
State U of New York Empire
  State Coll, NY — A,B
Syracuse U, NY — B

Human Ecology
Cornell U, NY — B
Marymount Coll of Fordham U,
  NY — B
Prescott Coll, AZ — B
State U of New York Coll at
  Oneonta, NY — B

Humanities
Adelphi U, NY — B
Bard Coll, NY — B
Buffalo State Coll, State U of
  New York, NY — B
Chaminade U of Honolulu, HI — B
Clarkson U, NY — B
Colgate U, NY — B
Cornell U, NY — B
Dominican Coll, NY — B
Dowling Coll, NY — B
Elmira Coll, NY — B
Hofstra U, NY — B
Houghton Coll, NY — B
Hunter Coll of the City U of
  New York, NY — B
Iona Coll, NY — B
Long Island U, Brooklyn
  Campus, NY — B
Marist Coll, NY — B
New York U, NY — B
Prescott Coll, AZ — B
Roberts Wesleyan Coll, NY — B
Sage Coll of Albany, NY — A
St. Thomas Aquinas Coll, NY — B
Sarah Lawrence Coll, NY — B
State U of New York Coll at Old
  Westbury, NY — B
State U of New York Coll of
  Technology at Alfred, NY — A
State U of New York Coll of
  Technology at Canton, NY — A
State U of New York Coll of
  Technology at Delhi, NY — A
State U of New York Empire
  State Coll, NY — A,B
Stony Brook U, State U of New
  York, NY — B
Syracuse U, NY — B
Union Coll, NY — B
United States Military Academy,
  NY — B
U of West Florida, FL — B

Human/Medical Genetics
Sarah Lawrence Coll, NY — B

Human Nutrition
Cornell U, NY — B
Rochester Inst of Technology, NY — B

Human Resources Management
Bernard M. Baruch Coll of the
  City U of New York, NY — B
Clarkson U, NY — B
Dominican Coll, NY — B
Excelsior Coll, NY — B
Fordham U, NY — B
Medaille Coll, NY — B
Nazareth Coll of Rochester, NY — B
New York Inst of Technology, NY — B
Niagara U, NY — B
Pace U, NY — B
Quinnipiac U, CT — B
Roberts Wesleyan Coll, NY — B
St. John Fisher Coll, NY — B
St. Joseph's Coll, New York, NY — B
St. Joseph's Coll, Suffolk Campus,
  NY — B
State U of New York at Oswego,
  NY — B

Human Resources Management and Services Related
Niagara U, NY — B

Human Services
Boricua Coll, NY — B
Cazenovia Coll, NY — B
Elmira Coll, NY — B

Hilbert Coll, NY — A,B
Medaille Coll, NY — B
Mercy Coll, NY — A
Metropolitan Coll of New York,
  NY — A,B
Mitchell Coll, CT — A
Mount Saint Mary Coll, NY — B
New York U, NY — A
Post U, CT — B
Quinnipiac U, CT — B
St. John's U, NY — B
St. Joseph's Coll, New York, NY — B
State U of New York Coll at
  Cortland, NY — B
State U of New York Coll of
  Technology at Alfred, NY — A
State U of New York Empire
  State Coll, NY — A,B

Hydrology and Water Resources Science
Cornell U, NY — B
Rensselaer Polytechnic Inst, NY — B
State U of New York Coll at
  Brockport, NY — B
State U of New York Coll at
  Oneonta, NY — B
State U of New York Coll of
  Environmental Science and
  Forestry, NY — B

Illustration
Pratt Inst, NY — A,B
Rochester Inst of Technology, NY — B
St. John's U, NY — B
Syracuse U, NY — B

Immunology
Cornell U, NY — B

Industrial and Organizational Psychology
Brooklyn Coll of the City U of
  New York, NY — B
Clarkson U, NY — B
Ithaca Coll, NY — B

Industrial Arts
Buffalo State Coll, State U of
  New York, NY — B
North Carolina Ag and Tech
  State U, NC — B
State U of New York at Oswego,
  NY — B

Industrial Design
Fashion Inst of Technology, NY — B
Pratt Inst, NY — B
Rochester Inst of Technology, NY — A,B
Syracuse U, NY — B

Industrial Electronics Technology
State U of New York Coll of
  Technology at Alfred, NY — A

Industrial Engineering
Columbia U, The Fu Foundation
  School of Engineering and
  Applied Science, NY — B
Cornell U, NY — B
Hofstra U, NY — B
New York Inst of Technology, NY — B
North Carolina Ag and Tech
  State U, NC — B
Rensselaer Polytechnic Inst, NY — B
Rochester Inst of Technology, NY — B
State U of New York at
  Binghamton, NY — B
State U of New York at Buffalo,
  NY — B

Industrial Production Technologies Related
Fashion Inst of Technology, NY — A,B

Industrial Safety Technology
Rochester Inst of Technology, NY — B

Industrial Technology
Buffalo State Coll, State U of
  New York, NY — B
Excelsior Coll, NY — A,B
North Carolina Ag and Tech
  State U, NC — B

State U of New York Coll of
  Technology at Canton, NY — A
State U of New York Inst of
  Technology, NY — B

Information Resources Management
Clarkson U, NY — B

Information Science/Studies
Bernard M. Baruch Coll of the
  City U of New York, NY — B
Briarcliffe Coll, NY — A
Brooklyn Coll of the City U of
  New York, NY — B
Buffalo State Coll, State U of
  New York, NY — B
The Coll of Saint Rose, NY — B
Coll of Staten Island of the City
  U of New York, NY — B
Cornell U, NY — B
DeVry Inst of Technology, NY — B
Elmira Coll, NY — B
Excelsior Coll, NY — B
Farmingdale State U of New
  York, NY — A
Fordham U, NY — B
Hofstra U, NY — B
John Jay Coll of Criminal Justice
  of the City U of New York, NY — B
Le Moyne Coll, NY — B
Long Island U, C.W. Post
  Campus, NY — B
Marist Coll, NY — B
Marymount Coll of Fordham U,
  NY — B
Medgar Evers Coll of the City U
  of New York, NY — B
Mercy Coll, NY — B
Monroe Coll, Bronx, NY — A,B
Monroe Coll, New Rochelle, NY — A,B
Nazareth Coll of Rochester, NY — B
New York Inst of Technology, NY — B
New York U, NY — B
Niagara U, NY — B
Pace U, NY — B
Quinnipiac U, CT — B
St. John's U, NY — B
St. Thomas Aquinas Coll, NY — B
Shepherd U, WV — A
State U of New York at
  Binghamton, NY — B
State U of New York at Oswego,
  NY — B
State U of New York Coll at Old
  Westbury, NY — B
State U of New York Coll of
  Agriculture and Technology at
  Cobleskill, NY — A
State U of New York Coll of
  Technology at Canton, NY — A
State U of New York Coll of
  Technology at Delhi, NY — A,B
State U of New York, Fredonia,
  NY — B
State U of New York Inst of
  Technology, NY — B
Stony Brook U, State U of New
  York, NY — B
Syracuse U, NY — B
United States Military Academy,
  NY — B
U at Albany, State U of New
  York, NY — B
West Virginia Wesleyan Coll,
  WV — B
York Coll of the City U of New
  York, NY — B

Information Technology
Canisius Coll, NY — B
D'Youville Coll, NY — B
Long Island U, C.W. Post
  Campus, NY — B
Marist Coll, NY — B
Nazareth Coll of Rochester, NY — B
Rensselaer Polytechnic Inst, NY — B
Rochester Inst of Technology, NY — B
St. Francis Coll, NY — B

Inorganic Chemistry
Cornell U, NY — B

Institutional Food Workers
State U of New York Coll of
  Agriculture and Technology at
  Cobleskill, NY   A

Insurance
Excelsior Coll, NY   B
St. John's U, NY   B

Interdisciplinary Studies
Alfred U, NY   B
Bard Coll, NY   B
Bernard M. Baruch Coll of the
  City U of New York, NY   B
Clarkson U, NY   B
Coll of Mount Saint Vincent, NY   A,B
The Coll of Saint Rose, NY   B
Cornell U, NY   B
Dowling Coll, NY   B
D'Youville Coll, NY   B
Elmira Coll, NY   B
Fordham U, NY   B
Hobart and William Smith Colls,
  NY   B
Hofstra U, NY   B
Iona Coll, NY   B
Ithaca Coll, NY   B
Keuka Coll, NY   B
Lehman Coll of the City U of
  New York, NY   B
Long Island U, Brooklyn
  Campus, NY   B
Long Island U, C.W. Post
  Campus, NY   B
Long Island U, Friends World
  Program, NY   B
Marymount Coll of Fordham U,
  NY   B
Mercy Coll, NY   B
Molloy Coll, NY   B
Mount Saint Mary Coll, NY   B
Nazareth Coll of Rochester, NY   B
New York U, NY   B
Nyack Coll, NY   B
Pace U, NY   B
Prescott Coll, AZ   B
Queens Coll of the City U of
  New York, NY   B
Rensselaer Polytechnic Inst, NY   B
Rochester Inst of Technology, NY   B
Russell Sage Coll, NY   B
St. Bonaventure U, NY   B
Sarah Lawrence Coll, NY   B
State U of New York at
  Binghamton, NY   B
State U of New York at
  Plattsburgh, NY   B
State U of New York Coll at
  Brockport, NY   B
State U of New York Coll at
  Oneonta, NY   B
State U of New York Coll of
  Technology at Canton, NY   A
State U of New York Empire
  State Coll, NY   A,B
State U of New York, Fredonia,
  NY   B
Syracuse U, NY   B
United States Military Academy,
  NY   B
U at Albany, State U of New
  York, NY   B
Vassar Coll, NY   B
Yeshiva U, NY   B

Interior Architecture
Fashion Inst of Technology, NY   A,B
Syracuse U, NY   B

Interior Design
Cazenovia Coll, NY   B
Chaminade U of Honolulu, HI   A,B
Marymount Coll of Fordham U,
  NY   B
New York Inst of Technology, NY   B
New York School of Interior
  Design, NY   A,B
Pratt Inst, NY   B
Rochester Inst of Technology, NY   A,B
Sage Coll of Albany, NY   A
School of Visual Arts, NY   B

Syracuse U, NY   B
Villa Maria Coll of Buffalo, NY   A

Intermedia/Multimedia
City Coll of the City U of New
  York, NY   B
Long Island U, C.W. Post
  Campus, NY   B
State U of New York, Fredonia,
  NY   B

International Agriculture
Cornell U, NY   B

International Business/Trade/Commerce
Berkeley Coll-New York City
  Campus, NY   A,B
Berkeley Coll-Westchester
  Campus, NY   A,B
Bernard M. Baruch Coll of the
  City U of New York, NY   B
Canisius Coll, NY   B
Chatham Coll, PA   B
Clarkson U, NY   B
Dominican Coll, NY   B
Dowling Coll, NY   B
D'Youville Coll, NY   B
Elmira Coll, NY   B
Excelsior Coll, NY   B
Fordham U, NY   B
Hofstra U, NY   B
Iona Coll, NY   B
Ithaca Coll, NY   B
Long Island U, C.W. Post
  Campus, NY   B
Marymount Coll of Fordham U,
  NY   B
Mount Saint Mary Coll, NY   B
New York Inst of Technology, NY   B
New York U, NY   B
Niagara U, NY   B
Pace U, NY   B
Post U, CT   B
Queens Coll of the City U of
  New York, NY   B
Quinnipiac U, CT   B
Rochester Inst of Technology, NY   B
St. Bonaventure U, NY   B
St. John Fisher Coll, NY   B
St. John's U, NY   B
State U of New York at New
  Paltz, NY   B
State U of New York at
  Plattsburgh, NY   B
State U of New York Coll at
  Brockport, NY   B
State U of New York Coll of
  Agriculture and Technology at
  Cobleskill, NY   A
Utica Coll, NY   B

International Economics
Bard Coll, NY   B
Fordham U, NY   B
State U of New York at New
  Paltz, NY   B
State U of New York at Oswego,
  NY   B

International/Global Studies
Adelphi U, NY   B
Chatham Coll, PA   B
City Coll of the City U of New
  York, NY   B
The Coll of New Rochelle, NY   B
Iona Coll, NY   B
State U of New York Coll at
  Cortland, NY   B

International Marketing
Pace U, NY   B

International Relations and Affairs
Bard Coll, NY   B
Canisius Coll, NY   B
Chaminade U of Honolulu, HI   B
Chatham Coll, PA   B
City Coll of the City U of New
  York, NY   B
Colgate U, NY   B
Coll of Staten Island of the City
  U of New York, NY   B
Concordia Coll, NY   B

Cornell U, NY   B
Elmira Coll, NY   B
Fordham U, NY   B
Hamilton Coll, NY   B
Hobart and William Smith Colls,
  NY   B
Houghton Coll, NY   B
Le Moyne Coll, NY   B
Long Island U, C.W. Post
  Campus, NY   B
Manhattan Coll, NY   B
Manhattanville Coll, NY   B
Marymount Coll of Fordham U,
  NY   B
Marymount Manhattan Coll, NY   B
Mount Saint Mary Coll, NY   B
Nazareth Coll of Rochester, NY   B
New York U, NY   B
Niagara U, NY   B
Pace U, NY   B
Quinnipiac U, CT   B
Rochester Inst of Technology, NY   B
Russell Sage Coll, NY   B
St. John Fisher Coll, NY   B
St. John's U, NY   B
Sarah Lawrence Coll, NY   B
State U of New York at New
  Paltz, NY   B
State U of New York at Oswego,
  NY   B
State U of New York Coll at
  Brockport, NY   B
State U of New York Coll at
  Cortland, NY   B
State U of New York Coll at
  Geneseo, NY   B
State U of New York Coll at
  Oneonta, NY   B
Syracuse U, NY   B
U of West Florida, FL   B
Utica Coll, NY   B
Vassar Coll, NY   B
Wells Coll, NY   B
West Virginia Wesleyan Coll,
  WV   B

Italian
Bard Coll, NY   B
Barnard Coll, NY   B
Brooklyn Coll of the City U of
  New York, NY   B
Columbia Coll, NY   B
Columbia U, School of General
  Studies, NY   B
Cornell U, NY   B
Fordham U, NY   B
Hofstra U, NY   B
Hunter Coll of the City U of
  New York, NY   B
Iona Coll, NY   B
Lehman Coll of the City U of
  New York, NY   B
Long Island U, C.W. Post
  Campus, NY   B
Mercy Coll, NY   B
Nazareth Coll of Rochester, NY   B
New York U, NY   B
Queens Coll of the City U of
  New York, NY   B
St. John Fisher Coll, NY   B
St. John's U, NY   B
Sarah Lawrence Coll, NY   B
State U of New York at
  Binghamton, NY   B
State U of New York at Buffalo,
  NY   B
Stony Brook U, State U of New
  York, NY   B
Syracuse U, NY   B
U at Albany, State U of New
  York, NY   B
Vassar Coll, NY   B
York Coll of the City U of New
  York, NY   B

Italian Studies
Columbia Coll, NY   B
Fordham U, NY   B

Japanese
Colgate U, NY   B

Hobart and William Smith Colls,
  NY   B
Sarah Lawrence Coll, NY   B
U of Rochester, NY   B

Japanese Studies
U at Albany, State U of New
  York, NY   B

Jazz/Jazz Studies
Bard Coll, NY   B
Barnard Coll, NY   B
City Coll of the City U of New
  York, NY   B
Five Towns Coll, NY   A,B
Hofstra U, NY   B
Ithaca Coll, NY   B
The Juilliard School, NY   B
Long Island U, Brooklyn
  Campus, NY   B
Manhattan School of Music, NY   B
Sarah Lawrence Coll, NY   B
State U of New York at New
  Paltz, NY   B
U of Rochester, NY   B

Jewish/Judaic Studies
Bard Coll, NY   B
Brooklyn Coll of the City U of
  New York, NY   B
City Coll of the City U of New
  York, NY   B
Hofstra U, NY   B
Hunter Coll of the City U of
  New York, NY   B
The Jewish Theological Seminary,
  NY   B
Lehman Coll of the City U of
  New York, NY   B
New York U, NY   B
Queens Coll of the City U of
  New York, NY   B
State U of New York at
  Binghamton, NY   B
State U of New York at New
  Paltz, NY   B
U at Albany, State U of New
  York, NY   B
Vassar Coll, NY   B
Yeshiva U, NY   B

Journalism
Bernard M. Baruch Coll of the
  City U of New York, NY   B
Brooklyn Coll of the City U of
  New York, NY   B
Buffalo State Coll, State U of
  New York, NY   B
Fordham U, NY   B
Hofstra U, NY   B
Iona Coll, NY   B
Ithaca Coll, NY   B
Long Island U, Brooklyn
  Campus, NY   B
Long Island U, C.W. Post
  Campus, NY   B
Marist Coll, NY   B
Marymount Coll of Fordham U,
  NY   B
Mercy Coll, NY   B
New York U, NY   B
Polytechnic U, Brooklyn Campus,
  NY   B
Purchase Coll, State U of New
  York, NY   B
Quinnipiac U, CT   B
St. Bonaventure U, NY   B
St. John's U, NY   B
St. Thomas Aquinas Coll, NY   B
State U of New York at New
  Paltz, NY   B
State U of New York at Oswego,
  NY   B
State U of New York Coll at
  Brockport, NY   B
Syracuse U, NY   B
Utica Coll, NY   B

Kindergarten/Preschool Education
Boricua Coll, NY   B
Buffalo State Coll, State U of
  New York, NY   B
Hofstra U, NY   B

A—associate degree; B—bachelor's degree

Hunter Coll of the City U of New York, NY — B
Long Island U, C.W. Post Campus, NY — B
Maria Coll, NY — A
Medaille Coll, NY — B
Mercy Coll, NY — B
Mitchell Coll, CT — A,B
New York U, NY — B
North Carolina Ag and Tech State U, NC — B
Prescott Coll, AZ — B
Queens Coll of the City U of New York, NY — B
St. Bonaventure U, NY — B
St. Joseph's Coll, Suffolk Campus, NY — B
St. Thomas Aquinas Coll, NY — B
Sarah Lawrence Coll, NY — B
State U of New York at New Paltz, NY — B
State U of New York Coll at Cortland, NY — B
State U of New York Coll at Geneseo, NY — B
State U of New York Coll of Agriculture and Technology at Cobleskill, NY — A
State U of New York Coll of Technology at Canton, NY — A
State U of New York, Fredonia, NY — B
Syracuse U, NY — B
Villa Maria Coll of Buffalo, NY — A
Wagner Coll, NY — B
West Virginia Wesleyan Coll, WV — B
Yeshiva U, NY — B

Kinesiology and Exercise Science
Buffalo State Coll, State U of New York, NY — B
Chatham Coll, PA — B
Coll of Mount Saint Vincent, NY — B
Hofstra U, NY — B
Ithaca Coll, NY — B
Long Island U, Brooklyn Campus, NY — B
Queens Coll of the City U of New York, NY — B
Skidmore Coll, NY — B
State U of New York at Buffalo, NY — B
State U of New York Coll at Brockport, NY — B
State U of New York Coll at Cortland, NY — B
Syracuse U, NY — B

Labor and Industrial Relations
Cornell U, NY — B
Ithaca Coll, NY — B
Le Moyne Coll, NY — B
Queens Coll of the City U of New York, NY — B
State U of New York Coll at Old Westbury, NY — B
State U of New York Coll at Potsdam, NY — B
State U of New York Empire State Coll, NY — A,B
State U of New York, Fredonia, NY — B

Labor Studies
Hofstra U, NY — B

Landscape Architecture
Chatham Coll, PA — B
City Coll of the City U of New York, NY — B
Cornell U, NY — B
North Carolina Ag and Tech State U, NC — B
State U of New York Coll of Agriculture and Technology at Cobleskill, NY — A
State U of New York Coll of Environmental Science and Forestry, NY — B
State U of New York Coll of Technology at Delhi, NY — A

Landscaping and Groundskeeping
Farmingdale State U of New York, NY — A
State U of New York Coll of Agriculture and Technology at Cobleskill, NY — A
State U of New York Coll of Technology at Alfred, NY — A
State U of New York Coll of Technology at Delhi, NY — A

Land Use Planning and Management
State U of New York Coll of Environmental Science and Forestry, NY — B

Laser and Optical Technology
Excelsior Coll, NY — A,B

Latin
Bard Coll, NY — B
Barnard Coll, NY — B
Brooklyn Coll of the City U of New York, NY — B
Colgate U, NY — B
The Coll of New Rochelle, NY — B
Fordham U, NY — B
Hamilton Coll, NY — B
Hobart and William Smith Colls, NY — B
Hunter Coll of the City U of New York, NY — B
Lehman Coll of the City U of New York, NY — B
New York U, NY — B
Queens Coll of the City U of New York, NY — B
Sarah Lawrence Coll, NY — B
U at Albany, State U of New York, NY — B
Vassar Coll, NY — B

Latin American Studies
Adelphi U, NY — B
Bard Coll, NY — B
Barnard Coll, NY — B
Boricua Coll, NY — B
City Coll of the City U of New York, NY — B
Colgate U, NY — B
Columbia Coll, NY — B
Cornell U, NY — B
Fordham U, NY — B
Hobart and William Smith Colls, NY — B
Hofstra U, NY — B
Hunter Coll of the City U of New York, NY — B
Lehman Coll of the City U of New York, NY — B
New York U, NY — B
Prescott Coll, AZ — B
Queens Coll of the City U of New York, NY — B
Sarah Lawrence Coll, NY — B
State U of New York at Binghamton, NY — B
State U of New York at New Paltz, NY — B
State U of New York at Plattsburgh, NY — B
State U of New York Coll at Brockport, NY — B
Syracuse U, NY — B
United States Military Academy, NY — B
U at Albany, State U of New York, NY — B
Vassar Coll, NY — B

Legal Assistant/Paralegal
Berkeley Coll-New York City Campus, NY — A
Berkeley Coll-Westchester Campus, NY — A
Briarcliffe Coll, NY — A
Bryant and Stratton Coll, Amherst Campus, NY — A
Hilbert Coll, NY — A,B
Maria Coll, NY — A
Marist Coll, NY — B
Mercy Coll, NY — B
Post U, CT — A,B
Quinnipiac U, CT — B

Sage Coll of Albany, NY — A
St. John's U, NY — A,B
Shepherd U, WV — A
U of West Florida, FL — A

Legal Professions and Studies Related
Hofstra U, NY — B

Legal Studies
Hilbert Coll, NY — A,B
John Jay Coll of Criminal Justice of the City U of New York, NY — B
Manhattanville Coll, NY — B
Maria Coll, NY — A
Marymount Coll of Fordham U, NY — B
Quinnipiac U, CT — B
Sage Coll of Albany, NY — A,B
St. John's U, NY — B
State U of New York, Fredonia, NY — B

Liberal Arts and Sciences and Humanities Related
Sarah Lawrence Coll, NY — B
Vassar Coll, NY — B

Liberal Arts and Sciences/Liberal Studies
Adelphi U, NY — A
Boricua Coll, NY — A,B
Buffalo State Coll, State U of New York, NY — B
Cazenovia Coll, NY — A,B
Clarkson U, NY — B
Coll of Mount Saint Vincent, NY — B
The Coll of New Rochelle, NY — B
The Coll of Saint Rose, NY — B
Coll of Staten Island of the City U of New York, NY — A,B
Concordia Coll, NY — A,B
Cornell U, NY — B
Dominican Coll, NY — A
Dowling Coll, NY — B
D'Youville Coll, NY — B
Elmira Coll, NY — B
Excelsior Coll, NY — A,B
Farmingdale State U of New York, NY — A
Five Towns Coll, NY — A
Fordham U, NY — B
Hilbert Coll, NY — A
Hobart and William Smith Colls, NY — B
Hofstra U, NY — B
Houghton Coll, NY — B
Ithaca Coll, NY — B
Keuka Coll, NY — B
Long Island U, Brooklyn Campus, NY — A,B
Long Island U, C.W. Post Campus, NY — B
Long Island U, Friends World Program, NY — B
Manhattan Coll, NY — B
Maria Coll, NY — A
Marymount Coll of Fordham U, NY — A,B
Marymount Manhattan Coll, NY — B
Medaille Coll, NY — A,B
Medgar Evers Coll of the City U of New York, NY — A
Mercy Coll, NY — A
Mitchell Coll, CT — A,B
Molloy Coll, NY — A
Mount Saint Mary Coll, NY — B
New York U, NY — A,B
Niagara U, NY — A,B
Nyack Coll, NY — A,B
Pace U, NY — A,B
Paul Smith's Coll of Arts and Sciences, NY — A
Polytechnic U, Brooklyn Campus, NY — B
Post U, CT — A,B
Prescott Coll, AZ — B
Purchase Coll, State U of New York, NY — B
Quinnipiac U, CT — B
Sage Coll of Albany, NY — A,B
St. Francis Coll, NY — A,B
St. John's U, NY — A,B

St. Joseph's Coll, Suffolk Campus, NY — B
Sarah Lawrence Coll, NY — B
Skidmore Coll, NY — B
State U of New York Coll at Oneonta, NY — B
State U of New York Coll of Agriculture and Technology at Cobleskill, NY — A
State U of New York Coll of Technology at Alfred, NY — A
State U of New York Coll of Technology at Canton, NY — A
State U of New York, Fredonia, NY — B
Syracuse U, NY — B
Union Coll, NY — B
Utica Coll, NY — B
Villa Maria Coll of Buffalo, NY — A
York Coll of the City U of New York, NY — B

Library Science
St. John's U, NY — B

Linguistics
Barnard Coll, NY — B
Brooklyn Coll of the City U of New York, NY — B
City Coll of the City U of New York, NY — B
Columbia Coll, NY — B
Cornell U, NY — B
Lehman Coll of the City U of New York, NY — B
New York U, NY — B
Queens Coll of the City U of New York, NY — B
State U of New York at Binghamton, NY — B
State U of New York at Buffalo, NY — B
State U of New York at Oswego, NY — B
Stony Brook U, State U of New York, NY — B
Syracuse U, NY — B
U at Albany, State U of New York, NY — B
U of Rochester, NY — B

Literature
Alfred U, NY — B
Bard Coll, NY — B
Bernard M. Baruch Coll of the City U of New York, NY — B
Cazenovia Coll, NY — B
City Coll of the City U of New York, NY — B
Columbia U, School of General Studies, NY — B
Elmira Coll, NY — B
Excelsior Coll, NY — B
Fordham U, NY — B
Hamilton Coll, NY — B
Houghton Coll, NY — B
Hunter Coll of the City U of New York, NY — B
The Jewish Theological Seminary, NY — B
Marist Coll, NY — B
Marymount Coll of Fordham U, NY — B
Nazareth Coll of Rochester, NY — B
Pace U, NY — B
Prescott Coll, AZ — B
Purchase Coll, State U of New York, NY — B
Quinnipiac U, CT — B
Sarah Lawrence Coll, NY — B
Skidmore Coll, NY — B
State U of New York at Binghamton, NY — B
State U of New York Coll at Brockport, NY — B
State U of New York Coll at Old Westbury, NY — B
Syracuse U, NY — B
United States Military Academy, NY — B
West Virginia Wesleyan Coll, WV — B

Logistics and Materials Management
Clarkson U, NY — B
Niagara U, NY — B
St. John's U, NY — B
Syracuse U, NY — B

Machine Tool Technology
Fashion Inst of Technology, NY — A
State U of New York Coll of Technology at Alfred, NY — A
Vaughn Coll of Aeronautics and Technology, NY — A

Management Information Systems
Bernard M. Baruch Coll of the City U of New York, NY — B
Chatham Coll, PA — B
Clarkson U, NY — B
Dominican Coll, NY — B
Excelsior Coll, NY — B
Fordham U, NY — B
Globe Inst of Technology, NY — A
Hilbert Coll, NY — A
Hofstra U, NY — B
Iona Coll, NY — B
Le Moyne Coll, NY — B
Long Island U, C.W. Post Campus, NY — B
Nazareth Coll of Rochester, NY — B
New York Inst of Technology, NY — B
New York U, NY — B
Polytechnic U, Brooklyn Campus, NY — B
Post U, CT — B
Rensselaer Polytechnic Inst, NY — B
Roberts Wesleyan Coll, NY — B
Rochester Inst of Technology, NY — B
St. John Fisher Coll, NY — B
St. John's U, NY — B
U of West Florida, FL — B
Yeshiva U, NY — B

Management Information Systems and Services Related
Fordham U, NY — B
Rensselaer Polytechnic Inst, NY — B
St. Bonaventure U, NY — B

Management Science
Cornell U, NY — B
Manhattan Coll, NY — B
Prescott Coll, AZ — B
St. Bonaventure U, NY — B
State U of New York at Binghamton, NY — B
State U of New York at Oswego, NY — B

Manufacturing Engineering
Clarkson U, NY — B
Hofstra U, NY — B
Rensselaer Polytechnic Inst, NY — B

Manufacturing Technology
Farmingdale State U of New York, NY — B
Rochester Inst of Technology, NY — B

Marine Biology and Biological Oceanography
Dowling Coll, NY — B
Mitchell Coll, CT — A
Sarah Lawrence Coll, NY — B
U of West Florida, FL — B

Marine Science/Merchant Marine Officer
Prescott Coll, AZ — B
United States Merchant Marine Academy, NY — B

Marine Transportation Related
United States Merchant Marine Academy, NY — B

Maritime Science
United States Merchant Marine Academy, NY — B

Marketing/Marketing Management
Berkeley Coll-New York City Campus, NY — A,B
Berkeley Coll-Westchester Campus, NY — A,B

Bernard M. Baruch Coll of the City U of New York, NY — B
Chaminade U of Honolulu, HI — B
Chatham Coll, PA — B
Clarkson U, NY — B
Cornell U, NY — B
Dominican Coll, NY — B
D'Youville Coll, NY — B
Elmira Coll, NY — B
Excelsior Coll, NY — B
Five Towns Coll, NY — A
Fordham U, NY — B
Hofstra U, NY — B
Iona Coll, NY — B
Ithaca Coll, NY — B
Keuka Coll, NY — B
The King's Coll, NY — B
Laboratory Inst of Merchandising, NY — B
Long Island U, Brentwood Campus, NY — B
Long Island U, C.W. Post Campus, NY — B
Manhattan Coll, NY — B
Marymount Coll of Fordham U, NY — B
Medaille Coll, NY — B
Mercy Coll, NY — B
Nazareth Coll of Rochester, NY — B
New York Inst of Technology, NY — B
New York U, NY — B
Niagara U, NY — B
Pace U, NY — B
Post U, CT — A,B
Quinnipiac U, CT — B
Rensselaer Polytechnic Inst, NY — B
Roberts Wesleyan Coll, NY — B
Rochester Inst of Technology, NY — B
Sage Coll of Albany, NY — A
St. Bonaventure U, NY — B
St. John Fisher Coll, NY — B
St. John's U, NY — B
St. Thomas Aquinas Coll, NY — B
Siena Coll, NY — B
State U of New York at New Paltz, NY — B
State U of New York at Oswego, NY — B
State U of New York at Plattsburgh, NY — B
State U of New York Coll at Brockport, NY — B
State U of New York Coll at Old Westbury, NY — B
State U of New York Coll of Technology at Alfred, NY — A
State U of New York Coll of Technology at Delhi, NY — A
State U of New York, Fredonia, NY — B
Syracuse U, NY — B
U of West Florida, FL — B
West Virginia Wesleyan Coll, WV — B
Yeshiva U, NY — B
York Coll of the City U of New York, NY — B

Marketing Related
Canisius Coll, NY — B
Mount Saint Mary Coll, NY — B
Pace U, NY — B

Marketing Research
Ithaca Coll, NY — B
Rochester Inst of Technology, NY — B

Masonry
State U of New York Coll of Technology at Alfred, NY — A
State U of New York Coll of Technology at Delhi, NY — A

Mass Communication/Media
Buffalo State Coll, State U of New York, NY — B
Chaminade U of Honolulu, HI — B
City Coll of the City U of New York, NY — B
Coll of Mount Saint Vincent, NY — B
The Coll of New Rochelle, NY — B
Excelsior Coll, NY — B

Five Towns Coll, NY — A
Fordham U, NY — B
Hamilton Coll, NY — B
Hobart and William Smith Colls, NY — B
Hofstra U, NY — B
Hunter Coll of the City U of New York, NY — B
Iona Coll, NY — B
Ithaca Coll, NY — B
Lehman Coll of the City U of New York, NY — B
Marist Coll, NY — B
Marymount Coll of Fordham U, NY — B
Marymount Manhattan Coll, NY — B
Medaille Coll, NY — B
Mount Saint Mary Coll, NY — B
New York U, NY — B
Niagara U, NY — B
North Carolina Ag and Tech State U, NC — B
Queens Coll of the City U of New York, NY — B
Quinnipiac U, CT — B
Russell Sage Coll, NY — B
St. Bonaventure U, NY — B
St. John Fisher Coll, NY — B
St. Thomas Aquinas Coll, NY — B
State U of New York at Buffalo, NY — B
State U of New York at New Paltz, NY — B
State U of New York at Oswego, NY — B
State U of New York at Plattsburgh, NY — B
State U of New York Coll at Brockport, NY — B
State U of New York Coll at Oneonta, NY — B
State U of New York, Fredonia, NY — B
U at Albany, State U of New York, NY — B
Yeshiva U, NY — B

Materials Engineering
Clarkson U, NY — B
Cornell U, NY — B
Rensselaer Polytechnic Inst, NY — B

Materials Science
Alfred U, NY — B
Clarkson U, NY — B
Columbia U, The Fu Foundation School of Engineering and Applied Science, NY — B
Cornell U, NY — B

Maternal/Child Health and Neonatal Nursing
State U of New York at Buffalo, NY — B

Mathematics
Adelphi U, NY — B
Alfred U, NY — B
Bard Coll, NY — B
Barnard Coll, NY — B
Bernard M. Baruch Coll of the City U of New York, NY — B
Brooklyn Coll of the City U of New York, NY — B
Buffalo State Coll, State U of New York, NY — B
Chatham Coll, PA — B
City Coll of the City U of New York, NY — B
Clarkson U, NY — B
Colgate U, NY — B
Coll of Mount Saint Vincent, NY — B
The Coll of New Rochelle, NY — B
The Coll of Saint Rose, NY — B
Coll of Staten Island of the City U of New York, NY — B
Columbia Coll, NY — B
Columbia U, School of General Studies, NY — B
Concordia Coll, NY — B
Cornell U, NY — B
Daemen Coll, NY — B

Dominican Coll, NY — B
Dowling Coll, NY — B
Elmira Coll, NY — B
Excelsior Coll, NY — B
Fordham U, NY — B
Hamilton Coll, NY — B
Hartwick Coll, NY — B
Hobart and William Smith Colls, NY — B
Hofstra U, NY — B
Houghton Coll, NY — B
Hunter Coll of the City U of New York, NY — B
Iona Coll, NY — B
Ithaca Coll, NY — B
Keuka Coll, NY — B
Lehman Coll of the City U of New York, NY — B
Le Moyne Coll, NY — B
Long Island U, Brooklyn Campus, NY — B
Long Island U, C.W. Post Campus, NY — B
Manhattan Coll, NY — B
Manhattanville Coll, NY — B
Marist Coll, NY — B
Marymount Coll of Fordham U, NY — B
Mercy Coll, NY — B
Molloy Coll, NY — B
Mount Saint Mary Coll, NY — B
Nazareth Coll of Rochester, NY — B
New York U, NY — B
Niagara U, NY — B
North Carolina Ag and Tech State U, NC — B
Nyack Coll, NY — B
Pace U, NY — B
Polytechnic U, Brooklyn Campus, NY — B
Purchase Coll, State U of New York, NY — B
Queens Coll of the City U of New York, NY — B
Quinnipiac U, CT — B
Rensselaer Polytechnic Inst, NY — B
Roberts Wesleyan Coll, NY — B
Rochester Inst of Technology, NY — B
Russell Sage Coll, NY — B
St. Bonaventure U, NY — B
St. Francis Coll, NY — B
St. John Fisher Coll, NY — B
St. John's U, NY — B
St. Joseph's Coll, New York, NY — B
St. Joseph's Coll, Suffolk Campus, NY — B
St. Lawrence U, NY — B
St. Thomas Aquinas Coll, NY — B
Sarah Lawrence Coll, NY — B
Shepherd U, WV — B
Siena Coll, NY — B
Skidmore Coll, NY — B
State U of New York at Binghamton, NY — B
State U of New York at Buffalo, NY — B
State U of New York at New Paltz, NY — B
State U of New York at Oswego, NY — B
State U of New York at Plattsburgh, NY — B
State U of New York Coll at Brockport, NY — B
State U of New York Coll at Cortland, NY — B
State U of New York Coll at Geneseo, NY — B
State U of New York Coll at Old Westbury, NY — B
State U of New York Coll at Oneonta, NY — B
State U of New York Coll at Potsdam, NY — B
State U of New York Coll of Technology at Alfred, NY — A
State U of New York Coll of Technology at Delhi, NY — A
State U of New York Empire State Coll, NY — A,B

A—associate degree; B—bachelor's degree

State U of New York, Fredonia, NY — B
Stony Brook U, State U of New York, NY — B
Syracuse U, NY — B
Union Coll, NY — B
United States Military Academy, NY — B
U at Albany, State U of New York, NY — B
U of Rochester, NY — B
U of West Florida, FL — B
Utica Coll, NY — B
Vassar Coll, NY — B
Wagner Coll, NY — B
Wells Coll, NY — B
West Virginia Wesleyan Coll, WV — B
Yeshiva U, NY — B
York Coll of the City U of New York, NY — B

Mathematics and Computer Science
Alfred U, NY — B
Hofstra U, NY — B
Ithaca Coll, NY — B
Long Island U, C.W. Post Campus, NY — B
Rochester Inst of Technology, NY — B
St. Joseph's Coll, New York, NY — B
U at Albany, State U of New York, NY — B

Mathematics and Statistics Related
Barnard Coll, NY — B
Canisius Coll, NY — B
Hofstra U, NY — B
New York U, NY — B
U of Rochester, NY — B

Mathematics Related
State U of New York at Buffalo, NY — B

Mathematics Teacher Education
Brooklyn Coll of the City U of New York, NY — B
Buffalo State Coll, State U of New York, NY — B
Chatham Coll, PA — B
City Coll of the City U of New York, NY — B
The Coll of Saint Rose, NY — B
Cornell U, NY — B
Daemen Coll, NY — B
Dominican Coll, NY — B
Dowling Coll, NY — B
Elmira Coll, NY — B
Hofstra U, NY — B
Hunter Coll of the City U of New York, NY — B
Iona Coll, NY — B
Ithaca Coll, NY — B
Keuka Coll, NY — B
Le Moyne Coll, NY — B
Long Island U, Brooklyn Campus, NY — B
Long Island U, C.W. Post Campus, NY — B
Manhattanville Coll, NY — B
Marymount Coll of Fordham U, NY — B
Molloy Coll, NY — B
Nazareth Coll of Rochester, NY — B
New York Inst of Technology, NY — B
New York U, NY — B
Niagara U, NY — B
Pace U, NY — B
Prescott Coll, AZ — B
Queens Coll of the City U of New York, NY — B
Roberts Wesleyan Coll, NY — B
St. Bonaventure U, NY — B
St. Francis Coll, NY — B
St. John Fisher Coll, NY — B
St. John's U, NY — B
State U of New York Coll at Brockport, NY — B
State U of New York Coll at Cortland, NY — B
State U of New York Coll at Old Westbury, NY — B

State U of New York Coll at Oneonta, NY — B
State U of New York Coll at Potsdam, NY — B
Syracuse U, NY — B
U at Albany, State U of New York, NY — B
U of West Florida, FL — B
Utica Coll, NY — B
West Virginia Wesleyan Coll, WV — B

Mechanical Design Technology
State U of New York Coll of Technology at Alfred, NY — A

Mechanical Engineering
Alfred U, NY — B
City Coll of the City U of New York, NY — B
Clarkson U, NY — B
Columbia U, The Fu Foundation School of Engineering and Applied Science, NY — B
Cornell U, NY — B
Hofstra U, NY — B
Manhattan Coll, NY — B
New York Inst of Technology, NY — B
North Carolina Ag and Tech State U, NC — B
Polytechnic U, Brooklyn Campus, NY — B
Rensselaer Polytechnic Inst, NY — B
Rochester Inst of Technology, NY — B
State U of New York at Binghamton, NY — B
State U of New York at Buffalo, NY — B
Stony Brook U, State U of New York, NY — B
Syracuse U, NY — B
Union Coll, NY — B
United States Military Academy, NY — B
U of Rochester, NY — B

Mechanical Engineering/Mechanical Technology
Buffalo State Coll, State U of New York, NY — B
Excelsior Coll, NY — A,B
Farmingdale State U of New York, NY — A,B
New York Inst of Technology, NY — A,B
Rochester Inst of Technology, NY — A,B
State U of New York Coll of Technology at Alfred, NY — A,B
State U of New York Coll of Technology at Canton, NY — A
State U of New York Inst of Technology, NY — B

Mechanical Engineering Technologies Related
New York Inst of Technology, NY — B

Medical Administrative Assistant and Medical Secretary
Monroe Coll, Bronx, NY — A
Monroe Coll, New Rochelle, NY — A

Medical/Clinical Assistant
State U of New York Coll of Technology at Alfred, NY — A

Medical Illustration
Rochester Inst of Technology, NY — B

Medical Laboratory Technology
Quinnipiac U, CT — B

Medical Microbiology and Bacteriology
Cornell U, NY — B
Quinnipiac U, CT — B
Wagner Coll, NY — B

Medical Radiologic Technology
Long Island U, C.W. Post Campus, NY — B
St. Francis Coll, NY — B
State U of New York Upstate Medical U, NY — B

Medicinal and Pharmaceutical Chemistry
State U of New York at Buffalo, NY — B

Medieval and Renaissance Studies
Bard Coll, NY — B
Barnard Coll, NY — B
Columbia Coll, NY — B
Cornell U, NY — B
Fordham U, NY — B
Hamilton Coll, NY — B
Hobart and William Smith Colls, NY — B
New York U, NY — B
State U of New York at Binghamton, NY — B
Syracuse U, NY — B
U at Albany, State U of New York, NY — B
Vassar Coll, NY — B

Mental Health/Rehabilitation
Elmira Coll, NY — B
Prescott Coll, AZ — B

Metal and Jewelry Arts
Hofstra U, NY — B
Pratt Inst, NY — B
Rochester Inst of Technology, NY — A,B
State U of New York at New Paltz, NY — B
State U of New York Coll at Brockport, NY — B
Syracuse U, NY — B

Meteorology
Cornell U, NY — B
State U of New York Coll at Brockport, NY — B

Microbiology
Cornell U, NY — B

Middle/Near Eastern and Semitic Languages Related
Sarah Lawrence Coll, NY — B

Middle School Education
Coll of Mount Saint Vincent, NY — B
Concordia Coll, NY — B
Elmira Coll, NY — B
Ithaca Coll, NY — B
Manhattan Coll, NY — B
Marymount Coll of Fordham U, NY — B
Medaille Coll, NY — B
New York U, NY — B
Prescott Coll, AZ — B
St. Bonaventure U, NY — B
St. John's U, NY — B
State U of New York Coll at Brockport, NY — B
State U of New York Coll at Cortland, NY — B
State U of New York Coll at Old Westbury, NY — B
State U of New York Coll at Oneonta, NY — B
U of West Florida, FL — B
Wagner Coll, NY — B
West Virginia Wesleyan Coll, WV — B

Missionary Studies and Missiology
Nyack Coll, NY — B

Modern Greek
Bard Coll, NY — B
Barnard Coll, NY — B
Brooklyn Coll of the City U of New York, NY — B
Colgate U, NY — B
Columbia Coll, NY — B
Fordham U, NY — B
Hamilton Coll, NY — B
Lehman Coll of the City U of New York, NY — B
New York U, NY — B

Modern Languages
Alfred U, NY — B
Bard Coll, NY — B
Coll of Mount Saint Vincent, NY — B
Elmira Coll, NY — B
Fordham U, NY — B
Hamilton Coll, NY — B

Hobart and William Smith Colls, NY — B
Long Island U, Brooklyn Campus, NY — B
Marymount Coll of Fordham U, NY — B
Nazareth Coll of Rochester, NY — B
Pace U, NY — B
Purchase Coll, State U of New York, NY — B
St. Bonaventure U, NY — B
St. Lawrence U, NY — B
St. Thomas Aquinas Coll, NY — B
Sarah Lawrence Coll, NY — B
Syracuse U, NY — B
United States Military Academy, NY — B

Molecular Biochemistry
Polytechnic U, Brooklyn Campus, NY — B

Molecular Biology
Bard Coll, NY — B
Clarkson U, NY — B
Colgate U, NY — B
Cornell U, NY — B
Hamilton Coll, NY — B
Long Island U, C.W. Post Campus, NY — B
Sarah Lawrence Coll, NY — B
State U of New York Coll at Brockport, NY — B
U at Albany, State U of New York, NY — B
Wells Coll, NY — B

Multi-/Interdisciplinary Studies Related
Adelphi U, NY — B
Barnard Coll, NY — B
Buffalo State Coll, State U of New York, NY — B
The Coll of New Rochelle, NY — B
Cornell U, NY — B
Hofstra U, NY — B
Ithaca Coll, NY — B
Long Island U, Brooklyn Campus, NY — B
Long Island U, C.W. Post Campus, NY — B
Long Island U, Friends World Program, NY — B
New York Inst of Technology, NY — B
Pace U, NY — B
Queens Coll of the City U of New York, NY — B
St. John Fisher Coll, NY — B
Shepherd U, WV — A
State U of New York at Buffalo, NY — B
State U of New York Coll at Potsdam, NY — B
Stony Brook U, State U of New York, NY — B
Vassar Coll, NY — B

Music
Adelphi U, NY — B
Bard Coll, NY — B
Barnard Coll, NY — B
Bernard M. Baruch Coll of the City U of New York, NY — B
Brooklyn Coll of the City U of New York, NY — B
Buffalo State Coll, State U of New York, NY — B
Chatham Coll, PA — B
City Coll of the City U of New York, NY — B
Colgate U, NY — B
The Coll of Saint Rose, NY — B
Coll of Staten Island of the City U of New York, NY — B
Columbia Coll, NY — B
Columbia U, School of General Studies, NY — B
Concordia Coll, NY — B
Cornell U, NY — B
Dowling Coll, NY — B
Elmira Coll, NY — B
Excelsior Coll, NY — B
Five Towns Coll, NY — A,B
Fordham U, NY — B

Hamilton Coll, NY	B
Hartwick Coll, NY	B
Hobart and William Smith Colls, NY	B
Hofstra U, NY	B
Houghton Coll, NY	B
Hunter Coll of the City U of New York, NY	B
Ithaca Coll, NY	B
The Jewish Theological Seminary, NY	B
The Juilliard School, NY	B
Lehman Coll of the City U of New York, NY	B
Long Island U, C.W. Post Campus, NY	B
Manhattan School of Music, NY	B
Manhattanville Coll, NY	B
Mercy Coll, NY	B
Molloy Coll, NY	B
Nazareth Coll of Rochester, NY	B
New York U, NY	B
Nyack Coll, NY	B
Purchase Coll, State U of New York, NY	B
Queens Coll of the City U of New York, NY	B
Roberts Wesleyan Coll, NY	B
St. Lawrence U, NY	B
Sarah Lawrence Coll, NY	B
Shepherd U, WV	B
State U of New York at Binghamton, NY	B
State U of New York at Buffalo, NY	B
State U of New York at New Paltz, NY	B
State U of New York at Oswego, NY	B
State U of New York at Plattsburgh, NY	B
State U of New York Coll at Geneseo, NY	B
State U of New York Coll at Oneonta, NY	B
State U of New York Coll at Potsdam, NY	B
State U of New York, Fredonia, NY	B
Stony Brook U, State U of New York, NY	B
Syracuse U, NY	B
U at Albany, State U of New York, NY	B
U of Rochester, NY	B
Vassar Coll, NY	B
Villa Maria Coll of Buffalo, NY	A
Wagner Coll, NY	B
Wells Coll, NY	B
West Virginia Wesleyan Coll, WV	B
Yeshiva U, NY	B
York Coll of the City U of New York, NY	B

Music History, Literature, and Theory

Bard Coll, NY	B
Cornell U, NY	B
Fordham U, NY	B
Hofstra U, NY	B
Nazareth Coll of Rochester, NY	B
Sarah Lawrence Coll, NY	B
Skidmore Coll, NY	B
State U of New York at New Paltz, NY	B
State U of New York, Fredonia, NY	B

Music Management and Merchandising

Five Towns Coll, NY	A,B
Hofstra U, NY	B
New York U, NY	B
State U of New York Coll at Oneonta, NY	B
State U of New York Coll at Potsdam, NY	B
State U of New York, Fredonia, NY	B
Syracuse U, NY	B
Villa Maria Coll of Buffalo, NY	A

Musicology and Ethnomusicology

Cornell U, NY	B

Music Performance

Bard Coll, NY	B
Brooklyn Coll of the City U of New York, NY	B
City Coll of the City U of New York, NY	B
Hofstra U, NY	B
Ithaca Coll, NY	B
Long Island U, Brooklyn Campus, NY	B
Long Island U, C.W. Post Campus, NY	B
New York U, NY	B
Queens Coll of the City U of New York, NY	B
Sarah Lawrence Coll, NY	B
State U of New York at Binghamton, NY	B
State U of New York at Buffalo, NY	B
State U of New York Coll at Potsdam, NY	B
Syracuse U, NY	B
U of West Florida, FL	B

Music Related

Long Island U, Brooklyn Campus, NY	B
State U of New York Coll at Potsdam, NY	B

Music Teacher Education

Brooklyn Coll of the City U of New York, NY	B
City Coll of the City U of New York, NY	B
The Coll of Saint Rose, NY	B
Concordia Coll, NY	B
Dowling Coll, NY	B
Five Towns Coll, NY	B
Hartwick Coll, NY	B
Hofstra U, NY	B
Houghton Coll, NY	B
Ithaca Coll, NY	B
Long Island U, Brooklyn Campus, NY	B
Long Island U, C.W. Post Campus, NY	B
Manhattanville Coll, NY	B
Mercy Coll, NY	B
Nazareth Coll of Rochester, NY	B
New York U, NY	B
North Carolina Ag and Tech State U, NC	B
Nyack Coll, NY	B
Prescott Coll, AZ	B
Queens Coll of the City U of New York, NY	B
Roberts Wesleyan Coll, NY	B
State U of New York Coll at Potsdam, NY	B
State U of New York, Fredonia, NY	B
Syracuse U, NY	B
U of Rochester, NY	B
U of West Florida, FL	B
West Virginia Wesleyan Coll, WV	B

Music Theory and Composition

Bard Coll, NY	B
Brooklyn Coll of the City U of New York, NY	B
City Coll of the City U of New York, NY	B
Cornell U, NY	B
Hofstra U, NY	B
Houghton Coll, NY	B
Ithaca Coll, NY	B
Long Island U, Brooklyn Campus, NY	B
New York U, NY	B
Nyack Coll, NY	B
Sarah Lawrence Coll, NY	B
State U of New York Coll at Potsdam, NY	B
Syracuse U, NY	B
U of Rochester, NY	B

Music Therapy

Molloy Coll, NY	B
Nazareth Coll of Rochester, NY	B
State U of New York at New Paltz, NY	B
State U of New York, Fredonia, NY	B

Mycology

Cornell U, NY	B

Natural Resource Economics

Cornell U, NY	B

Natural Resources/Conservation

Cornell U, NY	B
Prescott Coll, AZ	B
State U of New York Coll of Environmental Science and Forestry, NY	B

Natural Resources Management and Policy

Paul Smith's Coll of Arts and Sciences, NY	B
Prescott Coll, AZ	B
Rochester Inst of Technology, NY	B
State U of New York Coll of Environmental Science and Forestry, NY	B

Natural Sciences

Bard Coll, NY	B
Bernard M. Baruch Coll of the City U of New York, NY	B
Colgate U, NY	B
Daemen Coll, NY	B
Dowling Coll, NY	B
Fordham U, NY	B
Hofstra U, NY	B
Medgar Evers Coll of the City U of New York, NY	A
Roberts Wesleyan Coll, NY	A
St. Thomas Aquinas Coll, NY	B
Sarah Lawrence Coll, NY	B
State U of New York Coll at Geneseo, NY	B

Naval Architecture and Marine Engineering

United States Merchant Marine Academy, NY	B
Webb Inst, NY	B

Navy/Marine Corps R.O.T.C./Naval Science

Rensselaer Polytechnic Inst, NY	B

Near and Middle Eastern Studies

Barnard Coll, NY	B
Columbia Coll, NY	B
Columbia U, School of General Studies, NY	B
Cornell U, NY	B
Fordham U, NY	B
New York U, NY	B
Queens Coll of the City U of New York, NY	B
Sarah Lawrence Coll, NY	B
United States Military Academy, NY	B

Neuroscience

Colgate U, NY	B
Cornell U, NY	B
Hamilton Coll, NY	B
New York U, NY	B
St. Lawrence U, NY	B
Skidmore Coll, NY	B
Union Coll, NY	B

Non-Profit Management

Clarkson U, NY	B

Nuclear Engineering

Cornell U, NY	B
Rensselaer Polytechnic Inst, NY	B
United States Military Academy, NY	B

Nuclear Engineering Technology

Excelsior Coll, NY	A,B
United States Merchant Marine Academy, NY	B

Nuclear Medical Technology

Long Island U, Brooklyn Campus, NY	B
Long Island U, C.W. Post Campus, NY	B
Manhattan Coll, NY	B
Molloy Coll, NY	A
Rochester Inst of Technology, NY	B
State U of New York at Buffalo, NY	B

Nurse Anesthetist

State U of New York at Buffalo, NY	B

Nursing (Licensed Practical/Vocational Nurse Training)

Maria Coll, NY	A
Medgar Evers Coll of the City U of New York, NY	A

Nursing (Registered Nurse Training)

Adelphi U, NY	B
Coll of Mount Saint Vincent, NY	B
The Coll of New Rochelle, NY	B
Coll of Staten Island of the City U of New York, NY	A
Crouse Hospital School of Nursing, NY	A
Daemen Coll, NY	B
Dominican Coll, NY	B
D'Youville Coll, NY	B
Elmira Coll, NY	B
Excelsior Coll, NY	A,B
Farmingdale State U of New York, NY	A
Hartwick Coll, NY	B
Hunter Coll of the City U of New York, NY	B
Keuka Coll, NY	B
Lehman Coll of the City U of New York, NY	B
Long Island U, Brooklyn Campus, NY	B
Long Island U, C.W. Post Campus, NY	B
Maria Coll, NY	A
Medgar Evers Coll of the City U of New York, NY	B
Mercy Coll, NY	B
Molloy Coll, NY	B
Mount Saint Mary Coll, NY	B
Nazareth Coll of Rochester, NY	B
New York Inst of Technology, NY	B
New York U, NY	B
North Carolina Ag and Tech State U, NC	B
Pace U, NY	B
Phillips Beth Israel School of Nursing, NY	A
Quinnipiac U, CT	B
Roberts Wesleyan Coll, NY	B
Russell Sage Coll, NY	B
St. John Fisher Coll, NY	B
St. John's U, NY	B
St. Joseph's Coll, New York, NY	B
St. Joseph's Coll, Suffolk Campus, NY	B
Shepherd U, WV	A,B
State U of New York at Binghamton, NY	B
State U of New York at Buffalo, NY	B
State U of New York at New Paltz, NY	B
State U of New York at Plattsburgh, NY	B
State U of New York Coll at Brockport, NY	B
State U of New York Coll of Technology at Alfred, NY	A
State U of New York Coll of Technology at Canton, NY	A
State U of New York Coll of Technology at Delhi, NY	A
State U of New York Downstate Medical Center, NY	B
State U of New York Inst of Technology, NY	B
Stony Brook U, State U of New York, NY	B

A—associate degree; B—bachelor's degree

U of Rochester, NY — B
U of West Florida, FL — B
Utica Coll, NY — B
Wagner Coll, NY — B
West Virginia Wesleyan Coll, WV
York Coll of the City U of New York, NY — B

Nursing Related
Adelphi U, NY — B
Coll of Staten Island of the City U of New York, NY — B
Long Island U, Brooklyn Campus, NY — B
Long Island U, C.W. Post Campus, NY — B
New York Inst of Technology, NY — B
Roberts Wesleyan Coll, NY — B
St. Francis Coll, NY — B
State U of New York at Buffalo, NY — B

Nursing Science
Elmira Coll, NY — B
Long Island U, C.W. Post Campus, NY — B
State U of New York Upstate Medical U, NY — B

Nutrition Sciences
Cornell U, NY — B
New York Inst of Technology, NY — B
Russell Sage Coll, NY — B
State U of New York at Buffalo, NY — B

Occupational Health and Industrial Hygiene
Clarkson U, NY — B

Occupational Safety and Health Technology
Mercy Coll, NY — B
North Carolina Ag and Tech State U, NC — B
Rochester Inst of Technology, NY — B
Shepherd U, WV — A

Occupational Therapist Assistant
Maria Coll, NY — A
State U of New York Coll of Technology at Canton, NY — A

Occupational Therapy
Dominican Coll, NY — B
D'Youville Coll, NY — B
Ithaca Coll, NY — B
Keuka Coll, NY — B
Long Island U, Brooklyn Campus, NY — B
New York Inst of Technology, NY — B
Quinnipiac U, CT — B
Russell Sage Coll, NY — B
State U of New York at Buffalo, NY — B
State U of New York Downstate Medical Center, NY — B
Utica Coll, NY — B
York Coll of the City U of New York, NY — B

Office Management
Berkeley Coll-New York City Campus, NY — A,B
Berkeley Coll-Westchester Campus, NY — A,B
State U of New York Coll of Technology at Canton, NY — A

Operations Management
Clarkson U, NY — B
Excelsior Coll, NY — B
Farmingdale State U of New York, NY — B

Operations Research
Bernard M. Baruch Coll of the City U of New York, NY — B
Columbia U, The Fu Foundation School of Engineering and Applied Science, NY — B
Cornell U, NY — B
Long Island U, Brooklyn Campus, NY — B
Mercy Coll, NY — B

New York U, NY — B
United States Military Academy, NY — B

Ophthalmic Laboratory Technology
Rochester Inst of Technology, NY — A

Ophthalmic/Optometric Services
State U of New York at New Paltz, NY — B
State U of New York Coll at Oneonta, NY — B

Optical Sciences
U of Rochester, NY — B

Organic Chemistry
Cornell U, NY — B
Sarah Lawrence Coll, NY — B

Organizational Behavior
Manhattan Coll, NY — B

Organizational Communication
State U of New York Coll at Brockport, NY — B

Ornamental Horticulture
Cornell U, NY — B
Farmingdale State U of New York, NY — A
State U of New York Coll of Agriculture and Technology at Cobleskill, NY — A

Painting
Bard Coll, NY — B
Buffalo State Coll, State U of New York, NY — B
Cornell U, NY — B
Hofstra U, NY — B
Pratt Inst, NY — A,B
Sarah Lawrence Coll, NY — B
School of Visual Arts, NY — B
State U of New York Coll at Brockport, NY — B
State U of New York Coll at Potsdam, NY — B
Syracuse U, NY — B
West Virginia Wesleyan Coll, WV — B

Parks, Recreation and Leisure
Houghton Coll, NY — B
Ithaca Coll, NY — B
Mitchell Coll, CT — A
North Carolina Ag and Tech State U, NC — B
Prescott Coll, AZ — B
St. Joseph's Coll, Suffolk Campus, NY — B
St. Thomas Aquinas Coll, NY — B
Shepherd U, WV — B
State U of New York Coll at Brockport, NY — B
State U of New York Coll at Cortland, NY — B
State U of New York Coll of Environmental Science and Forestry, NY — B
State U of New York Coll of Technology at Delhi, NY — A

Parks, Recreation and Leisure Facilities Management
Paul Smith's Coll of Arts and Sciences, NY — A
State U of New York Coll at Cortland, NY — B
State U of New York Coll of Agriculture and Technology at Cobleskill, NY — A
State U of New York Coll of Technology at Delhi, NY — A,B

Parks, Recreation, and Leisure Related
State U of New York Coll at Brockport, NY — B

Pastoral Counseling and Specialized Ministries Related
St. John's U, NY — B

Pastoral Studies/Counseling
Houghton Coll, NY — B
Nyack Coll, NY — B
Roberts Wesleyan Coll, NY — B

Pathologist Assistant
St. John's U, NY — B

Peace Studies and Conflict Resolution
Colgate U, NY — B
Cornell U, NY — B
Fordham U, NY — B
Le Moyne Coll, NY — B
Molloy Coll, NY — B

Pediatric Nursing
State U of New York at Buffalo, NY — B

Perfusion Technology
State U of New York Upstate Medical U, NY — B

Personality Psychology
Cornell U, NY — B

Pharmacology
Hunter Coll of the City U of New York, NY — B
State U of New York at Buffalo, NY — B
Stony Brook U, State U of New York, NY — B

Pharmacy
Albany Coll of Pharmacy of Union U, NY — B
Long Island U, Brooklyn Campus, NY — B
St. John's U, NY — B

Pharmacy Administration/ Pharmaceutics
State U of New York at Buffalo, NY — B

Pharmacy, Pharmaceutical Sciences, and Administration Related
Albany Coll of Pharmacy of Union U, NY — B
Long Island U, Brooklyn Campus, NY — B
St. John's U, NY — B
State U of New York at Buffalo, NY — B

Philosophy
Adelphi U, NY — B
Alfred U, NY — B
Bard Coll, NY — B
Barnard Coll, NY — B
Bernard M. Baruch Coll of the City U of New York, NY — B
Brooklyn Coll of the City U of New York, NY — B
Buffalo State Coll, State U of New York, NY — B
Canisius Coll, NY — B
Chaminade U of Honolulu, HI — B
City Coll of the City U of New York, NY — B
Colgate U, NY — B
Coll of Mount Saint Vincent, NY — B
The Coll of New Rochelle, NY — B
Coll of Staten Island of the City U of New York, NY — B
Columbia Coll, NY — B
Columbia U, School of General Studies, NY — B
Cornell U, NY — B
Dowling Coll, NY — B
D'Youville Coll, NY — B
Elmira Coll, NY — B
Excelsior Coll, NY — B
Fordham U, NY — B
Hamilton Coll, NY — B
Hartwick Coll, NY — B
Hobart and William Smith Colls, NY — B
Hofstra U, NY — B
Houghton Coll, NY — B
Hunter Coll of the City U of New York, NY — B
Iona Coll, NY — B
Ithaca Coll, NY — B
The Jewish Theological Seminary, NY — B
Lehman Coll of the City U of New York, NY — B

Le Moyne Coll, NY — B
Long Island U, Brooklyn Campus, NY — B
Long Island U, C.W. Post Campus, NY — B
Manhattan Coll, NY — B
Manhattanville Coll, NY — B
Molloy Coll, NY — B
Nazareth Coll of Rochester, NY — B
New York U, NY — B
Niagara U, NY — B
Nyack Coll, NY — B
Prescott Coll, AZ — B
Purchase Coll, State U of New York, NY — B
Queens Coll of the City U of New York, NY — B
Rensselaer Polytechnic Inst, NY — B
Roberts Wesleyan Coll, NY — B
St. Bonaventure U, NY — B
St. Francis Coll, NY — B
St. John Fisher Coll, NY — B
St. John's U, NY — B
St. Lawrence U, NY — B
St. Thomas Aquinas Coll, NY — B
Sarah Lawrence Coll, NY — B
Siena Coll, NY — B
Skidmore Coll, NY — B
State U of New York at Binghamton, NY — B
State U of New York at Buffalo, NY — B
State U of New York at New Paltz, NY — B
State U of New York at Oswego, NY — B
State U of New York at Plattsburgh, NY — B
State U of New York Coll at Brockport, NY — B
State U of New York Coll at Cortland, NY — B
State U of New York Coll at Geneseo, NY — B
State U of New York Coll at Old Westbury, NY — B
State U of New York Coll at Oneonta, NY — B
State U of New York Coll at Potsdam, NY — B
State U of New York, Fredonia, NY — B
Stony Brook U, State U of New York, NY — B
Syracuse U, NY — B
Union Coll, NY — B
United States Military Academy, NY — B
U at Albany, State U of New York, NY — B
U of Rochester, NY — B
U of West Florida, FL — B
Utica Coll, NY — B
Vassar Coll, NY — B
Wells Coll, NY — B
West Virginia Wesleyan Coll, WV — B
Yeshiva U, NY — B
York Coll of the City U of New York, NY — B

Philosophy and Religious Studies Related
Pace U, NY — B
Roberts Wesleyan Coll, NY — B
St. John's U, NY — B
Sarah Lawrence Coll, NY — B
State U of New York at Oswego, NY — B
Syracuse U, NY — B
West Virginia Wesleyan Coll, WV — B

Photographic and Film/Video Technology
Rochester Inst of Technology, NY — B
St. John's U, NY — B

Photography
Bard Coll, NY — B
Buffalo State Coll, State U of New York, NY — B
Cazenovia Coll, NY — A,B
Cornell U, NY — B

Fordham U, NY — B
Hofstra U, NY — B
Ithaca Coll, NY — B
Long Island U, C.W. Post Campus, NY — B
Nazareth Coll of Rochester, NY — B
New York U, NY — B
Pratt Inst, NY — B
Prescott Coll, AZ — B
Rochester Inst of Technology, NY — A,B
Sage Coll of Albany, NY — A
St. John's U, NY — B
Sarah Lawrence Coll, NY — B
School of Visual Arts, NY — B
State U of New York at Paltz, NY — B
State U of New York Coll at Potsdam, NY — B
Syracuse U, NY — B
Villa Maria Coll of Buffalo, NY — A

Photojournalism
Rochester Inst of Technology, NY — B

Physical and Theoretical Chemistry
Cornell U, NY — B

Physical Education Teaching and Coaching
Adelphi U, NY — B
Brooklyn Coll of the City U of New York, NY — B
Canisius Coll, NY — B
Coll of Mount Saint Vincent, NY — B
Hofstra U, NY — B
Houghton Coll, NY — B
Hunter Coll of the City U of New York, NY — B
Ithaca Coll, NY — B
Long Island U, Brooklyn Campus, NY — B
Long Island U, C.W. Post Campus, NY — B
Manhattan Coll, NY — B
Mitchell Coll, CT — A
North Carolina Ag and Tech State U, NC — B
Prescott Coll, AZ — B
Queens Coll of the City U of New York, NY — B
St. Bonaventure U, NY — B
St. Francis Coll, NY — B
State U of New York Coll at Brockport, NY — B
State U of New York Coll at Cortland, NY — B
State U of New York Coll at Potsdam, NY — B
State U of New York Coll of Technology at Delhi, NY — A
Syracuse U, NY — B
West Virginia Wesleyan Coll, WV — B
York Coll of the City U of New York, NY — B

Physical Sciences
Bard Coll, NY — B
Colgate U, NY — B
Cornell U, NY — B
Fordham U, NY — B
Long Island U, Brooklyn Campus, NY — B
Mitchell Coll, CT — A
Rensselaer Polytechnic Inst, NY — B
Roberts Wesleyan Coll, NY — A
St. Bonaventure U, NY — B
St. John's U, NY — B

Physical Sciences Related
Hofstra U, NY — B
Stony Brook U, State U of New York, NY — B

Physical Therapist Assistant
Maria Coll, NY — A
New York U, NY — A
State U of New York Coll of Technology at Canton, NY — A
Villa Maria Coll of Buffalo, NY — A

Physical Therapy
Chatham Coll, PA — B

Coll of Staten Island of the City U of New York, NY — B
Daemen Coll, NY — B
D'Youville Coll, NY — B
Hunter Coll of the City U of New York, NY — B
Ithaca Coll, NY — B
Long Island U, Brooklyn Campus, NY — B
Mount Saint Mary Coll, NY — B
Nazareth Coll of Rochester, NY — B
New York Inst of Technology, NY — B
Quinnipiac U, CT — B
Russell Sage Coll, NY — B
State U of New York Downstate Medical Center, NY — B
State U of New York Upstate Medical U, NY — B
Utica Coll, NY — B

Physician Assistant
City Coll of the City U of New York, NY — B
Coll of Staten Island of the City U of New York, NY — B
Daemen Coll, NY — B
D'Youville Coll, NY — B
Hofstra U, NY — B
Le Moyne Coll, NY — B
Long Island U, Brooklyn Campus, NY — B
New York Inst of Technology, NY — B
Pace U, NY — B
Quinnipiac U, CT — B
Rochester Inst of Technology, NY — B
St. Francis Coll, NY — B
St. John's U, NY — B
State U of New York Downstate Medical Center, NY — B
Stony Brook U, State U of New York, NY — B
Wagner Coll, NY — B

Physics
Adelphi U, NY — B
Alfred U, NY — B
Bard Coll, NY — B
Barnard Coll, NY — B
Brooklyn Coll of the City U of New York, NY — B
Buffalo State Coll, State U of New York, NY — B
Canisius Coll, NY — B
Chatham Coll, PA — B
City Coll of the City U of New York, NY — B
Clarkson U, NY — B
Colgate U, NY — B
Coll of Mount Saint Vincent, NY — B
The Coll of New Rochelle, NY — B
Coll of Staten Island of the City U of New York, NY — B
Columbia Coll, NY — B
Columbia U, School of General Studies, NY — B
Cornell U, NY — B
Excelsior Coll, NY — B
Fordham U, NY — B
Hamilton Coll, NY — B
Hartwick Coll, NY — B
Hobart and William Smith Colls, NY — B
Hofstra U, NY — B
Houghton Coll, NY — B
Hunter Coll of the City U of New York, NY — B
Iona Coll, NY — B
Ithaca Coll, NY — B
Lehman Coll of the City U of New York, NY — B
Le Moyne Coll, NY — B
Long Island U, Brooklyn Campus, NY — B
Long Island U, C.W. Post Campus, NY — B
Manhattan Coll, NY — B
Manhattanville Coll, NY — B
New York Inst of Technology, NY — B
New York U, NY — B
North Carolina Ag and Tech State U, NC — B
Pace U, NY — B

Polytechnic U, Brooklyn Campus, NY — B
Queens Coll of the City U of New York, NY — B
Rensselaer Polytechnic Inst, NY — B
Roberts Wesleyan Coll, NY — B
Rochester Inst of Technology, NY — A,B
St. Bonaventure U, NY — B
St. John Fisher Coll, NY — B
St. John's U, NY — B
St. Lawrence U, NY — B
Sarah Lawrence Coll, NY — B
Siena Coll, NY — B
Skidmore Coll, NY — B
State U of New York at Binghamton, NY — B
State U of New York at Buffalo, NY — B
State U of New York at New Paltz, NY — B
State U of New York at Oswego, NY — B
State U of New York at Plattsburgh, NY — B
State U of New York Coll at Brockport, NY — B
State U of New York Coll at Cortland, NY — B
State U of New York Coll at Geneseo, NY — B
State U of New York Coll at Oneonta, NY — B
State U of New York Coll at Potsdam, NY — B
State U of New York, Fredonia, NY — B
Stony Brook U, State U of New York, NY — B
Syracuse U, NY — B
Union Coll, NY — B
United States Military Academy, NY — B
U at Albany, State U of New York, NY — B
U of Rochester, NY — B
U of West Florida, FL — B
Utica Coll, NY — B
Vassar Coll, NY — B
Wagner Coll, NY — B
Wells Coll, NY — B
West Virginia Wesleyan Coll, WV — B
Yeshiva U, NY — B
York Coll of the City U of New York, NY — B

Physics Related
Cornell U, NY — B
State U of New York at Buffalo, NY — B
State U of New York Coll at Brockport, NY — B
U of Rochester, NY — B

Physics Teacher Education
Brooklyn Coll of the City U of New York, NY — B
Chatham Coll, PA — B
City Coll of the City U of New York, NY — B
Cornell U, NY — B
Hofstra U, NY — B
Ithaca Coll, NY — B
Le Moyne Coll, NY — B
New York Inst of Technology, NY — B
New York U, NY — B
Pace U, NY — B
Roberts Wesleyan Coll, NY — B
St. Bonaventure U, NY — B
St. John's U, NY — B
State U of New York Coll at Brockport, NY — B
State U of New York Coll at Cortland, NY — B
State U of New York Coll at Oneonta, NY — B
State U of New York Coll at Potsdam, NY — B
Syracuse U, NY — B
Utica Coll, NY — B

Physiological Psychology/ Psychobiology
Hamilton Coll, NY — B
Medaille Coll, NY — B
Quinnipiac U, CT — B
State U of New York at Binghamton, NY — B
State U of New York at New Paltz, NY — B
Vassar Coll, NY — B
Wagner Coll, NY — B

Physiology
Cornell U, NY — B

Piano and Organ
Houghton Coll, NY — B
Ithaca Coll, NY — B
The Juilliard School, NY — B
Manhattan School of Music, NY — B
New York U, NY — B
Nyack Coll, NY — B
Roberts Wesleyan Coll, NY — B
Sarah Lawrence Coll, NY — B
State U of New York, Fredonia, NY — B
Syracuse U, NY — B

Pipefitting and Sprinkler Fitting
State U of New York Coll of Technology at Alfred, NY — A
State U of New York Coll of Technology at Canton, NY — A
State U of New York Coll of Technology at Delhi, NY — A

Planetary Astronomy and Science
Cornell U, NY — B

Plant Genetics
Cornell U, NY — B

Plant Nursery Management
State U of New York Coll of Agriculture and Technology at Cobleskill, NY — A

Plant Pathology/Phytopathology
Cornell U, NY — B
State U of New York Coll of Environmental Science and Forestry, NY — B

Plant Physiology
State U of New York Coll of Environmental Science and Forestry, NY — B

Plant Protection and Integrated Pest Management
State U of New York Coll of Environmental Science and Forestry, NY — B

Plant Sciences
Cornell U, NY — B
State U of New York Coll of Agriculture and Technology at Cobleskill, NY — A,B
State U of New York Coll of Environmental Science and Forestry, NY — B

Playwriting and Screenwriting
Bard Coll, NY — B
Fordham U, NY — B
New York U, NY — B
Purchase Coll, State U of New York, NY — B
Sarah Lawrence Coll, NY — B

Political Science and Government
Adelphi U, NY — B
Alfred U, NY — B
Bard Coll, NY — B
Barnard Coll, NY — B
Bernard M. Baruch Coll of the City U of New York, NY — B
Brooklyn Coll of the City U of New York, NY — B
Buffalo State Coll, State U of New York, NY — B
Canisius Coll, NY — B
Chaminade U of Honolulu, HI — B
Chatham Coll, PA — B

A—associate degree; B—bachelor's degree

City Coll of the City U of New York, NY — B
Clarkson U, NY — B
Colgate U, NY — B
The Coll of New Rochelle, NY — B
The Coll of Saint Rose, NY — B
Coll of Staten Island of the City U of New York, NY — B
Columbia Coll, NY — B
Columbia U, School of General Studies, NY — B
Cornell U, NY — B
Daemen Coll, NY — B
Dowling Coll, NY — B
Elmira Coll, NY — B
Excelsior Coll, NY — B
Fordham U, NY — B
Hamilton Coll, NY — B
Hartwick Coll, NY — B
Hobart and William Smith Colls, NY — B
Hofstra U, NY — B
Houghton Coll, NY — B
Hunter Coll of the City U of New York, NY — B
Iona Coll, NY — B
Ithaca Coll, NY — B
Lehman Coll of the City U of New York, NY — B
Le Moyne Coll, NY — B
Long Island U, Brooklyn Campus, NY — B
Long Island U, C.W. Post Campus, NY — B
Manhattan Coll, NY — B
Manhattanville Coll, NY — B
Marist Coll, NY — B
Marymount Coll of Fordham U, NY — B
Marymount Manhattan Coll, NY — B
Mercy Coll, NY — B
Molloy Coll, NY — B
Mount Saint Mary Coll, NY — B
Nazareth Coll of Rochester, NY — B
New York Inst of Technology, NY — B
New York U, NY — B
Niagara U, NY — B
North Carolina Ag and Tech State U, NC — B
Pace U, NY — B
Prescott Coll, AZ — B
Purchase Coll, State U of New York, NY — B
Queens Coll of the City U of New York, NY — B
Quinnipiac U, CT — B
Russell Sage Coll, NY — B
St. Bonaventure U, NY — B
St. Francis Coll, NY — B
St. John Fisher Coll, NY — B
St. John's U, NY — B
St. Joseph's Coll, Suffolk Campus, NY — B
St. Lawrence U, NY — B
Sarah Lawrence Coll, NY — B
Shepherd U, WV — B
Siena Coll, NY — B
Skidmore Coll, NY — B
State U of New York at Binghamton, NY — B
State U of New York at Buffalo, NY — B
State U of New York at New Paltz, NY — B
State U of New York at Oswego, NY — B
State U of New York at Plattsburgh, NY — B
State U of New York Coll at Brockport, NY — B
State U of New York Coll at Cortland, NY — B
State U of New York Coll at Geneseo, NY — B
State U of New York Coll at Oneonta, NY — B
State U of New York Coll at Potsdam, NY — B
State U of New York, Fredonia, NY — B
Stony Brook U, State U of New York, NY — B

Syracuse U, NY — B
Union Coll, NY — B
United States Military Academy, NY — B
U at Albany, State U of New York, NY — B
U of Rochester, NY — B
U of West Florida, FL — B
Utica Coll, NY — B
Vassar Coll, NY — B
Wagner Coll, NY — B
Wells Coll, NY — B
West Virginia Wesleyan Coll, WV — B
Yeshiva U, NY — B
York Coll of the City U of New York, NY — B

Political Science and Government Related
Cornell U, NY — B

Polymer Chemistry
Rochester Inst of Technology, NY — B
State U of New York Coll of Environmental Science and Forestry, NY — B

Portuguese
Brooklyn Coll of the City U of New York, NY — B
New York U, NY — B
United States Military Academy, NY — B

Pre-Dentistry Studies
Bard Coll, NY — B
Buffalo State Coll, State U of New York, NY — B
City Coll of the City U of New York, NY — B
Clarkson U, NY — B
Coll of Mount Saint Vincent, NY — B
D'Youville Coll, NY — B
Elmira Coll, NY — B
Fordham U, NY — B
Hobart and William Smith Colls, NY — B
Hofstra U, NY — B
Houghton Coll, NY — B
Keuka Coll, NY — B
Le Moyne Coll, NY — B
Marist Coll, NY — B
Mercy Coll, NY — B
Molloy Coll, NY — B
Nazareth Coll of Rochester, NY — B
New York U, NY — B
Niagara U, NY — B
Quinnipiac U, CT — B
Rensselaer Polytechnic Inst, NY — B
Roberts Wesleyan Coll, NY — B
Rochester Inst of Technology, NY — B
St. Bonaventure U, NY — B
St. Joseph's Coll, Suffolk Campus, NY — B
Sarah Lawrence Coll, NY — B
Siena Coll, NY — B
State U of New York at New Paltz, NY — B
State U of New York at Oswego, NY — B
State U of New York Coll at Brockport, NY — B
State U of New York Coll at Cortland, NY — B
State U of New York Coll at Geneseo, NY — B
State U of New York Coll at Oneonta, NY — B
State U of New York Coll of Environmental Science and Forestry, NY — B
Syracuse U, NY — B
Utica Coll, NY — B
Wagner Coll, NY — B
Wells Coll, NY — B
West Virginia Wesleyan Coll, WV — B
Yeshiva U, NY — B

Pre-Engineering
Medgar Evers Coll of the City U of New York, NY — A
Niagara U, NY — A

Roberts Wesleyan Coll, NY — B
Vaughn Coll of Aeronautics and Technology, NY — A

Pre-Law Studies
Bard Coll, NY — B
Buffalo State Coll, State U of New York, NY — B
City Coll of the City U of New York, NY — B
Clarkson U, NY — B
Coll of Mount Saint Vincent, NY — B
The Coll of New Rochelle, NY — B
Concordia Coll, NY — B
Cornell U, NY — B
Dominican Coll, NY — B
D'Youville Coll, NY — B
Elmira Coll, NY — B
Fordham U, NY — B
Hartwick Coll, NY — B
Hobart and William Smith Colls, NY — B
Hofstra U, NY — B
Houghton Coll, NY — B
Ithaca Coll, NY — B
John Jay Coll of Criminal Justice of the City U of New York, NY — B
Keuka Coll, NY — B
Le Moyne Coll, NY — B
Marist Coll, NY — B
Marymount Coll of Fordham U, NY — B
Medaille Coll, NY — B
Mercy Coll, NY — B
Molloy Coll, NY — B
Mount Saint Mary Coll, NY — B
Nazareth Coll of Rochester, NY — B
Niagara U, NY — B
Quinnipiac U, CT — B
Rensselaer Polytechnic Inst, NY — B
Roberts Wesleyan Coll, NY — B
Rochester Inst of Technology, NY — B
St. Bonaventure U, NY — B
St. Joseph's Coll, New York, NY — B
St. Joseph's Coll, Suffolk Campus, NY — B
Sarah Lawrence Coll, NY — B
Siena Coll, NY — B
State U of New York at Binghamton, NY — B
State U of New York at New Paltz, NY — B
State U of New York at Oswego, NY — B
State U of New York Coll at Brockport, NY — B
State U of New York Coll at Cortland, NY — B
State U of New York Coll at Geneseo, NY — B
State U of New York Coll at Oneonta, NY — B
State U of New York Coll of Environmental Science and Forestry, NY — B
State U of New York, Fredonia, NY — B
Syracuse U, NY — B
United States Military Academy, NY — B
Utica Coll, NY — B
Wagner Coll, NY — B
Wells Coll, NY — B
West Virginia Wesleyan Coll, WV — B
Yeshiva U, NY — B

Pre-Medical Studies
Bard Coll, NY — B
Buffalo State Coll, State U of New York, NY — B
City Coll of the City U of New York, NY — B
Clarkson U, NY — B
Coll of Mount Saint Vincent, NY — B
The Coll of New Rochelle, NY — B
Cornell U, NY — B
D'Youville Coll, NY — B
Elmira Coll, NY — B
Fordham U, NY — B
Hartwick Coll, NY — B
Hobart and William Smith Colls, NY — B

Hofstra U, NY — B
Houghton Coll, NY — B
Ithaca Coll, NY — B
Keuka Coll, NY — B
Le Moyne Coll, NY — B
Long Island U, Brooklyn Campus, NY — B
Long Island U, C.W. Post Campus, NY — B
Manhattanville Coll, NY — B
Marist Coll, NY — B
Marymount Coll of Fordham U, NY — B
Medgar Evers Coll of the City U of New York, NY — B
Mercy Coll, NY — B
Molloy Coll, NY — B
Nazareth Coll of Rochester, NY — B
New York Inst of Technology, NY — B
New York U, NY — B
Niagara U, NY — B
Quinnipiac U, CT — B
Rensselaer Polytechnic Inst, NY — B
Roberts Wesleyan Coll, NY — B
Rochester Inst of Technology, NY — B
St. Bonaventure U, NY — B
St. Joseph's Coll, Suffolk Campus, NY — B
St. Thomas Aquinas Coll, NY — B
Sarah Lawrence Coll, NY — B
Siena Coll, NY — B
State U of New York at New Paltz, NY — B
State U of New York at Oswego, NY — B
State U of New York Coll at Brockport, NY — B
State U of New York Coll at Cortland, NY — B
State U of New York Coll at Geneseo, NY — B
State U of New York Coll at Oneonta, NY — B
State U of New York Coll of Agriculture and Technology at Cobleskill, NY — A
State U of New York Coll of Environmental Science and Forestry, NY — B
State U of New York, Fredonia, NY — B
Syracuse U, NY — B
United States Military Academy, NY — B
Utica Coll, NY — B
Wagner Coll, NY — B
Wells Coll, NY — B
West Virginia Wesleyan Coll, WV — B
Yeshiva U, NY — B

Pre-Pharmacy Studies
Fordham U, NY — B
Le Moyne Coll, NY — B
Long Island U, C.W. Post Campus, NY — B
Roberts Wesleyan Coll, NY — B
West Virginia Wesleyan Coll, WV — B

Pre-Theology/Pre-Ministerial Studies
Roberts Wesleyan Coll, NY — B

Pre-Veterinary Studies
Bard Coll, NY — B
Buffalo State Coll, State U of New York, NY — B
City Coll of the City U of New York, NY — B
Clarkson U, NY — B
Cornell U, NY — B
D'Youville Coll, NY — B
Elmira Coll, NY — B
Fordham U, NY — B
Hartwick Coll, NY — B
Hobart and William Smith Colls, NY — B
Hofstra U, NY — B
Houghton Coll, NY — B
Keuka Coll, NY — B
Le Moyne Coll, NY — B
Marist Coll, NY — B
Molloy Coll, NY — B

Nazareth Coll of Rochester, NY — B
Niagara U, NY — B
Quinnipiac U, CT — B
Roberts Wesleyan Coll, NY — B
Rochester Inst of Technology, NY — B
St. Bonaventure U, NY — B
St. Joseph's Coll, Suffolk Campus, NY — B
Sarah Lawrence Coll, NY — B
State U of New York at Oswego, NY — B
State U of New York Coll at Brockport, NY — B
State U of New York Coll at Geneseo, NY — B
State U of New York Coll at Oneonta, NY — B
State U of New York Coll of Environmental Science and Forestry, NY — B
State U of New York, Fredonia, NY — B
Syracuse U, NY — B
Utica Coll, NY — B
Wells Coll, NY — B
West Virginia Wesleyan Coll, WV — B

Printmaking
Buffalo State Coll, State U of New York, NY — B
Pratt Inst, NY — B
Sarah Lawrence Coll, NY — B
State U of New York Coll at Potsdam, NY — B
Syracuse U, NY — B

Psychiatric/Mental Health Nursing
State U of New York at Buffalo, NY — B

Psychology
Adelphi U, NY — B
Alfred U, NY — B
Bard Coll, NY — B
Barnard Coll, NY — B
Bernard M. Baruch Coll of the City U of New York, NY — B
Brooklyn Coll of the City U of New York, NY — B
Buffalo State Coll, State U of New York, NY — B
Canisius Coll, NY — B
Cazenovia Coll, NY — B
Chaminade U of Honolulu, HI — B
Chatham Coll, PA — B
City Coll of the City U of New York, NY — B
Clarkson U, NY — B
Colgate U, NY — B
Coll of Mount Saint Vincent, NY — B
The Coll of New Rochelle, NY — B
The Coll of Saint Rose, NY — B
Coll of Staten Island of the City U of New York, NY — B
Columbia Coll, NY — B
Columbia U, School of General Studies, NY — B
Cornell U, NY — B
Daemen Coll, NY — B
Dominican Coll, NY — B
Dowling Coll, NY — B
D'Youville Coll, NY — B
Elmira Coll, NY — B
Excelsior Coll, NY — B
Fordham U, NY — B
Hamilton Coll, NY — B
Hartwick Coll, NY — B
Hilbert Coll, NY — B
Hobart and William Smith Colls, NY — B
Hofstra U, NY — B
Houghton Coll, NY — B
Hunter Coll of the City U of New York, NY — B
Iona Coll, NY — B
Ithaca Coll, NY — B
Keuka Coll, NY — B
Lehman Coll of the City U of New York, NY — B
Le Moyne Coll, NY — B

Long Island U, Brooklyn Campus, NY — B
Long Island U, C.W. Post Campus, NY — B
Manhattan Coll, NY — B
Manhattanville Coll, NY — B
Marist Coll, NY — B
Marymount Coll of Fordham U, NY — B
Marymount Manhattan Coll, NY — B
Medaille Coll, NY — B
Medgar Evers Coll of the City U of New York, NY — B
Mercy Coll, NY — B
Mitchell Coll, CT — A
Molloy Coll, NY — B
Mount Saint Mary Coll, NY — B
Nazareth Coll of Rochester, NY — B
New York Inst of Technology, NY — B
New York U, NY — B
Niagara U, NY — B
North Carolina Ag and Tech State U, NC — B
Nyack Coll, NY — B
Pace U, NY — B
Post U, CT — B
Prescott Coll, AZ — B
Purchase Coll, State U of New York, NY — B
Queens Coll of the City U of New York, NY — B
Quinnipiac U, CT — B
Rensselaer Polytechnic Inst, NY — B
Roberts Wesleyan Coll, NY — B
Rochester Inst of Technology, NY — B
Russell Sage Coll, NY — B
Sage Coll of Albany, NY — B
St. Bonaventure U, NY — B
St. Francis Coll, NY — B
St. John Fisher Coll, NY — B
St. John's U, NY — B
St. Joseph's Coll, New York, NY — B
St. Joseph's Coll, Suffolk Campus, NY — B
St. Lawrence U, NY — B
St. Thomas Aquinas Coll, NY — B
Sarah Lawrence Coll, NY — B
Shepherd U, WV — B
Siena Coll, NY — B
Skidmore Coll, NY — B
State U of New York at Binghamton, NY — B
State U of New York at Buffalo, NY — B
State U of New York at New Paltz, NY — B
State U of New York at Oswego, NY — B
State U of New York at Plattsburgh, NY — B
State U of New York Coll at Brockport, NY — B
State U of New York Coll at Cortland, NY — B
State U of New York Coll at Geneseo, NY — B
State U of New York Coll at Old Westbury, NY — B
State U of New York Coll at Oneonta, NY — B
State U of New York Coll at Potsdam, NY — B
State U of New York, Fredonia, NY — B
State U of New York Inst of Technology, NY — B
Stony Brook U, State U of New York, NY — B
Syracuse U, NY — B
Union Coll, NY — B
United States Military Academy, NY — B
U at Albany, State U of New York, NY — B
U of Rochester, NY — B
U of West Florida, FL — B
Utica Coll, NY — B
Vassar Coll, NY — B
Wagner Coll, NY — B
Wells Coll, NY — B

West Virginia Wesleyan Coll, WV — B
Yeshiva U, NY — B
York Coll of the City U of New York, NY — B

Psychology Related
Skidmore Coll, NY — B
State U of New York at Oswego, NY — B

Public Administration
Alfred U, NY — B
Bernard M. Baruch Coll of the City U of New York, NY — B
Cornell U, NY — B
Fordham U, NY — B
John Jay Coll of Criminal Justice of the City U of New York, NY — B
Long Island U, C.W. Post Campus, NY — B
Marist Coll, NY — B
Medgar Evers Coll of the City U of New York, NY — A,B
St. John's U, NY — B
Syracuse U, NY — B
U at Albany, State U of New York, NY — B
Wagner Coll, NY — B

Public Administration and Social Service Professions Related
Cornell U, NY — B

Public Health
Hunter Coll of the City U of New York, NY — B
St. Joseph's Coll, New York, NY — B

Public Health Education and Promotion
Ithaca Coll, NY — B

Public Policy Analysis
Bernard M. Baruch Coll of the City U of New York, NY — B
Chatham Coll, PA — B
Cornell U, NY — B
Hamilton Coll, NY — B
Hobart and William Smith Colls, NY — B
Rochester Inst of Technology, NY — B
Sarah Lawrence Coll, NY — B
United States Military Academy, NY — B
U at Albany, State U of New York, NY — B
Wells Coll, NY — B

Public Relations, Advertising, and Applied Communication Related
Rochester Inst of Technology, NY — B
State U of New York Coll at Brockport, NY — B

Public Relations/Image Management
Buffalo State Coll, State U of New York, NY — B
Hofstra U, NY — B
Iona Coll, NY — B
Ithaca Coll, NY — B
Long Island U, C.W. Post Campus, NY — B
Marist Coll, NY — B
Mount Saint Mary Coll, NY — B
Quinnipiac U, CT — B
Rochester Inst of Technology, NY — B
State U of New York at Oswego, NY — B
State U of New York Coll at Brockport, NY — B
Syracuse U, NY — B
Utica Coll, NY — B
West Virginia Wesleyan Coll, WV — B

Publishing
Rochester Inst of Technology, NY — B

Purchasing, Procurement/Acquisitions and Contracts Management
St. John's U, NY — B

Rabbinical Studies
Ohr Somayach/Joseph Tanenbaum Educational Center, NY — B

Radio and Television
Brooklyn Coll of the City U of New York, NY — B
Buffalo State Coll, State U of New York, NY — B
Fordham U, NY — B
Hofstra U, NY — B
Iona Coll, NY — B
Ithaca Coll, NY — B
Marist Coll, NY — B
Mercy Coll, NY — B
New York Inst of Technology, NY — B
New York U, NY — B
State U of New York at New Paltz, NY — B
State U of New York Coll at Brockport, NY — B
State U of New York, Fredonia, NY — B
Syracuse U, NY — B

Radio and Television Broadcasting Technology
Hofstra U, NY — B
Iona Coll, NY — B
New York Inst of Technology, NY — A

Radiologic Technology/Science
Manhattan Coll, NY — B
Quinnipiac U, CT — B
State U of New York Upstate Medical U, NY — B

Radio, Television, and Digital Communication Related
State U of New York Coll at Brockport, NY — B

Reading Teacher Education
City Coll of the City U of New York, NY — B
St. John's U, NY — B
State U of New York Coll at Cortland, NY — B
State U of New York Coll at Oneonta, NY — B

Real Estate
New York U, NY — B
St. John's U, NY — B

Rehabilitation Therapy
Ithaca Coll, NY — B

Religious Education
Houghton Coll, NY — A,B
The Jewish Theological Seminary, NY — B
Nyack Coll, NY — B
St. Bonaventure U, NY — B
West Virginia Wesleyan Coll, WV — B

Religious/Sacred Music
Concordia Coll, NY — B
Nyack Coll, NY — B

Religious Studies
Bard Coll, NY — B
Barnard Coll, NY — B
Brooklyn Coll of the City U of New York, NY — B
Canisius Coll, NY — B
Chaminade U of Honolulu, HI — B
Colgate U, NY — B
Coll of Mount Saint Vincent, NY — B
The Coll of New Rochelle, NY — B
The Coll of Saint Rose, NY — B
Columbia Coll, NY — B
Columbia U, School of General Studies, NY — B
Concordia Coll, NY — B
Cornell U, NY — B
Daemen Coll, NY — B
Elmira Coll, NY — B
Fordham U, NY — B
Hamilton Coll, NY — B
Hartwick Coll, NY — B
Hobart and William Smith Colls, NY — B

A—associate degree; B—bachelor's degree

Houghton Coll, NY | B
Hunter Coll of the City U of New York, NY | B
Iona Coll, NY | B
The Jewish Theological Seminary, NY | B
Le Moyne Coll, NY | B
Manhattan Coll, NY | B
Manhattanville Coll, NY | B
Molloy Coll, NY | B
Nazareth Coll of Rochester, NY | B
New York U, NY | B
Niagara U, NY | B
Nyack Coll, NY | B
Queens Coll of the City U of New York, NY | B
St. Francis Coll, NY | B
St. John Fisher Coll, NY | B
St. Lawrence U, NY | B
St. Thomas Aquinas Coll, NY | B
Sarah Lawrence Coll, NY | B
Siena Coll, NY | B
Skidmore Coll, NY | B
State U of New York Coll at Old Westbury, NY | B
Stony Brook U, State U of New York, NY | B
Syracuse U, NY | B
U at Albany, State U of New York, NY | B
U of Rochester, NY | B
U of West Florida, FL | B
Vassar Coll, NY | B
Wells Coll, NY | B
West Virginia Wesleyan Coll, WV | B

Religious Studies Related
Sarah Lawrence Coll, NY | B

Resort Management
Rochester Inst of Technology, NY | A,B

Respiratory Care Therapy
Long Island U, Brooklyn Campus, NY | B
Molloy Coll, NY | A
Quinnipiac U, CT | B
State U of New York Upstate Medical U, NY | B
Stony Brook U, State U of New York, NY | B

Restaurant, Culinary, and Catering Management
State U of New York Coll of Technology at Alfred, NY | A
State U of New York Coll of Technology at Delhi, NY | A,B

Restaurant/Food Services Management
Niagara U, NY | B
Rochester Inst of Technology, NY | A,B
Syracuse U, NY | B

Retailing
Syracuse U, NY | B

Romance Languages
Bard Coll, NY | B
Bernard M. Baruch Coll of the City U of New York, NY | B
City Coll of the City U of New York, NY | B
Colgate U, NY | B
Cornell U, NY | B
Dowling Coll, NY | B
Elmira Coll, NY | B
Fordham U, NY | B
Hunter Coll of the City U of New York, NY | B
Manhattanville Coll, NY | B
New York U, NY | B
St. Thomas Aquinas Coll, NY | B
Sarah Lawrence Coll, NY | B
U at Albany, State U of New York, NY | B

Russian
Bard Coll, NY | B
Barnard Coll, NY | B
Brooklyn Coll of the City U of New York, NY | B
Colgate U, NY | B
Columbia Coll, NY | B

Columbia U, School of General Studies, NY | B
Fordham U, NY | B
Hobart and William Smith Colls, NY | B
Hofstra U, NY | B
Hunter Coll of the City U of New York, NY | B
Lehman Coll of the City U of New York, NY | B
New York U, NY | B
Queens Coll of the City U of New York, NY | B
Sarah Lawrence Coll, NY | B
Stony Brook U, State U of New York, NY | B
Syracuse U, NY | B
United States Military Academy, NY | B
U at Albany, State U of New York, NY | B
U of Rochester, NY | B
Vassar Coll, NY | B

Russian Studies
Bard Coll, NY | B
Barnard Coll, NY | B
Colgate U, NY | B
Columbia Coll, NY | B
Cornell U, NY | B
Fordham U, NY | B
Hamilton Coll, NY | B
Hobart and William Smith Colls, NY | B
Syracuse U, NY | B
U at Albany, State U of New York, NY | B
U of Rochester, NY | B

Safety/Security Technology
Farmingdale State U of New York, NY | B
John Jay Coll of Criminal Justice of the City U of New York, NY | A,B
Mercy Coll, NY | B

Sales and Marketing/Marketing and Distribution Teacher Education
New York Inst of Technology, NY | B
State U of New York at Oswego, NY | B

Sales, Distribution and Marketing
Dowling Coll, NY | B
Long Island U, Brooklyn Campus, NY | B
Quinnipiac U, CT | B
State U of New York Coll of Technology at Alfred, NY | A
Syracuse U, NY | B

School Psychology
St. John's U, NY | B

Science Teacher Education
Alfred U, NY | B
Buffalo State Coll, State U of New York, NY | B
Canisius Coll, NY | B
City Coll of the City U of New York, NY | B
Coll of Mount Saint Vincent, NY | B
Concordia Coll, NY | B
D'Youville Coll, NY | B
Elmira Coll, NY | B
Hofstra U, NY | B
Hunter Coll of the City U of New York, NY | B
Iona Coll, NY | B
Ithaca Coll, NY | B
Le Moyne Coll, NY | B
Marymount Coll of Fordham U, NY | B
Nazareth Coll of Rochester, NY | B
Niagara U, NY | B
Prescott Coll, AZ | B
Queens Coll of the City U of New York, NY | B
Roberts Wesleyan Coll, NY | B
St. John Fisher Coll, NY | B
St. John's U, NY | B
State U of New York at New Paltz, NY | B
State U of New York at Oswego, NY | B

State U of New York Coll at Brockport, NY | B
State U of New York Coll at Cortland, NY | B
State U of New York Coll at Old Westbury, NY | B
State U of New York Coll at Oneonta, NY | B
State U of New York Coll at Potsdam, NY | B
State U of New York Coll of Environmental Science and Forestry, NY | B
State U of New York, Fredonia, NY | B
U at Albany, State U of New York, NY | B
U of West Florida, FL | B

Science Technologies Related
Maria Coll, NY | A

Science, Technology and Society
Cornell U, NY | B
Rensselaer Polytechnic Inst, NY | B
Vassar Coll, NY | B

Sculpture
Bard Coll, NY | B
Buffalo State Coll, State U of New York, NY | B
Cornell U, NY | B
Hofstra U, NY | B
Pratt Inst, NY | B
Rochester Inst of Technology, NY | B
Sarah Lawrence Coll, NY | B
School of Visual Arts, NY | B
State U of New York at New Paltz, NY | B
State U of New York Coll at Brockport, NY | B
State U of New York Coll at Potsdam, NY | B
Syracuse U, NY | B

Secondary Education
Alfred U, NY | B
Buffalo State Coll, State U of New York, NY | B
Canisius Coll, NY | B
City Coll of the City U of New York, NY | B
Coll of Mount Saint Vincent, NY | B
Concordia Coll, NY | B
Dominican Coll, NY | B
Dowling Coll, NY | B
D'Youville Coll, NY | B
Elmira Coll, NY | B
Fordham U, NY | B
Hofstra U, NY | B
Houghton Coll, NY | B
Hunter Coll of the City U of New York, NY | B
Iona Coll, NY | B
Ithaca Coll, NY | B
Keuka Coll, NY | B
Le Moyne Coll, NY | B
Long Island U, Brooklyn Campus, NY | B
Long Island U, C.W. Post Campus, NY | B
Manhattanville Coll, NY | B
Marist Coll, NY | B
Marymount Coll of Fordham U, NY | B
Mercy Coll, NY | B
Molloy Coll, NY | B
Mount Saint Mary Coll, NY | B
Nazareth Coll of Rochester, NY | B
New York U, NY | B
Niagara U, NY | B
Nyack Coll, NY | B
Prescott Coll, AZ | B
Roberts Wesleyan Coll, NY | B
St. Bonaventure U, NY | B
St. John's U, NY | B
St. Joseph's Coll, Suffolk Campus, NY | B
St. Thomas Aquinas Coll, NY | B
Shepherd U, WV | B
Siena Coll, NY | B
State U of New York at New Paltz, NY | B

State U of New York at Oswego, NY | B
State U of New York at Plattsburgh, NY | B
State U of New York Coll at Brockport, NY | B
State U of New York Coll at Cortland, NY | B
State U of New York Coll at Old Westbury, NY | B
State U of New York Coll at Oneonta, NY | B
State U of New York, Fredonia, NY | B
Utica Coll, NY | B
Wagner Coll, NY | B
Wells Coll, NY | B
West Virginia Wesleyan Coll, WV | B

Securities Services Administration
State U of New York Coll at Brockport, NY | B

Security and Loss Prevention
Farmingdale State U of New York, NY | B
John Jay Coll of Criminal Justice of the City U of New York, NY | A,B

Semitic Languages
Cornell U, NY | B

Sign Language Interpretation and Translation
Rochester Inst of Technology, NY | A,B

Slavic Languages
Columbia Coll, NY | B
Columbia U, School of General Studies, NY | B
Cornell U, NY | B
U at Albany, State U of New York, NY | B

Slavic Studies
Barnard Coll, NY | B
Cornell U, NY | B

Social Psychology
Cornell U, NY | B

Social Sciences
Adelphi U, NY | B
Bard Coll, NY | B
Cazenovia Coll, NY | B
Chaminade U of Honolulu, HI | B
Clarkson U, NY | B
Colgate U, NY | B
Coll of Mount Saint Vincent, NY | B
Concordia Coll, NY | B
Dominican Coll, NY | B
Dowling Coll, NY | B
Elmira Coll, NY | B
Fordham U, NY | B
Hofstra U, NY | B
Iona Coll, NY | B
Ithaca Coll, NY | B
Keuka Coll, NY | B
Long Island U, Brooklyn Campus, NY | A,B
Medaille Coll, NY | B
Mount Saint Mary Coll, NY | B
Nazareth Coll of Rochester, NY | B
New York Inst of Technology, NY | B
New York U, NY | B
Niagara U, NY | B
North Carolina Ag and Tech State U, NC | B
Nyack Coll, NY | B
Pace U, NY | B
Quinnipiac U, CT | B
Rensselaer Polytechnic Inst, NY | B
Sage Coll of Albany, NY | A
St. Bonaventure U, NY | B
St. John's U, NY | B
St. Joseph's Coll, New York, NY | B
St. Joseph's Coll, Suffolk Campus, NY | B
St. Thomas Aquinas Coll, NY | B
Sarah Lawrence Coll, NY | B
State U of New York Coll at Old Westbury, NY | B
State U of New York Coll of Technology at Alfred, NY | A

Majors and Degrees
Social Sciences

State U of New York Coll of
   Technology at Canton, NY   A
State U of New York Coll of
   Technology at Delhi, NY   A
State U of New York Empire
   State Coll, NY   A,B
Stony Brook U, State U of New
   York, NY   B
Union Coll, NY   B
U of West Florida, FL   B
Utica Coll, NY   B

Social Sciences Related
Adelphi U, NY   B
Cornell U, NY   B
Queens Coll of the City U of
   New York, NY   B
Sarah Lawrence Coll, NY   B
Skidmore Coll, NY   B
U of Rochester, NY   B
U of West Florida, FL   B

Social Science Teacher Education
Dominican Coll, NY   B
Elmira Coll, NY   B
Prescott Coll, AZ   B
State U of New York Coll at
   Oneonta, NY   B
U at Albany, State U of New
   York, NY   B
U of West Florida, FL   B
Utica Coll, NY   B

Social Studies Teacher Education
Brooklyn Coll of the City U of
   New York, NY   B
Buffalo State Coll, State U of
   New York, NY   B
Chatham Coll, PA   B
City Coll of the City U of New
   York, NY   B
The Coll of Saint Rose, NY   B
Daemen Coll, NY   B
Dowling Coll, NY   B
Elmira Coll, NY   B
Hofstra U, NY   B
Iona Coll, NY   B
Ithaca Coll, NY   B
Keuka Coll, NY   B
Le Moyne Coll, NY   B
Long Island U, Brooklyn
   Campus, NY   B
Long Island U, C.W. Post
   Campus, NY   B
Manhattanville Coll, NY   B
Marymount Coll of Fordham U,
   NY   B
Molloy Coll, NY   B
Nazareth Coll of Rochester, NY   B
New York Inst of Technology, NY   B
New York U, NY   B
Niagara U, NY   B
Pace U, NY   B
Queens Coll of the City U of
   New York, NY   B
Roberts Wesleyan Coll, NY   B
St. Bonaventure U, NY   B
St. Francis Coll, NY   B
St. John's U, NY   B
State U of New York Coll at
   Brockport, NY   B
State U of New York Coll at
   Cortland, NY   B
State U of New York Coll at Old
   Westbury, NY   B
State U of New York Coll at
   Potsdam, NY   B
Syracuse U, NY   B
Utica Coll, NY   B

Social Work
Adelphi U, NY   B
Buffalo State Coll, State U of
   New York, NY   B
Chatham Coll, PA   B
The Coll of New Rochelle, NY   B
The Coll of Saint Rose, NY   B
Coll of Staten Island of the City
   U of New York, NY   B
Concordia Coll, NY   B
Daemen Coll, NY   B
Dominican Coll, NY   B

Elmira Coll, NY   B
Fordham U, NY   B
Iona Coll, NY   B
Keuka Coll, NY   B
Lehman Coll of the City U of
   New York, NY   B
Long Island U, Brooklyn
   Campus, NY   B
Long Island U, C.W. Post
   Campus, NY   B
Marist Coll, NY   B
Marymount Coll of Fordham U,
   NY   B
Mercy Coll, NY   B
Molloy Coll, NY   B
Nazareth Coll of Rochester, NY   B
New York U, NY   B
Niagara U, NY   B
North Carolina Ag and Tech
   State U, NC   B
Nyack Coll, NY   B
Roberts Wesleyan Coll, NY   B
Rochester Inst of Technology, NY   B
Shepherd U, WV   B
Siena Coll, NY   B
Skidmore Coll, NY   B
State U of New York at Buffalo,
   NY   B
State U of New York at New
   Paltz, NY   B
State U of New York at
   Plattsburgh, NY   B
State U of New York Coll at
   Brockport, NY   B
State U of New York Coll at
   Cortland, NY   B
State U of New York, Fredonia,
   NY   B
Stony Brook U, State U of New
   York, NY   B
Syracuse U, NY   B
U at Albany, State U of New
   York, NY   B
U of West Florida, FL   B
York Coll of the City U of New
   York, NY   B

Sociobiology
Cornell U, NY   B

Sociology
Adelphi U, NY   B
Alfred U, NY   B
Bard Coll, NY   B
Barnard Coll, NY   B
Bernard M. Baruch Coll of the
   City U of New York, NY   B
Brooklyn Coll of the City U of
   New York, NY   B
Buffalo State Coll, State U of
   New York, NY   B
Canisius Coll, NY   B
City Coll of the City U of New
   York, NY   B
Clarkson U, NY   B
Colgate U, NY   B
Coll of Mount Saint Vincent, NY   B
The Coll of New Rochelle, NY   B
The Coll of Saint Rose, NY   B
Columbia Coll, NY   B
Columbia U, School of General
   Studies, NY   B
Cornell U, NY   B
Dowling Coll, NY   B
D'Youville Coll, NY   B
Elmira Coll, NY   B
Excelsior Coll, NY   B
Fordham U, NY   B
Hamilton Coll, NY   B
Hartwick Coll, NY   B
Hobart and William Smith Colls,
   NY   B
Hofstra U, NY   B
Houghton Coll, NY   B
Hunter Coll of the City U of
   New York, NY   B
Iona Coll, NY   B
Ithaca Coll, NY   B
Keuka Coll, NY   B
Lehman Coll of the City U of
   New York, NY   B
Le Moyne Coll, NY   B

Long Island U, Brooklyn
   Campus, NY   B
Long Island U, C.W. Post
   Campus, NY   B
Manhattan Coll, NY   B
Manhattanville Coll, NY   B
Marymount Coll of Fordham U,
   NY   B
Marymount Manhattan Coll, NY   B
Mercy Coll, NY   B
Molloy Coll, NY   B
Mount Saint Mary Coll, NY   B
Nazareth Coll of Rochester, NY   B
New York Inst of Technology, NY   B
New York U, NY   B
Niagara U, NY   B
North Carolina Ag and Tech
   State U, NC   B
Post U, CT   B
Prescott Coll, AZ   B
Purchase Coll, State U of New
   York, NY   B
Queens Coll of the City U of
   New York, NY   B
Quinnipiac U, CT   B
Roberts Wesleyan Coll, NY   B
Russell Sage Coll, NY   B
St. Bonaventure U, NY   B
St. Francis Coll, NY   B
St. John Fisher Coll, NY   B
St. John's U, NY   B
St. Joseph's Coll, Suffolk Campus,
   NY   B
St. Lawrence U, NY   B
Sarah Lawrence Coll, NY   B
Shepherd U, WV   B
Siena Coll, NY   B
Skidmore Coll, NY   B
State U of New York at
   Binghamton, NY   B
State U of New York at Buffalo,
   NY   B
State U of New York at New
   Paltz, NY   B
State U of New York at Oswego,
   NY   B
State U of New York at
   Plattsburgh, NY   B
State U of New York Coll at
   Brockport, NY   B
State U of New York Coll at
   Cortland, NY   B
State U of New York Coll at
   Geneseo, NY   B
State U of New York Coll at Old
   Westbury, NY   B
State U of New York Coll at
   Oneonta, NY   B
State U of New York Coll at
   Potsdam, NY   B
State U of New York, Fredonia,
   NY   B
State U of New York Inst of
   Technology, NY   B
Stony Brook U, State U of New
   York, NY   B
Syracuse U, NY   B
Union Coll, NY   B
U at Albany, State U of New
   York, NY   B
U of West Florida, FL   B
Utica Coll, NY   B
Vassar Coll, NY   B
Wagner Coll, NY   B
Wells Coll, NY   B
West Virginia Wesleyan Coll,
   WV   B
Yeshiva U, NY   B
York Coll of the City U of New
   York, NY   B

Soil Science and Agronomy
Cornell U, NY   B

Soil Sciences Related
Cornell U, NY   B

Spanish
Adelphi U, NY   B
Alfred U, NY   B
Bard Coll, NY   B
Barnard Coll, NY   B

Bernard M. Baruch Coll of the
   City U of New York, NY   B
Brooklyn Coll of the City U of
   New York, NY   B
Buffalo State Coll, State U of
   New York, NY   B
Canisius Coll, NY   B
Chatham Coll, PA   B
City Coll of the City U of New
   York, NY   B
Colgate U, NY   B
Coll of Mount Saint Vincent, NY   B
The Coll of New Rochelle, NY   B
The Coll of Saint Rose, NY   B
Coll of Staten Island of the City
   U of New York, NY   B
Columbia Coll, NY   B
Columbia U, School of General
   Studies, NY   B
Cornell U, NY   B
Daemen Coll, NY   B
Dominican Coll, NY   B
Elmira Coll, NY   B
Fordham U, NY   B
Hamilton Coll, NY   B
Hartwick Coll, NY   B
Hobart and William Smith Colls,
   NY   B
Hofstra U, NY   B
Houghton Coll, NY   B
Hunter Coll of the City U of
   New York, NY   B
Iona Coll, NY   B
Ithaca Coll, NY   B
Lehman Coll of the City U of
   New York, NY   B
Le Moyne Coll, NY   B
Long Island U, C.W. Post
   Campus, NY   B
Manhattan Coll, NY   B
Manhattanville Coll, NY   B
Marist Coll, NY   B
Marymount Coll of Fordham U,
   NY   B
Mercy Coll, NY   B
Molloy Coll, NY   B
Nazareth Coll of Rochester, NY   B
New York U, NY   B
Niagara U, NY   B
Pace U, NY   B
Prescott Coll, AZ   B
Purchase Coll, State U of New
   York, NY   B
Queens Coll of the City U of
   New York, NY   B
Quinnipiac U, CT   B
Russell Sage Coll, NY   B
St. Bonaventure U, NY   B
St. Francis Coll, NY   B
St. John Fisher Coll, NY   B
St. John's U, NY   B
St. Joseph's Coll, New York, NY   B
St. Lawrence U, NY   B
St. Thomas Aquinas Coll, NY   B
Sarah Lawrence Coll, NY   B
Siena Coll, NY   B
Skidmore Coll, NY   B
State U of New York at
   Binghamton, NY   B
State U of New York at Buffalo,
   NY   B
State U of New York at New
   Paltz, NY   B
State U of New York at Oswego,
   NY   B
State U of New York at
   Plattsburgh, NY   B
State U of New York Coll at
   Brockport, NY   B
State U of New York Coll at
   Cortland, NY   B
State U of New York Coll at
   Geneseo, NY   B
State U of New York Coll at Old
   Westbury, NY   B
State U of New York Coll at
   Oneonta, NY   B
State U of New York Coll at
   Potsdam, NY   B
State U of New York, Fredonia,
   NY   B

A—associate degree; B—bachelor's degree

Stony Brook U, State U of New
  York, NY   B
Syracuse U, NY   B
United States Military Academy,
  NY   B
U at Albany, State U of New
  York, NY   B
U of Rochester, NY   B
Vassar Coll, NY   B
Wagner Coll, NY   B
Wells Coll, NY   B
York Coll of the City U of New
  York, NY   B

Spanish and Iberian Studies
Barnard Coll, NY   B
Fordham U, NY   B

Spanish Language Teacher Education
Brooklyn Coll of the City U of
  New York, NY   B
The Coll of Saint Rose, NY   B
Daemen Coll, NY   B
Dowling Coll, NY   B
Elmira Coll, NY   B
Hofstra U, NY   B
Iona Coll, NY   B
Ithaca Coll, NY   B
Le Moyne Coll, NY   B
Long Island U, Brooklyn
  Campus, NY   B
Long Island U, C.W. Post
  Campus, NY   B
Manhattanville Coll, NY   B
Marymount Coll of Fordham U,
  NY   B
Molloy Coll, NY   B
Niagara U, NY   B
Pace U, NY   B
St. Bonaventure U, NY   B
St. John's U, NY   B
State U of New York Coll at
  Brockport, NY   B
State U of New York Coll at
  Cortland, NY   B
State U of New York Coll at
  Oneonta, NY   B
State U of New York Coll at
  Potsdam, NY   B
U at Albany, State U of New
  York, NY   B

Special Education
Buffalo State Coll, State U of
  New York, NY   B
Chatham Coll, PA   B
Coll of Mount Saint Vincent, NY   B
The Coll of New Rochelle, NY   B
The Coll of Saint Rose, NY   B
Daemen Coll, NY   B
Dominican Coll, NY   B
Dowling Coll, NY   B
D'Youville Coll, NY   B
Keuka Coll, NY   B
Long Island U, Brooklyn
  Campus, NY   B
Manhattan Coll, NY   B
Marist Coll, NY   B
Marymount Coll of Fordham U,
  NY   B
Medgar Evers Coll of the City U
  of New York, NY   B
Mercy Coll, NY   B
Molloy Coll, NY   B
Mount Saint Mary Coll, NY   B
Nazareth Coll of Rochester, NY   B
New York U, NY   B
Niagara U, NY   B
North Carolina Ag and Tech
  State U, NC   B
Prescott Coll, AZ   B
Roberts Wesleyan Coll, NY   B
St. Bonaventure U, NY   B
St. John Fisher Coll, NY   B
St. John's U, NY   B
St. Joseph's Coll, Suffolk Campus,
  NY   B
St. Thomas Aquinas Coll, NY   B
State U of New York at New
  Paltz, NY   B
State U of New York at
  Plattsburgh, NY   B

State U of New York Coll at
  Geneseo, NY   B
State U of New York Coll at Old
  Westbury, NY   B
Syracuse U, NY   B
U of West Florida, FL   B
West Virginia Wesleyan Coll,
  WV   B

Special Education (Early Childhood)
Canisius Coll, NY   B
Cazenovia Coll, NY   B
Keuka Coll, NY   B

Special Education (Mentally Retarded)
U of West Florida, FL   B

Special Education (Multiply Disabled)
Dominican Coll, NY   B

Special Education (Specific Learning Disabilities)
West Virginia Wesleyan Coll,
  WV   B

Special Education (Speech or Language Impaired)
Brooklyn Coll of the City U of
  New York, NY   B
Buffalo State Coll, State U of
  New York, NY   B
Ithaca Coll, NY   B
Long Island U, Brooklyn
  Campus, NY   B
Long Island U, C.W. Post
  Campus, NY   B
New York U, NY   B
Pace U, NY   B
State U of New York Coll at
  Cortland, NY   B

Special Education (Vision Impaired)
St. Francis Coll, NY   B

Special Products Marketing
Buffalo State Coll, State U of
  New York, NY   B
Quinnipiac U, CT   B
Rochester Inst of Technology, NY   B

Speech and Rhetoric
Adelphi U, NY   B
Dowling Coll, NY   B
Hofstra U, NY   B
Iona Coll, NY   B
Ithaca Coll, NY   B
Lehman Coll of the City U of
  New York, NY   B
Long Island U, Brooklyn
  Campus, NY   B
Marymount Coll of Fordham U,
  NY   B
Mercy Coll, NY   B
North Carolina Ag and Tech
  State U, NC   B
Pace U, NY   B
St. John's U, NY   B
St. Joseph's Coll, New York, NY   B
St. Joseph's Coll, Suffolk Campus,
  NY   B
State U of New York at New
  Paltz, NY   B
State U of New York Coll at
  Brockport, NY   B
State U of New York Coll at
  Cortland, NY   B
State U of New York Coll at
  Oneonta, NY   B
State U of New York Coll at
  Potsdam, NY   B
Syracuse U, NY   B
U at Albany, State U of New
  York, NY   B
West Virginia Wesleyan Coll,
  WV   B
Yeshiva U, NY   B
York Coll of the City U of New
  York, NY   B

Speech-Language Pathology
Brooklyn Coll of the City U of
  New York, NY   B

Lehman Coll of the City U of
  New York, NY   B
Pace U, NY   B
Yeshiva U, NY   B

Speech Teacher Education
Brooklyn Coll of the City U of
  New York, NY   B
Elmira Coll, NY   B

Speech Therapy
Iona Coll, NY   B
Queens Coll of the City U of
  New York, NY   B
State U of New York at New
  Paltz, NY   B
State U of New York Coll at
  Geneseo, NY   B
State U of New York, Fredonia,
  NY   B

Sport and Fitness Administration
Cazenovia Coll, NY   B
Ithaca Coll, NY   B
Medaille Coll, NY   B
Mitchell Coll, CT   A
New York U, NY   B
St. John's U, NY   B
State U of New York at Oswego,
  NY   B
State U of New York Coll at
  Brockport, NY   B
State U of New York Coll of
  Technology at Alfred, NY   A
West Virginia Wesleyan Coll,
  WV   B

Statistics
Barnard Coll, NY   B
Bernard M. Baruch Coll of the
  City U of New York, NY   B
Clarkson U, NY   B
Columbia Coll, NY   B
Columbia U, School of General
  Studies, NY   B
Cornell U, NY   B
Hunter Coll of the City U of
  New York, NY   B
New York U, NY   B
Rochester Inst of Technology, NY   B
State U of New York Coll at
  Oneonta, NY   B
U of Rochester, NY   B

Structural Engineering
Clarkson U, NY   B
Cornell U, NY   B
State U of New York at Buffalo,
  NY   B

Substance Abuse/Addiction Counseling
State U of New York Coll at
  Brockport, NY   B

Surveying Engineering
Cornell U, NY   B

Survey Technology
Paul Smith's Coll of Arts and
  Sciences, NY   A
State U of New York Coll of
  Technology at Alfred, NY   A,B

System Administration
Rochester Inst of Technology, NY   B
State U of New York Coll of
  Technology at Alfred, NY   B

System, Networking, and LAN/WAN Management
Rochester Inst of Technology, NY   B

Systems Engineering
Cornell U, NY   B
Rensselaer Polytechnic Inst, NY   B
Rochester Inst of Technology, NY   B
United States Military Academy,
  NY   B

Talmudic Studies
The Jewish Theological Seminary,
  NY   B

Taxation
St. John's U, NY   B

Technical and Business Writing
Clarkson U, NY   B
Farmingdale State U of New
  York, NY   B
Medaille Coll, NY   B
New York Inst of Technology, NY   B
Paul Smith's Coll of Arts and
  Sciences, NY   A

Technical Teacher Education
New York Inst of Technology, NY   A,B

Technology/Industrial Arts Teacher Education
Buffalo State Coll, State U of
  New York, NY   B
New York Inst of Technology, NY   B
St. John Fisher Coll, NY   B
State U of New York at Oswego,
  NY   B

Telecommunications
Briarcliffe Coll, NY   A
Ithaca Coll, NY   B
New York Inst of Technology, NY   B
Rochester Inst of Technology, NY   B
St. John's U, NY   B
State U of New York Coll of
  Agriculture and Technology at
  Cobleskill, NY   A
Syracuse U, NY   B

Telecommunications Technology
Rochester Inst of Technology, NY   B
St. John's U, NY   B

Textile Science
Cornell U, NY   B

Theater Design and Technology
Five Towns Coll, NY   B
Ithaca Coll, NY   B
Purchase Coll, State U of New
  York, NY   B
Syracuse U, NY   B

Theater Literature, History and Criticism
Bard Coll, NY   B
Cornell U, NY   B
Marymount Manhattan Coll, NY   B
New York U, NY   B

Theater/Theater Arts Management
Brooklyn Coll of the City U of
  New York, NY   B

Theology
Fordham U, NY   B
Holy Trinity Orthodox Seminary,
  NY   B
Houghton Coll, NY   B
Nyack Coll, NY   B
St. John's U, NY   B

Theoretical and Mathematical Physics
State U of New York at Buffalo,
  NY   B

Therapeutic Recreation
Ithaca Coll, NY   B
Mitchell Coll, CT   A
St. Joseph's Coll, Suffolk Campus,
  NY   B
State U of New York Coll at
  Brockport, NY   B
State U of New York Coll at
  Cortland, NY   B
Utica Coll, NY   B

Tourism and Travel Services Management
Dowling Coll, NY   B
New York U, NY   B
Niagara U, NY   B
Paul Smith's Coll of Arts and
  Sciences, NY   A
Rochester Inst of Technology, NY   A,B
State U of New York Coll of
  Technology at Delhi, NY   A,B

Tourism and Travel Services Marketing
Rochester Inst of Technology, NY   B
State U of New York Coll of
  Agriculture and Technology at
  Cobleskill, NY   A

Toxicology
Clarkson U, NY	B
Cornell U, NY	B
St. John's U, NY	B

Trade and Industrial Teacher Education
Buffalo State Coll, State U of New York, NY	B
The Coll of Saint Rose, NY	B
New York Inst of Technology, NY	B
North Carolina Ag and Tech State U, NC	B
State U of New York at Oswego, NY	B
U of West Florida, FL	B

Transportation and Highway Engineering
Cornell U, NY	B

Transportation and Materials Moving Related
Dowling Coll, NY	B
St. John's U, NY	B
Syracuse U, NY	B
United States Merchant Marine Academy, NY	B

Transportation Technology
Dowling Coll, NY	B
Niagara U, NY	B
North Carolina Ag and Tech State U, NC	B

Turf and Turfgrass Management
State U of New York Coll of Agriculture and Technology at Cobleskill, NY	A,B
State U of New York Coll of Technology at Delhi, NY	A

Urban Studies/Affairs
Barnard Coll, NY	B
Buffalo State Coll, State U of New York, NY	B
Canisius Coll, NY	B
Coll of Mount Saint Vincent, NY	B
Columbia Coll, NY	B
Columbia U, School of General Studies, NY	B
Cornell U, NY	B
Fordham U, NY	B
Hobart and William Smith Colls, NY	B
Hunter Coll of the City U of New York, NY	B
Manhattan Coll, NY	B
New York U, NY	B
Queens Coll of the City U of New York, NY	B
Sarah Lawrence Coll, NY	B
U at Albany, State U of New York, NY	B
Vassar Coll, NY	B

Veterinary/Animal Health Technology
Medaille Coll, NY	A,B

Veterinary Sciences
Mercy Coll, NY	B
State U of New York Coll of Technology at Alfred, NY	A
Wagner Coll, NY	B

Veterinary Technology
Medaille Coll, NY	A,B
Mercy Coll, NY	B
Quinnipiac U, CT	B
State U of New York Coll of Technology at Canton, NY	A
State U of New York Coll of Technology at Delhi, NY	A,B

Violin, Viola, Guitar and Other Stringed Instruments
Five Towns Coll, NY	A,B
Houghton Coll, NY	B
The Juilliard School, NY	B
Manhattan School of Music, NY	B
Sarah Lawrence Coll, NY	B
State U of New York, Fredonia, NY	B
Syracuse U, NY	B

Visual and Performing Arts
Bard Coll, NY	B
Barnard Coll, NY	B
Briarcliffe Coll, NY	A
Cazenovia Coll, NY	B
Columbia Coll, NY	B
Cornell U, NY	B
Ithaca Coll, NY	B
Long Island U, C.W. Post Campus, NY	B
St. Bonaventure U, NY	B
Sarah Lawrence Coll, NY	B
State U of New York Coll at Old Westbury, NY	B
Vassar Coll, NY	B

Visual and Performing Arts Related
Adelphi U, NY	B
Fashion Inst of Technology, NY	B
Long Island U, C.W. Post Campus, NY	B
Rensselaer Polytechnic Inst, NY	B
Sarah Lawrence Coll, NY	B
State U of New York Coll at Geneseo, NY	B

Voice and Opera
Bard Coll, NY	B
Five Towns Coll, NY	A,B
Houghton Coll, NY	B
Ithaca Coll, NY	B
The Juilliard School, NY	B
Long Island U, C.W. Post Campus, NY	B
Manhattan School of Music, NY	B

New York U, NY	B
Nyack Coll, NY	B
Roberts Wesleyan Coll, NY	B
Sarah Lawrence Coll, NY	B
State U of New York, Fredonia, NY	B
Syracuse U, NY	B

Watchmaking and Jewelrymaking
Fashion Inst of Technology, NY	A

Water Resources Engineering
State U of New York Coll of Environmental Science and Forestry, NY	B

Web/Multimedia Management and Webmaster
Rochester Inst of Technology, NY	B

Web Page, Digital/Multimedia and Information Resources Design
Medaille Coll, NY	B
Quinnipiac U, CT	B
Rochester Inst of Technology, NY	B
State U of New York Coll of Technology at Delhi, NY	B

Welding Technology
Excelsior Coll, NY	A,B
State U of New York Coll of Technology at Alfred, NY	A
State U of New York Coll of Technology at Delhi, NY	A

Western Civilization
Bard Coll, NY	B
Sarah Lawrence Coll, NY	B

Wildlife and Wildlands Science and Management
Prescott Coll, AZ	B
State U of New York Coll of Agriculture and Technology at Cobleskill, NY	A,B
State U of New York Coll of Environmental Science and Forestry, NY	B

Wildlife Biology
State U of New York Coll of Environmental Science and Forestry, NY	B

Wind/Percussion Instruments
Five Towns Coll, NY	A,B
Houghton Coll, NY	B
The Juilliard School, NY	B
Manhattan School of Music, NY	B
Sarah Lawrence Coll, NY	B
State U of New York, Fredonia, NY	B
Syracuse U, NY	B

Women's Studies
Barnard Coll, NY	B

Brooklyn Coll of the City U of New York, NY	B
Chatham Coll, PA	B
City Coll of the City U of New York, NY	B
Colgate U, NY	B
The Coll of New Rochelle, NY	B
Columbia Coll, NY	B
Columbia U, School of General Studies, NY	B
Cornell U, NY	B
Fordham U, NY	B
Hamilton Coll, NY	B
Hobart and William Smith Colls, NY	B
Hunter Coll of the City U of New York, NY	B
The Jewish Theological Seminary, NY	B
Nazareth Coll of Rochester, NY	B
Purchase Coll, State U of New York, NY	B
Queens Coll of the City U of New York, NY	B
Sarah Lawrence Coll, NY	B
Skidmore Coll, NY	B
State U of New York at Buffalo, NY	B
State U of New York at New Paltz, NY	B
State U of New York at Oswego, NY	B
State U of New York Coll at Brockport, NY	B
State U of New York, Fredonia, NY	B
Stony Brook U, State U of New York, NY	B
Syracuse U, NY	B
U at Albany, State U of New York, NY	B
U of Rochester, NY	B
Vassar Coll, NY	B
Wells Coll, NY	B

Wood Science and Wood Products/Pulp and Paper Technology
State U of New York Coll of Environmental Science and Forestry, NY	B

Woodworking
State U of New York Coll of Technology at Delhi, NY	A

Youth Services
Cazenovia Coll, NY	B
Medaille Coll, NY	B

Zoology/Animal Biology
Cornell U, NY	B
Quinnipiac U, CT	B
State U of New York at Oswego, NY	B
State U of New York Coll of Environmental Science and Forestry, NY	B

A—associate degree; B—bachelor's degree

Athletic Programs and Scholarships

Archery

Barnard Coll, NY	W
Columbia Coll, NY	M, W
Columbia U, The Fu Foundation School of Engineering and Applied Science, NY	M, W
Rensselaer Polytechnic Inst, NY	M, W
Syracuse U, NY	M, W

Badminton

Columbia Coll, NY	M, W
Columbia U, The Fu Foundation School of Engineering and Applied Science, NY	M, W
Mercy Coll, NY	M(s)
Rensselaer Polytechnic Inst, NY	M, W
State U of New York at Binghamton, NY	M, W
Syracuse U, NY	M, W

Baseball

Adelphi U, NY	M(s)
Bernard M. Baruch Coll of the City U of New York, NY	M
Briarcliffe Coll, NY	M(s)
Buffalo State Coll, State U of New York, NY	M
Canisius Coll, NY	M(s)
City Coll of the City U of New York, NY	M
Clarkson U, NY	M
Colgate U, NY	M
Coll of Mount Saint Vincent, NY	M
Coll of Staten Island of the City U of New York, NY	M
Columbia Coll, NY	M
Columbia U, School of General Studies, NY	M
Columbia U, The Fu Foundation School of Engineering and Applied Science, NY	M
Concordia Coll, NY	M(s)
Cornell U, NY	M
D'Youville Coll, NY	M
Dominican Coll, NY	M(s)
Dowling Coll, NY	M(s)
Farmingdale State U of New York, NY	M
Fordham U, NY	M(s)
Globe Inst of Technology, NY	M
Hamilton Coll, NY	M
Hartwick Coll, NY	M
Hilbert Coll, NY	M
Hofstra U, NY	M(s)
Iona Coll, NY	M(s)
Ithaca Coll, NY	M
John Jay Coll of Criminal Justice of the City U of New York, NY	M
Keuka Coll, NY	M
Le Moyne Coll, NY	M(s)
Lehman Coll of the City U of New York, NY	M
Long Island U, Brooklyn Campus, NY	M(s)
Long Island U, C.W. Post Campus, NY	M(s)
Manhattan Coll, NY	M(s)
Manhattanville Coll, NY	M
Marist Coll, NY	M(s)
Medaille Coll, NY	M
Mercy Coll, NY	M(s)
Mitchell Coll, CT	M
Molloy Coll, NY	M(s)
Monroe Coll, New Rochelle, NY	M
Mount Saint Mary Coll, NY	M
New York Inst of Technology, NY	M(s)
New York U, NY	M, W
Niagara U, NY	M(s)
North Carolina Ag and Tech State U, NC	M(s)
Nyack Coll, NY	M(s)
Pace U, NY	M(s)
Polytechnic U, Brooklyn Campus, NY	M
Post U, CT	M(s)
Purchase Coll, State U of New York, NY	M, W

Queens Coll of the City U of New York, NY	M(s)
Quinnipiac U, CT	M(s)
Rensselaer Polytechnic Inst, NY	M
Rochester Inst of Technology, NY	M
Shepherd U, WV	M(s)
Siena Coll, NY	M(s)
Skidmore Coll, NY	M
St. Bonaventure U, NY	M(s)
St. Francis Coll, NY	M(s)
St. John Fisher Coll, NY	M
St. John's U, NY	M(s)
St. Joseph's Coll, Suffolk Campus, NY	M
St. Lawrence U, NY	M
St. Thomas Aquinas Coll, NY	M(s)
State U of New York Coll at Brockport, NY	M
State U of New York Coll at Cortland, NY	M
State U of New York Coll at Old Westbury, NY	M
State U of New York Coll at Oneonta, NY	M
State U of New York Coll of Agriculture and Technology at Cobleskill, NY	M
State U of New York Coll of Technology at Alfred, NY	M
State U of New York Coll of Technology at Canton, NY	M
State U of New York Inst of Technology, NY	M
State U of New York at Binghamton, NY	M(s)
State U of New York at Buffalo, NY	M(s)
State U of New York at New Paltz, NY	M
State U of New York at Oswego, NY	M
State U of New York at Plattsburgh, NY	M
State U of New York, Fredonia, NY	M
Stony Brook U, State U of New York, NY	M(s)
Syracuse U, NY	M
The Coll of Saint Rose, NY	M(s)
Union Coll, NY	M
United States Merchant Marine Academy, NY	M
United States Military Academy, NY	M
U at Albany, State U of New York, NY	M(s)
U of Rochester, NY	M
U of West Florida, FL	M(s)
Utica Coll, NY	M
Vassar Coll, NY	M
Wagner Coll, NY	M(s)
West Virginia Wesleyan Coll, WV	M(s)
York Coll of the City U of New York, NY	M, W

Basketball

Adelphi U, NY	M(s), W(s)
Albany Coll of Pharmacy of Union U, NY	M, W
Alfred U, NY	M, W
Bard Coll, NY	M, W
Barnard Coll, NY	W
Bernard M. Baruch Coll of the City U of New York, NY	M, W
Brooklyn Coll of the City U of New York, NY	M, W
Buffalo State Coll, State U of New York, NY	M, W
Canisius Coll, NY	M(s), W(s)
Chaminade U of Honolulu, HI	M(s)
Chatham Coll, PA	W
City Coll of the City U of New York, NY	M, W
Clarkson U, NY	M, W
Colgate U, NY	M(s), W(s)
Coll of Mount Saint Vincent, NY	M, W
Coll of Staten Island of the City U of New York, NY	M, W

Columbia Coll, NY	M, W
Columbia U, School of General Studies, NY	M, W
Columbia U, The Fu Foundation School of Engineering and Applied Science, NY	M, W
Concordia Coll, NY	M(s), W(s)
Cornell U, NY	M, W
D'Youville Coll, NY	M, W
Daemen Coll, NY	M(s), W(s)
Dominican Coll, NY	M(s), W(s)
Dowling Coll, NY	M(s), W(s)
Elmira Coll, NY	M, W
Farmingdale State U of New York, NY	M, W
Fashion Inst of Technology, NY	M, W
Fordham U, NY	M(s), W(s)
Globe Inst of Technology, NY	M(s), W(s)
Hamilton Coll, NY	M, W
Hartwick Coll, NY	M, W
Hilbert Coll, NY	M, W
Hobart and William Smith Colls, NY	M, W
Hofstra U, NY	M(s), W(s)
Houghton Coll, NY	M(s), W(s)
Hunter Coll of the City U of New York, NY	M, W
Iona Coll, NY	M(s), W(s)
Ithaca Coll, NY	M, W
John Jay Coll of Criminal Justice of the City U of New York, NY	M, W
Keuka Coll, NY	M, W
Le Moyne Coll, NY	M(s), W(s)
Lehman Coll of the City U of New York, NY	M, W
Long Island U, Brooklyn Campus, NY	M(s), W(s)
Long Island U, C.W. Post Campus, NY	M(s), W(s)
Manhattan Coll, NY	M(s), W(s)
Manhattanville Coll, NY	M, W
Marist Coll, NY	M(s), W(s)
Marymount Coll of Fordham U, NY	W
Medaille Coll, NY	M, W
Medgar Evers Coll of the City U of New York, NY	M
Mercy Coll, NY	M(s), W(s)
Mitchell Coll, CT	M, W
Molloy Coll, NY	M(s), W(s)
Monroe Coll, Bronx, NY	M, W
Monroe Coll, New Rochelle, NY	M, W
Mount Saint Mary Coll, NY	M, W
Nazareth Coll of Rochester, NY	M, W
New York Inst of Technology, NY	M(s), W(s)
New York U, NY	M, W
Niagara U, NY	M(s), W(s)
North Carolina Ag and Tech State U, NC	M(s), W(s)
Nyack Coll, NY	M(s), W(s)
Pace U, NY	M(s), W(s)
Paul Smith's Coll of Arts and Sciences, NY	M(s), W(s)
Polytechnic U, Brooklyn Campus, NY	M, W
Post U, CT	M(s), W(s)
Pratt Inst, NY	M
Purchase Coll, State U of New York, NY	M, W
Queens Coll of the City U of New York, NY	M(s), W(s)
Quinnipiac U, CT	M(s), W(s)
Rensselaer Polytechnic Inst, NY	M, W
Roberts Wesleyan Coll, NY	M(s), W(s)
Rochester Inst of Technology, NY	M, W
Russell Sage Coll, NY	W
Sarah Lawrence Coll, NY	M
Shepherd U, WV	M(s), W(s)
Siena Coll, NY	M(s), W(s)
Skidmore Coll, NY	M, W
St. Bonaventure U, NY	M(s), W(s)
St. Francis Coll, NY	M(s), W(s)
St. John Fisher Coll, NY	M, W
St. John's U, NY	M(s), W(s)
St. Joseph's Coll, New York, NY	M, W

M—for men; W—for women; (s)—scholarship offered

St. Joseph's Coll, Suffolk Campus, NY	M, W
St. Lawrence U, NY	M, W
St. Thomas Aquinas Coll, NY	M(s), W(s)
State U of New York Coll at Brockport, NY	M, W
State U of New York Coll at Cortland, NY	M, W
State U of New York Coll at Geneseo, NY	M, W
State U of New York Coll at Old Westbury, NY	M, W
State U of New York Coll at Oneonta, NY	M, W
State U of New York Coll at Potsdam, NY	M, W
State U of New York Coll of Agriculture and Technology at Cobleskill, NY	M, W
State U of New York Coll of Technology at Alfred, NY	M(s), W(s)
State U of New York Coll of Technology at Canton, NY	M, W
State U of New York Coll of Technology at Delhi, NY	M, W
State U of New York Inst of Technology, NY	M, W
State U of New York at Binghamton, NY	M(s), W(s)
State U of New York at Buffalo, NY	M(s), W(s)
State U of New York at New Paltz, NY	M, W
State U of New York at Oswego, NY	M, W
State U of New York at Plattsburgh, NY	M, W
State U of New York, Fredonia, NY	M, W
Stony Brook U, State U of New York, NY	M(s), W(s)
Syracuse U, NY	M(s), W(s)
The Coll of New Rochelle, NY	W
The Coll of Saint Rose, NY	M(s), W(s)
Union Coll, NY	M, W
United States Merchant Marine Academy, NY	M, W
United States Military Academy, NY	M, W
U at Albany, State U of New York, NY	M(s), W(s)
U of Rochester, NY	M, W
U of West Florida, FL	M(s), W(s)
Utica Coll, NY	M, W
Vassar Coll, NY	M, W
Wagner Coll, NY	M(s), W(s)
Webb Inst, NY	M, W
West Virginia Wesleyan Coll, WV	M(s), W(s)
Yeshiva U, NY	M, W
York Coll of the City U of New York, NY	M, W

Bowling

Briarcliffe Coll, NY	M(s), W(s)
Buffalo State Coll, State U of New York, NY	M, W
Clarkson U, NY	M, W
Fashion Inst of Technology, NY	M, W
Globe Inst of Technology, NY	M, W
Marist Coll, NY	M, W
Rochester Inst of Technology, NY	M, W
State U of New York Inst of Technology, NY	M, W
State U of New York at Binghamton, NY	M, W
Syracuse U, NY	M, W
United States Military Academy, NY	M, W

Cheerleading

Bernard M. Baruch Coll of the City U of New York, NY	W
Colgate U, NY	M, W
Coll of Mount Saint Vincent, NY	W
Elmira Coll, NY	W
Fordham U, NY	M, W
Houghton Coll, NY	M, W
Manhattan Coll, NY	M(s), W(s)
Marist Coll, NY	M, W
Medaille Coll, NY	M, W
Mitchell Coll, CT	
Nazareth Coll of Rochester, NY	W
New York U, NY	M, W
Nyack Coll, NY	M(s), W(s)
Rensselaer Polytechnic Inst, NY	M, W
Rochester Inst of Technology, NY	M, W
Siena Coll, NY	W
St. Bonaventure U, NY	M, W
St. John Fisher Coll, NY	W
State U of New York Coll at Oneonta, NY	W
State U of New York Coll of Technology at Alfred, NY	M, W
State U of New York, Fredonia, NY	M, W

Syracuse U, NY	M, W
West Virginia Wesleyan Coll, WV	M, W

Crew

Barnard Coll, NY	W
Chatham Coll, PA	W
Colgate U, NY	M, W
Columbia Coll, NY	M, W
Columbia U, School of General Studies, NY	M, W
Columbia U, The Fu Foundation School of Engineering and Applied Science, NY	M, W
Cornell U, NY	M, W
Dowling Coll, NY	M, W
Fordham U, NY	M, W(s)
Hamilton Coll, NY	W
Hobart and William Smith Colls, NY	M, W
Iona Coll, NY	M, W
Ithaca Coll, NY	M, W
Long Island U, C.W. Post Campus, NY	M, W
Manhattan Coll, NY	M, W
Marist Coll, NY	M, W
New York U, NY	M, W
Rensselaer Polytechnic Inst, NY	M, W
Rochester Inst of Technology, NY	M, W
Sarah Lawrence Coll, NY	M, W
Siena Coll, NY	M, W
Skidmore Coll, NY	M, W
St. Lawrence U, NY	M, W
State U of New York Coll at Geneseo, NY	M, W
State U of New York at Binghamton, NY	M, W
State U of New York at Buffalo, NY	W(s)
State U of New York at Oswego, NY	M, W
Syracuse U, NY	M(s), W(s)
Union Coll, NY	M, W
United States Merchant Marine Academy, NY	M, W
United States Military Academy, NY	M, W
U at Albany, State U of New York, NY	M, W
U of Rochester, NY	M, W
Vassar Coll, NY	M, W

Cross-Country Running

Adelphi U, NY	M(s), W(s)
Alfred U, NY	M, W
Bard Coll, NY	M, W
Barnard Coll, NY	W
Bernard M. Baruch Coll of the City U of New York, NY	W
Brooklyn Coll of the City U of New York, NY	M, W
Buffalo State Coll, State U of New York, NY	M, W
Canisius Coll, NY	M(s), W(s)
Cazenovia Coll, NY	M
Chaminade U of Honolulu, HI	M(s), W(s)
City Coll of the City U of New York, NY	M, W
Clarkson U, NY	M, W
Colgate U, NY	M, W
Coll of Mount Saint Vincent, NY	M, W
Columbia Coll, NY	M, W
Columbia U, School of General Studies, NY	M, W
Columbia U, The Fu Foundation School of Engineering and Applied Science, NY	M, W
Concordia Coll, NY	M(s), W(s)
Cornell U, NY	M, W
D'Youville Coll, NY	W
Daemen Coll, NY	M(s), W(s)
Dominican Coll, NY	M(s), W(s)
Farmingdale State U of New York, NY	M, W
Fashion Inst of Technology, NY	M, W
Fordham U, NY	M(s), W(s)
Globe Inst of Technology, NY	M, W
Hamilton Coll, NY	M, W
Hartwick Coll, NY	M, W
Hilbert Coll, NY	M, W
Hobart and William Smith Colls, NY	M, W
Hofstra U, NY	M(s), W(s)
Houghton Coll, NY	M(s), W(s)
Hunter Coll of the City U of New York, NY	M, W
Iona Coll, NY	M(s), W(s)
Ithaca Coll, NY	M, W
John Jay Coll of Criminal Justice of the City U of New York, NY	M, W
Keuka Coll, NY	M, W
Le Moyne Coll, NY	M(s), W(s)
Lehman Coll of the City U of New York, NY	M, W
Long Island U, Brooklyn Campus, NY	M(s), W(s)

Long Island U, C.W. Post Campus, NY	M(s), W(s)
Manhattan Coll, NY	M(s), W(s)
Marist Coll, NY	M(s), W(s)
Medaille Coll, NY	W
Medgar Evers Coll of the City U of New York, NY	M, W
Mercy Coll, NY	M(s), W(s)
Mitchell Coll, CT	M, W
Molloy Coll, NY	M(s), W(s)
Nazareth Coll of Rochester, NY	M, W
New York Inst of Technology, NY	M(s), W(s)
New York U, NY	M, W
Niagara U, NY	M(s), W(s)
North Carolina Ag and Tech State U, NC	M(s), W(s)
Nyack Coll, NY	M(s), W(s)
Pace U, NY	M(s), W(s)
Polytechnic U, Brooklyn Campus, NY	M, W
Post U, CT	M(s), W(s)
Pratt Inst, NY	M, W
Purchase Coll, State U of New York, NY	M, W
Quinnipiac U, CT	M(s), W(s)
Rensselaer Polytechnic Inst, NY	M, W
Roberts Wesleyan Coll, NY	M(s), W(s)
Rochester Inst of Technology, NY	M, W
Siena Coll, NY	M, W
St. Bonaventure U, NY	M(s), W(s)
St. Francis Coll, NY	M(s), W(s)
St. John's U, NY	W(s)
St. Joseph's Coll, New York, NY	M, W
St. Joseph's Coll, Suffolk Campus, NY	M, W
St. Lawrence U, NY	M, W
St. Thomas Aquinas Coll, NY	M(s), W(s)
State U of New York Coll at Brockport, NY	M, W
State U of New York Coll at Cortland, NY	M, W
State U of New York Coll at Geneseo, NY	M, W
State U of New York Coll at Old Westbury, NY	M, W
State U of New York Coll at Oneonta, NY	M, W
State U of New York Coll at Potsdam, NY	M, W
State U of New York Coll of Agriculture and Technology at Cobleskill, NY	M, W
State U of New York Coll of Technology at Alfred, NY	M(s), W(s)
State U of New York Coll of Technology at Delhi, NY	M, W
State U of New York Inst of Technology, NY	W
State U of New York at Binghamton, NY	M(s), W(s)
State U of New York at Buffalo, NY	M(s), W(s)
State U of New York at New Paltz, NY	M, W
State U of New York at Oswego, NY	M, W
State U of New York at Plattsburgh, NY	M, W
State U of New York, Fredonia, NY	M, W
Stony Brook U, State U of New York, NY	M(s), W(s)
Syracuse U, NY	M(s), W(s)
The Coll of New Rochelle, NY	W
The Coll of Saint Rose, NY	M(s), W(s)
Union Coll, NY	M, W
United States Merchant Marine Academy, NY	M, W
United States Military Academy, NY	M, W
U at Albany, State U of New York, NY	M(s), W(s)
U of Rochester, NY	M, W
U of West Florida, FL	M(s), W(s)
Vassar Coll, NY	M, W
Wagner Coll, NY	M(s), W(s)
Webb Inst, NY	M, W
West Virginia Wesleyan Coll, WV	M(s), W(s)
Yeshiva U, NY	M
York Coll of the City U of New York, NY	M, W

Equestrian Sports

Alfred U, NY	M, W
Barnard Coll, NY	W
Colgate U, NY	M, W
Cornell U, NY	W
Dowling Coll, NY	W
Hartwick Coll, NY	W
Long Island U, C.W. Post Campus, NY	M, W
Marist Coll, NY	M, W
Marymount Coll of Fordham U, NY	W
Mercy Coll, NY	M, W
Molloy Coll, NY	M(s), W(s)
Nazareth Coll of Rochester, NY	M, W
New York U, NY	W

M—for men; W—for women; (s)—scholarship offered

Pace U, NY — M, W
Post U, CT — M(s), W(s)
Rensselaer Polytechnic Inst, NY — M, W
Rochester Inst of Technology, NY — M, W
Sarah Lawrence Coll, NY — M, W
Siena Coll, NY — M, W
Skidmore Coll, NY — M, W
St. Joseph's Coll, Suffolk Campus, NY — M, W
St. Lawrence U, NY — M, W
State U of New York Coll at Geneseo, NY — M, W
State U of New York Coll at Potsdam, NY — W
State U of New York at Binghamton, NY — M, W
State U of New York at New Paltz, NY — W
Syracuse U, NY — M, W
United States Military Academy, NY — M, W
U of Rochester, NY — M, W

Fencing
Barnard Coll, NY — W
Buffalo State Coll, State U of New York, NY — M
City Coll of the City U of New York, NY — W
Colgate U, NY — M, W
Columbia Coll, NY — M, W
Columbia U, School of General Studies, NY — M, W
Columbia U, The Fu Foundation School of Engineering and Applied Science, NY — M, W
Cornell U, NY — M, W
Hamilton Coll, NY — M, W
Hunter Coll of the City U of New York, NY — M, W
Marist Coll, NY — M, W
New York U, NY — M, W
Queens Coll of the City U of New York, NY — W(s)
Rensselaer Polytechnic Inst, NY — M, W
Rochester Inst of Technology, NY — M, W
St. John's U, NY — M(s), W(s)
State U of New York at Binghamton, NY — M, W
Syracuse U, NY — M, W
Union Coll, NY — M, W
United States Military Academy, NY — M, W
Vassar Coll, NY — M, W
Yeshiva U, NY — M

Field Hockey
Barnard Coll, NY — W
Colgate U, NY — W(s)
Columbia Coll, NY — W
Columbia U, School of General Studies, NY — W
Columbia U, The Fu Foundation School of Engineering and Applied Science, NY — W
Cornell U, NY — W
Elmira Coll, NY — W
Hamilton Coll, NY — W
Hartwick Coll, NY — W
Hobart and William Smith Colls, NY — W
Hofstra U, NY — W(s)
Houghton Coll, NY — W(s)
Ithaca Coll, NY — W
Long Island U, C.W. Post Campus, NY — W(s)
Manhattanville Coll, NY — W
Nazareth Coll of Rochester, NY — W
Quinnipiac U, CT — W(s)
Rensselaer Polytechnic Inst, NY — W
Rochester Inst of Technology, NY — W
Siena Coll, NY — W
Skidmore Coll, NY — W
St. Bonaventure U, NY — W
St. Lawrence U, NY — W
State U of New York Coll at Brockport, NY — W
State U of New York Coll at Cortland, NY — W
State U of New York Coll at Geneseo, NY — W
State U of New York Coll at Oneonta, NY — W
State U of New York at New Paltz, NY — W
State U of New York at Oswego, NY — W
State U of New York, Fredonia, NY — M, W
Syracuse U, NY — W(s)
Union Coll, NY — W
U at Albany, State U of New York, NY — W(s)
U of Rochester, NY — W
Utica Coll, NY — W
Vassar Coll, NY — W
Wells Coll, NY — W

Football
Alfred U, NY — M
Buffalo State Coll, State U of New York, NY — M
Colgate U, NY — M
Columbia Coll, NY — M
Columbia U, School of General Studies, NY — M
Columbia U, The Fu Foundation School of Engineering and Applied Science, NY — M
Cornell U, NY — M
Fordham U, NY — M
Hamilton Coll, NY — M
Hartwick Coll, NY — M
Hobart and William Smith Colls, NY — M
Hofstra U, NY — M(s)
Iona Coll, NY — M
Ithaca Coll, NY — M
Long Island U, C.W. Post Campus, NY — M
Marist Coll, NY — M
North Carolina Ag and Tech State U, NC — M(s)
Pace U, NY — M
Rensselaer Polytechnic Inst, NY — M
Shepherd U, WV — M(s)
St. John Fisher Coll, NY — M
St. Lawrence U, NY — M
State U of New York Coll at Brockport, NY — M
State U of New York Coll at Cortland, NY — M, W
State U of New York Coll of Technology at Alfred, NY — M(s)
State U of New York at Buffalo, NY — M(s)
Stony Brook U, State U of New York, NY — M(s)
Syracuse U, NY — M(s)
Union Coll, NY — M
United States Merchant Marine Academy, NY — M
United States Military Academy, NY — M
U at Albany, State U of New York, NY — M(s)
U of Rochester, NY — M
Utica Coll, NY — M
Wagner Coll, NY — M(s)
West Virginia Wesleyan Coll, WV — M(s)

Golf
Adelphi U, NY — M(s)
Barnard Coll, NY — W
Canisius Coll, NY — M(s)
Clarkson U, NY — M
Colgate U, NY — M, W
Columbia Coll, NY — M
Columbia U, School of General Studies, NY — M
Columbia U, The Fu Foundation School of Engineering and Applied Science, NY — M
Cornell U, NY — M
D'Youville Coll, NY — M, W
Daemen Coll, NY — M(s)
Dominican Coll, NY — M(s)
Elmira Coll, NY — M, W
Farmingdale State U of New York, NY — M
Fordham U, NY — M
Hamilton Coll, NY — M, W
Hartwick Coll, NY — M, W
Hilbert Coll, NY — M, W
Hobart and William Smith Colls, NY — M, W
Hofstra U, NY — M(s), W(s)
Iona Coll, NY — M(s)
Le Moyne Coll, NY — M(s)
Long Island U, Brooklyn Campus, NY — M(s), W(s)
Manhattan Coll, NY — M(s)
Manhattanville Coll, NY — M
Mercy Coll, NY — M(s)
Mitchell Coll, CT — M
Nazareth Coll of Rochester, NY — M, W
New York U, NY — M
Niagara U, NY — M(s)
Nyack Coll, NY — M(s)
Pace U, NY — M(s), W(s)
Post U, CT — M(s)
Queens Coll of the City U of New York, NY — M(s)
Quinnipiac U, CT — M(s)
Rensselaer Polytechnic Inst, NY — M
Roberts Wesleyan Coll, NY — M(s), W(s)
Shepherd U, WV — M
Siena Coll, NY — M, W
Skidmore Coll, NY — M
St. Bonaventure U, NY — M(s)
St. John Fisher Coll, NY — M
St. John's U, NY — M(s), W(s)

Ice Hockey
St. Joseph's Coll, Suffolk Campus, NY — M
St. Lawrence U, NY — M, W
St. Thomas Aquinas Coll, NY — M, W
State U of New York Coll at Cortland, NY — W
State U of New York Coll at Potsdam, NY — M
State U of New York Coll of Agriculture and Technology at Cobleskill, NY — M, W
State U of New York Coll of Technology at Delhi, NY — M, W
State U of New York Inst of Technology, NY — M, W
State U of New York at Binghamton, NY — M(s)
State U of New York at Oswego, NY — M
State U of New York at Plattsburgh, NY — M, W
Union Coll, NY — M, W
United States Merchant Marine Academy, NY — M, W
United States Military Academy, NY — M
U at Albany, State U of New York, NY — W(s)
U of Rochester, NY — M
U of West Florida, FL — M(s)
Utica Coll, NY — M, W
Vassar Coll, NY — M, W
Wagner Coll, NY — M(s), W(s)
West Virginia Wesleyan Coll, WV — M(s)

Gymnastics
Columbia U, School of General Studies, NY — W
Cornell U, NY — W
Hunter Coll of the City U of New York, NY — W
Ithaca Coll, NY — W
Rensselaer Polytechnic Inst, NY — M, W
State U of New York Coll at Brockport, NY — W
State U of New York Coll at Cortland, NY — W
Syracuse U, NY — M, W
United States Military Academy, NY — M

Ice Hockey
Barnard Coll, NY — W
Buffalo State Coll, State U of New York, NY — M, W
Canisius Coll, NY — M(s)
Chatham Coll, PA — W
Clarkson U, NY — M(s), W(s)
Colgate U, NY — M(s), W(s)
Columbia Coll, NY — M
Columbia U, The Fu Foundation School of Engineering and Applied Science, NY — M
Cornell U, NY — M, W
Elmira Coll, NY — M, W
Fordham U, NY — M
Hamilton Coll, NY — M, W
Hartwick Coll, NY — M
Hobart and William Smith Colls, NY — M, W
Manhattanville Coll, NY — M, W
Marist Coll, NY — M
New York U, NY — M
Niagara U, NY — M(s), W(s)
Paul Smith's Coll of Arts and Sciences, NY — M(s)
Quinnipiac U, CT — M(s), W(s)
Rensselaer Polytechnic Inst, NY — M(s), W(s)
Rochester Inst of Technology, NY — M, W
Siena Coll, NY — M
Skidmore Coll, NY — M, W
St. Lawrence U, NY — M(s), W(s)
State U of New York Coll at Brockport, NY — M
State U of New York Coll at Cortland, NY — M, W
State U of New York Coll at Geneseo, NY — M
State U of New York Coll at Oneonta, NY — M
State U of New York Coll at Potsdam, NY — M
State U of New York Coll of Technology at Canton, NY — M
State U of New York at Binghamton, NY — M
State U of New York at New Paltz, NY — M
State U of New York at Oswego, NY — M
State U of New York at Plattsburgh, NY — M, W
State U of New York, Fredonia, NY — M
Syracuse U, NY — M, W
The Culinary Inst of America, NY — M
Union Coll, NY — M, W
United States Military Academy, NY — M

Ice Hockey

U of Rochester, NY	M, W
Utica Coll, NY	M, W
Wagner Coll, NY	M

Lacrosse

Adelphi U, NY	M(s), W(s)
Alfred U, NY	M, W
Barnard Coll, NY	W
Briarcliffe Coll, NY	M
Buffalo State Coll, State U of New York, NY	M, W
Canisius Coll, NY	M(s), W(s)
Cazenovia Coll, NY	M, W
City Coll of the City U of New York, NY	M
Clarkson U, NY	M, W
Colgate U, NY	M(s), W(s)
Coll of Mount Saint Vincent, NY	M, W
Columbia Coll, NY	M, W
Columbia U, The Fu Foundation School of Engineering and Applied Science, NY	M, W
Cornell U, NY	M, W
Dominican Coll, NY	M(s)
Dowling Coll, NY	M
Elmira Coll, NY	M, W
Farmingdale State U of New York, NY	M
Fordham U, NY	M, W
Hamilton Coll, NY	M, W
Hartwick Coll, NY	M, W
Hobart and William Smith Colls, NY	M, W
Hofstra U, NY	M(s), W(s)
Iona Coll, NY	W(s)
Ithaca Coll, NY	M, W
Keuka Coll, NY	M
Le Moyne Coll, NY	M(s), W(s)
Long Island U, Brooklyn Campus, NY	W(s)
Long Island U, C.W. Post Campus, NY	M(s), W(s)
Manhattan Coll, NY	M(s), W(s)
Manhattanville Coll, NY	M, W
Marist Coll, NY	M(s), W(s)
Medaille Coll, NY	M, W
Mitchell Coll, CT	M
Molloy Coll, NY	M(s), W(s)
Nazareth Coll of Rochester, NY	M, W
New York Inst of Technology, NY	M(s)
New York U, NY	M, W
Niagara U, NY	M, W(s)
Pace U, NY	M(s)
Quinnipiac U, CT	M(s), W(s)
Rensselaer Polytechnic Inst, NY	M, W
Rochester Inst of Technology, NY	M, W
Siena Coll, NY	M, W
Skidmore Coll, NY	M, W
St. Bonaventure U, NY	M, W
St. John Fisher Coll, NY	M, W
St. John's U, NY	M(s)
St. Lawrence U, NY	M, W
State U of New York Coll at Brockport, NY	M, W
State U of New York Coll at Cortland, NY	M, W
State U of New York Coll at Geneseo, NY	M, W
State U of New York Coll at Oneonta, NY	M, W
State U of New York Coll at Potsdam, NY	M, W
State U of New York Coll of Agriculture and Technology at Cobleskill, NY	M
State U of New York Coll of Technology at Alfred, NY	M(s)
State U of New York Coll of Technology at Canton, NY	M, W
State U of New York Coll of Technology at Delhi, NY	M
State U of New York Inst of Technology, NY	M
State U of New York at Binghamton, NY	M(s), W(s)
State U of New York at New Paltz, NY	M, W
State U of New York at Oswego, NY	M, W
State U of New York at Plattsburgh, NY	M
State U of New York, Fredonia, NY	W
Stony Brook U, State U of New York, NY	M(s), W(s)
Syracuse U, NY	M(s), W(s)
Union Coll, NY	M, W
United States Merchant Marine Academy, NY	M
United States Military Academy, NY	M, W
U at Albany, State U of New York, NY	M(s), W(s)
U of Rochester, NY	M, W
Utica Coll, NY	M, W

Vassar Coll, NY	M, W
Wagner Coll, NY	M(s), W(s)
Wells Coll, NY	W
West Virginia Wesleyan Coll, WV	M, W

Racquetball

Columbia Coll, NY	M, W
Rensselaer Polytechnic Inst, NY	M, W
State U of New York Coll at Cortland, NY	M, W
State U of New York Coll at Geneseo, NY	M, W
State U of New York at Binghamton, NY	M, W
Syracuse U, NY	M, W
United States Military Academy, NY	M, W

Riflery

Columbia Coll, NY	M, W
Columbia U, The Fu Foundation School of Engineering and Applied Science, NY	M, W
Rensselaer Polytechnic Inst, NY	M, W
Syracuse U, NY	M, W
United States Military Academy, NY	M, W

Rugby

Barnard Coll, NY	W
Buffalo State Coll, State U of New York, NY	M
Canisius Coll, NY	M
Colgate U, NY	M, W
Columbia Coll, NY	M, W
Columbia U, The Fu Foundation School of Engineering and Applied Science, NY	M, W
Daemen Coll, NY	M
Fordham U, NY	M, W
Hamilton Coll, NY	M, W
Hartwick Coll, NY	M
Hobart and William Smith Colls, NY	M, W
Iona Coll, NY	M, W
Manhattan Coll, NY	M
Marist Coll, NY	M, W
Rensselaer Polytechnic Inst, NY	M, W
Rochester Inst of Technology, NY	M, W
Siena Coll, NY	M, W
St. Bonaventure U, NY	M, W
State U of New York Coll at Cortland, NY	M, W
State U of New York Coll at Geneseo, NY	M, W
State U of New York Coll at Oneonta, NY	M, W
State U of New York Coll at Potsdam, NY	W
State U of New York at Binghamton, NY	M, W
State U of New York at New Paltz, NY	M, W
Syracuse U, NY	M, W
Union Coll, NY	M, W
United States Merchant Marine Academy, NY	M
United States Military Academy, NY	M
U at Albany, State U of New York, NY	M, W
U of Rochester, NY	M, W
Vassar Coll, NY	M, W

Sailing

Barnard Coll, NY	W
Colgate U, NY	M, W
Fordham U, NY	M, W
Hamilton Coll, NY	M, W
Hobart and William Smith Colls, NY	M, W
Mitchell Coll, CT	M, W
Rensselaer Polytechnic Inst, NY	M, W
State U of New York Coll at Geneseo, NY	M, W
Syracuse U, NY	M, W
United States Merchant Marine Academy, NY	M, W
United States Military Academy, NY	M, W
Webb Inst, NY	M, W

Skiing (Cross-Country)

Alfred U, NY	M, W
Buffalo State Coll, State U of New York, NY	M, W
Clarkson U, NY	M, W
Columbia Coll, NY	M, W
Columbia U, The Fu Foundation School of Engineering and Applied Science, NY	M, W
Rensselaer Polytechnic Inst, NY	M, W
St. Lawrence U, NY	M, W
United States Military Academy, NY	M, W

Skiing (Downhill)

Alfred U, NY	M, W
Barnard Coll, NY	W
Buffalo State Coll, State U of New York, NY	M, W
Clarkson U, NY	M, W
Colgate U, NY	M, W
Columbia Coll, NY	M, W
Columbia U, The Fu Foundation School of Engineering and Applied Science, NY	M, W
Hamilton Coll, NY	M, W
Hobart and William Smith Colls, NY	M, W
Marist Coll, NY	M, W
Paul Smith's Coll of Arts and Sciences, NY	M(s), W(s)
Rensselaer Polytechnic Inst, NY	M, W
Rochester Inst of Technology, NY	M, W
Skidmore Coll, NY	M, W
St. Lawrence U, NY	M, W
State U of New York at Binghamton, NY	M, W
Syracuse U, NY	M, W
Union Coll, NY	M, W
United States Military Academy, NY	M, W
U of Rochester, NY	M, W

Soccer

Adelphi U, NY	M(s), W(s)
Albany Coll of Pharmacy of Union U, NY	M, W
Alfred U, NY	M, W
Bard Coll, NY	M, W
Barnard Coll, NY	W
Bernard M. Baruch Coll of the City U of New York, NY	M
Briarcliffe Coll, NY	W(s)
Brooklyn Coll of the City U of New York, NY	M
Buffalo State Coll, State U of New York, NY	M, W
Canisius Coll, NY	M(s), W(s)
Chatham Coll, PA	W
City Coll of the City U of New York, NY	M
Clarkson U, NY	M, W
Colgate U, NY	M(s), W(s)
Coll of Mount Saint Vincent, NY	M, W
Coll of Staten Island of the City U of New York, NY	M, W
Columbia Coll, NY	M, W
Columbia U, School of General Studies, NY	M, W
Columbia U, The Fu Foundation School of Engineering and Applied Science, NY	M, W
Concordia Coll, NY	M(s), W(s)
Cornell U, NY	M, W
D'Youville Coll, NY	M, W
Daemen Coll, NY	M(s), W(s)
Dominican Coll, NY	M(s), W(s)
Dowling Coll, NY	M(s)
Elmira Coll, NY	M, W
Farmingdale State U of New York, NY	M, W
Fordham U, NY	M(s), W(s)
Globe Inst of Technology, NY	M(s)
Hamilton Coll, NY	M, W
Hartwick Coll, NY	M(s), W(s)
Hilbert Coll, NY	M, W
Hobart and William Smith Colls, NY	M, W
Hofstra U, NY	M(s), W(s)
Houghton Coll, NY	M(s), W(s)
Hunter Coll of the City U of New York, NY	M
Iona Coll, NY	M(s), W(s)
Ithaca Coll, NY	M, W
John Jay Coll of Criminal Justice of the City U of New York, NY	M, W
Keuka Coll, NY	M, W
Le Moyne Coll, NY	M(s), W(s)
Lehman Coll of the City U of New York, NY	M
Long Island U, Brooklyn Campus, NY	M(s), W(s)
Long Island U, C.W. Post Campus, NY	M(s), W(s)
Manhattan Coll, NY	M(s), W(s)
Manhattanville Coll, NY	M, W
Marist Coll, NY	M(s), W(s)
Marymount Coll of Fordham U, NY	W
Medaille Coll, NY	M, W
Medgar Evers Coll of the City U of New York, NY	M
Mercy Coll, NY	M(s), W(s)
Mitchell Coll, CT	M, W
Molloy Coll, NY	M(s), W(s)
Monroe Coll, Bronx, NY	M

M—for men; W—for women; (s)—scholarship offered

Monroe Coll, New Rochelle, NY	M
Mount Saint Mary Coll, NY	M, W
Nazareth Coll of Rochester, NY	M, W
New York Inst of Technology, NY	M(s), W(s)
New York U, NY	M, W
Niagara U, NY	M(s), W(s)
Nyack Coll, NY	M(s), W(s)
Pace U, NY	W(s)
Paul Smith's Coll of Arts and Sciences, NY	M(s), W(s)
Polytechnic U, Brooklyn Campus, NY	M, W
Post U, CT	M(s), W(s)
Pratt Inst, NY	M, W
Purchase Coll, State U of New York, NY	M, W
Queens Coll of the City U of New York, NY	W(s)
Quinnipiac U, CT	M(s), W(s)
Rensselaer Polytechnic Inst, NY	M, W
Roberts Wesleyan Coll, NY	M(s), W(s)
Rochester Inst of Technology, NY	M, W
Russell Sage Coll, NY	W
Shepherd U, WV	M(s), W(s)
Siena Coll, NY	M(s), W(s)
Skidmore Coll, NY	M, W
St. Bonaventure U, NY	M(s), W(s)
St. Francis Coll, NY	M(s)
St. John Fisher Coll, NY	M, W
St. John's U, NY	M(s), W(s)
St. Joseph's Coll, Suffolk Campus, NY	M, W
St. Lawrence U, NY	M, W
St. Thomas Aquinas Coll, NY	M(s), W(s)
State U of New York Coll at Brockport, NY	M, W
State U of New York Coll at Cortland, NY	M, W
State U of New York Coll at Geneseo, NY	M, W
State U of New York Coll at Old Westbury, NY	M
State U of New York Coll at Oneonta, NY	M(s), W
State U of New York Coll at Potsdam, NY	M, W
State U of New York Coll of Agriculture and Technology at Cobleskill, NY	M, W
State U of New York Coll of Technology at Alfred, NY	M(s), W(s)
State U of New York Coll of Technology at Canton, NY	M, W
State U of New York Coll of Technology at Delhi, NY	M, W
State U of New York Inst of Technology, NY	M, W
State U of New York at Binghamton, NY	M(s), W(s)
State U of New York at Buffalo, NY	M(s), W(s)
State U of New York at New Paltz, NY	M, W
State U of New York at Oswego, NY	M, W
State U of New York at Plattsburgh, NY	M, W
State U of New York, Fredonia, NY	M, W
Stony Brook U, State U of New York, NY	M(s), W(s)
Syracuse U, NY	M(s), W(s)
The Coll of Saint Rose, NY	M(s), W(s)
The Culinary Inst of America, NY	M
Union Coll, NY	M, W
United States Merchant Marine Academy, NY	M
United States Military Academy, NY	M, W
U at Albany, State U of New York, NY	M(s), W(s)
U of Rochester, NY	M, W
U of West Florida, FL	M(s), W(s)
Utica Coll, NY	M, W
Vassar Coll, NY	M, W
Wagner Coll, NY	W(s)
Webb Inst, NY	M, W
Wells Coll, NY	W
West Virginia Wesleyan Coll, WV	M(s), W(s)
York Coll of the City U of New York, NY	M

Softball

Adelphi U, NY	W(s)
Alfred U, NY	W
Barnard Coll, NY	W
Bernard M. Baruch Coll of the City U of New York, NY	W
Briarcliffe Coll, NY	W(s)
Brooklyn Coll of the City U of New York, NY	W
Buffalo State Coll, State U of New York, NY	W
Canisius Coll, NY	W(s)
Chaminade U of Honolulu, HI	W(s)
Chatham Coll, PA	W

City Coll of the City U of New York, NY	W
Colgate U, NY	W(s)
Coll of Mount Saint Vincent, NY	W
Coll of Staten Island of the City U of New York, NY	W
Columbia Coll, NY	W
Columbia U, The Fu Foundation School of Engineering and Applied Science, NY	W
Concordia Coll, NY	W(s)
Cornell U, NY	W
D'Youville Coll, NY	W
Dominican Coll, NY	W(s)
Dowling Coll, NY	W(s)
Elmira Coll, NY	W
Farmingdale State U of New York, NY	W
Fordham U, NY	W(s)
Hamilton Coll, NY	W
Hartwick Coll, NY	W
Hilbert Coll, NY	W
Hofstra U, NY	W(s)
Iona Coll, NY	W(s)
Ithaca Coll, NY	W
John Jay Coll of Criminal Justice of the City U of New York, NY	M, W
Keuka Coll, NY	W
Le Moyne Coll, NY	W(s)
Lehman Coll of the City U of New York, NY	W
Long Island U, Brooklyn Campus, NY	W(s)
Long Island U, C.W. Post Campus, NY	W(s)
Manhattan Coll, NY	W(s)
Manhattanville Coll, NY	W
Marist Coll, NY	W(s)
Marymount Coll of Fordham U, NY	W
Medaille Coll, NY	W
Mercy Coll, NY	W(s)
Mitchell Coll, CT	W
Molloy Coll, NY	W(s)
Monroe Coll, Bronx, NY	W
Monroe Coll, New Rochelle, NY	W
Mount Saint Mary Coll, NY	W
Nazareth Coll of Rochester, NY	W
New York Inst of Technology, NY	W
New York U, NY	W
Niagara U, NY	W(s)
North Carolina Ag and Tech State U, NC	W
Nyack Coll, NY	W(s)
Pace U, NY	W(s)
Polytechnic U, Brooklyn Campus, NY	W
Post U, CT	W(s)
Purchase Coll, State U of New York, NY	M, W
Queens Coll of the City U of New York, NY	M(s)
Quinnipiac U, CT	W(s)
Rensselaer Polytechnic Inst, NY	W
Rochester Inst of Technology, NY	W
Russell Sage Coll, NY	W
Sarah Lawrence Coll, NY	W
Shepherd U, WV	W(s)
Siena Coll, NY	W(s)
Skidmore Coll, NY	W
St. Bonaventure U, NY	W(s)
St. Francis Coll, NY	W(s)
St. John Fisher Coll, NY	W
St. John's U, NY	W(s)
St. Joseph's Coll, New York, NY	W
St. Joseph's Coll, Suffolk Campus, NY	W
St. Lawrence U, NY	W
St. Thomas Aquinas Coll, NY	W(s)
State U of New York Coll at Brockport, NY	W
State U of New York Coll at Cortland, NY	W
State U of New York Coll at Geneseo, NY	W
State U of New York Coll at Old Westbury, NY	W
State U of New York Coll at Oneonta, NY	W
State U of New York Coll at Potsdam, NY	W
State U of New York Coll of Agriculture and Technology at Cobleskill, NY	W
State U of New York Coll of Technology at Alfred, NY	W(s)
State U of New York Coll of Technology at Canton, NY	W
State U of New York Coll of Technology at Delhi, NY	W
State U of New York Inst of Technology, NY	W
State U of New York at Binghamton, NY	W(s)

State U of New York at Buffalo, NY	W(s)
State U of New York at New Paltz, NY	W
State U of New York at Oswego, NY	W
State U of New York at Plattsburgh, NY	W
State U of New York, Fredonia, NY	W
Stony Brook U, State U of New York, NY	W(s)
Syracuse U, NY	M, W(s)
The Coll of New Rochelle, NY	W
The Coll of Saint Rose, NY	W(s)
Union Coll, NY	W
United States Merchant Marine Academy, NY	W
United States Military Academy, NY	W
U at Albany, State U of New York, NY	W(s)
U of Rochester, NY	W
U of West Florida, FL	W(s)
Utica Coll, NY	W
Wagner Coll, NY	W(s)
Wells Coll, NY	W
West Virginia Wesleyan Coll, WV	W(s)
York Coll of the City U of New York, NY	W

Squash

Bard Coll, NY	M
Barnard Coll, NY	W
Colgate U, NY	M, W
Columbia Coll, NY	M, W
Columbia U, The Fu Foundation School of Engineering and Applied Science, NY	M, W
Cornell U, NY	M, W
Fordham U, NY	M
Hamilton Coll, NY	M, W
Hobart and William Smith Colls, NY	M, W
Rensselaer Polytechnic Inst, NY	M, W
St. Lawrence U, NY	M, W
State U of New York Coll at Geneseo, NY	M, W
Syracuse U, NY	M, W
United States Military Academy, NY	M, W
U of Rochester, NY	M
Vassar Coll, NY	M, W

Swimming and Diving

Adelphi U, NY	M(s), W(s)
Alfred U, NY	M, W
Barnard Coll, NY	W
Brooklyn Coll of the City U of New York, NY	M, W
Buffalo State Coll, State U of New York, NY	M, W
Canisius Coll, NY	M(s), W(s)
Chatham Coll, PA	W
Clarkson U, NY	M, W
Colgate U, NY	M, W
Coll of Mount Saint Vincent, NY	W
Coll of Staten Island of the City U of New York, NY	M, W
Columbia Coll, NY	M, W
Columbia U, School of General Studies, NY	M, W
Columbia U, The Fu Foundation School of Engineering and Applied Science, NY	M, W
Cornell U, NY	M, W
Fordham U, NY	M(s), W(s)
Hamilton Coll, NY	M, W
Hartwick Coll, NY	M, W
Hobart and William Smith Colls, NY	W
Hunter Coll of the City U of New York, NY	W
Iona Coll, NY	M(s), W(s)
Ithaca Coll, NY	M, W
Keuka Coll, NY	W
Le Moyne Coll, NY	M, W
Lehman Coll of the City U of New York, NY	M, W
Long Island U, C.W. Post Campus, NY	W(s)
Manhattan Coll, NY	W(s)
Manhattanville Coll, NY	W
Marist Coll, NY	M(s), W(s)
Marymount Coll of Fordham U, NY	W
Mount Saint Mary Coll, NY	M, W
Nazareth Coll of Rochester, NY	M, W
New York U, NY	M, W
Niagara U, NY	M(s), W(s)
North Carolina Ag and Tech State U, NC	W(s)
Pace U, NY	M, W
Queens Coll of the City U of New York, NY	M(s), W(s)
Rensselaer Polytechnic Inst, NY	M, W
Rochester Inst of Technology, NY	M, W
Sarah Lawrence Coll, NY	W
Siena Coll, NY	W(s)

College	
Skidmore Coll, NY	M, W
St. Bonaventure U, NY	M(s), W(s)
St. Francis Coll, NY	M(s), W(s)
St. Joseph's Coll, Suffolk Campus, NY	W
St. Lawrence U, NY	M, W
State U of New York Coll at Brockport, NY	M, W
State U of New York Coll at Cortland, NY	M, W
State U of New York Coll at Geneseo, NY	M, W
State U of New York Coll at Old Westbury, NY	M, W
State U of New York Coll at Oneonta, NY	M, W
State U of New York Coll at Potsdam, NY	M, W
State U of New York Coll of Agriculture and Technology at Cobleskill, NY	M, W
State U of New York Coll of Technology at Alfred, NY	M, W
State U of New York Coll of Technology at Delhi, NY	M, W
State U of New York at Binghamton, NY	M(s), W(s)
State U of New York at Buffalo, NY	M(s), W(s)
State U of New York at New Paltz, NY	M, W
State U of New York at Oswego, NY	M, W
State U of New York at Plattsburgh, NY	M, W
State U of New York, Fredonia, NY	M, W
Stony Brook U, State U of New York, NY	M(s), W(s)
Syracuse U, NY	M(s), W(s)
The Coll of New Rochelle, NY	W
The Coll of Saint Rose, NY	M(s), W(s)
Union Coll, NY	M, W
United States Merchant Marine Academy, NY	M, W
United States Military Academy, NY	M, W
U of Rochester, NY	M, W
Utica Coll, NY	M, W
Vassar Coll, NY	M, W
Wagner Coll, NY	W(s)
Wells Coll, NY	W
West Virginia Wesleyan Coll, WV	M(s), W(s)
York Coll of the City U of New York, NY	M, W

Table Tennis

College	
Colgate U, NY	M, W
Columbia Coll, NY	M, W
Columbia U, The Fu Foundation School of Engineering and Applied Science, NY	M, W
Fashion Inst of Technology, NY	M, W
Rensselaer Polytechnic Inst, NY	M, W
State U of New York at Binghamton, NY	M, W
Syracuse U, NY	M, W

Tennis

College	
Adelphi U, NY	M(s), W(s)
Alfred U, NY	M, W
Bard Coll, NY	M, W
Barnard Coll, NY	W
Bernard M. Baruch Coll of the City U of New York, NY	M, W
Brooklyn Coll of the City U of New York, NY	M, W
Buffalo State Coll, State U of New York, NY	W
Chaminade U of Honolulu, HI	M(s), W(s)
Chatham Coll, PA	
City Coll of the City U of New York, NY	M, W
Clarkson U, NY	M, W
Colgate U, NY	M, W
Coll of Mount Saint Vincent, NY	M, W
Coll of Staten Island of the City U of New York, NY	M, W
Columbia Coll, NY	M, W
Columbia U, School of General Studies, NY	M, W
Columbia U, The Fu Foundation School of Engineering and Applied Science, NY	M, W
Concordia Coll, NY	M(s), W(s)
Cornell U, NY	M, W
Dowling Coll, NY	M(s), W(s)
Elmira Coll, NY	M, W
Fashion Inst of Technology, NY	M, W
Fordham U, NY	M(s), W(s)
Hamilton Coll, NY	M, W
Hartwick Coll, NY	M, W
Hobart and William Smith Colls, NY	M, W
Hofstra U, NY	M(s), W(s)
Hunter Coll of the City U of New York, NY	M, W
Ithaca Coll, NY	M, W
John Jay Coll of Criminal Justice of the City U of New York, NY	M, W
Le Moyne Coll, NY	M(s), W(s)
Lehman Coll of the City U of New York, NY	M, W
Long Island U, Brooklyn Campus, NY	W(s)
Long Island U, C.W. Post Campus, NY	W(s)
Manhattan Coll, NY	M(s), W(s)
Manhattanville Coll, NY	M, W
Marist Coll, NY	M(s), W(s)
Marymount Coll of Fordham U, NY	W
Mercy Coll, NY	M(s)
Molloy Coll, NY	W(s)
Mount Saint Mary Coll, NY	M, W
Nazareth Coll of Rochester, NY	M, W
New York U, NY	M, W
Niagara U, NY	M(s), W(s)
North Carolina Ag and Tech State U, NC	M(s), W(s)
Pace U, NY	M(s), W(s)
Polytechnic U, Brooklyn Campus, NY	M, W
Pratt Inst, NY	M, W
Queens Coll of the City U of New York, NY	M(s), W(s)
Quinnipiac U, CT	M(s), W(s)
Rensselaer Polytechnic Inst, NY	M, W
Roberts Wesleyan Coll, NY	M(s), W(s)
Rochester Inst of Technology, NY	M, W
Russell Sage Coll, NY	W
Shepherd U, WV	M(s), W(s)
Siena Coll, NY	M(s), W(s)
Skidmore Coll, NY	M, W
St. Bonaventure U, NY	M(s), W(s)
St. Francis Coll, NY	M(s), W(s)
St. John Fisher Coll, NY	M, W
St. John's U, NY	M(s), W(s)
St. Joseph's Coll, Suffolk Campus, NY	M, W
St. Lawrence U, NY	M, W
State U of New York Coll at Brockport, NY	W
State U of New York Coll at Cortland, NY	W
State U of New York Coll at Geneseo, NY	W
State U of New York Coll at Oneonta, NY	M, W
State U of New York Coll at Potsdam, NY	W
State U of New York Coll of Agriculture and Technology at Cobleskill, NY	M, W
State U of New York Coll of Technology at Delhi, NY	M, W
State U of New York at Binghamton, NY	M(s), W(s)
State U of New York at Buffalo, NY	M(s), W(s)
State U of New York at New Paltz, NY	M, W
State U of New York at Oswego, NY	M, W
State U of New York at Plattsburgh, NY	M, W
State U of New York, Fredonia, NY	M, W
Stony Brook U, State U of New York, NY	M(s), W(s)
Syracuse U, NY	M, W(s)
The Coll of New Rochelle, NY	W
Union Coll, NY	M, W
United States Merchant Marine Academy, NY	M, W
United States Military Academy, NY	M, W
U at Albany, State U of New York, NY	W(s)
U of Rochester, NY	M, W
U of West Florida, FL	M(s), W(s)
Utica Coll, NY	M, W
Vassar Coll, NY	M, W
Wagner Coll, NY	M(s), W(s)
Webb Inst, NY	M, W
Wells Coll, NY	W
West Virginia Wesleyan Coll, WV	M(s), W(s)
Yeshiva U, NY	M, W
York Coll of the City U of New York, NY	M

Track and Field

College	
Adelphi U, NY	M(s), W(s)
Alfred U, NY	M, W
Barnard Coll, NY	W
Briarcliffe Coll, NY	M(s), W(s)
Brooklyn Coll of the City U of New York, NY	M, W
Buffalo State Coll, State U of New York, NY	M, W
City Coll of the City U of New York, NY	M, W
Colgate U, NY	M, W
Coll of Mount Saint Vincent, NY	W
Columbia Coll, NY	M, W
Columbia U, School of General Studies, NY	M, W
Columbia U, The Fu Foundation School of Engineering and Applied Science, NY	M, W
Cornell U, NY	M, W
Farmingdale State U of New York, NY	M, W
Fordham U, NY	M(s), W(s)
Globe Inst of Technology, NY	M, W
Hamilton Coll, NY	M, W
Hartwick Coll, NY	M, W
Houghton Coll, NY	M(s), W(s)
Hunter Coll of the City U of New York, NY	M, W
Iona Coll, NY	M(s), W(s)
Ithaca Coll, NY	M, W
Lehman Coll of the City U of New York, NY	M, W
Long Island U, Brooklyn Campus, NY	M(s), W(s)
Long Island U, C.W. Post Campus, NY	M(s), W(s)
Manhattan Coll, NY	M(s), W(s)
Marist Coll, NY	M(s), W(s)
Medgar Evers Coll of the City U of New York, NY	M, W
Nazareth Coll of Rochester, NY	M, W
New York Inst of Technology, NY	M(s), W(s)
New York U, NY	M, W
North Carolina Ag and Tech State U, NC	M(s), W(s)
Pace U, NY	M(s), W(s)
Polytechnic U, Brooklyn Campus, NY	M, W
Pratt Inst, NY	M, W
Quinnipiac U, CT	M(s), W(s)
Rensselaer Polytechnic Inst, NY	M, W
Roberts Wesleyan Coll, NY	M(s), W(s)
Rochester Inst of Technology, NY	M, W
Siena Coll, NY	M, W
St. Francis Coll, NY	M(s), W(s)
St. Lawrence U, NY	M, W
State U of New York Coll at Brockport, NY	M, W
State U of New York Coll at Cortland, NY	M, W
State U of New York Coll at Geneseo, NY	M, W
State U of New York Coll at Oneonta, NY	M, W
State U of New York Coll at Potsdam, NY	M, W
State U of New York Coll of Agriculture and Technology at Cobleskill, NY	M, W
State U of New York Coll of Technology at Alfred, NY	M(s), W(s)
State U of New York Coll of Technology at Delhi, NY	M, W
State U of New York at Binghamton, NY	M(s), W(s)
State U of New York at Buffalo, NY	M(s), W(s)
State U of New York at New Paltz, NY	M, W
State U of New York at Oswego, NY	M, W
State U of New York at Plattsburgh, NY	M, W
State U of New York, Fredonia, NY	M, W
Stony Brook U, State U of New York, NY	M(s), W(s)
Syracuse U, NY	M(s), W(s)
Union Coll, NY	M, W
United States Merchant Marine Academy, NY	M, W
United States Military Academy, NY	M, W
U at Albany, State U of New York, NY	M(s), W(s)
U of Rochester, NY	M, W
Vassar Coll, NY	M, W
Wagner Coll, NY	M(s), W(s)
West Virginia Wesleyan Coll, WV	M(s), W(s)
York Coll of the City U of New York, NY	M, W

Ultimate Frisbee

College	
Columbia Coll, NY	M, W
Fordham U, NY	M, W
Hamilton Coll, NY	M, W
New York U, NY	M, W
Rochester Inst of Technology, NY	M, W
State U of New York Coll at Geneseo, NY	M, W
Union Coll, NY	M, W
U of Rochester, NY	M, W
Vassar Coll, NY	M, W

Volleyball

College	
Adelphi U, NY	W(s)
Alfred U, NY	W
Bard Coll, NY	M, W
Barnard Coll, NY	W
Bernard M. Baruch Coll of the City U of New York, NY	M, W

M—for men; W—for women; (s)—scholarship offered

Brooklyn Coll of the City U of New York, NY — M, W
Buffalo State Coll, State U of New York, NY — M, W
Canisius Coll, NY — M, W(s)
Chaminade U of Honolulu, HI — W(s)
Chatham Coll, PA — W
City Coll of the City U of New York, NY — W
Clarkson U, NY — M, W
Colgate U, NY — M, W(s)
Coll of Mount Saint Vincent, NY — M, W
Coll of Staten Island of the City U of New York, NY — W
Columbia Coll, NY — M, W
Columbia U, School of General Studies, NY — W
Columbia U, The Fu Foundation School of Engineering and Applied Science, NY — M, W
Concordia Coll, NY — W(s)
Cornell U, NY — M, W
D'Youville Coll, NY — M, W
Daemen Coll, NY — W(s)
Dominican Coll, NY — W(s)
Dowling Coll, NY — W(s)
Elmira Coll, NY — W
Farmingdale State U of New York, NY — W
Fashion Inst of Technology, NY — W
Fordham U, NY — W(s)
Globe Inst of Technology, NY — W
Hamilton Coll, NY — M, W
Hartwick Coll, NY — W
Hilbert Coll, NY — M, W
Hofstra U, NY — W(s)
Houghton Coll, NY — W(s)
Hunter Coll of the City U of New York, NY — M, W
Iona Coll, NY — W(s)
Ithaca Coll, NY — W
John Jay Coll of Criminal Justice of the City U of New York, NY — W
Keuka Coll, NY — W
Le Moyne Coll, NY — W(s)
Lehman Coll of the City U of New York, NY — M, W
Long Island U, Brooklyn Campus, NY — W(s)
Long Island U, C.W. Post Campus, NY — W(s)
Manhattan Coll, NY — M, W(s)
Manhattanville Coll, NY — W
Marist Coll, NY — M, W(s)
Marymount Coll of Fordham U, NY — W
Medaille Coll, NY — M, W
Medgar Evers Coll of the City U of New York, NY — W
Mercy Coll, NY — W(s)
Mitchell Coll, CT — W
Molloy Coll, NY — W(s)
Monroe Coll, Bronx, NY — W
Monroe Coll, New Rochelle, NY — W
Mount Saint Mary Coll, NY — W
Nazareth Coll of Rochester, NY — M, W
New York Inst of Technology, NY — W(s)
New York U, NY — M, W
Niagara U, NY — W(s)
North Carolina Ag and Tech State U, NC — W(s)
Nyack Coll, NY — W(s)
Pace U, NY — W(s)
Polytechnic U, Brooklyn Campus, NY — M, W

Post U, CT — W(s)
Pratt Inst, NY — W
Purchase Coll, State U of New York, NY — M, W
Queens Coll of the City U of New York, NY — M(s), W(s)
Quinnipiac U, CT — W(s)
Rensselaer Polytechnic Inst, NY — M, W
Roberts Wesleyan Coll, NY — W(s)
Rochester Inst of Technology, NY — M, W
Russell Sage Coll, NY — W
Sarah Lawrence Coll, NY — W
Shepherd U, WV — W(s)
Siena Coll, NY — M, W(s)
Skidmore Coll, NY — W
St. Bonaventure U, NY — M, W(s)
St. Francis Coll, NY — W(s)
St. John Fisher Coll, NY — W
St. John's U, NY — W(s)
St. Joseph's Coll, New York, NY — M, W
St. Joseph's Coll, Suffolk Campus, NY — W
St. Lawrence U, NY — W
St. Thomas Aquinas Coll, NY — W(s)
State U of New York Coll at Brockport, NY — W
State U of New York Coll at Cortland, NY — M, W
State U of New York Coll at Geneseo, NY — M, W
State U of New York Coll at Old Westbury, NY — W
State U of New York Coll at Oneonta, NY — M, W
State U of New York Coll at Potsdam, NY — W
State U of New York Coll of Agriculture and Technology at Cobleskill, NY — W
State U of New York Coll of Technology at Alfred, NY — W
State U of New York Coll of Technology at Canton, NY — W
State U of New York Coll of Technology at Delhi, NY — W
State U of New York Inst of Technology, NY — W
State U of New York at Binghamton, NY — M, W(s)
State U of New York at Buffalo, NY — W(s)
State U of New York at New Paltz, NY — M, W
State U of New York at Oswego, NY — W
State U of New York at Plattsburgh, NY — W
State U of New York, Fredonia, NY — M, W
Stony Brook U, State U of New York, NY — W(s)
Syracuse U, NY — M, W(s)
The Coll of New Rochelle, NY — W
The Coll of Saint Rose, NY — W(s)
Union Coll, NY — W
United States Merchant Marine Academy, NY — W
United States Military Academy, NY — M, W
U at Albany, State U of New York, NY — W(s)
U of Rochester, NY — M, W
U of West Florida, FL — W
Utica Coll, NY — W
Vassar Coll, NY — M, W
Wagner Coll, NY — W(s)
Webb Inst, NY — M, W
West Virginia Wesleyan Coll, WV — W(s)

Yeshiva U, NY — M
York Coll of the City U of New York, NY — M, W

Water Polo
Chaminade U of Honolulu, HI — M(s)
Colgate U, NY — M, W
Columbia Coll, NY — M, W
Columbia U, The Fu Foundation School of Engineering and Applied Science, NY — M, W
Fordham U, NY — M(s)
Hamilton Coll, NY — M, W
Hartwick Coll, NY — M, W(s)
Iona Coll, NY — M, W(s)
Lehman Coll of the City U of New York, NY — M
Marist Coll, NY — W(s)
Queens Coll of the City U of New York, NY — M(s), W(s)
Rensselaer Polytechnic Inst, NY — M, W
Rochester Inst of Technology, NY — M, W
Siena Coll, NY — W(s)
St. Francis Coll, NY — M(s), W(s)
Syracuse U, NY — M, W
Union Coll, NY — M, W
United States Military Academy, NY — M
Utica Coll, NY — W
Wagner Coll, NY — W(s)

Weight Lifting
Rensselaer Polytechnic Inst, NY — M, W
Syracuse U, NY — M, W
United States Military Academy, NY — M, W

Wrestling
Colgate U, NY — M, W
Columbia Coll, NY — M
Columbia U, School of General Studies, NY — M
Columbia U, The Fu Foundation School of Engineering and Applied Science, NY — M
Cornell U, NY — M
Hofstra U, NY — M(s)
Hunter Coll of the City U of New York, NY — M
Ithaca Coll, NY — M
Lehman Coll of the City U of New York, NY — M
New York U, NY — M
Rochester Inst of Technology, NY — M
State U of New York Coll at Brockport, NY — M
State U of New York Coll at Cortland, NY — M
State U of New York Coll at Oneonta, NY — M
State U of New York Coll of Agriculture and Technology at Cobleskill, NY — M
State U of New York Coll of Technology at Alfred, NY — M
State U of New York Coll of Technology at Delhi, NY — M
State U of New York at Binghamton, NY — M(s)
State U of New York at Buffalo, NY — M(s)
State U of New York at Oswego, NY — M
United States Merchant Marine Academy, NY — M
United States Military Academy, NY — M
Wagner Coll, NY — M(s)
Yeshiva U, NY — M

ROTC Programs

Adelphi U, NY	A(c), AF(c)	Lehman Coll of the City U of New York, NY	A(c)	Skidmore Coll, NY	A(c), AF(c)
Albany Coll of Pharmacy of Union U, NY	A(c), AF(c)	Le Moyne Coll, NY	A(c), AF(c)	State U of New York at Binghamton, NY	AF(c)
Alfred U, NY	A(c)	Long Island U, C.W. Post Campus, NY	A(c), AF(c)	State U of New York at Buffalo, NY	A(c)
Buffalo State Coll, State U of New York, NY	A(c)	Manhattan Coll, NY	A(c), AF	State U of New York at Oswego, NY	A(c)
Canisius Coll, NY	A	Maria Coll, NY	AF(c)	State U of New York Coll at Brockport, NY	A, N(c), AF(c)
Cazenovia Coll, NY	A(c), AF(c)	Marist Coll, NY	A		
Chaminade U of Honolulu, HI	A(c), AF(c)	Medaille Coll, NY	A(c)	State U of New York Coll at Cortland, NY	A(c), AF(c)
Chatham Coll, PA	A(c), AF(c)	Mercy Coll, NY	AF(c)	State U of New York Coll at Geneseo, NY	A(c), AF(c)
City Coll of the City U of New York, NY	A(c), AF(c)	Molloy Coll, NY	A(c), N(c), AF(c)	State U of New York Coll at Old Westbury, NY	A(c), AF(c)
		Mount Saint Mary Coll, NY	A(c)		
Clarkson U, NY	A, AF	Nazareth Coll of Rochester, NY	A(c), AF(c)	State U of New York Coll at Potsdam, NY	A(c), AF(c)
Colgate U, NY	A(c)				
Coll of Mount Saint Vincent, NY	A(c), AF(c)	New York Inst of Technology, NY	A, AF	State U of New York Coll of Environmental Science and Forestry, NY	A(c), AF(c)
Columbia Coll, NY	A(c), N(c), AF(c)	Niagara U, NY	A		
Columbia U, The Fu Foundation School of Engineering and Applied Science, NY	A(c), N(c), AF(c)	North Carolina Ag and Tech State U, NC	A, AF	State U of New York Coll of Technology at Alfred, NY	A(c)
		Pace U, NY	A(c)	State U of New York Coll of Technology at Canton, NY	A(c), AF(c)
		Polytechnic U, Brooklyn Campus, NY	AF(c)		
Cornell U, NY	A, AF	Pratt Inst, NY	A(c)	State U of New York Inst of Technology, NY	A(c), AF(c)
Daemen Coll, NY	A(c)	Queens Coll of the City U of New York, NY	A(c), N(c)		
Dowling Coll, NY	AF(c)			Stony Brook U, State U of New York, NY	A(c), AF(c)
D'Youville Coll, NY	A(c)	Quinnipiac U, CT	A(c), AF(c)		
Elmira Coll, NY	A, AF(c)	Rensselaer Polytechnic Inst, NY	A, N, AF	Syracuse U, NY	A, AF
Farmingdale State U of New York, NY	A(c), AF(c)	Roberts Wesleyan Coll, NY	A(c), AF(c)	Union Coll, NY	A(c), AF(c)
Fordham U, NY	A, N(c), AF(c)	Rochester Inst of Technology, NY	A, N(c), AF	U at Albany, State U of New York, NY	A, AF(c)
Hamilton Coll, NY	A(c), AF(c)	Russell Sage Coll, NY	A(c), AF(c)	U of Rochester, NY	N, AF(c)
Hartwick Coll, NY	A(c), AF(c)	St. Bonaventure U, NY	A	U of West Florida, FL	A, AF
Hofstra U, NY	A	St. John Fisher Coll, NY	A(c), N(c), AF(c)	Utica Coll, NY	A, AF(c)
Houghton Coll, NY	A(c)	St. John's U, NY	A	Vaughn Coll of Aeronautics and Technology, NY	A(c), AF(c)
Iona Coll, NY	A(c)	St. Joseph's Coll, Suffolk Campus, NY	A(c), AF(c)		
Ithaca Coll, NY	A(c), AF(c)			Wells Coll, NY	AF(c)
John Jay Coll of Criminal Justice of the City U of New York, NY	AF(c)	St. Lawrence U, NY	A(c), AF(c)	York Coll of the City U of New York, NY	A(c), AF(c)
		Siena Coll, NY	A, AF(c)		

A—Army; N—Navy; AF—Air Force; (c)—available through a cooperating host institution

Alphabetical Listing of Colleges and Universities

In this index, the page locations of the **Profiles** are printed in regular type, **Profiles** with **Special Messages** in *italics*, and **In-Depth Descriptions** in **bold type**.